Cultured Force

Cultured Force

*Makers and Defenders of the
French Colonial Empire*

BARNETT SINGER
and
JOHN LANGDON

THE UNIVERSITY OF WISCONSIN PRESS

The University of Wisconsin Press
1930 Monroe Street, 3rd floor
Madison, Wisconsin 53711-2059
uwpress.wisc.edu

3 Henrietta Street
London WC2E 8LU, England
eurospanbookstore.com

Printed in the United States of America

Library of Congress Cataloging-in-Publication Data

Singer, Barnett.
Cultured force : makers and defenders of the French colonial empire /
Barnett Singer and John W. Langdon
p. cm
Includes bibliographical references and index.
ISBN 0-299-19900-2 (cloth : alk. paper)
1. Colonial administrators—France—Biography.
2. France—Colonies—Adminstration—History.
3. Imperialism—History.
I. Langdon, John W. II. Title.
JV1811.S56 2004
325′.344′0922—dc22
2003021174
ISBN 0-299-19904-5 (pbk. : alk. paper)

ISBN-13: 978-0-299-19904-3 (pbk.: alk. paper)

Preface

Scholarship starts out as an exercise somewhat like what children perform with Tinker Toys or Legos: it becomes ever more complex, and you often continue because you started. Many times along the disorderly route you doubt your own utility, thinking of other seemingly simpler outlets like letter or songwriting; but here at the close, we believe we can claim some usefulness here. We cannot and are not about to declare this book the last word in scholarship on France's imperial effort, and on some of its key movers and shakers in the last several centuries. But we *have* put a lot of pivotal, fascinating figures and developments under one roof, and hope that we have achieved a certain interest and clarity. We hope too that those new to French imperialism can get a convenient, interesting introduction in this book, while scholars in the field may find themselves freshly stimulated by some of what we present and interpret. We haven't felt the need to consult or list every last bibliographical item remotely pertaining to the subject; but via archival, printed primary, and secondary sources mentioned, readers should get a sense of the extensive material available for such a study, some previously untapped. It is also true that certain chapters here are "sketches" or bridges, while others (chapters 2–5, 8) are more monographic—truly the heart of what we treat in this book.

My own [Singer's] previous efforts in French history included a good deal of social and intellectual history; but I suppose I got to the point of realizing that people able to do such things benefit from something primary called security and order, which perhaps kindled my interest in military history. Frankly though, I don't think I considered any such points at the outset of this project. I simply remember seeing names like Lyautey or Faidherbe given a line or two in classic French history texts like Alfred Cobban's or Gordon Wright's, and I finally thought I wanted to learn more about those names.

In 1989 I read one of the noted practitioners in this field, Douglas Porch (his popular-scholarly *Conquest of Morocco*), and started in with Lyautey's extensive, stimulating writings, as well as those who had worked on him. I then began moving backward to his mentor, Gallieni, along with the less admirable Joffre, then to Faidherbe, and eventually to Bugeaud (all pre-archivally at first). However, I never forgot buying Marcel Bigeard's great memoir (*Pour une parcelle de gloire*) at a *tabac* and devouring it on a Bordeaux park bench outside the archives there in the late '70s; so I would also go forward as well into the cauldron of France's last colonial stand in Vietnam and Algeria, a staple today of bestseller tables in French bookstores. I've often felt that ignorance is the foundation of learning, and what I learned from this project was how fascinating, cultured, aware, noble, and idiosyncratic, if sometimes brutal and certainly militarily adept the greatest French colonial figures were; and how being abroad often revealed their best selves. Bugeaud, Faidherbe, Gallieni, Lyautey, Bigeard—each gave a researcher huge surprises! Remember how Flaubert said that he was Madame Bovary? I think my biographical empathy at times attained that sort of pitch, and at the least, I certainly found it easy to remain interested in those who put themselves through so much.

Among the last memoirs I read before delivering a version of this manuscript was Hélie de Saint Marc's prize-winning autobiography, published in the mid-1990s and written by a man alive only due to a series of flukes.[1] What that memoir showed me was the poverty of our ideological terminology, our silly attempts to locate good, unsullied people on one side of the spectrum and bad on another, the anachronistic artificiality, if you will, of our interpretive one-note sambas. What do you make of a Saint Marc who read all the adventure writing he could as a boy, who in the Bordelais fought his fear and joined up as an authentic Resistant in 1941, before it became popular, and who then ran errands at the risk of his life, despising those who trafficked and learned to live with the Nazis? At one point he was put up by a lovely couple later tortured, but who never talked, and who died in deportation. Saint Marc, whose supposedly conservative father could never abide the yellow stars reserved for Jews, was himself arrested and deported to Buchenwald. As a skeletal figure he worked twelve-hour days in a tunnel underground, watched by the SS and their barking dogs, given little to eat, holding on to life by a thread. He was saved from deadly pneumonia by a male nurse who stole medicine for him, and by a Latvian Communist, who gave him food; and finally he returned home, a rare herring who had made it through such nets. Lost in the postwar world, and after graduating from the elite military school of Saint-Cyr, Saint Marc joined the Foreign Legion out of sheer idealism—for service in Indochina, a beautiful part of the world that never left him inside, despite the many comrades and indigenous friends he lost there to bullets, dysentery, even burial alive. And thence came Algérie française, and again, his prose on this area and period remains hauntingly right, as cultured as one can get, right up with any travel writer I've read. Saint Marc listened and debated the agony of the land, and was anything but dogmatic. Instead, he had the vulnerable maturity of one who had faced death for much of his life and who knew history—how conquerors had succeeded conquerors in this land, how sons dissipated what fathers had built, how people whose grandparents had cleared swamps and who invited him to eat on gorgeous plantations of fruit trees were as evanescent as the May fly.

After putting heart and soul into that last stand French colonial milieu, marrying there and having children, and hoping for a reconciliation of all sides, he joined the officers' putsch of 1961, described in chapter 8, paying for it with more years of prison. Not one of his lines in a French I've so hated translating is wasted or untasteful—and that was often true in the course of my research on Bugeaud, Faidherbe, Gallieni, Lyautey, and Bigeard as well. Translating any of them frequently seemed an abomination (and explains the many dollops of original French in our endnotes). In sum, can one simply call a man like Saint Marc who devoted himself to a series of ideals, and never without self-questioning (Valéry's *non sans réflexion*) a Rightist? A sometime Leftist? Or a what?

Among other things this project showed me was that true greatness and "constructivity" won't always fit neatly into our relatively untested, yuppie ideological categories—that contradiction and paradox were more the rule here. Isn't it time for *us* to become more supple and ecumenical, as regularly happened to imperial figures we discuss, given what they saw and learned abroad?

Greatness, however, is not our only subject here. The lower human qualities of brutality, jealousy, rivalry, political maneuvering, and self-centeredness are also part of the military-imperial saga discussed in this book. Having experienced the proximity of certain false personalities and read fine psychoanalytic work on them, I began to understand people like General Joseph Joffre psychologically, a minor figure in the colonies, but a major tragedy for France as its narcissistic, reprehensible chief of staff in World War I (see chapter 4). Yes, there was perhaps some autobiographical resonance here—but what historian doesn't indirectly put some of that into books and articles?

In fact, I've always felt that if I ever got to the point of appending a preface to this effort of over a decade, I would say something like: "Not for original family or milieu—too often fair-weather; but a bit like the imperial figures we study here for family of the world, which, however, includes colleagues, friends who were always there, my daughter, and two women who did so much for me (Judy in the early going, then for much the larger and more onerous part, Kathy), tolerating and facilitating my full immersion in this project."

After that, I would like to thank two professors of what I call the Belle Epoque of North American historians of France, John Cairns, who read two of my early papers on this subject, including one for me at a Society for French Historical Studies conference I couldn't attend; and Eugen Weber, who read the entire manuscript in draft, offering perceptive feedback. I also thank the great Lyautey expert, William Hoisington Jr., who read the manuscript as well, offering useful suggestions, especially on the "bridge" chapters. I thank those who hosted conferences and other fora allowing me to present various parts in much earlier drafts and versions; journal editors who also saw earlier versions and parts of what became this work; and on a number of research trips, the personnel of the Library of Congress and of the French archives—the Service Historique de l'Armée de Terre, Vincennes, the Centre des Archives d'Outre-Mer, the Archives Nationales, the Archives du Ministère des Affaires Etrangères, and the Bibliothèque de l'Institut (housing the Terrier papers indicated to me by an anonymous reviewer for the SSHRC); not to mention the new Americanized Bibliothèque Nationale. A separate thanks to personnel at the underutilized "Histoire Orale" branch at Vincennes. Closer to home, I thank the interlibrary loan desks of Brock and Niagara, the User Services department at Brock, and staff at a variety of other university libraries around this region. I also thank academic authorities both at Brock and Le Moyne who awarded grants for travel. I thank Donald Teale for helping us conceptualize the shape of this book and V. P. Schmidt for translation help, and am grateful for student assistance near the end of the project.

I would finally like to thank great military-colonial historians of France like Alistair Horne and Douglas Porch for giving us a path to follow—one that is hopefully useful and enjoyable to both scholars and lay readers alike. And hats off as well to the author of a lively recent synthesis in the field, Frederick Quinn.[2] But by and large I did much of this in relative isolation. Therefore, I would blame no one but myself for the many potential shortcomings here—or let us say that I will take majority blame, given that what you find here is mostly mine. I am well aware that we may be dealt some scholarly flak for our "revisionism," and also for the simplifications of chapters 1, 6, and 7, our bridge chapters. But these simplifications were quite purposive—there so that general readers would get a fairly straightforward sense of developments, rather than a consistent pitch of scholarly complexity that might be harder to follow.

Last but not least, I thank a co-author who is happily my opposite, and without whom I would never be in this position. To this good friend and stable human, John Langdon, I now cede the floor . . .

I [Langdon] must say that I have truly enjoyed working for a number of years on this intriguing project with someone who had embraced the field earlier. I too began as a social and educational historian of modern France, then became immersed in twentieth-century diplomatic history, particularly as applied to World War I and the Cold War. I have learned much from our collaboration, especially on the mentalities of those who built and defended the colonial empire of *la grande nation.* My late mentors, John W. Bush and C. Vincent Confer, would doubtless recognize much of themselves in some of these pages. But in the final analysis, the historian has nowhere to stand but in the present, and again, no one to blame for shortcomings but him or herself. My co-author and I accept those terms, and wish you, the reader, both enjoyment and enlightenment as you follow the story we set out to tell.

Cultured Force

Introduction

Biographical study is a relatively painless way to introduce people to an era's subtleties, and especially, to that too often simplified, misunderstood, but definitely important historical phenomenon called Western, and in our case, French imperialism. In the latter field we already know how important the individual was in making and helping to hold onto an extensive French empire made after 1830—how impetuous commanders abroad often mounted operations clearly in opposition to the home government's wishes or restrictions. In the literature on modern French imperial enterprises one thinks, for example, of Christopher M. Andrew's and A. S. Kanya-Forstner's *France Overseas: The Great War and the Climax of French Imperial Expansion*, arguing that for most of the nineteenth century "the main expansionist urge came not from Paris but from soldiers and sailors at the outposts of empire, prompted on occasion by missionaries and businessmen who had preceded them."[1] One thinks also of Kanya-Forstner's monograph, *The Conquest of the Western Sudan: A Study in French Military Imperialism*, showing how the process could become obstinately obsessive, and how figures like Bugeaud of Algeria had set the tone back in the 1840s, when "military insubordination was raised to the level of an art."[2] So *pace* Marx and Lenin, we now know how crucial and important it is to study individuals in the creation, extension, and protection of modern French colonies of different types.

We also have much better knowledge of key French proconsuls than we did even twenty years ago, knowledge that should make any researcher in the field aware of the nuances of these personalities. On Bugeaud of

Algeria (our subject in chapter 2), modern biographical treatments have modified earlier shibboleths showing him as merely brutal, especially in the Algerian conquest. (Perhaps the best example of the latter viewpoint is Patrick Kessel's persuasively spirited, ninety-page Marxian diatribe, *Moi, Maréchal Bugeaud* [1958].) The first biography to point the way toward revisionism was Antony Thrall Sullivan's *Thomas-Robert Bugeaud: France and Algeria, 1784–1849: Politics, Power, and the Good Society*.[3] In a compact book, Sullivan helped us note here how innovative Bugeaud's military theories were, precisely because they stemmed from his empirical intellectuality, deriving in part from innovative agricultural work in his home region of France. The latter was really his first love, before the conquest of Algeria claimed Bugeaud's initially reluctant attention. A subsequent biography, and the best we now have, Jean-Pierre Bois' *Bugeaud*,[4] continues the nuanced scholarly treatment of this figure, and is also devoid of ideological one-sidedness, and of the knowing cynicism that too often vitiates work on European imperialism and imperial figures. Sullivan first guided one of the present authors toward the numerous published collections of Bugeaud's fascinating speeches, letters, and military articles, but our analysis of them in chapter 2 goes deeper in terms of their quality. We also use archival sources that haven't been mined in the same way, or at all. Other important scholarly guides on Bugeaud include Kenneth J. Perkins, showing his paradoxically protective side vis-à-vis Arab culture and tribal administration, an emphasis later altered by those who followed him in Algeria.[5] And one should emphasize that it *was* Bugeaud, more than any other figure, who got the snowball of an extensive second French empire rolling.

For Faidherbe of Senegal and West Africa, the next great French proconsul of the nineteenth century and subject of chapter 3, we have a massive doctoral dissertation, Leland Conley Barrows' "General Faidherbe, the Maurel and Prom Company, and French Expansion in Senegal" (UCLA, 1974); but Barrows is quite patronizing to this important and deeply cultured figure, seeing him merely as the instrument of French merchants in Senegal. Barrows also wrote articles on Faidherbe,[6] but his views require much modification, and he never followed up with a book on the subject. The most recent and best biography of Faidherbe is the journalist Alain Coursier's *Faidherbe 1818–1889: du Sénégal à l'armée du Nord;*[7] but though well written, it suffers from a paucity of references and a sketchy bibliography. Our work, again including archival runs not previously used, should help fill a gap here, especially in English.

Gallieni, the next great French colonial figure of the nineteenth and early twentieth centuries, has received good biographical treatment,[8] though again, lack of proper referencing will be irksome to scholars. No one, however, has ever entwined his record and fortunes with those of the minor colonial figure Joseph Joffre, whose efforts were militarily disastrous for France. In chapter 4 we devote much space to their colonial careers, which dovetailed in Madagascar around the turn of the century; then a good deal more to tragic strategic differences between them after their imperial stints were done, both before and during World War I. We highlight Gallieni's superbly tasteful culture, a culture that informed his action, and contrast it to the thin culture (and character) of Joffre, a man mainly skilled at propaganda and networking. Again, our use of sources and new interpretations should hopefully help blaze scholarly trails here.

When it comes to Gallieni's principal disciple, Lyautey (treated partially in chapter 4 and extensively in chapter 5), there has been a plethora of monographic work. On this last major French proconsular figure abroad, we have André Le Révérend's biography *Lyautey*,[9] and his better-documented doctoral dissertation on Lyautey's literary proclivities, *Lyautey écrivain 1854–1934;*[10] William Hoisington Jr.'s *Lyautey and the French Conquest of Morocco*,[11] a fine military study based on exhaustive use of French archives; another exhaustive archival treatment by Daniel Rivet, *Lyautey et l'institution du protectorat français au Maroc 1912–1925*,[12] wishing neither to magnify nor to play down Lyautey, and especially, his enormous intelligence and sensitivity; Pascal Venier's *Lyautey avant Lyautey*,[13] a shorter archival treatment on Lyautey's early life and pre-Moroccan colonial activities; and Moshe Gershovich's *French Military Rule in Morocco: Colonialism and Its Consequences*,[14] a perhaps too careful, but important study, partially on Lyautey. This literature, however, focuses too exclusively on the Lyautesque translation into reality of terms like "direct" or "indirect" rule, or "associationism"; and again, we think we can claim some originality in interpretation and source use here.

So far the best among rare efforts comparing modern Gallic imperial figures is Douglas Porch's article, "Bugeaud, Gallieni, Lyautey: The Development of French Colonial Warfare."[15] But though stimulating and valuable, Porch compares only their versions of colonial warfare, not the etiology of their characters, literary-artistic sides, building activities, and so on. His book *The Conquest of Morocco*[16] does advance some characterological views of Lyautey, but these require nuance.

Ours is, in fact, the first work offering much implicitly comparative *psychological* analysis, showing how these people all suffered in varying ways and degrees during their childhoods, or at the least, possessed the common trait of wanting to exceed social, professional, and geographical boundaries back in France. But mainly, this will be the first comparative study from a *literary* standpoint, yet simultaneously, from a *military* one, permitting more flexible thinking on these issues, and on the legacy of these proconsuls in Algeria, Senegal, Vietnam, etc. For our book goes on to sketch the "heirs" to these earlier imperial leaders, showing how they impacted policy both abroad and in Europe. We conclude with a "last of the line" figure, Marcel Bigeard, an anachronistic throwback to the era of the proconsuls, fighting in the doomed hellholes of French colonialism during the 1940s and '50s. Bigeard had and has a fine, if autodidactic French culture and character (why disassociate the two, as moderns too often do?). But he is also known for a record of exceptional, innovative military achievement.

In America Alice L. Conklin has pointed the way toward a nuanced integration of French colonial-military and intellectual/cultural history in a fine monograph, *A Mission to Civilize: The Republican Idea of Empire in France and West Africa, 1895–1930,*[17] as well as in a thought-provoking article, "Boundaries Unbound: Teaching French History as Colonial History and Colonial History as French History."[18] In the latter Conklin says that "the field of French colonial history is renewing itself dramatically at the moment," and that we need to include more on the *culture* of colonialism in our courses. She has also led the "nuancing" brigade of today's colonial historians in other welcome directions. When France still had a thriving empire, it took terms like "civilizing mission" literally and seriously. But in a postcolonial era of demystification through the 1990s, such terms were often held to be devoid of true content, and a new conventional wisdom was that "Europeans [simply] masked their baser motives for colonies—greed, national pride, the quest for power—in claims to civilize the 'natives' beyond their borders." However, Conklin adumbrates a "paradox of liberal empire building" by elaborating *along* with the brutality, all the enlightened things that nations like France accomplished abroad. Her work has truly helped those studying European imperialism to begin modifying accepted beliefs or shibboleths that had swept the field in the past forty years or so.[19]

A fine session at the 2001 American Historical Association meeting in Boston illustrated this dramatic renewal in French colonial studies denoted by Professor Conklin. Called "Narratives of Exploration and Empire in Nineteenth-Century France," the session featured a paper by Matt Matsuda on French images of supposedly pacific absorption of Tahiti in the later nineteenth century; and another by Alice Bullard on French intellectual excuses for the persistence (or toleration) of slavery in Senegal. Between those papers Edward Berenson, director of the Institute of French Studies at New York University, showed the evolution of his own research. Once a social historian firmly in the camp of John Merriman, Ted Margadant et al., Berenson has "gone colonial," but in the biographical, cultural, psychological way alluded to above. His paper on "The Explorer as Hero: Pierre Savorgnan de Brazza and the French Third Republic," gave us a foretaste of a doubtless fascinating book to come. Brazza, despite a thick Italian accent, became a major French hero around 1880 due to his clash with Henry Morton Stanley in the Congo, allowing France to claim a part of that area. But Berenson skilfully melds intellectual with military-colonial history, showing how the French media of the time helped create the hero, managing images of Brazza in photographs that portrayed him as a republican Moses, and magnifying his appeal as a mobbed, barefooted lecturer home from his travails abroad to enthrall large audiences. We also see how this intellectual-cultural background impinged on the political environment, helping create a republican consensus about colonial expansion that we discuss as well in chapter 4.

What of our inner biases that allow us to interpret facets of colonialism in these ways? Vigorous audience comments at that session showed that "subtexts" are also becoming a wave of the future, that even beyond the biographical urge in French colonial studies comes the autobiographical—i.e., psychoanalytical proclivities that send historians in certain directions, and that will become increasingly aired. Meanwhile scholars of World War I have also embraced a multifaceted approach to their research that resonates with our own findings here. Again in chapter 4 we show how the culture of key "colonials" helped create contrasting styles of command in that conflict. The prospectus for an international conference on the First World War held at Lyon's Institut d'Etudes Politiques in September 2001 mentioned "shifts in methodology" in this domain too, and an "academic upheaval which has meant that isolated study of the military, cultural, social or economic facets of the war is no longer possible."[20]

Our research and views should therefore help bridge a customary gap between military-colonial and intellectual/cultural history. Yet no one has pursued the path of a comparative dichotomy in modern French colonial greats—Bugeaud, Faidherbe, Gallieni, Lyautey, and nonproconsuls like Bigeard—showing how these figures were both adept at the art of war, and, in varying degrees, marvelously knowledgeable about French and other cultures (Faidherbe, for instance, was a remarkable scholar of Greek, Latin, and a number of African languages). As Porch and others have shown, their militarism abroad could include outright acts of brutality, sometimes mirroring those of their opponents. In the case of the proconsuls these were seen in the infamous *razzias*—tree-cutting, burning of crops, and so on. However, incongruous as it may sound, the exquisite cultures, intellectuality, and sensitivity they possessed may *also* be readily noted in their copious, interesting writings, which we treat at length here. No one again has compared these figures in terms of blending a genuinely protective side, seen in all the salutary, practical innovations such as vaccinations or new justice systems they supervised abroad; along *with* military toughness, even ruthlessness.

There are of course many Napoleon-obsessed history buffs who may simply say: wasn't this the exact characterological mix already seen in that celebrated Franco-Corsican? It is indubitably true that the French Revolutionary and Napoleonic eras of conquest helped launch France's *mission civilisatrice* to spread its light abroad in a second, post-1830 colonial empire; and that our core proconsuls in various parts of Africa or Asia certainly considered this a part of their assignments, though never in any dogmatic sense. (For in varying degrees all considered it important as well to respect and protect local traditions, differences, and rights.) It is also true that Napoleon had been a kind of enlightened despot, acting to reduce feudal inequities, abolish serfdom, liberate subject peoples from arbitrary leaders, establish constitutions, build roads, monuments, and institutions, and extend educational opportunties at least for new elites. In all our great proconsuls there was something as well of this enlightened despotism in their imperial *oeuvre*. Like Napoleon too, the greatest French "colonials" we treat were all well-read. They loved and felt history, generally knew the ancients, wrote tastefully, thought philosophically, and had few illusions about human nature. Like the emperor all used their culture, rather than just parading it; none could be called pedantic. Yet none was in any way a conscious emulator of Napoleon, and there were crucial differences from Bonaparte.

For one thing, none worshiped war with nearly the intensity that Napoleon had. None could have countenanced the sacrifice of piles of men to further some grand idea or ideal. Even Bugeaud, who learned important military lessons fighting in Napoleon's armies, had been repulsed by the sheer suffering he encountered in Spain, as well as on the road to great Napoleonic battles like Austerlitz. Faidherbe was a wonderful military leader in Senegal in the 1850s, but at bottom, as much a scholar or engineer as a soldier. And though Gallieni liked to reread Napoleon's correspondence and memoirs, he had the same philosophy about colonial warfare as his acolyte, Lyautey, especially in French Indochina, then Madagascar: one must possess the "heat," and be able to threaten its use, precisely in order to *avoid* employing it whenever possible. Once used, force was merely the prelude to pacification, and to the improvement of life for as many humans as came under one's influence. Gallieni also used his own specifically colonial experiences and wisdom to avoid misapplying Napoleonic doctrines before and during World War I.

Lyautey is probably the best example of an almost schizoid combination of military-organizational acumen, shown in his colonial assignments, and a superb culture. But though he became an enlightened despot of the Napoleonic stamp in the French protectorate of Morocco, he was actually no great fan of the diminutive empire-maker in Europe.

Our best imperial figures did seem to mirror—again, if not to emulate—the best of Napoleon's military views: how to use the element of surprise, how to improvise and adapt, how to avoid getting hooked on plans, how to use head and instincts to outwit foes of greater numbers, and how thereby, to win low-odds victories. But according to Porch, they did so in ways that were distinctly colonial and therefore, original.[21] This military ability would continue to be seen in some of the last defenders of the French Empire in its final agony after World War II—figures like de Lattre de Tassigny and especially Bigeard, prominently discussed in the last part of our book. The greatest example of a minor colonial figure who *did* misapply Napoleonic elan and "attack philosophy" remains Joffre, France's lethal Chief of Staff for a good part of World War I. But the best of our modern imperialists seemed to reflect the best and avoid the worst of Napoleon's legacy.

Yet another significant difference between Bonaparte and the great colonials who followed his era was that the former never totally transcended his origins. One of Napoleon's failings derived from family feeling, impelling him to place relatives of varying quality at the heads of his satellite kingdoms of Europe. Our proconsuls were in some sense all unfamilial misfits, individual operants who became their full selves far from home (though Bugeaud would certainly have been known as a great agricultural reformer in his native region of the Périgord-Limousin had he not gone abroad to supervise France's conquest of Algeria). As well, none of our major figures suffered from a vendetta mentality, as Napoleon did, and we can see none, except for the stupidly optimistic Joffre, embarking on an operation remotely akin to the emperor's invasion of Russia.

Finally, Napoleon centered his power on Paris, continuing in the centralizing path of Louis XIV and other Old Regime monarchs; whereas our "makers and defenders" in colonial fora often opposed the big bad wolf of a far-off capital and its *a priori* assumptions, regulations, and views. They continually revised in light of what they encountered abroad, embodying a Lockean empiricism, where Napoleon was more Cartesian. From his Paris vantage point the latter liked to know exactly what was going on at a certain hour in every *lycée* of France; whereas our imperial personnel needed to know why this valley or clan in the middle of nowhere was different from that one, and what needed to be done on the spot, owing to local or regional variety, and to changing conditions. All these colonial leaders deeply distrusted Parisian bureaucratic thinking about a terrifically diverse and fluid French empire.

It would be simplistic, in other words, to make Napoleon a central part of some paradigm here. We have larger concerns in this book—one being to provide a more nuanced image of the French brand of colonialism, and of Western imperialism generally. A second is to offer some revisionist thinking about France's performance in war since 1815 or so. For when people hear of the modern martial French both in Europe and around the world, they too often assume that by and large they didn't fight very effectively. The debacle of 1940 at the hands of the Nazis, then nation-scarring defeats in their colonial empire of the '50s are fixed in many minds as representing perpetual (and simplified) French traits at war. In this book we again emphasize that some of France's key imperial figures—men of real culture and character—were also great military leaders; and more, that the French imperial effort itself was often quite a noble and utilitarian endeavor, and at the least, an interesting one.

In chapter 1, a background chapter, we treat distinctive personalities of the "First French Empire," men like Dupleix and La Bourdonnais in India—an empire largely lost by the end of the Napoleonic era. Then in subsequent chapters we move to the heart of our book with Bugeaud and his adherents in Algeria; Faidherbe in Senegal and West Africa; Gallieni in Sudan, Vietnam, and Madagascar; and Lyautey in those places and Morocco. We close our account with Bigeard, who as noted, fought in and against the death throes of France's empire in Indochina and North

Africa during the 1940s and '50s. We hope to show what these men and their adherents, sometimes misunderstood or undervalued at home until they directed energies outward, accomplished abroad, hoping also to dispel certain shibboleths that even now clog our vision of French and (really of all) Western imperialism. We will not paint with one sunny revisionist brush, but will at least qualify what too often comes out on historical pages in one, unrelievedly dark hue.

For on hearing the word "imperialism," too many automatically assume that it is invariably a bad thing, or at least always the same *kind* of thing. This view of imperial history is about as simplified as religious dogma. In actuality, there were rarely nirvanas before the Western colonial era. In fact, there were usually earlier forms of imperialism, such as Arab incursions into great swaths of Africa, which brought widespread slavery, among other things. In many disparate areas there were also frequent intertribal or clan rivalries, devastating internecine struggles that the advent of powers like the French (at least in the modern era) often helped attenuate. There were also crippling superstitions and frequently, ineffective medical procedures, which again Western standards altered, creating rapid population growth in such areas. Writers like Frantz Fanon averred that postcolonial eras of plenitude would invariably recapitulate some ideal pre-European harmony, which is a misleading perspective. Algeria, for instance, had large problems before the French, and would badly deteriorate after France's departure.

Much better than Fanon's intellectual mathematicism, as we might call it, is Chinua Achebe's nuanced evocation of traditional Ibo (or Igbo) society in *Things Fall Apart*. As many know, the book evokes a "world we have lost" of beautiful rhythms marked by reverence for the seasons, and a variety of religious festivals and customs; by folktales handed from generation to generation; by rules; and by special foods like roasted locusts. But it was also a world of medicinal superstition, and from today's perspective, a certain chauvinism in men who needed to rule multiple wives and children. This even included ritual murders of the latter, and of course "manly," but lethal tribal warfare. Achebe has the sensitivity to nuance on British colonialism, which shattered the old order, but also gave him a university education, and a language and culture to evoke the story of his own area. He continued to apprehend the complexity of a tragic postcolonial situation, where indeed British creation of something called "Nigeria" was partly to blame for the massacre and mutilation of Ibos in the late 1960s. Fanon notwithstanding, so also was the jihad of expansionist Islam.[22]

What needs to be emphasized is that imperialism of different stripes—
not simply modern *Western* imperialism—has been a constant of history.
The very language you are reading here is mainly a result of Roman imperialism and then of the Anglo-Saxon incursion into England, another form
of imperialism (over the Celts). One could also throw in the Norman
invasion and takeover of England in the eleventh century. Imperialistic
war made the language of Shakespeare, F. Scott Fitzgerald, and Churchill?
Unfortunately, there is something to this paradox, however inconvenient
it may sound.

Besides arguing the pervasive quality of imperialism in history, we
would again like to stress—at least from what we know of French and
other Western varieties—its paradoxical mix of positives and negatives. In
this opening chapter we have decided to show this by examining in a very
cursory manner certain "case studies" that seem to make our point.

To open, one might look at the founding of the Belgian Congo during
the 1880s. Belgium's involvement here started with King Leopold II's
support of the Welshman Stanley's expedition into the Congo in the late
1870s. Leopold then became sovereign of a gigantic Congo Free State,
ratified by the Berlin Congo Conference (or Berlin Conference on Africa)
between November 1884 and February 1885. Motivations included the usual
mix of enhanced national prestige, exploratory adventure, economic gain,
particularly from ivory and rubber, and "civilizing." Imperial-minded Belgians were proud that Leopold's Congo was some eighty times bigger than
the mother country, that it offered much scope for settlers and missionaries, and that their king was made more august by its acquisition.[23]

On the plus side the Belgians shed their own blood to rid the Congo
once and for all of Arab slave-traders who had replaced a once-vigorous
European trade. It also took modern machinery from Europe to blast
out copper or gold from Congolese mines that couldn't have been tapped
with indigenous technologies. On the minus side, cheap labor was recruited by coercion. As late as the 1920s there would be hardly more than
10,000 whites in the Belgian Congo, versus some 12,000,000 blacks. Among
the latter, shamanistic medicine had done little to alleviate scourges like
malaria, until European medicine brought quinine and other remedies.

But one certainly sickens learning of a Belgian training establishment
for elephant catching, which mobilized tribespeople to decimate these
animals in search of ivory tusks that, among other things, helped make
beautiful music in the concert halls of Europe. Just as sad was the Belgian proliferation of gunnery that eventually extirpated great gorilla and

chimpanzee populations, fascinating to foreign visitors as manifestations of our evolutionary past. Eventually, European steamers would be routinely plying the Congo River so "sportsmen" could jump off into the interior and shoot at these creatures.[24]

For some reason one feels almost as bad about the melancholy fate of these innocent animals as about the fate of humans in the area; but there is no question that the Congo became a sanguinary place for its people, especially due to the monumental greed and brutality associated with the rubber trade. This was the infamous "red rubber," collected by native sweat and blood. During the period from about 1892 to 1910 rubber was to Belgium and its Congo what cotton had been to Britain during the Industrial Revolution. Profits were for a time enormous. Rubber had been of little utility until the mid-nineteenth century, but with Goodyear's vulcanization process, allowing it to withstand heat and cold, and then in 1888 John Dunlop's invention of the first pneumatic tire, a great locomotion revolution in bicycles and automobiles began in Europe and America.

In the 1880s Africa provided only 5 percent of the world's rubber, but by 1900 the figure had risen to over 30 percent, and the Congo showed the most dramatic increase. Ironically, the Belgians had abolished slavery, but now terrorized Africans into going deeper and deeper into dangerous forests to procure rubber vines from the trees. At an extreme those who faltered were whipped, had hands cut off, homes burned, and spouses or daughters taken to hostage houses, where they were threatened or outright raped. At the very least the result was a total disruption of the rhythm of tribal lives. By about 1904, with rubber vines mostly gone in the Congo, these abuses were resounding in European ears, thanks to humanitarian obsessionals like E. D. Morel, who in that year founded the Congo Reform Association. By 1908 international protest forced the Belgian government to wrest control of the colony from its monarch. Even today oral histories of certain Congolese regions are rife with the memory of the rubber era that created so much suffering.[25]

And yet, was all of Belgium's influence in the Congo bad? It would be temptingly simplistic to say that it was, or to keep blaming the departed Belgians for intertribal slaughters that continue to rage on in countries once belonging to them. It is true that the Belgian Congo became anything but the high moral experiment Leopold II and his successor Albert had hoped it would be; also true that the mother country failed to nurture an elite that could adequately replace it. Still it wasn't all bad, nor the only "bad" on history's ample menu of imperial evils.

In the case of the great British colony of India we can again see historical positives and negatives plentifully intertwined. In chapter 1 we
discuss more extensively Britain's competition with the French over the
subcontinent, and its victory there in the eighteenth century. Then from
the nineteenth century British hegemony in India undoubtedly had pejora-
tive consequences, including economic exploitation, inequities, and some
brutality. But what of the positive aspects? What of British Governor-
General Wellesley's edict forbidding the drowning of female Indian children in the ocean off Saugur Island? Or British opposition to the Hindu
practice of *suttee*—the burning of widows on their husbands' funeral
pyres? Lord William Bentinck, another governor-general in India, finally
abolished *suttee* (1829), along with female infanticide, mutilation, and
torture, though these practices continued in remote areas. Then there was
the ostensibly religious practice of *thugi*, whereby robber groups would
ambush travelers, take their booty, and ritually strangle them to appease
the Mother Goddess Kali. To which one might counter, *et tu, Brute*, and
rightfully so. All religious pasts are full of intolerance, of which the European and British witchcraft craze constitutes only one of many horrifying
examples; but clichéd as it sounds, two wrongs hardly make a right. Gang
robbery had been a kind of epidemic in central and northern India, and
indigenous travelers were certainly happy to gain protection afforded by
the British.[26]

The two-edged sword of Western imperialism appears again when one
considers the spread of British technology in colonial India. Large industrial concerns supplanted local economies, leading to long hours for low
pay, and an English-dominated mercantile economy, whereby Lancashire
cotton mills received cheap raw material, then sold finished goods back
to the colony. On the other hand the railway boom in India, especially
from 1850 or so, had unintended effects. Railways had been built to transport British-made imports into India's far-flung regions and to bring
out coal and raw cotton more efficiently. But Indian passengers flocked to
these new conveyances, helping thereby to unify a giant subcontinent with
little potential of becoming a real country. The railways also made it possible to transport foodstuffs quickly to regions that had suffered periodic
famines. A British canal-building boom also helped accomplish the same
thing.[27]

What other British advances did great numbers of Indians see fit to use?
Dr. William O'Shaughnessy had the first Indian telegraph line laid in 1851,
and eventually far-flung cities were linked up—enhancing opportunities

for nationalism to take hold. The penny post was to the average person one of the biggest imperial miracles of all. Assuming one could read or write, or find someone to do so, Indians could now communicate with relatives in areas that had previously seemed like remote planets, which again helped instill a growing unity. Bad? If one deems the preservation of local cultures important—bad. But if one considers the formation of modern states and the enrichment of many lives worthwhile, then these contributions were good.

Equally two-edged were the effects of educational institutions that Britain sprinkled over India, creating an Anglicized Indian elite that included men like Gandhi and Nehru. Stanley Wolpert emphasizes the role here of T. B. Macaulay, "whose victory in the defense of English education for Indians accelerated demands for the demise of British rule by arming India's elite with the [very] words in which to call for it."[28]

Even the caste system, which the British again helped eradicate, becomes part of our "two-edged sword" argument. On the positive attributes of this old system J. H. Hutton notes: "[One's] caste canalizes [the Hindu's] choice in marriage, acts as his trade union, his friendly or benefit society, his slate club and his orphanage; it takes the place for him of health insurance, and if need be provides for his funeral."[29]

But certainly most would now condemn—as the British did—the indignities of Untouchability. Members of this group had to live in utter segregation, avoiding certain streets or if within earshot of higher caste Hindus, needed to cry out to warn of a polluting presence. Born to their condition by virtue of fate (karma), due to sins committed in an earlier life, they could at least look forward to the possibility of improvement in the next one. No wonder Gandhi warred against this disability, putting Untouchables (to the consternation of nauseated adherents) in his ashrams. In theory Untouchability was finally abolished by the Indian Constitution of 1949, but aspects of it have lingered on, and again, can one truly blame the British, who helped initiate its demise?[30]

Turning to another case study, Dutch imperialism in the Indonesian archipelago, we again encounter such two-edged themes. Here was another small European country eventually absorbing an area over fifty times its size and with a much higher population, a population that European technology and medical standards helped increase greatly. As usual, the Dutch had hardly been the first to crisscross these beautiful islands. Negritos, Chinese, Indochinese, and Malays were among earlier immigrants to the area. In the centuries after Christ, Hindus had proselytized in parts of

Indonesia, and during the Middle Ages it was the turn of a more successful Islam, brought by Arab and Persian merchants. (Today's Indonesia
still contains more Muslims than any nation in the world.) Much ethnic
intermingling occurred before the Europeans arrived in their age of discovery. These Europeans would include Portuguese and Spanish, then the
Dutch in the seventeenth century. In the next century, the English flexed
their military muscles, winning nearly all of this vast area. At the close of
the Napoleonic wars, however, they returned Java and other parts to the
Dutch, in order to concentrate on Malaya and Singapore.[31]

Economic concerns were one motivation for a sustained Dutch presence here. European demand for a tasty stimulant made them plant coffee
trees all around Java in ever-bigger plantations. One assumes that even
Marxists—possibly old Karl himself—took time out from their denunciations of imperialism to have a cup. In addition to coffee profits, much
money came into Dutch coffers from tea, cinnamon, quinine, indigo,
and especially tobacco, whose production in the East Indies grew tenfold
between 1870 and 1890. Not to mention sugar production that more
than doubled in that era (as did coffee itself), tin mining whose output
close to quintupled, and the beginnings of a great imperial motivator of
the modern era, oil. (From only 300 metric tons in 1889 the Dutch were
already producing some 363,000 by 1900 in this area.)

Was that meteoric leap in capitalist-imperialistic production on Java
and other Indonesian islands all bad? Again, one surefire indicator of
the relative beneficence of the Dutch presence was a dramatic population
increase. In Java alone, the population surged upward from 2.5 million
souls in 1800 to some 28 million a century later; and, after liberation from
the Dutch, to 63 million by 1961. The total population of Indonesia today
stands at over 160 million, making it the world's largest island nation, with
Java alone containing over 90 million people. Giant irrigation works introduced by the Dutch, producing more arable land, constituted one reason
for this development, railways another. Dutch hygiene standards also contributed—with progressive victories over plague, dysentery ("beri/beri"),
and other prevalent diseases.

In terms of decency Dutch imperialists in Indonesia ought to be ranked
quite high. They were truly tolerant of religion in the general region, and
even their war on the use of drugs by the indigenous, especially Malays,
does not strike one as totally illiberal, given that hemp smoking could
supposedly make these people depressed or violent (running "amok" was
the term employed there). But as in the Belgian Congo, Dutch gunnery

facilitated an increasing holocaust of animals, especially tigers, whose skins were exported to different palaces, and poor rhinos, whose horns were spiritually and medicinally used by Chinese and Javanese; not to mention the repulsive netting of birds like parakeets and cockatoos for use in China and Europe. Nearby Singapore became one of the world's greatest emporia for imperialism's silent victims. As a visitor to that city in the 1920s, Paul Morand, noted: "External and inexpiable prisoners of war, they arrive from the depth of the jungle and the tips of the trees, streaming towards a few Chinese shops that stink of the carrion of vultures, the musk of rats, the odor of civet cats rising in the smoke of incense burned to the protecting Buddha." Having his civilized cocktail at the Raffles hotel, Morand tried not to think too much of such animals ending up behind bars, seething in their trapped fury; but these silent victims of European technology and greed remain in memory to haunt us.[32]

By 1911 there were a good 80,000 Europeans in Indonesia, mostly Dutch. But nothing seems to promote eventual failure better than success—one of our themes as well concerning French imperial efforts; and once the Dutch had succeeded in the material realm, they then felt they had to uplift Indonesia morally. The "Ethical Policy," first proclaimed by Queen Wilhelmina in 1901, and translated into enhanced educational opportunities, would help create the usual indigenous elite to eventually expel an imperial power. The Dutch also made Malay Indonesia's official language, which along with common use of Dutch, aided in nationalistic unification. Dutch *Ethici* not only pushed for better educational facilities, but better credit, improved health programs, more autonomy for local authorities, and the reduction of opium use. The idea was to spread enlightenment, but the most important result was a staggering rise in anti-Dutch nationalism. Dutch Indonesia remained a rich colonial area up to World War II, supplying some 90 percent of the world's quinine, over 80 percent of its pepper, and a good 30 percent of its rubber, as well much sugar, coffee, and oil. But growingly, the same assault on shaky Western security occurred, as in many other colonial areas, and Communism made seductive inroads.[33]

During World War II Holland's colonial perishability was revealed by its ultra-rapid defeat at Nazi hands; but Indonesian inhabitants old enough to remember it still shudder at the new Japanese brand of imperialism that followed. After the war came the inevitable "packing-up" syndrome of tired Europeans, followed by an unstable but independent Indonesia since 1949, marked by Sukarno's leadership tending toward dictatorship, followed by General Suharto's bloody coup of 1965. (Both men, by the way, were typical products of the Dutch-created elite—Sukarno having studied civil engineering at the Bandung Technical Institute, and Suharto graduating from cadre school at Gombong.)

Moving finally to the proximate colonial case of French Indochina, which will garner much space in our book, we again confront similar paradoxes. In Vietnam the Annamese, who would dominate the future country, had themselves been incomers as a nomadic people, probably from Tibet. Around the time of Christ they occupied Tonkin or northern Annam, and their history would henceforth reveal both imitation of and resistance to Chinese imperialism, as well as their own expansionist tendencies southward. The Chinese had already begun colonizing Tonkin and Annam a couple of centuries before Christ, and totally annexed those areas around 180 A.D. The Annamese would then absorb Chinese ways, but try tenaciously to retain their own identity in the face of a more populous and sophisticated northern neighbor, revolting several times, with final success in 939 A.D.[34]

The period that followed was a confused one, with some fifteen Annamite dynasties and much warring among factions, not to mention imperialistic incursions by the Mongols (who sacked Hanoi in 1257), the temporary resurgence of the Hindu Chams (who sacked it in 1371), and others. The coming of the Europeans after 1600 coincided with increasing Annamite ventures southward toward Saigon, as well as their wars with contiguous Khmers and Laotians, and much pirating, massacring, and anarchy (some also perpetrated by Chinese or Cambodians). The Emperor of Annam remained mysterious and unpredictable. On the downside, the precolonial era was characterized by dynastic vicissitudes, an in-the-clouds mandarinate, widespread opium use, and supersitious medical standards before France intervened; on the upside, the Annamese were a tough, supple people, and their ceremonies of birth or marriage had wonderful depth and beauty.[35]

The last centuries before the French takeover were ones of intense feuding and almost constant war, in good part on north-south lines that continued into the twentieth century. But the Annamese also brought a certain coherence to the region, having partitioned Tonkin in the north and Cochin China in the south into separate states in 1673, successfully taken on the Hindu Chams, and then expelled the Cambodians from Cochin China. However, as late as 1820 their occupation there was confined to a relatively small part of the Mekong delta—poor rainfall and fear of malaria inhibiting a transfer of people from the bloated north to the less populous south. In 1820 much of what became Vietnam was still very poor, prey to Chinese usury and venal justice, and rife with mosquito-borne malaria that made lives in some parts predictably short. According to Edmund Roberts, a U.S. envoy traveling in Cochin China during the early 1830s, "the inhabitants [surrounding the bay] are without exception the most filthy people in the world." Leprosy, smallpox, bad teeth, and constant itching were undoubtedly exacerbated by an aversion to washing ("in the course of a whole month ... I have not seen a person bathe, although beaches abound everywhere"). Chronic rice shortages, fear of spirits, and despotic leaders certainly did not help.[36]

Would the French become perfect saviors there? Of course not. But in certain respects they *did* constitute an improvement over the turbulence of a Vietnamese past sketchily delineated here; and in much the same manner as seen in other colonial areas. As A. D. C. Peterson generalizes, "by Asiatic standards, the Western administrations of America, Britain, Holland or France have been probably the most just and certainly the most merciful in the [entire] history of the Far East."[37]

The first French presence in Vietnam was dominated by Catholic missionaries, but protection of these missionaries became in part a cover for expansion. During the nineteenth century a Catholic revival in France led to increasing proselytization abroad, and the French also wished to establish trade routes to China.

All this became the background for France's invasion of Cochin China, much of it absorbed by a treaty with the Emperor of Annam in 1862, including Saigon. (We provide more detail on all this in chapters 4 and 7.) Then it was the turn of contiguous Cambodia, and partly in the serendipitous way of all imperialism, there followed France's arduous conquest of coastal Annam and northern Tonkin from 1867 to its completion two decades later.

By 1899 a federalized Indochinese Union again revealed Western imperialism as the progenitor of unified national states. The French instituted a regime of both direct and supposedly indirect rule here, with a governor-general (often of high quality) at the top. Beneath, there was a Governor of Cochin China and four Residents-Superior of the protectorates of Annam, Tonkin, Cambodia, and Laos (finalized by 1907).

Under the French deltas of both north and south would become greater rice producers, thanks to a costly scheme of irrigation, especially an extensive canal system. The rubber industry under Gallic plantation owners (nicely glimpsed in the Catherine Deneuve vehicle *Indochine* of 1991) took off from a mere 300 tons of production in 1900 to some 70,000 by 1939. It is debatable, as we later show, how much good this French monopoly did for the average Vietnamese worker or peasant. The industrial north also began to mine and export much anthracite coal, tin and zinc; some cotton was spun in mills; and of course rice exports increased dramatically. In addition to modern irrigation systems, over 30,000 kilometers of roads, about half paved, and some 3,000 kilometers of railroads (by the 1930s) averted famines and allowed the population to explode. The relative beneficence of the French presence is again demonstrated not only by a good doubling of the Vietnamese population through to World War II, but by a huge increase in Chinese immigration to the area too. From a mere 45,000 in the southern province of Cochin China in 1880, the Chinese, attracted to French Saigon and environs, would number roughly 3,000,000 by 1936.[38]

The French made Hanoi and Saigon glittering cultural jewels, though the former outshone the latter. Hanoi had long been the Chinese and Anna-mite capital, where Saigon was almost an ad hoc Gallic progeny, "a French city flowering alone out of a tropical swamp in the farthest corner of Asia."[39] Little wonder that Hanoi became the more important administrative and cultural center, given its array of fine museums, a world-renowned Ecole française d'Extrême-Orient, fine medical facilities, and the Université de Hanoi, which along with the lycées trained a Vietnamese elite, including Ho Chi Minh and General Giap, students who would again learn to overthrow their teachers.

French medicine truly made an impact in preserving and increasing these lives that would revolt, and given that rice constituted a good nine-tenths of an average Vietnamese diet, so did agricultural benefits mentioned. As much as the Dutch helped make modern Indonesia, the French—with all the pros and cons tallied up—helped create what became modern Vietnam. How long should we blame them for the nation's contemporary problems and poverty?[40]

Moving over to another gem mentioned in that Franco-Indochinese diadem, Cambodia had perhaps most required a French protective presence. In fact without that presence its demise would certainly have occurred before the twentieth century. For despite a once great Khmer or Angkor Empire, at times ruling other swaths of Indochina, Cambodia was often prey to bigger and tougher neighbors. Once mired under the inevitable Chinese a millennium ago, the region then succumbed around

1500 to Thai, and later, Vietnamese incursions, which by the eighteenth century nearly made the very entity of Cambodia extinct. Only struggles between these neighboring jackals allowed a stricken prey to struggle on through the 1840s as a vassal of squabbling imperial rivals. The country's disappearance was only delayed by temporary division of a Thai-dominated western Cambodia from a Viet-dominated east.

Then came France. Searching for a route to the Chinese trade up the Mekong River, the French took Cambodia in the same somewhat serendipitous manner as it did other colonies. In 1863 it established a "protectorate" there, a term that may sound ironic, but in fact wasn't all euphemism. These accidental tourists would make Cambodia a mostly peaceful place for virtually a century. The French would flatly call Cambodians lazier and more submissive than the Vietnamese, and that ethno-impression, combined with one of a certain nobility, struck foreign visitors up until the 1950s and '60s. In his travel book of 1940, Osbert Sitwell called Cambodians the most beautiful race he had ever beheld, noting that they "possess the most exquisite manners, traditionally one of the marks and relics of any high civilisation that has passed away."[41] His postmortem may have been early, but would soon be corroborated. Sitwell added that without the French, whom the Cambodians treated well, they themselves realized they would soon be extinguished by more energetic neighbors. Peterson has called pre–Khmer Rouge Cambodia "a sort of charming museum piece, an Indo-Chinese Bali," and for Charles Fisher this was "an essentially unsophisticated and easy-going people . . . strangely remote from the achievements of their ancestors."[42]

The French brought economic prosperity, abolished slavery, fought venal tax rackets, and after 1904 basically chose Cambodian kings, thereby averting dynastic struggles and civil wars. Phnom Penh became a beautiful city with Gallic architecture, bars, cafés, villas, and courtyards, and contained a population of up to a half million souls.

Again, World War II had its impact, bringing a much tougher Japanese imperialism that controlled Cambodia partly by using Thai "clients," though Vichy France still maintained a presence, as it did in Vietnam. After the war Cambodian nationalism, the narcissistic ambitions of King Norodom Sihanouk, and French preoccupation with the Vietnamese quagmire—described in our chapters 7 and 8—led to complete independence by the end of 1954. By then Communist growth made the country's future unclear.

To continue sketching paradoxes that Western imperialism and postimperialism force us to consider, Cambodia in its Indian summer era under the God-king Sihanouk tried to steer between Americans and Vietnamese Communists during the 1960s. Allowing the latter their sanctuaries did not exactly endear Sihanouk to the Americans, and for a while, he severed diplomatic relations. In the spring of 1970, while he was abroad for medical treatment, a military coup ensued, and Cambodia basically split into two factions—the Khmer Rouge, supported by Chinese and Vietnamese Communists, and the pro-American side, led by General Lon Nol, who wanted the Viets out.

For those who require a refresher course, on April 17, 1975 the Khmer Rouge ended this ruinous civil war in triumphant victory, making people in Phnom Penh cheer vociferously. Was the trouble in the former French "Cambodge" over? As we know, it was only beginning. Of all the examples of a postimperial tumble from frying pan into a fire of immensely greater intensity, Cambodia provides the most poignant one, though Algeria, Uganda, and many others certainly rank high as well. For there now ensued what John Barron calls *Murder of a Gentle Land*—not at the hands of invading Vietnamese, Thais, French, or Americans, but of indigenous Khmer Rouge, who soon operated in a grisly manner. All possessions, including bicycles and autos, were confiscated, banks were abolished, and currency went up in smoke. So did the contents of great French libraries, if they weren't first tossed into the Mekong River. Quickly gone too were schools, temples, and even the postal system. Rapidly as well came the mass evacuation of a capital city swollen by civil war into a metropolis of some 3,000,000. At gunpoint masses of people were herded out—from hospital sickbeds, in pregnancy, none of that mattered. Bazookas rocketed into the houses of people who wouldn't leave. Thirsty infants in crushing heat cried amid executions and marches. Phnom Penh became a kind of ghost town, and thanks to the Big Brother-type "Organization on High," a huge experiment in instant ruralization and self-sufficiency turned rice fields where people labored into the infamous "killing fields." Here Khmer thugs laughingly murdered with plastic bags, bayonets, knives, axes, and guns, or to prove sadistic credentials, by pulling out nails or pinning ears to walls during lengthy interrogations, or extricating livers from live victims. With Phnom Penh in ruins and the entire country in agony, most Cambodians of 1977 might well have regretted France's vanished colonial regime.[43] Another imperialism, that of the Communist Vietnamese, would terminate the destruction of the Killing Fields at the end of 1978; but Cambodia has never truly recovered.

In sum, was Western, or French, imperialism all bad? Not if one looks closely at large parts of history in a variety of places. Was it all good? Of course not, and if in the following pages we stack our deck with some of the most interesting makers and areas of the modern French empire, we do so in part to right a tilted interpretational ship to a more balanced mid-point. As noted, we also wish perhaps to impart that one shouldn't gibe so readily at something that is relatively decent; much worse is always possible![44]

But enough tilting at interpretive windmills; on to what an American radio personality calls "the rest of the story" . . .

CHAPTER ONE

France's First Empire

Gains and Losses

Before embarking on the great age of post-Napoleonic proconsuls abroad, we must provide an overview of what we call the First French Empire, an interesting and crucial bridge to our main story of the nineteenth and twentieth centuries. The earliest French efforts to establish an overseas empire began when reports of Spanish imperialism in the New World, especially of Cortés in Mexico between 1519 and 1521, caught the attention of Francis I, the talented and impetuous French monarch of that era. The latter sent an Italian mariner Giovanni de Verrazzano on a voyage of exploration, and in 1524 Verrazzano apparently sailed up the eastern seaboard from Cape Fear to Newfoundland. His scouting expedition then prepared the way for Jacques Cartier, whose three voyages between 1534 and 1541 acquainted France with the Saint Lawrence River as far south as what became Montreal.

Following the death of Francis I, amateur explorers from towns like Dieppe, Honfleur, or Rouen tried to establish Gallic settlements in Madagascar, the Indies, and America; but searing religious wars that wracked France in the last quarter of the sixteenth century impeded any sustained colonial efforts.[1] After those wars ended, the great Samuel de Champlain explored the Acadian coast of today's Maritimes, founded Quebec City in 1608, and a year later sailed into the beautiful lake that bears his name. These exploits, among others, encouraged King Louis XIII's first minister, Cardinal Richelieu, to begin colonization of what was called New France—in theory, all territory between Florida and the Arctic Circle. But the French had neither cash nor interest to pursue such an ambitious course with any depth. Explorations like those of the Jesuit Father Jacques Marquette and his companion Louis Joliet, followed by the 1682 expedition of Robert de La Salle established French claims to the Mississippi Valley. Two decades later Antoine de Cadillac founded the settlement of Détroit, a crucial location for controlling the passage between Lakes Huron and Erie. But these were isolated, if significant colonial achievements, not least in economic benefits associated mainly with the fur trade.

More ambitious were French efforts to establish a foothold on the vast subcontinent of India. To that purpose Louis XIV and his industrious finance minister, Colbert, established in August 1664 the joint-stock Compagnie des Indes Orientales in August 1664. The idea was to project French power toward the Indies and outdo a great competitor, the Dutch, as controllers of the region's commerce.[2] After several abortive ventures, in 1670 the Compagnie acquired a small fishing and trading port in the Carnatic (the southeastern tip of India), called Pondichéry. Its hinterland was a cotton-producing region, and Shirkan-Loudi, governor of Cuddalore, allowed the French to begin settling there. Situated between the Ariankuppam River and the Indian Ocean, Pondichéry was strategically important, given the presence in the region of the Dutch, Portuguese, and particularly, the English.[3] Next came France's acquisition of Chandernagor in 1690 and Calcutta in 1701, and within three decades Pondichéry became a French colonial outpost with a population of 50,000.

During this period both French and English East India Companies played ambiguous, dual roles. Designed to increase the wealth of their nations, they also pursued political objectives in India with relative impunity, given the primitive nature of communication with the mother countries.

The French coveted a variety of commodities here, with textiles constituting 50 percent of the value of the India trade, including muslins, silks and cottons, and a quarter of the trade in spices, particularly pepper, essential for the preservation of meat. Incense, coffee, tea, and Bengali saltpeter rounded out a lucrative commercial menu. The profit margin on such Indian commodities was extremely high, running to 300 percent in silk, 400 percent in cottons, 420 percent in pepper, and 1500 percent in saltpeter.[4]

In the eighteenth century France's position in India would be fortified and expanded by the actions of a truly unusual figure, Joseph-François Dupleix. Born in France's Nord in 1697 and raised in Brittany, Dupleix had a father who was an official of the Compagnie des Indes, specializing in tobacco importation. After the early death of his mother, the young

Dupleix attended a Jesuit secondary school in Brittany, but worried about the boy's uncommercial proclivity for mathematics and other bookish subjects, his father packed him off to India in 1720, obtaining an appointment for him as counselor to the Compagnie des Indes in Pondichéry. Though Dupleix Senior was a wealthy man, his son arrived in India without a *sou* to his name. Both a dreamer and planner, Joseph Dupleix wanted to make a fortune here, seeking to augment French trade and the contents of his own pocket at the expense of the Compagnie's British rivals.[5]

Mounting in the Compagnie's bureaucracy, Dupleix was appointed director for Bengal in 1731, a position that put him in charge of the Compagnie's holdings at Chandernagor. He wasted no time shaking things up and turned out to be an astute and ambitious entrepreneur. Supervising a staff of fourteen, he built warehouses, brought expenses under control, and worked incessantly to increase the number and size of French vessels doing business with Bengal. Even so, Dupleix couldn't turn a real profit for France, partly due to the devastating Bengali cyclone of 1737, which destroyed many buildings, and to shipwrecks, which in the 1730s affected almost half the vessels chartered by the Compagnie. (Indian Ocean weather has always been known for its turbulent unpredictability.)

Despite such setbacks, Dupleix attracted a good deal of notice. He was a clever administrator with an eye and nose for money, a truly ambitious, if unscrupulous man who might be outthought but would never be outworked. He was also vain, emotional, arrogant, hot-headed, and self-righteous, managing to alienate virtually everyone with whom he worked, especially military officers.

In January 1742 he succeeded Benôit Dumas as Governor of Pondichéry, and just before that appointment married his best friend's widow, a "half-caste" of thirty-three who had already been married once as a young teen, producing eleven children, five of whom continued living with her and Dupleix. Born in Pondichéry, the French Governor's spouse spoke a number of regional dialects and became a valuable source of diplomatic connections for her husband. But like Dupleix she too was an inveterate intriguer, and almost as much of a know-it-all. The couple's skills would soon in fact be tested. For three years after Dupleix' assumption of the governorship, during the War of the Austrian Succession, the British began attacking French vessels engaged in the India trade. A neutrality agreement of 1701 had not been renewed, and Pondichéry found itself fatally squeezed between English forts at Cuddalore and Madras. Dupleix now wanted the French fleet to protect the city.

The fleet's commander was Bertrand François Mahé de la Bourdonnais, another quirky character of the sort our colonial story will keep bringing to the fore. Born in 1699, la Bourdonnais had grown up in the Breton port of Saint-Malo, and naturally focused his energies on the sea. As a teenager he embarked on voyages to the East, where he developed a passion for navigation and for a domineering mode of commanding those beneath him. At twenty-five the swashbuckling captain became part of a French fleet sent to relieve the town of Mahé in the Seychelles, which had fallen to the English. The French managed to retake the town in December 1725, thanks largely to a disembarkation raft designed by la Bourdonnais himself. This exploit gave the young man a decidedly swelled head, which in tandem with his violent, eruptive personality, made other people in the Compagnie despise him even more than they did Dupleix. Good relations between two such strong-willed figures would have constituted a minor miracle, but unfortunately for the French, no such miracle was forthcoming.[6]

In 1745 la Bourdonnais commanded French forces on Ile-de-France (today's Mauritius), a small island off the southeastern coast of Africa. By all accounts he ran this base well, overcoming tremendous obstacles in creating a jumping-off point to service and protect French holdings throughout the Indian Ocean. Meanwhile, Governor Dupleix wanted to stymie English raiders by taking Madras and dismantling Fort Saint-George, whose guns provided English ships a safe refuge. As long as Madras seemed out of danger, the English had agreed to refrain from attacking French Pondichéry; but Commodore Curtis Barnett broke that agreement, assembling a naval squadron to seize French shipping off the Carnatic coast. One of his prizes included a vessel carrying the lion's share of Dupleix' personal fortune, and this provocation stung the latter into summoning the man he execrated, la Bourdonnais, for the assault on Madras.

Together these two imposing personalities would have to plan the destruction of the English fleet, and their attack on Madras became a cooperative venture rendered more difficult by la Bourdonnais' tardiness in answering Dupleix' summons. The former only arrived in Pondichéry with his nine ships in July 1746, a few months after Dupleix had called urgently for help. Dupleix spent those months fuming, though given the distance between la Bourdonnais' base of Ile-de-France and the Carnatic, a delay of that proportion hardly seems outlandish. La Bourdonnais requested additional armaments, but Dupleix trimmed down his order by a third, preferring to spend the Compagnie's resources on his own militia to assault Madras by land. French military leadership here would be divided between these two very different, but eccentric personalities, Dupleix on land and la Bourdonnais at sea, with neither a clear-cut superior.

Fortunately for France, England's Barnett died unexpectedly after putting in at Fort Saint David, and his replacement, Edward Peyton, was a timid plodder. On July 6, 1746 la Bourdonnais' fleet confronted the English, fighting an inconclusive battle and absorbing 222 casualties to Peyton's 60. The French boats took refuge in Pondichéry, whereupon Peyton broke off contact, sailing away to Pulicat. Presuming incorrectly that Peyton was actually a clever strategist, la Bourdonnais feared that he was waiting for a French assault on Madras, at which time he would pounce upon the landing. Had he realized that the English were equally perplexed by Peyton's conduct, he might well have turned the tide here for the French.[7]

Instead, la Bourdonnais merely tested his adversary with a kind of naval demonstration of power off Madras. When Peyton heard of this on September 2, he promptly sailed to Bengal, which constituted desertion in the face of an enemy! La Bourdonnais made up his mind to proceed with an assault anyway, easily taking Madras; but instead of honoring Dupleix' pleas for the destruction of Fort Saint George, the money-hungry naval commander decided to return it to the English, in exchange for a bribe. Dupleix then accused la Bourdonnais of high treason, and the breach between the two became irreparable.[8]

That October, a cyclone pulverized Madras, forcing la Bourdonnais to pull back and repair his ruined ships. Dupleix remained in Madras in charge of ground troops, seeking assurances from the English that they would not contest French control of the port. Those who refused, like Governor Morse, were deported to Pondichéry. Among the recalcitrant was a soon-to-be great name in English colonial annals, a twenty-one-year-old bookkeeper named Robert Clive, who fled to the English base at Cuddalore, south of Pondichéry.[9]

In August 1747, the English decided to besiege Pondichéry itself, but Dupleix along with his spirited wife directed a skillful defense against a squadron commanded by Britain's Admiral Boscowen. When monsoon season arrived in October, the British reluctantly retreated, leaving Dupleix a hero to French and Indians alike. He returned to Pondichéry, greeted by a fifteen-cannon salute, but his moment of triumph would be brief.[10] For as part of the Treaty of Aix-la-Chapelle in 1748, ending the War of the Austrian Succession, France was forced to return Madras to England.

More significantly, Clive, who had played a notable role in the siege of Pondichéry, returned to Madras as food commissioner, and would henceforth become Dupleix' fatal nemesis.

The War of the Austrian Succession had convinced Dupleix of Pondichéry's vulnerability to attack, its survival during that conflict having depended entirely on ships bringing bullion and manufactured goods from France. The port's lack of a hinterland meant that the loss of even one ship there placed it in real danger. At this point too, the Viceroy of the Deccan died, and the French stuck their noses into a heated succession struggle. Their intervention resulted in a dramatic French victory at the battle of Ambur, due in large measure to the heroism of a dashing young captain named Charles de Bussy; but it would also represent a costly diversion of French effectives.[11]

After France's victory, the new Viceroy Muzaffar Jung rewarded the Compagnie with much land around Pondichéry, making it a self-sustaining entity no longer dependent on a seaborne lifeline. But Muzaffar had only wounded his dynastic rival Nasir Jung, not destroyed him, and the latter now raised a large army and counterattacked. De Bussy helped out and this time the usurper lost his life. The Viceroy then rewarded Dupleix, who had saved his life, with the governorship of an entire province. The French king Louis XV followed this promotion by making Dupleix a marquis into the bargain, and Gallic influence now extended over a significant portion of southern India.[12]

More than three decades on the subcontinent led Dupleix to the zenith of his career, controlling the interests of what was now optimistically renamed the Perpetual Company of the Indies; while simultaneously, he enjoyed the privileges of an Indian monarch. But the very duality of his status made him suspect back in Paris. Conversant though he might be with subcontinental affairs, he was dangerously out of touch with the home base and atmosphere. His own actions also played a role in his impending problems, for Dupleix had now charged the adept la Bourdonnais with treason, and after a summary trial, his rival was flung into the Bastille prison in Paris, March 1, 1748. The naval commander's "embastillement" would last three long years, until he finally obtained an acquittal and was released in February 1751.

This controversy involving two headstrong Bretons became the talk of the French capital, including of intellectuals like Voltaire, who ardently defended la Bourdonnais; and the Court itself was split on the issue.[13] All of which fixed the government's attention more squarely on the

Compagnie's role in India. The more Louis XV's ministers examined that role, the more suspicious they became, especially of the Compagnie's idiosyncratic director, Joseph Dupleix.

Dupleix' expansion into the Indian hinterland irritated the English as well, because of an obvious threat to their own holdings. All this occurred, in addition, against the background of the collapse in India of the Moghul empire, with Britain and France both supporting rival leaders—the French protégé Chanda Sahib opposed by England's man, Mohammed Ali. In 1751 the latter sought assistance from Robert Clive, who was now a captain in the British army. Responding assertively, Clive boldly attacked Arcot, capital of the Carnatic, while French troops were deployed elsewhere. Clive may not have succeeded in holding the city, but his skilled leadership delayed French recapture of Arcot for several months. Clive then returned to his base at Trichinopoly with his reputation as a tactical genius henceforth assured. Meanwhile the English reinforced their company, while Dupleix received nothing more from an ever cooler and more distrustful Paris.[14]

The beleaguered director was able to use his own wealth to hire troops, but his greatest liability proved to be a lack of adept military leaders. De Bussy was more than 600 miles distant, and Dupleix was left with the likes of Captains d'Auteil and Law de Lauriston, each lacking military qualities necessary to confront someone on the order of a Clive.

Uncertain of how to proceed, d'Auteil and Chanda Sahib decided to deploy numerically inferior forces on the island of Srirangam, across from Britain's garrison at Trichinopoly—a move which turned out to be catastrophic. D'Auteil refused to move toward Trichinopoly, contenting himself with bombarding the city from the island, and he was replaced by Lauriston, who was no more energetic. The British Company meanwhile sent out Major Stringer Lawrence to reinforce Clive, before the French could procure any needed reinforcements.[15]

In June 1752 Clive and Lawrence encircled the island, finally compelling the French to surrender. They then beheaded Chanda Sahib, and the way to Pondichéry's hinterland lay open to England's puppet, Mohammed Ali.[16] The disaster at Trichinopoly would surely have led to the fall of Pondichéry within a few weeks, but for a peace concluded at home. As it was, the events at Trichinopoly would be fatal to Dupleix' large ambitions in India. At this point he could still count on support from the Viceroy of the Deccan, and when a French ship arrived with 500 precious reinforcements, he set about searching for allies among other neighboring Indian princes. The energetic de Bussy was willing to come and help out, but the

English still decisively outnumbered the French. In 1753 Dupleix sent the Compagnie a detailed report, asking for more men to help him expel the British. But news of Trichinopoly finally reached the French capital, exhausting the Compagnie's patience with such a self-important representative abroad. In 1754 they recalled Dupleix from the post and part of the world that had become his obsession.

In retrospect, Dupleix' errors are easy for historians to ascertain. In the first place, the impulsive director should never have dispatched de Bussy to Aurangabad instead of keeping him closer to Pondichéry, where he was the only French soldier of real quality. In de Bussy's absence, Britain's Clive and Lawrence won a series of significant victories. This was the immediate reason for Dupleix' recall, and there is no question that he partly caused it himself.

His other errors were more conceptual than concrete. Dupleix had originally come to the subcontinent to seek a career working for the Compagnie, *not* to extend French civil authority over all of southern India. But that is exactly what he ended up doing, and with such single-mindedness that even the most obtuse of Englishmen could not have failed to detect a threat to their interests. In actuality Dupleix simply lacked resources and/or skills to expand French control beyond the vicinity of Pondichéry.[17]

Puffed up by his own bravado, the director had ensnarled France in an interminable war whose objectives were never clear to his employers. The Compagnie's investments in southern India sufficed to maintain the port of Pondichéry and the profitable trade that flowed through it; but to attempt a takeover of the entire Carnatic seemed nonsensical to authorities at home. Consequently, the Compagnie recalled Dupleix when they finally grew weary of an incessant drain on their resources. In today's world of the bottom line, corporate America would act no differently.[18]

Dupleix' mistakes handed Clive his first great opportunity, leading to the final destruction of French rule in India during the Seven Years War. But the French director had had successes as well, and these should not be overlooked. Dupleix had turned the hitherto puny port of Pondichéry into a commercial facility giving the Compagnie substantial profits in the short term, and the prospect of a sustained income in the long. The fact that Paris never truly comprehended his policies and actions should not strip them of all validity, although the entire Dupleix program *was* overly ambitious. To sum up, one can make a strong case for the dual nature of Dupleix' role in India—both commercial and military—as the central factor in his downfall.[19]

In the final analysis, Dupleix' Indian problems were due in good part to his own flawed character. Undeniably industrious, he could also be an insufferable nitpicker when dealing with subordinates. Versatile as an administrator, engineer, diplomat, and general organizer, he was also less than adept militarily, and had an unfortunate tendency to blame others for any setbacks on land or sea. He hated people who didn't stick to enterprises, yet would commit himself to unrealistic goals. He was a prig with a chip on his shoulder, and had a morbid, paranoid tendency to distrust other humans with whom he dealt.[20]

Dupleix' recall did not of course save India for France, as the disastrous Seven Years War of 1756–63 would soon end forever Gallic hopes of maintaining a strong presence on the subcontinent. Meanwhile, rivalries in the American wilderness west of the Thirteen Colonies, controlled by Indian tribes and with but a few hamlets on the Mississippi and Detroit rivers, and isolated forts, had begun the process of setting the rest of the world on fire. French-British skirmishes, then undeclared naval battles in the Atlantic, helped bring Austria's Queen Maria Theresa in for another round of the Austrian Succession against Frederick the Great of Prussia—this time on the French side. The French also counted on Russian involvement there. The Seven Years War of course became a horrendously wasteful conflict in Europe, and between France and Britain abroad, a kind of colonial Super Bowl.

In 1758 the French Compagnie dispatched a new military governor out to the Carnatic, Lally-Tolendal, and it proved to be that poor man's undoing. Lally's defeat by the British in 1761 would not only doom the French cause on the subcontinent, but ultimately, bring the end of his own life in a controversial execution.[21]

Arriving in Pondichéry in April 1758, Lally had prepared carefully for a vigorous campaign against the English, who nonetheless welcomed him with Clive's stunning victory at the battle of Plassey. That victory won all of Bengal for London, placing Lally at a serious disadvantage. He might then have cooperated with de Bussy, who still exercised much influence among princes of southern India; but his manner and actions alienated those who might have helped him. Launching an effort to retake the Coromandel coast, Lally at first succeeded, capturing Britain's Fort Saint David at Cuddalore, then Arcot. He received a million pounds from the Compagnie and substantial reinforcements, but his failure in early 1759 to take Fort Saint George at Madras proved fatal to his cause. In the following year, lacking sufficient naval support, Lally lost the battle of Mashlipatam and had to withdraw to Pondichéry, where the English besieged his men. In January 1761 he was forced to surrender Dupleix' beloved port.[22]

Defeated soon after in the Seven Years War, France was forced to sign the humiliating Treaty of Paris in 1763, ceding to Britain all its possessions in India, with the exception of small concessions at Mahé, Karikal, Yanaon, and Chandernagor. The concession of Pondichéry was only returned after two years of British occupation. The war had destroyed its fort, palaces, and the French city which surrounded it, and though France would continue holding this *comptoir* until 1954, Pondichéry never returned to its former glory under Dupleix. Its ruin spelled the end of French hopes to dominate the subcontinent, and Lally served as the government's most convenient scapegoat. Imprisoned in London for two years, he was then liberated and repatriated to France, but the French immediately threw him into the Bastille. In 1766 the Crown brought the unfortunate man to trial on charges of treason, based primarily on his surrender of Pondichéry. Then on May 6 judicial authorities convicted Lally, sentencing him to death, and three days later he was executed.

There had of course been precedents for such punishment, like the famous case of England's Admiral Byng; but Lally's execution disturbed many in France, including again, that great gadfly, Voltaire, who wrote a scathing account of the affair. Today the consensus among historians is that Lally lost in India not because of any treasonable inclinations, but because of crucial factors beyond his control. These included persistent interference by officers of the Compagnie, the poor and haphazard quality of French reinforcements, British control of sea-lanes leading to India, and of course Clive's considerable military ability.

But French failure in India was not considered final in that era. Several self-styled experts now pointed to the island of Madagascar as a potential steppingstone for the eventual reemergence of France as a major power on the subcontinent. France had been interested in this large island off the eastern coast of Africa since the days of Richelieu, but Louis XIV's minister Colbert had written it off, believing it too expensive to conquer. Shortly after the Seven Years War, a French soldier of fortune named Maudave wrote the Ministry of Colonies, urging colonization of Madagascar. Characterizing it as a valuable island with a variety of raw materials, including gold, Maudave felt that such a prize might serve as a staging area for the future reconquest of India.[23] The French government was unenthusiastic, suggesting that Maudave himself should assume all expenses for any such expedition. Scrounging up some cash, Maudave actually landed on the island in September 1768, but his shoestring expedition proved fruitless.

Stranger yet was the saga of Count Maurice Benyoski, a Polish nobleman in the service of Catherine the Great of Russia. In the late 1760s Benyoski was exiled to Siberia, either because of a torrid love affair or because of his participation in a Polish revolt against Russia. Managing to escape, he had made his way by 1770 to Canton, China, then en route back to Europe, stopped at Ile de France in the Indian Ocean and somehow, developed the same notion as Maudave—that Madagascar ought to be colonized. The French government was interested enough to provide this adventurer with arms, men, and ships to establish a trading post on the island. But Benyoski had larger ambitions, and after arriving on Madagascar in 1774, the Polish visionary urged more colonial schemes on the French, finally attracting the adverse attention of the minister of marine, Turgot, who reminded him of the limits of his mandate and ordered him to desist.

Ignoring the order, Benyoski expanded his trading post into a rather profitable agricultural colony. But on his return to France in December 1776, he found that French policy was to maintain the status quo in the Indian Ocean. The monarchy's expensive involvement in the American Revolution was a factor, and by 1783 the peripatetic Benyoski became disgusted enough to cross the Atlantic, seeking support from the state of Maryland. A few local officials in America led him on, and when he returned to Madagascar the following year with the idea of founding an American settlement there, Paris had had quite enough. The French Ministry suspected that Benyoski wanted to establish his own personal sovereignty on the large island (a suspicion confirmed by his expulsion of the French garrison and proclamation of himself as "emperor" in 1785); so the government dispatched a frigate with orders to capture the energetic count dead or alive. In May 1786 the French force from Ile de France caught up to this odd character and executed him.[24] As it turned out, France would not take full possession of Madagascar until 1885, when Britain recognized French ownership of the island in exchange for subsequent French recognition of a British Zanzibar. Madagascar will become a significant part of our modern colonial story in later chapters.[25]

The French had also blended their interests in India and Madagascar by recognizing the possible utility of the island of Réunion, or what was then called Bourbon. Lying due east of Madagascar, Réunion originally served as a stopping point on their main shipping route to India. Either the Dutch or the Portuguese had been the first Europeans to see the island (it first appears on a chart of around 1502).

In the mid-1640s the French began taking Réunion seriously, and small settlements of Malgache malcontents were dumped there between 1646 and 1657; but the French temporarily abandoned their colonization efforts when cyclones devastated the island in 1657 and 1658.[26] Colbert's creation of the Compagnie led to renewed occupation in 1663, at which time the first explicit mention of its usefulness occurs in the records. But by 1669, when the government gave up its plans to take Madagascar, Réunion no longer seemed so significant. Settlements did continue—a trickle of people coming to the island to run coffee and sugar plantations that in the eighteenth century became staffed with slaves; but the government neglected Réunion until the struggle for India heated up during the 1750s. After that the British also recognized the island's utility, ultimately trying to liquidate France's presence there during the Napoleonic era in 1806; but by this time Réunion along with Mauritius was so well fortified that it would take more than a token show of naval muscle to elbow out the French. Contemporaneously, coffee plantations (wrecked by storms in 1806–7) definitively ceded to those aimed at increased sugar production. In 1810, Britain's Colonel Keating would put ashore with a much stronger invasion force, inducing the French to capitulate. But when Napoleon's reign ended, Réunion was reunited with France as part of the Treaty of Vienna in 1815. When France finally got going on its conquest of Madagascar later in the nineteenth century, the island would prove significant as a naval base and staging area for that colonial assault.[27] In terms of name chronology (which we have simplified), the French had changed the island's designation several times, from Bourbon to Réunion to Bonaparte and back to Bourbon, before finally settling on Réunion again when the July Monarchy was overthrown in 1848.

Other islands in the western Indian Ocean also interested France because of their proximity to Madagascar. The Comoros, lying to the northwest between Madagascar and Tanzania, had been invaded and settled by several peoples long before Europeans set foot there. Predictably, the Portuguese were the first of the latter to do so, finding an eclectic mix of ethnic groups whose dominant religion was Shirazi Islam, but whose total numbers did not exceed 3,000. They brought back to Europe intriguing legends concerning the four islands. According to one, the throne of the Queen of Sheba had been stolen and hidden in a crater on these Comoros, and supposedly, Solomon's armies had eventually located it, returning it to Her Majesty.[28]

In 1843 France would gain a protectorate over the Comoros, when the Sakalava King, Andirantsouli, ceded the islands to Paris in return for an annual rent of 5,000 francs and French educations for his two sons.[29] At the time the islands found themselves under siege by slavers operating from Madagascar. The French military ran them off, suppressing a series of revolts, before dividing the islands into concessions they awarded to planters from Réunion. Sugar-planting and the importation of African slaves followed. But Réunion was more extensively developed, and the Comoros never became a highly significant French colony. Despite the endpoint of our chronology here, they truly belong to the haphazard character of a "First French Empire."

Northeast of Madagascar and due east of Kenya lie the Seychelles, mentioned in Arab manuscripts of the ninth and tenth centuries. Again, Portuguese mariners were the first Europeans to reach these uninhabited islands early in the sixteenth century, but in 1742 la Bourdonnais sent a man named Lazare Picault to explore them, hoping to utilize the islands in a future war with the British. The grateful Picault named one of the islands after la Bourdonnais, but in 1756 the French Crown took direct control of them, renaming them for the Viscount Moreau de Séchelles.

The first permanent settlement only occurred in 1771, when fifteen Frenchmen, seven slaves, five south Indians, and one African female arrived from Réunion. They were followed by refugees from France's failed outposts in India, and during the 1790s, by metropolitan Frenchmen fleeing the Revolution. Rumor had it that one could make a fortune in timber and tortoises here, and indeed some 13,000 shelled creatures had been shipped from the Seychelles by 1789; but there is no evidence that anyone in the population of 487 slaves and 104 free whites ever became rich.[30] Today's ecologists, however, would marvel at what the settlers of 1771 found there— an environment virtually unaltered since the Seychelles had first risen out of the ocean.

The year the French Revolution began (1789) the Seychelles attempted to declare independence from France; but the revolt was crushed by two French commandants, who ran the colony through the Napoleonic Wars, repelling a number of landings by British pirates. But following the Peace of Amiens in 1802, English naval commanders succeeded in blockading the Seychelles, moving in to stay in 1810, and taking formal possession by terms of the Treaty of Paris in 1814. The British would hold the Seychelles all the way up to 1976.[31]

Of course French colonial ambitions of the pre-Napoleonic era had extended well beyond the Indian Ocean. Moving from there to the South Pacific, we find that England's Captain Cook was not the only man interested in that idyllic expanse of land and sea; France's Louis-Antoine de Bougainville was another. Born to a judicial family in Paris, 1729, Bougainville's mother died in his infancy, and Louis was raised by the widow of a former Police Lieutenant, Hérault. Madame Hérault helped turn the boy into a Renaissance man—a classicist, artist, writer, and mathematician, as well as a swordsman, gambler, and devotee of the ladies. Destined for law, following family tradition, the young Bougainville instead went off to sea, becoming a top aide to General Montcalm in Canada during the Seven Years War.[32]

After that conflict he devised an abortive plan to occupy the Falkland Islands. In 1764 he arrived with two naval vessels, a small contingent of Acadians, and the title of governor, but both British and Spanish protested vigorously, and Bougainville withdrew.

Immediately following the Falklands fiasco, Bougainville received instructions to proceed to China by way of the South Seas, identifying en route territories that might be useful for French commercial expansion. For that type of voyage he required engineers, naturalists, astronomers, and hydrographers, in addition to able seamen, and in 1766 he returned to the port of Brest in Brittany to hire such a crew.[33] Later that year he left on a journey that would immortalize his name, becoming an acutely thorough observer of natural phenomena he beheld. Bougainville was also a fine observer of humans, though some of those observations would today be considered politically incorrect. For example, on truly wild Indians of the Argentine: "They are of the medium height, horribly ugly and nearly all show signs of skin disease. They have very swarthy complexions.... They pillage and massacre and carry off their surviving victims into slavery."[34]

Passing through the Straits of Magellan, Bougainville searched in vain for Easter Island, but kept sailing onward, claiming Tahiti, whose physical beauties astonished him. As for Tahitian women, he found that "their appearance ravished the eye and the heart, and all their gestures were harmonious." He went on to note: "Here the lot of women is sweet idleness and the art of pleasing their most serious occupation. These pleasure-loving habits of the Tahitians give them a noticeably gentle evenness of temper, which is only possible to people who have leisure and are happy."[35]

After Tahiti came the discovery of Samoa and a group of islands which Bougainville also claimed for France, naming them the New Hebrides. He then proceeded westward into waters that no European vessel had previously seen. Turning north from the Great Barrier Reef, he found the Solomon Islands and claimed New Britain, returning to France in 1769.[36]

Bougainville's exploits proved the French could sail the Pacific about as well as the English. Of the islands he claimed, Tahiti would finally remain a French possession, still a tonic vacation spot for tired Europeans. Those Tahitians Bougainville brought back with him to France, and stories he and his men told of unclad women offering favors to French sailors entranced the métropole, creating a long-standing Gallic fascination with the island. A tropical flower continues to bear Bougainville's name, as does the largest island in the Solomons.

In older age Bougainville wed a lady twenty years his junior (1780), but though it became a happy union, it began with his prolonged absence, fighting for America's revolutionaries. Bougainville did so admirably, then accompanied the Count de Grasse to the Caribbean for more naval engagements that ended badly; and back in France he had to defend himself against charges of naval incompetence. His main accuser was none other than de Grasse. But the storm dissipated, and Bougainville's lovely wife gave him several sons, and he seemed about to settle down, except that the French Revolution soon erupted, a conflagration Bougainville and his family would barely survive. In 1801 his second son drowned while swimming in a river, and then five years later his wife passed away, in good measure from a broken heart. One of Bougainville's other sons became a rear admiral, following his famed father's footsteps with more exploratory voyages, including one to Tahiti. At eighty-two the elder Bougainville passed away and his ashes ended up in Paris' Pantheon.[37]

Returning to eighteenth-century French voyages of exploration, sources disagree on the first discovery of New Caledonia. Bougainville had most likely passed it without stopping in 1768, and neither the British nor the French truly coveted the area. Tales of cannibalism abounded, and in later confirmation of such stories, the crew of a French vessel which landed there as late as 1850 would be killed and eaten. The French proved more persistent here than the British, with a certain Monsignor Douaré founding the first Catholic mission on New Caledonia in 1844, and Rear Admiral Febvrier-Despointes officially claiming the island for France in 1853. The French government of that era considered it an admirable site for a penal colony, and 40,000 prisoners would languish there between 1864 and 1897, many of them political exiles from the 1871 Paris Commune. Life on New Caledonia was reputedly brutal, and by the mid-1890s the French decided to ship their prisoners to the somewhat more humane confines of Devil's Island and the "dry guillotine" of Cayenne in French Guiana.[38]

France became interested as well in the Marquesa Islands, about 1,200 miles northeast of Tahiti. The Spanish explorer Alvaro de Mendaña de Neira had landed there in 1595, and his arrogance in dealing with inhabitants had provoked a bloody encounter. Alvaro named these islands for the Marquesa de Mendoza, then sailed away. In 1774 Captain Cook visited one of the twelve islands, and in 1791 the Frenchman Etienne Marchand charted these Marquesas. France took possession of the islands in 1842, establishing a fortress called Port Philippe. Clad in an odd costume, Admiral Dupetit-Thouars announced to a crowd of bemused inhabitants that he claimed the islands in the name of King Louis Philippe of France. He then beat the ground three times with his sword, ran the *tricolore* up a hastily improvised flagpole, and sang the "Marseillaise." The natives here, whose propensities included aforementioned cannibalism, were distinctly unimpressed, and the islands proved difficult to subdue. A series of violent revolts only ended with a French victory in the 1880s, and ever since, the Marquesas have played a very tiny role in world affairs, though the painter Gauguin is buried there.[39]

Financially speaking, the main locus for France's eighteenth-century colonial empire was centered on North America and particularly, the Caribbean. For many years France had held prized islands in the West Indies, and at the time of the Seven Years War, many influential Frenchmen considered those possessions more valuable than Canada. France lost the latter but was happy to recover these islands in the Treaty of Paris concluding the war.[40] During the twilight of the Old Regime the Caribbean constituted without any doubt France's most lucrative source of colonial profits. Guadeloupe, Martinique, and what became Haiti were home to hundreds of thousands of African slaves and some 20,000 whites who owned them. The Caribbean islands produced copious quantities of coffee and sugar cane, refined back home in the rich French port cities of Bordeaux and Nantes, before being shipped as finished products to other parts of Europe. In the eighteenth century European coffee and sugar demand grew by leaps and bounds, and the French took full advantage of these new tastes. By the final decade before the Revolution, Gallic trade with the West Indies stood at over 50,000,000 *livres*, nearly a quarter of their national income.

To backtrack, Columbus had been the first European to see Martinique and Guadeloupe (called "island of beautiful waters" by the Caribs) in 1493.

The pious Italian named the first Madaniña and the second Guadeloupe, consecrating it to Our Lady of Guadeloupe; but he never went ashore on either island until his fourth voyage in 1502, when he left a few pigs and goats on Martinique. Glutted with silver and gold taken from its colonial domains in South America, Spain ignored these islands for more than a century, and in 1626 the few Spaniards living on Guadeloupe were driven off by a Frenchman, Pierre Belain d'Esnambuc, who established a trading company there. He did the same for Martinique nine years later, by which time Richelieu's Compagnie des Isles de l'Amérique had dispatched two men, Jean du Plessis d'Ossonville and Léonard de l'Olive, to explore Guadeloupe.[41] D'Esnambuc, who had settled on Martinique, then entrusted that island to his nephew, Jacques-Dyel du Parquet, who purchased it from the Compagnie, developing it with Portuguese assistance into a prosperous colony. The cultivation of sugar cane came soon after.

In 1658 Louis XIV repurchased Martinique from du Parquet's children, placing it several years later under the control of the Compagnie des Indes Occidentales. His financial wizard Colbert recognized Martinique's great potential for wealth and did what he could to stimulate it, sending slave ships there from the Compagnie du Sénégal; but he could spend only limited amounts of money on this future economic goldmine, due to Louis XIV's costly European wars. In 1723 the French introduced Arabian coffee to Martinique, further enhancing the island's growing prosperity.[42]

Nearby Guadeloupe developed more gradually, with its colonists subduing Carib revolts by 1640, and it became part of the French monarchy's domains in 1674. The fate of these Caribs killed off by warfare, European diseases, and their inability to endure the rigors of plantation work was a melancholy one. During the early eighteenth century, Jean-Baptiste Labat directed the colony's fortunes, arming its black slaves to fight against English raiders, and spearheading the creation of the island's first sugar refineries. During the Seven Years War, Britain captured both Guadeloupe (1759) and Martinique (1762), but as seen, returned them to France in the 1763 Treaty of Paris. Two decades later, the War of American Independence drained French resources so much that the country hadn't money or energy to protect its significant Caribbean investment. It had already been difficult to prevent smuggling of timber or food items from British North America onto these lucrative islands; but when the United States attained independence, it became impossible. In recognition of this unpleasant reality, a decree of August 1784 essentially legalized trade between the French West Indies and the United States, setting aside the *Exclusif*, meaning traditional French monopoly rights over colonial trade.[43] Finding itself on the edge of its own revolution, the French government kept the decree secret for fear of riots in Paris, and when it became public anyway, French merchants clamored unanimously that this meant their commercial ruin!

Simultaneously, a significant antislavery movement had been developing in pre-Revolutionary France. The Enlightenment had taught Frenchmen to find slavery barbaric, and in 1788 the Society for Friends of Blacks was founded in Paris. The Marquis de Lafayette joined the group, as did a number of influential French thinkers of the time. Six years later, at the height of the Reign of Terror, the National Convention would free slaves in all French possessions. Since no one believed that a free-labor economy in the sugar islands could possibly turn a profit, the French would have to look elsewhere for colonial opportunities.

In 1802 Napoleon reestablished slavery, and a slave revolt on Guadeloupe ensued, ending in the disaster of Matouba, where antislavery rebels blew themselves up, rather than surrender to French forces under General Antoine Richepanse. The sugar islands were finally restored to France in 1816, following the Treaty of Vienna. Slavery there was eventually abolished in 1848, and in 1946 the islands would become French departments, though they are truly typical of the "First Empire."

France's largest Caribbean possession was also the scene of Latin America's first successful revolution, becoming one of the most fascinating and tragic parts of our story. On December 6, 1492 Columbus had landed on a large island he named Española, or "Little Spain." The original Arawak population there disappeared by the end of the sixteenth century through the same lethal combination of overwork, brutalization, and exposure to European diseases that was the case for other Indian tribes. Spaniards also enjoyed axing the heads off of Arawak men, women, and children, affording these unfortunates the dubious distinction of gaining martyrdom within the embrace of a new religion. Spain settled the eastern end of the island but paid little attention to it, leaving the western end to French pirates operating out of the Cayman Islands. In 1664 these unkempt black-guards established the town of Port-de-Paix (now Port-au-Prince), and the Compagnie des Indes Occidentales claimed the territory that year. In the Peace of Ryswick of 1697 Spain formally ceded the western third of the island to France, which promptly renamed the colony Saint-Domingue.

During the eighteenth century, Saint-Domingue became France's most prosperous Caribbean colony, its vaunted "Pearl of the Antilles." For exportation its planters grew not only sugar and coffee, but indigo, cotton, and cocoa. Slave laborers imported from Africa worked the fields, and French families owned virtually the entire colony. A *Code Noir* (Black Code) developed in the reign of Louis XIV regulated relations between these owners and slaves, theoretically permitting the former to cut off ears of slaves caught after a first escape lasting at least a month, or to brand them on their shoulders. A second escape attempt could bring leg crippling, and a third the death penalty. As many as 15 percent of imported slaves did not even survive the Atlantic voyage, and once in the "Pearl of the Antilles," suicide or infanticide were common. One can see why angered slaves in revolt later resorted to extreme measures. For punishments some planters used whips with angled hooks that badly cut up the skin. According to the Black Code fifty lashes was the maximum, but putting salt or aloe into wounds raised no eyebrows, nor did the cutting off of noses!

Despite the blood on slave owners' hands, and indirectly, on those of Enlightenment figures back home, sweetening and sipping their coffee while discussing high-minded ideas, the island's prosperity was undeniable. By 1789, partially reflecting liquidation of most French holdings in India, as much as two-thirds of the value of France's foreign investments derived from Saint-Domingue alone. Slaves numbering some 460,000 constituted 90 percent of a population of over half a million, with 30,000 whites and 28,000 free "mulattoes" making up the balance. Despite restrictions, or perhaps because of them, many of these mulattoes were upwardly mobile in the decades before the revolution. For slaves there was some relaxation of rigorous, repressive treatment in the sunset of the *ancien régime* during the 1780s. Some got to own their own land and even inherited estates from enlightened masters. Though parts of the *Code Noir* prescribed Catholic instruction and Sunday worship in churches, slave festivities replete with voodoo dances going back to Africa were a tolerated, even encouraged part of the island's ambiance. This social atmosphere was a complex one, ranging from aristocratic *grands blancs* and more self-made *petits blancs*, to a wide variety of "mulattoes," then to the hundreds of thousands of slaves who also exhibited much variety (due in part to how they were treated). Saint-Domingue might be the largest supplier of coffee anywhere, and its sugar cane planters "recognized as the most efficient and productive . . . in the world"; but in addition to this economic dynamism there was an easy-going sensuality, increasing tolerance and blending of peoples, and a unique Creole tongue, cuisine, and tone. More and more planters evaded French regulations, and some returned to France bringing slaves who would find freedom there. However, like the Old Regime in France itself, this was a society truly resting on a powderkeg, or as the Count de Mirabeau put it, on Vesuvius![44]

When on August 8, 1788 Louis XVI announced the convocation of an Estates-General, signaling the French Revolution's onset, slave owners of Saint-Domingue prepared to send thirty-seven representatives, of whom only six were eventually seated in the Estates. White and mulatto planters united in their reluctance to see the end of slavery, but encountered heated opposition from the Société des Amis des Noirs, and their own cohesion was anything but seamless: most whites wished to maintain the existing colonial order without alteration, while free mulattoes judged that the French Revolution promised *them* equality of treatment and freedom from discrimination.[45] News of the Bastille's fall (July 14, 1789) then provoked riots on Saint-Domingue by poor whites and in response, the creation of an assembly of wealthy white planters, excluding both poor whites and mulattoes. In the midst of this turmoil, contradictory instructions kept arriving from Paris, exacerbating divisions.

All of which was the background to an uprising of August 22, 1791, the famed "night of fire," when slaves in Saint-Domingue revolted against their masters. Black rioters wrecked hundreds of coffee plantations and sugar mills, and rebel control soon extended throughout the northern part of Española. Former slaves hung whites, shot them with their own guns, decapitated planters' children, and displayed the heads on their spears. They raped and murdered mothers and daughters alike, and within a matter of days had killed thousands, before whites began fighting back with equal savagery, including decapitations of their own, or breaking at the wheel.

The revolutionary situation on the future Haiti became complex, and there were agonizing conflicts within families. In some cases white fathers strangled bastard mulatto sons, or mulatto sons murdered white planter fathers. Meanwhile, slave armies continued to control the north.[46]

Of course power politics also played a role, as European opposition to the messianic goals of the French Revolution intensified. Spain joined other European nations in denouncing the Revolutionary Constitution of 1791 and insisted on the restoration of King Louis XVI to his former status, then directed the colonial government of its poorer eastern portion of Española to attack Saint-Domingue. Britain aided in the attack, but in support of the white planter aristocracy; while Spain supported the slaves *against* their masters, hoping thereby to take the entire island. This divided anti-French forces, and in August 1793 the French colonial administration on Saint-Domingue regained the initiative, emancipating all slaves under its control. The National Convention in Paris soon ratified that decision, and black rebels straggled back to the French side.[47]

In the Treaty of Basel France then obtained the eastern two-thirds of Española from Spain. But the antislavery movement had evolved in the direction of independence, and in 1797 the great Toussaint l'Ouverture, a former slave who had been a general during the 1791–94 uprising, established a military government over the entire colony.

Toussaint was the most noble black figure of this turbulent period. Born in 1743, he was already middle-aged at the time of the great slave revolt. His childhood on a quite liberal French plantation had been a happy one, with much reading of classical history and European literature. Toussaint's planter owner enjoyed stimulating the cultural tastes of the young man and conversing with him, eventually giving him forty acres to run, as well as the household staff. Nearing thirty, Toussaint was permitted to marry. He would then turn into both a fine military leader and a sincere Catholic, acting like a priest to his followers.

In the slave revolt Toussaint relied on his own martial intuitions, as well as on Spanish guerilla tactics. He tried his best—with no real success—to rein in the sadism of associates like Jean Jacques Dessalines, a black fighter who liked to gag foes inside chests, then saw the chests in two! Toussaint was the more disciplined leader, teaching slaves how to drill, care for arms, and march more indefatigably than European soldiers.

With the emancipation of early 1794 he made the decision to use his slave battalions in behalf of the French against the Spanish. By the fall of that year this astonishing new force successfully attacked the British, who paradoxically helped them modernize militarily; and in feudal fashion Toussaint rewarded his followers with plantations expropriated from white owners, who had long since fled. In a number of engagements these slave armies also had to fend off mulattoes. By 1797, as noted, Toussaint and his black army were powerful enough to establish a military government over the entire colony. Becoming much loved, he attempted to cooperate with the French, resisting pressures to declare outright independence. By September 1798 British forces were gone, and with the dawn of a new century, economic prosperity had returned to the island, its social peace tenuously maintained under Toussaint's authoritarian but popular rule.

At this point Napoleon Bonaparte turned his attention to the Caribbean. In 1799 French First Consul, and in 1801 Consul for Life, the thirty-two-year-old general wished to reassert French control of Saint-Domingue, dispatching an expedition of between 25,000 and 35,000 men on 86 ships, headed by his brother-in-law, General Charles Leclerc. Leclerc, known as the "little Napoleon," since he resembled Bonaparte, was Josephine's brother, who herself had grown up on Martinique as the daughter of a prosperous Creole sugar planter there. Leclerc was also married to Napoleon's sister, Pauline, an inveterate husband-cheater, whom he loved ardently till his death.

Leclerc's forces arrived on the island in February 1802, and blood soon spilled profusely, with General Rochambeau of American Revolutionary fame enthusiastically supervising the annihilation of blacks and mulattoes. On the other side Toussaint led a determined resistance, and Dessalines masterminded a scorched earth strategy, drowning Haiti's towns in a sea of fire and ash. In the midst of this savage fighting, Napoleon buttered up Toussaint with a personal letter, preaching the virtues of peace. Privately, Bonaparte wished to turn back the clock, reasserting French control here; but the ravages of yellow fever on his forces proved disastrous. Happy were French soldiers who died quickly; others suffered from cramps, aching heads that seemed about to blow up, and insatiable thirst. They would vomit blood, as well as a substance dubbed "black soup," then their faces turned yellow, and bodies were encased in malodorous phlegm, before death happily intervened.

Leclerc himself would perish of the disease at thirty, but not before he helped engineer a perfidious bargain with Toussaint, who was betrayed partly with the connivance of his black generals Dessalines and Christophe. Their aid helped facilitate Toussaint's easy arrest by the French, June 7, 1802.

France was nonetheless doomed on the island, and so was the land itself—destruction of plantations and plentiful soil erosion marking the beginning of Haiti's inexorable decline into future poverty. In a kind of death agony Rochambeau, Leclerc's successor, went crazy, ripping apart foes with dogs and even resorting to crucifixions. On the other side Dessalines fought both whites and blacks in his usual sadistic fashion. When England reinvaded the Caribbean in July 1803, Rochambeau surrendered to them within a short time. Resumption of the Napoleonic wars in Europe and Bonaparte's sale of Louisiana to the U.S. helped influence French withdrawal of their troops from the Caribbean.

Meanwhile, the noble Toussaint, transported to France, lived out his last days in a gloomy fortress high up in the Jura Mountains, where cold, damp conditions in his dungeon cell, as well as poor food, took a toll on his health. He became grey and coughed incessantly, finally passing away on April 7, 1803. But Toussaint had his posthumous revenge when on January 1, 1804, the island of Española declared independence, adopting its original Arawak name of Haiti. The first French colony to revolt successfully against the métropole, it would not be the last.[48]

Implicit throughout this chapter has been the contention that between 1515 and 1815, France never really developed anything that could be characterized as a master plan for colonial expansion. Dreams of glory, visions of profit, and quests for adventure never jelled into a coherent, overall strategy. Instead there were an eclectic series of ad hoc efforts to plant the French flag in various parts of the globe, most undertaken by ambitious individuals and entrepreneurs. Support from the mother country was poradic, due to the lack of any clear, consistent purpose directing France's colonial impulse. Military protection was often inadequate, especially in huge territories claimed by France, like "Louisiana," theoretically spilling from New France west to the Rockies and southward to the Gulf of Mexico. That territory simply contained too few Frenchmen, who had to rely overly on uncertain Indian alliances to curb the expansionistic appetites of British colonists. In 1763 France was forced to cede Louisiana to Spain (in exchange for Spanish aid during the Seven Years War), as well as land east of the Mississippi to English Americans, who would keep moving inexorably westward. Napoleon made a short comeback after his Egyptian debacle, getting Louisiana back from Spain in exchange for Tuscany and six warships; but the decimation of his troops on Saint-Domingue soured him on the idea of a resurgent Franco-American empire, and in his typically impulsive way he sold a huge amount of territory for what seemed an exorbitant price to the surprised Americans, but which of course turned out to be a steal. After Napoleon's final fall in 1815, most swaths of a first French Empire were lost to the English.[49]

Before the resumption of overseas expansion in 1830, to which we turn in our next chapter, France held only Guyane, Réunion, Saint Pierre and Miquelon, Martinique, Guadeloupe, and a handful of trading posts in India and on the Senegalese coast. Upon such a skimpy and fragile foundation, the French would then construct a new and greater colonial empire during the next hundred years. But in 1815 no one could have predicted such developments, for to all intents and purposes, France's empire was close to dead!

CHAPTER TWO

Bugeaud and the Conquest of Algeria

THE MAKING OF THE modern French empire begins with France's most famous conquest abroad, the one that created a great colony (and more than a colony), Algeria. When we consider the French absorption of Algeria, starting with localized expeditions to the Mediterranean coast in 1830, we will emphasize one great figure in particular—the man who took control in 1840, making an intermittent, half-hearted war into a fight to the finish, and French Algeria an enduring reality: Thomas Robert Bugeaud, our first Gallic proconsul of modern times.

Algeria had long been an imperial crossroads. Its Berbers probably came from the Middle East or possibly earlier, from Asia. There followed imperialisms of the Phoenicians, Romans, and Germanic Vandals, then the great Arab conquest of the seventh and eighth centuries, fueled by the proselytizing power of Muslim principles. Subsequent invasions in the eleventh century intensified a progressive Islamization and Arabization of the Berbers. We should not ignore a Byzantine presence, nor Spain's brief tenure here in the fifteenth century, on driving Moors from the home country. Then came the Ottoman Turks and their hegemony in Algeria; but by the beginning of the nineteenth century the weakening sultans eventually gave power here to *deys* (rulers) drawn from the janissary corps. These Ottoman *deys* governed Algiers and environs directly, and three other provinces around Constantine in the east, Oran in the west, and Medea in the center came under the control of *beys*.

The *deys* were anything but reliable or fair, and between 1671 and 1818 fourteen of thirty were assassinated. By the early nineteenth century both the Ottomans and their *deys* were in palpable decline, and the old corsair capital of Algiers was losing population. Kabyle revolts in the mountains also helped weaken Turkish administration of the hinterland.

How then did the French become involved in Algeria? They did so in the same somewhat ad hoc manner we have previously seen. In the late 1790s the French government bought a large amount of wheat from two Jewish middlemen in Algeria, but couldn't or at any rate, didn't pay for it. Interest owing on the debt mounted precipitously, and after Napoleon's fall, the *dey* and one of the surviving merchants presented a gigantic bill to the restored Bourbons. French authorities dragged their heels on payment, and in 1827 diplomatic relations between them and the *dey* snapped in a famous incident, when the *dey* Hussein struck the French consul at Algiers three times with a fly-whisk, then expelled him.

For three years France replied with a naval blockade, while the *dey* destroyed French trading posts and had his guns fire on French ships; then on the eve of the French Revolution of 1830 that toppled the Bourbons, France's Polignac government decided to invade. On June 14, 1830 a 37,000-man army under General Louis-Auguste de Bourmont disembarked at Sidi Ferruch, a sheltered Mediterranean beach twenty miles west of Algiers. Victory ensued, partially due to popular antipathy against the Turks, and Algiers fell to French forces. When Louis Philippe's July Monarchy took over from the deposed Bourbons, it simply inherited an Algerian problem, in the way Kennedy would be legated the Bay of Pigs by Eisenhower.

In fact neither the French king nor his ministers, not to mention Parliament were quite sure how to handle this new baby. There were, however, a lot of commanders left over from Napoleon's heyday who envisaged great things here; but for the next four years France basically confined itself to occupation of coastal areas, and on July 22, 1834 would create a new government-general of North Africa to run these territories.

Succeeding de Bourmont in Algeria under the July Monarchy was General Clauzel, who had vigorous ideas, but not enough support at home to enact them. On the edge of war with neighboring Morocco, Clauzel was forced to resign, leaving Algiers in late February 1831, and replaced by the mediocre General Berthezène. From the point of view of European colonists, Berthezène seemed too decent to the Arabs, and in December the French foreign minister replaced him with his own mistress' husband, the tough veteran, General Savary, Duc de Rovigo. This former minister of police under Napoleon harassed Arab chieftains until his death in the spring of 1833, while his wife presumably enjoyed herself back home. Two

successors to Rovigo, Generals Avizard and Voirol, tried to be more conciliatory, but the whole era was one of French uncertainty and tergiversation.

From about 1834 this wavering helped facilitate the rise of a new Arab
champion in Algeria who would attack both French and Turkish posts: Abd
el-Kader. In 1835 Marshal Clauzel returned to Algeria to fight Abd el-Kader,
but soon gave way to a new governor, General Damrémont. French Algeria, such as it was, now seemed to require a stronger, more skillful military leader to clean house; and that someone would be Thomas Robert
Bugeaud.[1]

Bugeaud has often been a dirty word among historians, frequently
equated with unremitting brutality and even by some, with an early form
of French fascism.[2] Here we conceive of him as the first of the modern
imperial figures who created France's "Second Colonial Empire," perhaps not quite in the class of great proconsuls who followed—Faidherbe,
Gallieni, and Lyautey—but a much more complex and significant man
than usually conceded. Though known for the pacification of Algeria,
and preparing for its future preeminence among modern French colonial
acquisitions, he also deserves to be known for other traits and achievements, particularly his great work in agriculture. The more we immersed
ourselves in Bugeaud's life, as well as in his copious military-colonial writing, the more we came to realize that here indeed was a certain greatness.[3]

Most obviously, we will argue here that Bugeaud was a military genius,
perhaps even in the class of such moderns as Guderian or Patton. It is easy
to overlook what an artist Bugeaud was in that domain—how much he
brought to the colonial theater from his prior Napoleonic experience, as
well as from managing a large estate and extensive lands; and how much
he fine-tuned in thought and writing the techniques he would use to make
an improbable French conquest of Algeria successful. Thanks to the breadth
of Bugeaud's military conceptions, and a keen sense of improvisation,
Algeria's absorption under his aegis was anything but accidental or lucky.

Bugeaud had the qualities of all great military thinkers and operants: a
true sense of how to bend plans and principles to circumstance; great
respect for his enemies and their terrains; and a knack for minimizing
his own material and human losses, and of knowing how *not* to rush into
grand maneuvers lacking any real utility. The portrait we give below is
of a man who certainly showed in action the ruthlessness for which he
is known, but who was also a surprisingly fine stylist in his copious writing, and in general, a successful self-made man who used sufferings he
had endured in his revolutionary childhood to later advantage. We find in

him a delicacy, and oddly, in someone known for toughness, a sensitive side, revealed throughout his life. Bugeaud was a hard worker, a family man, and a true agricultural innovator, and there are grounds for calling him an imperialist *malgré lui*. But once in Algeria, he cared more for the North African inhabitants he "pacified" than is generally known. In sum, he is a figure who needs to have a greater and different place in textbook accounts of French colonial history.[4]

The family background of Thomas Robert Bugeaud de la Piconnerie sounds superficially like that of French urban nobles of the eighteenth century, as described by Robert Forster in his *Nobility of Toulouse*.[5] But in fact it was quite complex. Born in 1784, the year Beaumarchais' Figaro announced the imminent demise of France's aristocracy, Bugeaud grew up as the youngest of seven children in a family that had only bought its robe noble office and title in 1729. This was anything but high nobility; the Bugeauds were a family on the rise, but with a definite ceiling above them. To remain noble they were forced to shell out another 6,000 pounds several decades after obtaining their office. The land they owned outside Limoges at La Durantie and La Piconnerie gave them some prestige, but not much income; nor did a small iron-making operation. As with the Habsburgs, marriage was a better way to rise in the world, and the match of Jean-Ambroise Bugeaud, Thomas' authoritarian, prickly father, with Françoise Sutton de Clonard in 1771 was a step up—bringing a large dowry, and linkage to a family of Irish lineage with important sword nobility connections in France. In the 1780s Jean-Ambroise preferred inhabiting his residence in Limoges to the one he had in the country. He was certainly tough with his seven children (of fourteen born). Most favored was his oldest son, Patrice, very much like his father and earmarked for the military. A second son, Ambroise, would become a naval officer, then came four daughters, and finally, the youngest, who no one would have pegged for national fame. Much as in Stendhal's *The Red and the Black*, the problem was what to do with this younger son, and had times remained normal we would almost certainly never have heard of Thomas, as his father had early on intended him for the clergy.

The social complexity referred to—one reason Bugeaud developed into a complex adult—came from both a robe noble and sword noble mentality in the family, mixed with some of the rusticity associated with the poorest French aristocrats of the countryside, the *hobereaux*. But one shouldn't leave out an outright peasant influence on this future lover of the land. For while Thomas' family lived in Limoges, the boy was placed

with a peasant wet nurse back at La Durantie, where he remained an unusually long six years, wearing wooden clogs, eating sharecropper soup,
and speaking *patois*.

Just as the Great Depression would catastrophically change things for
many in our century, so the French Revolution of 1789 was about to have
a major impact on the young Bugeaud and his future. Owing to its painful, profound effects, one could even say that the Revolution made him.
In 1790 the boy was summoned to Limoges in order to learn the arts of
gentlemanliness; but due to emigration of several Bugeauds, and to his
noble title, his father was thrown into prison in December 1792, then re-
incarcerated at the height of the Terror in December 1793. His wife was confined to her home and their possessions were inventoried for confiscation.
In early May 1794 authorities imprisoned Françoise, with the guillotine
still hungry for French victims.

Since his older brothers were out of France, the ten-year-old Bugeaud
was left with his sisters, holding what remained of the family fort. It was
no joke to be children without income, so his sisters made shirts, and the
boy hawked them in the city to keep body and soul together. The pluck
he would later show in battle was already on display. He and his sisters
also testified at a local revolutionary tribunal in behalf of their incarcerated parents, helping keep the guillotine at bay. Sister Phillis' attractions
to one of the questioners was probably one reason the axe didn't fall, but
finally, nobles with *émigré* offspring could defer the verdict no longer.
Slated for execution, the Bugeauds were only saved by the fortuitous fall
of Robespierre in the summer of 1794. Françoise was liberated in November, but mentally scarred by the experience. The boy went back to his
studies at the Ecole centrale in Limoges, and was cited at the prize ceremony of 1798. But the death of sister Thomassine while bearing a first
child broke her mother's heart, and Françoise died soon after. Bugeaud's
father, who had recovered his estate at La Durantie under the Directory,
became morose and more unpredictably violent, and for young Thomas,
life with him in Limoges was one of increasing abuse. Finally, the boy
walked more than fifty kilometers to La Durantie, joining sisters Phillis
and Hélène, and making it his home.

There, he continued the education of his early life, deriving an all-
important love of the country and of agriculture. From dawn to dusk
the Périgordian teenager fished and hunted with sharecroppers' children,
partly to help feed sisters, uncles, and aunts—most of the latter priests
and nuns—who were crowded into a dilapidated home. He continued

speaking *patois*, and became more attuned to the plight of poor share-croppers than a clichéd view of him might imply. From 1798 or so Thomas was mainly home schooled by his sisters, developing a penchant for reading and learning. And he enjoyed his newfound freedom to live and to consider his own future. The Revolution's impact on his parents and brothers had truly freed him from his provincial destiny; without it he would never have become the future architect of a French Algeria.

But at eighteen the young Bugeaud was finding La Durantie a hard go economically. His brother Jean-Ambroise was lost at sea in 1800, and in 1803 his abusive father died, leaving the boy virtually nothing. For a time Thomas thought of attempting the trade of blacksmith. But by the early 1800s a new whirlwind was making his gale-force appeal throughout France and Europe, and partly for economic reasons Bugeaud left La Durantie in 1804 to volunteer before call-up time for a recently created corps of grenadiers in Napoleon's Imperial Guard, arriving at Fontainebleau outside Paris at the end of June. He came to this new military existence with no great enthusiasm, and like great colonials who followed, didn't at all appreciate the restrictions of garrison life, nor the macho nature of his peers. While fellow soldiers went out in search of standard forms of hedonistic fulfillment, Bugeaud preferred to read, write letters in his barracks, or walk alone in the Forest of Fontainebleau. Like new entrants into a British boys' school, newcomers were immediately tested, and the perhaps Irish temper in Bugeaud provoked a duel against a more seasoned soldier who had ragged him. In it the young recruit managed to kill his tormentor, the first of several Bugeaud duels to end in such decisive fashion.

Yet Thomas generally remained bookish and cool-headed, again paradoxical, given a later reputation for colonial brutality. Pursuing his studies and filling out his culture, he paid tutors to teach him mathematics, foreign languages, and geography. In February 1805, after witnessing the Emperor's coronation, he and other *vélites* were moved to a new camp at Courbevoie, where part of the contingent was designated for the Italian theater. Bugeaud was among those left behind to continue manning the Imperial Guard. Avoiding pleasures available in town, he was, however, shocked by plentiful young women giving themselves and their pay to grenadiers for a few weeks' monogamy. His homesickness grew worse that spring, but by summer he was off to Boulogne, and a first view of the sea in Napoleon's ill-conceived invasion of England, called off after Bugeaud's participation in a few minor naval engagements.

Land battles were now in the offing, as Napoleon wished to gain the element of surprise against a resurgent Austria, buoyed up by its alliances with other powers. In September Bugeaud began a long march across the north of France, crossed the Rhine, and in mid-October joined in the Battle of Ulm. En route to the more famous and pivotal Battle of Austerlitz near the end of 1805, the sight of Napoleonic soldiers raping and vandalizing their way through the Austrian countryside became too much for the young man to bear. Having suffered from paternal aggression as a boy, this Candide found nothing stirring in sackings and other such byproducts of war, including heaps of battle-wounded he encountered at the zenith of the Emperor's glory.

After Austerlitz it was back to Courbevoie, where he arrived in February 1806, and in April he was made sublieutenant in the 64th Regiment of the Line. Passing through several camps and enduring a fair amount of boredom, Bugeaud began considering other careers. By fall, however, his regiment was again impelled eastward, arriving in untested triumph for the end of the Battle of Jena in October, then marching and fighting further east toward Poland. That winter, war in its full horror finally imprinted itself on the young Bugeaud's psyche. Led into battle by General Lannes at Pultusk a day after Christmas, witnessing soldiers lying unattended for days on the battlefield, and hearing them groan from painful wounds, made Bugeaud wonder about Napoleon's rationale for unlimited conquest. Bugeaud was himself wounded here, and a doctor's report several months later noted how painful he found it to walk or even move, though he enjoyed recuperating in Warsaw that winter, before regaining France in the spring.

On his first leave from the army, and basking in the good farming and familial life back in La Durantie, Bugeaud penned a letter of resignation to army authorities, which his sister Antoinette was supposed to mail and didn't. He then sent another one, but was ambivalent, and early in 1808 asked to be reinstated.[6]

In sum, the contradictory nature of a future colonial great had already begun manifesting itself. No matter how sensitive he might be about war, and no matter how attracted to the bucolic farming life, Bugeaud *was* a fine and courageous soldier. Rejoining the army, he was posted in the spring of 1808 to the 116th Regiment of the Line for duty in the Peninsular Campaign, one of Napoleon's graveyards-in-the making. On May 2 Madrid erupted in revolt, and Bugeaud took part in the savage French repression. Witnessing Spanish throat-cuttings and other manifestations of popular

fury, he began learning lessons here that he would later apply in North
Africa. After mastering the Madrid uprising, the French at first felt they
were at an end point; in fact the revolt was only beginning. At the end of
May Saragossa was the next city to erupt, and one French siege didn't
suffice, so a second commenced in December, with Bugeaud and his 116th
Regiment participating under Lannes by late January 1809. In savage street
fighting Bugeaud felt himself to be part of an inferno here, yet he also
began demonstrating qualities for which he is best known.

Of course Napoleon's "Spanish Ulcer" presented the same kind of
dilemma we will encounter again and again in this book: one may not like
war, but once in it one either responds in kind, or loses. In Saragossan
house-by-house fighting against "Godless" Napoleonic troops spreading
revolutionary ideals, Spanish Catholic fighters astounded Bugeaud with
their no-holds-barred manner of fighting. Bayonet tussles were awful, and
Bugeaud ordered French sappers to blow up goodly portions of the city.
Now when his troops took young women and nuns as mistresses, he was
no longer much bothered; this was war. (Some of the nuns apparently
thanked their conquerors for diverting them from their vocations.) Like
other future French colonials Bugeaud learned instinctively here that one
had to fight in the style of the foe. But the difficulties and sheer futility of
the Spanish campaign overwhelmed him too. On September 29, 1809 he
wrote his sister Phillis that he loathed the nature of this war. "We are
strong enough to beat the enemy, but not to pursue him after the victory,"
he noted. "This cursed Peninsula is so large and so mountainous, that . . .
what we have done till now is hardly of any use." Bugeaud repeatedly mentions in letters home the loss of good men around him, and the sensitivity he is generally not known for comes through over and over again in
these missives. To his sister Antoinette on May 10, 1808 he had written that
he loved and needed her letters to offset the horrors of a conflict where
French throats were getting plentifully slit—that he reread them every two
hours on days he received them. To Phillis from the inferno of Saragossa,
September 2, 1809: "I do not like to lose a moment in telling you anything
that happens to me, good or bad, because you take the same interest in
it as I do; it would, indeed, be treason against friendship not to tell you
everything." These letters to his sisters would often end with tender pro-
testations of love.[7]

Bugeaud was not too sensitive, however, to stop participating in tough
missions, and he regularly got promoted. By 1811 he was an acknowledged
expert on this new type of war in Spain, as well as a member of Napoleon's

Legion of Honor. As in Vietnam or Algeria at the very end point of France's imperial glory in the mid-twentieth century, the French got tentative control of Spain's cities, but not its countryside, where inhabitants gave a bitter preview of later nationalist, guerilla struggles. Rapes and plundering continued to bother Bugeaud, and one could call him ambivalent about the so-called glory of war right through to his departure from Spain, concurrent with the emperor's own demise in 1814.[8]

In fact, he felt little regret about Napoleon's fall, accepting with ease King Louis XVIII's promotion of him to colonel in June of 1814. There was nothing hypocritical about this, for Bugeaud found it easy to defend the fledgling Bourbon monarchy of a wound-salving Restoration era. He would always profess more loyalty to his country than to any dynasty or leader. Bugeaud also became a Knight of the Royal and Military Order of Saint-Louis, and by now had a mature sense of his own uniqueness, seen in the flourishing whirl of his signature in letters, and confirmed by copious praise of his military qualities found in his personal dossier.[9] Now commanding his own garrison, he felt his basic mission was to help the restored monarchy get on its feet and attain stability.

Yet when Napoleon whirled back through the French countryside during the Hundred Days, Bugeaud and his 14th Line Regiment came on side to fight bravely for an old boss against Austrian-Sardinian forces in Savoy. After Waterloo Bugeaud had the distinction of fighting in the last Napoleonic battle, and with characteristic verve. When that episode ended, he returned to the white flag and cap of the Bourbons, but was dismissed on half-pay from the army as punishment, though remaining a committed supporter of the monarchy.

As with Austria's Metternich, now set to dominate post-Napoleonic Europe, Bugeaud had had enough of revolutionary turbulence. In the era after 1815 he detested equally excesses wrought by Ultras of the far Right and by a far smaller contingent of ex-Jacobins on the Left. What he feared most was anarchy, for he had lived and suffered its pains. And the dangers were far from over; learning that he was marked for assassination by Ultras in a "White Terror," he ignored edicts taking away his weapons, including a hunting rifle, and went around armed. Bugeaud remained as much on parole through to 1830 as France itself was vis-à-vis a watchful Europe.[10]

In 1818 he decided to marry in the hard-headed, practical way one might expect from someone who had seen his young world and more recently, his military and economic position crumble. Bugeaud desired a woman of good character who could measure up to his sisters, particularly Phillis. After poring over the situations of a variety of prospects, he chose an attractive eighteen-year-old from an old and wealthy Dordogne family that could afford a handsome dowry. Elisabeth Jouffre de Lafaye found the idea of the match agreeable, love was in the air, but Bugeaud learned that winning over her father, a justice of the peace, was about as difficult as conquering Napoleon's enemies on the battlefields! Finally he won this battle too, receiving some 250,000 francs off the top, then roughly the same amount with the sale of one of his wife's Vendean properties. That gave Bugeaud enough cash to buy back La Durantie from his family, as well as other lands nearby, and he could henceforth indulge in perhaps his truest passion—agricultural improvement.

Living on the cusp of the Limousin and Périgord, an area as backward as any in the country, and with stubbornly poor soil, he certainly had his work cut out for him. Peasants in this region, many of them sharecroppers, often lived in squalid dwellings, used outmoded agricultural techniques, and had skinny, malnourished animals.[11] Like an inspired Turnip Townsend of the previous century, Bugeaud began fighting poor methods of these sharecroppers, who in bad years flirted with starvation—especially opposing their anachronistic use of fallow land. Planting clover for forage would allow animals to become bigger and produce more manure for crops. Up at dawn to work beside peasants in the fields and to combat the old habits to which many stubbornly clung, Bugeaud made La Durantie a model farm of the region; and had the Algerian problem not intervened, one could see Bugeaud well satisfied with a life devoted to clover and manure, better plows and plowing techniques, or to husbandry that made his cattle the envy of many. He also had plentiful oak, chestnut, fruit, and mulberry trees planted, the latter permitting him to kick-start a regional silk industry. Flaubert would teach us to scoff at all this in his famous agricultural show scene in *Madame Bovary*, but Bugeaud *was* an important agricultural innovator. In 1824 he brought together a number of farmers from the area, initiating a series of meetings in France's first *comice agricole*. From 1824 to 1841 he was president of his cantonal branch, and many *comices* around France followed his example, as well as that of his model farm of La Durantie. These annual cantonal fairs became significant regional events. At those he attended Bugeaud would give a speech, local musicians would play, and of course there were prizes for the best livestock. At least until the 1830s—when the French entered Algeria, not to leave till the early 1960s—Bugeaud's deepest obsession and vocation remained farming, and in his region he was likened to Cincinnatus, a true apostle of enlightened cultivation.

But if he considered himself in the Roman tradition of the noble on his lands, Bugeaud also heeded the Roman noble's responsibility of being ever ready to return to the army. All through his high "agricultural" period he never stopped staying abreast of military theories and improvements, and as the 1820s progressed, he truly craved forgiveness by the Bourbons, and a new assignment. In a letter written to the war minister in 1824, Bugeaud complained of seeing his finest years elapse away from an army he had considered a second family, and of not being able to serve the Bourbons and his fatherland. The same day he wrote another letter to the royal dauphin, begging unsuccessfully to be reinstated. Well connected, he contacted a spate of other important military and political authorities, but nothing worked.[12]

The Revolution of 1830 and the debut of the July Monarchy then became major turning points in the life of this imperialist-in-the making. First off, that upheaval replacing Charles X, Louis XVIII's Bourbon brother, with the Orleanist King Louis Philippe "gave him back his sword," as many biographers note, and Bugeaud was soon awarded command of a regiment of the line.[13] Then his renown got him elected as a member of the Chamber of Deputies for his home district of Excideuil in the Department of the Dordogne, and he would remain a deputy from 1831 to 1847. He was suddenly not in as bad odor as his old foes, the Ultras, were to a quite liberal Orleanist monarchy. After the 1830 revolution Bugeaud had thought of concentrating on army service alone, but soon found that heading up the 56th infantry regiment at Grenoble—despite the excitement his Napoleonic renown bred in young charges—constituted a jolt to the peaceful family life he had known in the Périgord.

For right after moving, his only son Léon Thomas was tragically carried away by what was called "brain fever," and in good part Bugeaud blamed himself, given a disruptive change in abode, climate, and environment. Since his marriage it might have seemed that the gods had been conspiring against him, and maybe more so, against his wife, bereft of distractive pursuits like farming or military concerns. Their first son, Léonard, had been born in 1820 but died in 1822, the year Marie, a first daughter, came into the world. A second daughter, Hélène, arrived in 1825, but there were miscarriages before and after her birth. One occurring in 1826 nearly carried off Madame Bugeaud, and repetitive bleedings she endured from doctors through the spring of 1827 couldn't have helped.

Then came this death of a son Bugeaud had desired so badly, Léon Thomas, nicknamed Léo. Earlier biographers seemed to ignore the psychological contribution of these terrible losses to both a paradoxical sensitivity in Bugeaud, and a progressive hardening of his character that ensued in the last two decades of his life, coinciding with his preponderant role in the conquest of Algeria. In the spring-summer of 1831, Bugeaud received a military promotion to brigadier general, then his election as a deputy; but his wife was still depressed by her loss and in poor health, though consoled by seeing her increasingly absent husband energetically concentrated on a new path in life.[14]

In Paris, however, Bugeaud found himself disgusted by the endless loquacity of French parliamentarians.[15] As a deputy in the Chamber he championed the necessity for agricultural improvements, believing that only the countryside could morally regenerate, and that incendiary city types ought to be sent out to rural areas to stem the tide of depopulation. Procuring subsidies to set up more *comices*, he hoped to fill all of France with them. Home at the end of parliamentary sessions, he would still supervise his own farm, speaking *patois*, and forcefully preach the virtues of clover. The locals loved him, and he became then and in the colonial future, "le Père Bugeaud." In a society focusing on inequities wrought by industrialism, and specifically, on the problem of poverty, Bugeaud thought it paramount to feed people more efficiently by using better farming techniques.

But as a man still associated with the military, Bugeaud was given a new assignment and hiatus in February 1833—supervising the guard of the Duchess of Berry, incarcerated at the citadel of Blaye for a recently failed coup in the west of France, attempting to restore the deposed Bourbons. Though he had been reluctant to take on the assignment, worrying about his still convalescing wife, Bugeaud and the mercurial duchess hit it off quite well. He remained perfectly diplomatic when it was discovered that she had secretly become pregnant by an Italian prince. In May she gave birth to a daughter, and in June Bugeaud accompanied her and the baby on board the *Agathe* to Palermo, where she was to meet her lover and retire to an orderly domestic life. The assignment completed, he was then happy to get a breather in the Périgord, having made a friend not only of this declawed Legitimist princess, but of King Louis Philippe himself, pleased with his job.[16]

Back in the Chamber of Deputies Bugeaud was now most fearful of Parisian Leftists and their revolutionary potential. A true Hamiltonian

type, he considered property-owning the only real source of societal stability. He also had a great fear of the press as a fomenter of instability, and
increasingly favored its repression, calling it a Hydra of a million heads,
spewing constant venom.[17] He especially loathed radical newspapers, in
league, he felt, with groups like Friends of the People or the Society of the
Rights of Man. He wanted the army to be copiously visible in the capital,
predicting some form of an 1848 revolution long before most did.

Members of both press and Parliament now got his goat, dubbing him
"the jailer of Blaye." From then on Bugeaud's battle with Leftist parliamentarians and journalists became intense. As he noted: "Yes, gentlemen,
the journalists are our new despots. They have replaced the high barons
of the feudal era. It is precisely because I love freedom that I don't want
to submit to their tyranny. We are willing to grant every indulgence to a
journalist who attacks ... the entire social order day after day, yet in my
view he is a hundred times more guilty than the wretch sent for ten years
to the galleys because of a single isolated act! Every day the postal system
distributes the most appalling poisons all across France."[18]

One instance of Bugeaud's rough and ready personality was a duel he
provoked in 1834, which again stemmed from his guardianship of the
Duchess, and unleashed grave consequences. In January of that year deputies were discussing military duties in the Chamber, and Bugeaud averred
that obeying orders was always a necessity in the army. At which point a
deputy on the Chamber's far Left—a lawyer by origins named Dulong—
asked whether one should obey to the point of being a "jailer." Dulong was
a colorful character, reputed to be the illegitimate son of the revolutionary politician, Dupont de l'Eure. He was certainly a different animal from
Bugeaud, and the latter predictably grew furious, especially after Dulong's
words made it to the *Journal des débats*. Demanding a letter of apology,
and not getting what he wanted, Bugeaud asked Dulong for a duel.

His preference was for the aristocratic sword, but apparently Dulong's
witnesses felt that would spell doom for their man. Bugeaud and his military seconds then proposed the sabre, and opposition witnesses refused
that option as well, which left pistols. On January 29 at 6 A.M. Bugeaud
met Dulong in the Bois de Boulogne. The general's resolve and aim were
sure, and his first shot hit Dulong above the left eyebrow, dropping him
to the ground. The deputy briefly came to, then fell back unconscious,
passing away the next day.[19]

Not to take the future colonial hero off the hook in this affair, one
should also look psychoanalytically at M. Dulong. Probably considering

himself an outsider, due to his illegitimacy, had he intentionally rattled a rather flimsy personality cage? Had he even masochistically helped cause his own death by picking on one of France's thinner skins? It is certainly worth considering. We should also remember that even Jacobin-Socialists of the era, such as Louis Blanc, saw these fights to the finish as perfectly acceptable. "Abolish dueling," said Blanc at one point, "and you create the dictatorship of insult."[20]

After this duel, politicians of the *juste milieu* rallied around Bugeaud as a kind of leader, and Louis Philippe was allegedly happy to have seen a vociferous republican so definitively silenced! Like Bugeaud the king had himself suffered from the Terror—his father, the Duke of Orleans, who renamed himself Philippe Egalité, nonetheless perished on the guillotine— and both were united by a constant fear of some sort of revolution redux.

The aftermath to the duel was, however, of more than anecdotal influence in French history, as the Left's fury over the killing provoked serious Parisian riots in April 1834. In fact a revolutionary situation had been in the French urban air for at least a year, as courageous workers daring to strike and join underground clubs felt the new regime ignored their economic misery and political marginality. Agitation in Lyon was then followed by an eruption in Paris, which was partly blamed on Bugeaud but more on the king, considered his supporter.

During those Paris riots of 1834 Bugeaud did take part in the repression along with several other generals. Ever since his war duty in Spain he was considered and considered himself an expert at "war of the streets." But he had absolutely nothing to do with the infamous, Daumier-immortalized massacre of men, women, and children in Paris' Rue Transnonain, with which he would nonetheless be connected for life. That was the sector of General de Lascours, who never accepted either responsibility or culpability. In fact Bugeaud was profoundly saddened by the atmosphere of civil war in the capital, doing his best to spare prisoners the ill treatment certain commanders obviously enjoyed meting out. The birth that year of a son who would finally make it out of infancy and live into adulthood also enhanced his more sensitive side.[21]

In Parliament a majority now voted for a beefed-up army as a palpable response to the appearance of barricades in the French capital. Then came the Fieschi bomb plot of 1835 against the king that killed or maimed over forty people, leading to the repressive September laws, which Bugeaud fully supported. Not only did revolutionary leaders like Blanqui and Barbès irritate him, but so did lawyers protecting them. Bugeaud wanted the death sentence for terrorists and began to see the king, who was busy dodging assassination attempts, as a kind of waffler.[22]

Oddly, however, the man who would intervene so decisively in Algeria remained mostly an isolationist in foreign policy through the 1830s. Polish or Ottoman-Egyptian problems that quickened romantic sympathies in France left him utterly cold. Bugeaud also feared the potentialities of an Algerian quagmire, which by the end of the decade would tie down over 50,000 French soldiers. Through the 1830s this soldier later known for forceful interventionism there had a curiously Maginot-type mentality. He was certainly a key proponent of the fortification of Paris, thinking that without such protection Paris would always be an enticing prize for foreign powers. Remembering Saragossa, he was intermittently obsessed with a repeat of house-to-house warfare in the capital. He also wanted to improve frontier garrisons to repress possible European invasions.

At this point our isolationist more or less stumbled into the Algerian hornet's nest that would make his lasting fame, as well as infamy. With the debate still heated on whether to fight to hold the Mediterranean coast, or embark on a fuller, deeper occupation, Bugeaud's name suddenly seemed like a French lifeline. In 1836 he was given temporary command of a new Algerian army corps at Oran, and instructions to march it to the Tafna River, taking command of troops there as well, before another march and attack on Tlemcen, hopefully ridding it of an enemy presence. Immediately Bugeaud revealed his directive energy here. As seen, previous governor-generals and/or military leaders had all shown glaring deficiencies. On arrival he found troops plagued by poor morale in a godforsaken area, where ravages of fever and dysentery and of Arab ruthlessness (cutting off prisoners' heads was routine) demoralized soldiers, making French suicides common. Immediately, an aroused Bugeaud convoked officers at his tent, disserting at length. He announced his intentions of reducing the large amount of baggage dragged by French troops, as well as their cumbrous artillery, which made them enticing targets. Mules could do much of that work now. One eyewitness says Bugeaud's first speech hit these men like the proverbial cold shower. Hardly there, he also got rid of deadwood leadership. And when he received critical newspaper articles in his bag of mail, he launched an immediate tirade at men who criticized superiors behind their backs to newspapers in Algiers and France, serving notice that such behavior would no longer be tolerated. The soldiers in Algeria soon realized that they were in the presence of a leader who could inspire. But Bugeaud also admonished those who cut down Arab olive trees to build fires for their soup, screaming that when it arrived, they would have their pay docked. That money would then be used to recompense inhabitants for damage done to their property. The terrible Bugeaud temper—perhaps a legacy of his red-headed Irish side—had already become legendary.

Camping on both sides of the Tafna in early June, and integrating his new recruits, he then marched a bulging army in pursuit of the redoubtable Emir Abd el-Kader, whose troops had been killing many Frenchmen, particularly in the rear of straggling columns. Marching to Tlemcen, which he secured, then descending the Tafna to its mouth, Bugeaud finally caught up to the emir July 6 on the banks of the Sikkak River. It was the first head-to-head battle with a determined will-o'-the wisp who had been nipping at columns and retreating, and for it Bugeaud reintroduced his old Spanish techniques from the Napoleonic era, putting his soldiers into the form of a V, and effectively pincering the enemy. In stunning fashion Bugeaud won, with Abd el-Kader losing between 1,200 and 1,500 dead to only 32 on the French side. Numerous prisoners were taken, remaining Arab-Berber troops took flight, and with this victory on the River Sikkak, Bugeaud had accomplished his Algerian missions: to secure a French post on the Tafna, to reach Tlemcen, feeding and securing it, and to prove the vulnerability of an emir who had not only seemed invincible to the French, but more importantly, to his own adherents.[23]

But in letters sent home to friends and politicians, the newly created lieutenant general remained ambivalent—with no illusions about the amount of pain it would take to subdue this vast area even temporarily. On his return to the Chamber of Deputies in Paris, he made a prophetic speech, warning that "in war, it's war with all its consequences; one cannot make a *demi-guerre*." Even more prophetically he opined that one day the French would have to leave this inhospitable place. He did try to hold his tongue, but felt he couldn't.[24]

The ambivalent Bugeaud was soon dispatched back to Algeria to explore the possibility of a peace, or truce. In March 1837 he arrived first to show force, then camped at Tafna to begin crafting a treaty with Abd el-Kader, whom he rather admired as the one man who could discipline and control Arab tribes, due to his combined military-religious authority. In numerous, long, elegant letters to Governor-General Damrémont and to the war minister in Paris, Bugeaud asked for autonomy in these delicate negotiations, where both force and delicacy were required. He impressed on the home administration how much money a peace would save paying the military, and how it might facilitate colonization, as well as commerce with the Arabs. The treaty was signed on May 20 and as it turned out, engineered a Franco-Muslim ceasefire in Algeria for over two years. But Bugeaud worried about finding the right military leader, both strong yet attuned to Arab customs, for the period after his departure. On the whole he harbored no illusions about the durability of this coup. As he put it, "in making this peace, I've in no way flattered myself that it will last forever, or even for very long." He went on to admit that he made the deal partly because the French government had pushed him to do so. For now the shaky truce allowed the French to stay dominant in key coastal towns of Algeria, while allowing the tenacious emir control of the interior in the province of Oran, and in its ports like Mostaganem. In a speech to the Chamber, June 8, 1838, Bugeaud concluded frankly: "I never was, and still am not, favorable to Africa; I think that Africa is a fatal present which the [Bourbon] Restoration has given us." In fact he was still afraid that Algeria was becoming the same kind of seductive mess that Spain had represented for Napoleon.[25]

Meanwhile, "hollow orators" in the French Parliament seemed ignorant about the costs of an inevitable new round of war in Algeria, treating it as a trifling enterprise. Politicians like the ex-poet Alphonse de Lamartine spoke in wonderful rhetorical flourishes, but with no practical applicability. "What ... can one hope for from these pompous windbags, these renowned statesmen?" wrote Bugeaud in a typical letter.[26]

Fallow time occurred whenever he could get back to cultivating his large garden at La Durantie, and while there for several months in 1839, he apologized to letter-writing friends like Genty de Bussy that he couldn't keep up with correspondence. In a letter to Genty of August 16, 1839, he remarked on the felicity of time spent at home, that he had been "perfectly happy for several months in my fields, or in the bosom of a dear family, enjoying perfect health." Here, his biggest concern was getting the right weather for his corn, potatoes, or apricots.[27]

But all through the 1820s and '30s he had also been adumbrating in pamphlets and other fora his military philosophy, slated for use in Algeria. The dichotomy between the cultured man of the plough and the man of the sword would continue the rest of his life. As a military theorist, Bugeaud was utterly without patience for leaders lacking a grasp of each little detail in war. Even in letters to journals like *Le spectateur militaire* he furnished such details in abundance on, for example, the disastrous use of long, invitingly cumbrous columns.[28] Ever shading and qualifying,

Bugeaud constantly recast his theories, depending on variables like terrain or size of battalions, and his work abounds with statistics and examples drawn from Napoleonic battles like Wagram or Waterloo.[29]

Whenever he saw hazy theories expounded in journals, Bugeaud would riposte immediately. In war "the right method consists in doing what is useful, appropriate, and possible," he wrote. In the same letter he excoriated the practice of using large, immobile squares (*carrés*), declaring that smaller ones were more effective, in that once pierced, fewer men would be lost. Better not to risk one's entire force on a single move. Good leadership of infantry also meant wasting fire only when close enough to make the enemy truly pay. "Nothing is more foolish or harmful than these random firings which lead to nothing," he said.[30]

His military writing also featured a theory of aggressive retreats, which he first learned in Spain and later employed in Algeria. To him soldiers shouldn't just retreat from battle like sheep; instead, he argued, one must shoot while withdrawing, then use the accidents of terrain to serve as hiding places, in order to keep pressure on the enemy's flanks or advancing columns.[31]

Nearing the end of the decade, it was clear that Bugeaud understood the particular exigencies of Algerian combat better than most. There one had to use eyes and ears to detect the enemy and stay quiet at night, not attracting disasters. Informal little bivouacs behind rocks were more beneficial than big chains of posts that could be easily infiltrated. No need to send reconnaissance patrols too far afield to find an enemy, he felt, for they would be easily picked off; better to let that enemy reveal itself first.[32]

Like every great colonial warrior to follow, Bugeaud was acutely aware of the limits of classroom preparation in a theater like Algeria. Forget the book learning; *you* make your own books here! he declared emphatically, almost exactly what Gallieni would later tell Lyautey in the north of Vietnam. Especially in the mountains of Kabylia, where attacks rarely came head-on, but instead were mosquito-like, French columns had to learn to protect each other, fighting not so much a massed, European-style enemy as his infrastructure—villages, hiding places, stores of food. Here war would most resemble the hunting Bugeaud had engaged in on his estate; waiting for the right moment to seize an elusive prey was the constant challenge. Being ruthless? That too was part of the eat-or-be eaten equation in a place like Algeria. Threats that seemed plausible could accomplish a good deal here.[33]

Despite all this military acumen, Bugeaud defended his Treaty of Tafna as a vital breathing space and viable alternative to a badly made war. Let Abd el-Kader grow richer and improve his army with better firepower; then he would only make himself more vulnerable, he argued. It was important, however, to stop and consider the potential costs of a full-scale conflict, which still made Bugeaud queasy. Concluding a long treatise full of supporting detail and statistics, Bugeaud averred that "it's a double disaster for the country to want a stupid conquest and to make war so stupidly that one never conquers." Already, he felt that the one chance for French durability in Algeria was colonization by the military, habituated to extreme heat, snow, fevers, and other rigors of the field, and not simply avid for personal gain.[34]

With the resumption of hostilities in 1840, and problems encountered by Governor-General Sylvain-Charles Valée, Bugeaud began to see advantages in becoming a possible replacement. The great turnover in French governors-general in Algeria during the 1830s had begun as well to win over a reluctant government to Bugeaud. In a matter of ten years there had been eight changes. The militarily adept Governor-General de Damrémont had unfortunately been killed by Turkish fire at the siege of Constantine, which then catapulted a reluctant Valée to the top spot. But Valée's problems fighting against Abd el-Kader in 1839–40, parliamentary critiques of his administration, soldiers' grumbling, his underestimation of diseases wrought by mosquitoes, and the fall of a ministry that protected him in Paris made him less and less attractive.[35]

The Algerian situation was now at its most critical point, for France's gingerly presence had emboldened Abd el-Kader into rallying and unifying tribes into a kind of rival state. The emir's appeal was partly the same as that of nationalists in Europe, like Giuseppe Mazzini. Abd el-Kader believed that he could regenerate Arabs and Kabyles who had writhed under a corrupt Turkish yoke for several centuries. But besides these ideas of an Arab *risorgimento*, he also connected into a long Islamic past that still honored its saintly *marabouts* and khalifs. His own Muslim credentials were quite impeccable—he prayed routinely, fasted weekly from before dawn to dusk, and in private life, was an ascetic avoiding the lure of treasure, the seductions of polygamy (he had only one wife at the time), stimulants, and though undoubtedly martial, the pleasures of sadism. He did, however, make peace with associates to whom torture was no stranger. On the other side this was the moment when the July Monarchy itself seemed in need of a *risorgimento*, of glory that would make it more popular, as witness the transfer of Napoleon's remains to the Invalides that year. Its surrender in the recent affair of Mehmet Ali versus the Ottoman sultan had certainly gone down badly, particularly with the idealistic young. In sum, this seemed to be the time for bold actions in Algeria.[36]

An undoubtedly bold Bugeaud at least benefited from the support of a major French politician of the era, Adolphe Thiers, though Thiers would only want him appointed as governor-general along with a civilian administrator as a kind of watchdog. As for the other great political name of the time, François Guizot, he had great faith in Bugeaud's military ability, yet also hesitated on an Algerian offer for the better part of a year. In part this Anglophile feared England's reaction to French expansion in the Mediterranean. Guizot's protector, Louis Philippe, wondered as well how Bugeaud would treat his royal sons in Algeria (it turned out that he would quickly earn their respect and even love). One should finally note some scandal in the air after the Treaty of Tafna, when Bugeaud procured *quid pro quo* money he used for roads and other electorally useful improvements in his home department of the Dordogne.[37]

Bugeaud, however, now saw himself as the one military leader able to win a kind of noble duel against Abd el-Kader, whom he called the new Jugurtha (of Roman times). Bugeaud felt the French were faced with three implacable choices in Algeria: to give it up, try to hold a few coastal towns, or go for broke and attempt conquest into the interior. The press, he believed, would cry out over total withdrawal, though for him that still represented a viable option. But he definitely thought retaining only a few coastal redoubts would prove counterproductive as well. Privately, the general continued to see the Algerian involvement as a kind of mistake, but he determined that conquering the interior was the best and only way to force some sort of resolution there.[38]

Finally nominated on December 29, 1840 as governor-general by the ministry of Guizot and Marshal Soult, Napoleon's old veteran of Andalusia; and after taking care of problems in his home region of France, Bugeaud arrived in Algiers February 22, 1841. He had no notion whatsoever of waiting to implement policies. Like FDR after his first inauguration in the Depression, the new governor-general would act with alacrity here. During his first proclamation in Algiers Bugeaud announced his goals of making the Arabs submit and flying the French flag over all Algeria; then military colonization and agricultural progress would follow. Staying in coastal towns alone, France would possess only the Algerian head, not the body, he said. A French conquest would facilitate the creation of something durable here. Unlike his predecessor Valée, and unlike a

General Joffre in World War I, Bugeaud then followed this proclamation by a tour of hospitals to see wounded soldiers and to feel the realities here.[39]

As the army's commander-in-chief Bugeaud had distinct advantages over the greatest of French "Africans," Generals Christophe Juchault de Lamoricière, a brave, innovative Arabic speaker, but a stubborn man, leading the French military in the province of Oran; Nicolas Changarnier, who commanded in the province of Algiers, and though also courageous, was considered fastidious about matters like dress, while a bit lax in battle preparations; and Louis Eugène Cavaignac, a valiant, but noninspirational republican, who would become a general in 1843. Bugeaud had experienced guerilla warfare up close in Spain and had written extensively on it, realizing that this was the wave of the future. He knew the importance of good intelligence gathering, of scouting patrols, and of small, mobile patrols here. He knew for certain that huge splatters of artillery fire would be wasted in Algeria, and wanted emphatically to end the use of long columns that created such appetizing targets. He knew that more pack animals and better supplies, especially of water, would allow the French to hold on more effectively, and also stressed the importance of better hospitals. Forts and other fixed emplacements would be reduced in number; the French would have to learn to live off the land here. Above all, mobility was the key, and by taking roads less traveled, Bugeaud hoped to reduce French casualties. In these bracing conceptions, the new commander had to tilt with more orthodox army personnel, as French colonial greats who followed would all have to do through World War I, and even in Vietnam and Algeria of the 1950s.[40]

Among Bugeaud's admirers were the king's sons, and one of them, the Duc d'Aumale, listened raptly to his apothegms and stories. Alexis de Tocqueville, who distrusted Islamic influence and feared English designs in the Mediterranean, also supported the new governor's military plans. In his memoirs the well-known soldier Marshal Canrobert recalled Bugeaud: "This sensitive, highly-strung person became the epitome of calm, maintaining a totally lucid, active intelligence when in danger.... In this superior soul character dominated all else." Canrobert went on to signal his tenacity and willpower, making one of the most astonishing statements we have seen on him: "You see, young man," he told his interlocutor Bapst, "I am eighty-five years old; I have seen all the great men of our century: Bismarck, Cavour and Thiers, Napoleon III, Victor-Emmanuel, and William I. *Eh bien!* Of all these men, the greatest in heart and character, and in the good he did for his country and countrymen, is Marshal

Bugeaud ... write it down and repeat that Marshal Canrobert is the person who told you this!"[41]

Such fulsome praise may raise modern scholarly eyebrows, but it comes from a credible source, making methods soon employed by Bugeaud in Algeria more comprehensible. And indeed, Bugeaud went into action immediately. He began abolishing the use of large, vulnerable camps, bringing in better chariots, mules, guides, and provisions, and started pushing army effectives from the 63,000 at Valée's retirement up to an eventual involvement of over 100,000. Still ravaged in places by epidemics, Bugeaud's soldiers, with packs lightened and better victuals, followed his new methods. No longer, for instance, would he permit underlings to lose lives by walking alone to take food to comrades on duty. Gone too were ineffective belts that did little to combat the scourge of dysentery. The old flannel kind was not high enough to cover the belly on marches, winding about the body only once. Once sweated up, soldiers soon found the device uselessly knotted, and would simply discard it en route. Now they were going to get a belt like the one used by the Arabs, a large wool one some three meters long, wrapped several times round the body to ward off chills.[42] To a friend, Bugeaud wrote April 16, 1841: "Some complain that I'm going too fast, my dear Genty.... One thing is certain: my *army* is happy."[43]

Bugeaud's first military goal was unambiguous: to rush directly for the emir's strongholds in the Oranais region. So in a beautiful May of 1841—coinciding with Tocqueville's first investigative trip to Algeria, shortened by dysentery—Bugeaud led a column from Mostaganem to take Abd el-Kader's new fortress capital of Tagdempt. Immediately, the emir fled, then a scorched-earth fire consumed a good deal of the town, with Bugeaud's troops finishing things off by destroying its walls. In other towns he did the same thing, en route to the second regional capital of Mascara, where the emir's cavalry claimed the heights around it. There too Bugeaud partly leveled the place, then garrisoned it permanently under a French colonel. During the French pullout, Abd el-Kader's troops attacked, but against the great proponent of aggressive retreats, and Bugeaud's success in replying tarnished the emir's formerly golden reputation among his followers. Some of the most famous French soldiers in Algeria had been involved in this campaign, but Bugeaud gave special praise to the fighting ability of Mustafa ben Ismaël, commanding indigenous cavalry for France. Other French battalions took more strong points in Algeria, but in those battles too, Abd el-Kader's charges simply annoyed them, and Bugeaud worried about the equivalent of Russian winter taking its toll here: searing heat, sending numerous French soldiers to hospitals or their beds.

After Bugeaud's wife and daughters made an enjoyable September visit to Algiers, the general resumed campaigns in the fall, realizing that Abd el-Kader's dancing and feinting, and the character of supporters who only provisionally surrendered, meant a long war here. The enemy tried to avoid, while Bugeaud's men—marching faster and farther—tried to find. He was up in the night to do battle along with his charges, and indeed, it was at the end of 1841 that Bugeaud strode out of his tent to fight the enemy, then realized he still had on his cotton nightcap! This scene worthy of Groucho Marx spawned a famous song, one that became a staple among Bugeaud's men, featuring the refrain: "Have you seen the *casquette* of father Bugeaud?" A fierce winter of 1841–42 scarcely deterred enthusiastic French operations that continued apace, and their efforts induced more and more tribespeople to surrender prisoners and animals in the mountains, as well as in the interior. Bugeaud himself took Tlemcen for good in January 1842, planning a link-up between the provinces of Oran and Algiers. By the beginning of summer he felt he had the slippery, but now less prestigious Abd el-Kader on the ropes. He wrote Thiers and others to the effect that the Muslim leader was like an ebbing storm that might still produce a few more lightning flashes, but would soon end. At the same time the governor refused to minimize challenges that would follow even a temporary French conquest, and his admiration of a great adversary reveals his own depth. To his friend Gardère, he wrote that the emir "strives against his ill fortune with grand energy and ability. He is really a master man, worthy of a better fate."[44]

By the fall of 1842 the French controlled the mountains between Tlemcen in the west and Constantine in the east, and found themselves ensconced on the edge of the Sahara. But Bugeaud never once underestimated his opponents' ability to reappear for new rounds of warfare. Early on he had endorsed the building of ramparts to protect new European villages, and foremost among parliamentarians interested in Algeria, Tocqueville continued giving approval to Bugeaud's leadership that he would qualify a few years later.

By the end of 1842 Bugeaud had discarded the wall idea, costing too many lives of too many men who were attacked while constructing it; and then its successor, the ditch or moat. He would live or die by his own methods, and now deemed a complete takeover of Algeria a real possibility. Treating with tribal chieftains, Bugeaud would be decent to the *soumis* (submissive), but pitiless with those who broke agreements to arm themselves for more resistance; and already some of the educated public back home was appalled. More and more tribes, however, surrendered. Treating them in feudal manner, Bugeaud forced their leaders to collect taxes as a guarantee of fidelity, and some of the chieftains seemed happy with the protection of Bugeaud's French.[45] Others were not, and he asked the home government if he might deport their hostile tribes perhaps to Martinique or Guadeloupe! Submissive Arab or Kabyle tribes-people—the latter, Berbers of the coastal ranges—would police themselves in Algeria, and be willing vassals. The Arabs themselves (it is too often forgotten) had been great imperialists; they knew the game. And Bugeaud would be just as firm with his own *colons* who stepped out of line and abused Muslims. In both French and Arabic notices were tacked up announcing the arrest of any European found beating up friendly inhabitants of Algeria.

The French, meanwhile, would build here, working to reduce diseases, enhance trade opportunities, and to some degree, assimilate. Trade, said Bugeaud, would have the same efficacy in Algeria as alcohol had had for the American Indian. It would overcome resistance, and so would more secure roads. A crucial need for dealing with the indigenous was interpreters who had courage, moral firmness, delicacy, but above all, linguistic skill in French, Arabic, Turkish, Kabyle, and even Persian. A series of meetings by a commission to set standards for interpreters rapidly led to modifications of those linguistic requirements. Eventually committee members felt that Arabic (written and spoken) was the one requisite language in Algeria, given that many Kabyle chieftains and even the common people used it. Because of the difficulty of finding suitable candidates, qualifications became ever more limber. Connecting in their idiom with tribespeople and notables remained the ultimate goal.[46]

But already, one of the main problems of Bugeaud's governorship had emerged—the paradoxical fact that dealing with tribespeople was often less complicated than dealing with opinion back home, including with the war minister's critiques. Marshal Nicholas Jean de Dieu Soult had a deservedly strong military reputation, but was now in the governor-general's estimation, a senile, stubborn old bureaucrat. Through the 1840s Bugeaud fought constantly over budgetary matters with Soult or with Melcion d'Arc, director of Algerian affairs at the War Ministry. Soult kept warning Bugeaud about parliamentary discord on these and other Algerian questions. Correspondence exchanged between Bugeaud and the minister or underlings in his office bulges in the archives. First off, Bugeaud sent detailed reports of his battles to Soult. There were all sorts of other affairs to deal with: for example, four members of a shipwrecked crew of a French ship, having to be ransomed from Kabyles in 1841. Bugeaud wrote repeated letters to Soult on the subject—how much money to pay, how to contact Sardinian and Spanish consulates (as the four sailors hailed from those places), and so on. Soult had his own recommendations on where to lodge prisoners, whom to execute, how to distribute and at what price confiscated animals, etc. His letters, reports, and directives often ran to twenty pages of sanctimonious rule making and precedent citing that irked Bugeaud, as well as his military subordinates.[47]

Bugeaud needed to push hard as well for promotions of army men he deemed worthy. One on whom he wrote Soult was another example of cultured force, Captain Rivet, who had been in Algeria ten years, lived among Arabs and knew their customs and language, and had organized and fought with tribespeople. Bugeaud said that few officers possessed this mixture of courage, knowledge of an area, and linguistic skill, and that Rivet ought to have command of a squadron of native cavalrymen (*spahis*). Bugeaud certainly knew talent. Eventually achieving the title of General Rivet, this enlightened officer would produce a beautifully written, almost courtly history of the Bugeaud years in Algeria, showing how the French were at pains to compensate fairly, to maintain customs, and above all, not to duplicate a Turkish system that had "always been repulsive" here. But where Bugeaud knew these people first-hand, the War Ministry in Paris didn't; so there were constant quarrels about such appointments and promotions, as well as demotions or transfers.[48]

As for hostile journalists Bugeaud's iterative term for them became "les Bedouins de Paris," worse to him than real ones. There was also the problem of a growing bureaucracy that proconsuls after Bugeaud would equally revile. In a letter to Genty of August 14, 1842 Bugeaud noted: "They seem to think that I have nothing else to do but paper-pushing: this is what I like the least and do the most!" To Thiers he would complain six months later of battling "wrongheaded, ill-conceived, or cowardly ideas, which from the French public enter our offices and translate into bad projects."[49]

The war? It was going better than dealing with functionaries, speculators, and adventurers arriving in droves. After French military successes newcomers settled in "this wasp's nest where all the dreamers and starvelings of France end up . . . all these pen-pushers, petty lawyers and swindlers, people who were . . . unable to make a go of it in the home country and have come to Africa to seek their fortune." Bugeaud still felt that the French could put something in place here that was fairer than the previous Turkish system, especially when it came to taxation and justice. But it would take constant work and policy making, for "here everything is urgent. Every minute there are new questions requiring immediate decisions."[50]

If the French were going to make it in Algeria, thoroughly was the only way; nothing and nobody could be allowed to impede the process. As the 1840s paced onward, Bugeaud increasingly found himself on a kind of colonial ship pulling away from the dock of mainstream opinion back home. The governor-general cared deeply about resettling Arabs on lands they could farm and grow to love—their own roofs overhead, their own gardens to cultivate. Yes, one used the sword here, but then came the plow. He also pushed for the resumption of *bureaux arabes*, by which Muslims through their notables would partially administer themselves, including local policing. These became a lasting institution, though in the early years Bugeaud's officers who worked in them generally knew Arabic, and were of higher quality and more sensitive than those of later genera- tions. Justice administered by the *bureaux arabes* was certainly fairer than that of the Ottoman Empire. There were twenty-one of these offices in place by April 1845. But at the same time as one endeavored to protect Islamic rights, one *also* needed a powerful, mobile French army to con- tinue providing security for Europeans. And already, Bugeaud seemed to consider that army as a higher power, and in some ways unaccountable to the home front.[51]

This mindset allowed him to justify and use extreme measures in his war against the Muslims—the aforementioned *razzias*, including crop and village burnings, livestock confiscations, or destruction of fruit trees. Such activity was repugnant but defensible to intelligent Frenchmen like Tocqueville; to some it was merely repugnant. For Bugeaud the two options here were to win at any price, or leave. "We're going to out-Arab the Arabs," as he would say. Humanists back in France might be aghast, but "it is to these *razzias*, which so horrified you, that we owe all our progress, and particularly, the security which made it possible for *you* to visit much of Algeria in such peace," he wrote. He would also remind those at home that some of Abd el-Kader's men had been resorting to worse terror, for instance, cutting off hands and feet of recalcitrant chief- tains. He stressed as well an immemorial Arab propensity for intertribal

warfare, revolt, and theft of both property and women as a virtuous manifestation of courage.[52]

By early 1844 Marshal Bugeaud considered the most onerous stage of
the conquest over. He had been awarded the title of Marshal the previous
summer by the French king, who had lost one son to this conflict and
received word of the exploits of another, the Prince d'Aumale. The twenty-
one-year old Aumale's capture of Abd el-Kader's personal retinue, the
smalah, in May 1843, was crucial, procuring 15,000 prisoners. Chased all
over the Oranais from the Mediterranean south to the desert, the emir
took refuge on Morocco's frontier; and much of the area he had formerly
dominated was now pacified. (Algeria's European population had shot
up by 20,000 in the past year alone.) In April 1844 Bugeaud made a
proclamation to tribes that were still resistant—a last humanitarian offer,
as he saw it. Many others had seen the advantages with us and deserted
the emir: why not you? he asked. If you refuse, he continued, "I will go
into your mountains, burn your villages and harvests, cut down your fruit
trees and ... I will be completely innocent of these disasters before God;
for I will have done enough to spare you from them!"[53]

But though weakened, Abd el-Kader was still avid for another round,
enjoying his refuge across the frontier. In Morocco he began preaching a
new Islamic crusade to win back Tlemcen, Oran, Mascara, even Algiers,
and in this period, there were numerous cross-border attacks on French
posts and allied tribes. Bugeaud's warnings, transmitted by his chief interpreter, Léon Roches, fell on deaf ears. Writing back, the emir spoke of God
and Islam, telling Bugeaud that even the weak knew how to blind a lion!
Nothing daunted, Bugeaud warned Morocco's sultan in June that France
was losing patience, and that it would take over Oujda near the frontier
as a temporary measure. If problems didn't cease, it might even go further into Morocco itself. On June 12 France's foreign minister, Guizot, gave
an ultimatum to Morocco's emperor, demanding that his troops stay out
of Algeria and Abd el-Kader be ejected from his country. That July another
of Louis Philippe's sons, the Prince de Joinville, led a flotilla of twenty-
eight French warships patrolling the Moroccan coast, then in early August
directed a naval bombardment of Tangier and Mogador.[54]

When Bugeaud decided to cross the Isly River at dawn on August 14,
1844, he was crossing a Rubicon en route to what became his hallmark
victory, perhaps France's greatest since the Napoleonic era. And he was
doing it in typical French imperial style by not waiting for instructions
from the War Ministry. In this celebrated Battle of Isly, Moroccan cavalry

emerged from the hills and hit the French from all sides. But Bugeaud's infantry and *tirailleurs* coolly fought back, and eventually the enemy took flight, with the French pressing on a great victory and cutting the foe's cavalry in two. Bugeaud was amazed by the valor of his men, and of their leaders like Caïd Mohamed ben Kaddour and General Marie-Alphonse Bedeau on the wings, not to mention the egregious Colonel Yusuf (born Giuseppe Ventini on the Island of Elba). Hijacked by pirates in the Mediterranean and made a mameluke in Tunis, where he studied Koran, Arabic, and Turkish, "Yusuf" subsequently escaped to Algiers and now proved his military worth. Some French groups had been outnumbered at least twelve to one in this battle, Bugeaud commented proudly. To him this victory was one of superior organization and planning over forces of far greater numbers, and a high point for the entire corps of "Africans"—"the consecration of our Algerian conquest."[55] Isly had shattered Abd el-Kader's Moroccan base, forcing him to take flight, and after the sultan's foot-dragging, produced a Treaty of Tangier with Moroccan authorities, acceding to French requests and making the emir an outlaw there. King Louis' appreciation was immediate. In a letter to the governor-general he described the deep emotions news of the victory had given him, and how Bugeaud ought to convey his great pleasure to the men in his battalions. The king then conferred the title Duc d'Isly on the grizzled African leader.[56]

Returning to France, Bugeaud d'Isly (as he henceforth signed letters) continued receiving much praise; in the midst of growing economic depression the July Monarchy had gotten a badly needed infusion of *gloire*. There were celebrations of the victory at Isly all over France. Letters of congratulation poured in to Bugeaud from old associates, including one who had known him thirty-six years and averred that "nothing you do astonishes me." On January 24, 1845 the Marshal followed Louis Philippe's address in the Chamber with a ringing speech of his own, saluting an overextended army that had done the impossible, marching and fighting in sweltering heat, and then, after three days rest, back working on its bridges and roads. Bugeaud made sure also to defend *razzias* in a war atmosphere so different from Europe. For in Africa there were no cities that constituted decisive takeover points and whose seizure ended conflicts. Here "there is only one vital striking point, and that is agriculture." The speech flowed on and on, a verbal river gathering all the obsessional imperial debris in the governor-general's mind. Again, he preached the virtues of military over civilian colonization, provoking laughs when he declared: "I could compare those who live along the coast under the civilian regime to badly-raised children, and those who live in the interior under military rule to well brought-up ones." But he meant it. And he warned realistically that in the post-Isly atmosphere the wine of victory could too easily becloud French heads, and that the whole Algerian problem would never be easy to resolve definitively. He spoke of several million Arabs, of whom virtually all adult males were warriors, concluding that there *was* hope for the future, but that the French could never afford to be weak here. He was soon infuriated by a government ordinance of April 1845 instituting a director of civilian affairs in Algeria, ostensibly to weaken his own authority.[57]

Meanwhile, Bugeaud managed to remain a dedicated family man, though the demands of his occupation made huge inroads into the attentions he could vouchsafe a wife and children. On his trip home he was so fêted that it cut into precious time he craved with his loved ones. In one of his earlier letters, sent to an ailing daughter at home, he wrote: "How sorry I am, my good Léonie, that you have been ill again. All the turns of your sickness have been running in my head. I see you in bed, I hear your fits of coughing, I see your cheeks flushed with fever, I feel your pulse.... I hope this letter will find you well, and that you will go to the watering-place at the end of May, and come and see your dear father in September, as he wants you to compensate him for his fatigues." He ended the letter by asking "Ninie" to write, and also to kiss her sister Marie for him. Again, the shibboleth view of Bugeaud seems to bypass this utterly human, even tender side he had. That tenderness also emerged in a letter he wrote his wife July 15, 1843, where he said he couldn't wait to see her, either back in France, or by her taking a trip to Algeria. "If you do not come," Bugeaud remarked, "I will come to you, I swear it; but let me entirely decide this great work. I will not say finish it, but put it in such a state that it will not go backward."[58]

Decisive results in the Algerian context were still not easy to achieve and indeed, after the flush of Isly had subsided, Bugeaud's "Africans" found themselves on the edge of one of their darkest hours. Another rebel chieftain in the line of Abd el-Kader, Bou Maza (the goat man), raised the standard of Islamic revolt among Kabyle tribes of the Dahra mountain chain in the north. The revolt spread, and Bugeaud gave carte blanche for repression to commanders of various sectors. A publicized atrocity, though far from the only one of the time, occurred in June 1845, when Colonel Amable Jean-Jacques Pélissier's soldiers penned part of the rebellious Oulad Riah tribe into a cave or really, the beginning of a series of grottos in the Dahra near Mostaganem. After attempting to procure a surrender, Pélissier's men started a fire at the mouth of the cave and perhaps unintentionally, suffocated 500 to 600 men, women, and children in the process. There were reports, however, of soldiers shooting at some of those trying to flee.

One often sees Bugeaud's name used in association with this tragedy, but in fact he was far away at the time. He would nonetheless endorse the action, as did virtually all other "Africans," failing to comprehend French parliamentary horror when reports of the atrocity surfaced. As noted, it was not the only incident of this kind. Mountain tribes that pillaged and murdered would often take refuge up on cliffs and finally, in caves. Pélissier was a man with some literary pretensions, and he composed an ultrarealistic report on what the bodies looked like the next day. Had Bugeaud been able to do so, he would certainly have suppressed that report; but news of the episode reached the Paris press, provoking the well-known brouhaha it did. Yet the governor-general continued to deem this a proper example to show other tribes in the mountains. In a letter to the war minister he said that Colonel Pélissier hadn't resorted to this action before trying every other possibility of conciliation, and noted unambiguously that "if the government consider that there is punishment to be awarded, it is upon me that it must fall." As for his "philanthropic" parliamentary colleagues, he felt they were plainly out of touch. Indecision, any show of weakness would be absolutely fatal in Algeria. To Thiers July 20, 1845 he revealed the schism that had now become so wide between métropole and "Africans," declaring in reference to the affair of the caves that "very few people in France can understand the cruel necessities of this inextricable war, with the added complication of a new people settling on the territories of the conquered." Not to give Bugeaud anything like full approval, one is again reminded that present writers and readers are here, in rather exalted circumstances, partly because many horrendous, unpardonable things were done to make today's "civilization," or what remains of it.[59]

Subordinates like Saint-Arnaud went completely down the line for Bugeaud, and so did General Cavaignac of the future June Days massacre of 1848 in Paris. In fact, they would do the same kind of thing to other tribes. There were all sorts of mini Abd el-Kaders to fight, fierce prophets like Bou Ali, Ali Chergui, Si Larbi, or Bel Bej. "I get utterly lost with them all," wrote a despairing Saint-Arnaud. Prices to be paid fighting such foes might include freezing to death or becoming an invalid for life, not to mention Arab torture. But French soldiers in Algeria had truly become a contingent with a mystique all their own. What commentators in Paris and visitors seemed to miss most was that one couldn't colonize without military security, and that it must be bought at a high ethical (or nonethical) price.

Bugeaud became so incensed by the government's inability to stifle criticism of his men, and by its attempts to limit his power with a new director of Algerian civil affairs that he went home in a huff to La Durantie in September 1845, leaving Lamoricière as interim governor. There were soon, however, more troubles to follow for the Duke of Isly. With the most feared Gallic commander away, Abd el-Kader and a band of warriors again crossed Morocco's frontier into Algeria, and in late September slaughtered an entire contingent of Frenchmen, including the courageous Colonel de Montagnac. One French company stuck in Sidi-Brahim, without water and with almost no food for three days, was also decimated. Bou Maza now pledged allegiance to a resurgent emir, and a large-scale insurrection resulted. Back in France Bugeaud, who had resolved *not* to return to Algeria until the government denounced press falsities on his policies, was stricken by this costly resumption of hostilities, and with Lamoricière and others clamoring for his return, decided reluctantly to go back to the fray. Before he left, he presented the war minister Soult a long shopping list from artillery to mules. But the governor had no certainty of a successful outcome. "If I don't succeed," he wrote pessimistically, "nothing in the world will be able to chain me any longer to this rock of Sisyphus."[60]

On arrival in Algiers October 15 Bugeaud rolled up his sleeves, telling *colons* that there would always be a price here, but that it was worth paying. In fact, another round of conflict with the Arabs, declared Bugeaud to the new war minister in November, was less bothersome than "this underhanded war waged against me in certain *bureaux*, and the bad ideas they have succeeded in pushing through." That new war minister replacing Soult, who resigned in November 1845, was General Moline de Saint-Yon. Saint-Yon was more appreciative of Bugeaud than his predecessor, but unfortunately, lacked Soult's clout both in governmental chambers, and with the king.[61]

Searching out Abd el-Kader, a massive manhunt countered by orders of the emir's councilors to slit the throats of French prisoners, again revealed Bugeaud to be a master tracker, never Cartesian or *a priori*, always sprouting in his mind and thence in communications to subordinates every possible route Abd el-Kader might take. This was what he did best. Harder to take was all "the [French] filth and folly that is thrown at my head," as he commented acidly in one letter. "Could they do worse if I had lost a hundred fights and all Algeria?" He went on to say that he took his revenge by military success; but the effect on his mental and physical health continued to grow worse.[62] Privately, his demoralization seemed almost complete, as, for example, when he wrote Guizot that "my time is past, that's clear." He added that his very success was his undoing, that now every amateur wanted to bring his own stone to this Algerian edifice. Advising Guizot to groom a successor, he declared that health and family would be the public reasons given for his eventual departure, but the real reason was that "I do not want to be the artisan of false ideas which generally prevail on the great questions of Africa." Bugeaud, however, never stopped caring about the area, and even as problems seemed at times insuperable, wrote Genty that he was still working from morning till night, and sometimes through the night. He also mellowed somewhat when it came to French politicians. A visiting parliamentary delegation, led by Tocqueville in November 1846, was treated respectfully, though the group seemed self-righteous. Proudly, Bugeaud showed off gardens his soldiers had planted, new roads, and hospitals. Tocqueville still admired Bugeaud, but they differed sharply on the issue of military versus civilian colonization. Another celebrated critic was Bugeaud's military rival, Lamoricière, recently elected as a deputy and also promoting a scheme of civilian colonization. Bugeaud's detailed response in the form of a pamphlet criticized "entrepreneurs of colonization" who would allow the worst elements (who by "laziness or *inconduite*" couldn't make it in Europe) to stream into Algeria. Prescient, he considered Lamoricière's idea of pushing the Arabs away the wrong route for the future. For Bugeaud, this was a country of "a bellicose people, admirably prepared for war"; better to learn to live with them side by side, allowing military *colons* to provide security. Then, via enriching cultivation and commerce, more and more Muslims would adhere to the French. Listen to the Lamoricières, and Algeria might become a long-term distraction weakening France's position in Europe![63]

After another massacre of several hundred French soldiers, Bugeaud again wrote Louis' chief minister Guizot (March 9, 1847), excoriating the War Ministry and its ill-conceived ideas that were making it hard to hold onto the conquest. But Guizot was himself none too healthy politically, and Bugeaud groaned: "I am already rather too old for the hard work of Africa." In a letter written to Thiers two days later, he repeated his hoarse-voiced obsession about the necessity of military colonization, and reiterated that he would soon leave North Africa for good. The whole issue was settled when Tocqueville, chair of a parliamentary committee voting on a special appropriation for Algeria and on Bugeaud's plans for military colonization, unanimously rejected the latter.[64]

Despite writing he saw on the wall, Bugeaud's last year in Algeria was a busy one. Military success had spawned many issues to decide on, including the clamor of indigenous job-seekers, sending beautifully-written Arabic letters to the marshal's office. These were laden with unctuous formulae ("May God conserve your long life," etc.). A typical letter lauded Bugeaud's military prowess, yet his cultured qualities as well. There were also many property or indemnity claims, making Bugeaud's correspondence with both the Finance Ministry in Algiers and the War Ministry in Paris thicker. It had all become too bureaucratic, and Bugeaud remained frustrated. Many claims appeared spurious to the Finance Administration, but still had to be checked in Paris. Some Arabic letters were even dispatched to King Louis Philippe, then relayed back to the governor. French confiscations from Abd el-Kader's *own* confiscations meant distributing money procured from sales of animals, an exhaustive process of establishing precise amounts and a list of deserving names. The result was ever more governmental forms to fill out. Trying to locate the right Islamic authorities to work with as intermediaries was also hard, as everybody seemed to be a *marabout* here! Bugeaud's administration had to deal too with thousands of tribespeople demanding a return to Algeria from Morocco, where their links to Abd el-Kader made them suspect. For that problem he blamed the sultan's "incredible apathy." Needless to add, land demands of European *colons* kept increasing as well.[65]

Exhaustion from all this, and the rejection of his most cherished policies, finally impelled the marshal to tender his resignation at the end of May 1847. In a farewell address to the *colons*, army and navy at Algiers (May 30), he emphasized the state of the colony when he had arrived, and how, despite Parisian foolishness, security was now established over a far greater area, with the Arabs themselves contributing, and bridges, buildings, water lines, and new villages in place everywhere. Bou Maza had given himself up to Saint-Arnaud in April, and though the surrender of Bugeaud's great opponent, Abd el-Kader, was still seven months in the future, it had become a foregone conclusion. Bugeaud's departure from North Africa was certainly big news, and one of the best descriptions comes from the Prince de Joinville, who noted dramatically: "I can still see his grand white head, as he stood uncovered on the bridge of the ship which bore him away, and passed slowly between the lines of warships, with their cannon thundering, drums rolling, bands playing the Marseillaise, and crews cheering wildly." Over and over Bugeaud had pleaded ill health, and with reason; but to Léon Roches he wrote that the main reason for his departure was the government's failure to confirm his view of military colonization. Repeating the same thing to General Charon, he noted that "I did not want to be the one to apply all the absurd ideas about colonization which ... will lead to the destruction of my work."[66]

Back home in La Durantie the former governor kept fighting these battles, less than a year before the Revolution of 1848 and less than two years, it turned out, before the end of his life. Bugeaud was still heavily consulted on African policy—too much so for his taste. In September 1847, the month when the Duc d'Aumale succeeded him as Algeria's governor-general, he wrote his daughter: "My house is never empty. Not only do they make me write unceasingly, but they nibble at my time and my provisions. A man is really unhappy if he has a little influence, or at least is supposed to have it." Discussing French imperial policy, Bugeaud still felt he had to combat the unobservant humanism of certain deputies in the Chamber. "If only there were no Arabs in Algeria, or if they resembled the effeminate peoples of India ...," he wrote d'Aumale.[67] He continued to deem civilian colonization more appropriate for the coast alone, and felt that inland Arabs would understand French military colonization as normal spoils of war; whereas others might be perceived as plain property thieves. Civilian immigration nevertheless proceeded apace—Spanish, Italians, Maltese, along with French—and obliterated Bugeaud's military emphasis. By 1847 there were over 100,000 Europeans in Algeria, but only some 15,000 lived outside coastal agglomerations; military colonization had never filled the breach. Bugeaud's Algerian ideals were consigned if not to total failure, at least to much modification. In any event he had now to worry about problems on the home front, rising unrest partly derived from economic dislocation, as well as the efflorescence of a new idea, socialism, along with what he saw as other domestic rackets.[68]

Speaking of rackets, Bugeaud himself seems not to have been politically pure either. Probably correctly, he was accused of committing electoral fraud to keep his parliamentary seat during the 1840s, though one should consult Sherman Kent's old book on July Monarchy electoral procedure to realize how normal all this was at the time. What the process generally involved, according to Kent, was plying regional electors with benefits like roads or hospitals, or even liquor, to keep a seat. The political "ins" of the

July Monarchy benefited from government patronage to do this to political "outs," and Bugeaud was certainly devoted to a regime that had made
him a deputy, lieutenant-general, marshal of France, and duke, not to mention Algeria's governor.[69]

Out of both his parliamentary seat and Africa on the eve of the Revolution of 1848, he could now look closely at the internal French scene, and
the prospect dismayed this expert on "street war." (Bugeaud even wrote
a manuscript on the subject.) Through 1847 and early 1848 he feared the
rising revolutionary tide, stimulated by a middle-class banquet campaign
against electoral restrictions, and hoped to show what he could do to stem
it. But Louis Philippe only reluctantly made him commander of Paris' military garrison after an initial massacre on the Boulevard des Capucines
of February 23, 1848 turned a riot into actual revolution. Given ensuing
fraternization of troops with the Paris masses, it became rapidly too late
for toughness without creating much carnage. When the king announced
a ministry of Thiers, Odilon Barrot, and Bugeaud, crowds of Parisians
shouted their displeasure at each name. To the name Bugeaud some called
out repeatedly "Transnonain!"[70] On February 24 Bugeaud wanted to attack
rioters in full Algerian-style force, using four columns of troops—one
under General Tiburce Sébastiani to penetrate the Bank of France area via
the Hôtel de Ville; another under his Algerian associate, General Bedeau,
aimed for the Place de la Bastille via the *grands boulevards*; a third to stop
the building of new barricades in the rear; and a fourth under Colonel
Jean-André Brunet to head across the Seine for the Pantheon. Only Brunet
attained his objective, while Sébastiani was halted at the Hôtel de Ville
and Bedeau was mired in thick crowds on the Boulevards Poissonière
and Bonne-Nouvelle, trying to reason with demonstrators—"a just man,
moderate, liberal-minded, as humane as though he had not waged war in
Africa for eighteen years," in Tocqueville's words. Increasing insubordination of garrisons mixing with crowds, then the intervention of middle-
class politicians, along with Bugeaud's own second thoughts and Louis'
hasty abdication, compelled withdrawal of these troops.[71]

Returning to La Durantie after the substitution of a provisional government for the former king, Bugeaud armed his servants and sharecroppers
against possible marauders. To his daughter in Algiers with her husband,
he wrote March 10, 1848: "My little darling, I was hungry to see you at La
Durantie; now I am both hungry and thirsty. How happy should I be to
have you and your husband here in the spring, to visit our fields and
woods. You would comfort me for the bitter deceit of politics." Even away

from Paris, Bugeaud was still parrying accusations concerning the Trans-nonain massacre, making him at times fear for his life. To the current war minister he wrote on March 28, 1848 about lies appearing in newspapers (hundreds of new ones now in circulation), as well as in club motions and anonymous letters. "Eh bien! monsieur le ministre," declared Bugeaud emphatically, "I did *not* go into that street." He added that it would be easy to conduct an official investigation on the subject, and "I am urgently requesting one to put an end to these rumors which disgust me." A day later in a letter to his friend Gardère he excoriated the organization of labor, and then to Léon Roches, now a *chargé d'affaires* in Tangier, he said this was 1793 all over again, minus the guillotine. He had always consid-ered himself a man of the people, said Bugeaud, but these communists and socialists were a mystifying new force, too utopian and unrealistic, and committing acts that even the Touaregs of Africa would blush at committing! To a colonel in Algeria he wrote on July 4 that the man was fortunate to be so far removed from a country where people were acting far worse than the Arabs, and to Thiers he declared that this was a clear fight between civilization and barbarism.[72]

During the June Days of 1848, however, it was difficult to discern which side was "civilized." Bugeaud took no part in the infamous series of fire-fights with workers on the Paris streets, but other Africa veterans played major roles. Besides the leadership of Cavaignac, one could mention Lamoricière, personally vengeful after being injured in the February fight-ing. At that time Tocqueville had called on "this singular person stretched upon his bed, and reduced to a state of immobility very much opposed to his character"—head smashed, arms punctured by bayonet thrusts, limbs bruised. But in the repression of June there was Lamoricière back heading troops on horseback, and never had one "seen a figure more re-splendent with aggressive passion and almost with joy." Lamoricière "gave his commands amid the whirl of bullets," gesticulating "in a sort of rage," says Tocqueville. One cannot imagine Bugeaud waging urban civil war and spilling so much Parisian blood with such pleasure. As for the rela-tively humane Bedeau, he was seriously wounded and almost killed on the first day of fighting.[73]

During the autumn Bugeaud remained depressed by the "Red Repub-lic," though the election of Louis Napoleon Bonaparte as president gave him some hope. Even after winning an Assembly seat in "partial elections" for the Department of Charente-Inférieure; and after receiving command of the Army of the Alps in late December, Bugeaud thought into early

1849 of action against the revolutionary regime. He wanted to publish his pamphlet on *The War of Streets and Houses*, due to what he considered military bungling that had produced thousands of casualties in the June Days, and the continuing influence of "demagogues and utopians of all colors," of "novateurs barbares." (The manuscript, however, remained unpublished and lost for almost 150 years!) He also kept worrying about how to improve life for soldiers in Algeria, writing the War Ministry about matters like better stretchers for the wounded—remaining a major cause of discomfort and death a century later in French Indochina.[74]

Bugeaud's health kept deteriorating, but few were prepared when an attack of Asiatic cholera sweeping across Paris suddenly killed him in 1849 at age sixty-five. His solemn burial at the Invalides concluded the career of a complex figure, one who might have become known as the Gallic Turnip Townsend; but instead, was ever linked to the creation of a French Algeria, which by this time was cut up into three departments. Aside from his great role in the creation of an *Algérie française*, Bugeaud can also be seen as feeding into the lineage of subsequent imperial figures—Faidherbe, Gallieni, Lyautey—to whom we turn in coming chapters. As well, he influenced a bevy of other French military leaders, who might loosely be called "Bugeaudistes," and who would play important roles in the country's future history, stimulated by the master's model.[75]

One such was Marshal Canrobert. Born in 1809, Canrobert grew up in a military family and had been enthralled in his youth by tales of Napoleonic glory. But as seen, Bugeaud also impressed him, in part with his military acumen in Algeria, where Canrobert first went in the 1830s; and more, by the force of his entire character.[76]

Another Bugeaudiste was General Louis Jules Trochu, who would prepare Paris for the siege of 1870–71 at the hands of the invading Germans. Trochu learned from other great Africans like Lamoricière, for whom he was aide-de-camp in the early 1840s, and the impulsive Changarnier, whose vanity led him to a clash with Bugeaud and removal from the colony, until he returned after the latter's departure. But Bugeaud remained Trochu's most enduring influence. Becoming aide-de-camp and secretary to the governor-general made him "the daily auditor . . . of the last great professor of war remaining in the country," he recalled.[77] For some five years from the time of the Battle of Isly, Trochu scarcely left the master's side, following him back to France and witnessing him and Guizot in têtes-à-têtes before the outbreak of revolution. Seeing Bugeaud ready to take command of Parisian troops in February 1848, then preempted by politicians, would also have an effect, he says, on his own actions in September 1870. Bugeaud's meetings with Guizot and the events that followed became "the great political lesson[s] of my life." Fittingly enough, Bugeaud expired in Trochu's arms in 1849.[78]

Another admirer was Count Pierre de Castellane, who in a memoir written during the Second Empire gives us another unambiguous appreciation of Bugeaud. "Who among us could forget this noble face and soul?" he wrote, adding that no one under his command could ever do so. He said the way the governor-general talked to soldiers went straight to the heart and inspired.[79]

Probably the most eccentric Bugeaudiste was Léon Roches, who went to Algeria in the 1830s, learned Arabic and elements of Islam, and then became secretary and interpreter to Abd el-Kader, feigning a conversion to Islam and endearing himself to the emir as "Omar," son of Roches. When he finally told Abd el-Kader the truth about his conversion, he was both guilty and fortunate to leave this magnetic father-figure, which then led him to Bugeaud. The first night he unfolded his story he was struck by "the general's frank and loyal nature." Roches became chief interpreter to the Army of Africa and Bugeaud's right-hand man in dealings with Arab sheiks through the period of the Battle of Isly, saluting the governor's humanity with certain tribes caught between the French and Abd el-Kader, and his diplomatic skill treating with their leaders. Despite a reputation for tactlessness, Bugeaud acted with an "exquise galanterie" that won over many chieftains. One night Roches introduced a down-at-heels Genoese sea captain he knew and liked, worrying about the man's ragged persona. Bugeaud invited the guest to dine, then reproached Roches: "Haven't you learned yet what I'm about? . . . that I place heart and good sense above the mind and science?" He went on to recall dinners with Dordogne peasants, where they spoke *patois* and taught him many useful things, unlike putatively classier types indulging in "hollow verbiage." He concluded to Roches that he ought to know that "I'm preoccupied by what's inside, not what's outside" (*du fond et non de la forme*). Struck by the marshal's "delicious simplicity," Roches realized why soldiers would so readily lay down their lives for him.[80]

A qualification to this view comes, however, from Lucien François de Montagnac, whose letters strip away much of the glamorous veneer of the Algerian adventure in Bugeaud's era. For nine long years Montagnac suffered deprivations and plain loneliness in North Africa that emerge in a collection of epistles put together by his nephew after his death. These letters become increasingly morbid. Writing a long one to his uncle Bernard de Montagnac (begun on December 19, 1841 and completed February 2, 1842), he complains poetically of the winter at Mascara: "But alas! The fine days have passed, and the livid figure of winter is mercilessly hurling its mantle of hoarfrost on our shoulders. Here we are in the ice and snow, experiencing intermittent thaws and rains; in short, the whole procession of this harsh season is trooping by with its pitiless horde of calamities."[81] Montagnac declares that leaders like Bugeaud might have talent, but underestimate actual difficulties endured by French soldiers in the field.

On May 31, 1845 he writes his uncle Bernard that "our strongest battalions don't even have 400 men. When we lose 500, we are sent 200 to replace them, and of *what*?" Two hundred men with "fear in their bellies"![82] On these pages being a French African seems to mean being part of a machine where men are expendable. Montagnac apologizes to his uncle for his inveterate depression, but in his next two letters it continues, as he discusses a year of hunting for the elusive Abd el-Kader, now protected by Morocco, and the frequent loss of comrades. He describes how generals like Bugeaud fight with each other, and mentions silly journalists at home who understand nothing of this miserable existence, where one chases (or more often) waits for a will-o'-the wisp in snows or blazing deserts for years on end.[83]

If anything, the death of Montagnac at forty-two, before he had experienced the domestic pleasures of life, only confirmed this sense of sadness about being an African. During the spring of 1845 he had finally received a brief convalescence break, but developments in Morocco brought him back early; and in late September, 1845, on a cavalry charge, he was hit in the head and stomach by bullets, tumbling off his horse, crying out in the last minutes of his existence, "Courage, mes enfants!"[84] A contemporary reader of Montagnac's letters comes away very moved.

In his history of the French Foreign Legion Douglas Porch touches on these matters, noting that "when he arrived in Algeria in 1840, Bugeaud found the army wasting away" in fixed positions, and was determined to make it more mobile. What of the cost? The Legion derived a lasting *esprit de corps* from the new staccato rhythm of Bugeaud's marches—living off the land, always on the move, and in any kind of weather. But what Montagnac complained of was confirmed by Charles-Nicolas Lacretelle, who joined up as a second lieutenant in 1843 (after Saint-Cyr), and who felt he was out marching a good 250 days a year! Another Legionnaire repeated the saw that Bugeaud's infantry men required "the thighs of a buck, the heart of a lion . . . and the stomach of an ant." Indeed, these men were often consumed by terrible thirst, and grew sickly and yellow from their privations; yet the *sine qua non* always remained their "ability to undertake [these] brutal marches."[85]

Which did not deter the many ardent Bugeaudistes, of whom one stands above the rest, the soldier a biographer has called "l'effervescent Saint-Arnaud." Born in Paris as Arnaud Jacques Le Roy, this impetuous young man graduated from the Lycée Napoléon (later Henri IV) with a new name he considered more dashing, Achille de Saint-Arnaud, then went on to embrace the African adventure. With the possible exception of Roches, Saint-Arnaud was Bugeaud's favorite protégé, and the love went both ways. For instance, in the discrepancy between Changarnier and Bugeaud, Saint-Arnaud came down clearly and unambiguously on the latter's side. Bugeaud rewarded him with much praise and with promotions he wrung from the Paris ministry.[86]

In Saint-Arnaud's fine collection of Algerian letters his praise of Bugeaud remains consistent. Many of these letters home were written to a favorite brother, a lawyer in Paris. In one of June 12, 1841 from Mascara, Saint-Arnaud wants to scream out how much the new governor is misunderstood and undervalued. "General Bugeaud follows a goal with a steadfastness as praiseworthy as it is skillful. . . . He is a wonderful man, my brother; people don't know him, they don't do him justice. He is truly a genius." Every day, says Saint-Arnaud, he discovers new qualities in his chief, though there are also defects—a certain brusqueness at times, and a dogged perfectionism. But "quelle conscience, quelle probité, quelle délicatesse de sentiments, quelle abnégation personnelle!" However, "they surround him with difficulties. Little cliques raise up obstacles in his path . . . and the press is constantly assassinating him. . . . I wish I were in France to shout this from the rooftops!"[87]

Bugeaud's influence helped Saint-Arnaud endure years of hard work, bad weather, and poor health in Algeria. In a letter to his brother of 1844 he mentions with a certain longing the Parisian life, while here in Tiaret he is fighting excruciating boredom and wilting heat mounting to fifty-two degrees centigrade. He fears he soon won't have the strength to stand up, let alone march.[88]

The price continued to be paid after the victory at Isly, where "the marshal showed what he could do in a big war" and where "the army's confidence in him has no limits." But still "we swelter, freeze, die in droves."

Saint-Arnaud's defense of Bugeaud continues, becoming a perpetual pre-occupation. Who else can save the royal family? he asks rhetorically in a letter to his brother of August 18, 1845. "There is only one sword that can save them, and that is the sword of the Duke of Isly. And they want to take Africa away from him!"[89] Enduring stomach pains, sometimes wishing for a post back home, or for games of whist by a cozy fire, Saint-Arnaud keeps mentioning his inspiration, quoting from Bugeaud's letters of encouragement. For example: "My dear Saint-Arnaud, I love you more than ever, because every day you prove . . . that you are an *homme de coeur* who acts intelligently." Citing these words to his brother in a letter of December 28, 1845, Saint-Arnaud comments that reading those lines felt like gaining the stars of a major-general![90]

Through 1847, the last year of Bugeaud's North African tenure, Saint-Arnaud continued to fight off recurring health problems. But his appreciation of Bugeaud remained intact, and in 1848 he still viewed him as the one man who could save France, "l'homme du pays." In June 1849 he heard that Bugeaud had been in Paris—to become a government minister? Or the army's chief of staff? "He would fit well anywhere," he confidently wrote home.[91]

Then later that month came the sudden, devastating news of Bugeaud's death from cholera, and Saint-Arnaud's emotional reaction remains the greatest encomium of any we have seen, for he was absolutely stricken. To his brother, writing on June 20, he said of Bugeaud's death: "To express my pain to you is impossible! I loved him as one loves a father, and never has a son felt such agony. Since the 17th I've been sick with chagrin." In his next letter of July 9, 1849 he added that "every day and night, I think about the marshal. My heart is bleeding. I regret his loss even more for France than for myself."[92] No mediocrity or mean spirit could ever receive such a confirming *cri de coeur*.

What of Bugeaud's imperial legacy? Certainly he was French Algeria's key maker, but another significant figure was a governor-general of the 1850s who also became a marshal of France, Jacques Randon. Randon extended the conquest southward toward the Sahara, which was costly and difficult, and by 1857 had also subdued the last great fora of resistance in the country's northeast—Little Kabylia (seaside hills), then Greater Kabylia (mountains). He also supervised the building of ports and communications, the digging of wells and mines; and more waves of colonization followed. On the minus side a new *cantonnement* policy of which Bugeaud would have disapproved impelled nomadic tribes out of areas where they predominated and into something like Arab or Berber reservations. This allowed heavier European cultivation of potentially rich farmland, and employment of Algerians as a kind of rural proletariat.

In the 1860s French Emperor Napoleon III, whose Second Empire had replaced the moribund Second Republic, wanted to launch a genuinely liberal policy for Algeria's Muslims, potentially including citizenship that would have permitted their continuing allegiance to Koranic law. In one *senatus-consultus* of 1863 he tried to change *cantonnement* back to the previous policy of allowing Muslims to retain what remained of their property (though colonists could still buy it cheaply); in another of July 14, 1865, he supported giving Algeria's Arabs and Berbers subject status and once in allegiance to France's Civil Code, they could then apply to become French citizens. But when his regime fell on the battlefield of Sedan in the Franco-Prussian War of 1870, that policy perished as well.

In the short run Algerian Muslims were astounded by the demise of "Sultan Napoleon III," and a great revolt led by Mohammed el-Mokrani followed—fires, pillaging, murder afflicting countryside and cities alike. All this was partly owing to el-Mokrani's disgruntlement at finding himself in deep debt and unable to pay, due to bad harvests. There had also been Algerian-Muslim resentment at being drafted to fight in a European war. In this serious threat to Bugeaud's Algeria the French lost over 2,000 men, but their own repression was savage, and reprisals particularly in Kabylia led to executions and much confiscation of desirable land, and the creation for good of a Muslim rural proletariat.[93]

It was the last great threat to French Algeria until the war of the 1950s that would sear the mother country to its core. Between 1871 and the first stirrings of an Algerian Muslim revolt at Sétif in 1945, there *were* minor disturbances; but basically a long afternoon of relative stability and prosperity ensued for the mixture of Francophone Europeans, who would eventually number 1 million. French civilian governors and their control of the colony had indeed obliterated Bugeaud's enlightened military emphasis. This civilian control did nothing to douse the potential powderkeg of Arab-Berber nationalism. Between 1911–19 efforts at reform of inequities that plagued Muslims largely came to naught, and a double electoral college still gave outnumbered *pieds noirs* control. The patient Muslims bided their time, swallowed resentments, and finally, embittered rebels would set off an explosion in 1954.

For good or ill Bugeaud *had* created the first great colony of a second French empire, opening the way for others. These included contiguous

Tunisia, where the French would engineer a military protectorate with its financially strapped *bey* in the early 1880s, partly to keep the Italians from becoming Algeria's neighbors; then to complete a North African hat trick, Morocco, extensively discussed in our chapter on Lyautey.[94]

Bugeaud was a fine example of "cultured force," and he best showed that culture in a remarkable three-volume work published the year after his death, and ignored by both Sullivan and Bois. The first volume of this *Histoire de l'Algérie française* begins with an exhaustive detailing of Algerian geography—its mountains, rivers, plains—and its climate, flora and fauna, and above all, its possibilities; and it never bores. The labored, loving quality of a Balzac gradually sweeping into one corner of Saumur in *Eugénie Grandet* is on display here in this tome; so is an important Bugeaudesque dialectic between past and future. He sees much that France can do in Algeria—where they might drain unhealthy swamps, procure salt, and combat epidemics; where they could plant or teach planting; where they might derive marble, iron, copper, maybe even diamonds from mines, all the while using history's best models. Buoying himself, and with no blind credulity, on accounts of Strabo, Herodotus, Sallust, Pliny, and the like, those ancient North African models for Bugeaud included Carthaginians, who, he says, had admirable democratic, commercial, and occupational virtues (though encouraging their women to give up children for ritual slaughter!). There were also positive aspects to consider in the region's oldest continuous inhabitants, Berber Kabyles, whom Bugeaud respected for their industry, cleanliness, and savage devotion to freedom; in Arab Bedouins; and less so, in Moors and Arabs of fixed abodes. But the civilization France really needed to match or exceed—and at its apogee—was ancient Rome's, for whom North Africa had become a prosperous granary feeding the central city of a vast empire. Here he admired the administrative acumen of a Caesar and Augustus, and the culture Rome spread. He moves onto Christians, and even finds in one Vandal monarch positive aspects, though his "successors ... imitated what he had done badly—his persecutions of orthodox Christians, his devastations and confiscations, just as they borrowed from Roman civilization its laziness, luxury, and vices."

In this past-future dialectic Bugeaud was perhaps warning that France must stay at its best here, or else. *Our* main point is the taste, sensitivity, even tolerance one paradoxically finds in this masterwork written by a tough military man. Bugeaud, for example, respected Kabyles for treating women better than did Moors, whose girls "only left their father's home

for a spouse's," or Bedouins, whose wives worked like beasts, while husbands took long rest or smoking breaks. Even on the Jews of North Africa
Bugeaud showed that tolerance and respect, much different from Vichyites
who would to some extent appropriate his name. He approvingly cites
"the great liberty" Jewish women enjoyed in Algeria, and quoting the Tal-
mud, mentions the excessive charity richer members of the community
must bestow on the poor, which he felt should be emulated by Europe's
Christians. He knew and supported the fact that France had liberated
these Jews from onerous restrictions under the Turks, and that in return,
they would become trustworthy adherents of the métropole; however, "it
might have been more politic to leave them for a time in a state of inferiority in order not to jostle so deeply Moor and Arab prejudices ...
which, though unjust, have nonetheless brought jealousies and a defiance
it would have been prudent to prevent." Even concerning the Arabs he
fought so sedulously he seems tolerant here of their marital habits, and
an admirer of *marabouts* like Abd el-Kader. With no rancor he notes how
Arab males of his era prize four things above all—horse, sword, language,
and father's name.[95]

One should not simply take for granted that, to use imperfect moni-
kers, this Davoût-Taine would then be followed by a Turenne-Littré. Something of the sort occurred, however, for France overseas, when Bugeaud
gave way to a second, and in some ways, greater and more cultured proconsul—Faidherbe of Senegal and West Africa. To this fascinating figure
we now turn.

CHAPTER THREE

Faidherbe of Senegal and West Africa

L OUIS LÉON FAIDHERBE, the next important French imperial figure of the nineteenth century, garnered his reputation primarily in the French pacification and absorption of Senegal, but also influenced the creation of French West Africa as a whole. Like other great Gallic proconsuls of his century he was something of a misfit who would find his truest métier and worth abroad, posted first to Bugeaud's Algeria in the 1840s, then to Guadeloupe, back to Algeria, and finally to his beloved Senegal in the early 1850s, where he made his name. After departing Senegal in the mid-1860s Faidherbe devoted the latter part of his life to scholarship and general writing on Africa, war duty in 1870–71 during the Franco-Prussian War, and then politics in the first decade of the Third Republic, before passing away in 1889.

Apart from his military and civil colonial achievements, it is the depth and originality of Faidherbe's extensive writings on Africa that place him in a class apart among modern French colonial figures. For someone so adept at the art of war, Faidherbe had a fine, humanistic mind, and there are grounds for calling him, as we do here, one of the most enlightened French imperialists.

Biographical studies of Faidherbe in the French language all leave something to be desired, as does the exhaustive dissertation we have on him in English by Leland Barrows. Barrows plays down Faidherbe's influence on the creation of French West Africa, seeing him as a person of rather limited aims, a man of definite accomplishments, but not really the Faidherbe of later legend.[1] This American's scholarship is impressive, but he is wrong when he sees Faidherbe as part of an end point in the history of earlier French imperialism, or when he attributes the frenzied colonization of Sudan during the 1880s to trends that had nothing to do with Faidherbe's earlier, pathbreaking efforts eastward through Senegal.

In fact Faidherbe was a pioneering "new model" imperialist of the mid-nineteenth century. According to Jean Martin, "he [Faidherbe] inaugurated completely new methods of colonization" and was "a pioneer, the technician *par excellence* of colonial expansion in black Africa." Martin Klein writes that "the scramble for Africa has often been treated as a phenomenon which suddenly manifested itself about 1880, but the expansive impulse was fully developed in Faidherbe's Senegal." R. L. Delavignette and Charles Julien have also noted that Faidherbe's Senegal was "a colony of a very new type, absolutely different from the Antilles and from Réunion or Algeria, which were the greatest models of the time."[2] Our view is that Faidherbe *did* give great impetus to French expansion in Senegal and then West Africa as a whole, and we hold that to some degree, future great imperial figures in areas like the Sudan, Tonkin, Madagascar, and Morocco were his progeny, especially Gallieni and Lyautey.

To provide hasty psychoanalysis of this unique colonial's childhood may seem too reductive, and more suspect yet are old-fashioned geographical determinants of character, making, say, Pyrenean origins somehow responsible for Gallieni or Joffre, though (as will be seen in the next chapter) they were so different. By the same token one could look at the grim seriousness of Lille and more generally, of the Nord as a determinant in the character formation of Faidherbe and possibly be exaggerating.[3]

But like de Gaulle Faidherbe *was* a man of the Nord, to which he would return after his experience abroad as a popular military commander during the Franco-Prussian War; and he *did* derive an important psychological effect by losing a strong father when he was only seven, getting enough paternity for a role model, yet clearly not enough to overwhelm him or to rein him in to a more conformist life at home. He was raised strictly yet lovingly by a mother whose economic straits weighed on the boy—she had recurring trouble keeping afloat in the trade of haberdashery. Was Louis Léon her favorite? This is difficult to affirm, but his copious letters to his mother from Africa certainly show the deep esteem in which Faidherbe held *her*. The only one of her five children impelled toward higher education, Faidherbe may have been a fitful student (excellent in mathematics, uneven in other subjects); but he could also see himself as different by vaulting ultimately to the Ecole Polytechnique, a French military and colonial forcing ground of the nineteenth century. Faidherbe got his education as Napoleon had done—using government largesse for his tuition. Once at Polytechnique, he apparently didn't play by all the rules, because a summary of his grades for 1840—which in those days, included such physiognomic assessments as "Face: oval; Hair: blond; Forehead: bare; Nose: medium; Chin: round"—noted under conduct: "very inattentive." The need to get away from the herd and be different was probably there in Faidherbe from the start—at these schools he attended, then in military garrisons to which he proceeded as part of an engineering corps, and even in the youthful idea he had of going to America to search for gold.[4]

His posting to Algeria in 1843 as a military engineer under the aegis of Bugeaud made Faidherbe see a future for himself outside France. These stints in North Africa (before and after the 1848 Revolution) began the real formation of his adult character, partly due to the fact that suffering helped make him wiser. Stuck in freezing water for hours in battles, he almost surely developed there the intermittent bouts of rheumatism and later, paralysis which became permanent in the last part of his life. He would have other health problems as well. In Guadeloupe, after his first posting to Algeria, Faidherbe developed skin problems, perhaps venereal in origins. In Senegal would come hepatitis, and later, chronic bronchitis. This physical suffering may have accentuated the sensitive side of Faidherbe, but he was also inherently artistic enough to be a fine sketcher of locals he saw abroad, and on friendly terms with French painters like Courbet.[5]

Returning to the North African experience, that period of his life taught Faidherbe much that would stand him in good stead later on in Senegal. Already he showed a fine appreciation for what he encountered around him, reflected in a spate of letters sent home, particularly during his second Algerian tour. (These weren't available to previous biographers.) At an oasis town of the Sahara, for example, he paints in words an Arabian nights atmosphere of palm and fig trees, a market piled high with dates, ostrich plumes, and other articles, debauched grand seigneurs drinking strong coffee or smoking hash, malevolent brigands who made their living pillaging caravans, beautiful but unwashed young dancers, and assassins lingering in cafés with glittering knives at the ready.[6]

On tough engagements, Faidherbe finds himself chasing an elusive enemy and enduring difficult long marches, amidst a hail of bullets. On a good day—two good ones in a row, mentions one of his letters—the French lose only a few men and kill a lot of the foe. Yes, "we have completely ruined a fraction of the Bemi'Salah, burned their houses, cut down their olive tree groves, and sacked their gardens" (as a lesson to tribes refusing to submit). Faidherbe blithely concludes that his health has also improved![7] He mentions the usual problems presented by lesser French talents around him, particularly one of his colonels; but in a letter to his mother, declares proudly that he got his vengeance when General de Saint-Arnaud praised him before an entire brigade, ordering the miscreant colonel to award Faidherbe a decoration he deserved. A few days later he notes how lucky he was that in their latest engagement a Kabyle bullet went right through his saddle.[8]

In the mountain country of Algeria, pacifying and if need be, laying waste villages to procure tribal surrenders, Faidherbe kept having the good fortune to miss bullets that wounded or killed soldiers around him. Whenever the French retreated, the enemy seemed to attack, rather like Bugeaud, or in our century, Mao. Reluctantly, Faidherbe killed back, or gave orders for killings. Certain Arabs were shaking down the previously submitted, burning their villages: 100 years later this would again be the game here. Faidherbe complained that his superiors always seemed to select him for difficult jobs and that the weather was a beast. In February 1852 he wrote from a tent up in thick snow that the French were preparing a tour de force not previously undertaken—a winter campaign in the mountains of Kabylia. Despite the weather they were trying to construct a road, with Faidherbe himself in charge of over 1,000 workers, supervising work from 6 A.M. till 5 P.M. Miraculously, his own health held, but not that of his precious horses. This area might be one of the most beautiful in the world, he said, but one really needed a strange disposition to put up with such a life, compared to how a person might live in France. On February 25, 1852 he wrote home in the midst of a bad storm at Bougie, commenting that one couldn't even see the man beside him. Already the French had lost 150 men on this expedition in Kabylia, and Faidherbe expected many more to die. In hospitals there were almost 600 wounded soldiers, and "every day they amputate the feet of five or six."[9]

On the edge of transfer to the part of Africa that would make his reputation (Senegal), how might one compare this Faidherbe-in-the-making to Bugeaud? According to Sullivan, "as a humanist and a savant Faidherbe differed markedly from Bugeaud and was clearly a precursor of the great scholar-administrators who governed the new French empire in subsequent decades." His complexity and elasticity, along with his strength, would also distinguish him, even among the best French colonial personnel.[10]

Those traits would certainly help him in Senegal, and Faidherbe's transfer there in 1852 as chief military engineer, then his assumption of the governorship in 1854 would alter both his life and French imperial history.
In London, en route to his new posting he wrote his mother perhaps his
most fascinating letter. That missive of October 1852 reveals Faidherbe's
admiration for the British "workshop of the world" at its zenith, but he
also finds London's houses somber and disappointing, and the English
mercantile spirit one-dimensional. "The lowliest French grocer is a poet,
an artist, and a savant compared to the English merchant—the English
have no interest other than profit," he declares confidently. Once their fortune is made, he adds, they haven't any idea of how to use it to procure
enjoyment. In the realm of fine arts the English also appear ignorant, and
in cookery "le rosbeef" represents a good half of the lot. Despite his admiration for Westminster Abbey, Faidherbe notes proudly that the British
have no buildings to compare with France's Louvre, Notre Dame, Tuileries,
or Versailles. Most of their palaces aren't even made of good materials,
adds this military engineer. Faidherbe also relates that he attended a dance
one night, only to be sharply irritated when his English partner danced
more slowly than the music; and he concludes that a second Norman conquest might just give these British some culture![11]

Instead of conquering England, Faidherbe would have to settle for a
tropical area not far from where the English were busy extending their
own West African domains. As soon as he arrived in the Senegalese town
of Saint-Louis on the Atlantic coast, he wrote his mother a long, detailed
letter about the trip down from Britain, especially how much he worked
during the voyage at translating Arabic. Then came a first exciting look
at the Isle of Gorée and at a region that would come to fascinate him:
Senegal.[12]

The name for this African area probably came from the Berber-derived
Zenaga, the name of the long river traversing the region. Racial and linguistic intermingling, continual conquests and assimilations, including
religious ones, and prevailing instability had been the key elements of
Senegalese history.[13] French commercial companies had begun trading on
the Senegal River in the seventeenth century, with only two coastal bases
here—Saint-Louis, founded in 1659 on an island at the river's mouth; and
the Isle of Gorée a bit farther down the coast, the latter pried from the
Dutch via Louis XIV's Treaty of Nimwegen of 1678. Commercially, the
French here traded useful items like kettles and cloths, as well as less
useful trinkets for what would become a commercial staple in Europe,

gum arabic. The slave trade had also been part of the equation, and one white traveler was astonished by black villagers who so willingly participated in it.[14]

Even these French bases were difficult to hold, given increasing British competition (no Norman conquest for them); and several times the French lost both Gorée and Saint-Louis to England, until their final return to France's jurisdiction in 1817. Other problems included the ravages of disease and poor supplies, and the fact that many came down here "to flee creditors or other personal and financial troubles at home." Moreover, the trading season lasted for only half the year. After trying to make a go of things in Senegal, most French incomers would turn tail and eventually return home. Yet travel writers and scientists were starting to see possibilities in the area; one well-known example for the eighteenth century was a book by Michel Adanson, whose *Voyage to Senegal* sparkled with exotic data. There were also an increasing number of freed African *habitants*, as they were called, and *métis* offspring of Frenchmen married to local women, creating a kind of regional elite. But except for a narrow swath of land on both sides of the Senegal River, the whole region had too much savannah to grow anything beyond the millet and groundnuts that already abounded; and with no real security inland from the coast, anything like an economic take-off lay in the future.[15]

A significant development in West Africa as a whole from at least the eighteenth century was the explosion of militant Islam, long present but becoming an ideological wildfire Faidherbe would have to confront with great force and ingenuity. Warrior clergy from Moorish, Peul (Fulani), and Toucouleur ethnic groups led the onslaught of a faith numerous black chieftains found too seductive or powerful to resist. These *marabouts* were not above using the slave trade to enhance their positions of power, confronting the "mutable morality" of the French, who by the early nineteenth century wanted to stop a practice in which they had once participated. From the late eighteenth century, Islamic jihads had been truly transforming Senegalese areas like Futa Jalon, Futa Toro, Bondou, and Khasso, with a spate of conversions and some anarchy resulting. Tribes like the Wolofs (or Jolofs) "dominated by this apathy of despair which terror and uncertainty about the next day engender" had become "the plaything of the Trarza Moors and chieftains imposed on them," according to two contemporary observers. Khasso too was a region full of anarchy before Faidherbe—anarchy that "always invades societies, great or small, lacking directing will." The area of Bambouk, reputedly gold-filled, also lacked security, and travelers were apparently killed there on the smallest pretext. Arbitrary Islamic violence, especially by the Moors, made some counter-vailing force necessary, in part for obvious economic reasons.[16]

It is certain that the old approach of attributing one overriding motive or another to imperialism simply won't explain French activity in this period, or Faidherbe. The Hobson-Lenin side, however, should not be denied its importance. Commerce did play a role in French West African expansion during the nineteenth century, especially as the search for a new economic base (given the demise of the slave trade) grew. Cotton was perceived as one key to the future in Senegambia, although it would never compete viably with the rest of the world's output, except for a short period during the American Civil War. The gum trade, however, took off sharply from the 1830s or so, given its use in the burgeoning production of textiles in Europe. Then came the advent of the peanut, which few until Faidherbe's time had viewed as a great staple of the future. By then, as Carrère and Holle put it, "the peanut is evidently destined to dethrone gum, the major product of Senegal ten years ago." In this economic prog-nostication they were proven correct. From the mid-nineteenth century peanuts were increasingly used in Europe to produce oil for cooking and for industry, and by the twentieth century the nut crop would become "at once the life and death of Senegal," accounting for about one half of cul-tivated land.[17]

It would be too easy, however, to see Faidherbe as a mere pawn of French economic interests—specifically, the cluster of Bordeaux merchants operating from Saint-Louis and Gorée on the Senegalese coast. But these merchants did have a hand in making him governor of an area that had only become an official French colony in 1848. Simply put, it looked like a well-recommended military man could defend their interests. The Bor-delais merchant Maurel's immediate "plan" (for Faidherbe to enact) was to wrest the gum market from Moorish control, including their specified ports of call and oppressive duties, putting it firmly under French juris-diction. Maurel also wanted better protection for merchants and French control of the new peanut crop. But this was no "plan" Faidherbe could simply adopt without his own modifications. Better forts to strengthen French trading posts along the river, enhanced exploration, and protec-tion on the banks of the Senegal were already in his mind, quite apart from the merchants' interests and pressures. Like Bugeaud, Faidherbe felt that Africans respected force above all else, but as he wrote in a letter to the naval and colonial minister in Paris, this situation covering over 400 leagues was complex, and a war here could easily last several years on a variety of fronts.[18]

A large thorn in the side of any neat economic plan formulated by French merchants was the Islamic tide, especially of El Hadj Umar Tall, whose rival brand of ideological imperialism would soon force Faidherbe to become more repressive in Senegal than might otherwise have been the case. "Islam is making daily progress," a travel writer, G. T. Mollien, had warned earlier in the century, and now the wildfire was being spread by someone of redoubtable force.[19]

Tall was born around 1794 in a village of the Toucouleur Futa Toro, an area in need of strong leadership, as it was often raided by Moors and other tribes. A firm Islamic background and his own abilities made the young man a *marabout* or holy man by 1825, impelling him first to Saint-Louis, then to Mecca, a rare thing to undertake when extensive travel still meant much travail. Studying hard for several years in Mecca, as well as in Medina and Cairo, and possibly in Damascus and Jerusalem too, Tall became a khalif, then concentrated his energies on a trek westward back to the Sudan for a holy war.

En route home he gained many Islamic converts, not to mention wives, and the confidence that continued success and death-defying beliefs bestowed. His saintly reputation went ahead of him into the Ségou and Futa provinces, but increasing wealth from slaves, gold trading, and plain racketeering, as well as an arms buildup, also cemented his power. Still, religion remained most important for him. Tall was a zealot unhappy with mixed religious practices in the western Sudan, and wanted to implement a purer brand of Islam in the region. (He could easily fit in many parts of today's Middle East.)[20]

By the time Faidherbe acceded to power, much of Senegambia was already within Tall's potential grasp, including Bambouk and Karta, and many chieftains had already given in to his considerable powers of persuasion. Tall's coffers bulged with booty, crops, and captives. So it was inevitable that he and Faidherbe would square off in West Africa, but not merely as economic rivals. Faidherbe simply did not want to see Umarian Islam triumph in this region, swallowing up many principalities of the Senegal valley east of Bafoulabé and other parts of western Senegal. More clearly, Faidherbe's goal was to end Umarian domination of the Middle and Upper Senegal River. But he realized what he was up against and was never one to underestimate an opponent. As he would note in his last book, and it still rings true in today's world, "wars of religion are pitiless, and fanaticism inspires a courage which retreats from nothing." In a letter home to his minister, he wrote anxiously of the prophet's influence, conceding that his opponent was a man of "high intelligence and rare energy," one who would provide implacable opposition to Europeans in the region.[21]

Tall's main forces were composed of Toucouleur and Peul tribespeople of the Futa provinces and Bondou, for whom Faidherbe had admiration, along with reservations. As he wrote, "the Toucouleurs (blacks mixed with Peul) are an intelligent and perfidious race; they have been made vicious by Islam, which has also made them as lying and thieving as the Moors."[22] As for Tall, he saw him as a man who cared nothing of famine and disorders he brought in his wake, and who was capable of doing anything to propagate his rigid ideals.

An interesting critique of Faidherbe's policy toward Tall and his successors by Yves-Jean Saint-Martin was itself tempered in the author's later work on Senegal. According to Saint-Martin in a book on the Toucouleur empire, Tall was en route to creating a true Islamic-Sudanese empire, a "fécond métissage" that would ultimately have proven benign. Faidherbe, says Martin, propagandized the notion of a civilizing France, contrasted to a more barbarous Islam, in order to get Paris behind his campaigns. In fact, Tall would largely have stayed out of the way of French interests, and his more relaxed successors would have done more good than they could in their brief reign to the east in Ségou and hinterland, before a final defeat at the hands of the post-Faidherbe French.[23]

This is a beguiling interpretation, but it underestimates the converting fervor of Tall's minions. As Thierno Diallo puts it, "With the infidels, the Peuls knew only one possible attitude: violence and war. Calling themselves and believing themselves invested by God with a sacred mission, they felt obliged to make war on the infidels." It was also a Muslim duty to take slaves to cultivate the land, which again confronted a more liberal French attitude on that issue.[24]

On the positive side, Islam attenuated dramatically the ravages of European liquor on chieftains and their soldiers, and imposed other moral standards. Eugène Mage, sent by Faidherbe in the 1860s to meet with Toucouleur Muslims, conceded that black Africa *was* semicivilized by the Islamic religion. Some say Faidherbe himself preferred a controlled Islam, feeling that it civilized more than the animistic beliefs of unconverted blacks. But Mage also had the chauvinistic sense that the French could do the civilizing much better here.[25]

Faidherbe certainly did not want to obliterate the Umarian empire entirely, one reason being the sheer impossibility of total search and destroy operations, exacerbated by two opposite seasons that greatly affected the river and its navigation. He also feared un-Islamized chieftains using *thiedos* (or *kiedos*), dynasties of black soldiers (originally slaves) to uphold their corrupt power. These *thiedos* were great abusers of alcohol and had less of a sense of fair play, he felt, than Muslims. Still he supervised much reconnoitering, learning the river in its many moods, and what kinds of vessels were most suitable for transporting war materials and men. If there *were* to be a showdown, it behooved the French to be prepared.[26]

For Umar Tall's threat was a real one, and by the mid-1850s the two sides were approaching a large-scale confrontation, with Tall not the only Islamic threat for the French to worry about. Simultaneously Faidherbe would also have to confront the fierce Moors or Mauritanians, led by their Trarza king, Mohammed-el-Habib. Faidherbe's ruthlessness here would partly be an ad hoc response to Moorish brutality. Like the Moors Faidherbe felt he had to become a village burner, if more sparingly; but these Moors also took women and children as prisoners, and would even cut some into pieces at festivals. Faidherbe knew that "it is by these cruelties that they make themselves so feared by the blacks." He wrote a lot about Moor leaders of the Brakna, Trarza, and Dawaish areas, all killing each other during the nineteenth century. Around 1800, when Brakna Moors were at war with the Trarzas, one leader apparently took the other's wife prisoner and sent her back minus nose and ears; the other also got herself taken prisoner and was returned without teeth. In his brutal response to such brutality, mixed, however, with diplomacy, Faidherbe was about to experience the same French dilemma encountered in Bugeaud's Algeria, and one that would dog his countrymen right down to the evanescence of the empire in the 1950s. But it should be added that the fight against the Mauritanians of Senegal was also more clearly economic than the one against Tall. As noted, Faidherbe and French or mulatto merchants wanted to wrest the gum trade from Mauritanian control and end the forced payment of exorbitant customs dues. This was one of the two big tests the governor faced in the mid-1850s.[27]

Tall remained the more daunting Islamic foe, and here the confrontation of two rival imperialisms was more clearly ideological. Even the seasons demarcated the two series of French campaigns—the dry season better for fighting Moors inland, the rainy season for navigating up the Senegal to meet Tall's Umarians. One by one chieftains signed protection

treaties with the khalif, and by 1855 Tall basically controlled eastern Senegambia. Only revolts that temporarily weakened him in areas like Karta,
and assorted tribal uprisings of Bambaras in 1855–56 allowed Faidherbe to
retain some optimism about a coming confrontation, while also occupying himself elsewhere with the Moors. The Umarian conquest of Karta
was, however, completed by early 1857, though to some degree, it was a
Pyrrhic one.

The French, using fortified Médine as their key position on the upper
Senegal, were all this time busy selling a message of tolerance and forming an anti-Umarian front. They also proffered gifts, another method of
gaining allies.[28] The way Faidherbe gathered help against both el-Habib's
Moors and Tall's Umarians is illustrated in frequent letters he sent to
princes, combining diplomatic flattery with threats. In one of May 1, 1855,
Faidherbe reminds the prince that "the Trarza [Moors] have pillaged and
burned a part of your country. . . . Pay close attention, you have around
you people sold out to the Moors and who are trying to make you quarrel with me." In a subsequent letter he tells the *damel* or local prince to
keep his *thiedos* in line or else (January 21, 1857). He also stresses attractive economic benefits, especially from an enhanced peanut and gum
trade with France. In one more letter of March 4, 1857, touchingly entitled "Governor to the chieftain of M'Pal and all the honest people of the
village," Faidherbe says he has been fighting the Moors for three years,
and that if the French had not done so, these "Moors, jealous of seeing
the peanut enrich you, would already be masters of all of Cayor, and
would have tried to make you slaves to force you to cultivate the peanut,
as they get gum harvested by your children that they have been able to
steal in their *razzias*." Faidherbe posed here as a champion of justice and
peace, and part of that was as genuine as the French protectorate idea we
will later discuss in its Indochinese, Malgache, and Moroccan varieties;
but his methods could also become as excessive as his opponents' (though
Tall's routine executions of African notables showed more open brutality). Faidherbe was probably sincere when at a banquet for French merchants he said in a rousing speech: "We are only making war in order to
obtain peace." Was it peace, he went on, to see the Trarzas kidnap 300 or
400 blacks at the end of their trading sessions? Was it peace to have their
brigandage extend right up to the gates of the French enclave of Saint-
Louis? Was it peace when the French couldn't cultivate anywhere in peace?
Or when commercial travelers were being assassinated up river because
they wouldn't hand over their wares? "Was it peace," he concluded, "when

France, that old and noble nation in the vanguard of world civilization for so many centuries, paid tribute to savage hordes who only a few years ago learned to stammer out the Koran?"[29]

By copying the Moors—taking herds of cattle, burning villages harboring traitors, nabbing prisoners or hostages, but also working with pro-French princes who wanted friendship—Faidherbe hurt the Mauritanian potentate el-Habib enough to obtain the "peace of the marabouts" by January 1857. Predictably, el-Habib broke that peace soon after, but French prestige, based on increasing allied strength, forced him to demand another peace agreement in 1858. Thus Faidherbe got what he wanted from the Moors—one of his key aims as governor. France now had protectoral authority over the Walo and several Wolof (Jolof) states as well. The Moor Trarzas and Braknas relinquished their political hold on the left bank of the Senegal, and Moor customs duties on the lucrative gum trade were replaced by a fairer 3–4 percent tax on the value of exported gum. In addition, they could now operate this gum trade only at French posts. The Trarza and Brakna confederations of Moors henceforth grew more tranquil, especially with the strong-arm accession in 1858 of the pro-French Sidi-Eli, replacing el-Habib.[30]

As for the more explosive Tall, Faidherbe continued to reply to him firmly when he could, but he had to get black chieftains to his side to build an anti-Umarian alliance system, particularly in states of the upper valley. Two rival systems were being frantically huckstered—Tall promising paradise, Faidherbe promising commercial protection and human rights. He also continued to buy as much aid as he could. Faidherbe kept massaging the home front as well, in copious, informative letters sent to the Ministry, keeping support in France constant; he was truly an adept publicist for the shaky colony of Senegal. In a letter of October 15, 1856 to the naval and colonial minister, he said of one area: "This Bondou is one of the richest countries for growing millet and corn; immense plains covered with grain stretch as far as the eye can see on both banks ... promising abundance." Faidherbe also made the home base aware of the price he and his men were paying for fighting redoubtable foes. In another letter he noted that "for five months we have not known what rest is! We are always on the move to present a front on all sides ... on forced marches without camp or supplies," attempting to snare enemies "hitherto considered uncatchable."[31]

France's confrontation with Tall came to a head when the latter decided to attack the new French fortress of Médine on the Senegal in April 1857.

Much mythmaking would surround this "siege of Médine," tardily, but dramatically relieved by Faidherbe's use of steam ships filled with reserves that came up river in July, when the water had risen. Inside the fortress the besieged led by the courageous *métis*, Paul Holle, were suffering from disease and conditions of near famine; but Faidherbe's troops finally succeeded in putting the Umarians to flight. Giving them chase, he employed a scorched earth policy, also making treaties of alliance as he went. Owing to other French victories as well, the Gallic position eventually became secure enough that Faidherbe was able to travel back to the mother country from September 1858 to February 1859. On his return he would force Tall to cease hostilities in August of 1860 and transport his Islamic imperialism away from western Senegal, now given over to what the khalif considered as infidels.

That Umarian departure, originating from Senegal's Futa province, would be a major undertaking, with some 50,000 people, or 20 percent of the population, accompanying him, and with famine conditions left behind. This famine was no more fortuitous than the disastrous lack of food in Stalin's Russia of the early 1930s, or in China during the Great Leap Forward. For the Umarians had made sure before departing to destroy great amounts of millet and other food stores, and the population in Bondou alone dropped by about a half. Tall left an area strewn with emaciated bodies on the roads and in the fields. But from then on the new Toucouleur Empire would be situated beyond the limits of Faidherbe's Senegal in modern Mali, though there would be revolts and attempts at reconquest through to the 1880s, and Futa itself remained unstable. Islamic-Toucouleur imperialism, passing from Tall to his son Ahmadou, would sanctify and mythologize this hegira east, rather in the way Boers later did their Great Trek, or Maoists their Long March. As David Robinson writes, "Bundu and Senegambia were polluted, the good Muslim must [now] take his family and property to the new jihadic society of the east." Home-burnings and kidnappings certainly helped induce the hesitant to make the trip. Robinson goes on to label this hegira a "watershed of nineteenth century ... Senegambian history." As for the French, they would no longer be second-rate, tolerated merchants in the region. In the future, Faidherbe's aim would be to buttress a secure French presence where it existed and contain the outlanders. Alliance treaties in areas like Futa Toro became part of that consolidation process. A frontier between French and Umarian spheres would be mostly maintained along the Senegal River from Bafoulabé to Médine, with the French possessing left-bank protectorates and interests, the Toucouleurs theirs on the right bank and in the east. But this French hegemony over the left bank would also give them a jumping-off point for the future, leading to the next great colonial actions here in the era of Gallieni—conquest of the western Sudan.[32]

After lifting the siege of Médine, Faidherbe could discreetly congratulate his soldiers for producing the prophet's humiliating flight, "to the great mortification of those who had believed him a supernatural power." This was henceforth a kind of harvest time for the French and for indigenous peoples under their sway in that part of West Africa. In the summer of 1858 Faidherbe wrote his minister that the French would soon be in "an excellent situation to exploit the riches of the country and to work for its development." A few days later he composed a sixteen-page letter to Prince Napoleon (the emperor's cousin) on the possibility of French expansion 250 leagues up river.[33] Recommending Faidherbe's promotion to colonel on October 20, 1858, the prince praised his great success in Senegal. In a note to Napoleon III he added that Faidherbe's governorship had replaced a previously passive French presence, marked by constant commercial blackmail, with one that was now strong and respected.[34]

What distinguished Faidherbe in this enterprise from a more rigid successor, Captain Jean-Bernard Jauréguiberry (between Faidherbe's first and second governorships), was his empiricism, his sense of how to alter Parisian directives, and yet his ability to stay friendly with the home base. As one historian remarked, "Paris did not attract him," but Faidherbe certainly knew how to deal with the ministries there.[35]

Just as he was able to get along with Parisian authorities, he also knew how to do so with local tribespeople.[36] Like the twentieth-century anthropologist Claude Lévi-Strauss he saw more complexity in so-called primitive cultures than surfaces might indicate, or certainly more than someone like a Jauréguiberry could discern. Most secondary authorities concur that Faidherbe was relatively free of racism in the European sense, one reason he would publicize this African area so well.

But Faidherbe was much more than a publicist; he was a true builder. His projects included the formation of a Bank of Senegal; construction of bridges over the river, then regular ferry service; and urban development of the capital of Saint-Louis—including paved roads that were essential in the rainy season, sidewalks, better disposal of waste, more latrines, stronger houses (brick replacing the straw that had been vulnerable to fire), quays, and attempts to assure a reliable supply of fresh water.[37]

Like the greatest of "new model" imperialists after him, Faidherbe realized that people here enjoyed pomp and circumstance, though balls, festivals, and firework displays he sponsored got him into some trouble with the French clergy in Senegal. So did his liberal views on *mariage à la mode* (temporary marriages between French soldiers and locals), as well as his creation of the soon-to-be-famous *tirailleurs sénégalais*, Senegalese sharpshooters with special uniforms and cachet, who would later become celebrated in World War I and endure well after that. But Faidherbe *was* emphatically supported by glowing economic statistics, due to the sharp growth of the gum and peanut trade, and the security provided by his military victories.

There are indeed grounds for calling him an enlightened despot in Senegal, as there are for considering Lyautey one in Morocco a half century later. On the enlightened side were the "Villages of Liberty" Faidherbe founded for emancipated slaves, and the way that he also fought to keep them from being recruited to the Caribbean. At one point he even threatened resignation over the issue. His school policy, however, was mainly elitist, though again, this so-called elitism, in addition to firming up alliances, was also an attempt *not* to rob the average native of his or her culture. Faidherbe's most elitist creation was the School for Hostages (Ecole des Otages), renamed School for Sons of Chieftains and Interpreters (1861). In 1860 these establishments had only twenty-five students enrolled; largely as a token of good faith or perhaps as a kind of insurance, two children from the father's family would be placed in French schools. These lay schools created for Muslims were to be a serious rival to Islam, and even Koranic schools had to receive Faidherbe's authorization; the influence of *marabouts*, or Muslim clergy, was now closely watched. But Faidherbe also created a Muslim tribunal, supervising better justice and fighting venality among both local people and French. (Secondary authorities agree that Faidherbe himself never made much money from his own positions and was not truly acquisitive.) To sum up, he managed to accomplish a good deal as Senegal's governor.[38]

By 1859 Faidherbe's administrative divisions came to three *arrondissements*, with capitals at Saint-Louis, the fort town of Bakel, and Gorée; but his imperialism here was mainly indirect. Futa, for example, was divided into four manageable states under regional leadership. Faidherbe instituted head taxes only where possible, and carefully watched his budget. Chieftains had considerable power in their areas of hegemony—over domains like taxation, justice, etc. It must also be said that they collaborated with the French in instituting forced labor, the equivalent of France's *corvées* that had died out at the time of the French Revolution.[39]

An entente with Tall in 1860 allowed the French to dominate Senegambia, giving the Umarians at least temporary sway over modern Mali to the east. In Bondou the French choice to succeed Tall, Bokar Saada, would rule from 1860 to 1885. Some rebuilding and recovery ensued there in the first decade after the region's devastation, and revenge for many was sweetest when Tall was killed in 1864 and his empire to the east partitioned.

But meanwhile, problems in the region of Cayor, where Faidherbe finally installed a puppet *damel*, and difficulties with the Paris ministry revealed his own continuing fragility in Senegal; and in 1861 he regretfully decided to resign his seven-year governorship. Health was one reason, disappointment with the colonial minister of the time, Chasseloup-Laubat, another. But what this resignation would also demonstrate was how much Faidherbe's methods contrasted with the more orthodox ones of his successor, the naval officer Jauréguiberry.

Starting in December 1861, Jauréguiberry became Senegal's governor for a year and a half, trying to fill large moccasins indeed, and not fully comprehending that Faidherbe's "imperialism" was but a loose network of alliances *cum* military protection for commercial interests. Unrealistically, Jauréguiberry treated Senegal as definitively conquered, and thus had problems from the beginning, including a full-scale revolt in Cayor, spearheaded by a militant new *damel* (Lat Dior), and a war in Futa Toro.

Jauréguiberry was a French Calvinist, which in his case gave him a puritanical, self-righteous rigidity. At the necessary game of public relations he simply couldn't match Faidherbe, thereby alienating authorities in France. He wouldn't emancipate slaves slowly and empirically, and more generally, couldn't adjust ministerial instructions to local conditions; he was too literal and by-the-book. His new *arrondissements* were a bureaucrat's dream; he wanted more direct rule of a kind that in Senegambia was unworkable. He also alienated commercial interests by severe decrees against land speculation, and drinkers by raising a tax on alcohol. Further, he bruised the egos of *laptots* (black naval hands), trying too rapidly to end their illiteracy, where it existed. The Senegalese sharpshooters did not like his "French-learning" edicts either, nor the ways in which he tried to discipline them.[40]

On the positive side Jauréguiberry could see ahead to the future greatness of the port of Dakar, and gave one of Faidherbe's great associates, Pinet-Laprade, carte blanche for its improvement. "Hasty, abrasive, and quixotic ... [Jauréguiberry] was also a prophet," writes Barrows.[41] The educational level of river captains and sharpshooters *would* eventually go up; the customs system *would* be transformed along his recommended lines; Dakar *would* become Senegal's greatest port. Unfortunately Jauré-guiberry wanted it all to happen too fast, operating in a doctrinaire manner here.

This doctrinaire quality was what cost him his position as governor. Where Faidherbe would only take revenues where possible, the new governor had provoked a revolt in Futa Toro by his overly thorough collection of head taxes. Jauréguiberry was also too zealous in repressing that revolt, incurring many casualties on the French side. After crafting a shaky settlement in Futa Toro, he was soon sent back to France by a minister he had repeatedly irritated.[42]

So Faidherbe, more rested now, returned to Saint-Louis for a somewhat reluctant second term as governor in July 1863. His main ideas included completing projects like the port of Dakar, sending explorers like Eugène Mage to treat with Umar Tall's successor, Ahmadou, and moving a French presence from the upper Senegal toward the Niger. He would also try to induce the British and Portuguese to leave their strongholds of Gambia and areas south of the Casamance. Mainly he wished to consolidate the string of trading posts and forts that facilitated French hegemony in Senegal. But he also had to worry about new revolts and brigandage in areas like Cayor.[43]

There was more brutality to be used against the chieftain Lat-Dior, a former ally who massacred French garrisons and was finally expelled from Cayor in the mid-1860s. The French employed usual methods of repression like village burning, destroying crops of collaborators, or kidnapping, and famine conditions would for a time result there. Faidherbe's restoration of the weak and habitually inebriated Madiodio as Cayor's *damel* was a definite error. Eventually Lat-Dior returned to his post, and Cayor remained anything but quiet, as his nephew began fighting the French in the early 1880s. Other new Islamic leaders like Maba Diakhow also portended difficulty as Muslim fomenters of jihad. "Maba's case," notes Barrows, "was only one example of what the future held for French rule in Senegal." There were also sporadic uprisings in parts of the hard-to-reach South from the 1860s through to the 1880s.[44]

But however transitory his results, Faidherbe had created a certain order and done much good in this general region of Africa. In his second administration he dismantled Jauréguiberry's more objectionable procedures in justice and government, as well as concessions given to the Trarzas;

made French businessmen more confident of security for their mercantile operations; and simplified the tax structure. Only progressively did
he abolish African slavery, realizing he could not do so in one fell swoop.
He also continued to promote the building of roads, telegraphs, and
new buildings, especially in Saint-Louis. Writing elegant letters home, he
remained on good terms with his colonial minister, and with Emperor
Napoleon III as well.[45]

What Faidherbe left in Senegal was both fragile and substantial, but
the area would also leave a good deal with him. Ill health and what he
deemed the comparative penny-pinching of Paris in the declining era of
the Second Empire eventually induced him to leave in May 1865; but possibly his scholarly curiosity, which required more leisure time, got the better of him as well. Maybe it was age, though he was still only forty-seven
years old. At all events Faidherbe returned to Algeria as a brigadier general, remaining there until the War of 1870 broke out between France
and Prussia. In Algeria he also began sifting through and evaluating his
Senegalese experiences, finally becoming a scholarly writer, an inclina-
tion he had too often had to bury at the hands of military and political
concerns.[46]

Faidherbe's curiosity and general empathy for Africa led in this period
to a veritable flurry of learned activity. Much of what he studied and wrote
came after his Senegalese stints, and especially after the Franco-Prussian
War of 1870; still, from the beginning he had never been the type to let
life pass by unobserved or unanalyzed. As much as he had come to Senegal to impose a certain outlook, he had also learned from the beginning
to take much account of the culture that existed there.

In Senegal Faidherbe had played a key role in making *Le moniteur du
Sénégal* and *Annales sénégalaises* his journals. The *Moniteur* became a
record of his military operations and economic gains, useful for public
relations. But these journals and the many articles Faidherbe contributed
to them also provide much interesting information on indigenous peoples
and tribal life, forming a chronicle of his time that one historian considers
"lively and rarely boring."[47]

To say that Faidherbe was part propagandist and part scholar may seem
contradictory, but such contradictions were part of his "new model" French
imperialism. Just after his first series of military campaigns Faidherbe
published a *Notice sur la colonie du Sénégal*, frankly aimed at the home
government as well as interested readers, and anticipating his bigger, better known work, *Le Sénégal*, which would bring the story up to the 1880s.

Succinctly Faidherbe discusses here the limits of the region, its history and governors, and the nature of its religions, customs, and races. His racial judgments are typical of his century, at once interesting and exaggerated. Of the Oulof (Wolof) and Sérer tribes, Faidherbe notes that "their dominant quality is apathy. They are mild, puerile and vain, credulous beyond words, feckless and inconstant." But they are brave too, supposedly because of undeveloped nervous systems, and prey to famine, because they sell too much of their millet. He gives readers factual summaries of subregions and groups previously mentioned—Moors, *thiedos*, Futa, etc. Despite sometimes naïve views, he also reveals a sense of balance. People of Futa may show "their lack of good faith, avidity, and propensity for theft," but on the positive side demonstrate a love of work, hatred of slavery, and concern for their area. What emerges here is Faidherbe's *own* intense love of the region.[48]

Much like a Balzac or Flaubert, Faidherbe balanced flights of intuition against copiously observed detail and plain practicality. For those reasons a primer he wrote on West Africa for schoolchildren of the 1860s remains interesting even now. His idea was to feed elite young Senegalese in school not just elements of European history and geography, but also data about their own region. In this text Faidherbe asked simple questions and answered them, noting lacunae in contemporary knowledge of Africa. An example of his precision: "5. What do we call 'Moors' in Senegal? We are accustomed to calling Moors in Senegal inhabitants, mostly nomads ... of the right bank of the river and of the Sahara in general." Moral judgments are also rife in the text. Asking his young readers what the *thiedos* are, he answers that they are "given to drunkenness, which degrades them a lot." And he makes errors, declaring, for instance, that cotton will become the key crop of the future in Senegambia. But however simple and at times erroneous, the information Faidherbe provides here indicates a far less Eurocentric mind than usually imputed to Western imperialists.[49]

In Bône, Algeria from December 1866 through to the fateful year of 1870, Faidherbe devoted himself steadily to ethnographic and archeological labors. Working on necropoli in 1869 he found 2,000 tombs at Mazuela, leading to a book on Numidian inscriptions.[50] Opening that short tome, one finds that Faidherbe now has an array of titles and learned societies beside his name. He says here that he would like travelers and soldiers to become more interested in such matters, citing other savants, like a Dr. Reboud, "botaniste distingué," who had helped locate a cache of Libyan inscriptions. Faidherbe's precisions on language and ethnographic history

(Libyan versus Punic), his knowledge of Egypt's past, and his speculations on how a Nordic influx south had influenced the Berber race before intermarriage with blacks hold more interest than the book's title may indicate. He is obsessed by conquerors and vanquished, and by what remains of ancient traits in tribes like the Touaregs; also by physical degenerations, especially in the Berbers.[51]

On language he shows extensive comparative learning, demonstrating, for example, how Phoenician, Arabic, and Hebrew employ consonants on the line and vowels outside as accents. His comparisons complete with printed samples become truly detailed here, showing his aptitude for linguistic scholarship.[52]

The new model imperialist is well on view in this parade of linguistic skill, and also in the reasons for it. One of those reasons was again, a plain curiosity that exceeded that of his average colonial predecessors or contemporaries. A second was Faidherbe's desire to acquaint travelers and soldiers with what seemed to be recalcitrant tongues. A third was once again his own care for these areas that he knew so well.

A Faidherbian vocabulary of 1,500 French words with equivalents in Wolof, Poul, Futa, and Soninké (or Sarakhollé) might again seem another dull pamphlet to open, as one of the present authors did in the Library of Congress during the 1990s; but Faidherbe's short summaries of where these languages were used, their general characteristics, and how they compared to each other turn out interesting even for the modern reader. The clarity of word charts and pronunciation guides would certainly have aided merchants or soldiers. Words Faidherbe chose to translate are generally not abstract—demeurer, démolir, divorcer some of the typical ones beginning with "d."[53]

A similar pamphlet from the 1870s is his *Le Zénaga des tribus sénégalaises*, a treatise on Berber languages. In the high age of European imperialism, this work is dedicated to Leopold II, King of the Belgians and founder of an association for the "civilization" of Africans. But the booklet *is* useful, giving details about the Berbers and then key elements of their grammar. The way Faidherbe makes allusions to grammatical constructs in English or German makes one think that like Gallieni, another multilingual imperialist, he would have been a far more aware commander of troops in World War I than the tragically provincial Joffre. (See the following chapter.)

In *Le Zénaga* Faidherbe clearly shows how to negotiate aspects of the languages—for example, pronouns and verb conjugations. No pedant, he yet alludes both to Western languages to help his readers, and to tongues like Kabyle and Touareg. He shows what is common among various Arab dialects, and locates derivations dating back 2,000 years; for example *iourmi*—meaning European (*roum* had meant "city of Rome.").[54]

His best linguistic work treats the Poul language, which had interested him since his assumption of the Senegalese governorship in 1854. Only after he left Senegal, however, did he have the requisite leisure to write about that language he had come to learn. And this work turns out again to be far more than a dull grammar book. At the beginning Faidherbe avows a debt to Charles Darwin, indulging his own fascination with evolution as a preface to the physiological origins of languages. This was a time when such amateur speculations could be taken seriously, and Faidherbe's views would reach many European societies of which he was a member, including ones in Berlin and London.[55]

Faidherbe's intuitions about languages are sometimes extreme, but they rarely bore a reader. For example: "It seems that energetic races make the greatest use of consonants. . . . In derivative languages, the disappearance of consonants is sometimes a consequence of the softening of manners and of a race." (If so, slurring Americans of the twenty-first century had better watch out!) Faidherbe notes how the French had made the Latin *pater* into *père*, and how Creoles found even that "r" too difficult, saying pé (for *père*). The Peuls and Sudanese blacks in general can't handle too many consonants either, he confidently adds.[56]

Faidherbe shows quite rightly that linguistic irregularities had derived over the centuries from the developing tastes of peoples, as "règles d'euphonie." Full of respect for how the Peuls had implemented words and constructs to adapt to surroundings, he observes correctly that "there are people who imagine that grammarians made the rules of languages." He moves to Latin to demonstrate how internal rhymes mirrored taste—"vinorum bonorum" or "deus maximus"—then returns to the Peuls, showing how they too have "a delicate ear." He is truly marvelous on onomatopoeia. "Ma" is the universal sound a child makes at the mother's breast— hence the Poul word *ioumma* for mother, not far from the French *maman* (or the English mom or mommy). *Niám*, the Poul root of *niamdé* for "to eat," is also onomatopoeic (reminiscent of the American "yummy").[57]

Certainly Faidherbe plays favorites, and reveals his prejudices without bothering to veil them, viewing the mixed Peuls as superior to the run of Senegalese-Sudanese blacks—their aquiline noses and sometimes reddish complexions (of Ethiopian origins) signs of an intelligence that, he avers, had made them masters of the region, never slaves. His linguistic comparisons clearly show such preferences. "As much as Malinké is hard, Poul is soft and harmonious," he writes. The elegance of their doubled consonants reminds him very much of Italian: *debbo* for woman, *bibbé* for children are good examples, and he salutes Poul complexity vis-à-vis other, simpler languages of the general region.[58]

The main thing this short book and its revised version show the modern reader is a super-observant man, respectful of the complexity of areas so different from those of his native France. Certainly Faidherbe remained involved with a European or classical heritage he also knew well—never did he become a pure Africanophile.[59] But he did have an unusually deep appreciation of regional or local cultures he encountered during his gubernatorial stints in Africa.

That observant nature in turn helped make him an effective military commander—the curious dialectic that is one of our main themes here; but the one European conflict that allowed Faidherbe to reveal his talents in this domain was the Franco-Prussian War of 1870–71, and it was such an early French defeat and gave him a role so late in the day that it hardly showed what he could do. Not until late November 1870 was he awarded command of the Army of the Nord, his home area, in replacement of General Bourbaki. The French disaster of Sedan was more than two months behind, and the Prussian General Manteuffel was now occupying large swaths of northern France. Quickly, Faidherbe eliminated drunkenness and lack of discipline in the motley French group under his command. His first idea was to retake Amiens, but he was afraid of ruining that city, perhaps in part because of its great Gothic cathedral. Winter came in for an early and heavy landing. Finally just before Christmas he fought against Manteuffel at Pont-Noyelles on the Somme. Battle was fierce here, including body-to-body use of bayonets, but the French lacked too many material necessities to adapt well to the freezing weather. Faidherbe also had to beg the War Ministry repeatedly for reinforcements.[60]

The value of his troops was mainly as an annoyance or irritant to the Prussians. He now began to retreat to a defensible line, and Manteuffel—like Tall—tried to avoid more head-on engagements with this foe. Instead the Germans held a line on the Somme, trying to bomb the strategically important town of Péronne into submission. Louis Cadot holds Faidherbe somewhat accountable for the siege that ensued there, making Péronne one of the worst hit towns or cities of the war. Information was poorly relayed, and Faidherbe arrived too late to relieve the pulverized town. Other battles of the North followed in aid of Péronne, notably at Bapaume, again in freezing temperatures. Here the French at least temporarily had successes. After that, Manteuffel again showed his respect for Faidherbe by staying away from him; but though Bapaume itself was retaken by the Germans, the siege of Péronne continued until its capitulation January 9. The result was much damage, with sick and homeless people all over the place, and quite a few prisoners of war taken. In capitulation the French also had to abandon their armaments to the Germans, as would one day be the case for the Czechs in a Nazi-occupied Sudetenland. Yet Faidherbe's troops, fighting both Prussians and winter, continued in desperate combat, even as the national collapse approached its final act. On slippery roads, trying to skirt superior Prussian forces freshly debouched by rail, Faidherbe and his troops had to accept battle on the heights of Saint-Quentin, retreating as effectively as possible against forces he estimated at double his own. He was, however, proud of the hard fighting of his troops, persisting right up to the armistice of late January 1871.[61]

Faidherbe remained a popular figure in a French region that had been spared the worst of Prussian pillage and rape. At least he had hurt the Germans a little and proven "that the Frenchman isn't a degenerate soldier." His opponents would also give him good marks for his military accomplishments.[62]

Faidherbe's soldiers seemed to have no qualms either about the aging colonial leader—by and large, they respected him greatly. And his African-bred empiricism also allowed him to perceive the nature of the next, more serious war to come. The German use of trenches and their practice of blowing up bridges over vital rivers had taught Faidherbe a lot, and his observation "that with today's firepower there is no more place on the battlefield for a squadron of cavalry" should have been tacked onto the walls of French war schools! This of course was only common sense, but common sense not many commanders would possess in 1914.[63]

As a well-known imperial figure and war hero, Faidherbe was now impelled against his better judgment into postwar French political life. Early in the period of the Paris Commune he departed the military, citing bad health and a need for total rest, although he would remain politically interested in things martial, supporting more efficient draft and mobilization plans. Elected in three departments for the interim Assembly, he chose to represent the Nord, but found his middling liberalism raised difficulties with both Catholic Right and neo-Jacobin Left. So he resigned, due also to the onset of paralysis, and returned to his research interests, which he preferred anyway. Like two future war ministers, Gallieni and Lyautey, used to untrammeled power abroad, Faidherbe would find French politics at home too full of irrelevant talk and deals.[64]

But he still had to fight a good deal during that decade. Money was a recurring problem for the colonial veteran, one reason the War Ministry made him a member of the Central Railway Commission in 1872 until his death—it paid a salary to a man with "no fortune." Faidherbe's dossier shows constant wrangles with authorities over pensions and even authorizations of where he was allowed to live. He was also angered by a government edict of 1873 revoking name changes of squares and streets that had taken place after the Franco-Prussian War—i.e., eliminating many *places* or *rues* Faidherbe. He wondered as well why he was the only commanding general of that war who had not received a military medal and was concerned that devoted inhabitants of the Nord would misconstrue the government's actions, or nonactions, on this issue.[65]

Another problem of the period was Faidherbe's continually deteriorating health, undoubtedly part of the "colonial price" we have seen people like Saint-Arnaud pay in Algeria. Inspection reports mention Faidherbe's virtually complete paralysis and his confinement to a wheelchair from the early 1870s. In one report for 1876 the inspector notes that Faidherbe is "stricken with a severe disease, so that he can no longer move, except in an invalid's vehicle"; and one of 1878 declares that "he can no longer walk and needs to be carried or put in a wheelchair to get around, even in an apartment" (though the inspector adds that he *does* possess superior mental faculties.)[66]

Despite these health problems Faidherbe returned to Parliament in 1879, this time as a senator, supporting the education of young women and perhaps contradictorily for some historians, a strong colonial policy. Leaving his wheelchair, he generally had to be carried up to speak. The discord of politics in that era, cresting with the popularity of War Minister Boulanger, disgusted him. But he continued to write, until a series of strokes laid him low at the end of the 1880s. His unpublished letters from the era become harder and harder to decipher. Alive long enough to hear—perhaps with some ambivalence—of new French successes in the Sudan, Faidherbe finally passed away at the end of September, 1889, and the last testimony to his relatively modern, open-minded intellect was that as a member of a "Society of Mutual Autopsy" he had legated his skull to science. (His wife, however, cancelled the bequest, burying him intact in the Invalides.)[67]

That wife, as well as his first one, both of whom gave him offspring, should also be mentioned in connection with this unusual French imperial figure. Some believed that Faidherbe indulged in what they referred to as Negrophilia by contracting a *mariage à la mode* during the early 1850s with a Sarakhollé tribeswoman, Dionkounda Siabidi (or in French, Dioucounda Sidibé), a woman who helped him learn the Poul, Wolof, and Soninké languages. He also had ideas on the creation of a mulatto race that would supposedly constitute a new African elite, contributing with his own son by Dionkounda, Louis Léon. The idea had been in the air before Faidherbe, partly due to the ravages of yellow fever in rainy season, which presumably a hardier Franco-African ethnicity might be better able to withstand in places like Senegal.[68]

Faidherbe probably also found exotic what was not so exotic to local people, including nudity symbolizing virginity there, vis-à-vis the clothed worldliness of married people. In an era of heavily attired Europeans this custom might have had exactly the reverse significance for Faidherbe.[69]

His social liberalism must also have played a role in his second marriage of 1858 to an eighteen-year-old niece, when he himself was forty. This young lady had lost her father at an early age, and Faidherbe had to beseech the War Ministry for permission to marry "ma nièce et pupille," Mlle Angèle-Marie Faidherbe, still living with his sisters who, he says, had largely raised her. Because of "Faidherbe's exceptional position," the War Ministry gave its approval, and the couple were married in Lille (during his leave home from Senegal), December 7, 1858. This union gave Faidherbe two more sons and a daughter, and his wife would also raise his son by Dionkounda. In later life War Ministry inspections would always call Faidherbe the father of four, not distinguishing between offspring of the two marriages.[70]

Thanks to a liberating colonial experience, Faidherbe had found what he needed in life and made a series of significant contributions. Like the great colonial figures he would influence, Gallieni and Lyautey, Faidherbe learned tolerance abroad and how morals are as relative as Diderot had announced in his *Letter on the Blind*. On the whole Faidherbe did want to replace African polygamy with European monogamy, but he also knew how tenacious the former was—in Cayor, for example, free men often had three wives, legally spending two or three nights in a row with each. They could also have slave concubines. A tolerant Faidherbe knew he could not eradicate such mores in a day.[71]

One final characteristic of this colonial figure was a lack of illusions

about French colonization, or, as in Bugeaud's case, a fear of it when commercialization became too dominant in its wake. Faidherbe flatly wondered whether the French could be anything but teachers in remote areas
like Senegal. Too few would actually go off and try to make an enduring
life there. Even in more developed Algeria a good two-thirds of immigrants (late 1880s) were now drawn from other European nationalities, he
noted, while the French were plagued by a low birthrate, due to libertine
proclivities and too much culture. (Bugeaud had also complained about
French culture, yet ironically he and Faidherbe were both marvelously
cultured themselves.)[72]

In his prognostications Faidherbe did foresee the possibility of enhanced tourism in the Senegal of the future. To Switzerland and Italy, and
now to Algeria went pleasure-seekers—why not to West Africa? His last
book, indeed, was something of a long brochure on how to get there and
what to expect. The weather was not to be feared, he said, since Senegal
was one of the healthiest of colonies, and even tornadoes there were more
"a distraction than a danger." Again one sees this imperialist as a kind of
publicity man, before guidebooks became standardized. In the very year
of his death a British-French treaty delimited the borders of Gambia and
Senegal, while by the turn of the century French West Africa would be
organized, with its capital the rapidly growing deep-water port of Dakar.
Faidherbe had truly been prophetic about Senegal's possibilities.[73]

Concluding, there were in this colonial figure enough contradictory
facets to justify the appellation of "new model" imperialist, especially
given those who preceded him. Suggesting that he presaged elements in
Gallieni and Lyautey, both of whom admired him greatly, does not, however, mean that there was an exact blueprint for the makers and defenders of a French Empire. As will be seen in the next two chapters, Gallieni
and Lyautey shared aspects of the Faidherbian mix of common sense and
romanticism, military toughness and aesthetic-scholarly curiosity, realism
and idealism, some of which we have noted in Bugeaud as well. Setting
aside comparisons, what Faidherbe created in West Africa and what he
put into print demonstrated at the least much that was useful, beneficial,
and enhancing. His life and work should receive attention as one more
biographical qualification of reductive, superficial notions that still pre-
dominate about nineteenth century French or European imperialism.

CHAPTER FOUR

Gallieni and Joffre

Colonials Tragically Intertwined

W HEN WE COME TO THE CASE of Gallieni, we encounter a proconsul who was one of France's greatest—and who ended up among
its most tragic, both for himself and for his country. Gallieni continued the "new model" mix of Faidherbe in a second French colonial
empire on extended missions to West Africa, Vietnam, and Madagascar.
He was a scholarly, literate, and sensitive man, well demonstrated in his
copious writings, yet also in the same league militarily as a Faidherbe
and Bugeaud. In this chapter we devote much space to the tragic endpoint
of Gallieni's extensive colonial resumé: i.e., the background and course of
World War I, France's worst ever, and his role in it.

Too often people have underestimated such a colonial background as
excellent preparation for a European war.[1] To be sure, the colonial milieu
also brought to the fore bumblers like the future French chief of staff in
World War I, Joseph Joffre, also an alumnus of West Africa, Indochina,
and Madagascar. Here we will discuss Joffre at great length as Gallieni's
antithesis, a man who came up a deceptively similar colonial route, but
who turned out sadly different.

Gallieni, by contrast, would put to good use his extensive imperial
experience when he became Governor of Paris at the outset of World
War I; but that he, rather than Joffre, would be most responsible for
saving the capital at the Battle of the Marne has been too little known by
lay people and too rarely acknowledged in general histories.[2] What makes
Gallieni's case tragic is that despite age and exhaustion he might have
saved France as well from what turned out to be its most Pyrrhic victory,
if only Joffre hadn't throttled his efforts and ideas.

Biographers frequently exaggerate Gallieni's ethnicity, particularly toughness deriving from his mother's Pyrenean and Corsican blood. Still, a multihued lineage helped dictate his future suppleness of character. His father was a Lombard born in the province of Milan and glad to become a part of Napoleon's Cisalpine Republic. Choosing France as his ultimate home, Gallieni's father entered the French army in 1829, ascending the ranks from the bottom. When posted to Saint-Béat near the Spanish frontier, he met and married Françoise Périssé from an old family in that region, and their famed son Joseph Simon was born there in 1849. Father Gaëtan Gallieni moved to a variety of garrisons around France with his family, attaining the rank of captain in the early 1850s, and decided to retire in Saint-Béat, eventually as its mayor. A naturally strategic place, Saint-Béat had been fortified by the Romans, and the young Gallieni loved the mountains of the region, learning skills there that would help make him the explorer he later became.[3]

Unfortunately, he didn't get his fill of this area nor of his many maternal relatives strewn around it; for at age eleven he was dispatched across France to the military college of La Flèche, a preparatory school for Saint-Cyr. Homesick, Gallieni initially rebelled there, but eventually matured into a serious type some would see as English in tone—and indeed, he later learned the English language, admiring writers such as Mill and Spencer, and esteemed English virtues. Having heard Italian at home, Gallieni found it easier to absorb foreign languages than did the run of ethnocentric Frenchmen of his era; and though he continued to dislike aspects of La Flèche, he managed to win the Latin prize there, as well as stand out in mathematics.[4]

Passing the examination to enter officers' school at Saint-Cyr in 1868, Gallieni soon became part of a generation deeply marked by the Franco-Prussian War. Of fourteen Cyrians in the naval infantry, four were killed, five wounded, two taken prisoner at Sedan, and three (including Gallieni) made it to Bazeilles, before being captured and imprisoned in Germany. Thanks to this incarceration Gallieni learned German language and culture, as de Gaulle would do in World War I—an awareness that again, would later be underutilized. Studying with a high school teacher, and conversing frequently in the language with a Bavarian officer, Gallieni also read much German literature or philosophy, particularly Schiller and Goethe. He also got to know the captive Englishman Kitchener, a volunteer in the French army during this war, and a man whose career would eerily parallel his own.[5]

Liberated, Gallieni was a changed man, a patriot and republican desiring the regeneration of his country. That was one reason he chose to serve in the colonial milieu. His first posting was as lieutenant of naval infantry to Réunion in the Indian Ocean, whence he embarked in April 1872, spending several years in idyllic surroundings—years he would never forget when troubles clawed at him later in life.[6]

His next posting to Senegal would make far more demands on Gallieni. The man who would become the model for many, including Lyautey, had several models of his own as he prepared in 1876 for his first colonial test—the great Faidherbe, as well as explorers like Mungo Park, whose territory he would now get to see first-hand.[7] For Gallieni was himself to become an explorer as well as an imperial figure on a continent now succumbing to the great European "scramble."

Dispatched to Dakar in December 1876 on board the *Parana*, he arrived in a colony where his countrymen still had a totally secure foothold only near the coast. The main idea of its governor, Colonel Brière de l'Isle (1876–81), was to make French commerce more secure deeper into the interior. But few explorers had ever reached these African depths, and of those, almost none had returned.

At first based on the Isle of Gorée, Gallieni fought garrison boredom by keeping a journal both in French and several foreign languages. Brière then gave him reconnaissance gigs and command of a "circle" in Thiès, and Gallieni rapidly proved himself the ideal diplomat to treat with African chieftains. In the summer of 1878 a wave of yellow fever, killing hundreds of Europeans around him, somehow spared him its ravages. That September he again traveled up the Senegal to parley with loquacious chieftains, and Brière was satisfied, making him head of "Indigenous Politics" at the outset of 1879. He also consented to allow Gallieni, who knew the Bambara language, to lead an expedition further into the interior. The mission was to travel to Médine on the Senegal River, then through hazardous country to the valley of the Niger, a region largely shut off to whites since the expeditions of Mungo Park, who had died in 1805. Redefined by the French as the western Sudan, this expedition would test Gallieni's abilities not only because of jungles, mountains, and intense heat, but also tribal conflicts. The ultimate French plan was to open commerce eastward, and possibly to conquer this western Sudan; then via a railway, to link the basin of the Senegal to that of the Niger, following up with a potential extension across the Sahara to Algeria—scarcely less bold a concept than Russia's trans-Siberian enterprise of the era!

Gallieni's chief adversary between Senegal and Niger would be the King of Ségou, Ahmadou, son of Umar Tall. Ahmadou's Toucouleur-Muslim despotism ruled over mainly Malinka and Bambara tribes, but most of these tribespeople loathed his imperial control. Unfortunately, they were too often busy fighting each other to offer effective resistance in the parts of a 300,000 square kilometer empire that Ahmadou reliably controlled—basically, along the right bank of the Niger River.

Now a captain, Gallieni prepared his expedition for early 1880. The idea was to woo tribespeople away from Ahmadou by signing treaties of protection and friendship, then procuring what seems a Bismarckian contradiction—protectoral accommodation with the despot himself, assuming he could reach him.[8]

Gallieni's finest book, *Voyage au Soudan français*, complete with drawings of animals and chieftains, discusses this expedition, and reading it, one notices first and foremost yet another acute colonial observer and highly literate man. Here one realizes that as much as any colonial milieu the western Sudan taught Gallieni to track changing data and to improvise—at many points a life-saving skill. As an amateur anthropologist he had to make distinctions in a hurry, noting, for instance, that the Sarracolet tribe were the region's commercial go-betweens; that for some tribespeople green pigeons and for others certain snakes were sacred; that the Peuls, the Toucouleur leaders, had different subdivisions; that Bambara and Malinka women, more than in Europe, were "things of the husband"; that Bambaras and Malinkas could be pried away with gifts and protection from Toucouleur domination; that some black chieftains were always sober, while others led all-night drunks on local *dolo*; that the region was rife with civil war, often between villages; that one might contain fierce inhabitants, while in the next, people were "gentle and reserved."[9] What Gallieni learned above all else was that great colonial lesson: to avoid simplistic, *a priori* generalizations.

And he loved the area, sounding almost Darwinian in his descriptions of, among others, chameleons ("the habitual color of the chameleon is of a vivid green, which, modifying itself according to the nuance of the object on which the animal is placed, becomes dark or light yellow or olive"). He enjoyed drinking water beside "a whole flock of cute little does," or hearing the "sonorous whinnying" of hippos. These observations stemmed from a love of natural beauty, but they were also necessary for sheer survival. It was a time when nocturnal lion attacks were always possible, when crossing rivers or rapids could mean death, and when the first rains of the winter season ruined roads and brought life-threatening attacks of fever.[10]

This Sudanese experience also developed Gallieni's soon-remarkable facility for assessing individual character and worth. Pierre Gheusi would remark that it took him a matter of minutes to measure a person's value, though Gallieni's estimates were not always foolproof. He would not, for example, ascertain the true nature of his future colonial subordinate Joffre until it was too late, to the detriment of many young French soldiers of World War I. But he did learn here how crucial the human element always was, discounting the old proverb that "no one is indispensable."[11]

To make treaties with difficult chieftains beset by rivals, Gallieni had to show that he could protect them from Ahmadou's onerous taxes and religious intolerance, and not least, from each other. Implementing such a policy required discerning in a hurry who had power and who was a mere figurehead; who could be relatively trusted and who couldn't. He had to know what gifts to proffer and how much stealing to put up with (since it was omnipresent). What he saw between the Senegal and Niger Rivers was what Faidherbe had already found in his more westerly sector—extreme anarchy wrought by despotic, whimsical rulers. Gallieni had to locate the best interpreters and guides, some of whom he came to care for as much as the few Europeans he took with him. One Bambara was an adept tracker, but too fond of cognac—each morning on the trip he begged for slugs of it. Yoro, Gallieni's African cook and general aide, was "vain, a liar, and a thief," according to his employer, but more skilled than the French doctor Tautain when it came to treating fevers.[12]

The ability to make order from disorder at high speed would be Gallieni's forte in the Paris region when the Germans approached in 1914, and it was a skill he began developing here. At a number of Sudanese villages he found depopulation and ruin in once prosperous areas, and however hypocritical the French "civilizing mission" may sound, Gallieni was sincere when he remarked: "It is for us now to substitute our benevolent influence [here]." This meant breaking up extortion rackets that forced Bambaras to hide their crops in case Toucouleur masters came to their villages, and it meant working with chieftains and preserving their ways. "We don't want territories, tithes, or captives" nor to "tamper with chieftains, customs, or religions," Gallieni concluded.[13]

For his expedition beginning February 4, 1880, he demonstrated another métier that became useful in 1914: outfitting or stockpiling (*ravitaillement*) of food, medicine, arms, and presents. Gallieni's convoy contained, among other things, fireworks, music boxes, parasols, and glassware as gifts, plus much ammunition and guns. His *tirailleurs, spahis*, guides, interpreters, and two French doctors also reflected that ability to prepare.[14]

Mounting the Senegal to Médine and Bafoulabé was the relatively easy part of the trip; then using compasses to make their way farther into the interior became an exercise in the art of intuitive exploration. We haven't space to show in detail the series of improvisations and gambles Gallieni's expedition became, how many times death threatened (ambushes, six-foot boas suddenly dropping into campsites), or how skilled a diplomat he was in making treaties of friendship with chieftains he encountered. Death came closest at two points—the first outside Dio in May 1880, where thousands of Beleri and Bambara tribespeople ambushed his already attenuated group and nearly massacred them, but for his guides locating a river ford, and fortuitous escape. The second was when the rainy season of fevers hit with full force.[15]

Nearing, then passing the Niger, Gallieni was down to a few rounds of ammunition and out of presents. Most of his pack asses were skinned by brambles or cliffs, and his *tirailleurs* and *spahis* had been much reduced in numbers. Looking dishevelled, he pressed on to have talks with Sultan Ahmadou in June, while intermittent diarrhea and fever attacks laid him and his comrades low. He had no certainty at all that summary execution did not lie in wait. Ahmadou kept him out of the holy city of Ségou, and instead, the group was lodged in a miserable village called Nango about twenty-five miles away—for ten agonizingly long months, as it turned out. Gallieni made sure to publicize the vengeful powers of a far-away France, but each morning he and his group still feared the possibility of decapitation. Food here was poor, water nondrinkable, and in June alone, a demoralized Gallieni had at least fifty attacks of fever, he says. The remaining French supply of quinine had gotten wet in river-crossings and lost effectiveness, so fever victims experienced waves of icy shivering alternating with burning fits, and also loss of appetite. Meanwhile, he and his fewer and fewer adherents had to wait "philosophically for the end of [each] fever attack." Gallieni would still be suffering its effects at the time of the Marne in 1914; but at least he was learning to overcome extreme odds.[16]

Waiting for the sultan to sign a protectorate treaty and let them go became a maddening experience. The sultan kept promising, but as Gallieni wrote, "we are victims of these habits of slowness and indolence of the Toucouleurs." On December 4 he mentioned five straight days of fever, with severe headaches and hummings in his ears. A sad January 1,

1881 came, and French conversations were focused only on departing this godforsaken trap. Then came news of a French rescue column at Kita, and Gallieni played power poker with the sultan. Chastened, and greedy for what he might procure from French benevolence, the latter finally signed the Treaty of Nango, March 10, 1881. By it France received its protectorate from the Niger's source to Tombouctou (though the treaty would be undermined both by Gallieni and by the sultan's own treachery). On March 21 Gallieni and the remnant of his group were finally permitted to leave, and once he made it back to Saint-Louis, he departed immediately for Bordeaux.[17]

In France Gallieni received decorations—a Legion of Honor and a medal from the Geography Society—as well as military promotion. The press wrote extensively about his expedition, and he got to meet celebrities like the engineer for the Suez Canal, Ferdinand de Lesseps. He also had time to digest the lessons of the Sudan and to write the above-mentioned book. Often he would remark that if he hadn't been a soldier, he would surely have been a writer; but really, like Caesar, he was both. He drew on both English and German literary models ("A man today who ... doesn't know German, I consider him as disarmed," he would later remark). There was and would continue to be a real symmetry to his existence, as he lived in a demanding colonial world, then returned to France to digest his experiences and write about them. Back home on this round he had time as well to look around for marriage prospects, and in 1881 met and soon wed Marthe Savelli. From a wealthy Corsican family, she was a musical and multilingual woman who would recognize Gallieni's "exquise délicatesse," and give him happiness (as well as two children). But inevitably, the craving for action got the better of him. Several years of get-well time on the island of Martinique, starting in 1883, eventually became a bore. In 1886 Lieutenant-Colonel Gallieni asked for another stint in Africa and duly received an assignment—this time as Supreme Commander of the French Sudan.[18]

The situation there remained anything but resolved. In the north, Ahmadou was still a problem, having relocated to a new capital, and in the south, another Muslim chieftain, Mahmadou Lamine ("the Marabout"), had raised a revolt. To confront the latter, Gallieni brought along his old infantry friend Vallière, previously in the Sudan with him, as well as Dr. Tautain, who abandoned a Paris medical practice to join the expedition. For troops Gallieni had a thousand Senegalese *tirailleurs*, a division of *spahis*, an artillery company, cannoneers, and also the latest in artillery.[19]

Gallieni began his main assault on Mahmadou's forces by splitting his company—one part setting out from Aroundou and the other from the chief French town of the Sudan, Kayes, December 12, 1886. The idea was to converge after a difficult march at Diane, the Marabout's stronghold. Again Gallieni sharpened skills here that he had garnered on his first trip. En route he still had to fight tenacious local customs, which included slavery, and eventually he would capture a group of women belonging to Mahmadou and marry them off, with his top seventeen Sengalese *tirailleurs* receiving their top seventeen choices. "We know with what facility native women in Senegambia change master," commented Gallieni. He also fought the use of torture, such as by a tribe of Bondous who cut off an ear, hand, and foot of a typical unfortunate, who was then roasted over a fire.[20]

Gallieni made a great reputation among tribespeople by combating Mahmadou's practices of village burning, murdering notables, or taking women and children as captives. Here he continued learning how to protect, as he would protect Parisians in 1914. His idea was to instill instruments of civilization that were hard-won and rare benefits in such an area. As he said at one point during the Senegal-to-Niger railway project, whose construction he supervised, "I felt a real satisfaction when I took the train at Dakar that was to lead us to Saint-Louis." Soon, one could painlessly cross the "Thieves' Ravine" that had always terrified merchants.[21]

Eventually both of Gallieni's aggregations reached Diane, hastily evacuated by Mahmadou, who left his Koran and sandals behind. Thus far there had been no French casualties. En route Gallieni made a number of new treaties with chieftains, who pledged to close their villages to Mahmadou; but as good faith, they had to give up sons to attend French schools as "hostages." France's protectorate was then extended considerably southward. But Gallieni remained forceful with those who revolted, including Mahmadou's vengeful son, Soybou, captured, then executed with full military honors. In Gallieni's view French weakness would never do here. Friendship treaties in various states or subregions now allowed traders security, and the building of roads, hospitals, and new villages followed.

On May 12, 1887 Gallieni signed a reinsurance treaty with the other major potentate, Sultan Ahmadou, permitting the French protectorate to continue in all areas under his current and future domain. In fact Gallieni considered pagan tribes like the Bambaras surer allies than these sultans, whose word seemed as shaky as a Frenchman's health under the pitiless sun of extended marches. But he also went to work on another Islamic potentate, the "Almany" Samory Touré, whose Sudanese sway extended down to Guinea and the Ivory Coast. A French envoy, Captain Péroz, went to meet this sultan surrounded by courtesans, and by fierce warriors ready to decapitate a French representative at the flick of a finger. But France's pre-1914 Republic then had numinous sway both at home and abroad, and Gallieni sent a tough letter to the sultan, and finally a treaty was signed there too. Of course as Chamberlain would learn in the late 1930s, treaties made were only as strong as forces that could compel compliance. And indeed, Mahmadou promptly rebelled again, holing himself up with 2,000 warriors in a well-fortified citadel. Gallieni led a surreptitious, rapid assault, then Mahmadou ran with about 100 supporters left, was wounded, and subsequently died in captivity. Forts, gardens, roads, and sewers followed in areas he had dominated, and on balance, Gallieni had created a miracle of organization and security in a now large French West Africa. Faidherbe had begun the process, but Gallieni and the Republic he represented had a much wider-ranging prestige among West Africans, who could now cultivate in more peaceful conditions than they had previously known. On the negative side the French would keep pushing at great expense eastward toward modern Chad, searching for a kind of El Dorado that never quite panned out. And Samory, the last rebel leader, would torment them throughout the 1890s. But Gallieni had more than done his job.[22]

Back in France again the colonial warrior was even more celebrated this time, and at thirty-eight, after brief command of a naval infantry regiment in Toulon, entered Paris' Ecole de Guerre. In the capital he completed a second book on the Sudan, but avoided discussions of his exploits abroad. Living in the Latin Quarter, he instead absorbed exciting developments in French culture, meeting and admiring figures like the Socialist leader Jean Jaurès, and staying current with literary trends. He also savored the pleasures of family life. From his stint at the Ecole de Guerre he emerged as a member of the General Staff, and a colonel in April 1891. Soon after, he became head of the French Colonial Army Corps. But the bureaucratic atmosphere of Paris depressed him as much as it did our other proconsuls, and Gallieni also felt anxious over reports that his successor, Louis Archinard, was imposing a more blatantly military conception of the Sudan protectorate than he would have liked. To Eugène Etienne, undersecretary of state for colonies, and soon leader of the *Parti colonial* pressure group in the Chamber, Gallieni bluntly criticized the

unlimited and costly expansion advocated by Archinard and his adherents. He was duly appointed to a commission that would set limits on
this expansion, but reappointment of Colonel Archinard to his position
of command impelled Gallieni toward some other challenge abroad. That
challenge would be the Tonkin of northern Vietnam.[23]

Because of its importance then and in the latter part of our account,
and to our story on both Gallieni and Joffre, we truly need to amplify
here on the series of people and events that led to such a deep French
involvement in Southeast Asia. The Tonkin was the last and most difficult
of three French protectoral areas of Vietnam to be absorbed—with southern Cochin China first, followed by central Annam. As noted, the French
had initiated a modern empire here rather as accidental tourists. Initially
there had been missionaries, supported variously by French regimes,
depending on their values. Those proselytizers certainly suffered, as did
Vietnamese Catholics they had converted, branded as infidels and even
cut in half by the emperor of Annam, Tu Duc, who took the throne in
1847. France's Napoleon III, married to an ardent Catholic in the early
1850s, felt he had to reply to such mistreatment; but he was pressured as
well by mercantile and naval interests. Their operations of the late 1850s
in Vietnam made him hesitant, especially given the ravages of disease on
French soldiers and sailors, dying in droves from cholera, dysentery, and
a variety of fevers, or living with gangrenous arms or legs requiring amputation. The minister of the navy and colonies, Chasseloup-Laubat, was
nothing daunted. To some degree he was in fact the key figure who pushed
Vietnam on Napoleon III and thence on his successors. Under Chasseloup's
sway, a French admiral moved inland from the sea, managing to occupy
the southern town of Saigon in 1861. More Frenchmen then sailed up the
Mekong into its fertile delta, and by 1862 Emperor Tu Duc had given the
French three provinces in the rice-rich Saigon region of Cochin China.
Worrying about a rebellion up north, he needed the French for now.
But already Napoleon III feared a deeper commitment here. Tu Duc also
worried that France desired all of Vietnam; in 1862 he tried to placate
them not only with the three provinces granted, but also by allowing a
French protectorate over all six provinces of Cochin China (southern
Vietnam). Hoping for a lucrative route up the Mekong to southwestern
China, the French had settled for protectorates en route—typical ad hoc
Western imperialism.

In 1863 Admiral Pierre Paul Marie Benoît de la Grandière (how they
named them then) absorbed contiguous Cambodia as a protectorate, and

in 1867 decided before consulting with Napoleon III simply to take over the other three western provinces of Cochin China in order to protect that protectorate. (Bridge players might see this as imperial crossruffing!)

French naval officers continued to wonder whether the sinuous Mekong would be commercially navigable from its delta in Cochin China up to the rich Chinese province of Yunnan. To learn the answer Admiral de la Grandière, Saigon's French governor, put together an exploratory voyage led by Captain Doudart de Lagrée, and with an impetuous young lieutenant in tow, Francis Garnier. Starting out in June 1866 they found the voyage difficult, due to sandbars and rapids, and in southern China Lagrée died, leaving the way open for an obsessed Garnier to continue down the Yangtze River to Shanghai and thence back to Saigon. Another Frenchman who thought the extension of empire was an antidote for decline at home, Garnier was moved to write about his experiences, bringing out his *Voyage d'exploration* in 1873.

By then he knew that the Mekong wasn't a useful commercial route to China; however, the Red River, which started up in Yunnan and wound down through northern Vietnam to Haiphong on the Gulf of Tonkin, seemed more suitable. Once again, an historian sees people, not abstract forces, largely making this French empire. In the early 1870s a merchant named Jean Dupuis picked up the ball of expansion (when at that point the idea of a French advance into northern Vietnam might yet have perished). An arms salesman to a warlord in Yunnan province, Dupuis decided to spurn the overland route and instead sail the Red River to sell his arms, before bringing back return cargo. He received support and a loan from Admiral Jules-Marie Dupré, then French governor in Cochin China. But Paris, still reeling from defeat in the Franco-Prussian War, was fearful of moving northward into what was then a Vietnamese state (outside Cochin China). And indeed, such a voyage would receive no authorization from Emperor Tu Duc.

Ignoring these problems, Dupuis led his expedition up the Red River to Yunnan, selling his arms and returning to Hanoi with copper and tin. He concluded that this river would indeed be commercially navigable all the way to China's southern provinces. Emperor Tu Duc at the capital city of Hué predictably protested this unauthorized voyage into a Tonkin which harbored rebels against Annam. Dupuis wanted to make the trip again, but local mandarins stopped him. However, Admiral Dupré decided *he* would take Tonkin once and for all, endeavoring to open up the trade route to China and at the same time, outdo the British.

Unfortunately, Tonkin at the time was in a bad state. The Taiping Rebellion in China, a long, bloody conflict, had pushed Chinese rebels downward into North Vietnam, where they lived off the land. Tu Duc called for help from the Chinese government, but the soldiers dispatched instead joined the bandits, whom the French would dub "Black Flags." These problems gave Admiral Dupré a pretext for intervention. Dupré felt he had to get France into the region fast, before other European powers imposed their own order on this unruly Chinese border region. Exceeding the wishes of a rather timorous Paris still on parole after the great German victory, Dupré decided in the typically obstreperous way of colonials abroad to build on Dupuis' voyage by sending that explorer and veteran of the Mekong, Garnier, to Hanoi, ostensibly to obey Tu Duc and get Dupuis out. In fact he would begin the conquest of the Tonkin. (Dupré gave him 200 French soldiers and a few Annamese for the expedition.)

On arrival in Hanoi Garnier noted how sloppily the city was held and presumed that the surrounding Tonkin, already chafing under Tu Duc, was ripe for the picking. Here was another of those quixotic French administrator-explorers in a long line reaching back to Dupleix, whom in fact Garnier admired. Both he and Governor Dupré agreed that at least the Red River delta should be freed of bandits, and that the river should be opened to international commerce all the way up to China.

In Hanoi this little potentate issued an ultimatum for inhabitants to give up their arms and open the river to trade, asking also for the reduction of Vietnamese tariffs to aid European commerce. Failing assent, there would be an assault on the city's citadel. Local mandarins ignored the ultimatum, so Garnier attacked, taking the citadel with no loss of French soldiers. So far imperial expansion up here had come easily. Garnier then moved eastward, obtaining victories in Tonkin's delta, and getting more troops from Saigon, as well as Vietnamese Catholics and opponents of the Emperor to his side. After a month he had taken the area between Hanoi and the Gulf. In late December the emperor wished to sue for peace, but at the very moment when largely Chinese Black Flags were entering the fray. Pirates of this type had long occupied the Gulf of Tonkin, terrorizing inhabitants, selling women and children, and offering loot to the Chinese government that protected them. Garnier was too caught up negotiating with Tu Duc's representatives to respond properly. Hearing of a Black Flag march on Hanoi, he charged ahead of his men to meet the enemy, lost contact with the main body of his forces, and was killed by a volley of fire at the Paper Bridge just beyond the city. Dead at thirty-five Garnier had become another French colonial martyr—one more embodiment of a perhaps anachronistic, crusading chivalry and romanticism abroad. But because of his premature death, France's conquest of Tonkin would be deferred about a decade.

For Admiral Dupré now knew he must pay for exceeding Parisian constraints and losing Garnier, whom he blamed posthumously for misinterpreting orders! The home front promptly admonished Dupré to suspend this attempt to conquer Tonkin, and instead, to craft a more reliable treaty with Tu Duc in Hué. On his side the Emperor viewed French strength as something to be used. Dupré appointed a cultured, pro-Vietnamese Frenchman, Paul Louis Philastre, for the negotiations. Although he had worked alongside Garnier in the civil service of Indochina, Philastre was very different. Sensitive to Asian culture, he had become a great translator of Chinese and was not blinded by French claims to civilizational superiority. As head of judicial affairs in Cochin China, he wanted Vietnamese law to thrive, fearing that French alterations of local mores would one day arouse nationalistic antipathy.

By 1874 France had procured its treaty with Annam's emperor, some of it simply ratification of what existed. France remained sovereign of Cochin China, and three new ports, as well as the Red River itself, were to be opened to commerce. Annam in turn would obtain French military aid to help repel incursions into its territory. As a man of his word, Philastre got Dupuis ejected from Hanoi and French forces pulled out of Tonkin. The emperor had made an accord ceding the south, which would of course remain longest in the western camp, in order to retain the north.

It was all shaky, however, and the Red River continued harboring pirates. China kept putting its nose into Vietnam, as it would in the next century. Faced with such foes, Tu Duc played a double game of placating both Chinese and French. He also took revenge on Vietnamese Catholics who had fought alongside Garnier, laying waste their villages and killing thousands. And though theoretically guaranteeing free European commerce on the Red River, he sabotaged the agreement in practice by allowing Black Flags and other bandits to hijack cargoes, making it anything but an ideal trading route. He also began calling China the area's suzerain, summoning troops to help keep order in the north.

Back in France the political front was divided on a deeper involvement in this quite miserable land so far from the métropole. In fact the whole decade from 1874 to 1884 would be a difficult one for France in Indochina. Annam's Emperor Tu Duc kept using his vassalage under China to hamper the French, to whom he was also nominally pledged! Surrounded by larger powers, mandarins had always been two-faced, and the result was that Tu Duc continued making trade on the Red River precarious, as well as persecuting indigenous Christians. The Emperor also offered increased support to the vicious Black Flags.

By the end of the 1870s the French Opportunist Party had become the majority in Parliament, and these moderate liberals were also proponents of renewed Indochinese expansion. In 1879 a first civilian governor of Cochin China, Charles le Myre de Vilers, began setting his sights on the north, fearing that rich anthracite deposits up there might be granted as concessions to competitors like the English. As usual, these proponents of imperial expansion needed a rationale, and here the 1874 Treaty filled the bill. By it the French were theoretically permitted to help Tu Duc repress any disorders in Tonkin, which seemed to include the plentiful bandits operating there. So Le Myre received a green light from Paris to protect Vietnamese "sovereignty." Then, after the relatively easy establishment of a Tunisian protectorate in 1881, the Opportunist government felt overwhelmingly that it had had enough of Tu Duc's gambits, and that it was time to establish a true protectorate in Annam, as well as a stronger presence in Tonkin. A parliamentary vote to spend money on an expedition allowed Le Myre to appoint Commandant Henri Rivière as the new Garnier.

In 1882 Rivière left Saigon with his French forces, shot up the Red River, reached its delta, then arrived at the citadel town of Hanoi. Did it all sound familiar? It was, but Rivière was no Garnier. A naval officer with literary ambitions who had known writers like Flaubert and written fiction, he simply hadn't Garnier's exploratory passion. In his mid-fifties Rivière had tired of the Vietnamese climate, as well as of its people. He also needed to be careful in Tonkin, given increasing Chinese distrust of French designs there. There were, as well, new divisions back in Paris and no precise instructions for Rivière, not to mention negotiations going on between a still duplicitous Tu Duc and Peking.

By this time the minister of the navy and colonies (a ministry that kept being renamed in the nineteenth century) was the same Admiral Jauréguiberry who had had such ambitious ideas in Senegal. Despite the fact that it could mean war with China, Jauréguiberry favored a French takeover of Tonkin. Economic reasons were not the primary motivation; more important was national honor, and what Joseph Schumpeter would label an atavism—France's need to beat other potential European competitors to the punch. Were these nations akin to little boys outdoing each other in the schoolyard? Perhaps, but with more significant consequences for the future.

When the Opportunist leader Jules Ferry, a patriotic Lorrainer and creator of a secular public school system at home, became French premier for a second time in the early 1880s, he supported the idea of French control of Tonkin. Ferry was pushed as well by commercial interests, as he disliked seeing the richest part of northern Vietnam under the Chinese; but also by soldiers and sailors, and swaths of French public opinion. A domestic liberal, Ferry felt he had to be tough abroad (compare to Truman or Kennedy in the next century).

Meanwhile, Rivière took Hanoi's citadel, reoccupied the area between that city and the sea, grabbed the northern coal mines, and vanquished Black Flag pirates at Nam Dinh. But in an ambush of May 18 involving both Chinese pirates and Annamite partisans, he became another martyr. To show French weakness here they carried his head around Tonkinese villages. It was the first swallow of a long summer, ending at Dien Bien Phu in 1954. But an intensely patriotic French Chamber continued supporting costly military action there.

Just a few days before Rivière's death, Ferry and his majority in the Chamber had voted over 5,000,000 francs to mount a larger expedition, hopefully to establish a protectorate in the parts of Vietnam still requiring one. He then sent new reinforcements to the Tonkin, and French troops also besieged the forts of Annam's capital at Hué, compelling Tu Duc to sue for peace just before his death in July. That death without heirs then ignited a turbulent power struggle, providing the French more pretext for expansion.

In August 1883 the French fleet led by François Harmand, operating on the Perfume River near Hué, admonished the Vietnamese to give up in two days, or else. Before receiving a response, French gunships started firing heavily. The chief mandarin there began negotiating with Harmand, and France finally received a protectorate for all Vietnam, except for Cochin China in the south, which was a full French colony.

Of course nothing was yet final here. France now had a military presence and functionaries in place to supervise Vietnamese imperial authorities in matters like defense or trade. Harmand was the man who divided Vietnam into three French areas—Tonkin, Annam, and Cochin China—and who preferred calling its people "Annamites." But the Chinese were angry, dispatching numerous soldiers southward into the Tonkin, which led to an undeclared Sino-French war. By the end of the year the French had already put over 20,000 men into this quagmire, under the overall orders of Admiral Amédée Courbet, and three other generals leading land operations.

One column went up the Red River valley to affront the Chinese, while the other two fought in the Black River area. It now devolved upon Courbet and his associate, General Bouet, to try and expel both Black Flag pirates, and though still kept secret from the French public, regular Chinese troops from the Tonkin. Patiently during that spring of 1884 French soldiers mopped up town after town of the Red River delta.

But the Chinese became ever more hostile, and in Parliament at home so did Georges Clemenceau, leading the far Left. French diplomats also worked at cross-purposes, negotiating separately with the Chinese. Ferry still retained a large parliamentary majority for what he called both a French civilizing mission, but also the commercial jumping-off point for a potential market of 400,000,000 Chinese. Here was an alternative to protection-strangled, shrinking markets of Europe! Ferry also believed that conquest of the Tonkin was necessary simply to protect Annam— the domino-like imperial extensions in Southeast Asia were becoming similar to those of French West Africa. What he played down was this undeclared war with the Chinese. Some say that Eisenhower's actions engendered later American involvement in Vietnam; might they go further back to those of Ferry? For without that determined French politician of the Third Republic the Americans would never have undertaken what they later did here.

Reluctantly, the Chinese made an agreement to withdraw troops from Tonkin, supposedly ceding to France's hegemony; then they treacherously attacked a relaxed contingent of French troops in late June at the post of Bac-Le, a contingent that had thought withdrawal was already a fact. Ferry again demanded Chinese withdrawal from Tonkin, and a huge indemnity for French losses in this ambush—the amount of which he would downsize as the year wore on. Ferry was also pushed by glory-seekers like Courbet into other actions against China, while fearing a widened war that might antagonize the English, whom he needed to resupply the French fleet in Chinese waters. He nonetheless permitted Courbet's forces to shell China's only arsenal, Foochow, an operation that also sank or burned twenty-two Chinese ships, and killed 2,000 Chinese soldiers and sailors. By October 1, 1884 Courbet's squadron was off the island of Formosa, near the fortress town of Keelung. Courbet attacked Keelung and won, wanting to build it up as a French base. He then asked Indochina's governor-general Paul Bert, formerly Ferry's right-hand man in educational reform at home, for someone to supervise the fortification process on Formosa. Bert procured him a captain of naval artillery, who wasn't right for the job, and Courbet telegraphed Paris directly, demanding a specialist in military engineering. The Naval Ministry consulted the War Ministry, and in late December 1884 they appointed Joseph Joffre to the position.

The portly Joffre arrived off Formosa in the middle of February 1885, and Courbet, a fellow Polytechnique graduate, immediately set him to work fortifying the base at Keelung. Joffre's assignment was to build roads to and from Keelung in order to bring transports of materiel, and to lodge French military personnel. This was no picnic, for Keelung was as yet a muddy, roadless mess, particularly when rainy season approached, and lethal fevers became prevalent. Shelling had ruined most inhabitations there, so Joffre had to supervise the building of new barracks for French soldiers, while original inhabitants ran up to surrounding mountains. There were as well some 20,000 Chinese soldiers who were always ready to ambush by night, cutting the throats of French soldiers or sailors, whose heads made valuable prizes.

As we will see, the narcissistic Joffre was a great maker of connections, and he certainly did well with Courbet, eventually gaining a Legion of Honor through the latter's recommendation. But conditions were anything but pleasant, with oppressive heat by day, and at night the constant fear of Chinese armed with Mausers or Hotchkiss machine guns cutting their way into compounds. There was also plenty of tuberculosis, typhoid, and dysentery to lay men low or kill them; but Joffre would live a long, charmed life, and somehow seemed immune to such maladies.

Courbet received French detachments as reinforcements, bad boys at home who had been enrolled in the Bataillon d'Afrique as a penalty for getting in trouble with the law. Here they demonstrated real courage. There were also misfits or draft-dodgers from German or Austrian armies who arrived as part of a Foreign Legion detachment, and fought bravely too. Their military protection allowed Joffre to do his job in relative peace. He built redoubts to hold off opposing fire, trenches, and a series of barricades, forts, and artillery depots. The result was what the French called a *camp retranché*, the same eerie term to be used at Dien Bien Phu in the 1950s. This one became a well-defended spot, with new roads leading into surrounding jungle (of course not cut out by the well-fed Joffre, but by Legionnaires and African battalion men working under him).

Having secured Keelung, Courbet next decided to attack the Pescadore islands in the middle of the Formosa canal, a good base for hitting China's coast. Several French ships went there at the end of March 1885, with Joffre part of the expedition, and a heavy assault knocked out forts, leading to the capture of a number of Chinese villages.

Ferry meanwhile kept at the Chinese about the payment of an indemnity. As noted, he continued to auction the price downward, but the Chinese government, still helping the Black Flags in Tonkin, refused to pay. And French opinion at home began souring on this Far Eastern adventure, with an approving majority in Parliament becoming slimmer. Some held that all this imperial activity played Bismarck's game of making the French forget about the lost provinces of Alsace and Lorraine.

Just when secret negotiations were about to get the weakened Chinese to agree to a French protectorate in Tonkin and without indemnity, Ferry was confronted by news of a French disaster in northern Vietnam. On March 28, 1885 the French took Lang Son near the Chinese frontier, and a French general was wounded in the process. One Colonel Herbinger, quite soused at the time, believed a full-scale Chinese onslaught was taking place and ordered a French retreat from the town. The French left behind ammunition and other materiel and escaped up to the surrounding mountains. And though Herbinger had totally miscalculated, and there was really no threat here, news of a massive "defeat" reached France, one that seemed to portend a tail-between-the legs flight from the entire Tonkin. To some at home this *ruée* from Lang Son seemed akin to Sedan of recent memory. In fact the engagement was nothing like that disaster, nor like the one that would occur here in 1950 (treated in chapter 7); but it emphatically seemed to many parliamentarians that France had gotten itself in too deep. On the point of signing his agreement with the Chinese and asking Parliament for 200,000,000 more francs to subsidize military operations in the Far East, Ferry was turfed out of his ministry on January 30, his majority dissipated. He was also chased by a Paris mob that called him "le Tonkinois," and nearly pushed into the Seine River. Ferry never returned to political prominence, and an assassin's bullet a few years later shortened his life. But the agreement *was* signed, and the French had their Vietnamese threesome of Cochin China, Annam, and Tonkin. It was now up to soldiers like Gallieni to defend this large French presence, particularly in a still vulnerable north.[24]

Revolts continued, and the French punished the recalcitrance of the new teen emperor and his mandarin regent. During the summer of 1885, they wrecked the imperial palace in Hué, burned the imperial library, replaced the dissident emperor with his brother; but also saw the mandarin and his charge make it to the mountains and inspire continuing dissidence. In 1887 came the formation of a French Indochinese Union, composed of Cochin China, Annam, Tonkin, Cambodia, and within six years, Laos. But widespread revolts and disorders continued, and the home front was so divided that at one point the colony persisted by only a four-vote majority in Parliament.

The Resident or Governor-General of Annam-Tonkin, Paul Bert, found this nascent imperial milieu wracked by renewed pirate activity, partly stimulated by pure hunger. The bandits would operate protection rackets on entire villages of Tonkin's Red River delta, or simply sack them, carrying off women, children, and livestock for sale in China's Yunnan province. They would then return with opium and munitions. In addition to the growing contingent of thugs, there were authentic liberationist groups popping up, forerunners of the Viet Minh in the next century. The French remained confused on how to respond. Bert began educating a Vietnamese elite to become part of France's governmental process and also tried to replace hidebound mandarins with a new set of notables. But his most pressing problem was making Indochina pay for itself, aware that Paris would not continue to foot the bill. His "associationism" seemed to diminish revolts in Annam-Tonkin, but they then picked up again under his successors.

The next strong governor-general here was Jean-Marie de Lanessan, if perhaps too rigid. In his administration of the 1890s Lanessan went back to the mandarins as a support for the French, and instituted building activity; but deficits continued. So did the problem of civil-military squabbles on the French side, and the ever terrifying menace of brigandage. This is where our hero of the French Sudan came into the picture.

In 1892 Colonel Joseph Gallieni left France for a still turbulent Tonkin, where he would truly solidify his famous "oil patch" method of pacification—starting with French military strongholds, then civilizing with schools, gardens, or medical establishments, while also allowing locals to assume more responsibilities. But the area was plagued with anarchy, thanks to these mostly Chinese brigands attacking European posts, interfering with railway construction, killing men, women, and children, confiscating harvests, and burning villages, then disappearing over the border, aided by customs authorities blackmailed into connivance. On arrival Gallieni was awestruck by the landscape and climate, gray and Breton-like compared to the sunny Sudan. He also found the Annamese tougher and more "closed" than African blacks he had known. Again, he had to learn quickly to distinguish ethnicities here, and to locate the major lords of pillage, especially among the Black Flags.

Assuming temporary command of a 3rd Regiment of Tonkinese sharpshooters, Gallieni began his work of tracking these ruffians, and also setting up a string of French fortifications along China's northern frontier. On December 1, 1893 he was made commander of the "Second Military Territory" in that mountainous region where brigandage thrived. Demanding carte blanche powers from the governor-general, Gallieni put together three columns in January 1894, preparing to converge on a pirate stronghold where European prisoners were being held. With 1,600 men under his command he was ready to go off into country, which though very different, was scarcely less forbidding than the Sudanese landscape he had previously fought to pacify.[25]

That first expedition was crowned with success when Gallieni's soldiers surprised the brigands in their hideout, killing their chieftain and about fifty warriors, freeing prisoners, then securing the countryside around it. Here he learned what Joffre wouldn't in the colonial milieu: how to use stealth and surprise as key battle elements, and how to prevent needless losses. From now on men under Gallieni's orders punished any incursions from China by giving immediate chase, forbidding pirates to regain the frontier. At the same time Gallieni began attending meetings with Chinese authorities, doing the best he could with rich food they offered, and procuring a treaty of May 19, 1894 that made border supervision more effective.

Fortified by the arrival of a great disciple, Hubert Lyautey, Gallieni went out on continual inspection tours and pirate hunts. A second major expedition against a brigand chief named Baky in April 1895 was another successful operation of three columns, converging on a seemingly impregnable mountain hideout. Lyautey planted the French flag in triumph, before Gallieni led a careful retreat. This expedition allowed the French to extend a more secure frontier with China to the west.

But an even more redoubtable pirate leader, "Dê Tham," was busy terrorizing other parts of Vietnam. At the same time back in Hanoi Lyautey realized that Gallic bureaucrats in Asia and in the jealous higher reaches of the French army in France were set to tie Gallieni's hands. A new governor of Indochina had succeeded Lanessan, and Lyautey did everything he could to place Gallieni in charge of a new expedition. But Gallieni knew

that such an expedition through deep forests would present grave difficulties. By early November Lyautey jubilantly announced the procurement
of 500 soldiers and 110 rifles for his mentor. Again, Gallieni put together
three columns, each subdivided into four aggregations, and after giving
Dê Tham a first ultimatum to surrender his forts and men, then a second,
the French groups began hacking their way through the woods November
29. The best they could do was reduce the number of warriors in the area,
allow railway construction to pick up again, and enhance security; but
due to bureaucratic constraints that had delayed the operation, there was
no possibility of ensnaring this Dê Tham, who slipped away. In any event
French army authorities had already decided to remove Gallieni from
Indochina, saddening a slew of admirers from Lyautey to Marshal Sou,
who openly sobbed at the colonel's recall.

And indeed he was back in his south of France by mid-February 1896.
At least he had rendered broad swaths of the Tonkin safer for Vietnamese
peasants, who had endured years of extortion there. And he had broad-
ened what one might call his "colonial culture." When he met Chinese
authorities, Gallieni was surprised by their tolerance and the civility of
their customs, though they seemed more militarily inclined than the
Annamese. As Marcel Bigeard would do fifty-odd years later (chapter 8),
he learned to eat the way people did in this area of the world, abandoning meat for rice, vegetables, and fruit. And on the whole, Gallieni left
Indochina with a sense of fulfillment and accomplishment.[26]

Within ten years French Vietnam would be more or less pacified, partly
thanks to his labors. One should also note the courage of Foreign Legionnaires fighting these bandits, and decimated by disease as well. By the turn
of the century Tonkin was truly under French jurisdiction in the form
of military "circles." A crucial factor allowing retention of the area until
the 1950s would also emerge at this time—fiscal responsibility. Under
Governor-General Paul Doumer, kicked to Indochina by conservative
pressure because he had had the temerity to introduce an income tax pro-
posal in France, the colony finally began paying for itself. Arriving in the
summer of 1897, this Gallic Alan Greenspan fought huge budget deficits
by bringing in astute French advisors, making customs and tax collection
in Vietnam more efficient, and above all, creating French monopolies on
the production and sale of items like salt, alcohol, and opium. The latter
hadn't previously been a central economic player here, but a new refinery
to produce a faster-burning kind got more Vietnamese hooked. At some
points opium would garner one-third of France's income here. Add to

that huge increases of rice exportation by large-scale French enterprises in the delta; the take-off of a rubber industry after Doumer's departure (really from around the beginning of World War I); the growth of substantial profits from the Hongay coal mines of the north; much building activity, which Doumer had initiated in the form of roads, railways, opera houses, and the like; and for good or ill, France would last so long here that it could give the Americans a dubious inheritance.[27]

Back home in 1896, after four long years in Southeast Asia, Gallieni was again enjoying family life on the future Riviera, bicycling with his children or trimming vines in his garden. He also needed to recover from renewed attacks of the yellow fever that had first afflicted him in Africa.[28] But due to his military-colonial talent he would as usual be jolted out of his "down time," already earmarked for the next French problem area abroad, Madagascar, which like the Sudan before his arrival was in a state of definite anarchy.

This huge island, bigger than France, the Netherlands, and Belgium put together, had seen the rise of a Merina or Hova kingdom (of largely Malaysian ancestry) that dominated the central plateau and highlands, then spread outward to control some two-thirds of Madagascar by the nineteenth century. Merina culture and language attained hegemony, and they held power by playing off two imperial and religious rivals, Catholic French and Protestant British, then by accepting Christian education offered by English missionaries. But revolts, wars, and intermittent persecution of European Christians made stability tenuous, and in 1882 France revived its claim to a protectorate over the Sakalava kingdom dominating the island's western regions. Disputes followed, and a Franco-Merina war led to the declaration of a French protectorate over all Madagascar (1885), which the English would recognize in exchange for acceptance of their own protectorate over Zanzibar in 1890. But under a rather insipid French resident general, Laroche, much bloodshed followed. Anarchy reigned in Madagascar's south and more crucially, in the west, where the Sakalava, of Bantu origins, buried young and old alive, and committed other atrocities at the behest of their sorcerers, pillaging right into the heart of the Merina-dominated central region. Interference with French commerce, and continuing poor relations with Imerina royalty finally impelled France to send a contingent of troops in January 1895, occupying the city of Tananarive (today's Antananarivo) that September. A treaty was made with the Merina queen, Ranavalona III, but French annexation efforts met with an anti-European, anti-Christian, protraditionalist revolt called the *Menalamba*. The French had trouble stemming this insurrectionary tide, as the island's affairs now passed from France's Ministry of Foreign Affairs to the Colonial Ministry in Paris. Squabbles at home and in the French army ensued, as a mix of Madagascar's famed crimson soil and French blood shed by soldiers and civilians created a "Red Cemetery"; and at this juncture the French Chamber of Deputies surprisingly voted in August 1896 to make the island a full colony.

As Stephen Ellis notes, "the first governor of the new colony of Madagascar would have to be in charge of both civil and military forces," and be of unusual caliber, given conditions here. That someone was Gallieni, rapidly promoted to general and arriving on the island in September 1896. The gravity of a wide-ranging uprising against the French—including burning of villages right up to Tananarive's suburbs, and destruction of churches and temples—gave him carte blanche power. And as commander in chief and governor-general of the fledgling colony, he exercised that power immediately, despite having written weeks earlier: "I know nothing of Madagascar." Perhaps too promptly, he arrested an aunt and uncle of the Merina queen, who also called herself queen of Madagascar, and a general who was her minister of the interior, all considered rebel supporters. By mid-October the two men were condemned to death and shot. Soon after, the aunt, a princess, was deported, in late February of the next year the queen was herself sent into exile on Réunion, and the Imerina monarchy abolished. Learning of this unilateral decision, French government officials erupted in anger, but Gallieni's offer to resign, roundly rejected, calmed their ire. In a letter he noted how free he felt of Parisian strictures in this war against the insurrectionists. As he said, "I don't preoccupy myself either with texts or regulations. I go straight to my general goal: bring back peace; Frenchify the island." Many today and even then would reject such goals, but taking initiatives in the colonial context before it was too late would again help Gallieni win at the Marne in 1914. This was also the era of high French moralism; and somehow, Gallieni's almost puritanical brand of authority reminds one of the Americans at *their* moral apogee, circa the Berlin Blockade of 1948. Gallieni, however, had fewer illusions here than in Sudan or Tonkin, realizing that many areas on this island were ones "where one had to create everything"—and where ill health and general disorder both seemed endemic problems.[29]

Again, he had to act as a kind of enlightened despot here. Having welcomed Lyautey to Madagascar and given him an operational command in the north, then the assignment of neutralizing a rebellious chieftain,

Gallieni felt free in May 1897 to undertake a first tour of the island. He inspected French strongholds and got to know Madagascar's complexities first-hand, as he had done in the Sudan and Tonkin. Organizing the Imerina into territories, he established circles of French military authority within those territories. Tananarive became a secure base for pacification operations extending farther and farther afield. Unable to enforce fully Laroche's edict abolishing Malgache slavery, which enraged Merina nobles, given that system's comparative mildness, Gallieni worked to enforce its abolition in a de facto manner, humanizing conditions of work on farms or in homes. Wherever possible, he eradicated feudal inequities, aided by popular insurrections against Merina nobles by subject peoples like the Betsileos, who generally revered him. On a subsequent inspection tour of September 1897 in the island's southeast, he was mobbed by these tribespeople, freed from Merina or Sakalava masters. More and more former dependants of the nobility now cultivated their own gardens, their own fields. Gallieni was happy to grant them their freedom, then pacify as many parts of the island as he could under a beneficent French umbrella, while working with and buttressing new elites (which the Merina, however, would again grow to dominate). To sum up, Gallieni's "oil patch" theory meant a series of protective French military strongholds, then palpable improvement of life in terms of farming techniques, or the building of schools, roads, etc. To fight leprosy, tuberculosis, syphilis, and other ailments, he pushed for the creation of medical establishments and for rudimentary hygienic standards. He also rooted out tribal pillaging, reformed corrupt finances and tax structures, and worked to reduce venal justice.[30]

But things went less smoothly here than in his previous colonial efforts. Certain areas of Madagascar like the Sakalava west or the south were harder to pacify than others; but perhaps worse was the fact that a burgeoning French colonial establishment at home now dispatched him too many functionaries who seemed to be in the way. As for Bugeaud the perspectives of Parisian bureaucrats nauseated Gallieni—they just didn't understand a young colony, he wrote, and strangled initiatives with "regulations, good maybe for the métropole or old colonies, but bad here." He also disliked moral criticisms of his French soldiers who took temporary Malgache wives.[31]

For a second group that truly aggravated him here was the missionaries—Catholics and Protestants—and their constant rivalries. A secularist, Gallieni tried his best to placate these people, but it took a lot out of him, particularly given the school choices he allowed Malgaches, one being lay institutions on the order of those found in France. He never trusted the national sympathies of British Protestant missionaries, but near to his departure, the expulsion of religious orders from France also led to a disconcertingly large number of ultra-Catholic missionaries moving to the colony, and they seemed hardly better.[32]

There were also difficulties presented by interracial, regional groups that had descended from Arab, African, and Asian immigrants to the island. And the perennial problem of finding good military personnel remained as well. Hubert Lyautey was of course the great exemplar. Part of the problem was poor communication with these soldiers, due to a lack of roads, rail, and telegraph. Financial allocations were also insufficient. Little wonder that as early as January 1899, Gallieni was complaining that he had had enough of this French imperial existence. To Joseph Chailley, he wrote January 15, 1899 from Tananarive that "I am truly fatigued and it would be better . . . that I give way to someone less overloaded than me. This colonial life wears you out quickly." In another letter to Chailley on November 15 he complained of all the French business types exploiting locals here, and of functionaries getting too comfortable as well. As he put it, "Tananarive has an ideal climate; life is easy here and so the bureaucrats like it a lot."[33]

Gallieni's detailed confidential report of 1899 on Madagascar—really another book—radiates true humility, emphasizing how much was still lacking on the island in terms of transportation and communications, health care, and general organization. New problems for French settlers, continued last bubblings of the *Menalamba* revolt, as well as the delicate state of Franco-British relations in the aftermath of their confrontation at Fashoda necessitated a trip back to France for diplomatic consultations. Gallieni wanted especially to procure funds for more highway and railway building, and for the construction of a large naval base at Diego-Suarez.[34]

First he enjoyed some vacation time in the south of France, waiting until the fall to take on the capital. But in Paris he felt truly out of place, complaining about life there, which he found agitated, expensive, and pretentious. The man who would become a hero to the city's inhabitants during World War I declared that "I have nothing of a Parisian's temperament." Dealing with politicians and government officials was simply not his cup of tea. The winter dragged on, depleting his finances, and due in part to shifting political sands, it took him a long time to obtain the funds he felt the colony required.[35]

But he continued to inspire, packing the Sorbonne with thousands of students when he came there to speak. His disciples were numerous. One, Paul Ellie, who had followed him from Tonkin to Madagascar, said he enjoyed the colonial life where so much needed to be done and where Gallieni's brand of ingenuity and energy seemed such a necessity. If the general pushed his men, he also pushed himself—up to fifteen hours a day—and Ellie became vividly attached. Capitaine "X," another acolyte, admired his adaptation to vegetarianism, his powers of observation, and mainly how he had so rapidly created relative peace and salubrity in areas of prior disorder. And Henry Charbonnel noted that a school gift of Gallieni's second book on the Sudan, ardently read and reread, made him a colonial soldier as well.[36]

The greatest of Gallieni's disciples was Lyautey, the subject of our next chapter; the most spurious, that colonel in the engineering corps, Joseph Joffre, future butcher of French soldiers in World War I. On returning to Madagascar in the summer of 1900 Gallieni tapped the latter to fortify the base of Diego-Suarez, a key to the island's defenses due to its bay and mountains—especially to counter possible British maritime incursions. He was soon pleased with Joffre's work and with his plans for a road to the south. But unfortunately he had little else to go on for his opinion of the man.[37]

Joffre of course would become known, mistakenly so, as France's savior during World War I. But anyone who has read historians like Alistair Horne, A. J. P. Taylor, or Barbara Tuchman realizes that in fact he would prove to be downright lethal in the position of supreme authority he would hold during that conflict.[38] Yet the flip side of the historiographical coin—Joffre depicted as an empty-headed idiot—will not quite do either. In our view Joffre had a psychological disorder which, like its stronger cousin, psychopathic behavior, was easily masked: narcissism. To our knowledge this important aspect of a minor colonial figure, but future head of the French general staff in the Great War has never been explored.

Narcissists are grandiose personalities who live for constant feedback and flattery. Almost too good to be true, they present themselves as having things always together and suffering from no problems. (Apparently, Joffre would constantly smile during the worst periods of wartime.) Because they are flatterers such people *seem* to care about others; but inside, they are only interested in keeping their images intact and have no genuine interest in others. They simply use people to work for them and to buttress their egos. Unable to see themselves in error, they always blame others for whatever goes wrong, sedulously backbiting, while also feathering their own nests. Narcissists are prone to anger and defensive behavior when those they idealize or use disappoint, show weakness, or have the temerity to outdo them.[39]

Narcissism stems particularly from a mother who made her child "special"; instead of actual love such a child receives kudos only for what is gained or projected to the world. Gilles and Catherine Joffre had eleven children, of whom Joseph was third oldest; but the two above him died at ages three and four, leaving him as first hope of a rural family in the southwest of France, where Joffre's father and grandfather had both been coopers. Though the family was in decent circumstances, and most of the eight beneath him did quite well also, Joseph Jacques Césaire became his parents' first prizewinner, especially in mathematics and science, on a march upward through the Collège de Perpignan and the Ecole Polytechnique in Paris. Simultaneously, Joffre was a rustic-looking, awkward provincial, ragged in the wider world for his Catalan accent. Undoubtedly he received less actual love and more kudos than siblings lower down the scale, all of which became the perfect recipe for a personality disorder that would later surface vis-à-vis his former colonial boss, Gallieni, during World War I.[40]

Like all narcissists Joffre would be a great collector (or stimulator) of flatterers, and testimony to his physical splendors, career abilities, and general character abounds. A typical description of his reassuring physique comes from Georges Blanchon: "Big, with a large chest, voluminous head, a vast square forehead accentuated by the shaggy eyebrows [and] ... a strong mustache ..."[41] Another officer recalls Joffre of the Marne as nothing less than a Greek deity—"Atlas carrying the celestial vault on his shoulders."[42]

Hagiographic treatments of the Great War era and after often mention the luminous sun and sky over Joffre's native region as determinants for his character. Emile Ripert made a pilgrimage to his birthplace of Rivesaltes and allowed himself to be carried off by its supposed effect on the cooper's famous son. From the Pyrenees came, for example, Joffre's reputed humility. But let us give the floor to the enthusiastic M. Ripert: "The wine of glory could not make the head grow big in a man who, from childhood, had absorbed the divine liqueur the sun provides the fields of Rivesaltes."[43]

In actuality Joffre was *far* less distinguished a colonial than either Gallieni or Lyautey, both of whom he knew on Madagascar. To backtrack, after the Franco-Prussian War Joffre had worked on various projects at

different garrison towns around France, through to the mid-1880s. Then
he went to the Far East as an engineer-captain, where he came under the
orders of Courbet, taking part in the Formosa campaign and rising to
chief engineer for the defense of Hanoi. As we have seen, this builder and
fortifier did work that apparently passed the test. But he was also adept at
making connections. After he participated in the Siege of Ba-Dinh of 1887,
he returned to France in October 1888 as attaché in the cabinet of the
director of engineering at the War Ministry. There followed commands at
different engineering regiments, and a post in 1891 as Professor of Fortifications at the Artillery and Engineering School of Fontainebleau.[44] According to Emile Mayer, Joffre imparted no great enthusiasm there.

But in 1892 he was sent back to the colonial milieu in order to supervise the building of a railway in French West Africa. The next year he
became part of the volatile situation involving Archinard and his cohorts
who wanted to flout Parisian constraints (particularly of a new Colonial Department split off from the Naval Ministry) and push eastward.
After Archinard's dismissal for too much independence of mind, Etienne
Bonnier took over his command, acting out a long-held dream of capturing Tombouctou. Here is where Joffre came into a rather doubtful scheme,
one that Bonnier had tried to keep secret from civilian superiors. On
December 26, 1893 Bonnier would lead one group of barges down the
Niger, while Joffre was asked to lead a supplementary column of French
soldiers overland from Ségou in the western Sudan 470 miles east to Tombouctou. On January 10 Bonnier's group arrived at Tombouctou, then a
couple days later, moved toward Goundam, where they camped and were
ambushed by Touaregs. The results were serious enough to justify Parisian
fears of such hastily conceived operations (operations of which Gallieni
too would have disapproved): Bonnier, ten of his officers, and sixty-eight
tirailleurs, among others, were killed searching for their El Dorado.

Already the government had dismissed both Bonnier and Joffre from
their commands, but Joffre would always land on his feet, and this expedition showed that well. Instead of remaining persona non grata, he ended
up capturing Tombouctou with his column, massacring the Touaregs who
had killed Bonnier, winning a Legion of Honor, and returning to France
as a hero promoted to lieutenant-colonel. His report called in an English
version My March to Timbuctoo discusses that expedition, showing how
he and his men had departed December 27, arriving in Tombouctou February 12. En route he kept the diary that forms the basis of this book, first
published in the Revue de Génie in 1895. His recitation of the campaign is

orderly and minute, as befits an engineer. That Joffre and guides were able
to skirt lakes and wind through hills and generally forbidding terrain reveals his practical skills. His descriptions of Tombouctou and its society
and economy are useful, as are those of operations against the Touaregs.
He plays up considerably the extent of routing of the enemy, and his optimism about a greater French presence in the area seems little different
from his later optimism during World War I. For in fact this capture of
Tombouctou would stimulate the military to keep fighting its way eastward at great expense in money and men through the 1890s, ending with
Captain Marchand's famous jaunt across Africa to Fashoda, where war
nearly broke out with the British. The capture of Samory finally occurred
as well at the end of the decade; but the famous remark of President Félix
Faure made in 1898 at the time of Fashoda remains apposite: "We have
behaved like madmen in Africa!"[45]

In his colonial *oeuvre* Gallieni was certainly a conqueror as well, but
prouder of his efforts at pacification. By contrast Joffre lived for glory
or kudos, a trait present in his African success and which would also
come to the fore in World War I. Unfortunately, his published report on
Tombouctou failed to reveal his true character.

On the island of Madagascar, to which he was assigned at the turn of
the century, Joffre's character was still easy to hide from a great colonial
who could usually evaluate people so readily. Again, the problem was that
as both commander in chief of the French Occupation army and governor-
general, Gallieni was too inundated with work (done with his usual high
standards) to notice well what a comparatively unimportant subaltern was
like as builder and fortifier of the naval base at Diego-Suarez. As seen,
Gallieni was obsessed with both pacifying and improving life on Madagascar, and he had too many groups or people to mollify. He had to deal
with colonists streaming in, and decide who should have how much land,
how many natives should be allowed to attend new schools, and how
hard to crack down on indigenous slavery, alcohol, and even drug use. He
needed to fight epidemics, initiate vaccination campaigns, and supervise
railway building, hospital construction, and agricultural improvement in
regions which varied greatly in their ecological or climactic conditions.
He needed to stay abreast of ethnic differences and reduce tribal conflicts.
There were also those wrangles with missionaries, and with sharp lawyers set in a Wild West atmosphere to ensnare the locals. He needed to
gain trust of the Malgaches and simultaneously write his long, meticu-
lous reports to the Colonial Ministry in Paris. As well he had to make

intermittent tours of the island. After 1900 it all became more difficult, as a vociferous Paris press and some politicians blamed Gallieni for what seemed like every business failure or unhappy government worker on Madagascar. He was watched more closely, and ever more hamstrung. His family's presence from 1902 helped, but sadly, he was too busy and remote to see Joffre for what he was.[46]

Meanwhile, Joffre was in love with a married woman, and supposedly overwrought too by the recent deaths of his parents, his stint in Diego-Suarez beginning in January 1900 is generally seen as a form of relief for a mind full of anxiety. Hagiographic biographers love to play up all the great things he supposedly did there until he departed in April 1903.[47]

But again, Joffre did little compared to Gallieni or even Lyautey, who had finished off his pacification process of the difficult south. Joffre of course made sure to send long, self-congratulatory reports on his work at Diego to the governor and delegated onerous work to subordinates. Among other things, he took credit for the reduction of thefts. He exhorted locals to grow more rice and got out to visit certain villages. But unfortunately, Diego was only one cog in a large colonial wheel and one among too many concerns crowding Gallieni's mind.[48]

In 1903 Joffre, the savvy careerist, returned to France and began mounting a hierarchy of commands. He also married a second time in 1905. His first wife, a widow six years his senior with two children, had died in pregnancy after their marriage in 1873. How real Joffre's supposed grieving into the 1880s was remains open to doubt. Finally in 1897, as the acclaimed hero of Tombouctou, he was home to look up an early love he had lost to a rival. Henriette Penon, who had married Lucien Lozès, also had two children, but while still married took up with a newly decorated Joffre. Here the narcissist's competitiveness shows quite clearly. A third child was born. Joffre had competed with a rival, helping to destroy a marriage, which, however, took a long time (given the era) to end in divorce. After that finally occurred, he married Henriette in 1905, never doubting the paternity of his daughter, Germaine. He would often say that "she's a Plas," referring to the maiden name of his pious mother.[49] Joffre certainly treated his offspring well, and Germaine became a devoted daughter, his only one, given Henriette's later miscarriage.

While Joffre was finally winning his love, Gallieni was turning away from colonial life. After a short-lived insurrection in the south of Madagascar, led by disgruntled sorcerers, and continuing critiques from Paris, Gallieni left the island in June 1905, glad to be gone. He was pleased by what he had done for the Malgaches, blending a new allegiance to France (when holidays like July 14 resonated almost religiously) with protection of local cultures and leaders. He had helped make life easier and more peaceful for many people. But like Bugeaud he was depressed by the quality of European incomers that the large island was attracting. He would now become a former colonial of considerable renown, compensated by living back at the family home in Saint-Raphaël, and having the leisure to consider his experiences and how they might relate to French army policy. He had a library that would grow to over 7,000 volumes and resumed his omnivorous reading. (Of his future nemesis, Joffre, it was said that he could hardly read maps, let alone books!) Gallieni loved history and was astounded by how little people ever learned from its vast storehouse of lessons; but he also enjoyed reading social theory, biography, and the work of literary masters like Corneille, Balzac, Dickens, and Voltaire, whose style he esteemed. In fact Gallieni's own enlightened progressivism, and the sure taste and clarity one finds in his copious correspondence and reports seem somewhat reminiscent of a Voltaire, minus the mordancy. But he tried as well to keep up with the latest trends of the Belle Epoque in art and music.[50]

He also continued writing, contemplating his Madagascar experience, but going farther back too. There was much correspondence to keep up with, but new projects as well. One book that he composed in that prewar period was for children, *Un Noël au Soudan*, recalling his captivity in Nango. This interesting little illustrated book shows an imperial influence on literature that would culminate in the famous Babar series.[51]

From 1906 to his full retirement in 1914, Gallieni's military positions included command of a corps in Clermont-Ferrand, then another in Lyon. In 1908 he became a member of the Supreme Council of War, and also made colonial tours of inspection. In this poignant period before history's greatest war, Gallieni demonstrated more than average prescience, and at least by 1911 knew what some did not yet accept—that war *was* inevitable, and that the Germans would definitely march through neutral Belgium. From 1911 to 1914 he kept demanding the crucial reinforcement of Maubeuge and the manufacture of more heavy artillery.[52]

But too many underestimated him. Charbonneau cites an important member of the General Staff who dismissed Gallieni as *merely* a colonial— a builder, not a tactician. Yet this "colonial" seemed to foresee the reality others were plainly ignoring. Already he knew the importance of air reconnaissance, to be used so dramatically for the turnaround of the Marne. In vain he was also trying at War Council meetings to overcome Colonel de Grandmaison's unquestioned dogma of *offensive à outrance*. Most important, as Leblond notes, "he had the psychology of the Germans." He was obsessed with the German frontier, traveling there frequently, and possibly for that reason, knew France's prospective Lorraine offensive (Plan XVII) would fail. As he direly told Leblond, "for forty years ... we have ignored everything about foreign arms ... English nullity, and especially, the formidable German preparations."[53]

In 1911 came Gallieni's recommendation of Joffre as the army's chief of staff, a major turning point for the country's fortunes. From the time of his marriage Joffre's career had been on an upward track, culminating with a position on the Supreme War Council in February 1910. A year later Adolphe Messimy, the new war minister, consulted Gallieni on who should become chief of the recently reorganized General Staff, replacing General Michel. One of Michel's handicaps had been a quite proper hesitancy about the offensive dogma of Ferdinand Foch and his zealous adherent, Grandmaison. But in the opinion of a number of army people, including Gallieni, Michel also lacked the qualities of a potential war leader. Messimy was impressed by Gallieni's imperial credentials, giving him a first shot at the position; but nearing retirement, the great proconsul refused the offer, calling himself a career colonial, which he felt would provoke controversy among metropolitan army officers, and also needlessly ruffle Michel's feathers. Messimy then asked Gallieni about a substitute and he recommended General Pau, a fine, one-armed officer, who was, however, too clerical for the era and who wanted to name other generals of the Right. Some accounts hold that there was another choice as well. Then came Joffre, whom unfortunately neither Gallieni nor Messimy knew well enough. With the exception of Tombouctou Joffre had had no real experience of military leadership; but his republican, even freethinking views, his orthodox military ideas, and his good-natured, quiet demeanor seemed unimpeachable. So Gallieni recommended Joffre, verging on damning with faint praise. He called his former subordinate a good worker—methodical and precise—and the appointment was made. Later, both he and Messimy would have great regrets, once they saw the falsifying chief for what he was. In fact, Messimy's regrets lasted into the 1930s, and "hundreds of times" he would wonder whether he should have pushed Gallieni harder to take the position, despite the latter's impending retirement date of April 1914.[54]

Before the conflict Messimy tried several times to rectify matters; meanwhile in his diary, Gallieni groaned about the whole General Staff (March 2, 1914), decrying its sloppy, misguided war preparations. A month later he derisively mentioned Joffre's girth: "In the Bois [de Boulogne] I see Joffre in front of me. He sure is big and heavy!"[55]

Just before the conflagration Gallieni's official retirement from the army coincided with the sickness and death of his wife, and the onset of depression. On April 26 he had mentioned "dark thoughts" ("des idées noires") in his diary; on July 30 after her death, "an immense void."[56] Unlike so many he knew that a major war would be a disaster, and just before it, had talked of offering the Germans his beloved Madagascar in exchange for Alsace-Lorraine and a Franco-German entente! But given increasing dangers looming on the horizon, he began pestering Joffre for suitable employment, and his former subordinate kept the great military talent waiting. Repeatedly, Gallieni warned the French General Staff to improve its Belgian defenses, as well as those on the left bank of the Meuse. Finally, at the eleventh hour, he was pulled out of mothballs by President Poincaré (July 31), the latter pressured by Messimy, who was again war minister. They now gave Gallieni the title of assistant (*adjoint*) to Joffre, with the idea that he would eventually replace him. This did not, of course, endear Gallieni to his former colonial subaltern, who kept him isolated from policy making through August, finally quashing the decision. As initial French plans failed, and the Germans hastened toward Paris, Gallieni chafed. But Messimy's last important move before leaving the War Ministry was to name him military governor of Paris, August 26, 1914, in replacement of General Michel. It turned out to be the perfect position—one where Gallieni's colonial lessons of materiel-scrounging, fortification, coordination, and general attention to detail could be profitably employed.[57]

Meanwhile, Joffre relied on an ill-fated Plan XVII, which would make Germany's "swinging door strategy" in conjunction with the Schlieffen Plan a near success. One major French offensive was to go directly across Lorraine, seconded by a lesser thrust through Alsace—with Germany as the objective. Another would affront the Germans in Luxembourg or the Belgian Ardennes, depending on their route of attack. General Michel had planned to defend France all along the Belgian border, and we have noted Gallieni's vain warnings about that frontier as well. But Joffre gravely ignored the possibility of a German advance through the heart of Belgium, though to be fair the Belgian government itself minimized this possibility. Joffre and his assistant Edouard de Castelnau also underestimated the size of a German army committed to such an advance. He and Castelnau figured the main attack would come through the more southerly Ardennes, which ironically happened one war later.

Suffice it to say that when hostilities began, Joffre's futile offensive in Lorraine August 14–20 was exactly what the German doctor could order, and was broken at immense cost to the French. Meanwhile the German rush through Belgium and down into France took a much wider end-run than he had anticipated. Joffre ordered a tardy retreat south, and was fortunate that Germany's chief of staff Moltke removed divisions from his right to help out in East Prussia. He was also fortunate that the Germans came across plucky British resistance at Mons and Le Cateau, and Belgian stubbornness. But the enemy was still ahead of schedule to get down to Paris, strangle it, then strike Joffre's troops from the rear in Lorraine as they abutted mountains, the Meuse River, and machine guns in their advance (hence the swinging-door). During the retreat Joffre had already dismissed over twenty French generals, including Lanrezac, who had never trusted Plan XVII in the first place; here was an example of the chief's lethal narcissism in action.[58]

Gallieni's remarkable book, *Les mémoires du Général Gallieni*, published posthumously, makes clear in an unself-serving way what a rapid debacle 1914 could have been for the French, no less than 1870 or 1940. But in very little time (redolent of Churchill and his aviators in 1940) the great pro-consul did much to avert that collapse. Already disgusted with the General Staff's ignorance about the Belgian invasion, its costly Lorraine thrust, and its Napoleonic dogma, he knew at the end of August that in the capital "we still have [only] a few days." On August 30 Gallieni scratched in his diary: "I have the impression that he [Joffre] considers Paris as sacrificed." The next day Alexandre Millerand, the new war minister, told him that Paris would indeed be taken by the Germans. Gallieni's actions became feverish—curfews, reinforcement of siege artillery, forges at work round the clock in the streets of Paris, trenches dug on the city's periphery, and coordination with Bourgès-Maunoury's 6th Army, which Joffre reluctantly gave him September 1.[59]

Like the fine leader he had been in the Sudan, Tonkin, and Madagascar, an aged Gallieni now hustled sloppy bureaucracy to get ready fast for the Germans. Constantly moving, he visited forts and military people, and requisitioned autos and taxis as early as August 29, cutting through conflicting jurisdictions. Racing out into the near provinces on September 1, he beheld a scene normally associated with 1940—roads clogged with refugees, mattresses, and carts, and ill-coordinated French armies. He couldn't believe the speed of the Germans and the corresponding pusillanimity of France's General Staff. The defense of Paris became his obsession. Having made a detailed study of the 1870 siege and attended to *ravitaillement* in the colonies, he set sheep and cattle grazing in parks, and worked on keeping the water supply pure, since dead soldiers on battlefields outside Paris polluted it. He was very hard on Paris bakers, giving them directives worthy of Robespierre, whose Committee of Public Safety he admired. He also attended to the "moral defense" of the city, specifically criticizing the excesses of alcoholism (an "evil ... that saps the whole country"). And Parisians amply returned his love and care. With the Germans only days away and the government busy departing for Bordeaux, Gallieni lauded the capital's "belle attitude."[60]

Gallieni's detailed reports make a perfect contrast to Joffre's, where empty generalities abound. When he fortunately received the aid of Maunoury's 6th Army, Gallieni's orders became terse and realistic, given the national emergency at hand. His letter of September 2, 1914 to Maunoury mentioned the necessity of destroying bridges over the Seine and Oise Rivers. Meanwhile Joffre clung to his plans of retreat too far south. Gallieni's metronome beat much faster. Responding to one of Joffre's telegrams, he repeated what "I have told you in three telephone conversations"—that far more reinforcements were required, or Paris would fall. Joffre replied that he needed to retain certain cavalry corps for his continuing retreat.

But on September 3 Gallieni's finest hour began. This was the day that announcement of the government's departure to Bordeaux hit Paris' walls, and his calm (the word so often imputed to Joffre) helped prevent a mass exodus. September 3 also saw the beginning of a fatal German military shift which Gallieni, *not* Joffre, first noticed. Rushing down from Senlis to Paris, the 1st German Army suddenly and dramatically changed direction, ignoring the capital and trying to execute its trap strategy a bit too early. According to air reconnaissance reports, the German General Alexander von Kluck was turning southeast, "offering the flank to an attack by the armies of Paris," a change calling for a prompt French counterattack. However, Joffre's idea of a retreat south of the Seine and toward the Yonne remained stubbornly intact. Seizing the reins, Gallieni realized that "minutes were [now] hours ... days and even years." He wanted all troops available for a counterattack—*today*, not later. With Maunoury's 6th Army, and with 60,000 men plus a new Algerian division of 20,000, he certainly had a force to punch back with at the invaders. By adding reinforcements, he hoped he could significantly increase his counterattack instrument. Considering nothing but the *patrie*, a latter-day Jacobin, Gallieni was inspired by "great examples given by our Men of the Convention and, closer to us, by Gambetta" (of 1870). The Germans had executed the mayor and other hostages at Senlis, and Gallieni knew their takeover of the Paris region would cause much damage. They had become the Germans of the twentieth century; it was now or never. Yet Joffre communicated on September 3 to Gallieni that no new move was required! On September 4 Gallieni nonetheless rallied Maunoury's 6th Army, giving a counterattack order. Tardily, and after repeated telephoning, a reluctant Joffre finally climbed on board, later fabricating prior directives to make it look like he had foreseen the Marne rebound much earlier. Documents revealing the meretriciousness of his claim remain in French army archives at Vincennes.[61]

It was the vivid Gallieni who had police eject passengers from Paris taxis, sending their drivers to the front. Joffre wanted to give direct orders to the 6th Army, but his old colonial boss briefly kept the chief at bay. Judith Cladel saw in Gallieni of this period the "burning inspiration of the artist";[62] but unfortunately, Joffre's dallying even after Gallieni rallied him made the ensuing victory of the Marne a lesser one than it might have been. For Joffre kept Britain's Commander Sir John French too long in the dark, withheld necessary troops from Gallieni, and instead of launching the counterattack on September 5, waited—and even then, Gallieni had to tell him the right spot to hit![63]

The first French counterattack came on the Ourcq, but on September 6 began the true Battle of the Marne. On September 7 and 8 the taxis came up in force to aid Maunoury with reinforcements. While the issue was still in doubt, Joffre found time to thank Gallieni (September 7). But once the Germans were in retreat, the chief's narcissistic jealousy became activated, and on September 8 Gallieni received word that he could no longer give orders to the 6th Army, "cutting short all my intentions and initiatives." Maunoury on the plateau over the Ourcq had Germany's von Kluck on the ropes; the added divisions Gallieni had demanded in vain, as well as more heavy artillery, might well have pushed the enemy from France, rather than simply behind the Aisne River and then trench lines of the fall.[64]

This was obviously a significant moment of the war, in terms of the many men who would be subsequently slaughtered. But on September 11 Joffre definitively removed his former colonial superior from any further command role, when the German retreat might still have been exploited. The Germans were permitted to cross the Aisne River and to hold a line there September 14. The race north to the sea and the war's costly trench stalemate were consequences of Joffre's failure to press home a stunning victory, and more fundamentally, of his palpable jealousy of Gallieni.[65]

But even after sacking this great colonial figure, Joffre might well have gained a reprieve, if only he had known how to act with prescience and alacrity. For by September 14 the Germans were plainly exhausted. By using trains to skirt the foe on foot and soon digging and defending its weak positions with machine guns; and by helping the gallant Belgians tie down a German army at Antwerp, Joffre might well have avoided the "Boche" occupation that would elicit a parliamentary inquiry after the war. Of course Joffre rationalized his every error. He took too long even to understand the nature of "the race" (to the Channel). A. J. P. Taylor puts it most clearly: "The Germans scratched holes in the ground, set up machine guns. To everyone's amazement, the advancing Allies hesitated, stopped."[66]

Joffre continued, however, to accept applause for the Marne, using it as a kind of unlimited credit card to reinforce his power for the next two years at least. In the fall of 1914 *Le Temps* published a version of the battle written by GQG (Grand Quartier Général). "My name," wrote Gallieni bitterly in his diary, "is not even pronounced there, not even in connection with the requisition of the automobiles." In December he lamented that the official report of the General Staff also said nothing of him in connection with the Marne victory.[67]

One prime creator of the Joffre myth was Maurice Gamelin, who "served Joffre as a complex mix of executor, prompt, inspiration, critic and conscience."[68] Gamelin helped coordinate Joffre's lethal offensives of 1915, and since mediocrity learns from mediocrity, Gamelin would later make his own lethal errors in 1940 as France's commander in chief against the Nazis. From the beginning, this amanuensis was a first-rate publicist for Joffre at the Marne, continuing in that role up until his death. In a book written after the Second World War he pretends Joffre had conceived the counterattack on August 25, 1914. As Joffre's *chef de cabinet,* then his faithful aide at GQG, Gamelin had been in a position to see all! Yet at GQG, as he boasts proudly, "we lived an almost monkish life," the same type of existence Gamelin would live at Vincennes *sans* radio communications when the Nazis invaded in 1940. He snipes at Gallieni's memoirs, which note that Joffre's orders for the Marne counterattack had "three different dates written over each other."[69]

Our talk with M. Devos, former head of the army's archives at Vincennes, was instructive here. Devos remembered strict censorship on the Gallieni side during the interwar era, and in historical work produced at Vincennes as late as 1939, Joffre's legend was allowed to prevail. One Colonel Huillier, for example, declared in a typed report, *La bataille de la*

Marne, that only Joffre oversaw everything, and was therefore the great architect of the victory.[70]

Outside GQG many others helped Joffre maintain the façade. Typical was Jules Jusserand, French Ambassador in Washington, writing the French Ministries of War and Foreign Affairs September 15, 1914, exulting about the Marne and proclaiming "Bravo Joffre."[71] This Marne propaganda and credit-taking would permit Joffre to get away with many more errors in the war; but from our point of view, just as revealing of his narcissism was a lack of regret for anything he ever did. This is easily perceived as one approaches the close of volume 1 of Joffre's war memoirs and notices no mention at all of the copious casualties the French sustained through 1914 alone. He was best at propagandizing his own value, and that unfortunately, is what this mediocre former colonial had learned abroad.[72]

Not everyone, however, accepted the Joffre version of the Marne. Clemenceau, Kitchener, and von Kluck himself would all salute Gallieni's underpraised role in the victory. "If he was English," remarked Kitchener, "[Gallieni] would be covered in glory."[73]

But glory was not what Gallieni desired, especially in such a dire atmosphere. The adulation of the Parisians discomfited him, and in an unfeigned way, he deprecated fame. What obsessed him was what Adolphe Goutard has called the "unexploited victory" of the Marne—the consequent race to the sea, the creation of an unassailable German front, and the occupation of ten of "our richest departments." Not only was Joffre's jealousy to blame, but so was that of French politicians, now back from Bordeaux. Gallieni tried unsuccessfully to remain above and beyond "these sterile discussions, these intrigues,"[74] but they bothered him terribly.

Through the fall of 1914 the spurned proconsul continually criticized GQG's complacent optimism. The self-satisfaction of both military authorities and politicians aggravated him greatly, given French battle deaths that had already reached epidemic proportions. As early as October 1914 he criticized Joffre's idea of a breakthrough on the trench front (*la percée*), an idea that would cost many lives through 1915. "We will not pass," he told Leblond, "we will not make a 'hole.' Joffre is too content to be in the trenches!" Gallieni was meanwhile asking repetitively for a command at the front, but received nothing.[75]

With the first fall of the war over, some 300,000 French soldiers already dead, and trench lines firmly in place, Joffre kept exhorting his soldiers to be better humans and to give more. In an instruction of December 20, 1914 he complained that one must add to military training "very strong moral training," as though that would keep his men alive in the face of machine guns. "[We must] develop in young soldiers the qualities of tenacity and patience, which are among the most important elements of modern combat," he added.[76]

Gallieni's more appropriate *j'accuses* reached deaf ears among French notables who counted. His popularity was mostly with the common people of Paris, not where it would help alter disastrous military policies. But he was right. What he said about GQG is now orthodoxy in accounts like Alistair Horne's, even if it wasn't then. Compare Gallieni, January 19, 1915: "The General Staff is still the same: it's a chapel [living] outside of realities" to Horne: "Isolated in its palace at Chantilly, GQG lived amid an atmosphere of back-stabbing intrigue reminiscent of the court of Louis XV at Versailles." Joffre's outlook was indeed dangerous, and as Gallieni penned in his diary January 30, 1915, "[Joffre-inspired] optimism every-where; the Germans, one fine day, we don't know why, will leave."[77]

Not only did he know they wouldn't, but like Churchill, he realized a way needed to be found to avoid more costly losses on the Western Front. Before the end of 1914 Gallieni was already considering a back-door series of operations to end the trench stalemate—entering southern Europe perhaps via the Dardanelles. Here again he was thwarted, and once more by his colonial subordinate. From the end of February 1915, Gallieni was vociferously advocating the idea of taking Constantinople, rushing into lands of the Austro-Hungarian Empire, gaining the element of surprise, and keeping Bulgaria from joining the Central Powers (which it would soon do). But Joffre dismissed this as "Gallieni's crazy ambition," reas-suring the politician Aristide Briand that *he* could still pierce the trench lines directly on the Western Front. As a sop in March 1915, Gallieni was offered the wounded Maunoury's army, now reduced to inaction; but he refused, desiring a command that would involve him in fighting. Through 1915 his interviews and diary entries remain those of an obsessed man reduced to waiting, while the flower of French youth was being trampled in huge numbers by Joffre's offensives.[78]

For 1915 was an unrelievedly tragic year, and due to repeated attacks into the German lines that ended in costly failures, Joffre was certainly the key culprit. His unregenerate narrative for that year (in his memoirs) remains scandalous reading. The tone of complete optimism and togeth-erness contrasts totally to someone like Gallieni, who worried himself literally to death over those slaughters.[79] One reason Joffre could be so re-lentlessly chipper was because he kept himself far from the front, clinging

to his vaunted routines. His legion of sycophants agree on Joffre's amaz-
ing calm that even today is found in texts as a concomitant of military
ability. For Blanchon "France is a country of equilibrium, but General
Joffre is even more balanced than it." The diplomat Gabriel Hanotaux
marveled at Joffre's serenity before the Marne, and an aide, Jean Fabry,
also extolled his *sang-froid*, not surprising, since he avoided battlegrounds!
For Gabriel Terrail Joffre was simply "master of his nerves," and for Henry
Bordeaux he stood out by his placidity.[80]

During this worst war in history, Joffre only shattered his habitual *bon-
homie* when someone near him worried too overtly about disasters that
never seemed to faze the chief. To one who anxiously pointed out that
the French army was heading for catastrophe, Joffre let some of the narcissist's underlying brutality show, banging a fist on the table: "And you,
sir," he replied, "don't you believe in France?" At another point General
Alexandre had a bad night of worry and again a well-rested Joffre punctuated the morning with a thump on the table, cutting off his interlocutor.
"So, you too, you're like the others. When *I* tell you we *will* get them[?]"[81]

Joffre's admirers placed much emphasis on his unvarying maintenance
of routines, which we could again lay to a narcissist's selfishness. Someone who truly cared about the impact of the war would have been more
peripatetic—pacing during the wee hours, leaving his Chantilly chef to
visit the fronts more often, and improvising. Not Joffre. Already as a school
boy he had had a fine appetite, exults René Benjamin, and nothing that
happened in the war changed that. Emile Hinzelin noted that "his life is
regulated with mathematical precision," providing in detail the great man's
menus during the crucial days preceding the Marne. Joffre's dinner for
September 3 was leek soup, beef sautéed Lyonnais style, roast chicken,
salami in butter, watercress salad, cheese, and fruit; being French, his
lunch was equally large. Benjamin was not wrong to dub him "the first
fork of the French army." All through the period of Verdun, far from the
big guns and tumult, Joffre continued to retire to bed at ten o'clock each
night. When someone came to ask about a battle's progress, the person
received an invariable answer from his aide: "Joffre is sleeping." To do a
good job, Joffre himself averred, one *had* to eat and rest one's fill. Why he
had been following this regime for some fifty years! Millions of casualties,
men fighting off rats and lice, screams as gangrenous legs were lopped off
without anesthetic—none of that altered Joffre's habits. But then he made
sure to avoid not only battlefields, but hospitals.[82]

When the odd hagiographer had the good fortune to penetrate into his office, a simple uncluttered environment also bespoke Joffre's unvarying routine and again drove some to paroxysms of worship for the former "hero of Tombouctou." Alphonse Séché was one of these visitors. "It is here that *he* works, that *he* reflects, that *he* orders," raved Séché. Owen Johnson, an American who obtained a wartime meeting with Joffre, called him "a Cincinnatus, a man of the type of Grant and Lincoln, sobered by responsibility, haunted by the nation's sorrows." Joffre then revealed his putative humility by playing this down, declaring: "I am simply one citizen of the Republic."[83]

It remains difficult to understand how so many were taken in by all this, but narcissists sedulously cultivate surface impressions they make (almost totally false), and obviously Joffre did a fine job at it. To him the 1915 offensives that decimated a generation of French youth were invariably good ideas ruined by other people and by the elements. "On two occasions," he writes, "in the Argonne in May and in Champagne in the autumn, we failed by only a narrow margin to achieve very large results. If news of our preparations had not leaked out, if the fine weather had continued, if fleeting opportunities had been seized by local commanders, Heaven knows how far back we might have been able to drive the enemy." Yes, "the success [in Champagne, March 1915] was in itself small and incomplete, but it seemed to mark the first stage on the road to victory," comments Joffre. And there again the rain unfortunately intervened.[84]

Learning to talk back to such propaganda took too much time in World War I, for many bought into Joffre's rationalizations. In a May offensive of 1915 in Artois, "it was the late arrival of our reserves which prevented us from following up properly the magnificent success of the first day." But by the end of May, "we had captured 6500 yards of trenches to a depth of between 3000 and 4500 yards." Joffre is even egotistical enough to quote from his insane battle orders, which after the war constituted damning evidence. Before another doomed offensive of September 1915 he said to his soldiers (soon to be cannon fodder): "The time has, therefore, arrived for us to make a victorious attack, and to add another page of glory to those already inscribed with the names of the Marne, Flanders, the Vosges and Arras."[85] As one concludes the story of a bad year, there is no hint of remorse for the myriad French casualties he had needlessly created.

If Joffre had an overarching plan during 1915, it was to breach the German salient near Noyon by attacking its two sides—roughly, Artois in the north and Champagne in the south. The First Battle of Champagne from December 1914 to the end of March 1915 was, however, anything but one battle, but rather, a chain of futile attacks, including ones the British felt compelled to initiate as aid; for example, at Neuve-Chapelle March 10. In April the French lost a pack of men trying to break through at Saint-Mihiel, and even the glorified war history put out by the army shows the lack of gain from all these engagements. Yet Joffre called it all wonderful![86]

Before each new effort he put out a blitz of generalities, and from each bloody failure kept pretending he was honing techniques for the ultimate breakthrough. In fact he was killing off an entire generation. After more heartbreaking losses in Artois, a typically longwinded report of May 20, 1915 told reserves how to push forward as much as possible (Joffre underlines all this for emphasis). Another long note for generals of June 19 repeats Joffre's view that one must not only crush the first line of trenches, but subsequent lines too. *There* of course was the rub; the Germans were getting used to allowing the French through no-man's land and into the first line of trenches, only to pulverize them from a second or third.[87]

In the summer of 1915 Joffre briefly halted this nonsense to confer with the British, whom he dominated. His plans for more fall offensives in Champagne could *not* be called off, he warned, and English diversionary assaults were absolutely necessary. So that fall the British would lose their own thousands helping Joffre up the trench line at Loos, in a gritty area of mining cottages and slag-heaps.

If he weren't killing and wounding so many young men, Joffre's patronizing lectures and banalities—to soldiers, the British, and the War Ministry—would be almost comical. To the latter his missive of October 3, 1915 on the recent Champagne assaults first apologizes for not going into more technical detail, implying that it would be too recondite to comprehend. Then he gives a much-iterated lecture on how one mounts one of these offensives. Needing to assign blame elsewhere, the narcissist thinks indiscretions in conversation might perhaps have tipped off the enemy, and of course there was always the weather.[88]

As a generation perished in the trenches, Joffre kept sermonizing about its moral attributes, or the lack thereof, garrulously repeating himself on group solidarity, will power, signs of respect, discipline, and other qualities vital for taking German bullets. He even had the cheek to suggest that future operations be undertaken on the model of his failed Champagne offensives.[89]

In order to hold their positions, commanders under Joffre had to parrot such generalities—and most did in reports reaching the chief or his aides.[90] Joffre or an assistant would approvingly blue pencil the odd line in this profusion of meaningless verbiage. But there were some courageous reports containing critiques, part of an atmosphere where Parliament was starting to watch Joffre more carefully. General Berthelot, Commandant of the 32nd Army Corps, noted what couldn't be done in an attack, drawing attention to problems like friendly fire catching one's own troops from behind. A report written November 7 by Major Méalin, commanding the 16th Rifle Regiment, noted—and the reader underlined—that "a single battalion cannot pierce several lines where there are still defenders." Basically, this major was saying that *any* offensive of the Champagne or Artois genre was doomed. Born in Avignon in 1874, Abel Léon Méalin had worked his way up to major (*chef de bataillon*), receiving a Legion of Honor October 3, 1915. Soon after the report he was removed from service. Another critical one was from General Jules Compagnon, Commander of the 64th Division of Infantry, emphasizing respect of the weather. Contradicting his chief, he remarked: "Maybe it's better to postpone the attack itself when weather is unfavorable, even if artillery preparation has already begun." Better, he continued, to lose munitions than to "risk a sacrifice of men out of proportion to desired results. Men . . . are getting difficult to replace."[91]

Thankfully, politicians like Viviani and Briand also began to see through Joffre and recognize Gallieni for what he was, begging the latter in October 1915 to be war minister. But the old colonial flatly demurred, citing health problems. What his imperial past told him to shun was the endless palaver he would encounter in French politics. He would have much preferred Joffre's position, but parliamentarians found it too risky to sack a still legendary figure. So on October 30, 1915 Gallieni reluctantly gave in to the pressure, becoming a minister in Briand's cabinet. Leblond remembers a few rays of initial hope he had in being taken off the shelf.[92]

Others also had new hopes after the appointment. A letter from a soldier named Thierry seemed to breathe a sigh of relief—one of thousands that would pour into Gallieni's office. Addressing it to "Mon Cher Ami," Thierry congratulated the colonial hero, wishing him a speedy recovery from poor health, then discussed his own situation: "As for myself, I wonder why I am still alive. I have come from a furnace the likes of which I could never have imagined!" Thierry found the recent offensives a "gaffe," where no sooner was a position taken, than the Germans would retake it—and at awful cost to the French. On January 22, 1916 Colonel Messimy wrote a secret report to the President of the Republic, advising that no more Joffre-type offensives be permitted. A deputy in the Chamber wanted to form a commission to review *all* military operations from the beginning of the war, deploring the General Staff's bullying of Parliament. He declared "himself unable to admire blindly what our generals have done since [the Marne and the Yser]."[93] Obviously more and more people were beginning to unravel Joffre's web of propaganda.

And not only the French. Distinguished British authorities felt they too had been suckered by the chief, particularly to participate in the fall offensives after the failure of those in the spring, where Germany had introduced poison gas. The British were irritated as well by Joffre's continued hostility to the idea of a Dardanelles offensive, which had required the element of surprise. A note of October 18, 1915 circulated by Lord Selbourne to his cabinet colleagues of October 18, 1915 and another by Lord Esther six days earlier both lamented the fact that the Dardanelles expedition might have been less disastrous had Joffre not opposed it from the beginning. (The chief's foot-dragging on a subsequent Salonika campaign helped create a disaster there too.) Selbourne and Esther supported the creation of a commission to control Joffre's direction of the war.[94]

Had the German generals Hindenburg and Ludendorff not pressured the defensive-minded General Falkenhayn to initiate an attack on Verdun early in 1916, Joffre's removal might well have happened earlier. For one thing he became commander in chief of all French armies on December 2, 1915, not simply ones in the north and northeast; so he could finally be made accountable for all reverses. And by the end of that year French casualties (dead and wounded) were nearing 2 million.

Meanwhile, despite failing health and rising at five each day, Gallieni did his job the one way he knew how—thoroughly. But what joy he had was tempered by melancholy and skepticism. All through his career people had called on him late—Sudan, Madagascar, Paris in 1914, and now in the thick of this decimating trench conflict. Why had they waited for all those battle deaths to make this appointment? he wondered. His obsessions wouldn't leave him. To Foch he said half-seriously that they ought to dynamite the Ecole de Guerre after the conflict. To Pierre Gheusi he complained of this political "prison ship" he was on, of constant arguments that led nowhere. But he did confront debaters, rising in the Chamber, for example, to discuss the abuse of military recommendations it took fifty bureaucrats to read. Predictably, Clemenceau loved his forthrightness, while others found the imperial alumnus too outspoken. Some argue, however, that Gallieni now had enough prestige to push for Joffre's demise. Instead, he maneuvered to give Castelnau more power of decision in the field (sabotaged of course by Joffre) and fruitlessly for now, to reorganize the high command under enhanced government control.[95]

One of his particular bugbears was the endless tangle of bureaucratic paper—"diminishing *la paperasse*, I think of nothing but that," remarked Gallieni. In the colonies, Leblond noted, he had always had to combat "the slowness, [wrought] by negligence or malevolence, induced by paper from the home country." Now he trimmed an extensive bureaucracy wherever he could, but he was also coughing continually, and this battle too was not easily winnable. He told the Chamber that bureaucracy governed France; privately, he sputtered of government functionaries: "What a foul race!"[96]

Gallieni, however, still considered Joffre the greatest danger to France and declared that "we will die of the General Staff." He was also plain fatigued. Doctors' visits multiplied and his nights were agitated. Gallieni felt too different in training from Briand and the rest, and again, colonial empiricism was the reason; what could Briand have learned of life in the Chamber? Whereas, "continual nomads, we [imperial figures] are accustomed to look around ourselves. . . . Now in this office (*boîte*) of Loménie de Brienne . . . I feel ill at ease: I liked the tropical forests better!"[97]

But a huge German assault launched on Verdun in February 1916 then intervened to overshadow such concerns. And there again Joffre had played a lethal role in what turned into a mini-holocaust. For all through 1915 he had allowed a war of attrition to work to enemy advantage, emboldening Falkenhayn, the enemy's chief of staff, to try this coup de grâce. Joffre's egotism had stripped the fort's governors of their independent powers; and on August 5, 1915 Verdun—just inside the German line and of strategic and historic significance—came under the chief's direct orders. Within days he made the government declass Verdun's series of twenty forts, reducing the whole area to a "fortified region." *Pace* the great Séré de Rivières, whose fortress construction had truly aided France in 1914, Joffre's view was that these forts were now anachronisms, and that armies in the field could better defend them than their own arms. Consequently, through the fall he removed a great amount of heavy gunnery and men from Verdun. General Coutanceau, Verdun's governor, tried to oppose some of these moves by the chief and was fired. In December General Herr wrote a letter to one of Pétain's commanders on his fears of an attack at Verdun and its poor defenses, and GQG later nearly had him executed for it! That December Gallieni also got wind of Verdun's sloppy defenses, including lack of rail lines and a poor trench network in the area, some rotting and collapsed. Supported by Clemenceau, the war minister wrote Joffre about the matter, receiving a prickly reply from a man who felt such critiques would hurt army spirit. Joffre even solicited the names of supposed traitors, presumably so that he could wreck their careers; while Gallieni considered him a pure liar concerning Verdun's insufficiencies.[98]

In sum, Joffre, the quintessential example of a mediocre excolonial, was as responsible as anyone for an impending tragedy, among the greatest of the war. Ignoring intelligence reports that streamed in from German deserters about a planned offensive, he neither allowed a pullback of the trench line, definitively abandoning the fort, nor made sufficient preparations for its defense. Only heavy rains kept the Germans from attacking a week earlier than their thunderous opening assault of February 21, 1916. It seems clear that Joffre was now set to give up on, or at least to neglect Verdun. But on February 24 an incensed Briand came to Chantilly, dragging the large commander from his sacred bed and demanding that Verdun be defended at all costs. French morale and Briand's ministry would be the casualties of his indifference! So Joffre rallied, but too late. By early March a key outer fort, Douaumont, had been basically handed to the Germans and Vaux soon followed. The seesaw effort to hold Verdun through the spring killed and maimed much of what remained of the French army, creating a large number of casualties, and pushing surviving soldiers toward mutiny.

Yet Joffre's prestige was so great that he remained in power throughout the disaster. As war minister, Gallieni was too burdened with parliamentary intrigue, bad health, and bureaucratic reorganization to take down Joffre right at the beginning of the prolonged battle. Then it became too late to act, before his own impending resignation.[99]

Joffre's memoirs on the Verdun tragedy contain no surprises. Again, the author aided by ghostwriters feels he never made a mistake, and seems to have discerned no real suffering either. His "duty," he recalls, was to remain at Chantilly, "far from the scene of action," and to eat his meals on time and get his rest; for "the Battle of Verdun offers one more proof that in all the affairs of war nothing is more important than the way the command is exercised."[100] The most moved he apparently got was remembering ceremonies that took place *after* the slaughter—the conferral, for example, of a Legion of Honor on the entire town of Verdun (or what remained of it) in September 1916: how fine President Poincaré's speech was, how affecting it all was. Pinning a medal on the retiring General de

Langle's lapel seems also to have moved him. Sounding like something out of *Candide*, Joffre could only see German failure at Verdun (how many prisoners and guns were taken), not the hundreds of thousands of his own soldiers who were dead or wounded. He considered Verdun a test of nerves for all France that had been surmounted, an examination that had been passed.[101]

The reality was so different as to defy rationality. But Joffre seems to have been little interested in the almost indescribable sufferings his men endured. In narcissistic fashion he either acted as a cheerleader far from the game, or denigrated the heroes of Verdun for their continued moral shortcomings.[102]

One of Napoleon's aphorisms—"he who knows how to flatter knows how to calumny"—remained apposite for Joffre's behavior patterns during this conflict. Empty flattery (a substitute for concern) continued to gush out. In one general order, Joffre congratulated French soldiers for having ruined all enemy plans (at a cost of over a million dead to that date). Yes, "you vanquished them on the Marne, stopped them on the Yser, beat them in Artois and Champagne." And now you've broken the German effort of five months at Verdun! And "la Victoire est certaine!" he declared confidently.[103]

From at least the first German attack on Verdun Gallieni had meanwhile lost his appetite, and his nights remained agitated. He said to Leblond that Joffre was a jealous peasant; he might have said worse.[104] While the onset of the protracted tragedy did not change Joffre's routines at all, it did help bring death to a more high-strung and caring man. Gheusi says that Gallieni was devoured by Verdun. He tried to arrange rest leaves for distraught soldiers and free them from taxing exercises, but he had not long either for the War Ministry or for life itself. What time remained was mainly consumed in political irrelevancy. In the month Verdun began, a typical day for Gallieni was clogged with meetings—a deputy, a senator, another senator, tête à têtes with Kitchener, a general, an admiral, the *contrôleur général* (twice), receptions, and so on. "What wasted time!" he called it all.[105]

Citing an infection in his urethra and an impending operation, but also stung by political opposition to his army reforms, Gallieni started mentioning resignation in early March. (Since he was hardly eating and totally fatigued, we can now assume he had cancer.) Over strenuous objections from politicians like Poincaré, he left the Ministry on March 17, fighting now to live. Typical diary entries include: "vomiting at night"

(March 19); "cough with vomiting" (April 2); and "overwhelming fatigue" (April 15).[106]

As doctors prepared a first prostate operation, Gallieni was busy reading English favorites like George Eliot and Thackeray, but still worrying about Verdun. The operation without anesthesia of April 20 seemed successful. By May, however, Gallieni had no recovery of appetite or energy. Doctors performed a second operation May 18, and hemorrhaging now sounded his death knell. Though he never gave up his will to hang on, even receiving a direct blood transfusion from his chief doctor, he passed away May 27, 1916, inquiring before the end about the *poilus* at Verdun. Ironically, he died almost simultaneously with Britain's own colonial hero, Horatio Herbert Kitchener.[107]

First and foremost an imperial proconsul Gallieni had a background more valuable for the Great War than most understood. He was unique, and unique people do not always receive the positions they should have. Gallieni was among the best formed by a certain time and experience in the Sudan, Vietnam, and Madagascar; he was sensitive, organized, and tough all at once. But greatness requires recognizers with the power and integrity to employ it properly, and due mostly to his jealous ex-subordinate, this didn't happen.

Of course Joffre was still very much alive, trying to wrest credit from General Nivelle for the final October recovery at Verdun.[108] But its dénouement coincided with an equally massive tragedy. When Sir Douglas Haig became British commander in chief at the end of 1915, Joffre had already won him over to the value of offensives, and specifically to an attack on the sixty-mile front in the valley of the Somme. Joffre's original idea was to use two French armies and one British army—forty French divisions, twenty-five English. But by spring 1916 the Verdun massacre had become too costly, so Joffre forced Haig to hurry up his date for a diversionary offensive the British weren't at all sure about. The date for the start of the offensive became July 1, 1916, and the French now provided far fewer divisions than promised. Britain would thus take the lion's share of a slaughter that had already lost its raison d'être. As is well known, the Germans possessed several well-fortified lines and were dug in to a depth of forty feet, ready to respond in force. Little wonder that British losses on the first day of the Somme campaign were the greatest of any day of the war.

Is it surprising that Joffre's memoirs congratulate himself for pushing Haig into this massacre?[109] Or that he again shows no remorse whatsoever

for British soldiers lost, 20,000 of whom perished on the first day of battle? Luckily, Joffre kept Haig's energy level up throughout the campaign.
"During the whole month of August I frequently called Sir Douglas Haig's
attention to the necessity of putting more vigour and continuity into our
attacks," recalls the well-fed cheerleader.[110]

That fall it was thankfully almost curtains for Joffre's direction of the
war effort. Maxime Weygand, right-hand man to Foch, noted that with the
arrival of Gallieni at the War Ministry confidence in Joffre had diminished,
and with General Rocque's assumption of the position it disappeared—
poor old Joffre was undermined! In his own memoirs Joffre makes his dismissal sound like *the* tragedy of the war. Another Joffre-conceived offensive on the Somme for the spring of 1917 would *certainly* have finished the
Germans, but of course the politicians undercut him. Joffre specifically
blamed Briand, Minister of War Rocques, and in a more gingerly way
(owing to his colonial celebrity), the next war minister, Lyautey, who broke
the bad news to him. Then he savaged his successor Nivelle for making
the costly mistake on the Aisne in 1917 that would doubtless have been his
own on the Somme. For "if we had had the firmness to renew and amplify
the battle which the winter had interrupted [on the Somme], the Germans
would have been crushed.... The men who saved them have a heavy
responsibility to bear in the face of History."[111] But not M. Joffre? He of
course could never answer such a paltry customer as History.

Making fun, however, of the old colonial simply obscures his criminal-
ity. It is tempting to laugh, for example, at his reluctance to use new-
fangled devices like the telephone.[112] It is easy to make fun of his inability
to read maps or his reluctance to check battlefield terrains. But more
serious is the lack of care about suffering that all this betrays. Can one
see Gallieni going into such exaggerated detail on all the nonsensical ceremonies Joffre attended during the war? (It is a narcissistic trait to stick
august people—or their images—onto one's own, rather as one adorns
a Christmas tree.) Look how good King George of England was to Joffre,
King Albert of Belgium too. Why, as his memoirs emphasize, "the highest orders were bestowed on me by our Allies: Knight Grand Cross of
the Order of the Bath, Cross of St. George, Grand Cordon of the Order
of Leopold, all of which, in my person brought honour to the whole of
the French army."[113]

After being sacked December 13, 1916, then given the temporary position
of chief military advisor to the government, Joffre was forced to resign
completely within two weeks. But Lyautey, an astute war minister, assuaged

the former chief's wounded vanity, getting the government to award him the ceremonial title of Marshal of France (December 27), the first created in almost fifty years.

In the spring of 1917 Joffre found a new treasure trove of validating ritual on a mission to America. The idea was to spread good will in the country of a new ally, as well as military intelligence (in Joffre's case a true oxymoron). The general would travel with other public figures and five officers, including Lieutenant François de Tessan to keep and write an account. For the war minister who followed Lyautey, Paul Painlevé, "the *Vainqueur de la Marne* could bring to the new soldiers of liberty, the fruit of his glorious experience." And from the beginning of his long diary Tessan kept the legend aloft. On board ship "Marshal Joffre is always calm, thoughtful, and smiley." Part of that may have been due to the handsome remuneration he was receiving—his normal French salary, a monthly indemnity of 20,000 francs a month, and a generous expense account for food. But Joffre would also be remunerated by a deluge of American testimonials. In his French exposés on the art of war at West Point, his speech at the Senate, where he replied to thunderous applause "I don't speak English," and responses to detailed questions Wilson put to him May 9 through an interpreter (Jusserand) at the White House, Joffre could not have imparted much that was militarily useful. But the American heart—both press and people—gushed out to him. Greeted everywhere by thick crowds, rubbing shoulders with the great at Mount Vernon or the Library of Congress, wined, dined, or paraded with mayors, university presidents, and labor leaders, buttered up by dailies in each city he visited ("Joffre Captures Chicago" screamed a typical headline), awarded honorary degrees, compared to historical figures like Washington, and generally idolized, why would Joffre even consider revising his self-conception?[114]

If anything, his military advice to the Americans expressed in customary generalities may have rendered his hosts more careful than they need have been. When, for instance, Wilson asked Joffre how many generals he ought to send to France, the great firer said that "one must envisage the case where perhaps ten generals out of twenty will be incapable of suitably exercising their command and will have to be dismissed."[115]

Once back in France he continued sending letters of advice to leaders like Pershing. In June 1917 the latter met with Joffre, admiring his name and reputation, but not appreciative of the fact that "a sort of tutelage [was] contemplated, which also made it objectionable." At Chaumont in mid-October, 1917 Joffre inspected American troops, continuing to offer patronizing nuggets of advice. Pershing remained an admirer, but was adamant that U.S. troops maintain their independence.[116]

In 1918 Joffre received a fresh apotheosis by election to the Académie française (February 14, 1918) and a formal reception December 19, attended by Presidents Poincaré and Wilson, as well as the French literary elite. Only a rare Academician dared pick at the legend. The novelist Paul Bourget remarked: "So Marshal, you're still winning the Battle of the Marne?" To which Joffre replied with ersatz humility: "I know nothing of that, but what gives me pleasure is that it *was* won."[117]

In the *après-guerre* era the former chief of staff made the rounds at banquets for war wounded, inaugurations of monuments, and the like. Louis Madelin once asked if he had had any doubts during the retreat before the Marne. And of course the man who had had to be persuaded by Gallieni to undo that retreat replied: "Never." He likened it to his march on Tombouctou, never doubting that "the little soldiers of France" would do as well at the Marne as his colonial soldiers had in the Sudan.[118] There were still no clouds in Joffre's sky, either present or past.

In 1920 he began a series of official voyages to several European countries for more ceremonies and medals—in Rumania, Portugal, Spain. Then in 1921 President Millerand called on him to spread his magic to the Far East. So that fall he embarked for Japan, French Indochina, Singapore, and Siam, giving out decorations and gifts, shipping home the loads of presents he in turn received, and of course redoing his Marne routine at numerous receptions.[119]

Meanwhile, Joffre's postwar correspondence was enormous. From around France and the world came letters and requests for pictures, autographs, help with widows' or war-woundeds' pensions, or recommendations for decorations. Some of the letters from the United States are interesting—for example, Henry and Polly Ehrlich of Brookline, Massachusetts to Joffre, December 24, 1926: "My sister and I collect autographs of famous men and women and would like very much to have yours." Odder is the letter of William and Robert Charles of Clayton, Missouri to Marshall [sic] Joffre, February 24, 1927: "Dear Marshall Joffre: We are twin brothers of thirteen and are much interested in the subject: 'Was Dickens Interested in Music?' We are getting up a book of famous persons' opinions on this subject and, as you have probably taken up the study of Dickens...." How deluded they were to think Joffre would have read Dickens. In the same year James Gaffney of Brooklyn wrote "The Hero of the Marne" (January 24), enclosing an article on animal heaven and desiring his opinions on the subject.[120]

Joffre meanwhile lived a nice life, dividing his time in the 1920s between a winter residence in Paris and summers at a country place in Louveciennes. He would attend meetings at the Ecole militaire or the Académie, and work on correspondence or on dictating and examining drafts of his memoirs. He also read newspapers, but avoided material questioning his war record.[121]

One reason letters in the archives crescendo from 1926 seems to have eluded biographers. It was due to Joffre's special position that year as President of the Committee for the Revival of the Franc. In French history texts we hear of Poincaré saving the franc, but the use of Joffre's prestigious name to get financial contributions to shore up the currency is little known. Subscriptions to the fund for amortizing the French debt poured into his office, not only from France but from around the world. Contributions with letters came from veterans' associations, trade unions, groups of bank tellers, businesses like the Paris Macy's, as well as individuals galore. Among the most touching was a letter, contribution, and poem addressed to the "victor of the Marne" June 6, 1926 by Pierre-Cyrus Alberge. In it the ailing little franc finally wakes up, eats its gold, and cries out its renewed health! In these archival files there are pages and pages of recorded contributions from Quebec addresses alone. Ph. Rosen of the Papèterie de la Bourse in Paris said in a letter of June 1, 1926 that he would print 120,000 illustrated cards for free to distribute as "propaganda" to all Parisian schools. Contributors to the fund gave up days, even weeks of their salary. Meanwhile, Joffre's replies were generally mass-produced, but his letter of June 4, 1926 to René Hersouin of Paramount's Publicity Service in Paris not only thanked the company for its money, but noted how much "I enjoyed seeing again the nice film of the *Châtelaine du Liban*."[122]

Such accolades he received in abundance could not have hurt the old hero's large ego; but his last public appearance came in June 1930. Leg pains, then an amputation, followed by a coma culminated in Joffre's death, January 3, 1931. Which of course provoked another flood of encomia, both from within the country and from others, not to mention colonies of the French Empire.[123]

Joffre had been most effective at self-publicity, but far less so at caring about actual people in mortal danger or admitting his errors in wartime. The unaltered, unregenerate nature of one of history's most dangerous narcissists seems the appropriate place to close here. To reiterate, it is best to see this once minor colonial figure *neither* as the great leader of World War I that many used to think he was; nor as a mere peasant fool, as certain historians would later argue. Rather, we view him as psychologically dangerous in the position he finally arrived at, plunging hundreds of thousands of innocents into a needless pool of death, and suffering no remorse at all for it. In such a post how differently that cultured colonial soldier, Gallieni, would have done.

Bugeaud of Algeria (Musée de l'Armée)

Faidherbe of Senegal and West Africa (Musée de l'Armée)

The great Gallieni (Musée de l'Armée)

The lethal Joffre (Musée de l'Armée)

The incomparable Lyautey (Musée de l'Armée)

Bigeard standing tallest at Dien Bien Phu (courtesy Marcel Bigeard)

Bigeard in the Algerian *bled* (courtesy Marcel Bigeard)

French North Africa

FRENCH EQUATORIAL AFRICA (AEF)

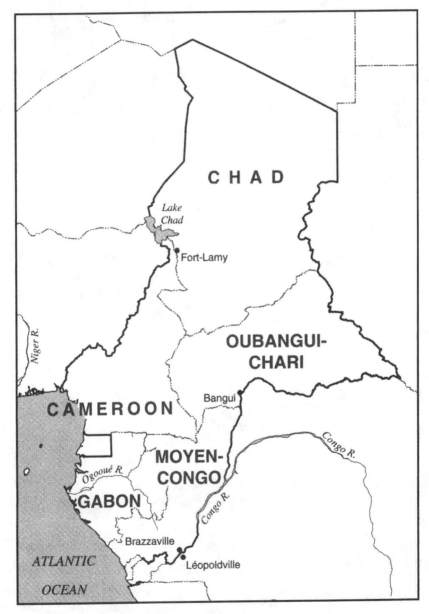

French Equatorial Africa (AEF), French West Africa (AOF), and Madagascar

FRENCH WEST AFRICA (AOF)

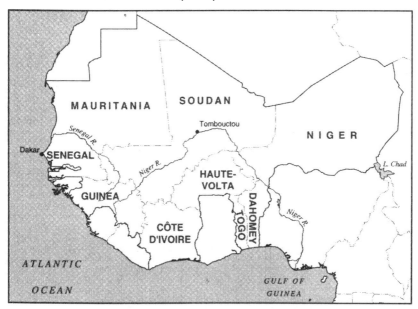

MADAGASCAR

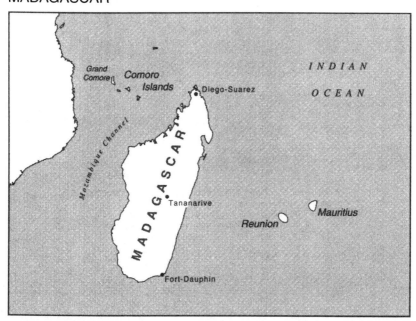

French Indochina

Lyautey

Prince of Proconsuls

I N LOUIS-HUBERT-GONZALVE LYAUTEY (1854–1934), last of the great
French proconsuls of the nineteenth and early twentieth century, we
have a figure much more like his mentor Gallieni than a Joffre. This
chapter will explore Lyautey's complexity and emphasize what the colonial effort meant to him, and what he imparted to it in Vietnam, Madagascar, Algeria, and especially Morocco through to the mid-1920s. Here
we will find a romantic who sought in the colonies a poetic outlet unavailable at home; yet like Faidherbe, a practical realist who located opportunities to build abroad that were equally unavailable in France, at least
in the military. We will see that Lyautey's brand of imperialism was partly
defined by what he feared most: formalism, hierarchical rigidity, Parisian
governmental strictures, and "mandarinism." We will consider the tradi-
tionalism and Catholicism of a man who never surrendered his aristocratic
conservatism, yet had far more tolerance and flexibility than such an affili-
ation usually implies, especially the longer he was abroad.

Lyautey was both quintessentially French, yet never really at home in the
métropole. He had the unique, isolated psyche of the artist, an insatiability
of conception that only colonial life could appease (and even then, only
when problems did not overwhelm him). Once again, his childhood and
background explain a good deal here and fortunately, quite a number of
biographies exist on a man so made for them. On his early life the best,
as noted, is a monograph of the 1990s by Pascal Venier. We have used some
of the same sources, as well as others, but our treatment offers added and
more complex psychological insights on this supremely cultured, yet militarily capable imperial figure.[1]

What is obvious from reading any Lyautey biography is how great an influence sickly, confined early years had on a person who in adult life wanted to use colonial activity for escape and the opportunity of doing good, untrammeled. Born in Nancy in 1854 to a stern family of soldiers and administrators on his father's side, and an aristocratic, more artistic one on his mother's, Lyautey at eighteen months was watching a parade celebrating the Prince Imperial's baptism. Suddenly he fell from the rusted railing of a second-story window on which his nurse had placed him and which unexpectedly gave way. His tumble earthward would have killed him had he not struck the shoulder of a *cuirassier* en route to the pavement, and the only immediate consequence seemed to be a nick in the forehead. But persistent back and internal pain ensued, and after an operation performed by a Parisian doctor, Lyautey was literally swaddled in plaster of Paris for two years, remaining in bed full-time. Immobile, and even when he began walking at six, still dependent on crutches, the boy was obviously deprived of a physically normal childhood. He did not even approach that normality until ten or so, continuing to wear a metal contraption until the age of twelve, and suffering hearing loss as well.

One consequence was that Lyautey became the object of much tender, feminine attention, accentuating the tasteful, intuitive side of a character best seen in his outpouring of many fine letters from abroad. But his childhood weakness also provoked a Theodore Rooseveltian desire to establish manly competence, intensifying a preoccupation with things military, stimulated as well by examples around him. His preeminent role model here was a paternal grandfather who showed his grandson the damaged hand he had received from frostbite in Napoleon's Russia, as well as the scar from a Cossack's lance. That grandfather had also commanded an artillery corps in Algeria under Bugeaud and became an important general. Much like Stendhal's Sorel (of *The Red and the Black*), the young Hubert was a voracious reader and dreamer; yet perhaps due to these battle stories he heard, and the military posters or lithographs he beheld at houses in his extended family, he would grow into an active, if aesthetically inclined military man. And one who oedipally found his own father, an engineer, too stodgy, and from whom he would always clearly differentiate himself.

To some degree, Lyautey would synthesize a practical, sober, and military paternal side with the more artistic-romantic side of his mother. Not only was that mother a significant influence, but even more so was her sister, Berthe de Grimoult de Villemotte. If Lyautey developed a complex of uniqueness in his adult life, if he became a tasteful, flashy, somewhat over-the-top, artistic personality, it wasn't his mother (whom he called a *femme d'intérieur*), but this maternal aunt who was more at the root of it. Having no children of her own, Aunt Berthe loved Lyautey like a son and took care of him a good deal in those crucial first six years of his life. His favorite aunt was a royalist, as well as a Catholic, yet open to new ideas, extremely well read, and a devotee of vivid, stimulating conversation with the many intelligent people she knew. Young Hubert found her company irresistible and would always adore her, and it is fair to conclude that she, more than anyone, helped him liberate himself from the expectations of his milieu. His regional origins also had their influence on him—his father's Franche-Comté and the Normandy, and especially Lorraine of his mother's side, which gave him special pride.[2]

As befitted a child of the elite, Lyautey went off to study at the Lycée of Nancy, where he befriended likeminded students like Antonin de Margerie, son of a university professor. Within his group of friends, the young Lyautey pledged himself to the daring ideological stripe of Legitimist Royalism (under the Second Empire). Yet when the group played at war games, Lyautey rapidly worked himself up to Emperor Napoleon III by a coup wrought with toy pistols! Some of the older members of his family weren't amused by his airs, but this was already the Lyautey who would forge his own style and path abroad.

The history of his time certainly intensified that generational obstinacy. For after studies both at the lycée in Nancy, then Dijon, whence his father, a specialist in bridge construction, had moved, Lyautey would become part of the generation of 1870, profoundly shattered but at the same time, mentally toughened by the great French defeat. In 1872 he chose to enroll at the Rue des Postes, an elite Jesuit preparatory institution, and by year's end had made it into military school at Saint-Cyr.[3]

Unfortunately, the young Lyautey found Cyrien routines and dogma too restrictive, to say the least, preferring the intoxicating social Catholicism of Albert de Mun, whom he met in 1874, and who helped spawn Munian groups at both Saint-Cyr and the Ecole Polytechnique. From there the young man went to the General Staff School in Paris, but was bored by some of the teaching he received. An ardent twenty-year-old, he found memory work and other rote learning tedious, partly due to his own high standards. In this crucial era he began unloading some of the hothouse royalism, Catholicism, and provincialism of his youth, though it did not shed easily. A note of 1875 shows his guilt at missing his prayers eight days running. Lyautey, however, had definitively entered a period of doubt, on which he approvingly quoted Lacordaire: "I have an extremely religious soul and an unbelieving mind."[4] His spiritual changes were facilitated by intellectual discoveries of thinkers like Plato, Descartes, or Balzac, by de Mun's social Catholicism, and above all, by his impatience with the routines of Saint-Cyr and of garrison life.

One really needs to linger on these years, more than is often done, for in the youthful Lyautey one already sees the contradictory sides of a complex imperial personality. The extensive notes he took in a number of courses (more demanding due to post-1870 educational changes in France) reveal Lyautey's industry. Reading moldy notebooks still in his papers, any former student will find his work ethic self-punishing, as if nothing was ever enough. Was it the influence of all those distinguished ancestors that made him never satisfied with his own efforts? Of a tremendously accomplished paternal side, in particular? Or was it the recent defeat? For whatever reason, the work Lyautey put into his notes on hygiene, topography, geography, artillery (with tasteful drawings), entrenchment, metallurgy, philosophy, and especially, language study, including translations from German into French, reveals an important part of his personality.

But at the same time the artistic, theatrical side of him kept popping through as well. The conflict this created in the youthful Lyautey became at times overwhelming. First off, he was still a Catholic, immersed in religion. Bear in mind too that France on the morrow of 1871 was a serious country indeed. So Lyautey sums up his life in those years as one of "storms, hopes and shattered hopes, fears and assurances." But despite all the rules, and the enormous expectations of family and teachers who considered him a model student, Lyautey's romantic, self-absorbed quality kept making him hear a special voice inside. In long, Péguyesque, obsessional sentences scribbled in his "Daily Notes," he remarks at one point that "there is nothing at the bottom of my life other than *me, me, me,* an absolute egotism." For if "I love my friends, and I do have them, I'm interested in myself above all"—to "get rated highly, appreciated, judged well. I am on a continual theatrical stage ... I live in myself ... I admire myself ..." Feeling unvalidated, as he says, and skating rings around potential competitors, "I view myself in all possible positions, and I live in a mystical, imaginary, and fictive life where I am the principal personage, where everything relates to me, where I shine in every way ... because I own things, because of who surrounds me; ... I am thirsty for all satisfactions of the soul, of thought, of vanity, including frivolous vanity." One could literally quote hundreds of these self-absorbed pages, nor should one terminate discussion of Lyautey's *sui generis* complex without mentioning as well his relationship with another student, Prosper Keller, about whom he also wrote extensively, and whom he treated in a self-confessed capricious, mercurial manner. What Lyautey's writing on his relationship with Prosper reveals is both a suffocating need for affection and confirmation by others, as well as a need to get away and be unique.[5]

Finally, this itchy-footed young man got a chance to see the world, traveling to Algeria, which he had heard about in his grandfather's martial tales. A first brief leave from his cavalry regiment in the late 1870s was followed by a longer North African stint with a regiment of hussars from 1880–82. For Lyautey the latter two years in both city and raw countryside flew by. There he grew into the man he would become, turning into a fine officer, and already, a leader of men. To appreciate what going abroad meant for this lover of the exotic, one has to dip into his many marvelous letters sent home in that era. Stimulated, even intoxicated by new surroundings, he wrote compulsively to family and friends. From one spot in Algiers (1882) Lyautey described "a real hole, no gas, no Café de la Paix, no theater, no music, no society life, but ... poetry bursting forth from everywhere."[6] Earlier on, he had written his father a typically exultant letter from Biskra: "Magical day; impossible to close one's eyes without seeing light, blue sky, wonders and more wonders!" Calling himself a lover of light, Lyautey had obviously located in Algeria what a once swaddled child could not have found in darker Lorraine. Was the landscape here arid? Of course it was, "but all this aridity is flooded with such color, the foregrounds are so pink, so purple, so golden, and the backgrounds so violet or blue ... that it's a fairyland at every minute, worth all the beautiful but drab landscapes of our gray-skied Europe."[7]

In Algeria he preferred the open country of desert, mountains, and plains to the cities, partly the difference between being a bureaucrat and a soldier out on mission. In Algiers of 1881, where he became ill from typhoid fever, he sputtered about office routines, noting, "there's decidedly but one life that suits me, and that's life in the open air." Painstaking administrator though he was, Lyautey liked to be away from his desk and out in the elements, especially in a youth that wished to burst its shackles. He found Algiers too full of Parisians and too much a replica of the métropole—"cafés, boulevards, strolling, toilettes ... a Frenchified city, all asphalt and stores." But there he also made Arab contacts and worked hard at learning the language. With the tireless linguistic industry

of a Faidherbe, Lyautey carefully translated from and into Arabic, artisti-
cally printing vowels and consonants, making long, careful lists of words,
phrases, and grammatical constructs, just as he did for other tongues like
German, English, and even Chinese.[8]

Returning to the somber Vosges of Lorraine was surely a letdown; but
Captain Lyautey then received a paid leave of several months to accompany his intellectual aunt on a trip to Italy, telling the War Ministry that
he would study military organizations and other pertinent data, and once
back, present them a formal report. En route he loved Austria, enjoyed
meeting the Royalist pretender, the Count of Chambord, then had more
surging emotions in the company of Pope Leo XIII at Pontifical Mass
in Rome's Sistine Chapel. In letters sent home Lyautey scooped up detail
after detail, observing, feeling, and digesting. But his more routine report
to the Ministry on organization of Italian cavalry, their harnessing techniques, and other such matters was also well received. The Ministry concluded that he had used his leave conscientiously.[9]

Getting away had revealed to Lyautey what he might become—and also
how he could be stimulated to produce an epistolary deluge from abroad,
ultimately making him one of France's most compelling letter-writers.
Leaving the métropole began showing him that no orthodoxy would
ever quite suffice. This Catholic's reading now included positivists and
Darwinians, and his former faith had clearly become modified. Moving
to different French garrisons, he became a more committed Republican,
particularly after Chambord's death. By the late 1880s his humane and respected command of a squadron at Saint-Germain-en-Laye outside Paris
got him noticed. Lyautey was good to his men, giving them books, billiard
tables, writing paper. In his five years there he also became a sought-after
salonnard in the nearby capital, protégé of the politician and leading literary light, Eugène-Melchior de Vogüé. Chez different hostesses Lyautey
rubbed shoulders with other young literary talents, including the neurasthenic M. Proust. Letting himself go, Lyautey also began to formulate
views on the encrusted institution of the French army, which he felt was
burdened with useless dogma and traditions.

Ironically, he also received glowing inspection reports from that army
he wished to reform, and almost all predicted a great future for him. But
Lyautey hadn't yet won anything close to celebrity, until his friend Vogüé,
who wanted to write on army reform, asked for Lyautey's thoughts on
the subject. Instead, Lyautey produced his own impassioned work, and the
result, which he could not as an officer sign, appeared as "Du rôle social

de l'officier dans le service militaire universel," in *Revue des deux mondes* (1891), catapulting him to the beginnings of a maverick notoriety.[10] Very quickly, people in the know figured out the author's identity. In this piece Lyautey criticized the formalism and triviality of French military formation, considering the service a matchless but often wasted opportunity for regenerating the young and thereby, a nation. Suddenly notables by the score—politicians, philosophers, clergymen, even Germany's Kaiser Wilhelm II—wished to correspond with or meet this daring theorist.[11]

But in 1894 at age forty, the proverbial age of midlife crisis, Lyautey was unsure quite how to proceed. He was no longer young, and though he had gotten his feet wet colonially, it was now or never for a real chance at achievement abroad. He knew for certain that he disliked bureaucratic strictures in France. Mired in command of the 7th Cavalry Division near Paris, and deeply craving action, he was soon to get it—and perhaps for the wrong reason. The French chief of staff, Mouton de Boisdeffre, counted Lyautey as a friend, but probably considered his controversial views an irritant. Lyautey requested a transfer to Indochina and Boisdeffre granted it, which pleased his subaltern. Boarding a ship at Marseille in the summer of 1894, the middle-aged Lorrainer suddenly found he could breathe again, and was soon busy writing numerous letters home.

In Saigon he met the governor-general Jean-Marie de Lanessan, whose philosophical sophistication and views on working with local notables made Lyautey instinctively like him. Formerly a professor of medicine, and a published expert on colonial affairs, Lanessan helped impress on Lyautey the utility of French protectorates. Suddenly Hubert felt at home here, inducing him to write a number of times about wasting his prior years in France—"ten years lost in . . . family or bureaucratic clichés," as he noted in a letter to his sister. His childhood, despite its positive aspects and tender beauties, had been a hothouse of shibboleths and formulae, of protection from "rudes contacts," and almost from life itself. He was glad as well to be away from the searing two-France division (Catholic versus anticlerical), about to rip the country apart in the Dreyfus Affair, and which he felt compartmentalized people. Colonial life seemed a much healthier melting pot.[12]

With Lanessan Lyautey traveled north to Hanoi, and the governor impressed upon him the need to get along with the area's mandarins and traditions. In a Tonkin replete with shakedown artists Lyautey became an interim army chief of staff. Just as he had madly studied Arabic en route to Algeria, he now immersed himself in Asian history and customs.

Putting in long days working on problems of kidnappings and general terror, and how to respond militarily or diplomatically, he was back in an enthusiastic mode, admiring soldiers in the field who in a matter of months seemed to learn far more about life here than they would back in France.

Lyautey at first had a sense of greenness compared to such men who had matured so quickly out in the elements. In a letter to the head general in Hanoi, he frankly avowed these insecurities: "I fully appreciate, mon Général, all the weight of the responsibility you have given me, and I would like to believe I am capable of handling it."[13] Then, after about a month in the north, the colonial "rookie" had one of the defining moments of his life—a first meeting with by far his greatest influence, Gallieni, commander of the Second Military Territory of Northeastern Tonkin. The two hit it off immediately. Eagerly, Lyautey showed Gallieni his books— one a series of "Staff Recommendations," another a "Course of General Tactics"—and solemnly Gallieni wrapped them in paper and string and essentially told Lyautey to file them under "Garbage." The colonial hero emphasized that here one learned from people, and from conditions in the field.[14] As seen, Lyautey rapidly grew to idolize this mentor, and was soon freed to accompany him as his chief of staff on pirate-chasing operations. He saw how Gallieni inspired both French and Annamese, and how rapidly he could get people to build or rebuild here. Rolled up in blankets, they would talk away at night—or really, Lyautey would listen to Gallieni's vast storehouse of experiences. Here, wrote Lyautey, "I drink in his Sudanese secrets . . . Contact with this hero . . . gives me a foretaste of the joys of action, erasing all the bitterness of stagnant suburban garrisons."[15]

Lyautey was glad to find his antibureaucratic, anti-Parisian impulses confirmed by such an experienced proconsul. Basically, Gallieni told Lyautey to bypass most directives he received from France. For instance, to pay for sheds needed to keep food from rotting, Gallieni couldn't await the long process of ministerial confirmations from Paris; instead, he laid heavy taxes on Chinese gambling houses that had been a drain on local purses. Let the Ministry grumble!

In the wilds, the two would now be scaling cliffs or traversing thick forests. As Gallieni's chief aide, Lyautey also had to scrounge enough rice to feed all the men. Gallieni would never let personal sentimentality get in the way of results, and with difficulty, Lyautey found the rice. On a 1,600-foot climb up a cliff to a pirate hideout, he found himself on a ledge looking over a dangerous abyss, with bullets humming around his head. Yet he loved it! The French pursuers grabbed a fortress, the pirates escaped,

and Lyautey described it all in letters home that would later form glittering published collections. It was art emerging from isolation and from
extreme circumstances. Climbing or sliding down steep gorges, fighting
cutthroats, and mastering his vertigo, Lyautey extolled the benefits of
muddling through: "Hands scraped, feet aching, but truly delighted by
vanquishing difficulty," he scribbled at one point. Getting back to a bed
with sheets after months of bivouacs and tough operations in the field
would be a contrastive "debauchery" for him.[16]

Lyautey also learned from Gallieni how to pace himself in Indochina.
Evenings after pirate-chasing, he wanted to talk feverishly of the next day's
operations, but Gallieni preferred to discuss John Stuart Mill or some
other writer. It was best to allow one's batteries to recharge. And Lyautey
was every bit as bookish as the master. In letters home he would implore
friends to dispatch him classics and also the latest publications. In one
he asked Max Leclerc to ship him some Vigny, Baudelaire's *Fleurs du mal,*
books by the historian Lavisse, and an up-to-date art catalogue. To Vogüé
he would later write in 1901: "Don't begrudge me your letters ... the
downside of my job is solitude. You in France can't imagine the loneliness
of a colonial leader."[17]

Even if Lyautey and Gallieni couldn't eliminate all the brigands they
chased in Vietnam, simply dislodging them from certain areas brought
enhanced security, which was always their primary goal. Where before
Annamese couldn't easily cultivate in fertile valleys, now they were able to
do so. Here was that protective side of French and other western imperialisms that is so easily forgotten. Before the Gallieni era, these peasants
often had to escape up cliffs to miserable caves, eluding rape and pillage.
But Lyautey also knew that nothing here would last forever, and that if
the French became too satisfied with a bureaucratic veneer established in
Indochina, they were courting disaster. He could not have been more
prophetic. He was aware that despite gorgeously poetic landscapes, safety
for inhabitants was the primary consideration here, and he took paternal
delight in creating that security. He was stupefied when he met Vietnamese
peasants the French had liberated from protection racketeers, informing
him that for the first time in twenty years they could now harvest all their
grain; and he realized what many at home took for granted: "Before disserting on forms of national life, one must first make [that] life secure."[18]

Back again in Hanoi as interim army chief of staff, Lyautey was able
to elaborate what would become his method—building up an area with
roads, agriculture, and markets, while making it militarily unavailable to

brigands. French authorities now believed they could do that right up to
the Chinese border. Lyautey first worked with Lieutenant-Colonel Vallières,
Commander of the Third Military Territory, on a sensitive diplomatic
mission to meet with a Chinese mandarin. That mission turned out so
successful that the French would have regular relations with the Chinese
on all frontier problems, help in watching markets for arms purchases, and
hopefully, Franco-Chinese cooperation in pursuing pirates on both sides
of the border. Lyautey was proud of this entente, crafted in a region where
such Chinese authorities had formerly been accomplices of the pirates.
There would now be better organization of French frontier posts as well.
Vallières was certainly happy to have such a man working for him, writing
his superior in Hanoi to "express my gratitude for the dispatches of Commander Lyautey to the Third Territory.... This officer was able to work intelligently and actively, warding off potential dangers." Vallières was pleased
with Lyautey's organization of sectors where people had previously been
afraid to show their heads, and thought his diplomatic mission to the mandarin Hoang-Van-Cao had been accomplished in exceptional fashion.[19]

When Gallieni left during the fall of 1896 to put out the next colonial
fire in Madagascar, it was expected that Lyautey would continue on as a
top commander in Tonkin. But a new governor-general, and especially
new military superiors took getting used to, and Lyautey wrote his mentor that he remained at his disposition. So Gallieni pulled the right strings,
and in January 1897, after two years up in Tonkin, Lyautey went off to join
him in a very different colonial theater. In Tonkin he had enjoyed going
from "the unknown to the known, from the inorganic to the organic,
from the vague to the actual," and now looked forward to the same kind
of enterprise on Madagascar.[20]

After a long, thoughtful sea voyage, Lyautey arrived in March, and was
given a red-carpet welcome by Gallieni, as well as instant responsibilities.
Great chiefs make great demands, and Gallieni wanted Lieutenant-Colonel
Lyautey to take care of roughly one-third of the island, the northwest of
the Imerina, where a number of chieftains were still in revolt. The key rebel
chieftain to put out of commission was one Rabezavana, and Lyautey's
troops, including Algerian, Malgache, and Senegalese sharpshooters, went
into action immediately. But aside from Lyautey's military and organization skills, his psychological sensitivity in negotiations also facilitated
Rabezavana's surprising surrender on June 2. Along with his warriors
Rabezavana came personally to give himself up, all of them flinging down
their rifles. The rebel chieftain even handed Lyautey a ring that had been

a symbol of his former power. Many peasants, formerly terrorized, gathered quizzically around the new French leader, but Lyautey surprised them by sparing Rabezavana's life, despite the latter's subsequent efforts at escape; to their extreme wonderment, he even gave the fallen chief a territory to run under the French, taking wind out of the sails of the entire *Menalamba* revolt.

As proconsul of this large northwestern swath of Madagascar, Lyautey reported regularly to Gallieni, whom he saw infrequently, in long, elegant letters. Despite a continuing campaign to extend pacification throughout the Sakalava regions extending to the west coast of the island, Lyautey was also obsessed by road building, town building, vaccinations, hygiene, etc. The poet in him continued to appreciate inspiring landscapes, sunsets, and other beauties he beheld; but he also loved meeting grateful Malgache women, children, and men who thanked him for his work. In a letter of 1898 he apologized to his sister for going on and on about everything, but "I'm so gripped by this task of creation, I live for my roads, villages, fields, flocks, nurseries." Opening formerly closed routes in the newly created Fourth Military Territory, and helping bring the entire Sakalava country under French control by the end of 1898, he had wasted little time here.[21]

On a trip back to France with Gallieni, an exhausted Lyautey arrived in May 1899 to find the country tapped out as well from the Dreyfus Affair, which discouraged him. (Lyautey was a rare army man of his class who had been an unqualified Dreyfusard.) In the main he did not like this home milieu. More and more, he saw the colonial life as a "school of energy" or "school of the outdoors," and would unblushingly liken what the French could do in Africa or Tonkin to the American pioneer epic. The imperial life could blow away inherited mustiness, rejuvenating the French mind and heart, as it had done for him.[22] A regenerated France would then become a country equal to Germany; it would be a nation rejecting the lure of decadence.

All this was the background to another important essay Lyautey produced in 1900, *Du rôle colonial de l'armée*, on those themes, and on what became the "Lyautey method." But despite his growing colonial fame he found that Paris' salon life no longer attracted him. So with Gallieni he returned to Madagascar in June 1900, the two having gotten the Ministry to procure a loan for the struggling colony, and authorization to fortify a naval base at Diego-Suarez, discussed in the last chapter. In fact Lyautey's extensive Paris contacts had helped get Joffre his position there, in addition to the monies Gallieni needed for Madagascar.

Colonel Lyautey, as he had become February 6, 1900, was now starting to taste real power, given supreme command of the southern territories of Madagascar (another third of the island). Much of that area also
remained unpacified. His headquarters would be the Betsileo capital of
Fianarantsoa, and from there he wrote his sister on November 17, 1900:
"I am forty-six years old tonight; the age Colonel Gallieni was when I
met him six years ago. He was a colonel, I am a colonel. He commanded
the most important territories of Indochina, I command a third of Madagascar.... He had faith in his star, I have faith in mine."[23]

For the next couple years Lyautey would mostly be on the road, fighting, building, creating, and inspiring, not least in numerous speeches. He
worked hard as an efficient administrator, yet his literary side continued to
show in many beautifully written letters. Gazing out from Fort Dauphin,
created by the French at the island's southern tip in the era of Louis XIV,
he wrote Vogüé (July 5, 1901): "From the balcony of my veranda tonight
it's marvelous. I won't try to describe it for you ... the combination of the
rising moon, the subsiding sea, palm trees etched against ... the sunset
still blazing behind, the high top of the *pic* Saint-Louis."[24]

The romantic Lyautey is best located in these epistles home, while the
pragmatic administrator can be seen in long reports he wrote on his work
around the island, generally for Gallieni. In one of February 26, 1901, running to some twenty pages, the Supreme Commander of the South summarized conditions encountered on a long reconnaissance mission from
the forested zone of the east to Midongy in the south. He had already
subdivided areas and had capable subalterns send him *their* reports. He
knew which tribes were "submissive" and which ones weren't, and pacified
areas most susceptible to backsliding. Even near Fort Dauphin the French
had to counter a long tradition of "people whose chief occupation was
cattle theft and plunder of coastal traders." The answer was first force and
nettoyage (clean-up), but then what would become the Lyautey method:
namely, "making administration as economical as possible, relying on
local leaders, reducing effectives, and neglecting unproductive regions."
About to leave in 1902, Lyautey wrote a final, exhaustive report on all the
provinces under his jurisdiction, stressing how fragile this recent French
presence was in areas used to constant brigandage and under no previous
administrative-fiscal regime. These reports were anything but a general-
ist's collection of theories; rather, they were empirical reviews of which
area and which notables were best handled in which ways.[25]

In Tonkin and especially Madagascar Lyautey had accomplished his tasks and had a wonderful dress rehearsal for the way he would soon operate in Morocco. He had helped rebuild villages and even aided in the creation of cities, presaging later achievements in Rabat and Casablanca. Unfortunately more Lyauteys would not be easily found in the colonial theater. Gallieni's "exit letter," congratulating him on completing his mission in Madagascar, praised his keen intelligence, indefatigatible activity, and leadership skills that facilitated the island's economic development. He hoped the government would now summon Lyautey to preside over some other challenging imperial milieu, making sure a month later to advertise his protégé's verve by sending a long letter on his work in the south to the War Ministry. In fact southern Madagascar was now so well organized and pacified that Gallieni was able to suppress its command. On March 9, 1903 he would write another glowing letter, supporting Lyautey's promotion to brigadier general, which would indeed come to pass in October.[26]

But only after a traumatic period back in France, during which Lyautey discovered how hard it was to go home again. Sent to command the 14th Regiment of Hussars at Alençon on October 1, 1902, he poured out his trapped anguish in letters describing a much superior and more fulfilling colonial life. Now he had to run this little regiment in France, plagued with trivial tasks! Once more Lyautey felt stifled. In the aftermath of the army's besmirchment during the Affair, people told him to play by the rules, keeping pen and mouth fastened shut. However, that brought on a state of torpor that made him want to burst! He knew he had only to await October 1903 to be permitted retirement, and he thought seriously of taking it, moving into politics or perhaps business.

Thankfully, the summer of 1903 brought a gust of change to Lyautey's becalmed personal ship. En route through Paris he dined with Jules Charles-Roux, the colonial lobbyist; and at that dinner, Algeria's new Governor-General Charles Jonnart poured out his own worries about rising anarchy on the frontier between Algeria and Morocco, ill-defined since Bugeaud's time. The region was now prey to numerous guerilla attacks. On a recent trip to see the Figuig palm groves there, Jonnart had himself been snared in an ambush, for which some French soldiers paid with their lives to save him.

Jonnart had just become governor-general of Algeria in 1903, and the ambush that nearly killed him was only one of several murderous incidents, making him consider more imaginative reactions. At dinner he asked Lyautey to describe his work with Gallieni fighting pirates of the Tonkin, and Lyautey elaborated on his method—military security, followed by enticing local populations with institutions of peace and prosperity. Jonnart began to see this as a possibility for Algeria's unruly South Oranais.

In August another attack by "jihadic" warriors killed thirty-six French soldiers, and survivors in the area feared imminent sabotage of rail and telegraph installations. Jonnart now pressed the War Minister to appoint someone of special verve to pacify this area. Why not Lyautey of Tonkin and Madagascar?

The appointment was duly made, though improperly translated code at first kept Lyautey in the dark on the reason for his dismissal from his regiment. He traveled to Paris, and at a bistro near the Gare Montparnasse opened the newspaper to a surprising headline—Lyautey to command at Aïn-Sefra! Though he had had prior hints about receiving the appointment, this must have constituted a moment of perfect happiness for him.

On the boat trip from Marseille that happy mood persisted, but the general who met him coolly at Oran was nothing like Gallieni. Taking a train southward to the French post of Aïn-Sefra, Lyautey had the general's warnings still in his ears about the mess he was inheriting. Aïn-Sefra was pretty enough, nestled high between a plateau and the beginning of the endless Sahara; but subalterns told Lyautey what *couldn't* be done here, not what could. All moves required lengthy confirmation from either Oran or Paris. Immediately, Lyautey toured the region, observing overloaded columns operating according to fixed regulations. Bugeaud would have been distressed by their vulnerability to attack, and so was Lyautey. Temper rising, he took an impulsive train trip to Algiers to meet with Jonnart, telling him flatly that he wanted carte blanche from the War Ministry to pacify the border area his way. Anything less, and he would leave Algeria, presumably to retire. Within a month Jonnart got to work on such authorization.[27]

Of course Lyautey's problems with Paris were far from over, and this would be a continuing theme for him, as it had been for his predecessors. Theodore Zeldin mentions colonial administrators ignoring Parisian telegrams for years on end; with Lyautey it was more a constant tussle, though he tried to do as much as possible without informing either the Quai d'Orsay or Rue Saint-Dominique back in Paris. His early hatred of rules at Saint-Cyr, of what he called *l'esprit de bouton* had ripened in the colonial milieu. Like Bugeaud, Lyautey felt he not only had to win victories over native rebels, but over the home base.[28] As he had written his sister in 1895, to accomplish anything abroad, "one must break all [their] suffocating rules." That sense of having his hands tied by the capital would haunt him even at the moment of his greatest triumphs. So in 1903, from Aïn-Sefra, he began directing "clean-up" expeditions without real Parisian approval, landing him in hot water with military authorities back home. Yes, "the Paris offices are in a panic, I know, and I'm having great fun with it," he added. In a less amused tone Lyautey would write Max Leclerc on April 21, 1904: "No one lays a brick [here] without Paris studying, verifying, and regulating the matter a year in advance."[29]

To understand Lyautey's pacification campaigns in the borderland of the South Oranais, we must now try to make some sense of that unstable land abutting Algeria and increasingly, in European news through to World War I. Morocco (al-Maghreb, meaning "the farthest west") was at the time a state in name only, with a sultan who could not command the allegiance of all tribespeople from his capitals in Marrakech, Meknès, and Fez. The forbidding ranges of the Rif Mountains on the Mediterranean and the vast High Atlas chain harbored dissident Berbers, while pirates from the Barbary Coast had long felt free to attack European shipping. At the turn of the century the country was anything but tamed, and quite different in its astonishing geographic variety from neighboring Algeria.

The golden age of a Moorish Islamic empire had lasted from the eleventh to the fifteenth century, but then, coincident with the arrival of Europeans, there began a long slide downward. In 1900 Morocco was still largely cut off from modernity. Theoretically a leader of both secular and religious realms, the sultan possessed only one gunboat, showing the limitations of his power. People supposedly under his rule were often barbaric, but so was he. One manifestation of this barbarism was the practice of the sultan and other Moroccan chieftains of proudly displaying salted heads of prisoners they had slain or mutilated.

Morocco's main towns were very primitive compared to European ones. Tangier had the most Europeans and was just across the water from Spain, but even there snake-eaters, omnipresent bribery, and polygamy abounded. Though Morocco seemed deceptively empty in large swaths, the interior capital of Fez was hard to get to (unless you wished to take your life into your hands), and had a cloistered quality, marked by narrow, dirty streets, and gates that literally shut each night. Europeans found lowland Arabs often deceitful to deal with, and in general preferred the roughly 60 percent of Moroccans considered Berber highlanders; but the latter were recalcitrant too. After the "Scramble for Africa" this closed-off country barely clung to its independence. What kept it from being absorbed by one European nation or a condominium of several—as had happened on

virtually the rest of the continent—was geography, Berber and Arab feroc-
ity, Islamic hostility to Christian Europeans, the lack of any compelling
material inducement here, except for strategic location, and intrapower
bickering. A final aid was the division in France between a gradualist Quai
d'Orsay and colonial soldiers, particularly on the Algerian frontier, who
were eager to teach Morocco military lessons via incursions.[30]

Between 1875 and 1894 a fairly strong sultan, Moulai-Hassan, had been
able to control the forces of centrifugal anarchy that made Morocco so
volatile; but on the death of that potentate, the country became even more
potentially explosive. A child king Abdul Aziz took over in 1894 and until
1900 the real ruler was the Grand Vizier Ba-Ahmed. After the vizier's death
there followed an unusual favorite, the Scotsman "Kaid" Maclean. The
young sultan became corrupted by modern leisure toys like bicycles, ten-
nis rackets, and cameras, and by the presence of plentiful British soldiers
of fortune. But traditionalists in the Maghreb worried about a European
dilution of Islamic doctrine and began an anti-European, anti-Christian
campaign, especially Bou-Hamara, nicknamed the Rogui (or "Pretender"),
who called himself the sultan of all dissident tribes. From 1902, when he
returned to Morocco after trips through Tunisia and Algeria, the Rogui's
popularity grew by leaps and bounds; he was supposed to possess mirac-
ulous, Rasputin-like powers, and many peasants believed in his magic. In
Algeria's border country he became a powerhouse, along with the Algerian
guerilla leader Bou-Amama. More and more believed the Rogui's claims
to be Allah's true sultan. He also kept a plentiful supply of salted heads,
and was an adept collector of arms money, not only from Algerian Arabs,
but from Spanish businessmen desiring minerals concessions. The puerile
Abdul Aziz underestimated him, and at the end of 1902 his troops were
soundly defeated en route to Taza. In the following years the Rogui,
making Taza his base, kept eluding the sultan, gaining more influence,
particularly in northeastern Morocco. Dissident mountain tribes of the
bled el-siba (unpacified regions) were also seduced. And there were other
nailers of the sultan's coffin, like the adventurer Moulai el Raisuni. By 1905
the sultan was even challenged by his half-brother, and Morocco was in a
state of true anarchy.[31]

For some time the French had considered occupying parts of this unstable land, but governments and minds at home were divided. In the
post-Bismarckian era Germany wasn't keen on such moves either, and the
English waited until 1904 to disabuse themselves completely of the idea of
Morocco becoming a second Egypt.

As for Lyautey, he hoped to subdue the influence of both the Rogui and Bou-Amama, the two most influential rabble-rousers, then apply his method in this tumultuous border region. Happily, Jonnart helped him bypass the métropole's usual regulations and restrictions. Lyautey's commandant at Oran, a divisional general he would eventually replace, also seconded his efforts.[32] These men were important allies in Lyautey's war with Paris, and against government rules, he occupied Béchar, south of Aïn-Sefra, but just inside Moroccan territory. Hastily renaming it Colomb for a French officer killed in the area, Lyautey was allowed to hold it—somehow Parisian authorities trusted that "Colomb" was in Algeria! Later it was called Colomb-Béchar, and from this strategic post, holding the key to the region's mountain passes, Lyautey could more effectively hamper marauders.

In June 1904 Bou-Amama left that southern region and migrated up to northern Morocco's Ras-el-Aïn (or Berguent), a watering town providing a convenient jumping-off point for operations southward. Lyautey immediately reassured people there that he would protect them by military occupation. But the sultan complained to French representatives in Fez, Paris ordered the Algerian governor-general to force Lyautey's evacuation from Berguent, and the latter predictably blew a fuse. Withdrawal, he felt, would gravely loosen French influence over the region's people, who would also be prey to the Rogui's and Bou-Amama's savage revenge. He warned the War Ministry (July 1904) that this could become a scene of utter disaster. Paris shot back that its order stood, only he might withdraw his troops in gradual stages. Lyautey's ever quick temper now prompted him to threaten resignation, an old Gallieni stratagem. Simultaneously, he asked Jonnart for help, finally locating him on vacation in Belgium. Hurrying to Paris, Jonnart impressed upon Prime Minister Combes the gravity of losing Lyautey's inspiring presence on an unstable colonial frontier. After a few months of deliberation the battle was won, and France's army was permitted to remain there in tandem with the sultan's troops.

In this Saharan area many Arabs were now taking to Lyautey's dramatically noble ways—including a purple and gold burnous he wore over his uniform and a tiger skin on his saddle. He had his desired foothold in Morocco (who knew where that might lead?), and his soldiers were infected as well by his bee-like activity. Lyautey's letters homeward flew out thick, fast, and elegant. His post at Aïn-Sefra was really a court, and he comported himself there like a feudal seigneur. Galloping around on fine horses with the fancy saddle and billowy burnous, he seemed to be making himself into a hybrid sort of lord not readily found elsewhere in the French military hierarchy.

By the end of 1905 a string of fortified posts protected the Algerian borderlands. Formerly a dangerous area, the South Oranais was now at relative peace, and visiting French politicians were impressed by Lyautey's accomplishments. Harvests were secure, the Arabs more loyal, and Lyautey's new law courts made even recalcitrant Berbers more amenable. The French foreign minister Théophile Delcassé, once opposed to Lyautey, found himself defeated.

One of the key reasons Lyautey did so well here was his unusual openness and sensitivity to Arabs and Islam, and his studious engagement with the language. Early in his career we saw how he had worked hard to learn Arabic. From his first trips to Algeria, he loved sitting on Arab mats, drinking their strong coffee, eating their food, and adopting parts of their garb. In Morocco he would even go to hear court cases in Arabic.[33]

Which again should make us qualify the way we generally conceive of Western imperialism. Too few see colonies as places that modified or attenuated European preconceptions; but that is exactly what happened to Lyautey abroad, for he became tolerant and even admiring of certain aspects of Islam, and of other religions such as Judaism. In a letter of 1903 to Paul Desjardins from Aïn-Sefra, he exulted: "The more I advance, the more I feel I'm liberating myself; each year I have the pleasure of casting off a prejudice."[34]

Meanwhile, on the international stage, France and Britain had now set aside differences, forming an entente, which henceforth allowed France a free hand in Morocco. But the aggressive Germans wanted to be heard from on these developments. One result was their challenge of France's special role in Morocco, and the conference they instigated on the matter at the Spanish town of Algeciras (January-April 1906). But the conference only confirmed France's significant relationship with the Maghreb. Things were looking up for Lyautey too. In 1907 he became divisional commanding general at Oran, with jurisdiction over the entire frontier and of operations into Morocco.

However, Morocco continued its anarchic ways and early in 1908 there was fighting at the gates of Casablanca, as well as throughout the entire Chaouia region. The weak Abdul Aziz had lost too many followers; his half-brother Moulai Hafid, egged on by a powerful kingmaker, Madani el-Glaoui, was a stronger, more traditional Islamic proponent of jihad, and many flocked to his side. Attacks on French and other foreigners in

Morocco increased, so Lyautey occupied another chunk of land around Oujda, the capital of northeastern Morocco, and supported a progressive occupation of the entire Chaouia led by General d'Amade. On trips home to see Prime Minister Clemenceau, who understood such *enfants terribles*, Lyautey pushed his policies. In May 1908 Lyautey became France's first high commissioner for the entire Moroccan-Algerian frontier, giving him greater power to work with local authorities on both sides of the border, centralize the police, and so forth. By the summer of 1908 he had eastern Morocco more or less in Gallic tow; but western Morocco remained unstable. A massacre of French workers in Casablanca and the final flight of Sultan Abdul Aziz to a French pension in Tangier, allowing a more anti-European Moulai Hafid to take the throne in August 1908, charged the atmosphere even more. The Rogui then challenged the new sultan, until caught, caged, and murdered in September 1909. To fight such rebels, Moulai Hafid burdened himself with unpayable debts.[35]

Through 1908–09 Lyautey still had to battle the Quai d'Orsay, as well as French authorities in Tangier. He also had to contend with jealousy of his special powers as High Commissioner, especially emanating from General Bailloud, a commander in Algiers. At one point, frustrated and depressed, Lyautey apparently considered suicide. But the Rogui's fall and more revolts allowed French reoccupation of Moroccan positions they had given up, making his spirits soar again in 1910. Certainly he had done the essential here, pacifying and organizing the Algerian-Moroccan frontier—a job that now seemed basically completed. He was in fact quite satisfied to return to France as commander of the 10th Army Corps at Rennes, knowing he might never return.

Before doing so, Lyautey decided to wed on October 14, 1909 Madame Inès Fortoul, the widow of an artillery colonel who was the son of Napoleon III's Education Minister. Madame Fortoul had two sons in the army, was President of the French Red Cross, having just organized a branch in Casablanca, and possessed enough intelligence and vigor to make Lyautey a fine companion. It had been a long time coming. Lyautey had considered himself too idealistic and obsessive to make a decent husband, and of course he was often out in the middle of nowhere. Perhaps the fear of suffocation, deriving from childhood, and an early surfeit of feminine attention, may have played its role in this deferral of marriage.[36] But here he was at the ripe age of fifty-five, contracting what André le Révérend has called a "mariage de raison." However Le Révérend also notes how close these two minds and souls were, and how much of a "First Lady" Madame

Lyautey became when he reached the colonial heights, not only occupying herself with maternity wards and old folks' homes, but indefatigable
as well on horseback in the countryside.[37]

A remarkable source on Inès' mentality has been ignored by historians:
her papers, which show her from early on to have been, like Lyautey, a
keen student in school, lauded especially for long, spirited compositions.
There is also a massive correspondence there between her and her late
husband Joseph Fortoul, who served in the Tonkin between December
1882 and 1885. Inès' letters to that terribly missed husband run to perhaps
1,000 pages! And they are marvelous—full of anguish from the moment
he drove away from her in Vincennes. In her words these letters are one
long sob, in which she simply can't shake the sadness of being "left"—
an imperial or wartime predicament historians have too often bypassed
(though older feminists like Helena Swanwick didn't). This mother of two
small children mentions her liver problems, violent headaches, fevered
dreams of an absent husband getting killed in battle, and suicidal thoughts;
but she also professes her deep love constantly, filling the pages with clear,
bold handwriting. Like Lyautey's epistles, hers are often long but never
dull. Whenever she sent a letter she felt was on the short side, she apologized profusely. In sum, Inès was an emotional, sensitive, aware person,
and like her celebrated new husband, always gilding the lily, feeling she
had never given enough. No wonder they were drawn to each other.[38]

All that notwithstanding, Douglas Porch has quite aggressively signalled
what for him was the real reason for Lyautey's longtime deferral of marriage: his putative homosexuality. There is no question that the imperial
adventure was made for outsiders of all sorts, and that abroad, one *could*
get away from the prying eyes and ears of France's *esprit de clocher*. But
Porch offers little concrete evidence and no conclusive footnote on the
matter, and it seemed to have little bearing on our story, until a French
tome appeared on this subject in 1998, seductively titled *Lyautey-Charlus*
(Charlus being a homosexual character in Proust's *Remembrance of Things
Past*). The author, Christian Gury, is a French lawyer and amateur literary
historian, and his book is in large part a profuse pasta of quotations,
almost all of which seem to have no or at best, tangential relevance to his
single-tracked theme. Those quotes run the gamut from André Gide to
Joan Rivers! Chatty, intellectual, cynical, and ultimately tedious, Gury also
uses some of the same quotations we have chosen from Lyautey's writings—on his love of beauty, poetry, Arab decor, the young and their potential; but twirling and twisting these, he really misses Lyautey's essence, as

he would have Gallieni's, and more, the entire character of an era. That Lyautey was theatrical, that he loved pomp and circumstance—no question. But that he cared about larger matters, that he wanted to build and ameliorate life for many people, that he was truly intelligent, intuitive, and prescient politically, and unusually industrious—none of this appears here. As for the *pièce de résistance*, the fact that Proust and Lyautey for a time had frequented the same salons, and that Proust may have put something of Lyautey's face or gestures (but how much is open to a variety of interpretations) into Charlus—again, this fisherman never quite gets into port with his catch. Whatever he in fact *was*, Lyautey certainly demonstrated much more in his actions than what Gury's book suggests.[39]

Of course Lyautey's social class *was* a kind of prison, and like the aristocratic hero and heroine respectively of two great Somerset Maugham short stories who fall for servants ("The Treasure" and "The Human Element"), Lyautey probably needed someone "other" for the possibility of a liaison. Previous to his marriage to an aristocrat, who like him, was idiosyncratic for her class, one should mention Lyautey's link to Isabelle Eberhardt, a Russian woman of mixed Armenian-German-Jewish heritage who grew up in Geneva, wandered through Europe, migrated to Algeria, smoked *kif,* took a medley of lovers, converted to Islam, then married and eventually discarded a *spahi* sergeant. Dressed in mannish clothes, Eberhardt nomadically wandered around the South Oranais, where her rebellious nature and searching intellectualism drew her to Lyautey. For several months they had all-night sessions, at the least of talk, until a flood blew away her house and took her already unhealthy life in late October 1904. But Lyautey also used Eberhardt's supposedly "maraboutic" powers for diplomatic links to Arab chieftains, and his work always came first.[40]

After his departure from North Africa, Oran's Chamber of Commerce compared Lyautey's legacy to that of his illustrious predecessor, Bugeaud.[41] Back in France, and doubtless sobered by the influence of marriage, he seemed determined now to play by the army's rules, volunteering to take a course to prepare him for his command position in Rennes. Rennes was the decidedly un-Parisian, Breton city where from the beginning of 1911 Lyautey would enjoy a year and a quarter of respite, commanding his corps and considering a move upward toward the General Staff, under his old associate, Joffre.

But in Morocco, tribal leaders continued to gang up on the new Sultan Moulai Hafid, especially in Fez. A rival sultan besieged that town, adding influential French voices to the call for a protectorate. The new French foreign minister was inexperienced enough to defer to a new war minister, Maurice Berteaux, who in turn was nudged by a leading colonial propagandist, Eugène Etienne. (Berteaux would soon be nudged as well by an airplane wing while watching an aviation exercise, and be killed in the process.) Finally, the French decided to reply militarily to the Siege of Fez, arriving in May 1911, ending the siege, then marching out against a new pretender, Moulai Zayn. Had they used this turmoil merely as justification for the implementation of a Moroccan protectorate, which would then link up with both Algeria and Tunisia, creating a formidable French North Africa?

Certainly the Germans thought so, and in July of that year their famous gunboat *Panther* steamed to Agadir on Morocco's Atlantic coast to challenge the French, and to blackmail them. In order to avert war, France reluctantly awarded Germany a slice of its Congo, and by an agreement of November 1911, the Germans henceforth permitted French control of Morocco, pleasing neither public at home, and fueling an imminent descent toward world war. But with Germany no longer a threat, the French by 1912 were finally ready to impose a protectorate over the majority of an unruly Morocco (mainly English pressure would get Spain a smaller piece in the northeastern part). After threatening abdication, Sultan Moulai Hafid at Fez was forced to accept by the end of March, after which riots again convulsed that city and the countryside.

Due to this more serious "Second Siege of Fez," the new French War Minister, Alexandre Millerand, as well as Prime Minister Poincaré knew they needed to appoint a first Resident-General of Morocco with real military and diplomatic ability. After some debate they finally chose Lyautey over General d'Amade, another fine colonial soldier, and it would become the role of a lifetime.

Departing from Marseille, and after a stop in Algeria, proceeding to Casablanca, an enthused Lyautey recruited talented French soldiers en route, giving them new assignments. Like Bugeaud or Gallieni he was not one to wait. Via Meknès his group found its way to besieged Fez, where the new resident-general contemplated swift reprisals, then began his usual policy of making friends with local notables. He met with the sultan, but while at a ball that evening the bullets began flying. By the next morning French artillery had miraculously driven away the rebels, yet the neurasthenic Moulai Hafid, increasingly seduced by the possibility of abdication and living off a French pension away from this murderous wasp's nest, began complaining. Lyautey tried to rally him and the Quai d'Orsay trembled—for the protectorate was not yet accepted by all European governments; but Hafid was bent on locating the easy life. Lyautey investigated another brother to replace him, Moulai Yussef, a quiet, religious type; and after negotiations, the deal was made. A smooth departure of Hafid was engineered for a cheering populace, and he left Fez in August 1912. With a new sultan installed, inaugurating a tradition of loyalty to France that would persist through two world wars, Lyautey set up his resident-general's headquarters in Rabat, and so began another era of feverish activity.

Here the old Lorrainer had found his quintessential milieu and imperial zenith. Possibly due to the steadying influence of marriage, and certainly to the extensive responsibilities he now had, this was the most pragmatic period he would know—stretching from the assumption of the protectorate in 1912 through a problematic and often militarily costly wartime period to his departure from Morocco in 1925. In the words of Jean Martin, Lyautey "would write in this country he so loved the finest page in French colonial history," ultimately transforming an anarchic, primitive cauldron into a more orderly and prosperous modern nation.[42]

Lyautey's first worry here was riotous Fez—its abandonment beyond discussion, as he wrote from the besieged city; but by the summer of 1912 that problem seemed under control. Revolts in the south under a new pretender, el-Hiba, then threatened Marrakech, to which Lyautey went with the new sultan, bringing a healing touch to the city. El-Hiba's men promptly took flight. By 1913 Lyautey had one Moroccan area completely pacified, a second semi-pacified, and a third still unconquered. His methods of indirect rule emphasized alliances with *grands caïds*, especially the lords of the Atlas in the south who controlled passes through the mountains. He also surrounded himself with topflight French military-administrative talent, including three tough colonels (at that point), Charles Mangin, Henri Gouraud, and Paul Henrÿs, as well as three others who had followed him from his days in Aïn-Sefra. Lyautey foresaw continuing resistance in the Middle Atlas Mountains, and hoped to hold on to a line that would prevent its spread into "useful Morocco." French forays against Zaïan Berber resistance in that area began under Henrÿs, while the aggressive Mangin, future "butcher" of World War I, outran Lyautey's leash to the south, eventually grabbing Kasbah Tadla against his wishes. (Imperialists still making it up as they went along!) Stung by critiques at home, Lyautey impelled General Franchet d'Espérey to rein in Mangin, but both would soon be in Europe anyway.

Meanwhile Berber resistance continued to the north, and in the spring of 1914 a French march began toward Taza. This was the crucial point at which eastern Morocco was cut off from the west by rebel tribes that held Taza, and this "last stone of the French edifice in North Africa" was taken in May 1914, seemingly uniting a Gallic Algeria and Morocco. But the tough Zaïans of the Middle Atlas continued to resist French hegemony. That spring-summer Henrÿs again had to advance against them, shakily taking Khénifra, then punching outward from there. The Zaïans kept retreating into the Middle Atlas, and Henrÿs looked forward to winter, forcing them down to the plains. (It strikes one how tenacious these French soldiers were at their nation's fragile zenith!)[43]

Seeing proverbial light at the end of the military tunnel, Lyautey simultaneously began work in Morocco on things he cared about—a proper justice system, new buildings to be harmonized with local traditions, construction of roads and railways, and development of the modern port city of Casablanca. A first major loan from the French government was finally approved in 1914, to be paid back in sixty-five years at 4.6 percent interest. As his nephew Pierre Lyautey put it, the resident-general was "working twenty hours out of twenty-four," and by 1914 French Morocco seemed on the edge of a tenuous stability. Lyautey, with black and silver burnous flowing on the purebred horse he rode, and with his seigneur's court, was certainly popular with many of its inhabitants.[44]

Then came the outbreak of World War I, France's greatest challenge perhaps in its history, and a significant one for Lyautey's Morocco as well. On hearing the news of a generalized conflict, he was one of the few Europeans to consider it immediately as disastrous. In his own colonial bailiwick redoubts like Taza and Khénifra would rapidly become vulnerable, and all of Lyautey's talents as a great persuader would be necessary to hold Morocco, soon to be denuded of numerous soldiers bound for the trenches. Another problem was that in but a few years under the protectorate, a French population of immigrants searching the good life had quickly grown. A positive consequence was the wartime recruitment of many of these middle-aged civilians to man regiments and at least *appear* to locals like real soldiers. Lyautey's regional commanders, Generals Brulard, Gouraud, and (now) Henrÿs, fought Zaïan Berbers and others, crisscrossing the land, and trying to maintain peace in bellicose areas. Unfortunately, they frequently had only attenuated or amateurish effectives at their disposal.

Brutally put, the French idea was now to hold positions of the pacified areas in Morocco, avoiding as best they could more costly military engagements in an unpacified *bled el-siba*. More than ever it was the time for Lyautey's "politique des grands caïds"—disarming local populations and vesting in Arab or Berber notables enhanced power under a beneficent French umbrella. But this only worked with real efficacy in areas south of Marrakech, or in cities like Casablanca. Lyautey had the good sense to abandon ideas of conquering tough mountain areas, and finally too, the eastern Tafilalet, an oasis region near Algeria that the French had initially thought they could absorb. But his fears about holding onto any French presence in wartime Morocco never abated.[45]

At least an over-burdened Paris henceforth allowed him a mostly free hand in the protectorate, and money for buildings, roads, or railways became easier to procure. Given the gigantic amounts being spent on artillery or uniforms in Europe, these sums now seemed pittances to the home ministries. Staggering urban transformation resulted—especially in centers like Rabat. Writers like Fanon would be critical of what Lyautey considered essential to the protectorate: building European agglomerations outside medinas, thereby allowing the old to coexist with the new. Even in new architectural creations, Lyautey supervised the blending of traditional Moorish with more European motifs.

To guarantee security in the protectorate during wartime, Lyautey closely surveyed German consulates, nationals, and agents in North Africa. In full view of the local people he used German prisoners-of-war to help construct roads, showing continued French strength. His persistent fear was of German propaganda emanating from the Spanish part of Morocco and really from neutral Spain itself, just across the water. Already the Spanish had given him trouble before the war concerning the projected building of a French railway line from Fez to Tangier. Now the Germans, he alleged, were blackmailing these Spanish, who were unusually weak. He also feared a "Germano-Islamic" linkage, seemingly dangerous because of the entry of Turkey into the war, and the growth of Constantinople as a base for propaganda operations throughout North Africa.[46]

Despite his talent for dissimulation, Lyautey knew that some Moroccan leaders would notice how weakened France was militarily, and he felt their agitation might make a dangerous harvest. Among those leaders was the pampered former sultan, Abdul Aziz, whom Lyautey had supported in his dark days of 1907–8. Aziz now represented one center of opposition

against both the French and Moulai Yussef, particularly in the mountainous north, where some were again proclaiming him sultan. In internation-
alized Tangier his presence was a danger; Lyautey warned the Spanish that
they should not receive him as royalty, for he could truly stir up pro-
German sentiments in Morocco. The man was a congenital liar agitating
potential dissidents, and still in contact with the rebel leader, el-Hiba.
Moulai Hafid, the other former sultan and Abdul Aziz's brother, seemed
a less dangerous threat. His neglect of Islamic customs made him un-
popular with Moroccans, who also remembered his cruelty and heavy
taxes. He was now traveling in Spain, hoping to elude French surveillance,
and Lyautey flatly warned the French Foreign Ministry that it would be
best to nab him as soon as possible, keeping him in France for the rest of
the war.[47]

The German-Turk alliance and "German-Islamic" propaganda would
remain key preoccupations for Lyautey throughout the conflict. Frantically, he beseeched Paris not to underestimate his repeated telegrams on
the subject. When the Turks proclaimed a Holy War, the paradoxical result
was the firming up of Moroccan support on purely religious grounds for
the French army![48]

Yet the protectorate in this era was by no means out of the woods. As
1915 wore on, so many French and native soldiers had been sent to Europe
that "only degenerates and outcasts" (as Lyautey called them) remained
in Morocco. Exhausted, he wrote the War Minister Millerand on June 11,
1915 of France's fragility in Morocco. "You have no idea of the daily effort
I must make with the sultan," he declared, "and with the *grands caïds*
and tribes, to maintain their confidence in our ultimate success." Because
of the Turkish threat, material and moral erosion of the military in the
French protectorate was dangerous. But that very fragility, as noted, helped
get Lyautey the funds he needed to keep building. His old romanticism
and poetic lyricism were mainly on hold now. As he said at the outset of
the war, "no more dreams but construction sites." And some would indeed
see the Morocco of Lyautey's tenure as one large construction project,
including the building of a modern port of Casablanca. But the Resident
still feared what would accompany this sudden modernization—too many
immigrants, too many money-seekers. He also continued to fear the erosion of indirect rule; the Moroccan model was still better than the Algerian one, he declared, and a bill before the French Chamber in 1915 offering
potential citizenship to all native soldiers from the three North African
colonies struck him as wrong-headed. His view was that *indigènes* must

be allowed to remain who they were in terms of customs or religion. The French were not here to assimilate.[49]

On a trip to the mainland in 1915 to pressure the government for a loan, Lyautey saw close-up Joffre's tragically ill-conceived military leadership. He had no illusions about the high command, especially after visiting the front and witnessing the human cost of a *guerre à outrance*. Lyautey had himself lost many close friends and family members to the slaughter. By late 1916, with the protracted tragedies of Verdun and the Somme concluding, the Moroccan Resident's ability to organize, streamline, and improvise looked attractive to a beleaguered French government. Back in Morocco, he received a surprising telegram of December 1916 from Prime Minister Briand, asking him to become France's new war minister. His temporary replacement as resident-general would be General Gouraud. With mixed emotions, Lyautey hesitated, then like his now dead mentor Gallieni, reluctantly accepted, taking a submarine over to Gibraltar, followed by a train ride through Spain, and up to a French political arena he had always loathed.

And indeed, he soon found himself hampered in Paris by new regulations, making the position of war minister something of a committee. In such an atmosphere he simply couldn't be himself. General Nivelle's confident plan for one more assault on the Aisne left him deeply shaken, and in early 1917 Lyautey tried in vain to warn Poincaré and Briand of its insanity. But the war minister's days were filled with paralyzing audiences—deputies, senators, prefects, ministers—that angered and distracted him. At a conference in Rome, he witnessed Allied disunity and a continuing ignorance of battle conditions. Already in January he thought of resigning his post, unless reforms gave him more power; but too many cooks spoiled the broth here, and after only eleven weeks in his position, Lyautey engineered his own fall by refusing to share military secrets with Parliament, some of whose members hooted his speech on the subject. That very day he penned a resignation statement, vacating the War Ministry in mid-March. Taking the cure at Vichy, Lyautey then left to regain his post as Morocco's Resident, at a time when Nivelle's failed offensive had produced another pile of needless casualties and for the first time, serious French mutinies. By the end of May Lyautey arrived back in Casablanca, and was soon reensconced at his familiar helm in Rabat.[50]

But wartime problems dragged on in Morocco. Lyautey mentions costly skirmishes around the country, including with persistent, if disunited Zaïans; a continuing dearth of good soldiers, which necessitated the creation of native-staffed *goums* (auxiliaries); and the enduring influence of

German-Islamic propaganda. Apparently the Germans were still plying dissident sheikhs with money, and working different areas. Typical German propaganda tracts found in Morocco during the last year of the war included one printed in Damascus: "Rise up, oh servants of God, the Most High has called for a holy war. Drive these French dogs from your country!" But by the end of the conflict this hadn't occurred, in good part due to Lyautey's policies.[51]

During the *après-guerre* era Morocco became a popular French colony to visit or read about, and what one might call the Age of Babar began—not least in an explosion of popular novels, travel accounts, or children's books on all of North Africa, greedily gobbled up by a French métropole proud (save for the far Left) of what intrepid Frenchmen had accomplished there. People now found it conveniently easy to travel to this new, relatively safe part of the empire. Casablanca was a large, prosperous port with a vertiginously growing amount of tonnage handled, and the discovery and exploitation of seemingly unlimited phosphate deposits in other parts of the protectorate promised riches. In a time of economic take-off, Lyautey had to invite and make his peace with big French industrial and financial concerns. A laudatory report of February 19, 1921 emanating from France's current war minister, Louis Barthou, called Morocco's Resident one of the great artisans of French colonial glory.[52]

In the same year Lyautey became a marshal of France, enhancing his celebrity status; but he himself was far from sure of anything like final stability in the protectorate. A series of letters he wrote to Henry de Castries after World War I reveal his increasing pessimism. There were still a number of revolts to suppress and areas needing pacification or repacification. And because of French manpower problems, occupation troops had to be downsized after the war, with as many as 40 percent now Africans. Lyautey kept telling the ministries back home that eventually more and more would take over here; but he also saw that sheer misery might attract recruits of doubtful quality and for dubious reasons. Lyautey's problematic health, already experienced during the war period, when he had suffered from "angio-colite" marked by fevers, shivering, vomiting, and chronic dysentery, continued as well into the early 1920s. Afflicted with liver and gall bladder trouble, he at one point seemed near death, and Moroccans prayed ardently in their mosques, while he went to Paris for an operation.[53]

Nearing the end of an illustrious colonial career, Lyautey feared that his departure would signal the "Algerianization" of Morocco and relegation of inhabitants there to the status of second-class pawns. There was even talk of unifying the three North African entities under a single administration, which made him irate. Short of that, there was much pressure to make administration more direct and to allay settlers' land hunger. Often prescient, Lyautey feared French underestimation of Islam in the twentieth century, hoping that France would continue to protect Moroccan religious customs and institutions, partly via a complex court system that respected not only sultanic and Islamic law, but also Berber and Jewish law, as well as that of the French. A new Native Policy Council in the protectorate debated how to do these things. Other problems it had to contend with included the naming of *caïds*, as well as economic resentments in Fez vis-à-vis more prosperous coastal cities and commercially competitive towns near French army emplacements (like Taza and Meknès). Yet another problem was upgrading the education of Moroccan elites and ordinary people. Debates on such matters, including with his right-hand man, Urbain Blanc, were taxing to Lyautey. The man who had made a positive impression both on French colonial soldiers, as well as on many, if not all Berbers and Arabs, still found himself on prickly terms with official Paris. "I feel that among them," he wrote, "from the Elysée Palace to Finances and the War Ministry, through the Quai d'Orsay, there is no one from whom one can hope for a hearing. It's just a void."[54]

During this bittersweet era in his life Lyautey seemed to take stock, and though he had already done genealogical work during the Belle Epoque, he brought it all together after the war in a Proustian romp called *Souvenirs de famille* .... No one has gone deeply enough psychologically here. If Lyautey was exhaustive writing about his various ancestors, great-grandparents, uncles, aunts, and so on, it was partly because in adulthood he had never replicated the warmth of a childhood in a large extended family. Being childless, he perhaps wanted to populate his present with numerous people of the past. Was there not also a wish here for the justification of his *sui generis* complex? And for a good situation in posterity's longer view?

In the hundreds of pages that we have in his papers, Lyautey is marvelous on the complex social classes in his background, which influenced him: open-hearted nobility prone to self-ruin, peasantry vaulting into the bourgeoisie, etc. He is marvelous as well on different regional influences, showing his pride at not having a drop of blood in him from south of the Loire! He knows which people (mainly Lyauteys) had fewer political proclivities, which ones were artsier (mainly his mother's side), which were

womanizers, and who had suffered in the Revolution (including the guillotine). The apogee of that thronged childhood lovingly discussed here was
a celebration at Montrambert of grandmother and grandfather Lyautey,
for whom Hubert was the favorite grandchild. He remembers in detail
what everyone wore and what everyone did there. In fact, he remembers
everything! About one of his great-uncles, flattened by the 1870–71 debacle,
he notes that his finger was henceforth stuck on a page of Thiers describing Napoleon's glorious battle of Jena.

One tragic event that crucified Lyautey, as he put it, but which also
quickened this Proustian desire to memorialize was destruction of the
family home early in World War I, where Lyautey had transferred the
bulk of his papers and material reminders of his past: Crévic in Lorraine.
Knowing the name Lyautey, the Germans had apparently asked directions
to the chateau, then dousing it with gas, leveled it by fire. As a boy Hubert
had spent vacations there with extended family, then unfortunately, made
it the repository between 1911–13 of all he had carefully collected, partly
so that he could leave it intact to a favorite nephew, Pierre. Now it was
gone, but a remarkable eighty-seven-page memoir he wrote after the war
details everything that was once there, room by room! This included pictures, swords, canes, even a crutch Lyautey had used as an incapacitated
child. It also included correspondence with Gallieni, and many books left
to him by a variety of family members, and which he had once lovingly
read. It included correspondence between his parents and earlier family
letters; a drawer full of *assignats,* the currency of the Revolution; a Louis
XV desk, pistols, and many other mementos of historical and personal
significance. In the way he had of always gilding the lily, Lyautey seemed
to recall virtually all he had once owned. Was this need for *objets* again a
kind of sublimated wish for children?[55]

Whatever it was, the loss of Crévic, combined with postwar problems in
Morocco, and declining health made the Resident wish to retire on a number of occasions. Key challenges inducing Lyautey to stay a little longer in
colonial harness were the military delineation of a "useful Morocco," then
the outbreak of a surprising Rif revolt, originating in Spanish Morocco,
which comprised only 7,700 square miles (the French zone extended to
over 154,000). The frontier between the two protectorates was rugged,
mountainous, and often ignored by Moroccans, and consequently, France
would become involved in a rebellion that in principle was directed solely
against Spain from this alpine terrain.[56]

When war broke out in the Rif, Lyautey's eventual opponent was a man who had little initial desire to take on France as well. Mohamed ben Abd el-Krim el Kattabi had been born around 1882 in a village near the Mediterranean. He and his younger brother then attended Spanish schools in Melilla, setting them above those schooled in the Rif, and Abd el-Krim became one of the few pupils from there to attend university at Fez; his brother, a bright young man, went to Madrid to study mining engineering. This education certainly gave them elite status.[57]

By 1914 their father had become an outspoken opponent of Spanish administrative practices in the Rif, and though he supported Spain's army against a German-instigated revolt during the war, the Spanish considered him dispensable. When he died an unpleasant death after a meal of poisoned eggs in September 1920, Spanish authorities took credit for the deed. They apparently thought his death would end Rif agitation against their rule, but reckoned without his gallant sons.[58]

In the summer of 1921 Abd el-Krim, invoking the memory of that dead father, began his revolt against Spain with an army of between 3,000 and 6,000 Moroccans. Thus began the protracted and bloody Rif War, mounted against a country whose great colonial days were over, and which hadn't taken its portion of Morocco as seriously as the French, clinging only to coastal agglomerations.[59]

Against Abd el-Krim Spain could deploy a force of 70,000 plus future reinforcements from the mother country. But their irregulars inflicted two devastating defeats on the Spaniards, enabling him to proclaim a Rifian republic in 1922. He was also supported by British mining interests looking for concessions in the Rif, and by anti-Lyautey French leftists, hoping for a diminution of their country's colonial empire. At a cost of many lives, the Spanish failed to dislodge Abd el-Krim in 1923, and under the dictatorial General Primo de Rivera, their disaster continued through 1924. By then Rivera considered giving up Spanish Morocco itself, but France would now become involved, and the war henceforth took on a different character.

How did this occur? One problem was that the territory Abd el-Krim claimed for his Rif republic crossed a poorly defined boundary between Spanish and French Morocco. When border villages inside the French zone began supporting Abd el-Krim in 1924, Lyautey grew apprehensive, yet counseled against direct military action. His garrison in Morocco had been reduced to 65,000 men, and Henri Poeymirau, his most energetic subordinate since assuming General Henrÿ's command in 1916, died of septicemia that year, after having sustained a grave battle wound several years earlier. But the colonial lobby in Paris wanted Abd el-Krim put out of business, whereas to Lyautey, nothing would be more likely to make the man a North African hero than a French attack![60]

Abd el-Krim himself seemed ambivalent about combat against French soldiers, issuing statements like the following: "I recognize that the French have given Morocco order, security, and economic prosperity; but I shall bring the same benefits, with the further advantage that I am a Muslim, and so it will be from a leader of their own faith, and not from an infidel, that the Moroccans shall receive these blessings."[61] France responded by directing Lyautey to put military pressure on the rebels, and he duly moved troops into a fertile agricultural region across the Ouerha River, a "police operation" compromising both Abd el-Krim's food supply and his prestige. So early in 1925, on a roll against Spain, he decided to fight the French, though a war against two European powers was hardly one he could hope to win. His strategy was to move against Fez and Taza; possession of the former would inspire all Moroccans to rally to his banner, while taking the latter would sever French communication lines.[62]

On April 13, 1925 Abd el-Krim launched an initial attack, and a few hours later, hit French posts just north of Taza. Breaking Gallic lines, the Rifians found themselves by the end of the week a mere twenty miles north of Fez. The audacity of their offensive dazzled border tribes, causing consternation among the French, who had underestimated the enemy, partly due to their contempt for the Spanish army it had been fighting.[63]

Lyautey, however, was no underestimator of anyone, and demanded reinforcements from Paris. Replying sharply with what he had, his military direction kept Abd el-Krim from taking either Fez or Taza.[64] During the remainder of 1925 fighting consisted primarily of skirmishes and raids, irritating but not fatal to the French cause; and a typhus epidemic in the Rif also hurt the rebels.

But engagements remained savage, and Rifian rebels manifested no benevolence toward the enemy. In an assault on France's post at Aulai, three weeks of incessant mortar fire reduced defenders to a catatonic state, with attackers throwing battered French corpses under the windows of blockhouses so that they might decompose within sight and smell of the garrison. Being captured meant standard treatment at the hands of Rif warriors: systematic mutilation, followed by death from slashing.[65]

These favored mutilations—lest we ignore what still occurs in the Middle East—included gouging out eyes, chopping off fingers and toes, and filling the mouths of corpses with torn-off genitals. Of course the Spanish routinely severed the heads and genitals of *their* victims too. French and Spanish planes were also willing to bomb villages whose sole occupants they knew to be women and children, and to shell towns when people were attending evening prayers at the mosque. One should add that the summer of 1925 was a very hot one, with daytime temperatures often exceeding 120 degrees Fahrenheit. That heat took its toll on both Europeans and Rifians, but probably hurt the latter most.[66]

By late June France had finally stabilized the situation, and negotiations opened in June 1925 in Madrid. Lyautey had always wished to cooperate with Spain, and the two countries now agreed to allow each other's forces pursuit of the enemy across their respective zones. But with the prospect of protracted negotiations the war dragged on. In June Abd el-Krim threatened Taza, Lyautey ordered all Europeans evacuated, and the French held the line. Taza's defense owed a good deal to a flamboyant Gallic warrior, Captain Henry de Bournazel, who dared the Rifians to kill him by wearing a bright red tunic in action. Bournazel was an anachronistic throwback to the age of chivalry, attracted to Morocco like many by Lyautey's model. Impatient with his own country's limitations, he had arrived in 1921 and rapidly fallen in love with North Africa's endless horizons, the Arab language, and action in battles, where he became a legend. Moroccans would say that bullets ricocheted off him and back at the enemy, and that he possessed the *baraka* later imputed to Bigeard in Algeria. But such *baraka* or good fortune was not ubiquitous, and many French posts fell into rebel hands. Rif rebels were able thereby to capture sizable stocks of munitions and guns.[67]

Paris was now ready to take these rebels seriously, but not to dispatch necessary reinforcements without examining the situation on the spot. The chief reason was growing dissatisfaction with the most important figure in French Morocco: Lyautey himself.[68]

For the French high command of the mid-1920s now held the aging colonial in some contempt, considering him a dinosaur whose tactics in Africa were outmoded holdovers from a simpler time before the Great War. Their desire was to put to use lessons they had learned fighting the Germans in World War I, and they had only lagged on that because of their underestimation of both the Rifians and their Spanish foes.[69]

In July 1925 Parisian authorities sent a generalissimo of the French armies, the great war hero Philippe Pétain, to Morocco as inspector general, and Pétain endorsed Lyautey's pleas for reinforcements. On his return to France the government promised an additional 100,000 troops for Morocco.

But Pétain was interested in a more massive and extensive retaliation against the Rifians that would also repress other rebellious tribes; whereas Lyautey had been far more careful, worried about alienating Moroccan sympathies. Pétain won the day, undermining Lyautey so skillfully that the great proconsul's recall was being bruited by August. Pétain himself would return to Morocco as supreme field commander, disposing of these new troops, which added to the 200,000 deployed by the Spanish, would constitute a striking force placing the Rifs and anyone allied with them at peril.

Despite his age and health, Lyautey had the feeling of being sacrificed by his government once he had built up a relatively successful protectorate. The overly emotional prose of Jacques Benoist-Méchin on the Resident's recall has more than a grain of truth in it: "Does the Government believe it has simply relieved him of his command? A serious mistake! It has snatched away the very best part of him, his reason for living, the country without which his existence no longer has meaning."[70]

At the moment of departure, amidst the precariousness of this Rif War that bothered him deeply, Lyautey was leaving Morocco with death in his soul, as he put it. He hated all the new military organization and bureaucracy being wheeled into place, and without so much as a consultation with the old proconsul! Lyautey had a taste of what the new Morocco would be like when he talked excitedly with his successor, Pétain, shortly after the latter's arrival in 1925 to supervise military maneuvers. The departing resident-general remarked how useful it was to work on the protectorate's thorny problems after midnight, whereupon Pétain, checking the time (it was ten p.m.), said abruptly that he was going to bed.[71]

Lyautey's concerns were anything but exaggerated. From now on no one would have the enlightened power he had wielded in Morocco, due to a division that would henceforth obtain between resident-general, shorn of any army leadership role, and the supreme military command position. Lyautey's mechanisms for dealing with Moroccan leaders, such as the Direction des Affaires Indigènes, and his consultative Chambers of Commerce and Agriculture for both French and indigenous people remained in place; but residents-general who succeeded him would be more arbitrary and less sensitive to both Berbers and Arabs. The French bureaucracy would also grew precipitously—from some 6,500 functionaries in Lyautey's last year as Resident, to almost 20,000 in 1932, swallowing up 57 percent of the budget that ran the protectorate. Lyautey had inaugurated a number of taxes to supplement French loans—trading and monopoly licenses, levies for road maintenance, and taxes on consumer items like tea or sugar. Thanks to those taxes, which were quite reasonable, he had kept his colonial craft afloat and maintained solvency. But after his departure indebtedness in Morocco would rapidly worsen; the French became too comfortable with what he had done so much to create. As in other imperial fora, educational institutions Lyautey had inaugurated also helped arouse rising expectations and ultimately, nationalism in Moroccans of the elite who attended them.[72]

In early October 1925 the aging proconsul departed on a liner from Casablanca, and at Gibraltar two British torpedo boats escorted his ship into the Mediterranean, its crews applauding on deck. But Lyautey's reception in Marseille was surprisingly perfunctory—no prefect or mayor on hand, no flags, no military escort. There were, however, some grateful *caïds* to greet him there.[73]

In France he spent goodly swaths of his remaining years at his late aunt's home in Thorey, Lorraine with his wife. (The ancestral abode of Crévic would have been too difficult to rebuild.) Lyautey resolved now to put his energy into gathering notes, letters, and reports he still possessed from a long career, asking the War Ministry for the collaboration of other officers. For a romantic, he had certainly kept his files and personal affairs with pathological precision.[74]

But however reflective about the past, Lyautey was also unusually prophetic about the future. Writing to Vladimir d'Ormesson just after World War I, he said he was worried by two contemporary powers he felt must be watched: Germany and, astonishing at that point, Italy. He talked already of a "consortium italo-prussien," and how when the Americans "are gone we will be terribly isolated." Needless to say, few possessed such an effective crystal ball that early. In 1929 Lyautey was still warning France to stay strong, but it was not a popular message of the time.[75]

In the declining period of his life, Lyautey began making his way back to the Church, though as late as 1927 he did not consider himself part of the flock. His faith only came back in 1930, when he took Easter communion under the aegis of Abbé Patrick Heidsieck, one of his disciples.[76] Still, as we have emphasized, one can hardly call Lyautey a typical Catholic imperialist, for the colonial context taught him an ecumenical tolerance that never left him.

Between Paris, where he now spent roughly half the year, and Thorey, where he roosted in summer and fall, Lyautey preferred the village in Lorraine. There he knew everyone, and with his wife, built up the estate and grounds, giving a good deal of time to people around him. In Paris he kept up a vigorous correspondence and received many visitors, not least his favorite nephew Pierre, who frequently called on his uncle. That particular relationship again deserves more psychological analysis than one obtains elsewhere. The correspondence between famed uncle Hubert and nephew Pierre went back to 1898, when Lyautey was in Madagascar, and runs to almost 400 letters exchanged. Lyautey was the mystical colonial, talking seductively of far-off lands to his young nephew, yet always making the boy feel important for letters *he* sent. Uncle Hubert would address him as "Mon petit Pierre chéri" or "Mon bon cher Pierre," and the warmth on both sides endured. Lyautey congratulated his nephew on his progress through a variety of schools, including the prestigious Ecole libre de sciences politiques just before World War I. Meanwhile, Pierre followed his uncle's colonial career in the newspapers, effusively congratulating him on new promotions or assignments. Lyautey became a father figure to Pierre, and undoubtedly a source of connections. After serving in World War I Pierre's postwar letters to his uncle in Morocco are written on Ministry of Finance letterhead, then from the office of the *Haut Commissariat* for Syria and Lebanon (in Paris), and finally, before Lyautey moved back home, on letterhead for a national committee on foreign trade. Along with Auguste Terrier Pierre was a key Parisian contact during Lyautey's postwar years in Morocco. Finally, by the last half of the 1920s, they could enjoy each other's company in Paris, working on projects together.[77]

Lyautey also attended meetings of the Académie française, which he didn't mind, since he presumably had stimulating company there; and then there were those of the Supreme War Council, which he often missed. Impelled by Premier Poincaré, he also became general commissioner for an upcoming International Colonial Exposition in the capital, testimony to France's newest "digestive" period, as one might call it. Lyautey took the position seriously, traveling to a variety of French cities to visit their Chambers of Commerce, and to other expositions in cities like Antwerp. His correspondence on the exposition was extensive in the several years before it opened. Lyautey hoped that pavillions devoted to various imperial areas would demonstrate the utility of a "Greater France," especially with the Depression and foreign policy problems looming. The Exposition opened in 1931, amid great pomp and circumstance. This was the 100th anniversary of the Algerian invasion and the 50th of France's takeover of Tunisia. Eight million visitors arrived at the site in the Bois de Vincennes to watch parades of native and French troops—with head counts of almost

300,000 some weekend days, coming to see Arab *souks*, ersatz Moorish palaces, and a reconstructed Angkor Wat temple. But rising nationalism and inequities abroad, including forced labor in various parts of the empire, revealed an underside to the French colonial enterprise. Maybe when something becomes too enshrined (witness our contemporary proliferation of awards or halls of fame), it is really on the way out, as Lyautey found himself to be during these last years of his life.[78]

In fact the France of the late 1920s, and particularly of the ideologically divisive '30s, increasingly repelled him. He had always warned against what he considered a congenital French weakness—their fondness for argument, debate, and dangerous disagreements. Nearing the end of his life, he found much more of that around than he liked. He would refer to a saying about two Germans or two Englishmen coming to an area and immediately forging a *Verein* or trust, while two recently-arrived Frenchmen would start a quarrel! A variation of the story has two Englishmen, two Germans, and two Frenchmen stranded on a desert island. The Englishmen create a bank, the Germans a barrack, and again, the French start an argument.[79]

Lyautey lived long enough to witness a dangerous civil war atmosphere in his country, the chasm between Right and Left growing wider, as Hitler rearmed across the Rhine. He himself had moved more to the Right, but no position satisfied him, and a year before his death he noted that "every day brings me a growing distaste for France."[80] On July 27, 1934 Lyautey died peacefully, and a year later his coffin was on board ship from Marseille, bound for Casablanca. Many then turned out to witness his burial with full military honors in Rabat. The deceased colonial had indeed come back to a beloved land; but in 1961, with a decidedly postcolonial French era at hand, his remains were returned for reburial to the Invalides in Paris, where they continue to occupy a prominent place.[81]

May we be forgiven for concluding that despite the transience of Lyautey's Moroccan policies, his failure to make indirect rule work in any sure or final sense, his evident theatricality, and his rah-rah, insatiable demands on engineers, workers, and other associates, he *was* a great man? May we reiterate that greatness is a rare and important human quality, which in the colonial context (as well as in a terrible European war) could produce at least some good? This is where we choose to close on the last and among the greatest of our cultured, yet militarily adept French proconsuls, with a more uncertain colonial era to follow.

CHAPTER SIX

Heirs to Lyautey

ALTHOUGH LYAUTEY LIVED until the 1930s he was definitely a colonial figure of the pre-1914 period, when his ideas were formed. The big dividing line, with a new, more problematic era to come for France after the age of proconsuls, was the Great War itself, and its impact can scarcely be overstated. For the empire's subjects the war's slaughter had weakened the myth of French and even European invincibility. As well, colonial peoples themselves had contributed their own sons to the war effort, since bloodletting on the Western Front forced the French and British to rely more and more heavily on volunteers raised in the colonies. A young man who survived the fighting returned home conscious of the equal vulnerability of whites and nonwhites to machine guns, artillery shells, land mines, or poison gas. He also chafed at discrimination he had suffered in the mother country's armed forces, and often was a trained killer who now knew how to use modern weapons. It would be increasingly difficult for the French to keep people like this loyal to the old colonial ways.[1]

In this chapter we discuss interwar challenges to the French Empire, particularly in Morocco and to a lesser extent in Syria, then go on to new problems raised by France's defeat at the hands of the Nazis in 1940. The latter part of the chapter treats the struggle of Gaullists versus Vichyites in various parts of the empire during World War II, as well as the role of the British and of local leaders. It also shows how issues that came out of the Second World War presaged a move toward colonial autonomy after that conflict.

To hold on to its imperial domains, Paris relied on a threefold military establishment: the Armée Métropolitaine, the Armée d'Afrique, and the Troupes Coloniale (or La Coloniale). The exclusive mission of the Armée Métropolitaine was to defend France, Algeria and, in practice, the rest of North Africa.

When created in 1830, the Armée d'Afrique had originated as the Army of Northwest Africa. It garrisoned all three French North African colonies, consisting of these components: *chasseurs d'Afrique* (metropolitan cavalry); *zouaves* (metropolitan infantry); the Foreign Legion; *spahis* (indigenous cavalry); *tirailleurs* (indigenous infantry); *goums* (Moroccan irregulars) and *compagnies sahariennes* (Saharan camel companies). Because of its heavily North African nature and orientation, deployment of this army outside the Maghreb was unwise. That task fell to La Coloniale, explicitly colonial troops who undertook the defense of *Afrique Occidentale Française* (French West Africa), *Afrique Equatoriale Française* (French Equatorial Africa), all of French Indochina, and remaining portions of the French Empire. Created in the seventeenth century to garrison French colonies, until 1900 La Coloniale was known officially as *Troupes de Marine*, a name it resumed in 1957. By 1940 it also incorporated local outfits like the *tirailleurs sénégalais, tirailleurs malgaches,* and similar Pacific and Indochinese units. It was supplemented when possible by "Coloniale Blanche," volunteer metropolitan regiments.[2]

After World War I defensive doctrines gained great prestige in French military thinking, at least in terms of future European war; whereas colonial combat was subject to no such restrictions. There the enemy were not Germans but native forces, allegedly inferior to the French. Generals like Pétain and Gamelin, justly maligned after 1940 for their ossified defensive mentalities, displayed no such attitudes when fighting Africans. They had modern technology on their side, and when fighting abroad, they meant to use it.

In Morocco Lyautey's military successor Pétain now sought an overwhelming victory against the Rifians, using France's technological superiority, and openly differing with Lyautey's idea of subduing the foe by indirect means and retaining the goodwill of Moroccans. Pétain was the great hero of Verdun and so his strategy won the day.[3]

It turned out, however, that Lyautey's idea of ruling Morocco through indigenous elites *also* helped Pétain against Abd el-Krim. Nearly all key tribal leaders in the country remained loyal to France, and several contributed a total of 5,000 men to the French army. Lyautey's erstwhile protection of the sultan paid dividends as well: since Abd el-Krim was attacking the French, to many Moroccans he appeared additionally to be attacking its sultanate.[4]

In September 1925 the hero of Verdun advanced with seventy-two battalions along a broad front, and within a month had expelled Abd el-Krim from nearly all of French Morocco. In the midst of the fighting, on September 24, Lyautey gave up his post as resident-general. Simultaneously, the Spanish carried out an amphibious landing in Alhucemas Bay, intending to penetrate the Rif from the coast rather than from inland areas. The French were skeptical, given their dim view of Spanish military prowess. But the landing on September 8 proved successful, and within a month the Spanish had consolidated a beachhead, garrisoning it with 13,000 men. The fighting at Alhucemas launched the career of a small, but tough Spanish colonel named Francisco Franco, who rode white horses in the face of the enemy and had a number of them shot out from under him.[5]

France's premier Paul Painlevé meanwhile tried to negotiate with the Rif Republic, while fighting during the rainy season was put on hold; but his government fell in February 1926, and Pétain had undermined his efforts anyway. Abd el-Krim then asked for peace terms, and public opinion in France, which had come to view the Rifians as heroic underdogs, forced Paris and Madrid back to the bargaining table. But the Europeans presented terms so stringent that his only choice was to refuse them. He especially wanted to hold onto his prisoners as bargaining chips, and also needed time to allow them recuperation from ill treatment. In April a joint Franco-Spanish offensive—both nations' forces imbued with vengeful verve—then cleared much of the Rif, squeezing Abd el-Krim's remaining forces into a tight corner. On May 18 one of the Rifian leader's associates revealed his whereabouts to the French, and hoping to save the lives of his family and advisors, Abd el-Krim surrendered the next day.

Pétain's strategy in the Rif War did raise some military eyebrows in France. Among others a talented junior officer, Captain Jean de Lattre de Tassigny, of whom more later, denounced this deployment of excessive equipment and manpower, asserting that his superior had in fact been re-fighting the Great War here. In de Lattre's view, departure from Lyautey's traditional colonial deployment of flying columns rendered French forces "slow and cumbersome," while misleading those forces into thinking that huge material advantages could be more decisive than speed, mobility, and training. Pétain of course zealously defended himself, retaining a substantial military reputation in France.[6]

And what of Abd el-Krim? Clearly he had represented a nascent Moroc-can—or at least Berber—nationalism strong enough to disrupt the French protectorate, yet incapable of attaining his dream of independence. Still, his efforts were as meaningful as those later undertaken in Indochina by the Viet Minh leader Ho Chi Minh. For the next twenty-one years the French interned Abd el-Krim with a number of family members on Réunion, and then in 1947, en route to a more comfortable exile on the French Riviera, the ship carrying him and his family stopped at Port Saïd on the Suez Canal. Somehow he was able to jump ship, requesting asylum in Egypt, which King Farouk granted, and there he remained until his death in 1963.[7]

On the whole we should not romanticize the tenacious Rif revolt, nor even emphasize its anti-Frenchness. Abd el-Krim's primary motive had been sheer revenge, and his main enemy the Spanish, who had gravely dis-appointed him. These Berbers knew that Spain possessed no treaty with Moroccans and had merely "sublet" a part of the protectorate from the French. Amongst themselves too Rifians had long been prone to murder-ous blood feuds. As a commentator of the 1920s noted: "from childhood the Rifi boy [was] taught to make war and to hate." A fine Matisse paint-ing, "The Standing Rifian" of 1912, shows the angry pride of a people who regularly captured foreigners, and had taken part in the conquest of Spain during the early Middle Ages. The Arabic word "rif" meant edge or border, and in the mountains these tribespeople inhabited a culture of vendetta predominated, where anything like kindly justice was unknown. This was why so many streamed into the French protectorate after their leader was captured; they recognized that they would be treated more fairly there, and in fact they were.[8]

More revolts, however, transpired in Morocco, and to master them, French officers augmented use of native troops to fight against their own—beginning with a pacification campaign of 1926 south of the Taza "stain." Tribespeople pushed up to the High Atlas Mountains saw Europeans claim lands below, where they had formerly lived. The result was looting and kidnapping, including the capture of Resident-General Steeg's nephew in 1927, who was released several weeks later, when the price was right. A series of French reprisal campaigns under the zealous Colonel de Loustal was launched in 1929, advancing up into the massif of Ouel el-Abid in the Middle Atlas. There were also pressures emanating from French Algeria to punish rebels in the Tafilalet near the border, busy ambushing soldiers and sabotaging installations there.

Paris was ambivalent about losing men trying to stem this rebellious tide, but in 1930 War Minister André Maginot came down to Morocco to consult with top military leaders about the feasibility of a stronger offensive strategy against dissidents. These French soldiers in Morocco included General Antoine Huré, a veteran of the Rif conflict and since 1929, commander of the region of Marrakech; Colonel, then General Henri Giraud, who commanded in the Algerian-Moroccan "confins," as they were designated; and Colonel de Loustal, commander of the Tadla territory. Maginot impressed on his interlocutors both a Parisian sense of fatigue with Moroccan rebellions, and a feeling that any large-scale operations here had better develop quickly and definitively, in order to free French army personnel from patrolling the Atlas should the Germans start another round up north. Loustal escorted Maginot to an observation post in the Middle Atlas, and apparently made a final deal. The war minister whose name is synonymous with France's defensive skein of fortifications begun in 1929 ironically authorized full offensive operations in Morocco. Acting in concert with the Army's Commander in Chief Weygand, his purpose was to unify the protectorate completely under French authority, destroying all rebellious enclaves and strongholds, especially in the Atlas Mountains. A deadline for completion of operations was set for the winter of 1933–34.

Under General Huré a first series of attacks in July 1931, emanating from the south, began encircling rebel strongholds in the Atlas highlands. In a memoir on the campaign Huré cited the theories of both Lyautey and Bugeaud, favoring a combination of French officers in Affaires Indigènes, heavily used Moroccan partisans, but also the latest in artillery and aviation. The enemy included *marabouts* with great influence over local populations, including one who had married women comb his long locks each morning, then kept a single hairdresser behind for special attention, thereby honoring her husband. These Berber women also took an active role in stockpiling arms, rolling boulders down cliffs at the enemy, or exhorting their husbands to fight more assiduously.

In late 1931–32 a successful French reoccupation campaign ensued in the scrubby Tafilalet—partly revenge for the debacle sustained here in 1918, and cutting off important linkages to the highlands. Lyautesque improvements there followed, including road building. More operations through 1932 continued to be successful, if costly, and by the end of that year the Great Atlas contained only scattered areas of resistance. In 1933 the French prepared to launch a last major effort, respecting M. Maginot's timetable. Generals Giraud and Catroux, later at odds in World War II, both won their fame during this action, making extensive use not only of Moroccan *goumiers* and *spahis* but of the Foreign Legion, whose losses were unlikely to provoke parliamentary inquests back in Paris.[9]

In total, France's final human bill for the entire series of campaigns in Morocco through the end of pacification (in 1934) came to 8,628 men killed. Among the dead was the flamboyant, chivalric Bournazel, an almost masochistic target in his bright red *dolman,* sprayed by bullets in 1933 while scaling a cliff in one of the last recalcitrant Atlas regions left (the Bou Gafer), and mourned by his men who idolized him. Such sacrifices— with Legionnaires among the bravest—ended most insurrection in the colony, allowing the French to retain the Atlas and its peaks, and placing the protectorate more firmly under their control. The last region to be won over was the Anti Atlas of the southwest in 1934. By that year the French Empire in all North Africa stood at its zenith, and as Huré concluded triumphantly, "for the first time in its history Morocco was unified and pacified, from the Rif to the Sahara, from the Ocean to the Atlas." No one could imagine a nationalist challenge that would seriously disrupt this imperial zenith across the Mediterranean. Only a military defeat of the métropole could make such a disruption feasible, but of course in but a few years Nazi Germany would stand ready to instigate just that.[10]

French Morocco at its pre–World War II apogee continued to reveal the two-edged sword qualities of European imperialism generally. Lyautey's support of feudal notables meant the perpetuation of and even an increase in corruption, and did nothing to allay plotting and feuding among *caïds.* An influx of French institutions, education, press, and radio bred an urban elite attracted to rebellious nationalism, and an attempt to create a truly functional Berber justice system (*à la française*) made Moroccan cities erupt.[11] But the standard of living in the protectorate increased greatly, due to an industrial take-off, which was not all to France's benefit. Some argued that diverting so much money and energy toward the infrastructure of empire meant the French could never compete with the renascent Germans, more concentrated on building up their own nation's power.

During the 1930s there was still a kind of Wild West atmosphere in Morocco, where adventurous French could imitate nineteenth-century Americans as pioneers, especially outside the big cities. Perhaps most altruistic and useful was France's dispensation of medical treatment, either at ultramodern new hospitals in urban centers, or via doctors and nurses selflessly curing people out in the elements (including numerous vaccinations of those lying prostrate from various diseases). Free doctors' examinations in the protectorate increased from 1.3 million in 1919 to 7.5 million in 1939. Vaccinations against malaria, typhus, and smallpox also increased dramatically, to the point where there were 820,000 given in 1938 alone. The usual rise in the indigenous population resulted—roughly doubling from 1912 through to the outbreak of World War II. We should also remember the benefits to Europeans who settled in this, as in other parts of the empire. The victory of germ theory on the edge of World War I, and the growth of imperial branches of the Pasteur Institutes afterwards played a great role in the diminution of tropical diseases.[12]

Guy Delanoë writes affectingly of his mother, a "doctoresse" answering Lyautey's call and coming to Morocco in 1913 to work at a new hospital there. His father then arrived in 1915 from a position at the Pasteur Institute in Paris, spending the interwar years in the protectorate's Mobile Health Group. This meant riding around on horseback in the countryside, accompanied by Moroccan nurses, and vaccinating people, classifying rats and fleas (key elements in the transmission of plague), and even at night examining blood samples under a microscope in his tent, using primitive coal lamps for light. The boy too would become a doctor in the country where he was born in 1916, and where just about all his boyhood friends were Moroccans. Delanoë grew to love the two cultures, ways, and languages, learning to speak Arabic fluently. Here is one human example among many of a cultural symbiosis that Lyautey had yearned to create here.[13]

But one must finally call this whole moment in French Morocco a transient one. For one thing the French military would steadily weaken through the 1930s. In addition, a new sultan who had come to power in 1927 and was at first a rubber stamp of the French would later vouchsafe partial sympathies to a rising nationalist movement. Residents-general who followed Lyautey also helped provoke that nationalism by rejecting his indirect methods of "association," in favor of more direct, Algerian-style administration. Under three diplomats, Theodore Steeg (1925–29), formerly Algeria's governor-general; Lucien Saint (1929–33), and Henri Ponsot (1933–36), French bureaucracy increased in what Lyautey would have seen as a parasitic, deleterious manner. Edouard Moha, sighing for Lyautey's genuine love of the Moroccan people and their customs, considers Steeg Lyautey's antithesis, a man who allowed a frenzy of land expropriation and real estate speculation to overwhelm his predecessor's ideas, exacerbating a gulf between the two peoples that would end tragically. As for Saint, who had cut his protectoral teeth as Tunisia's top authority from 1922–28, he was "a firm, authoritarian, and soulless government functionary." In 1936 a military man and former Lyautey associate, General Charles Noguès, took over from Ponsot as resident-general; but although "esteemed and appreciated by the Sultan, and respected and listened to by most pashas and caïds ... he couldn't reach the masses." In the estimation of Colonel Bel Madani, similar in viewpoint to Moha, none of these residents-general through wartime came close to matching Lyautey's peripatetic curiosity about everything happening in the protectorate. The first resident had constantly visited schools, hospitals, souks, and construction sites, and was always open to hearing complaints from Arabs or Berbers. Those who followed either wouldn't or couldn't do that, and in addition to the violence of rural revolts in the early 1930s, a growing nationalist movement led by urban elites presaged worse to come.[14]

Thankfully, we have a nuanced, scholarly corrective to the latter view on Noguès provided by William Hoisington, Jr.—on a figure he considers Lyautey's truest heir. Assuming the resident-general's position in September 1936, Noguès in Hoisington's view was inspired by Lyautey's love of the country and its people. (In 1909 he had worked with the master on the Algerian-Moroccan frontier.) He also benefited from good connections via marriage to Suzanne Delcassé, daughter of the Belle Epoque foreign minister, and after serving during the Rif conflict, had become a general partly due to Steeg's support. After a brief sojourn in France he returned to Morocco in 1929 on Lyautey's recommendation, as Saint's director of Affaires Indigènes. Then, after assuming positions in France and Algeria, he reluctantly accepted the Moroccan residency, under Popular Front pressure; but with his price tag a return to Lyautey's combination of civilian and military authority, which he duly received.[15]

Noguès had his work cut out for him, trying to stem a rising tide of urban, Islamic-inspired nationalism, and working with notables, not least the two-sided sultan Sidi ben Yussef, later to become Morocco's first king. Like Lyautey in World War I Noguès again had to be wary of rising German influence in neighboring Spanish Morocco during the Civil War era. In his part he oscillated between liberalizing, for example, temporarily permitting more freedom of the nationalist press, and getting tough, including the forced exile of rebel leaders and military incursions into riotous urban medinas. He also had to combat the effects of worldwide Depression (complete with Grapes of Wrath-type drought in large swaths of Morocco). Noguès responded with a flurry of reforms—tax breaks for business, credit to farmers, subsidized irrigation projects, and support of wheat and other cooperatives—paid for by imaginative wangling of money from Paris, already spending considerable sums at home. Noguès also had to fight to get Morocco's oranges or sardines, as well as its industrial products, sold abroad, overcoming not only the métropole's hesitations, but in an era when Casablanca had become a skyscrapered metropolis, competing directly with nations like the U.S. and Japan. The Germans were pressing for Spanish-Moroccan bases, Mussolini wanted the Mediterranean as an Italian lake, and in sum, an existential crunch from a variety of sides gravely challenged Noguès in France's last heyday here, a challenge he accepted with tenacity.[16]

The greatest problems emanated from a growingly militant nationalist movement in urban agglomerations within the protectorate; but Morocco was not the only site of violent French encounters with the Islamic world in the interwar period. We also need to consider French mandates of the Middle East, particularly in Syria, where a serious uprising had occurred in the era of the Rif revolt.

To provide a very brief background, after World War I destroyed the Ottoman Empire, Emir Faisal had established a Hashemite kingdom composed of Syria, Lebanon, and Palestine. But peacemakers at the Paris conference allowed Britain to claim a territorial mandate over Palestine and Transjordan, while (reflecting secret wartime dealing) France took Syria and Lebanon, in the same way they received former German colonies of Togo and Cameroon as African mandates. The exiled Faisal would meanwhile become a later King of Iraq.[17]

France's claim to mandate control of Syria and Lebanon was based on extensive investments in those Ottoman areas before World War I; advanced educational institutions, largely under the aegis of the Catholic Church; and its own idea of "moralizing" and teaching those who would one day be ripe for independence. There was also a small, but strong colonial pressure group that believed French greatness after the terrible losses of World War I lay in the empire's continued strengthening and expansion. They hoped to develop certain industries abroad and to derive raw materials like cotton from places like Syria, reducing imports from the Americans, among others. They felt too that securing a base in the eastern Mediterranean would help defend North Africa and repel propaganda that streamed there from the Middle East. Finally, there was a continued French attempt to prove themselves worthy peers of the colonial British, an old story.[18]

Technically of course these temporary "mandates" were not supposed to become part of a French Empire; but in actuality the French High Commissioner in Beirut could administer them any way he chose. The first three French generals, all military heroes from World War I, who became high commissioners set a tone here: Henri Gouraud (1919–23), Maxime Weygand (1923–25), and Maurice Sarrail (1925). The one-armed Gouraud, Lyautey's associate in Morocco before winning a reputation in the Great War, hoped perhaps outlandishly to copy his mentor's methods here, bringing a number of Lyautey's administrators over from Morocco. By 1921 France had also plunged a large amount of soldiers into the Levant, dividing Syria and Lebanon into four states, one of them occupied by a minority Islamic sect, the Druzes. This state of Jabal became a hotbed of nationalist sentiment, with its leaders calling for reunification of the four states into an independent Syria. Until 1922 Selim al-Atrash, Jabal's governor, cooperated with the French, when Gallic forces looted the home of his relative, Sultân al-Atrash, in retaliation for the latter's involvement in a rescue attempt of a Druze accused of plotting the French High Commissioner's murder. Selim died in 1923 and a French colonel replaced him as governor, an appointment requested by the Druze leadership.

This colonel, Gabriel Carbillet, was passionately devoted to the improvement of Jabal, and during his first year as governor, modernized impressively, circumventing traditional feudal authorities, but also inadvertently offending a proud, traditional people. Carbillet's road-building, sanitary innovations, irrigation systems, and schools required stringent tax collection and use of forced labor. He also tried to implement a land reform program, thereby alienating the Druze elite, and the interested peasantry was simply too intimidated to offer its support.[19]

All of which accompanied an unfortunate change of France's high commissioner. General Maxime Weygand, who took the position in 1923, got along well with the Syrians, helping France to reduce its forces from a peak of 71,000 to some 15,000 soldiers. But when a Leftist government came to power in France (1924), Weygand's Catholicism offended Paris, and his anticlerical, Left-oriented replacement, General Albert Sarrail, had no skill whatsoever in dousing the mounting fires of Syrian nationalism. The French government failed to realize that Weygand's Catholicism had made him valuable in Damascus, since Syria's Catholic community constituted France's sole dependable base of political support there. Sarrail, on the other hand, was an abrasive martinet, utterly lacking in diplomacy or tact.[20]

In April 1925 a delegation of Druze leaders obtained a meeting with him, and it went badly. The Druzes stated their case against Carbillet, observing that the March 1921 Franco-Druze agreement stipulated that the governor of Jabal should be a Druze. Sarrail might have pointed out that the Druzes themselves had elected Carbillet, which could have cooled tempers; but instead, he denounced the 1921 agreement as worthless, defending Carbillet, who quickly lost his position. Carbillet's replacement, Captain Raynaud, then ran afoul of the powerful Atrash family, which drafted petitions denouncing both Raynaud and Carbillet. These petitions arrived in Beirut and promptly vanished. In Suwayda, Jabal's capital, mass demonstrations against French rule now broke out, and on July 11 Sarrail invited five Druze leaders to a conference in Damascus; but on their arrival his French aides arrested and deported them. The result was a full-scale Druze rebellion.

Sultân al-Atrash summoned the faithful for an armed uprising, and on July 21 his forces routed a French column at Kafr. Seventy survivors made it back to Suwayda, and the Druzes then besieged them there. The French General Michaud led a 3,000-man strike force to relieve Suwayda, but on the way a Druze ambush cost it more than 800 men, as well as supplies, ammunition, artillery, and 2,000 rifles. French rule in Syria teetered on the brink of disaster.[21]

The destruction of the Michaud column brought new recruits to Sultân al-Atrash, who demanded an independent Druze state, and the uprising spread rapidly throughout Syria. However, in contrast to Abd el-Krim's Rif revolt, the Druze rebellion lacked a nationally recognized leader. By early September 1925, Paris had dispatched sufficient reinforcements to equip a column, headed by General Gamelin, Joffre's former right-hand man in World War I, who in 1939–40 would command all French armies in Europe. On September 24 Gamelin managed to relieve Suwayda, though he couldn't hold onto it. From October 18–20 a grave incident took place in Damascus' Maydan quarter, where rebels disarmed the *gendarmerie* and set several public buildings ablaze. Gamelin responded by withdrawing his troops from the quarter, then without warning anyone but French residents, thoroughly bombarded it. That action in Damascus caused much damage and loss of life before its termination October 20, and world opinion turned clearly hostile to the French.[22]

This series of events led to Sarrail's recall and his replacement by Henri de Jouvenel, a senator and editor of the Paris daily, *Le Matin*. Before Jouvenel could assume office, however, events in Damascus had intensified the revolt's appeal. France responded by arming Christian civilians, further embittering Syria's Muslims. But by the end of 1925 it was clear that the rebellion had crested and that Sultân had no hope of defeating France. Jouvenel preached the need for peace, but this war would be ended militarily, not politically.

Jouvenel now offered the Druzes an autonomous government and a constitution, but the Atrash family demanded more—Syrian home rule and total French military withdrawal. Had the diplomatic Jouvenel been Weygand's replacement in 1924, the entire affair might have been averted in the first place; but now he weakened the rebellion's morale by offering amnesties, while continuing to pursue coercive options. Significant military operations were delayed until spring 1926, though Jouvenel noted with interest how world opinion turned against the Druzes following their terrifying activities against Christians in Lebanon.[23]

Gamelin then received the go-ahead to resume shelling the Maydan quarter of Damascus in May, and by August the district was emptied of rebels. In April consolidation of France's position in southern Lebanon enabled it to assault the Jabal itself, and by June it expelled the rebels from their base. From then until October the French methodically rooted out remaining rebel strong points, and tactics used paralleled Pétain's in the Moroccan Rif. Aircraft and armor abounded, and bombardment of Damascus in 1926 proved lethal, with the Druze rebellion terminated by the spring of 1927. Gamelin's decisive colonial victory truly boosted his career prospects, but of course with deleterious consequences to ensue in 1940.[24] The French had lost approximately 2,500 here; the Druzes nearly 10,000.

Two key lessons suggest themselves to historians. First, the French had allowed the revolt to get out of hand, clearly underestimating the power of rising Arab or Islamic nationalism. Second, the Druzes were unable to stimulate a sympathetic movement in France, and without that, no Druze victory was possible, and Syrian independence would have to await the end of World War II.

The bottom line was that despite these challenges, the 1930s would bring no outwardly significant or decisive changes to the French empire. On the whole France remained in control, granting some reforms and slightly increasing citizenship (especially in black Africa), and enhancing investment abroad. There were all sorts of economic plans hatched in the métropole during the 1930s, which in some cases helped augment colonial production, especially of cocoa or coffee. But the depression also forced peasants in Tunisia and Algeria to sell land for a pittance, exacerbating the drift toward cities and the creation of makeshift shantytowns (*bidonvilles*). In terms of convoy labor used to build railways and a variety of structures in Africa, black veterans of World War I were allowed to avoid such work roundups and were able to procure administrative positions. During the Popular Front era (1937–37) a Parliamentary Commission of Inquiry began an investigation into conditions of forced labor, as well as the status of women and children in French overseas territories. Rights to form unions and to strike increased in the empire. But Martin Thomas has also emphasized the "frustration of reform" and repression of dissidence—a good illustration being the Daladier government's shutdown in 1938 of Habib Bourguiba's Néo-Destour Party in Tunisia. French fear of and restrictions on Islamic institutions, especially law courts, as well as low rates of imperial school attendance also contributed to colonial problems in a period of rising expectations. But Nicola Cooper's summary of French attitudes toward Indochina at the end of the decade applies to the entire imperial edifice of that era: "On the eve of the Second World War belief in Empire was thus strong in metropolitan France. Official rhetoric, colonial policy and cultural interpretations . . . all appeared to support the . . . perpetuation of French colonial rule."[25]

Then the métropole's own roof began shaking. Hitler's lightning invasion of Poland on September 1, 1939 initiated a new and devastating conflict for the homeland. Gamelin may have had imperial experience and successes, but as a European military leader in 1939–40, he unfortunately seemed cut more from the cloth of his old mentor, Joffre, than from that of a Gallieni. The precipitous fall of France in the late spring of 1940 to marauding Nazi Panzers and aircraft stunned everyone, including inhabitants of the colonial world, and henceforth, *la grande nation* lay prostrate at Germany's feet.

Paul Reynaud, former colonial minister at the time of the Exposition of 1931 and premier before Pétain took over France's leadership at Vichy, wanted to continue the war against Germany from the North African empire. So did his energetic undersecretary of war, Charles de Gaulle. But Pétain refused to consider that option, and nearly all French officers agreed with him. Most loathed the British, who had refused to send additional fighter planes to help France in its desperate battles over the Meuse River in mid-May, and that hatred was then confirmed by a tragedy largely occurring *outre-mer* in early July.

The problem can partially be traced to the fact that France's navy had been modernized just before World War II, to the point where Churchill himself marveled at its improvement. The navy's commander in chief, Admiral Jean-François Darlan, was a wily Gascon determined that this fine war instrument should never fall into enemy hands. After the humiliating armistice it was France's lone bargaining chip, and Vichyites like Darlan wanted neither the Axis powers nor the British to have it. But Churchill could not countenance such stubbornness in the face of Nazi might, for the French navy was still fourth strongest in the world and potentially of great utility to an already powerful enemy. From before the armistice Churchill had been urging the French to sail these valuable ships away from Germany's potential grasp to ports in Britain, America, or the French colonial empire. He believed such an action might then have led France's empire to do the right thing, and for the right side. But Darlan kept his own counsel, awaiting events. So did Admiral Marcel Gensoul, in charge of France's Pearl Harbor—the deepwater naval base at Mers el Kébir a few miles west of Oran off Algeria's coastline. Enjoined again to get the fleet out, if possible, to British or New World ports, or failing that, to scuttle, Gensoul instead readied himself in a hurry for the event that would rankle many Frenchmen of that generation.

In addition to seizing French ships already anchored in British Channel ports or at Alexandria, the Royal Navy struck mercilessly on July 3 at Mers el Kébir, sinking or crippling much of the fleet there. Only one battle cruiser (the *Strasbourg*) slunk away to Toulon, along with five destroyers. At dawn on July 6 British aircraft finished the job. Approximately 1,285 French sailors were killed in the operation, including 997 on the battleship *Bretagne* alone. France's failure to budge on the issue would remain symptomatic of its wartime stubbornness vis-à-vis *any* big power, especially in North Africa. That committed protectorate-holder, Noguès of Morocco, was typical here, commandeering arms to counter Germans, Italians, British, and finally the Americans—*anyone* who might threaten his Morocco. And only reluctantly did he bend to Vichy, particularly to its institution of a supra–North African authority under Weygand in Algiers. Watching Germany for any moves, and playing the Pétain government like a fiddle, a busy Noguès cut bureaucracy in Morocco, but was quite decent to Jews; continued prying money for improvement of the ports of Casablanca and Agadir, and the building of power plants, dams, railway extensions, and the like; and also obtained crucial oil supplies from the Americans. If many authorities of the French Empire were monkeys in the middle during this conflict, they could be headstrong ones.[26]

Meanwhile, having flown to England on June 18, 1940, another headstrong Frenchman had decided not to return home, electing to represent a Free France abroad. Charles de Gaulle broadcast his emotional appeal over the BBC to the French army and people, claiming that his country had lost only a battle, not the war, and urging France to continue fighting Germany wherever it could.

What scant, unmitigated support *le grand Charles* enjoyed in the military came from French colonial officers, considering Germany to be France's logical enemy even after Mers el Kébir. But two days after his June 18 broadcast, de Gaulle received a first pledge of support from Chandernagor, one of France's five commercial *entrepôts* remaining since the days of Dupleix in India. The New Hebrides, a Franco-British condominium, came over on July 27, and New Caledonia followed. None of these sources of support amounted to much, and de Gaulle really set his sights on Africa, which would give his movement both manpower and important military bases.[27]

One enticing location was French Equatorial Africa, known as AEF (Afrique Equatoriale Française). While most French colonial officials were devotedly Anglophobe, those of AEF feared Germany more than Britain.[28] AEF consisted of four colonies: Cameroon, Chad, Moyen-Congo, and Oubangui-Chari. A fifth colony, Gabon, wasn't actually affiliated but formed part of the same African region. The governor of Chad in June 1940 was Félix Eboué, about to become the first significant colonial official supporting de Gaulle's Free French.

Born in Guyane (South America) in 1884, Eboué came from a solid background—his mother strongly ambitious, his father the manager of a gold mine there, and the boy a bright, adept student, anticipating a career in the French civil service. Graduating from a lycée in Bordeaux with high marks, he chose the colonial branch, although a black Creole possessing a baccalauréat could then have his pick of any department. Attending the Ecole Coloniale in Paris, during the following decades Eboué served in Oubangui-Chari, Martinique, the Sudan, and Guadeloupe, before becoming lieutenant governor of Chad, a dusty, impoverished colony in French Equatorial Africa.[29]

The largest of the four colonies of AEF, Chad boasted a total population of 2 million people. But the governor's house in Fort Lamy was a crumbling cement structure lacking electricity and running water, though it did have an old refrigerator powered by oil. However France's swift defeat by the Nazis made such deficiencies unimportant. In the summer of 1940 Eboué faced a difficult decision: should he follow Vichy and take Chad out of the war, or answer de Gaulle's appeal and join up with him?

To make such a decision it helped that Madagascar's governor-general,

Marcel de Coppet, and Pierre Boisson, governor-general of AEF, had both issued their own proclamations on June 18 that France would continue the war. One factor giving Eboué pause, however, was the predicament of two of his sons, taken prisoner in France by the Germans. Another was that by June 25 Boisson realized that colonial officials in North Africa were intent on following Pétain; he could not see how AEF could continue the war if North Africa were either neutral or openly hostile to de Gaulle. On June 27 Vichy helped him decide, naming Boisson high commissioner for all of Tropical Africa. Coppet was replaced in Tananarive by Léon Cayla, governor-general of French West Africa and a firm Pétain supporter. De Gaulle attempted to sway Boisson, but the latter would have none of it. On July 6 he accepted his new appointment, refusing to continue the war abroad. In Fort Lamy Eboué and his staff now prepared to dissociate themselves from both Boisson and Vichy.

A number of other considerations made that choice easier. Most Frenchmen in Chad feared that if they adopted a position of neutrality, they would sooner or later be absorbed into the Italian colony of Libya, bordering Chad to the north. London also pressed Fort Lamy for a favorable decision, and Eboué knew well that Chad's commerce passed through British Nigeria en route to the Atlantic. Moreover, as a black he could hardly be expected to endorse Nazi racism, and as a socialist who had been influenced in that direction by Jean Jaurès, he despised Vichy's general political orientation.

Discreetly, Eboué replied to British inquiries that he was committed to continuing resistance, and on July 4 asked the British governor-general of Nigeria to send representatives to Fort Lamy, ostensibly to discuss liaison between the neighboring colonies. When they arrived the following day, Eboué came to the point: could Britain supply arms and aircraft to Chad if it rejected the armistice? The British response was noncommittal. But in early August de Gaulle and Churchill finally reached agreement on the creation of "Fighting France," a force of volunteers designed for combat against Germany and to be financed by London. So on August 26, 1940, in a ceremony in Fort Lamy's Hôtel de Ville, Eboué announced Chad's support for de Gaulle. Vichy's Minister of Colonies immediately replaced Eboué, but the action was fruitless since the man succeeding him was not permitted to fly into Fort Lamy. Eboué's coup had been successful, and de Gaulle rewarded him for his actions, making him governor-general of AEF that October. Eboué would offer Fighting France unswerving support, often using an old soccer term (a sport at which he excelled)—"play the game!" He would continue playing for de Gaulle's side until a premature death from pneumonia in 1944.[30]

Meanwhile in late August 1940 Cameroon went Gaullist in a bloodless coup, led by an upwardly mobile colonel, then governor and general, Leclerc. Cameroon's strategic reserves of oil, gold, tungsten, mica, and titanium were henceforth at the disposal of Free France. The country flanked Chad on the southwest and with forces in British Nigeria, defended Eboué from Vichyite landings.[31]

As soon as word arrived confirming the Gaullist Leclerc's coup in Cameroon, a new takeover bid hit Vichyite forces on the Congolese river between Léopoldville and Brazzaville, and mounted against the latter town. Once successful, the Gaullist Colonel Edgar de Larminat declared himself governor-general, proclaiming that "the men of the French empire will remake France," redeeming their country's name.[32]

On August 30 Oubangui-Chari joined de Gaulle as well. That left only Gabon, but its capital Libreville proved a tough nut to crack, and Gabon became the only spot in AEF where bloodshed occurred during the Gaullist takeover. In October Free French forces sank two Vichy ships and a submarine, with one Captain Saussine going down with his boat, and Governor Masson hanging himself on a ship carrying him back to France.[33]

All these actions won Free France a territory of 1.7 million square miles, more than 6 million people, and natural resources of great value. Larminat attributed victory to Europeans and Africans living in AEF, characterizing the Africans here as "a noble race." Regrettably, Larminat himself would meet a tragic end more than two decades after his African exploits and a distinguished career, defying de Gaulle over Algerian self-determination and putting a bullet into his head.[34]

Assisting these men in their efforts was AEF's status as a particular kind of French colony. In 1940 there were two main types of colonies. A colony à legislature possessed typical European democratic institutions, sending deputies to the French National Assembly. These colonies followed Pétain at once, since he was the duly elected premier; for them there was no real question of abandoning Vichy. A colony à décrets was ruled by executive decree, lacking democratic institutions, and AEF was such a colony, which helps explain why Eboué could exercise such decisive leadership, and why local elected officials could not prevent the coups carried out in Cameroon, Moyen-Congo, and Gabon. When the identity and policies of the top men changed, the colonies automatically fell into line at once.[35]

It should be underlined that Free French control of AEF was not merely symbolic. Chad was essential to the functioning of the Takoradi air route from the British Gold Coast (later Ghana) to Egypt, facilitating the supply of reinforcements and materiel to the eastern Mediterranean. But AEF was not as crucial to German hopes as French West Africa or Afrique Occidentale Française (AOF), which in turn was not as important as North Africa. In strategic terms, the closer a colony or region was to the Mediterranean or North Atlantic, the more valuable it became to Germany's war effort.

By this logic French West Africa (AOF), and particularly Senegal with its port facilities at Dakar, constituted a major prize. Immediately following the armistice its governor-general, Cayla, wondered whether to withdraw from the war or continue to fight. But the sinking of the French fleet at Mers el Kébir and coveting of the navy at Dakar left Britain with few friends in AOF. In any event, Cayla soon joined the less important colony of Madagascar, and was replaced by Pierre Boisson, who (as seen) became Vichy's High Commissioner for Black Africa. Boisson had lost a leg fighting Germany in World War I, and had no love for that country, but was still convinced that the only way to protect AOF from Axis occupation was to follow a policy of Vichyite neutrality.[36]

In September 1940 the British high command had prepared a naval expedition against Dakar (code-named Operation Menace), demanding Free French participation, but was ready to cancel the operation when Vichy rapidly reinforced its naval squadron there. Dakar was both a naval base and busy commercial port, providing the best harbor facilities on the west coast of Africa between Casablanca and Cape Town, not to mention a fine airfield. So de Gaulle urged Britain to get on with the attack. Allied naval forces bombarded the city September 23–25, but Boisson directed a seven-ship flotilla for Vichy, easily repulsing the attempted landing. All that was achieved by the Allies was the death of many Africans and French inside Dakar, which did nothing to improve de Gaulle's image in AOF. The memory of this Dakar fiasco would remain in the minds of many people critical of de Gaulle during wartime, making both British and Americans wary of his Free French leadership.[37]

As for Boisson, a master of "studied ambiguity," he would succeed in keeping AOF neutral until the success of Operation Torch altered Vichy's position in Africa in late 1942. He then backed Admiral Darlan's efforts to negotiate with the Allies, and after Darlan's murder, cast his lot with General Giraud. Boisson would retain his antipathy for de Gaulle, finally resigning after the latter's visit to Dakar in June 1943, and following his arrest in Algiers that December by Gaullist authorities, spent the rest of the war in prison.[38]

The Dakar debacle and its effects scarcely deterred de Gaulle, as he kept soldiering on, establishing the Council for the Defense of the Empire at Brazzaville October 27, 1940. This Brazzaville Council provided him with a territorial base independent of London; indeed, he set up the Council without even notifying Churchill. But over the winter of 1940–41 Free French prestige had fallen in Africa and with the British, now as ambiguous about them as they were about Vichyites they were hoping to convert. Improvement of Vichy's navy and closer collaboration with the Germans (including Nazi pressure to permit their entry into North African ports) also factored into the equation. So for the time being, the Free French would have to suspend potential African operations, until a new opportunity arose—not in Africa, but in the Middle East.[39]

There, the possibility of Syrian and Lebanese independence had been put on ice with the onset of World War II, and once the armistice was signed, the Levantine mandates passed under Vichy's control. Considered wishy-washy by Vichy, Gabriel Puaux was to be replaced as high commissioner in Damascus during the fall of 1940 by Jean Chiappe, a convinced collaborator, whose enthusiasm for the Axis cause led him to conclude erroneously that since Italy possessed air superiority over the Mediterranean, it would be safer for him to travel from France to Syria by air, rather than by sea. In fact, his untimely death came from the Italian air force's misplaced fire, striking his plane! Chiappe's replacement was General Henri Dentz, a fervent French defeatist and Anglophobe, whose presence in Damascus at the end of 1940 became the catalyst for Britain's resolve to intervene in Syria.[40]

Britain's Syria policy would especially target Dentz' willingness to permit Axis forces access to installations there. De Gaulle had different motivations for getting involved: Syria's strategic location and high-quality French bases made it an attractive prize for him, though his general Free French patriotism still extended to every part of the empire under Vichy's sway. But if the British seemed likely to intervene anyway, Gaullist cooperation would become mandatory.[41]

To coordinate with his lukewarm ally, de Gaulle first sent a reliable operative to Jerusalem in order to make contact with British authorities there. This was General Georges Catroux, a maker of Moroccan military policy in the early 1930s and by now, a cultured diplomat with much expertise in Asian affairs. In June 1940 Catroux had been French governor-general of Indochina, but supported de Gaulle. After France's surrender Japan had ordered him to close the border between China and Indochina, preventing French arms from falling into the hands of Chiang Kai-shek, whom Japan was fighting. Catroux resisted, but was eventually forced to comply, whereupon he demanded airplanes and weapons from Vichy for defense of Indochina against Japan. Pétain's government accused him of exceeding his authority, replacing him with Admiral Jean Decoux (see chapter 7); so Catroux caught a ship for Africa to join up with the Free French.[42]

He had already known de Gaulle when they shared a German POW camp in 1916 and now saw clearly where his duty lay. Though he had three and soon four stars on his shoulder to de Gaulle's one, he had no trouble subordinating himself to his junior in both years and rank; for him de Gaulle *was* France, including France abroad. And de Gaulle's links to the British didn't bother him at all. An elegant man with sure taste, Catroux was no Anglophobe, admiring Churchill's greatness in the era of the Blitz and able to get beneath the laconic exteriors of other British authorities he met. In Jerusalem during the fall of 1940 he conversed with the high commissioner in Palestine, Sir Harold MacMichael, who was Lord Curzon's nephew, but talented in his own right. The latter's overriding hope was to keep relative peace between Arabs and Jews. In a discreet way he favored Catroux' idea of an operation northward, but also knew that sharing borders with Lebanon and Syria meant getting along with Vichy authorities there. He even gave Catroux his bust of Napoleon for luck. While there, Catroux also assessed the French clerical community of Jerusalem, priests mostly pro-Vichy, some orders of nuns less so. He then traveled up the coast to Haifa, where a couple of Free French renegades maintained a radio post in a Jewish home, countering Vichy propaganda in the Mideast. His findings, which he then reported to de Gaulle at Fort Lamy, led Catroux to conclude that if the Free French arrived with overwhelming force, they would encounter minimal resistance in Syria. But if they seemed ill prepared or hesitant, they would fail miserably.[43]

Catroux returned to his base in Egypt, where most French who taught or worked in the Suez Canal administration were Vichyite, and he met with British authorities there. Taking to the airwaves in Cairo to ask French people in Egypt and the Middle East to follow de Gaulle, he was countered by the Levantine high commissioner's appeal for the French to remain "Vichy." Catroux had nothing but contempt for this General Dentz, considering him incompetent and partially responsible as Sarrail's former aide for provoking the Druze revolt of the mid-1920s. Catroux also tried to get Weygand to raise French North Africa, especially with the British crushing the Italians in Libya; but the seventy-four-year old general would have none of it. Catroux even appealed directly in a note to Dentz of February 1941, asking him to support de Gaulle. A few days later he was condemned by Vichy's Riom Court to death for these treacherous actions. Catroux would confess later that he still had illusions about the hero of Verdun, not wanting to realize that Pétain lacked any will whatsoever to take on the Nazis.

A more important wartime leader with his own hesitations about the Free French was General Archibald Wavell, commander of British forces in the Near East, whom de Gaulle and Catroux urged to intervene as soon as possible in Syria. But already running operations in Greece, Libya and Ethiopia, Wavell had no stomach for a fourth, particularly one requiring French cooperation! As long as Dentz' Vichyite forces appeared to be leaving the British alone, they seemed to posed no direct threat, and Wavell worried more about defending the Suez Canal and Palestine from Rommel's seemingly irresistible advances.

All this changed dramatically when Rashid Ali took Iraq into the Nazi camp on May 2, 1941, needing weapons stockpiled in Syria to resist a possible British countercoup. But the status of Free France had also been changing. By early 1941 they were providing units to stand with English fighters against Rommel's Afrika Korps, and sending a column under Leclerc from Murzuch to Kufra in North Africa. Moreover, at Vichy the Anglophobe Darlan offered support for the Afrika Korps in Tunisia, as well as Middle Eastern bases from which German bombers could reach British oil refineries in Iran. If Syria were placed at Nazi disposal, Hitler might then move south through Palestine to take the Suez Canal via its eastern back door. Belatedly, the British concluded that they must try to bring Syria into the Gaullist camp.[44]

On May 12, 1941 Royal Air Force planes attacked Syrian airfields, and Vichy authorities quickly realized that an operation was afoot. Catroux, designated to be Free French high commissioner for the Levant, issued repeated appeals for desertion of his countrymen. On May 25 the British sealed the border between Syria and Palestine, and Dentz tried to avoid invasion by removing nearly all Germans from Syria; but his actions had no impact on London, given the ability of the Nazis to return at any time.[45]

On June 8 a collection of Australian, British, Free French, and Indian forces invaded Syria and Lebanon from the south, streaming up the coast. Thousands of Catroux' pamphlets fluttered down from the skies, containing a "Manifesto of Free France." The Allies disposed of 20,000 men and 70 aircraft, against Dentz' 30,000 soldiers, 80 tanks, and 90 planes. De Gaulle authorized Catroux to issue a proclamation, stating that Free France would guarantee Syrian and Lebanese independence following the war, though in fact Gaullists were no more independence-minded than Vichyites.[46] This declaration helped win local support, but had no discernible impact on Vichyite forces, who fought doggedly under Dentz. These soldiers wanted to prove to Berlin that Vichy France was a faithful ally (failing which, the Germans might carry out reprisals against North African colonial entities, among others). Again, the British had underestimated Vichy's ability to fight back in the empire—"as at Dakar, so in Syria," in Martin Thomas' words.[47]

But Dentz was now wedged into a tough spot. To resist indefinitely, he needed both reinforcements and air support, which could only be provided by Vichy's Axis allies. However, if Dentz was an Anglophobe, he was certainly no Germanophile, and Hitler didn't press the matter, since Berlin was then concentrating on its imminent Operation Barbarossa against the Soviets and feared committing more than minimal forces to the Middle East. If Syria was lost, they could always come back some other time to mop it up again. Meanwhile, Britain's failure in Operation Battleaxe (Wavell's offensive in the western Sahara) liberated additional troops for use against Damascus. So Free French and Indian units entered that city on June 21, a day after Dentz asked for armistice terms.[48]

After more bitter fighting, Beirut fell July 10, and the two sides agreed to an armistice on Bastille Day; but that agreement proved unacceptable both to Vichy and to de Gaulle. Dentz would surrender only to the British, and de Gaulle opposed England's willingness to permit Vichyite forces repatriation in French ships. In his memoirs he would characterize the armistice as "a pure and simple transmission of Syria and Lebanon to the British."[49] Alone de Gaulle's position was, however, a weak one, and Syria could not have been kept out of Nazi hands without a sizable British occupation force there.

Dentz returned to Vichy and would later be brought to trial for treason in April 1945, receiving the death penalty. But France's provisional president de Gaulle granted him clemency, and Dentz died in prison that December. As for Catroux, he took over in the Levant, then became Free French national commissioner for Muslim affairs in 1943, proposing to de Gaulle reforms designed to head off the appeal of Arab nationalism in the French Empire as a whole. His proclamation of November 10, 1943, stating that the era of colonial domination was drawing to a close, strikes a modern-day reader as prophetic. And a key Free French promise would prove reliable, when Syria and Lebanon gained independence at the end of World War II, rather more quickly, however, than de Gaulle actually desired. In fact he derived from this enterprise another reinforcement of his chip-on-the-shoulder distrust of the British that would influence his later policies. De Gaulle would eventually maintain that both Major-General Sir Edward Spears, Britain's minister plenipotentiary to Syria and Lebanon during the war, and Prime Minister Churchill had undercut the French here, stimulating Arab nationalist appetites to be greater than what the French approved. As for Catroux he maintained his loyalty to Churchill, but found the supposedly Francophile Spears an obstinate foe in the Levant—bumptious, quarrelsome, and "immeasureably vain."[50]

However inconvenient, the English had been quite necessary to *le grand Charles*, and the Syrian campaign had demonstrated that *any* German intrusion into a French colony during the war was likely to provoke a British response. De Gaulle could at least view this operation as a kind of comeback after the failed invasion of Dakar, and so increasingly, would black Africans. But on the larger military scale Germany's invasion of Russia, as well as Japan's attack on Pearl Harbor turned the Middle East into but a minor theater of World War II.[51]

De Gaulle continued to believe that Free France needed its empire, both to resist German domination and to rebuild France as a great power following the war. His failure at Dakar and his noncrucial success in Syria did not diminish his notion of the colonies' strategic centrality. But Catroux, whom he respected as he respected few others, worked to transform his views. Eboué, to whom he owed a good deal, did the same thing as well. Both were visionaries who recognized that the prewar relationship between métropole and empire was now significantly altered. In November 1941 Eboué, as governor-general of AEF, had convened all colonial leaders subject to his authority to discuss postwar French policy in Africa. European leaders would henceforth be forced to consider the wishes of the continent's inhabitants, given more than 100,000 African recruits for Free France, the huge supplies of food they had turned over, and the territorial base from which de Gaulle could operate. Eboué and his commission of leaders produced an innovative statement that called for a more enlightened policy toward Africans, for one day soon these peoples would surely govern themselves. And de Gaulle started listening.[52]

Evidence of his attitudinal change would, however, take almost two years to surface, partly due to his hurt at being excluded from key operations in the French Empire—the first one on Vichy-held Madagascar. Japan's brushfire success in Southeast Asia, including the fall of Singapore in February 1942, convinced the British that even Diego-Suarez' fine harbor wasn't out of that Asian power's reach. Control there was strategically vital for communications with India via the huge Indian Ocean. But Churchill and British army leaders remembered Free French intelligence given them before Dakar, and decided to invade Diego on May 5, 1942 without de Gaulle, who would have loved to fight orthodox Pétainistes there. The British would only cut in the Gaullists when their operation was successfully terminated, including by a push inland. But on the latter they took their time, hurried somewhat by a Japanese submarine attack May 30 on one of their ships anchored off Diego. It then required a few months to absorb the entire island, and meanwhile, Churchill kept General Paul Legentilhomme dangling—a man who believed he could be the Free French Gallieni here. De Gaulle's anger also boiled as the British continued foot-dragging through 1942 on a change of authorities in Madagascar, despite a fine showing by Free French Legionnaires in the desert against Rommel at Bir Hakeim. None of this was pure Francophobia—simply wartime caution. For Britain still hedged bets on both Gaullists and Pétainists, pending future reunification of the French Empire; nor did they want to provoke a Vichy build-up before a new, more major operation, one that would be even more painful for de Gaulle.[53]

Stalin had of course been needling his allies to start liberating the west, and two weeks after Montgomery's artillery barrage against Rommel's forces at El-Alamein, Operation Torch began November 8 on the beaches of French North Africa—again, minus de Gaulle, kept in ignorance prior to the invasion. This Anglo-American offensive was primarily conceived of as a U.S. operation, given Vichy's Anglophobia stimulated by Mers, Dakar, and then Madagascar. The unblemished knights from across the Atlantic would presumably be able to proselytize easier here. And indeed, Algiers under General Alphonse Juin surrendered easily on the first day of fighting (to a mixture of American and British troops, supported by the British navy). But landings to the west at Casablanca (all-American and under George Patton, wearing pearl-handled Colt pistols) and at Oran (American troops and British naval escort) encountered tough French resistance. Though casualties were unexpectedly high, both cities naturally fell in a matter of days, and the question then became: which Frenchman should lead the North African sector of the empire back to the Allies' good graces?

Neither Roosevelt nor Churchill felt de Gaulle's time had yet come, due to his arrogance, and the fact that his presence might spark a French imperial civil war. At that point they may have been right. The United States first set alternative sights on General Henri Giraud, imprisoned by the Germans in 1940, and finally, with pieces of rope sent by his wife in jam tins and knitted together, shinnying over 100 feet to escape from the Castle of Konigstein in April 1942. Brought to North Africa on a British submarine, Giraud seemed a viable candidate as the new unifier of a liberated French North Africa. He had already cozied up to the Americans, hoping that their aid could take the region from the Axis. His chance had now come; or had it?

Fortuitously, the opportunistic, but talented Darlan was himself in Algiers just before Torch, visiting an ailing son in hospital there. American Commander in Chief Mark Clark now inclined toward using Darlan. Summoning the latter, Clark enjoined him to promote a ceasefire in all of French North Africa, or—pounding the table for effect—he would clap him into prison! Darlan was pressured by Vichy not to accept, but Clark held firm, while a number of French military leaders were on the point of squabbling like cats. Finally, Pétain gave all North African authority to Noguès, then sent a secret message to Darlan that he was only bowing to German pressure. The rivalries among Darlan, Giraud, Noguès, and Juin irritated Clark, who rather like Bogie telling the French in his bar to "lay off politics," said he would arrest them all if they could not agree! On November 13 under these threats, and with Darlan's engineering of a ceasefire, they acceded to a solution. Darlan became high commissioner and commander in chief of Naval Forces for French North Africa; Giraud commander in chief of Ground and Air Forces; Juin commander of the "Eastern Sector"; and Noguès commander of the Western Sector, while also remaining (for now) as resident in Morocco. Eisenhower found this compromise workable, figuring that Darlan might be able to deliver the French fleet in Toulon to the Allies, an urgent matter, given the Nazi dissolution of France's Unoccupied Zone November 11 and their imminent arrival at the big naval town, not to mention threats to Tunisia as well. However, Pétain's commander in Toulon, Admiral de Laborde, spurned Darlan's broadcast entreaties to get the fleet out of harm's way. Darlan did help place French leadership in West Africa behind the Allies, including thereby, the vital port of Dakar and air bases. He also helped switch allegiances of some 120,000 French troops in North Africa. But the fleet at Toulon never sailed out of the Nazi trap. Instead, Laborde (the wartime vise finally tightened on what remained of a proud navy) elected to scuttle just before the German arrival. As Henri Noguères would say of this bevy of two battleships, seven cruisers, twenty-nine destroyers, two submarines, and one battleship cruiser settling to the bottom of Toulon's harbor, it was a classic three unities tragedy, completed within twenty-four hours and in one place.

The sinking of these ships was at least better than German appropriation; but American satisfaction at its North African arrangements was now mitigated by outrage at home and in England over Darlan's appointment, which a backpedaling Roosevelt labeled temporary. Fernand Bonnier de la Chapelle, a young Royalist resistant linked to the Gaullist de la Vigerie brothers, made it temporary indeed, assassinating Darlan on Christmas eve, 1942. The Americans then gave the ball of leadership to Giraud, who became high commissioner for all French North Africa; but even they realized that Giraud lacked the prestige to lead in the empire for anything like the long term. Churchill nonetheless impelled a reluctant de Gaulle to meet with the new appointee at Casablanca in mid-January 1943.[54]

De Gaulle was the one to come out in good odor, his prestige in imperial France rising vertiginously through 1943. Even after the six-month fight for Tunisia against Rommel that position was secure. In this case a bad decision led to a good outcome: the British and Americans should probably have extended their invasion of November to that sector of French North Africa, precluding an Axis takeover at the end of 1942, and all the hard fighting that would persist until May 1943. They should also have called the German bluff when at first, Axis forces were rather thinly arrayed there. But the Americans and English (Montgomery's 8th Army entering from Libya in February with battle-hardened Aussies, New Zealanders, Greeks, Palestinian Jews, and even Free French in tow) finally overcame a much strengthened Axis army. In the end the Allies took "a large bag" when Tunis ultimately fell in May, including as many as 250,000 prisoners. The legendary Afrika Korps, now shorn of Rommel, was through.[55]

By that point de Gaulle was the big name everywhere in the empire. On June 3 the French Committee of National Liberation reconvened in Algiers with seven members, including de Gaulle and Giraud as coleaders. In early October Gaullists liberated Corsica, and then on November 8, General Giraud finally resigned from the committee, leaving de Gaulle as its president. The tall French leader had outlasted his competition and was now alone at the top, seconded by associates like Emmanuel d'Astier de la

Vigerie. But at the same time, stirrings of nationalism in the empire as a
quid pro quo for approval made him rethink his imperial positions. In late
1943 the first public evidence of this attitudinal change was revealed. On
December 8 he issued a proclamation on the future of French Indochina,
pledging greater sensitivity to local traditions, and greater access to state
services and employment. Four days later, in a speech in the Algerian city
of Constantine, he mentioned equality of opportunity and the brother-
hood of peoples. Reforms soon improved voting rights and representation
for Algeria's Muslims, arousing postwar expectations. Then in January
1944 de Gaulle opened the Conference of Brazzaville, speaking of France's
civilizing mission, its obligation to develop its colonies economically, and
its duty to bring progress and dignity to those who had labored so diligently on its behalf.[56]

Looming in the background were the overt and moralistic anticolonial sentiments of President Roosevelt and other American authorities. It
was clear that Washington would work to undermine French colonialism
after the war, so de Gaulle now had to act quickly. Brazzaville gave him
an opportunity to define the terms and set the agenda for postwar French
imperial policy. For the moment he even benefited from a certain latitu-
dinarianism on the part of the French Left, including Communists.[57]

But in the end, the Brazzaville Conference failed to provide a coherent
and feasible blueprint for the future. At the core of this failure lay what
Dorothy Shipley White calls "the Great Inconsistency." The conference
seemed to allow Africans greater future freedom managing their own
affairs, yet deny them the opportunity of autonomous development outside a French colonial framework. Already, there was a split in the Gaullist camp between those emphasizing reform and a quickened timetable
for independence, versus those who wanted to turn back the imperial
clock.[58]

So despite its appeal to *le grand Charles*, the formula adopted at Brazzaville did not serve France very well. Future governments in the postwar
era would have to pick and choose which aspects of the conference agenda
to emphasize. France's Constitution of 1945 would attempt to meet the
Africans halfway, but its rejection by voters led to the drafting of a second
document, opposing meaningful colonial reforms. Passage of this version
would have grave consequences for French rule not only in Africa but as
we will see, in Indochina.

Yet many Africans did remember de Gaulle as a savior, a war leader
whose heart was with them and whose words had moved them. For such

people, as would be seen on his return to power in 1958, he always remained "the man of Brazzaville." Brazzaville represented a kind of historical watershed, focusing attention on the empire's defects and openly acknowledging France's debt to its colonies. And it constituted a key stage in the evolution of de Gaulle's own perspective on imperial matters. That perspective would continue to evolve after the war in one fundamental direction: toward colonial autonomy. However, this was not quite the end of France's colonial greats or greatness. There would be more cultured military men aplenty whom the mother country would hurl into its last great imperial conflicts to come![59]

CHAPTER SEVEN

The Twilight of French Colonialism

ERMANY'S SURRENDER ON May 8, 1945 ended more than the Second World War; it also ended the prewar French colonial system. If anyone in France thought that the empire could simply reemerge without change, events of V-E Day in Sétif, Algeria would soon teach them differently. There a French victory parade degenerated into violence, with Algerian attacks on the *colons* provoking a massacre in return, and estimates of Algerian casualties ranging from 6,000 to 45,000.[1] Africans who had fought for France and in some instances been decorated by de Gaulle were now unlikely to ignore imperialistic discrimination. As was the case after World War I, only more so now, they would henceforth take their European military training and put it to good use, with results that would ultimately shake an empire, especially as this chapter will emphasize, in Vietnam, as well as in North Africa.

Brazzaville had certainly altered the vocabulary of French colonial rule. Jacques Soustelle was France's last minister of colonies, serving from November 1945 through January 1946, and Marius Moutet, who replaced him, became "minister of overseas France." This change in terminology underscored the emphasis placed at Brazzaville on assimilation of the colonies into France; after 1946 there would in theory be only one France, part of which lay overseas.[2] But it remained to be seen whether this reflected a true alteration in French attitudes, or mere window-dressing.

Curiously, the first serious challenge to French colonial rule did not come from North Africa, as perhaps was expectable; after the first Algerian eruption of 1945, things stayed relatively stable there into the early 1950s. Instead, the main challenge now came from Asia. Few Indochinese had fought for

246

France in Europe, but a significant number during the war had joined a resistance organization known as the Viet Minh, fighting occupying Japanese forces and pledged to seek Vietnamese independence.[3] The Viet Minh's unwillingness to accede to renewed French colonial domination after World War II then resulted in the prolonged and costly Indochinese War.

As noted in chapter 1, and elaborated on in chapter 5, present-day Vietnam was originally composed of three regions, running from north to south: Tonkin, Annam, and Cochin China. To reiterate and add more background on their eventual differences, French-Catholic missionaries had made inroads into the area during the eighteenth century. In the French Revolution, French India raised volunteers for the forces of a Vietnamese prince, who won a civil war and became Emperor Gia Long in 1802. When his son ascended the throne in 1820, France was starting to show interest in Southeast Asia, and in the 1840s the July Monarchy, using the emperor's treatment of Vietnamese Catholics as a pretext, pressed for closer relations. By the 1850s, in the reign of Emperor Tu Duc, French troops arrived in Cochin China along with the Spanish to chastise the Vietnamese for their supposed persecution of missionaries. But when the Spanish left in 1862, the French remained in the three eastern provinces of Cochin China and a few years later absorbed the other three.

Cochin China became a colony ruled directly from Paris, with representation in the Chamber of Deputies. Twenty-two years later, as seen, the French invaded Annam and Tonkin, and the emperor's death in 1883 followed by the Treaty of Hué (1884) transformed those areas into French protectorates. But Tonkin was administered as a colony, while the French ruled in Annam indirectly through the emperor and his officials.[4]

We have seen too how under these varieties of French rule colonial populations increased—Vietnam's by more than 100 percent. The Institut Pasteur opened a branch in Indochina, where researchers studied tropical infections, vaccinated inhabitants, and worked on problems of sanitation. Throughout the region the French built modern hospitals and had thousands of acres of marshland in Cochin China drained and made available for cultivation. They also shored up and expanded the Red River delta dike system. Roadways were extended, especially the "Mandarin Road," which became Colonial Highway 1, running north to south by the South China Sea coast; and the French supplemented that road with a Trans-Indochinese Railway. Meanwhile, both Saigon and Hanoi, with their busy and exciting Rue Catinat and Rue Paul Bert respectively, were greatly amplified, beautified, and though the word sounds perhaps naïve, civilized.[5]

Despite these impressive developments, the vast majority of Indochinese peasants remained poor. French-financed improvements extended their lives, bettered their chances of surviving infectious diseases, and increased their agricultural output; but Gallic rule in Indochina used the colonies mostly for the benefit of the mother country.

The French traditionally kept the region economically top-heavy and militarily feeble, a situation Georges Mandel tried to alter when he became minister of colonies in 1938. But Mandel's plans for economic invigoration through manufacturing, and for military strengthening by creation of an Indochinese national army won little support in Paris. Mandel, however, located an ally in General Catroux, whom he called out of retirement to become governor-general. Under Catroux' leadership the French began building a naval installation at Cam Ranh Bay in 1940; however, when the Japanese arrived in June, French authorities had no choice but to accept their terms.

As mentioned in our previous chapter, Pétain's government then dismissed the pro–British, pro–de Gaulle Catroux with what Joseph Buttinger described as "monumental bad taste," replacing him in July 1940 with Vice Admiral Jean Decoux.[6] Japan meanwhile used Southeast Asia as a staging area for its conquest of the Malay Peninsula and Burma, and Indochina chafed under Vichy. As the French were simply administering the area for Japan, resistance movements like the Viet Minh began winning more converts. That organization opposed both Vichy and Tokyo, though it was not anti-French in any cultural or economic sense. It should be added that Decoux engaged in quite a remarkable wartime balancing act, namely between a far-off métropole now taking little interest in the area, and the Japanese. Somehow he placated the latter, offering a series of reforms to the Vietnamese, and in difficult circumstances, supervising construction of roads and canals, which helped to bring many more acres of rice fields under cultivation. He was also as authoritarian as any Vichy governor in the empire.

When de Gaulle replaced the Pétainist regime, he was frankly improvising, sending a new general, Mordant, to Indochina, one who possessed nothing like Decoux' experience and tact. It was the first of a series of ill-advised appointments. Somehow the Japanese distrusted the new Decoux-Mordant tandem, and after torturing and decapitating some French officers, they took over Vietnam in a lightning coup March 9, 1945. The French presence was now liquidated, though the Viet Minh assisted French families by giving them food and shelter, until Allied planes could transport at least some of them to China. The rest remained huddled there. Here was the beginning of the Vietnam War in all its varieties; for now the door truly seemed open for Ho and the Viet Minh to assume power after an impending Japanese surrender, which looked likely, given the terrific pounding of Japan from the air by the Americans.[7]

When that surrender occurred after the dropping of America's atomic bombs, Ho Chi Minh quickly raced into the vacuum, taking control in Hanoi and Saigon, and spreading tentacles (though his group was still small) into the countryside, which had suffered from Japanese rapacity, a terrible famine, and floods. The anticolonial Americans were warmish to the Viet Minh, the Japanese had given them piles of arms, the population was promised redistribution of land—what Russian and Chinese Communists had previously promised—and the future looked relatively bright for Ho and his charges. Even as the Potsdam Conference decided in August 1945 on a temporary partition of liberated Indochina into a northern zone under the Chinese and a southern zone under the British, Ho told his people that independence was right around the corner.

He had reckoned without a France that wanted spiritually, morally, and mentally to avenge and wash away the stain of the 1940 defeat! And for some reason it assumed that it could reestablish antebellum authority in Indochina without any significant hardship. *Quelle illusion!* A key problem remained one of personnel. Admiral Decoux languished in a Japanese prison, then was recalled by de Gaulle to France, where he was flung into another one. Other government functionaries of the Pétain era were replaced by Gaullists lacking experience in Asia. Admiral Georges Thierry d'Argenlieu would become high commissioner for Indochina with a mandate to restore French sovereignty, regardless of cost; but there were complicating factors, not least the arrival of British forces in southern Vietnam on September 12 and the entry of Chinese troops into the north a few days later. Martin Thomas believes this "disastrous Allied partition of Indo-China at Potsdam in August 1945 set a match to the powder keg of frustrated Vietnamese aspirations and French impatience to resume unfettered colonial power."[8]

Intriguingly, the French underplayed Ho Chi Minh's proclamation of Vietnamese independence in the main square of Hanoi on September 2, 1945. Born in Annam as Nguyen Sinh Cung in 1890, Ho was a graduate of the French lycée in Hué, a merchant seaman, and a pastry chef who had apprenticed under the famous Escoffier in London, and since 1919, an agent of the Communist International. He had tried unsuccessfully for admittance to the Paris Peace Conference in order to present demands for Vietnamese self-determination there. In 1929 he founded the Indochinese Communist Party, and from its creation in 1941 became the heart and soul of the Viet Minh. Ho's proclamation of Vietnamese independence appeared to have the tacit support of the United States, but the French government thought it could dislodge his provisional government once it brought sufficient forces back to Indochina.

That would take time, one reason for British and Chinese intervention in Vietnam. These British forces under General Douglas Gracey were instructed to disarm Japanese soldiers and do nothing else. But Gracey also decided to weaken Viet Minh authority in the south, instituting a curfew and a shutdown of Vietnamese newspapers on September 21, and giving a green light to French aggressivity. The Viet Minh responded by promoting a general strike, shutting down Saigon, then massacring a good 150 French and Eurasians, showing what it would become. All this paved the way for the resumption of French rule here.[9]

Gracey's unilateral decision to rearm the few French soldiers remaining in the country and to assist them would have large consequences indeed. Anglo-French cooperation enabled the latter to occupy the chief government buildings in Saigon, ousting a Viet Minh–dominated Committee of the South. On October 5 General Leclerc, new commander in chief of French forces in Indochina, entered Saigon with considerable reinforcements. Twenty days later he began liquidating Viet Minh resistance, expecting to reconquer Cochin China within a month. It took somewhat longer, but by January 1946 with French effectives up to 30,000, the region was secured and the Committee of the South had gone underground.[10]

It was, however, a different game in the north, where the Viet Minh government still ruled. After Japan's surrender, de Gaulle appointed Pierre Messmer, then Jean Sainteny as chiefs of intelligence there. From the outset two central problems confronted Sainteny. First and most obvious was French military weakness. Paris might have been able to reclaim its position in Tonkin if it had been able to place troops there in August; but the difficulty was assembling a fleet necessary to move them halfway around the world on short notice. The second problem was that although it was theoretically possible for Sainteny to negotiate some agreement with the Viet Minh, it is difficult to conceive the form such a bargain might have taken.[11]

Another factor complicating the situation in Tonkin was the presence of a large Chinese army there. The Allied decision to allow Chinese occupation of Tonkin and Annam had a highly positive impact on the Viet Minh cause. For even Chiang's China had no sympathy for European colonialism, and as Ellen Hammer observed, "The Chinese had not nurtured Vietnamese nationalist movements on Chinese soil for so long in order to oust the first independent regime which had ruled Viet Nam in sixty years."[12]

However, these Chinese were also a ragged bunch living off the land and looting, and Ho himself wanted them out as soon as possible. Oddly, he and the French briefly found themselves in complete agreement, and French General Raoul Salan was able to negotiate the withdrawal of Chinese forces (Chiang Kai-shek granting them a free shot at getting back the Tonkin in return for concessions in China). The accord was signed in February 1946, and the Chinese finally departed in the summer, leaving a power vacuum, which the French army hoped to fill.[13]

But the difficulty of subduing Cochin China had persuaded General Leclerc that existing French forces were insufficient to carry out a military conquest of the north. Leclerc feared that any nationwide insurrection would simply destroy French influence in Indochina; while Marius Moutet, minister for overseas France, worried about the safety of the 25,000 French residents in Hanoi, whose lives would be threatened if France failed to create some kind of an entente with the Viet Minh.[14]

That understanding took the form of the shaky Ho-Sainteny Accords, signed by these two men on March 6, 1946. The accords defined the Democratic Republic of Vietnam as "a free state ... forming part of the Indochinese Federation and the French Union," and promised a plebiscite on unification of the Tonkin, Annam, and Cochin China. The Viet Minh granted permission for the French army to replace the Chinese in the north, and these troops would then withdraw in stages, so that by 1952 no units with offensive capabilities would presumably remain in Vietnam. In a much-cited phrase Ho noted that he found it preferable to inhale French doo-doo in the short run, rather than that of the Chinese for a longer haul. Knowing history, he feared the Chinese might get used to a Vietnamese occupation and stay put; whereas the French in an era of waning colonialism would never be able to hold on for long.[15]

Curiously, each side justified these accords by claiming temporary weakness. Leclerc's sober estimate of French capabilities was matched by the comments of Vo Nguyen Giap on Viet Minh insufficiencies of the time. Born in 1912, and a graduate of the Lycée Albert Sarraut and the University of Hanoi, founded by the French progressive Paul Bert, Giap had been a history teacher at a private school before World War II. His special pleasure was teaching Napoleon's battle strategies. Despite acquiring a French culture, Giap detested those who had provided him with it, as Decoux' Vichy authorities had guillotined his sister-in-law for terrorist activities during wartime, and also allowed his young wife to die of malnutrition while in prison. In December 1944 Giap formed the first combat units of Viet Minh guerillas, but in a rousing speech on March 7, 1945 declared their willingness to bargain because they were not yet strong enough to fight the French.[16]

Ho Chi Minh was himself disappointed by these accords, telling Sainteny that "I wanted more than that. But I understand that you cannot have everything in a day."[17] At least the accords called for an eventual military withdrawal from Indochina and termination of a French imperial presence there. Leclerc had not simply drunk champagne with Ho *pro forma*, but was actually prepared to implement that agreement, realizing what the military costs of anything more would be. Regrettably for both the French and American futures, his tenure in Indochina soon ended. On July 14, 1946 Leclerc left his post to become inspector of land forces in North Africa, where he would die in a plane crash the following year.[18]

His departure then allowed the more rigid Admiral d'Argenlieu to undermine the accords, which he viewed as an equivalent of the Munich agreement (and of course that capitulation would obsess Kennedy and Johnson as well). D'Argenlieu now contemplated a colonial war to overturn them. Here was one of de Gaulle's inexperienced appointees, a defrocked monk sent to Indochina with *a priori* ideas about an area he didn't know at all. Since the minister for overseas France, Moutet, was a man lacking backbone, prospects for calling d'Argenlieu to order were slim. A French commission on war crimes visited Lang Son, site of a wartime massacre of French soldiers by the Japanese, and got into a skirmish with the Viet Minh on November 20, 1946. That day fighting also erupted in the main Tonkin port of Haiphong, and though it stopped on November 22, d'Argenlieu ordered Colonel Debès, French commander in Haiphong, to make an example of Viet Minh troops there. The next day Debès gave the Viet Minh commander an ultimatum, then struck by land, sea, and air, destroying the Vietnamese quarter of Haiphong and killing more than 6,000 people, mostly civilians. This regrettable operation opened the way to a prolonged tragedy.[19]

And yet, on December 12 Ho Chi Minh observed in *Le Monde* that "neither France nor Viet Nam can afford the luxury of a bloody war, and to reconstruct on ruins would be catastrophic." By that time, however, Hanoi's streets were already running red with the blood of both sides. D'Argenlieu's subordinate, General Morlière, demanded on December 19 that the Viet Minh militia surrender its weapons, and they responded that night by cutting off Hanoi's power and water, then attacking French positions. The French counterattacked and barely missed capturing Ho, which again might have averted long-term involvement and tragedy for themselves and ultimately, for the Americans.[20]

It is clear that Viet Minh forces had launched the attack of December 19, and to the French government this placed them in the wrong. Some believed Ho had broken the Ho-Sainteny Accords, while others suspected a split in the Vietnamese government between Ho's moderates and extremists supporting Giap. But in actuality, Admiral d'Argenlieu had himself undermined the accords, insisting on showing off France's military might in Haiphong. And behind all this was a French Fourth Republic of constantly changing ministries, alternating between toughness and liberality abroad.[21]

So the French went to war in Indochina, and quickly found that they were in deep waters there. The old Socialist Léon Blum, who had become France's premier, applied his lucidity to the problem and in January 1947 offered command of all French forces to Leclerc, still alive at that point. D'Argenlieu was livid with rage, but need not have worried. Leclerc unfortunately rejected the offer, as he rejected the suggestion of Blum's successor, Ramadier, that he become high commissioner in Indochina. He was simply too careful a man to accept such assignments, fearing that Paris would undermine anything he might try to accomplish in this part of the world.[22]

The French then went on to fight a nineteenth-century colonial war in Indochina through to 1954, utilizing an expeditionary force enhanced by volunteers from North Africa, Indochina, and the Foreign Legion. The officer corps, however, was French. The idea or hope was that the Indochinese people could somehow be reconciled to French rule, either through persuasion or coercion. On the other side Ho and Giap would use much coercion of their own and were prepared to sacrifice many Vietnamese bodies, figuring that the French would eventually tire of a war of attrition.[23]

In February 1947 Paris did what it should have done a year earlier: it recalled d'Argenlieu, and Ho declared his government's willingness to accept independence within the French Union. French Communists and Socialists favored negotiations with him, but the right wing insisted on reaffirmation of Indochina's colonial status, and the MRP, a centrist party holding the balance of power in France, sided with the Right. Complicating matters, that party began to back Vietnamese Emperor Bao Dai, a playboy and expert bridge player, but never a viable alternative to the Viet Minh.[24]

On March 8, 1949 Bao Dai signed an agreement with French President Vincent Auriol by which France recognized Vietnamese independence within the French Union. In that year a new united Vietnam replaced Tonkin, Annam, and Cochin China as one of three Associated States of the French Union—along with less populous and important Laos and Cambodia. French forces would retain their bases and the right to move freely about the country, and the rights of French property holders would theoretically remain secure as well.[25]

But a weak Bao Dai proved to be no less frustrating to the French than the stronger Viet Minh. On the surface Bao behaved like a French puppet, but his maneuverings revealed more complex sides to his character. His root feeling was that no permanent settlement of the Indochina War was possible without Viet Minh involvement, especially with a great Communist victory looming up north in China. That victory of 1949 would change Ho's attitude dramatically. Between 1946 and 1949 Ho had frequently indicated that he would permit continuation of French influence in Vietnam, provided the French accepted Vietnamese independence. Now, with a victorious Chinese Communist army over the northern border, and the prospect that it could supply the Viet Minh with unlimited weaponry, Ho changed his tune. (What all this meant in human terms for our "cultured soldiers" will emerge more clearly in the next chapter.)[26]

The United States meanwhile had to this point kept its hands off the Indochina War. But after Mao's victory and the outbreak of the Korean War in June 1950, the Truman administration would begin viewing the conflict in Vietnam as part of an organized Communist movement threatening freedom in all of Asia. Henceforth came the prospect of massive American financial and military aid to underwrite the French war effort, aid which proved crucial to continued French campaigns here. By 1954 more than half the funding for the entire French defense budget would be supplied by Washington.[27] But Chinese Communist support of the Viet Minh had a more important impact on the fighting, for Ho could always look forward to reequipment with modern weapons and to the advantages of having steady supplies stream downward from the north.

To ensure this supply route, Giap launched a series of assaults in northern Tonkin along Colonial Route 4, the principal French highway running parallel to the Chinese border. This crucial 300-kilometer road was all that protected virtually the rest of Indochina from motorized divisions descending from the Communist north. Along that highway were a series of vulnerable garrison towns—the major ones being Cao Bang and Lang Son; vulnerable too were convoys of French trucks trundling artillery and other heavy materiel along a route made for Viet ambushes from secure hide-outs perched on cliffs towering above it. French patrols preceding these convoys tried to entice enemy fire, but not always with success, and truck rides that were really crapshoots often ended with blown-up, charred vehicles littering the road, their cargoes pillaged. One attack of September 1949 on a French convoy of fifty trucks killed 140, and the price for keeping this border presence intact became inordinate.

When France's General Revers came here on an inspection tour of May-June 1949, he recommended evacuations, causing divisions and scandal in Paris. General Robert Blaizot was set to pull out of this expensive sector, but was replaced by a new commander in chief there, General Marcel Carpentier, seduced by the opinions of another Marcel, General Alessandri, who advised against abandonment. But powerful Viet Minh forces in the region made the case for French evacuation by a series of assaults on these garrison towns, the first on primarily Moroccan companies at Dong Khe in late May 1950. Alessandri ordered paratroopers dropped in to take it back, but the odds were overwhelmingly against them. In the next, more important Viet Minh attack on Dong Khe September 16–18, elite Legionnaire paratroopers were decimated. Only then did the French decide on a definitive withdrawal plan, but late in the day, given a huge, China-facilitated enemy build-up in the area. Reinforcement of French troops at Cao Bang (derived from smaller garrisons) was dubbed Task Force Bayard, and placed under Lieutenant Colonel Marcel Le Page. The idea was for that group to march on Dong Khe and regain it in early October; while the rest of the Cao Bang garrison would then evacuate their positions, taking Route Coloniale 4, and hopefully link up with Le Page's column. It was a desperate plan, punctuated by arguments at the top between Generals Charpentier and Alessandri (the latter still against retreat, and perhaps more correct at this point). There was also poor co-ordination between the column marching for Dong Khe, and one preparing to blow up ammunition and leave Cao Bang in early October to cover thirty-three miles for the link-up. Had robust Legionnaires been permitted to zip into Dong Khe by surprise that column might have survived; but Le Page held them back overnight, and by the next morning the Viet

Minh were more numerous and ready for the kill. Le Page might still have
pulled back to That Khe. Instead, his men were ordered to leave Dong
Khe's environs, and by October 5 had blundered into a valley where they
found themselves without food or drink, and with only a few arms; and
surrounded by Viet Minh.

Charton's column meanwhile made it out of Cao Bang at midday October 3, weighed down by civilians designated as partisans, and lumbering
along Route Coloniale 4. Indigenous people left behind by reluctant
Legionnaires, including women and children trying to hook their fingers
onto departing trucks, would become the enemy's victims, and a source
of lingering shame for soldiers like Saint Marc, rivaling his Buchenwald
nightmares for years on end. Informed of Le Page's problems, Charton's
group was told to vacate the main route for a trail that ended up as bush.
The result was that both Le Page's and Charton's contingents had headed
into lethal ambushes prepared by fifteen well-armed enemy battalions.
North Africans ran away screaming, disorder spread, Charton was wounded
and taken with some 300 Moroccan *tabors*, the elite 1st Foreign Paratroop
Battalion (BEP) was decimated so badly it would have to be almost
entirely reconstituted for later use in Algeria; and altogether, the French
army lost a horrendous 6,000 to 7,000 men dead, missing, and wounded
here, including heavy losses among officers, and in courageous companies
of Moroccan sharpshooters and *goums*. Evacuation from the other key
point on Coloniale, Lang Son, formerly a beautiful, Frenchified provincial
capital of 100,000 inhabitants, but now much depleted, was also costly in
terms of materiel. Departing soldiers there abandoned 11,000 tons of shells
and cartridge rounds, 4,000 machine guns, and 600,000 liters of oil, rigged
for destruction by a man named Forster—except his detonator didn't
work, and the Viet Minh received a marvelous gift. A panic redolent of
1940 ensued everywhere in the region. The next item on the Viet Minh
menu was the all-important Red River delta, and the fall of Hanoi seemed
imminent. Civilian evacuations from the entire Tonkin were ordered, and
the French in Vietnam found themselves at their most dangerous crossroads yet.[28]

At this juncture, with the "disaster of Cao Bang" prominently featured
in the home front's media, the government of René Pleven made General
Jean de Lattre de Tassigny commander in chief in Vietnam *and* high
commissioner, giving him large powers indeed. De Lattre's orders were
unambiguous: to save not only Hanoi, but the entire French presence in
Indochina! It was a huge assignment, a contract demanding more trumps

than the French perhaps possessed; but then de Lattre was anything but ordinary. A look at his imposing, extensive military resumé shows this well.

Jean Marie Gabriel de Lattre de Tassigny was born in 1889 in the ultra-Catholic Vendée of France. At nine he went to board at the Collège Saint-Joseph in Poitiers, studying there for six years, before transfer to the Collège de Vaugirard in Paris and the Ecole Sainte-Geneviève in Versailles to prepare for a military career.[29] However, at the officers' school of Saint-Cyr, de Lattre, like his illustrious predecessors, found instruction tedious and uncongenial to anyone with a spark of originality.

He fared better at the cavalry school in Saumur and was then commissioned in the 12th Dragoons. In the Great War de Lattre was seriously wounded by a German lance, recovered, and in 1915 was transferred from cavalry to infantry in response to Joffre's request for officers to fill slots vacated by the dead.

Captain de Lattre of the 93rd Vendean Infantry Regiment served at Verdun in 1916 and was wounded again there; but by 1917 he was back commanding a battalion in Nivelle's ill-fated offensive on the Aisne River. The 93rd Regiment was nearly wiped out on the Chemin des Dames, but de Lattre survived to participate in Foch's offensives of the fall of 1918. He was twenty-nine at war's end, a respected leader, and thoroughly intolerant of military mediocrity.

Back home he struck up a friendship with another great Vendean, Georges Clemenceau, then in 1921 requested and received an assignment to Lyautey's Morocco. The colonies had never constituted the optimal path for advancement in the French army, but a young man who wanted to see action after the Great War was more likely to find it in the empire than in Europe. In Morocco de Lattre was posted to the staff of the legendary General Poeymirau, serving there until the latter's death from septicemia, then distinguished himself in the Rif conflict by his energy and ability to improvise. We have also seen that his critique of methods employed by Pétain did not pass unnoticed in France.

In 1926 Commandant de Tassigny returned to France, met and married a woman eighteen years his junior, and decided to prepare for the Ecole de Guerre exams, which he passed. After completion of that two-year course he obtained several posts in metropolitan France, ending up on the staff of General Weygand in 1933. In 1935 de Lattre took command of an infantry regiment at Metz, performing his duties with such distinction that in 1939 he became one of France's youngest brigadier generals. September 1939 found him chief of staff of the 5th Army in Strasbourg, whose armored commander was de Gaulle. In January 1940 de Lattre left the 5th Army for command of the 14th Infantry Division, deployed southwest of Sedan. Four months later, on May 13, Heinz Guderian's panzer armies smashed through the Ardennes, breaking the French lines at Sedan. The fate of France was sealed, but de Lattre and de Gaulle were two men who kept their heads as the disaster unfolded.[30]

De Lattre remained in France, then in July 1941 at Weygand's request assumed command of French forces in Tunisia. But already suspected of Gaullist leanings, he impeded Axis efforts to resupply Rommel's Afrika Korps through Tunis, and in February 1942 Vichy recalled him to Montpellier. On November 11 that year, three days after the Allies landed in North Africa, and the very day the Germans began occupying the south of France, he was arrested. Tried at Lyon in January 1943 on charges of treason against the French state, he was sentenced to ten years imprisonment.

De Lattre entered his cell at Riom under heavy guard, but still had friends in the army, and on September 3 several helped him escape. Squeezing through the bars of his window, he then climbed down a rope ladder, falling to the ground. After six weeks in hiding he was smuggled out of France aboard a British plane, and in December 1943 flew from London to Algiers to meet de Gaulle, becoming commander of the French army in Algiers. He then played an important role in the liberation of France and the end of the war with Germany.

At war's end this military powerhouse flatly asked de Gaulle to make him chief of the General Staff, so that he might effect serious military reforms; but de Gaulle hesitated six months, before deciding on the appointment. In March 1947 a furious de Lattre lost the office to General Revers, and the government dispatched him to South America as head of an economic mission. Surviving a plane crash in the foothills of the Andes, he ended up having a delightful time there. The following spring he was promoted to inspector general of the Armed Forces and in October 1948, commander in chief of Land Forces in Western Europe. Surprisingly, this man now left that post for the quagmire of French Indochina.[31]

It was the very moment when the catastrophe of Cao Bang loomed large, and de Lattre now moved with the energy of a Gallieni to save Hanoi. In the long run his object was to keep the French in Indochina, and to do so he knew he would have to fight conventional battles with Giap. The latter in fact welcomed his new adversary on January 14, 1951 by launching an assault on a French base fewer than forty miles from Hanoi. But a day later de Lattre hatched a powerful counteroffensive, driving off the Viet Minh and creating 6,000 casualties. He also forced its high command to reconsider its strategies.[32]

In the following six months, de Lattre moved forcefully on several fronts. First, he pushed for the creation of an independent Vietnamese army in support of France, then beefed up protection of the Red River delta. In March he flew to France to present a request for additional reinforcements, including NCOs and trained officers for the new Vietnamese army. At this time he also met with America's General Eisenhower, discussing strategy with him. In April de Lattre returned to Vietnam, taking truly personal command of French defenses there. Already planning a trip to Washington to lobby the Americans for additional aid, his flurry of activity reversed a decline in French morale, giving an impression that France might be able to salvage its position in Vietnam after all.[33]

Then the famed general's life fell apart. On the night of May 29–30, 1951 his only son Bernard, commanding an infantry company at Ninh Binh, was surprised by a heavy barrage of Communist mortar fire. The legendary French "pirate of the Delta," Roger Vandenberghe, already wounded by bullets or mines six times in this war, came in to help with a group that included beloved Vietnamese. But he himself was wounded again here, and his company lost nineteen men.[34] The battle ended as a French disaster, punctuated by the death at three in the morning of Bernard de Lattre himself.

Learning the news, his celebrated father was stunned, and though he ordered a massive, vengeful barrage on the enemy, nine months later he would himself be dead of cancer, evidence perhaps of an immune system weakened by grief. In the months left to him de Lattre did manage to visit Washington to persuade the Joint Chiefs of Staff to dispatch additional materiel to French Indochina, and the trip was successful. (Some might even see his selling job of Indochina's strategic importance to the Americans as one of the key early precursors of a later U.S. involvement.) De Lattre returned to Saigon on October 19, 1951, but lacked his customary vigor and panache. His physical condition was by that time declining rapidly, and a checkup in Paris revealed that he was suffering from terminal cancer. On November 20 he returned to Paris, undergoing surgery the following month, and passed away on January 11, 1952, the same day he was made a marshal of France.[35]

De Lattre's demise highlighted France's predicament in Asia. She was now fighting for two things: the salvation of Indochina from communism and the continued presence of Vietnam within the French Union. Everyone realized that French resources were inadequate to the first task, and de Lattre had attempted to compensate by insisting on developing a Vietnamese national army under Bao Dai, talking Washington into footing a good deal of the bill. In terms of the French Union France now worried about falling dominoes—not only in Asia, but in places like Rabat, Tunis, and Algiers.[36]

De Lattre's death rid General Giap of his most formidable adversary, giving the Viet Minh commander some breathing space, and the latter now prepared a two-pronged strategy. First, he sent guerillas into the Tonkin delta to affront the French, who responded by surrounding the area with more fixed installations, tying down more than 80,000 of their troops. Increasingly, the heavily populated delta became a costly congeries of French positions in or by villages mostly controlled by the Viet Minh, where the same two-facedness of inhabitants to be seen in the American war already obtained. By day most villagers remained silent and "know nothing," but sometimes became actively involved guerillas by night. The Viet Minh submerged themselves in water, breathing through bamboo, then hit hard at French emplacements with explosive-filled bangalores and a variety of other arms. In a fruitless cycle large-scale French operations would then be unleashed. Second, Giap began threatening Laos with his main group, compelling the French to defend that part of its empire with forces of equivalent size.[37]

Giap had not come to this decision easily. But French operations in different parts of Vietnam, particularly the South, made him cast his eyes around for a place to deliver the coup de grâce. He knew that a full-scale operation in the northern delta would cost him too many losses. Apparently he learned from a French newspaper in the summer of 1953 that France feared defending Laos most, which helped produce his heavy advance in that direction.

Giap's pressure on Laos then convinced French Commander in Chief Henri Navarre, who followed de Lattre's replacement, Salan, to impede Viet Minh communications in the area, by creating a French base at Dien Bien Phu, a vital road junction between Laos and Tonkin. On the plus side Dien Bien Phu possessed a good airstrip. Moreover, there were only two major routes for Giap's advance on Laos, and by decoding Viet Minh radio messages the French knew that his main forces would go through Dien, before trying to take the Laotian capital by January. One French problem, however, was that Dien Bien Phu lay in a valley thirteen miles long by seven wide, and the Viet Minh could easily occupy the heavily forested mountains surrounding it. Regrettably, Navarre overlooked several other key problems as well. Dien Bien Phu lay at maximum operational distance from French airbases of the northern delta, some on the outskirts of Hanoi. The French also refused to believe that Giap could deploy anti-aircraft guns, or that his artillery could reach this strategic point from the mountains. They basically underestimated or refused to consider how he would bring supplies some 400 kilometers from the Chinese frontier, using an army of a good 75,000 indefatigable coolies. (Of course all who worked for Ho and Giap *had* to be indefatigable!) Add to these oversights French failure to camouflage the base, and it is easy to comprehend the eventual debacle that would occur there.[38]

One more problem was the appointment of Navarre himself (May 8, 1953). Having fought in the Rif War of the 1920s and in World War II, then affected to a relatively quiet Algeria of the late '40s before becoming chief of staff to the commander of NATO's ground forces in Europe, Navarre was totally without experience of Indochina. But Prime Minister René Mayer of a Fourth Republic that had tired of this war was happy to have appointed such a man here. Scornfully labeled the "air-conditioned general," Navarre inspired little confidence in soldiers who had been suffering in the field. The replacement of Salan, who knew the Far East so well, by a man who didn't know it at all was the tragedy within a subsequent tragedy. Navarre himself realized his limitations, and had only taken the position reluctantly. The departure of top military brains associated with de Lattre compounded the problem. So did the contradictory policies of Jean Letourneau, who had been minister of overseas France from October 1949 to June 1950, then minister with special responsibility of Indochina from July 1950 to May 1953. Letourneau compounded powers in a way that really wasn't feasible, remaining both a French minister and becoming high commissioner as well. He then removed his expertise, leaving just when Navarre was taking over. One should also note the concomitant ending of the Korean War, and a sense that things should be on hold in Indochina until general negotiations resolved that conflict too. Not to mention a continuing hope that "Vietnamization" (what the French called *jaunissement*), less realistic than the later Nixon variety, except in southern Vietnam, might make a final denouement more palatable.[39]

It is simplistic to place all blame for the impending disaster on Navarre alone, though an *ex post facto* investigation led by General Catroux would award him majority responsibility for the eventual debacle. But once his plan was readied, visiting military experts from the United States and

Britain concurred on its efficacy, as did much of the press back home in France. Starry-eyed visitors included well-known names like Graham Greene and France's minister of defense, René Pleven. But the visiting Army chief of staff General Blanc, who knew Indochina better than Pleven, saw the Viet Minh in command here, not the French, and wondered how all these men parachuted into the basin would ever make it out. Another officer, Colonel Bastiani, considered it ludicrous to use a build-up here to interdict Giap's move toward Laos. Others warned that French aircraft would have a devil of a time bringing in supplies.

The *cuvette* or basin of Dien was really like a long stadium surrounded by thickly forested mountain heights commanded by the enemy. The entrenched camp's bottom was shorn of its vegetation, and trenches were dug that would become susceptible to flooding. Soldiers mired here began hoping by January 1954 that there would actually be no major enemy assault on their uncomfortable positions. They also began to doubt French opinion back home. One man wrote a letter back to his wife January 31: "France will never thank [these men], will not render honor to their memory, for the French seem ashamed of this war. France isn't worthy of its soldiers fighting in Indochina."[40]

There was in this dug-in prelude to Dien Bien Phu, where some 12,000 men simply waited, a strange recapitulation of so much of France's military history: in dangerous sortie operations that winter, which led to nothing, echoes of the 1870 siege of Paris and futile exit attempts against the encircling Germans. In the muddy, insular trench atmosphere, and in an idealistic effort to stay the course, World War I, and more particularly, Verdun. In the conception of walling off the Viets from Laos, the Maginot Line of the '30s; in the interminable, grubby waiting game of December, January, and February, with the hope against hope that maybe the enemy was impressed and wouldn't attack in force, the Phony War of 1939–40 preceding the Nazi onslaught in the spring. And maybe more generally, there was all this French delicacy, intelligence, and civilization (letters home show it well and so does our more human material of the next chapter), beautiful ideas in the helmets of those who seemed like Ravels and Debussys ready to be hit by Wagnerian forces of what would indeed become a kind of *Götterdämmerung*!

On March 13, 1954 the patient Giap finally unleashed a no-holds-barred assault against Dien Bien Phu, quickly revealing how gravely Navarre had miscalculated. Viet Minh artillery reached French installations with ease, while their antiaircraft batteries kept its air force at bay. After three days of enemy shelling, the airstrip was *hors de combat,* and Giap's artillery could now destroy anything attempting to move across it. On March 16 the Communist leader sent in suicide units composed of men with high explosives strapped to their bodies. The latter cut their way through Dien's barbed-wire perimeter, blowing themselves up when injured.[41]

Giap's decision-making rendered the battle a logistical tussle in which he held all the high cards. With their airstrip shut down, the French could resupply Dien only by parachute drops under heavy antiaircraft fire (see the next chapter for what this meant). That kind of operation gave the garrison only half the daily supplies required for survival, and so the outcome was clear after the first several days. The battle was also crucial for Giap, and one he took very seriously, because it coincided with the opening of the Geneva Conference that would seek a general negotiated settlement in Indochina.[42]

On March 20 General Paul Ely, now French chief of staff, flew to Washington at the request of Joint Chiefs of Staff Chairman Admiral Arthur Radford. The French knew they could only relieve Dien Bien Phu with air power, and since they now lacked it themselves, Washington's top brass seemed to be the only ones able to provide more. In the course of their conversations Radford suggested that three tactical nuclear devices might be sufficient to prevent the Viet Minh from overrunning the base! This idea got as far as President Eisenhower's desk, before he putatively dismissed it with the statement, "My God, you boys must be crazy. We can't use those damned things on Asians twice in ten years!" There was much discussion in Washington of how to help the French at Dien Bien Phu by more conventional means; but Ely found in his hosts—particularly in that staunch anti-Communist John Foster Dulles—an anticolonial bias lacking nuance. Secretary of State Dulles and President Eisenhower also hesitated due to the Geneva talks, defeatism in Paris, and American war-weariness after its protracted Korean conflict. There were nonetheless meetings with important Congressional members on the subject, and consultations too with Churchill and Anthony Eden. If the British and their Commonwealth had come on board, the French would probably have gotten their assistance from the air; but Britain had been burned enough across the Channel in the twentieth century and felt it best to await the Geneva talks. So in the end nothing came of Radford's promises to Ely, and the 11,000 or so left alive at Dien out of a French garrison of 20,000 surrendered on May 7, most to die subsequently. It was really the end of a French Vietnam.[43]

Perhaps their colonial venture in Indochina had been doomed for a long time, yet there remains a slim possibility that France lost its last chance for a decent settlement simply because of the human factor—the fact that General Jean de Lattre de Tassigny had died too soon. However one interprets this problem, what remained was a South Vietnam, bloated by a good million refugees from the North, henceforth clinging to its fragile, non-Communist existence via an American lifeline, not a French one.

More important to France, the Viet Minh's destruction of the French Empire in Indochina now sent shock waves through North Africa, which had given many men to fight in Vietnam, soldiers who had been observing France's military problems there with more than polite interest. World War II had already accelerated tendencies toward independence in both Morocco and Tunisia. Together with Algeria, the jewel in France's North African colonial crown, conflicts in these imperial areas would tear France apart in what remained of the 1950s and end its Fourth Republic.

French control of Morocco had begun to ebb in 1943, when its tenacious resident, Charles Noguès, fresh from resisting the Americans following their invasion of North Africa, escaped to Portugal, where he remained for a decade to avoid a sentence of twenty years hard labor and confiscation of his property by a French court. His successor, Gabriel Puaux, was former high commissioner in Syria and Lebanon, but not of Noguès' caliber. The year 1943 was also significant for a meeting at Casablanca of Sultan Ben Youssef with the anticolonial American President Roosevelt. To de Gaulle's annoyance, the two discussed Morocco's eventual independence, and their conversations facilitated the growth of an Istiqlal (Independence) Party. Calling for independence under a constitutional monarchy, Istiqlal worked publicly to that end, while the sultan operated behind the scenes. But as noted, governments of the Fourth Republic had no intention of dismantling the French Empire. Strikes broke out across Morocco early in 1947, and on April 7 Senegalese troops killed hundreds in Casablanca, while French police stood by. This Casablanca Massacre then led to the appointment of the controversial Alphonse Juin as new resident-general.[44]

In Morocco's French community General Juin's appointment was greeted with joy and relief, for they felt that here was a man who knew how to deal with Arabs, and they granted him a level of adulation denied even to Lyautey. Juin *had* had martial exploits, beginning his career in the Moroccan *tirailleurs*. He had served on Lyautey's staff, had been *chef de cabinet* for Resident-General Saint, and had been a commander of all French forces in Morocco. He had also led the Free French expeditionary force in Italy during 1944. More, he was intelligent, and putatively fluent in no fewer than eight languages—French, English, Spanish, Italian, German, Russian, Arabic, and Berber.[45]

Juin's failings, in other words, could not be attributed to stupidity but rather, to a somewhat haughty nature and a narrow political education. Born in Algeria of modest origins (his father a gendarme, his mother from a rather poor Corsican family), Juin had been educated in Bône and Constantine. There he imbibed the *pied noir* contempt for Arabs, an attitude reinforced by his wife Marie, who hailed from Constantine's upper bourgeoisie.[46] In her husband's entourage she excluded people offering any opinions contrary to her own, and throughout Morocco it was known that she idolized Eva Perón. Juin himself was already a hypersensitive, even paranoid man with regard to his personal dignity, reacting swiftly to any perceived slight. Though jovial, he often manifested a calculated rudeness, designed to close off discussions by burying opponents' arguments in a flurry of scorn.

In Morocco, however, the desire for independence could not be argued away, and through his own arrogance Juin helped set in motion the destruction of his mandate. The French outlawed Istiqlal, but the organization went underground, and its appeal kept growing. The French tried to undermine the sultan, bestowing favors on the pasha of Marrakech, Thami el-Glaoui, whose family had been at odds with the sultan's for centuries. But el-Glaoui was a poor leader, and his sycophantic behavior offended many Moroccans, tipping fence-sitters in Istiqlal's direction.[47]

By the early '50s the situation deteriorated rapidly. Serious urban rioting swept Morocco late in 1952, and the French cracked down with police sweeps and torture of suspects. In August 1953 they kidnapped the sultan and his family, exiling them to Madagascar. In his place the French installed a puppet ruler, someone even less attractive than el-Glaoui. The former sultan became revered as a Moroccan martyr, and the drive toward independence intensified. Istiqlal terrorism provoked not a French military response, but the actions of *Présence française*, a militia formed by French settlers there to terrorize dissident Moroccans. It was apparent that the French government would either have to grant Morocco independence, or embark on full-scale repression using massive forces.[48]

Events occurring at the time in Vietnam made the choice an easier one. In the aftermath of Dien Bien Phu, Pierre Mendès-France came to power as the Fourth Republic's premier, pledging to end the Indochina War in one month.[49] Using the Geneva Conference as his mechanism, he succeeded in extricating France from its Asian quicksand in July 1954. The outbreak of war in Algeria that November, coupled with unrest in Tunisia, left his government with only one decision concerning French Morocco. Mendès opened negotiations with the exiled sultan, permitting him to return late in 1955, and the following spring, Paris and Rabat signed agreements terminating the French protectorate as of March 2, 1956. The sultan promised to maintain good relations with France, a promise he would keep. As for Juin, his career petered out at the end of the Algerian War.[50]

Mendès also tackled the Tunisian problem simultaneously with the Moroccan one. On July 31, 1954 he issued the Declaration of Carthage, proclaiming Tunisian independence in principle, and initiating negotiations aimed at translating it into practice. Three years of talks ensued, ending with the release from French prison of Habib Bourguiba, leader of the nationalist Néo-Destour Party, on June 1, 1957. Two days later agreements creating self-government in Tunisia were signed, and final independence came on March 20, 1958. But Tunisia, like Morocco, was by this time only a sideshow, not the main colonial event.[51]

From 1946 to 1954 Vietnam had been that main event, and shortly after the conclusion of the war the new one became the most important part of French North Africa, Algeria. Many young Algerian Muslims had fought zealously during World War II for Free France, including Ahmed Ben Bella and Belkacem Krim, the latter from rugged Kabylia who, it was said, had mastered more than a hundred ways to kill a man and personally experimented with every one of them! These men and others like them carefully watched the war in Indochina, and the impact of France's 1954 defeat was stunning. Losing to the Nazis was one thing, but for the mother country to drop a showpiece colony to a collection of Vietnamese irregulars spoke volumes. The Algerians considered themselves racially and probably religiously superior to Asians, and took the lesson at once: if *they* can defeat the French, they reasoned, so can we. The result was the formation of an underground organization that would swallow up others of a different orientation, the Front de Libération Nationale, or FLN.

At one minute past midnight on November 1, 1954 (All Saints' Day), the FLN struck simultaneously at forty-five places throughout Algeria, hijacking buses, bombing stores, and killing Europeans in cities like Bône and Algiers, as well as in smaller towns. This was the beginning of the Algerian War, destined to cost a large number of lives, split France in two, destroy the Fourth Republic, and resuscitate de Gaulle's political career. It would likewise serve as a backdrop for the incredible exploits of a great French soldier, Marcel Bigeard, to whom we turn in the next chapter.

CHAPTER EIGHT

Bigeard

Last of the Line
in Vietnam and Algeria

ARCEL BIGEARD IS THE perfect, even quintessential example of the last of many things—a certain *noblesse oblige* revealed in French colonial milieus, devotion to something much larger than oneself, and a fine intellect to go with firm character and military excellence. His story is radiant but tragic, since many of the soldiers he mentions in extraordinary memoirs largely on his service in Indochina and Algeria of the '40s and '50s perished there—and with more than a few ideas in their own helmets. Bigeard's narrative humanizes and renders more palpable our discussion concerning the demise of the French colonial empire, showing that some of these men, however doomed, became the "best and brightest" of their countrymen. Here we examine the career of France's most decorated soldier, first fighting the Nazis in World War II, then during long stints in the Vietnam and Algerian debacles that scourged France through the 1950s, and which remain powerful issues there today. We treat a man from the lower classes who left school at fourteen, yet rose to the highest reaches of a hidebound military system as a four-star general—not via degrees or connections, though increasingly he realized the value of the latter; but by an imposing series of operational master-pieces resulting from courageous leadership, assiduity at getting the best from his men, celerity in decision making, intelligence, and incredible self-discipline. Finally, we discuss a man with real respect for those he fought and protected, and those of other cultures from whom he learned.

Today we are supposed to play down race or physiognomy, but a writer like Balzac would have noticed instantly what a beautiful animal Bigeard was—in his face and in his taut, yet supple carriage, what a romantically noble leader he could be, even in the many unromantic places where he would fight. However, he had not started out as an imperial figure—nor would he ever become anything like a proconsul. Yet it was during this final chapter of French imperialism in Indochina and Algeria that Bigeard made a legendary reputation, and deservedly so. Truly he was the last of the line, as unique as the great colonials we have treated here, yet somehow quite similar in his characterological mixture.

Cultured force? Bigeaud had and has exquisite manners—right down to the incredible alacrity with which a man showered by correspondence answers letters; and as for culture, he has written or edited over a dozen books. In the old path of Bugeaud, Faidherbe, Gallieni, Lyautey, here again is another expatiator, recaller, analyzer, and observer, but possessing a slangy, terse, yet elegant voice all his own. Like Bugeaud in particular, Bigeard was a great military theorist; but there is much more to him than just the military side. In his writing he has an acute sense of personality differences, and is a great observer of cultural trends as well.

Of course General Paul Aussaresses' interviews and first memoir of 2001 (on which more below) touched off yet another media brushfire concerning torture in Algeria, raging as we brought this manuscript to completion. Bigeard's role in Algeria was largely in operations of the *bled* (outback), but all this besmirched the army as a whole, not least Bigeard, object of nonsensical slander dealt with in our final note. The need to get special permission to see certain archives was another problem, and the tardy availability of inventories at Vincennes (December 2001) on the Algerian conflict, while blessedly useful and used here, also make a fuller exposition of that section something for another day. Hopefully ours may help point researchers in certain directions.

Saul Bellow once remarked that distinguishing is a higher mental activity than explaining, and when it comes to Bigeard in Algeria, his differences from people like General Massu with whom he somewhat fell out truly need to be distinguished. Our generation of baby boomers has created an atmosphere of indiscriminate tearing down, of deconstructing, of making anyone and everyone in the public realm very clay-footed indeed. The opposite shoal perhaps equally to be avoided is hagiography. However, a first, belated phone call to Bigeard revealed within minutes why so many young men were willing to live in hellish conditions and die in droves at his side. The voice of this survivor in his mid-eighties was strong, full, and urgent. Here was a man without a minute to waste, worried about the lack of a French military response (vis-à-vis English or Germans) to

Osama bin Laden's devotees, still burning for his country at the end of 2001, and like Gallieni, an instant appraiser of personalities, and though much consulted, apparently suffering no fools gladly. This and subsequent calls confirmed Bigeard's self-made tenacity, making clear how inspirational he would have been to his charges. They also showed his coruscating, quicksilver, in-a-nutshell intelligence, and how he invariably begins conversations *in medias res* and without needless preamble. They drove home as well his exquisite *gentillesse,* his French generosity, his heart (and that's "a real fine place to stawt," as Mr. Manilow would have it), his deep curiosity. Especially when it came to today's America, Bigeard listened carefully, obviously hoping to use what seemed to matter. Here, in sum, was a thoroughly healthy ego, in absolute contrast to that of a Joffre. But on to Bigeard's extraordinary story, one that in its detail reveals so much about this twilight era of the French empire.

Born in 1916 in the patriotic province of Lorraine—and a growingly anachronistic patriotism would remain one of his driving forces—Bigeard was the product of parents whose psychological shaping helped create a winner, continually eluding difficult circumstances. His father, a railway worker, was quiet, but industrious; his mother, domineering, demanding, but fair, and always wishing her son top-of-the line, accepted no excuses.

At fourteen Bigeard quit school to help these parents financially, taking a position in a bank and doing well there. Then, with no initial enthusiasm he began his future vocation in September 1936, when military service sent him on a train to the Maginot Line and the garrison of Haguenau. Already he had that same sense of cramped impatience with French provincial routines that had impelled earlier proconsuls outward, and in fact was much moved hearing a rebroadcast of Lyautey's funeral in the 1930s. The young Bigeard dreamt of a wider world, empathizing especially with French athletic achievements, at which he himself came to excel (cycling, boxing, running, shooting). He also idolized celebrated French aviators like Jean Mermoz and Hélène Boucher, both to be killed. And he devoured articles about living in colonial milieus like Indochina, with pictures of glamorous women and men in evening tuxedos, part of "la France conquérante, maîtresse de son empire." If at first military service was not really to his taste, he certainly toughened himself there. On returning home he was a stronger young man, ready to affront the Germans, when they came calling at the end of the decade.[1]

Back on the Maginot Line at the outset of World War II, Bigeard wanted badly to repel the enemy, and in the debacle of May-June 1940 fought well, trying to reassure higher-ranked soldiers afflicted with defeatism. There ensued the humiliating armistice and on June 22 as well, encirclement of his own regiment, though he continued fighting until the Nazis finally captured him.

Taken by train to a German prison, Bigeard got to see the enemy's "gods of war" first hand; but in each camp he inhabited thought only of escape. He was initially lodged in an elite *Oflag* for officers, but felt it would be easier to flee a more populated camp. Fortuitously he was transferred to Stalag 12A at Limbourg, where some 15,000 prisoners from various parts of Europe languished, bunked according to background in abodes of roughly 500 each. At the camp's heart was a barrack for those who had made previous escape attempts. When the Nazis asked for farmers, Bigeard and a handsome Parisian, Jean Bled, decided to volunteer, taken fifty kilometers from the stalag and marched out each morning at six to dig and hoe. Bigeard grew strong from the work, benefiting as well from the attentions of a German *fräulein,* his boss's daughter-in-law, bereft of her husband away on some front. Having plotted their escape, Bigeard and Bled snipped wires on the patriotic date of July 14, 1941, walked a week and a half, succeeded in crossing the Rhine, bypassed Trier, and got almost within smelling distance of their homeland. But one night at three in the morning they unfortunately abutted a new guard post the Germans had just erected that day after a recent escape in the area by Polish officers. It was the end of Bigeard's first try.

Taken back again by train, he was now placed in a tiny castle cell on 500 grams of bread a day and a pitcher of water. After a few weeks of that regime, Bigeard dropped ten kilos, writhing from hunger. But once relocated to Stalag 12A and its barrack of the escapees, he kept thinking of bolting again. Finally, Bigeard located a new pal he could trust there, Gérard Masbourian, who had attempted his own escape in June and been apprehended at the Luxembourg frontier. Masbourian wanted to try the same route again, now knowing which guard posts to avoid. Athletic and strong, he impressed Marcel, and together they executed their plan September 22, 1941, unscrewing a barrier in the middle of the night and hoping to slip off alone. Instead they were followed by almost the entire barrack, with German searchlights and machine guns soon ending a tragicomic escape attempt number two.

This time Bigeard rated a beating, along with reduced rations, and the whole barrack was threatened with deportation to a concentration camp if anyone tried again. None of which deterred him. Bigeard and Masbourian now felt their only chance would be to join a work convoy, and despite their record, Germany's recent, huge involvement in Russia and need for manpower gave them an opportunity. Affected to a group of French volunteers working in an aircraft parts factory, they were shunned as interlopers, and able thereby to hatch plans alone. They also got in shape unloading heavy materials all day. Masbourian met a German waitress who procured them civilian clothes, which at the right moment they hoped to change into from prison garb. Bigeard also learned that the building housing showers for prisoners neighbored a garage where German workers parked their bicycles. Again, the idea was to loosen some screws, choose another significant date (November 11, 1941) for exit, and slip out by night via the garage, taking bicycles en route.

This time only one other French group of two sniffed out the plan and followed, taking its own direction. Though hesitant at first about the weather, Bigeard and Masbourian actually got help from a freak, early snowstorm petalling everything white, and which probably saved them. For after an entire night of travel they found they had gone in a circle, arriving back near their starting point, only a few kilometers from the factory. Nazi patrols had meanwhile gone southward to search for their quarry. Eventually the unnoticed pair got themselves on a line due west, pedaling in snow and cold, overwhelmed by hunger and fatigue, and nearly nabbed in one village before dawn, when a German policeman noted a nonfunctioning back light. Mumbling German words, the two walked their bicycles to the first corner, and after turning it, flung caution to the winds and rode away.

Very tired, they eventually reached the Rhine, where they slept, then the next morning mingled with a flow of German workers crossing the bridge. On the other side Bigeard's now-damaged bicycle was discarded, then his friend's too, and they walked some forty-five kilometers toward Trier—a precursor to Bigeard's later exhausting marches in Vietnam and Algeria.

The next problem was traversing the Moselle, which they managed to do by pilfering a fisherman's rowboat, and hand paddling against a strong current. On November 20 they found themselves at the spot on Luxembourg's frontier where Masbourian had formerly been caught; this time he knew to avoid the main road, figuring it preferable to crawl over the frozen rails of a train track crossing a bridge and the frontier, while guards hopefully stayed inside their warm hut. Thankfully they did.

Risk-taking and good fortune continued as the escapees carefully avoided

Nazis in this tiny occupied country, and after ten kilometers, famished, had to decide between a farm that might be billeting German soldiers, or an inn. Masbourian's decision to choose the inn was the right one. There the pair told the truth, and were luckily served hot milk and bread by a waitress, who warned them to decamp fast—German soldiers often came in here. Later that morning they stopped at another house, and again, came up lucky, when a Resistant doctor there steered them to a nearby farm. Here they were cleaned up and fed, then slept for forty-eight hours.

Rejuvenated, and in new clothes, the resourceful duo were then led to the French frontier area, a bewildering maze of factories, train tracks, and barriers. Uncertainly snaking their way through, they came upon a worker, asking tentatively, "Sprechen Sie Deutsch?" The delicious answer was: "Je ne comprends pas." They had made it to France.

As if in a piece of fiction where everything works out, the future man of *baraka* (literally "blessing") was shepherded with his pal to a café where two French policemen, both Resistants, took them down to a cellar for a bath and rest, before sending them off on a nervous train ride through Lorraine. Though armed with new papers, the pair still realized that any thorough German examination might mean the end. What emotions Bigeard nonetheless had seeing his home turf swim by outside the windows and then on the quai of one town, witnessing his own sister and her husband! Getting out, he warned them to keep still, received the togs of a French railway worker, and in that outfit would arrive back in his hometown of Toul.

At the door of the house his father had built, Bigeard met his marvelous, tough mother, always expecting her son's low-odds victories and helping thereby to create the future legend of French Indochina and Algeria. Here too was his next-door neighbor and childhood sweetheart Gaby, who would remain another lodestone. But it wasn't safe here; Bigeard's first German farm boss had come to visit his parents, meaning Nazi authorities, including the Gestapo, might do so as well. Reluctantly leaving by night after a few days, Bigeard and Masbourian made their way on a train from gritty Lorraine, glutted with Nazis, to the Unoccupied South and the comparative ease of Nice by the sea, where Masbourian's parents lived.[2]

Here, both Bigeard and Masbourian were decorated and given back pay, which came in handy when Gaby arrived to marry Marcel in early 1942. Right after the wedding, military authorities then decided to send him to French West Africa—from Marseille to Dakar, with one short stop in Casablanca, a trip that in itself presented danger, given English and German naval activity in the Mediterranean and Atlantic. Without his bride Bigeard arrived by early March in Faidherbe's Senegal, an area still under Pétainist influence, and where laid-back colonials at first distrusted a newcomer who had fought and escaped the Nazis. Bigeard was dispatched to Thiès, and thence to Bandia, where he became head bookkeeper, then via long solitary marches at sun-up started to infect others with his enthusiasm. This led to a section command, and to something he would accomplish many more times abroad—transformation of those around him by his own hard work and example. He also had a soccer field and sports club built, which Africans willingly joined. Inevitably, his section became top-of-the line, making other deadwood leaders grumble. Six months of nocturnal mosquito fighting led to bouts of malaria, then the resourceful Gaby pulled strings and made the trip—again over dangerous waters—to join her husband. She and Marcel enjoyed a blissful, extended honeymoon in the forest, playing a few records on an old phonograph in their simple digs, where local people came to sing and dance too.

In the outside world nothing, however, was holding still, as the Americans landed in North Africa November 8. Tardily, the AOF dropped its allegiance to Vichy, and Bigeard's Senegal moved to the camp of Admiral Darlan, then after his assassination, to Giraud. *Tirailleurs sénégalais* were henceforth transferred in droves to fight in North Africa, and Marcel patiently awaited his turn.

In October 1943 he and others were sent to Meknès in Morocco, where soon after, French agents working for the British sought volunteers for an eventual parachute sortie into Occupied France. Few volunteered, but already Bigeard's philosophy was "toujours présent," and he willingly traveled to freed Algiers for demanding training under the English, learning to jump, climb cliffs, handle explosives, and kill, both armed and unarmed. No Anglophobe, he was particularly inspired by a man named Bill Probert, a veteran of Tobruk.

After the Normandy invasion the time for Bigeard's own participation in France's liberation neared. As "Commandant Aube" he mounted the *Halifax* in Blida August 6, 1944, flying with lights out across the sea toward France, Probert beside him. They would then parachute into the lush, mountainous Ariège of southwestern France. When it came time to yell "Go!" the future dean of "para" warfare naturally went first; however, his baptismal jump ended ignominiously in a tree. Near Foix the jumpers then linked up with Resistants, where the Gestapo were still torturing.

Among maquis here Bigeard would work with a group of Spanish anar-
chists led by one Royo, who at first insisted on strip-searching Bigeard
and cohorts, then grew to like and trust the Frenchman. Clad in civilian
clothes, and with a commemoratively significant cover name of Marcel
Bugeaud, bank employee, Bigeard went to Foix, checking out Resistance
activity there.

An initial operation against the Germans holed up in a secondary
school in the city was crowned with success August 19, when the regnant
Nazi colonel surrendered to Bigeard on condition that he and his men were
kept from Spanish hands. Liberated Foix predictably went crazy, then came
vigilantism and the settling of scores that so marked France of that era,
and which disgusted Bigeard, as did a precipitous boom in Resistance
credentials. There was another, tougher battle ahead against marauding
Russian "Mongols" recruited by the SS, whom Bigeard almost alone suckered into a trap, then, running for his life, drew onto the high road, where
they were picked off from the heights by Royo, Probert, and company.
Royo now wanted Bigeard to help him take Andorra, followed by nothing
less than Franco's Spain! But the Lorrainer sensibly demurred, and would
hear that this appealing Spaniard, a quixotic idealist right out of Orwell's
Homage to Catalonia, would later die for his cause.

By mid-September a decorated Bigeard departed the Ariège, wheel-
ing a confiscated Mercedes up to Paris, a city he had never seen before.
People adorned with ersatz Resistance laurels were plentiful here too, and
the twenty-eight-year-old Bigeard didn't like the atmosphere at all. But
he did locate a bistro where he had a dance with the famous Edith Piaf
(her own wartime record of dubious quality). That fall he then drove his
Mercedes with white parachutes daubed on its sides to foggy Lorraine.

Thence to the Bordelais to set up a cadre school near the beach town
of Arcachon for the Forces Françaises de l'Intérieur, and soon his group
acquired *une gueule terrible*—"para" training, boxing, explosives, and shooting on the English model. This type of training would become Bigeard's
hallmark, and he found command to his taste, though the end of the
European war in May, then America's atomic bombs of August precluded
any actual fighting against Germans or Japanese. Bigeard, however, was
ready to serve elsewhere. That elsewhere was first a regiment in Germany,
where he had to be patient with those who had come up via more orthodox routes, including Saint-Cyr, and who initially patronized him. Here he
followed orders of Lieutenant-Colonel Jean Gilles, later his one-eyed superior in Indochina and Algeria. Rapidly he advanced, and was "toujours

présent" when the colonial milieu soon called. Bigeard felt the French government must have reasons for wanting to regain a hold on Vietnam, and though saddened to leave his pregnant wife on the quai at Marseille, he volunteered to be a part of it.[3]

Sailing on a hot and uncomfortable American "victory ship," he arrived with his battalion in November 1945 near Cape Saint Jacques, before traveling up river to Saigon. Bigeard first embarked on operations up and down Cochin China for four months under General Leclerc, whom he admired. He also came to esteem Indochina's clean villages and hard-working people, as well as its fighters, whom he emulated.[4]

From reconquered Cochin China and Annam he then migrated north to Hanoi, a different milieu, not least owing to the presence of Ho's self-proclaimed Republic up there. While French authorities dickered with Ho's Communists and with the occupying Chinese, Bigeard and his cohorts kept fit via sport and marching, but also at evening dances with Vietnamese "taxi-girls" in tight dresses. He himself was tempted by a young escort, but receiving a telegram from home about his new daughter Marie-France, realized that one couldn't cheat and ruin what later came to be called his *baraka*.

Bigeard predictably ran afoul of authorities who seemed only too happy to remain in this beguiling, insulated city. He craved action and by the summer of 1946 got it, receiving a transfer up to the high country, arriving first at a crossroads of northwest Tonkin, one day to be France's end of the line here—lovely, mosquitoless, strategically important Dien Bien Phu. Here Annamese, who had never liked the area's Thais, were bent on conquest under Ho's banner, and a new group of volunteers under Bigeard had to protect the Thai, a people whose ways and elegance he loved immediately. Bigeard now knew the large differences among Tonkin's subregions—the Red River Delta containing four-fifths of its inhabitants, the Middle Region, and this High Region. After fighting only briefly in rice paddies of the delta, a key area for the French, Bigeard and his men would be mostly up in the Thai country east of Dien Bien Phu and west of the Red River, along the crucial Route Coloniale 41. Here difficult, mountainous or forested terrain dictated conditions of fighting. Route Coloniale 41 had to remain open, and Viet Minh guerillas kept at bay from a placid population.

Learning to subsist on a diet of rice and little else, and whipping into shape his Thai volunteers and some Frenchmen left over from more peaceful colonial days, Bigeard began having astonishing successes, though to be sure, this was that illusory period before the Chinese Communist victory of 1949 made the match uneven. For now a combination of guts, determination, and ingenuity could still win, almost as in the chivalric Middle Ages. Embracing the Thai barefoot style, "je me sens increvable" ("I felt unpuncturable"—or less literally, invincible), he recalls. All French greats abroad had believed in their destinies, and so we hear Bigeard go on to describe himself in that era: "*Quelle forme!* Thirty years old, tireless, a real *fauve*."[5]

He also reminds those who don't know Western imperialism that his men were greeted as liberators by this "fière et attachante population."[6] Though he soon lost the old French colonials who had been on probation for being here under Vichy and were sent home, he was given five top-flight officers as replacements to lead recruits in battle. Bigeard's missions continued, as Ho Chi Minh broke the semitruce December 19, hitting Hanoi and making the war an open one.

For about a year Marcel remained in these northern highlands, through to September 1947, eventually spearheading the recovery of nearly the entire "black Thai country" from Vietnamese guerillas. With an artist's sensitivity, as well as punchy French slang, he sketches the traits of officers he worked with, and of later ones who would come from France, almost all destined to perish. For example, Lieutenant Guilleminot was "solid as a rock, tremendous drive, big mouth, adored by his men ... believes in his star, will be killed in Algeria ten years later." Another sublieutenant, handsome and sad, would last only a few more weeks here. Yet another named Bréau was a "playboy [who] speaks often of his mother, whom he venerates, and will be killed in an ambush."[7] Climbing cliffs, fighting off mosquitoes or bloated bloodsuckers that feasted on them, or picking up malaria from drinking in streams, the group reeked and hurt plenty, but took clumps of Communist prisoners. Shouting à la Viet and often attacking at dawn (after grueling night marches), Bigeard's men assaulted enemy strongholds. A successful mission to take the region's de facto capital of Son La in early January 1947 made that his base from which to radiate further afield.[8]

Captain Bigeard and his charges continued fighting in breathtaking mountains and valleys, or cut their way through tangled brush to meet a tenacious foe. But protected villagers also helped his men build bamboo enclaves, and their gratitude, along with a need for money, facilitated some marriages—one Thai father even offering Bigeard his own daughter! The flattered French leader cited his spouse back home.

Venturing further from Son La to overcome more Viet Minh strong-holds, and frequently guided by Thais, Bigeard left positions gained as transient garrisons that would later be lost. In isolated circumstances, evac-uating wounded who had to endure four or five-day ordeals, these French soldiers were living a life at the antipodes from Sartre's and de Beauvoir's in Paris of that era. The long marches, with mosquitoes perpetually attack-ing, began wearing down even a nominally indefatigable commander. A light grenade wound in the back and disease also contributed to that fatigue, and after two years Bigeard would have a leave foisted upon him, relinquishing his toughened company to a captain who soon ran it into the ground—the pattern that would be repeated a number of times through his remaining years in Indochina, then North Africa.

About to be separated from men he had formed, Bigeard's emotions ran riot. Two years of living like a beast without his wife, and fighting almost without interruption, made him look forward to his impending rest time in France, but not without guilt for those remaining behind. By plane he traveled from Son La to Hanoi, then came the Hanoi-Paris run of three days in that era. On arrival at Orly, September 20, 1947, an emo-tional Marcel beheld Gaby with their daughter, Marie-France, in her arms, and broke down. Lodged in a hotel near the Gare du Nord, which became another tradition, Bigeard was astounded by the Paris bustle, yet thought continually of his men in Vietnam.[9]

He then traveled across France to the old train station at Toul, encoun-tering his happy sister, his father dying of cancer, and of course his mother Sophie, "still solid and authoritarian."[10] During several months of Lor-raine winter, recovering slowly from the effects of dysentery and malaria, Bigeard rejected rich food in favor of boiled rice and meat, had trouble wearing shoes after bare foot marches, remained guilty about being away from the fray, and finally, demanded a return trip.[11]

Already possessing eleven *croix de guerre,* he certainly had laurels to rest on; but he got his wish, affected to the 3d Colonial Battalion of Para-troop Commandos for supervision of training in the Breton seaside town of Saint-Brieuc, and when ready, for renewed service in Vietnam. Bigeard liked his new officers here, including one who became his assistant, Vallet de Payraud, "très vieille France," and an inveterate ladies man, receiving the nickname "le Vicomte."[12] He did not, however, care for his superior, Commandant Ayolles, an egotistical, mercurial personality, who seemed to bring out the worst in his men. Bigeard on the other hand was a fierce distinguisher of personalities, rapidly aware of which recruit needed what treatment. One named Chevret was a "beau garçon" who received a flood of female correspondence, another was the Rocky type, another sad and quiet, and so on: most were there for adventure, and doubtless, for the role they might play in France's martial regeneration after the collapse of 1940. Some had also joined up to avoid unemployment, mine work, exacting families, or delinquency in a world that didn't yet value it. All coveted a prestigious red beret and paratroop credentials.[13]

Bigeard certainly pushed his men hard. Two "titis parisiens" who sauntered to the capital for a forty-eight-hour leave decided to enjoy themselves a few extra days, and on their return Bigeard disciplined them in his forthright manner: "Je les mets K.-O.," as he noted.[14] Those Parisians would, however, follow him for years, one to be killed at Dien Bien Phu, the other trying to escape after imprisonment there.

By the spring of 1948 the hard training of a first stage was done; now came a move to an air base in southern Brittany for paratroop jumps. Romantically, Bigeard suggested they all march some 120 kilometers from Saint-Brieuc down to this base near Vannes. Starting at dawn, he led the way, setting his usual pace through the region's villages. Gaby and Marie-France arrived to occupy primitive digs, and jumps onto prickly Breton terrain or the cement of airstrips toughened recruits. These "paras" developed their own swagger, way of walking, way of being, and really, a mystique emanating in good part from their leader. It was again part of a France pulling up national socks after the debacle of 1940 that still weighed on many young minds.

Finally the one-third or so who had gained para diplomas possessed a requisite Bigeardian aura. In October they were taken down to Fréjus in the South of France, where everyone was herded and readied for Madagascar, North Africa, and yes, for Vietnam. Paras of the 3d Colonial soon found themselves on a Mediterranean quai, surrounded by family members some would never see again, then sailed from Marseille on the *Pasteur*, a converted liner, toward a colonial quagmire, mingling on board with another company of paratroopers from the Foreign Legion.[15]

In Saigon Bigeard ran into careerists who would return to France with little experience of war here, and rapidly got away from them, as if from a bad odor. They would never be to his taste. Ayrolles' hysterical rigidity, making recruits fearful of everything that moved, also continued to repel him. But Bigeard had to grit his teeth and wait—never his forte.

He got his chance for autonomy when one of Ayrolles' units was ordered to join a miscellaneous group heading up to the Tonkin. Asking to head the unit, Bigeard received the approval of a chief who was glad to rid himself of an irksome subordinate. On arrival December 11, 1948, Bigeard had another look at Haiphong, with its women and soldiers cavorting together at the Café du Commerce. Here he met with Commandant Romain-Desfossés, whom he instantly liked, and the man who had prepared the group's military tasks. He also met Pierre Château-Jobert, a superior he liked less and who would backbite Bigeard all the way through the Algerian period. The latter's conception of war, complete with heavy gunnery, tanks, and other accoutrements more proper to a European conflict, disgusted Bigeard, as he spent a dirty month fighting in the rice fields and paddies of the delta. Bigeard's group, augmented by Moroccans, Legionnaires, and members of other regiments, was here to support artillery-aviation operations, a type of war he didn't favor in Vietnam. Like Norman Schwartzkopf in this part of the world two decades later, he would see much in the French military hierarchy that displeased him. He himself preferred to fight à la Viet.[16]

Bigeard took opportunities to lead where he could. First Romain-Desfossés was injured in the thigh, so Bigeard replaced him in his functions. Then on January 16 Château-Jobert gave Bigeard's company a shot at parachuting into Yen Chau, one of the places he had conquered on his first tour of the northern Thai country. He was given another crack commando group of fifty more parachutists, and the strengthened contingent went off in eight aircraft, for their leader, an emotional fly-over of an area he knew well, including Route 41 snaking below. He was back to Sisyphean operations, trying to retake villages and towns previously held, then besieged by a constantly moving, feinting enemy. Flying in a lead Dakota over splendid mountains and valleys punctuated by isolated settlements, Bigeard led his group in an initial "Go!" before fluttering down, some to hard landings on dried-out rice paddies.

Here he took de facto command from those like the Corsican Commandant Paccioni who outranked him. Leaving retaken Yen Chau to his assistant, Payraud, Bigeard helped march out those who had been wounded, an arduous trek along Route 41, where he watched constantly for ambushes. There followed more long marches to meet the enemy, and in blistering heat. Paccioni had underestimated enemy strength, and 100 Viets soon snared Bigeard's men in an ambush; this time "we are the prey, they the hunters."[17] The French replied in force, but Bigeard now began soul-searching about this entire Vietnamese involvement, especially given an imminent Chinese Communist victory to the north.

His idea was henceforth to cut up his group into commando columns, each under one of his officers, going off in various directions to affront the enemy—genesis of the Challe Plan in Algeria many years later. Heat, hunger, mosquitoes, and if wounded, being jostled on horrid stretchers, while fearing Viet Minh capture and torture were givens here. Arduous operations yielded results, gradually clearing the area; but the loss of Bigeard's esteemed associates took a continual, emotional toll. One Lieutenant Huillier's death was followed in mid-March by that of Bigeard's co-rider in a jeep, his beloved "Vicomte," raked by the fire of a sudden enemy ambush. Bigeard barely made it out of that one, rolling into a rock-filled ravine and playing dead until reinforcements came. In the process he wounded his shoulder, later requiring hospitalization and morphine—an injury that would bother him for years. Six months of operations made the Thai country more secure, but Bigeard felt this sad human price always within him.[18]

He was now given command of a new unit to be called the 3d Thai Battalion. Headquartered back in Son La, with its rebuilt chief residence and villas reminiscent of pre–World War II imperial ease, and with an obstinate Gaby arriving to share his life at least intermittently here, Bigeard's mission was to hold some 10,000 square kilometers of rugged territory, for which he was awarded another fresh contingent. This group included a hero from a previous tour in Indochina who had escaped Viet captivity: Godard, a bony para, excellent with the Thais; and Bôle de Chaumont, "lieutenant racé, de qualité, curieux de nature," and who in turn esteemed Bigeard.[19]

By October 1 the battalion was officially constituted, formed of five companies, a valley for one, a valley for another, under lieutenants Bigeard trusted. With difficulty, they again cleaned out large swaths of the *pays Thai*, trying to win over populations that included the Meo (also known as the Hmong), fiercely independent opium cultivators in the mountains, who had originally come from as far off as Siberia.[20] To avoid Bigeard, many Viet Minh moved into adjoining Laos. In the area he controlled roads became safer, and there were plenty of defections to the French side (the Thais especially disliking Communist Tonkinese); but north of the border a Chinese Communist victory henceforth granted Giap technical support, along with ready asylum.[21]

Bigeard continued to be put off by comfortable administrator types visiting his secured areas, though at first he didn't mind one visit from a seemingly understanding General Alessandri in early March 1950. Alessandri, however, dropped a bomb; Bigeard was again to be relieved of his latest command and transferred. (The ostensible reason was his irrepressible habit of speaking his mind—in this case, on local trafficking of currency and opium.)[22] Devastated, the paratroop leader first turned angry, then wept in his room. His officers sent off a collective letter, petitioning for his reinstatement, but to no avail. With tears still in his eyes Bigeard consumed a last meal, realizing the area wouldn't hold; and indeed, his successor who arrived to flags at half-mast would not last long there.

Ever and again in history, from Themistocles to Churchill, it strikes one how badly we treat our great. Back in Hanoi with its "taxi-girls," bars, and numerous Chinese, Bigeard felt out of place. Both in the northern capital and in Saigon, French soldiers who had suffered in the field were often repelled by the sight of officers enjoying sleeker circumstances in these big cities.[23] Impulsively Bigeard sent a letter of resignation to his army superior, but the commander simply tore it up, knowing a good thing. French authorities told Bigeard to take two weeks with his wife by the beautiful Bay of Along, before starting a new command. Somewhat mollified, and digesting the *plat du jour* offered, the Bigeards enjoyed jogging, swimming, and good meals, as well as romantic strolls by "this famous bay, one of the wonders of the world."[24]

Then came another battalion to put in harness for operations in the delta, mostly composed of loyal Vietnamese, as well as Frenchmen like Leclerc's son. In Lyautesque fashion Captain Bigeard called himself a *caïd* among these Tonkinese who brought their families and possessions; but they were amazed to see him march step by step with them for entire nights. Leading by example would remain his forte. With a base at Haiduong, where Gaby occupied a villa, eight tough months of operations followed. More Viets were killed and more arms taken, and Bigeard's men slept in rice paddies of a region very different from the high country. Dodging enemy mines and having a sixth sense about impending ambushes, including one where he floored his jeep and tossed grenades to save his skin, Bigeard found it hard to blend such warfare—growingly difficult as the enemy insinuated itself into village life—with a domestic existence. He would be mourned once again by men he had to abandon by the end of that year.

Bound for France on another leave, Bigeard departed November 12, 1950 on the luxury liner *La Marseillaise*, arriving in other-worldly Paris that December. Here the battered warrior enjoyed seeing his daughter, Marie-France, buying her whatever he could afford. Then in Toul, with father and sister both dead (the latter passing away from her first delivery), he was saddened again by the inevitable downside of an imperial existence—not having been able to give his sister a last hug before her untimely death. Four more winter months passed in gray Lorraine. Driving his refurbished Mercedes, helping his mother with her orchard, buying his own place, and recovering from dysentery and malaria, Bigeard thought continually of Vietnam, guilty that he could not have given more, that "this thankless war does not permit sharing."[25]

General de Lattre de Tassigny had by now arrived in Indochina as commander in chief and high commissioner, and Bigeard was eager to serve under this "King Jean," a dynamo directing set-piece battles offered by the enemy during the winter and spring of 1951. But Gaby was clearly opposed to another round, hoping to see her husband return to a placid banking career!

In March 1951 Bigeard was nonetheless back in Brittany, where he discussed matters with the one-eyed Gilles, who bluntly offered two possibilities: heading up a new battalion for future service in Vietnam, or becoming part of Colonel Gilles' staff on his return to Tonkin. Flatly, Bigeard demanded the former. In return, Gilles first demanded his subordinate work six boring months in office administration, sifting through dossiers. Gaby and Marie-France came down to Vannes, Bigeard kept other bureaucrats at arm's length, jogging religiously each morning; and the months managed to pass. One positive emerged: Marcel got to look at the index book of promotions, realizing that it was at least as much who you knew as experience in the field that allowed one to advance in the army.

In September 1951 Gilles left for Vietnam, giving Bigeard command of the 6th Battalion of Colonial Paratroopers. He also offered him a glowing recommendation that would bring a fairly rapid promotion. Bigeard went to Saint-Brieuc on the Channel to use most of a year prepping these men for a theater where our "grand, exceptional de Lattre [was] getting bogged down, despite his brio."[26] The new contingent included "Leroy, called Polo ... a beau garçon," married to a teacher; Trapp, "tall, dry ... a rock, demanding of himself and of his men"; Lepage, "Breton, stocky, serious, tenacious," about to get married; and de Wilde, very religious, almost saintly. The two "titis Parisiens" returned as well, along with other promising recruits, among whom a man named René Sentenac, with "admirable guts, athletic, and strong," and who would perish in Algeria's desert.[27] Was Bigeard wrong to call this a young elite? Are *we* wrong to see some of the era's best Frenchmen here, trying to do the impossible in what remained of their empire?

Again, an inspirational leader produced excellence by putting his charges through rigorous training, and was himself promoted to major in January 1952. With Gilles gone Bigeard now had the future General Pierre Langlais above him in Brittany, not his cup of tea. But the new battalion developed its *esprit de corps,* and in late June departed Brittany for what had become an increasingly tough gig, given the Korean stalemate, de Lattre's death, and the growing effect of Communist Chinese arms, much of it captured American materiel. Leaving Gaby and Marie-France behind on the quai, along with other weeping family members, Bigeard and his men boarded the *Pasteur* in July—for death, as he remarks laconically.[28]

A good source that shows how lethal fighting in Vietnam had now become is a first published collection of letters sent to Bigeard by old combatants, or surviving family members. One French soldier who fought in a murderous extension of the same battle in May 1951 that killed Bernard de Lattre noted in a letter the superior firepower of the Viet Minh, and the fact that the French were outnumbered here ten to one! With a bullet in his leg this courageous soldier made it out of the inferno, and was loaded with medals from other, similarly difficult operations.[29]

However, Bigeard's men en route to "Indo" still had hopes, or perhaps illusions. Reaching Saigon near the end of the month, they then traveled up to Haiphong, embracing "once again this Tonkin, so sad, sober, captivating."[30] On the quai Bigeard met Lieutenant-Colonel Ducournau, a great leader under whom he was happy to serve, and who would eventually make it to four-star general, before later punching out in an Algerian helicopter accident. He also met the man setting military policy here, General de Linarès, who informed him that this was a different Vietnam from the one he had previously known—Giap's forces now stuffed with modern hardware and no longer simply guerilla warriors.[31]

Bigeard commanded a battalion augmented by other parachute company members, headed by a rich kid from Lyon whom he instinctively liked. On August 10 he reported the "boutique" in operational shape. Sent first to the area of Vinh Yenh, a key to Giap's designs against Hanoi, Bigeard's 6th remained there two months, effecting raids against the enemy. Ranks were swelled by more soldiers of varying backgrounds, including a former Resistant who had been liberated from Buchenwald, as well as by Tonkinese and other Asians. Bigeard wanted nothing left to chance, though he couldn't prevent the pain from landing on his pistol after one jump in October. He would subsequently have to parachute onto his left side to avoid a badly bruised right hip.

By this time the walkie-talkie had become a favored mode of communication for "Bruno," his radio moniker. (It should be noted that the French had a fondness right through to Dien Bien Phu for speaking "en clair," meaning the Viets could listen in as well, sometimes, however, to disinformation.) "Bruno" and his men were now called on to execute a dubious plan in an ever more dubious war, basically a replay of a plan used successfully the year before against Giap, but which General Salan tried tardily to cancel in the hands of Gilles and Linarès, knowing that lightning wouldn't strike twice. In response to a great offensive of two Viet Minh divisions pushing through Thai country toward the Mekong and Laos, Bigeard's aggregation was to grab the area around Tulé (or Tu-Lê), thirty kilometers west of threatened Nghia Lo, before linking up with other groups and pushing outward against the enemy. They would then help evacuate other French-Thai garrisons of the High Region.

A wave of Dakotas took off, and the 6th parachuted, arriving on the evening of October 16 in what rapidly became a trap. On Bruno's orders, they unrolled barbed wire and dug in thoroughly, while hearing the ominously near thunder of Viet assaults pounding Nghia Lo to the east, which fell on the evening of October 17. It was only a matter of time before the enemy reached the 6th here. Bigeard had sent out reconnaissance soldiers and placed different companies on various salients, realizing that bad weather would prevent any relief from the air, and that no breakout (the strategy his chiefs from afar preached) was yet feasible. Instead, the French and their Vietnamese or Thai units would have to absorb a massive attack. On October 20 a deafening explosion of mortars and grenades announced the enemy's arrival at Tulé, but Bigeard's men surprised them by firing back in force. Giap's charges kept at it, knowing that with some 10,000 soldiers, they possessed immense numerical superiority. In fact they easily pinned down French forces who grew hungry (having endured over a day without food), tired, and desperate. Overruling orders from high-ups that came to his radio, Bruno in the night darkness hung in with his fellows amidst this persistent, murderous firing.[32] At the base of jungle-covered mountains, the 6th Paratroopers kept replying gallantly, but after heavy losses retained only one pass at Tulé.

More brave acts were to be executed in this unsung land. A chaplain, Father Jeandel, would soon be captured here and held for two years by the

Viets, enduring horrors he might have avoided by not waiting to aid the wounded. But injured men littered the premises, some crying out for days, hoping for water, and instead, being eaten while still alive by rats or vultures. (The Viets only took the lightly wounded as prisoners.) Dead on the 20th included Sergeant François Guérin, who from dawn that day had valiantly resisted superior forces, and even when wounded by a grenade, had refused to leave the fight and get medical help, before another bullet ended his life; and Sergeant Roger Letourneux, who under heavy fire had managed to effect liaisons with detachments on other salients, before being killed.[33]

With dead and wounded multiplying so rapidly in this lethal mouse-trap, and bad weather still precluding aid from the air, Bigeard now hatched the idea of a low-odds escape march, headed in stages for the Black River to the southwest. Somehow, he and a contingent of French and Asian troops managed to slip out in the darkness to begin an arduous trek in perilous mountain country, knocking into rocks or roots, fording streams, and carrying wounded on stretchers. Some had to walk with fractured limbs or even bullets inside, and no one was rested; yet miraculously, they made the first stage of this endurance test—the valley emplacement of Muong Chen and its rice fields.

Here they stopped only briefly, knowing the enemy was on their heels. Bigeard figured he needed about three hours get-ahead time, and to that end left behind another brave sacrifice group of some eighty Thai irregulars under Master Sergeant Peyrol and Sergeant Cheyron, who would unload a sound and light show of grenades and artillery on the enemy, hopefully persuading them that the entire battalion was there for the taking. The rest continued marching back up into cliff country, dropping equipment as they went, some asleep and still pushing feet forward, others dying of exhaustion. At midnight those still going heard the last explosion at Muong Chen behind them; the sacrifice group had procured them their precious three hours.[34]

At Ban Hoc Bigeard's tattered forces finally met the 56th Vietnamese battalion sent there by Linarès, blithely eating lunch. For one so often critical of superiors Bigeard appreciated this Linarès, who as best he could had been following grueling exploits on the ground from his B-26 overhead. Yes, this was "a general as I like them, human, generous, worried about his men," Bigeard would note. Utterly tired, and suffering from malaria and leech bites, he and charges also realized their present haven was an ephemeral one; the Viet Minh could not be far behind.[35]

Reluctantly, they had to leave again, taking along their new comrades of the 56th. After marching over eighteen hours they had finally accomplished a second stage in Lance Armstrong style, bivouacking at Ban It Ong in the late afternoon, where they ate with villagers, washed, and had a little more breathing space. Bigeard's idea was to stay the night and leave at dawn, but Thai reconnaissance told them the pursuing Viets were only a few hours behind. Ever the improviser, Bruno pried his men off the ground where they lay supine, forcing them back at 9 P.M. onto the endless piste. On a moonless night they marched blindly, picking up those who fell from fatigue, men almost clutching men ahead of them so as not to get lost; and after midnight they reached an arm of the Black River, the Nam Chien, whose icy waters they then had to ford, linked in human chains. They now located a telephone line, which felt like manna, leading them directly to the Black River position where freedom lay; but the last hour was a tense one. Finally they made it to the blessed river, using Thai-piloted canoes to cross, before locating a safer refuge. Bigeard and his section were the last to traverse the water at three in the morning.[36]

A wounded, tired mess of a much reduced battalion was then taken by truck to recuperate at Son La; while on Morane aircraft an equally battered Bigeard went off to report to his superiors—Gilles, Linarès, and Ducournau—on this improbable escape from an enemy outnumbering his men a good ten to one. There had in fact been a reporter-photographer named Corcuff on the march, who ultimately brought the story of this dramatic exploit to the French papers, marking the beginnings of Bigeard's future fame. As recompense, he at least received some rest time, and what remained of his battalion was decorated en masse in Hanoi. He and his men proudly presented arms and received citations from the minister of the Associated States of Indochina. Bigeard himself was called *un chef prestigieux* and his men were praised for "an extraordinary physical effort," creating a "page of glory" for the colonial parachute corps as a whole. But as Bigeard noted dryly, Giap wasn't one to let an enemy rest on its laurels. After the receipt of decorations Bruno's last speech to the battalion urged them to remain modest, to consider only the future, to avenge their dead, wounded, and vanished, and to remember their collective motto—"who dares wins," to which Bigeard added, "we must hold on."[37]

In early November news reached him that constituted more than a footnote to this Tulé exploit. Having asked for posthumous decorations to be conferred on the sacrifice group left behind at Muong Chen, Bigeard now received word of a miracle. The thirty-four-year old Sergeant Peyrol had himself felt, as Bigeard did, that death at Muong Chen against well-armed elements of a 312th Viet Minh division was a certainty. It saddened Peyrol that the very day Bigeard designated him as leader of this suicidal rear guard was his daughter's birthday back home in Verdun. Peyrol had a warm bottle of champagne on hand, but to toast what? His own death, it seemed. After tossing their last grenades at the enemy, and losing half their contingent of Thais, Peyrol and Cheyron located a path they had previously cut into the brush, and on a happily dark night, they and the remaining Thais somehow made it into the jungle.

The Viet Minh then sent two companies to give chase, and for twelve days there ensued a parallel escape saga worthy of a movie made for today's nostalgic youth. River crossings, scaling of mountains, and on empty stomachs, gamble after gamble ensued. At one point a thirsty Peyrol got a scratchy response on his radio, but something in his gut told him to switch it off, the right move, as it turned out. It was in fact a Communist transmitter, posing as a French one. Nearing the Black River his ever-decreasing group almost smacked into a Viet Minh platoon using the same trail, requiring five hours of mute immobility, until they passed. On November 5 the lead Thai scout announced a first view of the river, but due to a strong current, swimming across was impossible. A Thai tribesman there also warned the group about Viet Minh patrols along the banks, telling them to remain in the trees; at dusk he would bring them rice. Again, Peyrol wondered about this offer, as these poor people could grow relatively affluent receiving Viet Minh pay-offs for French soldiers, arms, and radios. But at nightfall the rice arrived, a happy meal washed down with muddy river water. The next day the tribesman found the right part of the river for crossing on homemade rafts. But Bigeard's French were no longer on the other side; they had long since vacated the premises and been decorated. Instead, there were more Viet Minh patrols here, and when Peyrol and his group heard voices, they thought they were finished. Happily, it was a French rescue column. Of eighty-four men constituting the rear guard at Muong Chen, an exhausted sixteen had made it, including Peyrol holding his lucky champagne bottle, and now crying on the ground.[38]

That was still the way for these cultured warriors: Sisyphean challenges in the ebbing era of European imperialism that wouldn't end. So it was soon back to the delta—the "useful Tonkin" as the French called it—to fight again against Giap's crack soldiers, threatening Hanoi-Haiphong. And Bigeard returned to his routine of leading charges on early-morning marches, figuring that being in shape had helped in the Tulé escape and might again. Plague-like, the Viet Minh swarmed over country that Bruno's men had twice cleaned out. But he kept dropping from lead aircrafts for jobs where a dozen of his men might fracture bones in the jumps alone. One such injured included his lieutenant Rocher, who appropriately enough, struck a rock. On to more long marches, receiving numerous typed orders from above, working with other crack battalions, repulsing waves of attacks. Then Christmas in Hanoi, and just before New Year's 1953 arrived, with the consumer society starting to dawn in France, Bigeard was still thinking the queasy old colonial thoughts—how nothing quite lasted here, how everything was "éternel recommencement."[39]

A back-and-forth fight against the Viets, as it hewed to its close, became slightly more comfortable, thanks to infusions of American equipment and air support noted in our previous chapter. Among other things this support made evacuations of the wounded more expeditious, a big problem at Tulé. In 1953 Bigeard's *boutique* found itself back in the High Region, where Giap had been busy reconquering in swaths, and where the French objective was to regain ground previously secured. Marcel returned in late February to his old headquarters: "Sonla ... encore Sonla ... toujours Sonla," as he would write.[40] Arriving with his men under a cold rain, he was saddened to see its citadel and hospital destroyed, and his old villa roofless. "It's a known fact that one must never return to where one was happy," he remarks, sighing at all the work and fighting he and his men had put in there for nothing.[41]

Abandoning Son La, Bigeard regretfully saw a favored associate and alumnus of Tulé, Captain Pierre Tourret, go off to head his own paratroop contingent; but as if providentially, he now met another brother-figure at arms. For the 6th were at this point ordered to link up with a battalion led by a man who became Bigeard's friendly rival, Jean Bréchignac—"cyrard ... tough, feared, admired."[42] Both groups had to cover each side of Route Coloniale 41, fighting off an increasingly cocky enemy, and with heart-rending losses the price. On March 29 they began "Operation Adolphe," successfully completed April 3. Hoping in uncharacteristic fashion for rest time in Hanoi, Bigeard was instead dispatched next on a Dakota to Luang Prabang in Laos, where the photographer Pierre Schoendoerffer joined him, before later being captured at Dien Bien Phu. "Quel chic garçon!" recalls Bigeard.[43] He now had to go up the Mekong River, enduring more terrible marches and firefights. No wonder he later wrote one of the present authors: "Yes, I have seen and suffered a lot." But due primarily to Bigeard the Viet Minh momentarily ceased their Laotian offensives.

Having passed five more tough months in the field, the hawk-nosed, peripatetic commander finally received his respite in Hanoi. It was the end of May 1953, and the unfortunate change at the top we have discussed took place at that moment—General Salan replaced as commander in chief by Navarre. Salan, who had spent fifteen years via six stints in "Indo," starting back in the 1920s, then through the era of Leclerc and de Lattre, and who intimately knew its geography and people, the evolution of Viet Minh capabilities, and the need for Bugeaudesque improvements in French positions and tactics had given way to a know-nothing. On June 9 Bigeard's battalion presented arms to the new *Généchef.* Salan had also removed associates like Linarès, whom the men respected, and Navarre was now seconded by General René Cogny as commander of land forces in the Tonkin. Bigeard soon found himself working under this ill-fated Cogny— "grand, traits réguliers, bel homme, polytechnicien, très séduisant," in his fine French; but despite good looks and military attainments, too weak to countermand Navarre.[44] Bitterly, our paratroop ace had to digest the fact that plans or no plans, much of the black Thai country was again back in enemy hands. "Five years of hell to end up like this!" remarks Bigeard ruefully.[45] Young ladies in Hanoi (not the night-life town that Saigon was) beckoned what remained of a much-decorated battalion, but Marcel avoided them.

On July 14, 1953 came a poignant national holiday in the northern capital, with a parade before Navarre, Cogny, and Gilles, and a big crowd on hand. Leading his "boutique" through Hanoi's still Frenchified streets, Bruno was vociferously applauded.

But a few days later it was back to business in a series of Dakotas for Operation Lang Son or "Hirondelle," with 2,000 paras under Bigeard and Tourret jumping, then marching. These marches were dangerous in and of themselves—one tough enough to kill three of Bigeard's men from exhaustion beneath a relentless sun. After a short prayer from the chaplain, the bodies were rolled into a ravine. The goal was to destroy by a surprise *raid aéroporté* extensive arms depots in the area. There were potential snags—damaged bridges too weak for tanks, the necessity for road-clearing in a number of spots, possible mines, and above all, capricious weather, which in this case complied for the airmen, but also felled 102 soliders with heat stroke. However, "Operation Hirondelle" became yet another hard-won success for a 6th Battalion that received the toughest assignments in an area that had been evacuated in panic, before de Lattre's advent. From captured Viets paras nabbed a thousand pieces of Skoda artillery, Molotova trucks, Russian cigarettes, 18,000 liters of gas—so much for the shibboleth of independent Communist movements. Bigeard, however, did not overestimate the lasting significance of the victory. An exultant Navarre might think his charges had turned a corner, but Bruno deprecated this Navarre, considering him vastly inferior to leaders like Ducournau or the late de Lattre. Still, he continued executing orders received from above. He also collected marvelous new associates, including a reserve officer named Jacques Allaire, who had had one leg 50 percent atrophied by polio, was fearful at first of Bigeard's reputation, but would prove to be a "devil of a man [who] kept surprising me with his ardor."[46]

Three more months of fighting Viet Minh passed in the delta, and Bigeard, trying to recall it all, feels he can't do justice to what he went through. Even for the men themselves, there must have been such a feeling of "lastness" here—not just in the French imperial venture, but more generally, in certain aristocratic and chivalric notions dating back to the Middle Ages.

Briefly back in Hanoi, then given three derisory weeks in France, Bigeard returned to the fray, unaware that the end was nigh. Navarre's plan, as seen, was to reoccupy Dien Bien Phu as a base of operations barely ten miles from the Laotian border, but ominously far from the delta perimeter and Hanoi. The French commander in chief hoped perhaps against hope that when the enemy tried a full-scale invasion of Laos, it would shatter disastrously against a fortified Dien en route. Hence he would plunge his best men into this valley fortress, a basin punctuated by salients, hoping to entice the Viet Minh into a direct assault. In retrospect Bigeard thinks the project was something hatched in an office, ignoring actual conditions. Pure Joffre, one might add.

On November 19 the paratroop leader was called in to meet with Cogny. The next day in "Operation Castor" three para battalions, including those of Bigeard and Bréchignac, were to jump into Dien Bien Phu, taking it back from the enemy, before embarking on a great buildup and the reoccupation of two nearby airstrips. The top brass was, however, vague about how many Viets would be down below to meet them. If too many, it would be prudent to bolt for Laos, they declared. In fact the French were surprised by the numbers they had to fight, and the Viet Minh too would be jolted by the sudden incursion. Jumps occurred, going slightly askew due to the wind, and in a first engagement, with the 6th bearing the brunt while Bréchignac's men were several kilometers away, 115 Viets were killed, versus almost a dozen on the French side. These human prices remained a steep price to pay. Among the dead was one of the "titis parisiens," whom Bigeard then wrapped up in his parachute and solemnly buried along with other French dead here. Bigeard's clear, detailed report on the operation did not spare the higher command, noting that a better strafing job before the jump would have been useful, along with a longer, more thorough briefing for his battalion. The tightness of the drop zone was another problem, as was radio contact between battalions. He congratulated his men, including "autochtones," for their courage fighting the Viet Minh in tough, body-to-body combat; but again, why no indication of what was to come?[47]

Augmented by several other para groups, Bigeard's 6th stayed three weeks in Dien Bien Phu, still involved in hard fighting on November 27th, and done with their job by December 11. Meanwhile, Navarre had compounded his errors by evacuating the only other fortified French emplacement of the region due north, Lai Chau. Cogny had issued dire warnings since August concerning that move, noting that surrender of Lai Chau "without enemy pressure" would have a negative effect on partisans and French friends, and could induce a kind of panic. Awaiting Viet moves, and reinforcing Lai Chau with a new Thai battalion would make more sense. But Navarre overrode these objections, gambling all on Dien, which Giap would duly surround with men and materiel over the next four months. In the south meanwhile the enemy remained more indulgent, avoiding major battles, but harassing with bullets, mines, and traps, nailing down French troops for protection of installations, and for roads and railways leading out of Saigon to various parts of Indochina.[48]

French soldiers were siphoned off as well by Viet incursions into Laos, where Bigeard himself flew at the end of December. His mission was to reinforce country surrounding the air base of Séno, with Bréchignac now under him, and a battalion of North Africans too. Again, he and fellow soldiers marched arduously, heavily outnumbered by an ambushing enemy early in January at the village of Ban Song, from which they made a breakout, somewhat on the order of Tulé. Attacking the flown coop, Viet Minh soldiers were then pulverized by the French from the air. Another feint brought more enemy losses, and Ban Song became a new chapter in Bigeard's saga, attracting Giap's attention.

As he marked his wedding anniversary January 6, 1954, during this operation, Bigeard felt anything but confident about the future. Would he even *see* his family again? The worry was more than legitimate. The high command might crow about this latest victory, but he knew that each temporary failure only taught a tenacious foe how to tighten the noose, and that kudos or a twentieth *croix de guerre* could not prevent that impending final result.[49]

Remaining at the base of Séno until February 20, members of the 6th repaired shattered nerves with sports, shooting, and mock commando marches. There were also more citations. On February 14 Bigeard turned thirty-five, and at five in the morning was awakened by a volley of automatic gunfire and grenades, only his paratroopers wishing him happy birthday. What he called his second family moved him greatly that day.

Good, bad, or in-between, the French colonial era in Vietnam was nearly done, as Communist guerillas now hit other vital air bases. At one, Cat Bi, in the Red River Delta near Haiphong, there was a noble confrontation between Bigeard, whose 6th Battalion was sent there in early March to guard planes from enemy fire, and "Félix" Brunet, a star airman who ran the base. Brunet was a wily veteran of thousands of hours of flights, some downright scary, given equipment of the day, weather conditions, and enemy fire. In salty, unvarnished language Félix informed Bigeard that he didn't need paratroopers here, urging them to leave; to which Bruno remembers retorting, "if you're spoiling for a fight, I'm completely at your service."[50] The next night the Viet Minh attacked, and after blowing up a few planes, were thrown off by a combined effort, sparking a strong friendship between these two powerhouses, lasting until Brunet's death in Algeria.

Scenting the kill, Giap was now of course readying his great barrage of Dien Bien Phu. Poor preparations on the French side and the enemy's command of the heights above the valley augured badly for the French. Navarre hoped to liquidate the Viet Minh in Cochin China and Annam with operations like "Atlante," while staying on the defensive here in Tonkin—a bit of the old Schlieffen scenario—and only later striking hard up north. But would there *be* a "later"? Having mostly defeated the French in the Tonkin delta, Giap was more than willing to take on their forces at Dien Bien Phu. Between November 20, 1953 and March 13, 1954, the Communist military leader surreptiously encircled the valley, in part by the use of tunneling techniques that would later become famous in the war against the Americans. French Dien Bien Phu was no more ready for an attack that mid-March, 1954 than Joffre's Verdun had been in 1916.

On the evening of March 13 Giap's assault began on a series of French

strong points, starting with Béatrice, which fell rapidly. On March 15 it was
Gabrielle's turn, leading to the suicide of the French artillery commander,
Colonel Piroth, his disgraced honor—that musty, anachronistic word—the
reason. Summoned to Hanoi, Bigeard received orders from General Cogny,
who as noted, was too weak to alter Navarre's plan—to jump a second time
into Dien Bien Phu March 16, using his crack battalion as reinforcements
for already significant losses of Legionnaires, Algerian sharpshooters, and
other troops there. Ambivalent about the plan, and knowing his men were
beat after so many months of fighting, Marcel replied that he would
follow orders. Privately, he thought this might be the final death trap for
what superiors called an *unité d'élite*. Bigeard's right leg was also hurting
badly from an earlier jump, but he still felt that "my debut as a 'legend'
had to be earned."[51]

Trying to ignore his throbbing leg, he arrived safely along with over
600 confrères in the battalion, and was soon yelling on radio in the strong
point of Isabelle. His first take here? Twelve thousand men mired in mud,
and "a dirty impression of death." Martial Chevalier procured him a jeep,
in which he zigzagged to avoid enemy shrapnel, en route to the command
center. Bigeard then entered the citadel, where "it was raining shells," and
in an underground vault greeted Lieutenant-Colonel Langlais and Colonel,
soon General Christian de la Croix de Castries, Dien's overall commander,
whom Bigeard considered a "grand seigneur."[52] Imprisoned in World War
II, then wounded by a mine during the Italian campaign, and among
other things, a former world champion in the high jump, Castries had
been a disciple of de Lattre. He was also a ladies' man, and some believed
he had named salients at Dien Bien Phu for former mistresses. Right now
he was "worried but neat, clean-shaven, impeccably dressed, [and] always
the gentleman." But Bigeard didn't think he quite knew what to do here.[53]

Not appreciating the huddled anxiety of these commanders, Bigeard
next zipped his jeep to the foot of Eliane 4, where his *boutique* was dug
in. On Eliane 1 there was an Algerian battalion and on Eliane 2 one from
Morocco. In this sector he met Captain Dédé Botella commanding his
own parachutists, a North African who had had one leg shortened in the
Liberation of France; and this comrade in the "paratroop Mafia" offered
scant hope. Bigeard's men hunkered down, but unfinished French preparations, poor leadership, and the quality of the opponent weighed on his
heart. Somehow other French soldiers felt that Bigeard's arrival was a tal-
isman of good fortune, figuring that the great improviser must have a high
card up his sleeve. It was pure magical thinking. Bigeard did countermand

orders from Langlais that he deemed ill advised, and the two nearly came to blows. Finally, Langlais let Bigeard run his own show.[54]

Early on Bigeard knew he needed rapid improvement in his leg to function here, and consulted with Dr. Paul Grauwin, soon to be overwhelmed with injured patients. Grauwin examined the swollen calf, suspecting inflammation, possibly including phlebitis. Limping, Bigeard begged the doctor to make him walk at this crucial juncture, and Grauwin duly injected a mixture of Novocain and penicillin into the femoral artery. On subsequent mornings Bigeard would take time when he could to procure more treatments, and his leg and walking improved.[55]

A week of patrols through March 27 revealed the lay of the land. Dantesque, poorly prepared battles ensued, and Bruno screamed on radio, but often to no one at the other end. Deaths came quickly. Paratroopers and Foreign Legionnaires fell in droves, and so of course did plentiful Viet Minh; but they were easily reinforced.

With the loss of more strong points, offering Giap command of the whole camp, a first success at Dien Bien Phu was Bigeard-manufactured—his counterattack west of the main fortress on March 28, blunting the enemy's ferocious advance. Bringing together five separate battalions, and associates he could trust like Tourret and Piroth's replacement, Colonel Vaillant, valuable arms were taken from the fleeing Viets. But the price was more French losses, like that of one of Bigeard's favorite lieutenants, Michel Le Vigouroux, of whom he recalled: "A young officer, among so many others, who disappeared with a smile on his face, while our great chiefs slept in Hanoi beds and were perhaps making love!"[56]

Back at Eliane 4 Captain Botella hugged and congratulated his fellow paratrooper. But Bigeard realized these were only ephemeral successes, for Giap was determined to crush his opposite numbers due to Dien Bien Phu's strategic value, and for leverage at Geneva. Only with significant reinforcements would the French retain a slim chance for victory. Bigeard's paratroopers were sent to reinforce threadbare troop emplacements on different salients, but sadly, just as the Viet Minh launched a series of heavy attacks on the evening of March 30, leading to the rapid fall of Dominique 1 and 6 and Eliane 1. At which point an idealistic Langlais sent Bigeard and his men into Eliane 2 with other units, an engagement that became exorbitant in human cost. (The 1st Colonial Paratroop Battalion dropped from 641 men on March 30 to 394 in a matter of days.) Frantic, Langlais demanded help from Hanoi, but Cogny offered reinforcements in dribs and drabs—never enough to count, only to create more dead and wounded. A furious Bigeard orchestrated a counterattack and regained Eliane 1 at high cost, and Botella's, then Brèche's men held it—for now. In early April Bigeard, surrounded by haggard survivors and numerous dead, their legs and arms sticking out all over, beheld an "apocalypse" around him.[57] His best and brightest, dying in droves, had no idea that Navarre and Cogny were busy arguing back in Hanoi, then were hardly able to speak to each other!

Tightening the net, Giap now had salients from which to dominate remaining French targets, particularly Huguette 1. When he was later told to retake it, Bigeard figuratively feigned deafness; another good bunch would founder in the attempt. This entrenched war was simply not his dish. In a brief respite from April 6 to April 10, Bigeard and Botella went for a bath in the river with another French lieutenant, the latter unfortunately hit by stray fire, dying in Bigeard's arms, and leaving a wife and two children back in France. Bruno's emotions ran riot, but he still hoped he could bluff the Viets, and that the Americans would come in to help.[58]

With massive artillery assaults Giap now set about taking the lot, and Bigeard on radio with his filial, beloved officer Fromont was frantically holding, then bang—no more Fromont, killed by bullets to the head.[59] Langlais and Bigeard were now co-commanding. Geneviève de Galard, a devoted French nurse here, warned Bigeard not to visit the hospital and its horrors, otherwise he might be incapable of returning to battle. Dr. Grauwin kept imploring Bigeard to end this butchery. The battalion's retaking of Eliane 1 on April 10, then a scrap for Huguette on April 18 brought more costly losses, and after that cruel month, the first several days of May saw the divestiture of Huguette 4 and 5, which were held by Moroccan and Foreign Legion troops, and Dominique 3. By May 7 the last Elianes— 2, taken out by a well-prepared Viet mine which blew men and weapons into the air, 4, and "that damned Eliane 1"—were gone.[60]

Despite a hail of French citations, medals, and hasty promotions, Giap knew he had won, and a newly-promoted Lieutenant-Colonel Bigeard, huddled in the citadel with Langlais drinking coffee and smoking cigarettes, knew as well. The French were expiring in mud, the dead were everywhere, the wounded groaned in trenches. Generals in Hanoi had called for a ceasefire. Bigeard was in tears at his last radio communication with the "great Bréchignac," who would be captured clutching his weapons. Botella's final radio message was: "Cette fois, c'est foutu (this time, all is lost). Adieu, Bruno."[61] Castries had tried to get Bigeard to run, but he wouldn't, not with any of his men still alive. The French burned documents, exploded

cannonry, and then "a great calm, the silence of death, hung over the citadel, under a beautiful, clear blue sky."[62] Like a Verdun or Gulag survivor,
Bruno felt ashamed to be alive amid so many dead. He caressed the forehead of Galard, "the angel of Dien Bien Phu," nursing the wounded to the
end, her uniform unrecognizable from a heavy mixture of blood and mud.
Bigeard's faithful secretary, Martial Chevalier, wept. The Viets arrived with
roughly the same cry the victorious Nazis had used, hurrying the defeated;
here it was "Dehors, maolen, maolen!"[63]

Survivors whom Bigeard had whipped into shape back in Brittany and
led to glory at Tulé limped or passed away around him: Trapp with his broken leg expired on the spot; Lieutenant Bourgois had already been killed,
Le Boudec, wounded four or five times, was barely holding on, de Wilde
was wounded and near death, and Sergeant Sautereau would perish, as
befitted his name, like a crushed grasshopper on an escape attempt. There
were men with one leg, one arm, or worse, awaiting their fate. Of Bigeard's
original battalion of some 800 elite paras, no more than forty still remained—the rest dead or missing. The thirty-nine-year-old Bigeard was
himself led away by wiry little soldiers the French had once underestimated.
On a death march stretching as much as 500 miles from the fortress, many
captives would perish (estimates run to over 8,000), or become crazed
(Langlais, among others). Ranks meant nothing on "this endless path with
each person's last thoughts inside, which they alone will ever know."[64]

Craving a hospital bed, Bigeard and the rest were instead forced to
walk endlessly, or drop. At one point the Viets tried to get the bedraggled
French to return to Dien Bien Phu for camera shots and Bigeard refused;
better to die. Their tough captors desisted. But on 800 grams a day of
smelly, oil-cooked rice, the French remnant felt plenty stricken.

Eventually Bigeard was packed off to an officer's camp, and before he
left, the faithful Martial Chevalier handed him the rest of his cigarettes.
The calvary was not yet over. Bigeard and other officers, like Lieutenant-
Colonel Voineau, missing an eye from combat, were now jostled in a
Molotova truck along Route Coloniale 41, with no room to move, and
dysentery and malaria riddling their insides. In Son La, where he had once
been a somebody, Bigeard was ironically incarcerated in his own roofless
villa. Escape attempts into the brush almost surely meant death or recapture. Yet Bigeard, "Brèche," Voineau, and Tourret decided collectively to try.
Tourret was nabbed before he even got out, and the others in the forest,
lacking food and water, and hoping to raft over the Red River, were not
solid. With his one eye and bad stamina, Voineau was a liability, and the

group was easily snared. For days Bigeard and the photographer Schoendoerffer, caught in another escape attempt, were bound back to back, then
brought to a new camp. There followed brainwashing and empty stomachs, hardly cheering; but still faithful to his 6 A.M. *footing*, as he called
it, Bigeard would remark offhandedly: "I'd known worse, and one gets back
into shape."[65] Captors grilled their captives about American aid to the
French, and Bigeard forthrightly brought up Chinese Communist support
of the Viet Minh. With rations sharply cut, some thought again of escape.
Vaillant was sick and dying, while Langlais remained in a state of break-
down. Cigarettes rolled in old *Humanités* (the French Communist newspaper a young Ho Chi Minh had once devoured) were a jeering irony.
Sometimes the captives had to parade before Russian cameras, demonstrating the results of Western decadence. Bigeard also knew bitterly that
back "in France, they could surely care less and are getting ready for vacation," while "perhaps the best [are being] lost in this Tonkinese jungle."[66]

Meanwhile, some old faces came by, including Chevalier, down to forty
kilos after several escape attempts. Occasionally a little chicken or a goat
Bigeard boiled three times and served made mealtimes more palatable.
However, with Mendès-France's Geneva negotiations picking up steam, the
Communists started feeding their prisoners better, wanting to liberate
them after four months' captivity in relatively decent condition. They also
took Bigeard away for private talks about Tulé and other battles, ever the
students. Drinking a delicious cup of Nescafé, he felt bad that he couldn't
bring cups of it to his buddies. More tragedies ensued: a weakened associate, Ducroix, died in Bruno's arms; while Chevret, one of his lieutenants,
disappeared forever in another escape attempt. Bigeard couldn't forget
the many others who had already perished on the march along Coloniale
41, pants frequently bloodied from dysentery. Never would he forgive the
Viets for all the deaths they caused due to this forced marching of feeble
captives, withholding food when it counted.[67]

Finally came freedom on September 4, 1954—with a big dinner in Hanoi
offered by Cogny for Castries, Langlais, Lalande, Pazzis, and Bigeard. Why
hadn't the bigwig generals been at Dien Bien Phu? Bigeard asked straight
off, ever the critic of military hierarchy. Why not have let the doomed
make a run for it earlier? Or parachuted Bréchignac's men in when it
might still have made a difference?[68] Not wishing to hear such things, the
chiefs shunted the liberated down to Saigon, where Bigeard danced with
a beautiful Vietnamese girl in an otherwordly atmosphere, given what he
had been through.

There ensued a long, delicious flight homeward with other survivors like "Brèche" and Tourret on board. At Paris' Orly airport in tearful reunion were his wife, eight-year-old Marie-France, and Bigeard's wartime buddy, Bill Probert. And Bigeard himself wept. They put up at their old Hotel Terminus, where once Pétain had lodged a mistress, and Bigeard went to visit Madame Ducroix in Paris, mutely angry at not seeing her dead husband return.

And thence to Toul for another round there too. Naturally Sophie Bigeard asked her son—ever the domineering, demanding progenitor of a military success—why he had let himself be imprisoned in the first place! Already one of France's most decorated officers, Lieutenant-Colonel Bigeard had no answer.

In December Bruno escaped cold Lorraine for the sunnier Riviera, passing through Paris and traveling southward with Bréchignac. They stayed at a military center, meeting Langlais (now married), Allaire, Le Boudec, and other alumni of a catastrophe. The old parliamentarian Le Provost de Launay invited Bigeard to a cocktail party. But mainly he kept to a diet of rice, and the guilt of survival plagued him badly. That guilt was also part of a general letdown, as the French were busy packing up in North Vietnam. There people streamed from Hanoi, Haiduong, and Nam Dinh to the collection point of Haiphong, with frantic directives from Cogny's office warning that security couldn't be guaranteed after February 1, 1955. People were put up at a few remaining hotels and in abandoned *lycées*, *collèges*, seminaries, or cinemas. A number of businesses like pharmacies, bakeries, laundries, refrigeration and port operations were basically requisitioned by Cogny's Forces Terrestres of North Vietnam to smooth flights, while people boxed up what they could with a final deadline of April 15— Operation Ozymandias, as one might call it, before a putatively "Democratic Republic of Vietnam" took over.[69]

Meanwhile, wanting command of another battalion, Bigeard was instead given a teaching job at the General Staff School (Ecole Supérieure de Guerre) in Paris. Anti-Parisian bureaucracy, like the proconsuls, and just as disdainful of hazy military theory, Bigeard made it plain that he would prefer a shot at Algeria, where a full-scale revolt had begun. But he did offer an emotional lecture on Dien Bien Phu, and of course greatly interested his audience on that controversial topic. And he continued performing his ritualistic seven kilometers of jogging each morning at six. After meeting Le Provost de Launay, he and Gaby were promptly transferred from their mournful hotel room to a splendid apartment on the Boulevard

Lannes, named for one of Napoleon's most courageous marshals, and the street where Piaf then lived, and where another French icon, Brigitte Bardot, would one day reside as well.[70]

Then came maneuvers in Germany, and finally in 1955 Bigeard met General Jacques Massu, flatly demanding North Africa. Other generals counseled a patient rise in the hierarchy and acquisition of suitable diplomas; but Bigeard ultimately got what he wanted—command of the 3rd Battalion (later Regiment) of Colonial Parachutists. "Adieu Paris, adieu Place Joffre. God, please arrange that I never return!" he remembers saying to himself.[71]

On October 24 he was on a plane south, set to embrace a new arena of adventure, with Viet Minh warnings still in his ears, to the effect that Algeria would turn into France's next imperial graveyard. But light-heartedly, he told Gaby that this wouldn't exactly be Vietnam! After all, Algeria was an extension of France—not to worry ...

Truly this *was* more than a typical French colony, but rather, a place where as early as 1848 so many Europeans had arrived that the northern part became three departments of France itself. The south was an endless Saharan frontier, and conquest in that direction was again reminiscent of the pioneering Americans. Waves of immigration, consisting of French, as well as Spanish, Maltese, Italians, and others produced what used to be called a melting pot, and a stubborn *pied noir* character—though that rather patronizing term wasn't popularly used till quite late in the colony's history. In this group there obtained a feeling of both superiority and inferiority, and in fact, *pieds noirs* often felt more at one with the majority they dominated than with mainland French; yet they were also hardliners on retaining electoral inequities and their own untrammeled power. Enduring malarial fevers, they had drained the Mitidja swamps in the Algiers region, creating a fertile plain perfumed by fruit trees. They were often hardworking and inventive in the vast vineyards they cultivated, or on estates devoted to other crops; stately, fragrant eucalyptus they profusely planted made the region more attractive. They also felt they had employed and enhanced the Muslim population. However, despite their industry, they were equally capable of indolence on sun-scorched beaches fronting the glittery Mediterranean, or in people-watching cafés on the boulevards of big coastal cities, particularly following World War I, when frenzied building and the advent of amenities made urban populations boom. To be sure Algiers was always the dominant *pied noir* city, with more Spanish-oriented Oran an interesting rival.

But this historical sketch is too slender and reductive. When one reads Louis Bertrand's novel *Le sang des races* from his "Cycle Africain," one derives a better sense of the richness, youth, untidiness, romance, and imperfectly shaken kaleidoscope of a *pied noir* melting pot in Algeria, but one where ingredients were anything but firmly melded as late as 1920. Here the Spanish weren't just Spanish, but Andalusian, Castilian, Sevillian, and each with lingo and ways to contribute to a French culture that was more limber and elastic than in the métropole. The Italians were Sicilian, Calabrese, Neapolitan, Piedmontese, and each group again had different proclivities and speech patterns, and was perceived in varying ways. Sometimes they worked from well before dawn at humble occupations—stone breaking, railroad building, muleteering, while other times they succumbed to the café and to *amours passagers* in seductive Africa. The height of Bertrand's novel involves a young Spaniard and a badly married French woman from Champagne, who despite her "elite" status (which this Rafael approvingly notices in her beautifully kept home) has had an empty life extending from childhood through a loveless marriage to a drunk *colon* in Medea. In a *Madame Bovary*–type scene of seduction she finally overcomes her religious *pudeur,* giving herself to Rafael, amid the raucous, joyful *tintamarre* of an Arab wedding next door. Rafael then leaves her, returning to Algiers, which he likes less than the refreshing, open South; but on a trip back to his home country of Valencia, he finds that his Spanish cousins have it less well off than in Algiers. The place Bertrand describes and which he knew well seems to him at this *pied noir* apogee anything but old; rather, this part of North Africa would have a long, European-led future—one of refurbished, enhanced *latinité* reclaimed from those who had putatively broken the civilization of ancient Rome here.

To some degree this was an an arriviste's mythologizing about that culture; but in another book Bertrand shows with apposite detail the European fever of building where once there had been ruins, and also an obsession about recovering those ruins—of archaeological digs à gogo: basilicas here, Roman baths, aqueducts, villas there, descended during long centuries into dusty, under-the-sand oblivion. North Africa had once been a "centre de latinité" and could become so again. Let construction sites be multiplied, but at the same time, let all Roman or Christian ruins be excavated by loving, Faidherbian soldiers, by priests and students, protected, preserved, and . . . the sky was the limit![72]

Writing in the mid-1930s Gabriel Audisio, an intellectual leader of the "Ecole d'Alger," echoed this notion, denoting Algiers in particular as "one vast construction site," and approving the mix of peoples there—particularly the Latins, "tous les frères de l'olive." Yes, "this race has no reason to envy the young Americans of our cinema," he proudly added, implying that here was a younger and better America in the making. In Algeria Audisio beheld a radiant synthesis of complex elements, all "cemented by French culture," and with a bright future on the horizon.[73]

Those views ignored rapid *pied noir* alterations—particularly, the furthering of a Francophone melting pot and of comforts, seen by the 1940s in Albert Camus' great novel, *The Plague*, set in Oran. Splattered snail-like on a plateau by the ocean, Camus' Oran has a fussy, punctilious, and more "educated" aura than in Bertrand's earlier optic. If responses to the plague mirror French attitudes in Occupied France of World War II, Camus also seems prescient here about Algeria on the eve of catastrophe—comfortable Oran at first unable to face the growing evidence of disease, killing rats galore, then humans. For Camus wars, like plague outbreaks, were surprise events, not supposed to happen, not meant to shatter plans, futures, certitudes. Too many, including academic humanists, refused to face the facts. Camus' seriousness here seems a foil for *pied noir* insouciance on the edge of a catastrophe that had now arrived, and which soldiers like Bigeard would have to confront.[74]

But this great military man was also coming to an imperial milieu where Muslims themselves had perhaps less unity amongst themselves than Europeans. The numerical majority in Algeria consisted of Berbers and/or Kabyles of the mountains, a growing minority, Arabs of the lowlands, and mixed in-betweeners. The French worked with and identified traditional, Westernized, and Islamicized elites. Offspring of the traditional elite (families of the "great tents") were, however, finding themselves outclassed by poorer children on French school benches, and rivalries weakened them as well. The old bourgeoisie of the cities descended from Moorish families had lost economic clout since the 1840s, and all in all, the colonial power knew these so-called elites would never persist if French sway diminished too much.

The hardworking Kabyles fascinated the French as a civilization unto themselves. They were considered extremely egalitarian, which also translated into family versus family or village versus village vendettas, when someone tried to rise above the norm; very sensitive to matters of honor; and full of proverbial wisdom. Kabyles in turn marveled at French individualism, when for them the village was all; but they were also adept at imitating and evolving. In theory Islam was a kind of ideological glue in Algeria and so was rising nationalism; but even there a gulf yawned between hard-shell rebels, and assimilationists drawn to French culture and institutions, such as Ferhat Abbas, a Sétif chemist married, like many, to a French woman. These "évolués" would take time integrating with other firebrands in the Algerian revolt, and French would long remain a preferred *lingua franca.* As for Islam, especially among the Kabyle young there was a growing anticlericalism, and even among the old their religious practices were less pronounced than those of the Arabs. In sum, here was a complex society on a powderkeg, yet one that for so long had seemed invulnerable to any significant disruption.[75]

After the first salvoes of war on All Saints' Day of 1954, that long afternoon of relative Algerian tranquility ended. Coming on a significant festival day, this outburst caused surprise and much damage, followed by a tough first winter for growing French forces. In their revolt for independence, the nationalist Front de Libération Nationale (FLN) along with its military arm, the Armée de Libération Nationale (ALN) henceforth kept the terror ante high—cutting off noses or lips of suspected Muslim "collaborators" associated with the French, not to mention throat-slittings of *caïds* and *pieds noirs,* and even the stuffing of sexual organs into mens' mouths, such as had occurred in the Rif War.

For now the Oranic (extending outward from Oran) and the Algérois hinterland of Algiers were relatively quiet. The FLN initially concentrated on a poorer, more isolated Algeria—the Aurès Mountains and Constantinois. In his great memoir (yet another extremely cultured fighter), Hélie de Saint Marc evokes the Algerian east he encountered in operations— "rude, grave, spartiate." Here were the dry Alps of burning summers and freezing winters, a North Africa, as he puts it, that seemed tired of its own past. Roman ruins constituted an outdoor museum that gestured and tugged at even the most hardened Legionnaires. In fact Saint Marc could still feel old Roman soldiers and Numidian peasants walking here, and Saint Augustine too. This was the forgotten Algeria—a striking contrast to more fertile and built-up areas nearer the coast.[76]

French authorities at home were confused on how to proceed with this revolt, oscillating between rigor (voting a state of urgency for Algeria April 3, 1955, which permitted enhanced military-police cooperation and troop increases), and hopeful clemency. But the summer of 1955 showed that the revolt and its repression—ostensibly a "police action"—had turned into a full-fledged war. FLN attacks were now planned for the entire Constantinois. The main one aimed at the "coquette subprefecture" of Philippeville by the sea was only stymied by a military figure whose name would finally make headlines in France at the dawn of the next century: Paul Aussaresses. One has to linger on this Aussaresses (formerly a man in the shadows), because despite all the newspaper articles that have come out on his controversial activities during the Algerian conflict, his own memoir of 2001 remains a fundamental primary source, oddly revealing another of our "cultured forceful," whose spare, elegant French prose drips humanistic taste all the way, even if to a degree cowritten. Indeed, Aussaresses tells us he was the offspring of a father who was a historian and friend of Colette, advancing in the prefectoral and ministerial ranks, then heading a big provincial newspaper. His bright son, Paul, took a first prize for Latin translation at a *lycée* in Bordeaux, then in higher education majored in Latin, Greek, and philology, and later learned Arabic. All of which, he says, "rather predisposed me to a quiet university career."[77]

But World War II intervened in his academic career, and Aussaresses chose the Resistance. In Algeria in 1941, then Morocco in 1942, he became a secret agent. Hurtling on night aircrafts over France and parachuting, he realized what could happen to him, knowing of comrades who had had fingernails and teeth pulled out by the Nazis. In Tunisia of 1943 he fought pitched military battles where much of his section was slaughtered, then like Bigeard parachuted into the Ariège near the end of the war, helping liberate that pretty region. Garbed as a German soldier, he also fluttered down near Berlin in April 1945, only to be arrested by the Soviets and nearly executed as a fascist! Like Bigeard too he was then in Indochina, giving a parachutist regiment with a secret service coloration (the 11th Choc) its own cachet.[78]

In Philippeville of 1955 Aussaresses' supervisor Colonel de Cockburne made him an "information officer," but no one quite told him how to proceed. He nonetheless procured talented assistants. One was a Muslim named Issolah, whose family had been in the French army for generations. Issolah himself had enrolled at eighteen, and in Vietnam his battalion of sharpshooters had been wiped out. In Algeria his command of Arab and Berber dialects and his guttiness appealed to Aussaresses. Another *adjoint*, Pierre Misiry, hailed from a French family that had migrated to Tunisia, also knew Arabic, had enrolled in the army at eighteen, and been a para in Indochina.

Aussaresses had never worked with the police before, and now had to learn its different branches. Direly, they described the nationalist-terrorist threat in Algeria, and how under-equipped they were to combat it. Aussaresses began weaving a web, as he puts it, of informants, drawing especially on café patrons and even those of brothels. The police taught him

methods used to threaten informants that would become controversial—
coups mostly sufficient, then water filling lungs, and at an extreme, electric shocks. Cockburne was truly sickened, calling this the *sale guerre* it
would henceforth be labeled. Aussaresses realized his superior wouldn't
last long here. For the side being investigated and interrogated was distinguished by utter callousness when it came to human life. One FLN
leader, dubbed "le petit Messaoud," had been a trafficker in various
sordid things, as well as a pimp. In Aussaresses' estimation, he was quite
typical. Via mobster tactics such men became forces to be reckoned with,
needing only to be ruthless. Combating them were agents like the courageous Issolah, having nocturnal coffees with top FLN, and an information
web that became ever more complex.

On June 18, 1955, a date symbolic for former de Gaulle adherents, the
FLN set off seven bombs in Philippcville at the same hour, burned cars,
and smashed store windows. In one street a Muslim pal of a *pied noir,*
pressured by the rebels, split his friend's skull with an axe. The victim
lying in hospital then groaned out his attacker's name. For the first time
Aussaresses himself applied "constraint," trying to establish the man's contacts; but in this case he got nothing.

Aussaresses realized that FLN hunkered down in the country, and
largely impervious to air assaults, had to vacate their rural lairs to procure
victuals in Philippeville. He now got police to comb the town's grocery
stores, as well as pharmacies, watching for bulk purchases of foodstuffs or
bandages. His intelligence network then unearthed a huge daylight attack
set for Philippeville August 20, 1955, coinciding with a U.N. resolution in
favor of the FLN mounted by several Third World nations. It turned out
that this was only one of a series of ruthless attacks to take place in the
Constantinois. The plan was to take a middling Algerian port town hostage
and cause much human damage there.[79]

Philippeville's mayor pooh-poohed the report, and when the Army was
informed, a commanding lieutenant didn't believe it either. Aussaresses
nonetheless warned him to have his men go through normal paces up to
zero hour, for any change in routines would be a tip-off. Two days before
that date Aussaresses knew many FLN were already in cellars around
Philippeville, and had also commandeered the town's taxis. (He thought
of Gallieni before the Marne.)

At midmorning on August 20, a trigger-happy police commissioner proceeded to an arrest outside town, and along with Issolah and Misiry, then
had to fend off a hive of 500 *fells* shooting at them, while their women

urged them forward with screams. Issolah grenaded an FLN truck loaded with Molotov cocktails and bound for Philippeville, and the truck blew with its cargo. Somehow these men then made it back to town. It was 11:30 A.M. At 12:00 sharp an attack with more screams unfolded on Aussaresses' headquarters, but he and his men replied with machine guns, chasing the rebels back to a bistro, whence they had come. Bullets assailed the French from every side, and assaulting the café was no easy task. Finally Aussaresses and Misiry smoked out the defenders with grenades.

Outside, the battle continued to rage in a town somewhat denuded of population due to the attractions of the beach. In an almost surreal way rebels kept advancing on Philippeville's streets, apparently fearless. When they fell to defending fire, no one bothered to pick them up. The top leaders just ran, leaving behind these expendable dead or wounded. Aussaresses would later discover that their frontline fodder was composed of peasants liberally plied with hashish. By his patient intelligence gathering he had saved thousands of civilians from death or mutilation; but massacres outside Philippeville ended up more costly.

At an iron pyrite mine some twenty kilometers to the east, about 2,000 Muslims had been living and working in peace with 130 French-speaking Europeans, receiving the same pay and benefits. The FLN considered this an ideal target for their violence. At twelve noon on August 20, two fellahin groups attacked both the mine and homes of el-Halia, where women were warming up mid-day dinners for their husbands. The mine's defenses included a stockpile of machine guns, but the man with the key had gone to the beach! In crushing heat a horrible chain of events then unfolded. Two *pied noir* workers, managing to elude the hackers, reached an army camp ten kilometers away. Yelling and sobbing, they told of babies splattered against the walls, and housewives being raped, then disemboweled (*étriper* in the more elegant French). Captain Robert Perret, a Bigeard alumnus, had 200 young soldiers on hand who had hardly fired guns before. But they were ordered to retake the mine, while a couple of T6 airplanes would provide support from above. Somehow the recruits did admirably, but it was too late. Off the bat they found thirty-five dead bodies, and numerous wounded. When Aussaresses beheld children cut into pieces, throats slit, skulls crushed, and women's stomachs degutted or heads severed, he truly saw the nature of this war. Previously, Muslims and Europeans had lived easily with each other here. Now given booze and grass, and the right to pillage *pied noir* homes, ordinary people had turned into sadistic killers. This was what French authorities now had to fight—

in the highest reaches, a dashing general, André Beaufre, and Algeria's intellectual governor-general Jacques Soustelle.

Like Aussaresses Soustelle was another humanist confronted by jarring reality. A Protestant from France's Cévennes, he had been a distinguished ethnologist and linguist specializing on the Aztecs and at one time professor at the Collège de France, before becoming a top member of de Gaulle's wartime resistance, and later, Minister of Colonies and head of the Rassemblement du Peuple Français (RPF) party. Instructed by Interior Minister Mitterand to launch a series of reforms in Algeria when he took office in January 1955, Soustelle toured the country, and felt that social and economic innovations *could* work here. He didn't give up on those ideas, but was definitely converted to a harder line after witnessing victims of these massacres. A direct view of European women or children lying in hospital with fingers or other appendages cut off, and throats sliced was quite enough.[80]

As for Bigeard, immediately after his arrival in this suddenly dire North Africa of 1955, he met what he called the "grandes gueules" (or big shots) of the French army. Bigeard, Massu, and Gilles found themselves in an airplane together, checking out the landscape below, and discussing options. Then encountering his new battalion at Ouled Rahmoun, Bigeard beheld a sloppy, lifeless "boutique" consisting of 1,200, though as usual, he felt he could make them rapidly better. Cashiering troublemakers, the fearful, and the drinkers, offering transfers to all wishing to leave, he spent the next two months getting the rest into shape. One soldier, Lenoir (nicknamed Bébert or la Vieille), would be his assistant for almost five years, smoking a pipe and dressing like his boss. The terrain would be different here, but it was back to an old routine of sports, long marches, and impeccable attire, including the legendary paratroop "lizard" cap, designed by Bigeard himself. An enthusiastic young recruit named Guy Cado wrote his parents November 9, 1955: "We are finally going to march in the footsteps of Lyautey and Bugeaud. . . . Still believing!"[81] (A believing Cado was killed a few days later.)

Bigeard's superior here was Beaufre, distinguished in World War II, a supple military thinker, and one who gave his talented subordinate autonomy. As usual, Bigeard's description can be savored: "Le général Beaufre est beau, racé, distingué."[82] Beaufre's own style of warfare was both mobile and psychological, and he had earned a reputation as a relentless pursuer of FLN in the area east of Constantine. While together, he and Bigeard became a perfect match.

Not long on the scene Bigeard saw the problems facing him—terrorists bullying without limits, and too many appeasing *colons* and Muslims paying them off. Clearing the Bône-Philippeville road for safer trips, he soon became the Europeans' darling in that region, but poor leadership remained a French problem. Bigeard knew that too many army men avoided night operations, going after rebels by day, but giving them a free nocturnal pass. He also felt these leaders failed to teach young recruits or draftees how to mingle with the population, and how to exploit localized matters like family problems or ethnic rivalries. Bigeard thought in Lyautesque terms of the importance of the doctor and teacher, and of creating a true entente in a variety of regions. He began airing his views on these deficiencies, and his chiefs responded by using the 3d Para for increasingly tougher assignments. Counteracting conventional ideas, Bigeard mounted night attacks, and using the element of surprise, procured smashing military successes. As with Bugeaud, his great enemy was "immobilisme." Bigeard and his men rapidly became a kind of model in eastern Algeria, which Alistair Horne would call "a crack force, one of the most effective in the Western world."[83] Confidence grew, and when Langlais visited, both he and Bigeard agreed that this kind of war is "like camping and almost a vacation compared to what we've been through [in Vietnam]!"[84]

Flying back to Paris on a Caravelle, Marcel had three days with Gaby at the inevitable Hotel Terminus and a talk with Gilles and other "gros bonnets." General Lorillot, Algeria's commander-in-chief of the time, now wanted Bigeard's men for new pacification efforts in the Constantine region. With Martial Chevalier, his old Indochina secretary, back, Sentenac, an escapee from Dien Bien Phu, and Lenoir, a newer brother-figure at his side, Bigeard felt guardedly optimistic.

In late February 1956 his contingent, swelled by a fourth company under Captain Florès (nicknamed "Bir Hakeim"), fought in Kabyle villages west of Bougie, filled with rebels. Bigeard's idea was to act quickly here, yet be humane with civilians. An innovator in the use of helicopter warfare, his Bell became an airborne headquarters. Village after village was liberated, and Bruno's paras on furlough in Bône, marching in raw-boned formation, became famous, as well as attractive to young Bônoises. One general complained of these "gorillas" whooping it up too much, but Bigeard knew the hypocrite himself had a propensity for whisky and women. The general invited Bigeard's paras to a ball, and they partied till the wee hours of morning. At 6 A.M. Bigeard got his grumbly men outside for sport— "the girls, the whisky [to be] eliminated in sweat," as he said.[85]

Soon it was back to business. Summoned to see Beaufre, Bigeard heard about Algerian deserters from the French army who had murdered loyal *tirailleurs*, stolen a sizeable cache of arms, and were now six to eleven hours distant. How to find them before they reached safety in Tunisia? The chances seemed low, but Beaufre had faith in his subordinate. Quickly, Marcel scanned the map, putting himself in the escapees' shoes, and realizing that their leader had had French army training in Vietnam, and would therefore follow certain procedures, like using main roads. Bigeard sent several of his companies in different directions to search, and to find suitable places for awaiting the quarry. He himself grabbed a helicopter to scurry over high mountain country, and "Bir Hakeim" radioed that he thought he had found the escapees. Bigeard's *boutique* was hustled into action, and within five hours 126 rebels were dead, 15 *tirailleur* hostages freed, and a large quantity of munitions recovered. Arriving by helicopter, Beaufre was surprised and impressed.[86]

From then on helicopter use became all the rage, too much so in less empirical hands, and generals came down from coastal cities to check out Bigeard, who, more ominously, made the pages of *Paris-Match* and newspapers back in France. Beaufre soon located another mission for his star—up in the mountains. Rebels here had been shaking down civilians and sabotaging train tracks and other installations. Beaufre gave Bigeard all the firepower and helicopters he wanted for the operation. Starting near the Tunisian border—such borders a growing problem because of decolonization creating terrorist havens—Bigeard's battalion turned regiment searched five days, though interrupted in the midst of operations by a chopper debouching Beaufre and a gaggle of journalists. Again, success was followed by media hype.

Decidedly this would be a journalists' war, for Algeria was more accessible than Vietnam, and there had been improvements in aviation. This boded ill for the French effort, and played a key role in their eventual loss of Algeria. While the rebel side promoted a regime of closed information, the French permitted all manner of critiques. But France's government officials also busied themselves countering FLN propaganda. It wasn't hard to do: shakedowns of the most repulsive variety became standard from the time of the Philippeville massacres. A government translation of a collective letter from Muslim notables of several villages (February 1956) showed them "crying out their distress" at "ruined roads, blown bridges, houses of poor, innocent *fellahs* and schools burned down, not to mention inhuman *égorgements* committed on innocent *fellahs* and even on their . . .

mules, cattle, sheep." The letter was a plea for French help, but the FLN
kept ratcheting up the terror, and over wider and wider territory, partly
an attempt to eradicate more moderate nationalists like Messali Hadj's
Mouvement National Algérien. A long document of 1956 from Socialist
Minister-Resident Lacoste's office noted rebel fines imposed on Muslim
smokers—5,000 francs for a first offence, 10,000 for a second, and for a
third, death. Included as well are chilling photographs of missing noses
due to this infraction. Muslim readers of French newspapers must supposedly pay 10,000 franc fines when apprehended. There were blanket
orders to kill dogs that might offer civilians protection, and refusals could
bring 10,000 franc fines, then a throat-slitting of the dog and a forced
pet meal for its master! There were fines for attending movies, shopping
at French pastry shops, and of course for working as "collaborators" in
the homes of *colons.* There were other monthly collection rackets, large
ransoms demanded for automobiles stopped on the roads (as much as
200,000 francs), and threats of death to Jewish merchants unless they paid
substantial fines as well. A kind of segregation was preached by the FLN,
and their own pamphlets averred that Muslims consorting with French
or Jews might be legitimately killed. On the body of one man murdered
in April 1956 was a note declaring, "we don't want those who walk with
France." Fires to health facilities, grenades thrown at synagogues, and by
government count, 231 schools destroyed between November 1955 and the
end of April 1956, not to mention 259 train lines and 19,000 telephone
poles sabotaged—this was the reality. Muslims were forced out of villages
to do the dirty work, while rebels might rape their women. And of course
"the Kabyle smile"—cut-off members jammed in dead men's jaws: all
this represented plenty of "material," and a serious atmosphere as well for
Bigeard's pacification efforts that continued frantically all over the "Beaufre
zone." And *yet,* through June 1956 "the reputation of the *casquettes* grows,
the press mentions us daily, and the fellahin wonder what kind of fiends
they are dealing with."[87] Among those back home who noticed too, the
novelist Joseph Kessel came down for a few days to interview this demon,
then published a magazine piece that Bruno compulsively reread.

Bigeard's effectiveness was, however, the progenitor of troubles with
his own superiors, confronted with new ideas and repetitive successes
emanating from an energetic underling. In early June 1956 his 3d Régiment Parachutiste Colonial was sent to fight in the Nementcha Mountains
against tribesmen who had always been tough up here, including against
Rome's legions. For the operation Bigeard was given a new boss, General

Vanuxem, a former *baroudeur* in Indochina; but this "Vanu" was decidedly no Beaufre. Once an associate of de Lattre, "he's no *tendre* ... for
him, to hell with losses, only results count," as Bigeard would note.[88] In a
night operation where Bruno's men took the full brunt of a surprise
attack, then surprised the rebels back by pursuing at 3 A.M. in difficult
country, before ensnaring and crushing them, the 3d obtained a success
nearly ruined by Vanuxem and another general coming to interfere. This
galled Bigeard, particularly when he and his men had become nauseous
in aircraft hurtling over mountains, hurt their sides skinning up cliffs,
done without rest, put bodies on the line against suicidally tenacious warriors, improvised their way to victory, and then had to endure the arrival
of waddling brass full of suggestions! "I don't like to feel these big shots
around me, showing up by helicopter all fresh, when we haven't slept for
two nights," he recalled disdainfully.[89]

In the good colonial tradition Bigeard again learned to disregard or
modify orders from above, when he could. He was also plain angry at
losses of precious men that he couldn't prevent, due to these ill-conceived
operations ordered by superiors. Concluding a report on Vanuxem's
maneuvers, in a region where previous ones had failed, "I wasn't soft on
the command, specifying that it was absurd to throw units into this kind
of terrain without information and valid maps." He also minced no words
concerning Vanuxem's gratuitous views and didacticism.[90]

In the Nementchas for more missions, Bigeard, now accredited with
Arab *baraka*, somehow misplaced it on June 16, 1956, sustaining a grave
wound against a rebel band of Chaouia warriors. The bullet pierced his
chest a few centimeters above the heart and went out his back. Helicoptered to an infirmary, then stretchered onto a Dakota, Bigeard was flown
to a hospital in Constantine. The surgeon there said he was fortunate
to be alive, recommending total rest. But anxious about his men still in
the mountains, Bigeard rose at six the next morning for exercise, to his
doctor's consternation, who feared a hemorrhage. The surgeon then sent
his celebrated patient back to France.[91]

There he found himself big news indeed, and paparazzi jostled Gaby
at the airport with their flashes, along with more welcome Bigeard veterans, worried about their old leader. Thence to the Hotel Terminus, where
flowers and telegrams clogged his room. Then he went off to Toul for
convalescent rest, walking by the beautiful Moselle in June, or fishing
with Gaby, but with many journalists or other visitors pestering him there
too, not to mention sacks of mail arriving from admirers. Wound or no

wound, his chiefs also reacted harshly to the report Bigeard had issued on operations in the Nementchas, and their jealousy wasn't diminished by news that their subordinate would come to Paris for July 14 celebrations, where he would be made grand officer of the Legion of Honor by the President of the Republic. Since he had to put up with a journalistic plague, Bigeard didn't mind using it to explain exactly what he and his paras had been trying to do in Algeria. General Gilles in Paris told him to cool this putative publicity seeking, but Bigeard retorted sharply that he hadn't looked for it; it had found him.

In Paris on Bastille Day, with Gaby and Marie-France by his side, Lieutenant-Colonel Bigeard made the cover of *Jours de France,* while the newspaper *France-Soir* featured an article on him by Kessel. Photographers snapped profusely, and the great para parade on the Champs-Elysées was attended by over 100,000 Parisians, with Bruno in the lead and vigorously applauded. Receiving his decoration, he then dined afterwards with Gilles, who had spirited him away to a chic restaurant. But even here he was mobbed and applauded, and Gilles would not forget. The next day Bigeard was invited for a tête-à-tête at the Elysée Palace with President Coty, where he warned that the French must work fast in Algeria, since time was on the rebel side. He also "emptied his bag" about too many colonels sitting in Algiers' offices, and too few in the field, versed in the techniques of guerilla warfare.[92]

Back in Toul Bigeard was brought to earth by the blackened facade of his home, product of a tarring-machine that had exploded. No snob, he cleaned up himself, but couldn't wait to regain his cohorts in Algeria. And indeed, he soon returned with Gaby to their Paris hotel, said another goodbye, and went off to join the *boutique* in the Nementchas, where almost providentially, his captains successfully wound up their latest operation an hour later. It was a good new start, and Bigeard also looked forward to leaving the mountains to join other paras for duty in the impending Suez operation. The French knew how significant Egyptian President Nasser's backing of the FLN had been in this war, and for them the canal's nationalization was something of an excuse, as perhaps it was for the Israelis, to settle scores. But while awaiting the call in seaside Bône, Bigeard jogged early in the mornings, ignoring danger, though warned by his old pal, Allaire, who wanted to guard him. On September 5, 1956, at six in the morning Bigeard was running in shorts on a quai, when suddenly three Arabs burst forward, shooting him at point-blank range. Bigeard struggled to his feet, staggered after the assassins, who ran, then collapsed in the street. A French driver stopped, but refused to take him to hospital for fear of soiling his seats with blood. Luckily, a passing Arab driver did. Bigeard's right arm was shattered by two bullets, but more worrisome was a third that had entered his body near the liver. Ending up in a plaster body cast, the paratroop commander required a tough operation and was again, fortunate to survive. Gaby came down, his old fellow escapee from the Nazis, Masbourian, also arrived at his bedside, and French magazines played up the latest on the man of *baraka*. Suez meanwhile ended up a Gallic fiasco, due to the co-opting energies of the superpowers, and Cairo continued giving the FLN untrammeled support.[93]

Recovering, though sore in his right arm, Bigeard found himself affected with his regiment at the start of 1957 to Sidi-Ferruch on the sea west of Algiers. Minister-Resident Lacoste along with Algeria's new commander in chief Salan (nicknamed "the Mandarin" for his Indochinese past and inscrutability) had now decided to fight back in the cities, particularly Algiers. Unable to prevail by battling paras in the outback, the FLN from mid-1956 used bombs and other instruments of terror in Algeria's capital, where a large media presence could publicize such acts, and where Europeans would hopefully be provoked into reprisals.

Some believe it all started with the French guillotining of two top rebels June 19 (one of whom had killed eight civilians in an ambush). Ramdane Abane, the most single-minded of FLN leaders, then declared that 100 French civilians would be killed for every rebel guillotined. Between June 21 and 24, 1956, Saadi Yacef, second in command to Larbi Ben M'Hidi in the ZAA (Zone Autonome d'Alger), had his FLN henchmen gun down forty-nine civilians on the city's streets. From June through August attacks of all varieties grew more frequent, especially the setting off of powerful bombs in cafés and other urban fora. These explosions became an almost daily occurrence, and the population grew paranoid. Yacef's idea was to use women to carry, then place these explosive devices, for they were less likely to be noticed or frisked, especially with hair dyed blond to resemble Europeans. *Poseuses de bombe* included a number of middle-class women like Hassiba Ben Bouali, Zohra Drif, and Djamila Bouhired. How the bourgeoisie has sown the seeds of its own disasters—Marx certainly correct there! On September 30, 1956, a Drif bomb (concealed in a beach bag under a table) hit the Milk Bar at the corner of the Place Bugeaud; while Bouhired's exploded at the Cafétéria on the Rue Michelet, both popular spots with the young. Shattered glasses shot lethal shards all over the place, especially in the Milk Bar, limbs were torn off, and police had to rein in a population shouting for revenge. On October 6 an illegal bomb laboratory belonging to the Algerian Communist Party was located, their product slated for the FLN; but other bombs were being copiously manufactured elsewhere, and with constant refinements (some no bigger than cigarette packs, as Bigeard remembers). In early November three exploded—at a bus station, a Monoprix department store, and on a bus respectively—creating more dead and mutilated. On October 14 came the arrest of the controversial Fernand Yveton, a Communist militant working at a gasworks factory, caught in the act of placing a bomb; he then admitted another would explode at 6:30 P.M. Paul Teitgen, secretary-general of the Prefecture of Police, arrived and spent an afternoon sweating blood, though refusing to strong-arm the suspect into telling exactly *where* the device was located. His Resistance memories of the Gestapo and Dachau played a role in his hesitation. Luckily the bomb failed to function, but had it done so, thousands might have been victims of a massive gas explosion. Bigeard, among others, wonders what Teitgen (who would resign his position) could have told victims shorn of an eye, arm, or leg, not to mention their anguished families. Just before Christmas another bomb placed on a school bus killed and maimed a number of children.

There were in addition plentiful assassinations of both French and Muslim notables. Among the most notorious was the murder December 28 of Amédée Froger, mayor of Boufarik and head of Algeria's Federation of Mayors, an "ultra" on French Algeria but also a respected Muslim veteran of World War I, shot to death by Ali la Pointe, once a pimp, card-shark, and criminal in the Casbah, now Ben M'Hidi's associate. At the funeral site a bomb exploded, but luckily, the procession of mourners arrived slightly late. Again, police had to suppress European reprisals. By the end of 1956 urban terror in Algiers was at its height—bombs mostly reserved for *pieds noirs*, knife and gun attacks for Muslims. Salan and Lacoste feared the shaken down Casbah might soon overwhelm French *quartiers*. The regular police weren't adequate here, particularly when Ben M'Hidi promoted an impending general strike of commercial establishments, threatening to paralyze the city. There would also be pressure to keep 35,000 Muslim children out of school. Salan wasn't sure how far to go repressing such activity, nor was General Massu, back from Suez; but on January 7 Lacoste gave Massu complete autonomy as "superprefect" and commander of operations here. Massu knew the appointment was hardly a gift and that he would later be criticized. But he summoned four crack regiments from his 10th Parachutist Division, including Bigeard's

3d, each to patrol a different sector of the city. Bigeard's was given the pivotal task of establishing checkpoints and conducting house-to-house searches in the hardest part of the city to control, the western sector, including the Casbah. Especially with a strike so close at hand, and the Casbah so full of hiding places, the whole assignment seemed outlandishly difficult in a large metropolis.[94]

An even harder task befell another reluctant soldier, the future General Aussaresses. After working in Philippeville Aussaresses had been happy to receive a transfer to England, where he trained for Suez. But Bigeard's men kept him out of that engagement. For when the former information officer regained Algeria, he was invited by the 3d RPC at Bône to jump first as their honored guest. Unfortunately, the chute they gave Aussaresses had been garbled in storage, only opened just above the ground, and the secret service agent was flattened and lay stunned, his vertebral column smashed, while he watched Bigeard's paras flutter peacefully downward. Shunted to military hospitals in Algiers and Paris, Aussaresses was plastered up à la Lyautey, saddened at missing Suez.

By the time he recovered, Algiers had become *the* hot spot, and when Massu was made superprefect there, he wanted the best associates possible. Back in late August 1955 the general had visited Captain, later Colonel Mayer in Philippeville, asking with perplexity how that attack had been repelled at a cost of only two dead. Mayer led him to Aussaresses, and Massu remembered. Now he pressured him to do in Algiers what had formerly been done in Philippeville. Repelled by the prospect of this "sale boulot," Aussaresses told Massu to find someone else. But as he puts it, Massu wasn't one to be rolled in flour by a subaltern. Here was an offer a distraught Aussaresses knew he couldn't refuse—otherwise, he would have to leave the army, and what remained of an ideal that had guided him since World War II.[95]

Massu's other top *adjoint* was Lieutenant-Colonel Roger Trinquier, his long-time confidant, and sophisticated when it came to these "extravagant situations." Massu trusted both Trinquier and Aussaresses, though as the latter remarks, both were as nonconformist as one could be in the army. Aussaresses really blamed Massu's chief of staff, Colonel Yves Godard, for this new appointment. In 1948 Godard had maneuvered to take over Aussaresses' 11th Choc, wishing to designate its former leader as second in command. The blunt retort was that you don't make a man vicar in the parish where he was once head priest. As new *chef* of the 11th, Godard supposedly turned out a phony with men who had loved the Aussaresses blend of "anarchy and rigor, *bohème* and asceticism." Now Godard was giving him a big pile of dirty garments to launder, and at top speed.[96]

Meeting Massu on January 8, 1957, with death in his soul, as he says, Aussaresses knew he was in the presence of "a great captain"—an alumnus of Moroccan campaigns, of Leclerc's African division in World War II, and a legend in the French reoccupation of Hanoi, 1946. Aussaresses tried again to withdraw, but Massu dubbed him "the man of the situation." He then drove him around Algiers, and Aussaresses was blown away by this spectacular Gallic-Arab San Francisco by the sea. The city was an anomaly of almost a million inhabitants, but with the majority Europeans. Massu then got him an office at the prefecture, and in a whisper, told him to work fast, otherwise *pieds noirs* might torch the entire Casbah! Massu said flatly that the French would have to be pitiless here, and Aussaresses grasped his meaning. His usual stylish answer: "Je comprends, mon général." Massu especially stressed the importance of breaking the strike slated to start January 28, but Aussaresses pleaded the lack of an information network. His prior work in Philippeville counted for nothing here. Massu mentioned a police file of terrorists, and via an old Philippeville contact Aussaresses laid hands on it; but it was only a small start. Regimental arrests and denunciations would bulge his terrorist Rolodex; but this was a huge city compared to a provincial subprefecture. A camp for distinguishing suspects (some rapidly released) was set up outside Algiers, and others to the south. The leopards, as paras were called due to their garb, now appeared everywhere, and dead bodies left on the streets showed the populace renewed French determination here.[97]

Aussaresses began having his associates comb bars and brothels to find suspects. Putting together a staff of twenty noncommissioned officers, he didn't mince words about their responsibilities. One suspect, Babaye, had been corralled by the FLN in the mountains, then cornered in a para operation, and fought tenaciously, before deciding to join the French side. Aussaresses also developed a second, secret team, in case the first one were investigated. Trinquier helped by putting together a census in Algiers and having soldiers go around to homes, asking the number and names of inhabitants. Residents who seemed absent for unusually long times would be called in for questioning. When known terrorists were killed summarily, Aussaresses' staff was evasive with visiting brass.

As for Bigeard this army man knew too that the policing he had never wanted to do would produce criticisms; but he did a repugnant job the only way he knew how—with thoroughness, alacrity, and fairness. He was especially effective in gathering information through the entire chain that led from street terrorists sometimes up to the diplomatic heights. Just before the strike Yacef got his young women, including the European daughter of a well-known Communist, to place bombs at a student hangout, *L'Otomatic,* and directly across the Rue Michelet at *La Cafétéria,* as well as at a nearby *brasserie,* the *Coq Hardi.* When the first two exploded, curious patrons at the *Coq* came to the window, and were then nailed by the third bomb placed there. Flying glass opened veins and arteries, with five dead and sixty wounded the result, mostly young people. In reaction Massu instituted a 9 P.M. curfew, giving instructions to shoot violators.

Then came Plan Champagne to break the general strike. Via the combined work of Aussaresses, Trinquier, and the regiments, including Bigeard's, the announced stoppage of Monday, January 28 failed within a day or two. Had it lasted a projected eight days, it would undoubtedly have made the FLN's case before the U.N. and in large sectors of world opinion—i.e., that the rebel group was overwhelmingly popular with Muslims. The paras simply snatched idled workers from their homes, taking them back to their jobs, so that trolleys, gas, or electricity would still function. When dockers struck, Aussaresses replaced them with prisoners from one of his camps, who did the work more efficiently and were remunerated at regular rates. The paras also took children from their homes, escorting them back to school, and bashed in metal shutters of storefronts, forcing merchants to reopen (Bigeard remembers some whispering that they wanted a cop nearby to protect them). On the whole a concerted, massive effort in counterinsurgency made this first Battle of Algiers a military success; but the home front in France split acrimoniously over the army's repressive methods, especially the use of torture about which Aussaresses obviously writes most authoritatively. On March 21 Salan was summoned to Paris to testify about this interrogation procedure. Bigeard himself despised the round-ups, and the bitterness shows in his subsequent comments: "I did not like this period, [the French] so strong against a few bombs, some firearms and killers, and yet, [our] children, pretty young girls, innocent young men dying, while others had arms and legs torn off."[98]

The regiments had been doing an extraordinary job, though as Bigeard says, he never knew the fate of those arrested and passed onward; but lethal bombs still took tolls. On Sunday, February 10 two Algiers stadiums jammed with soccer fans succumbed to explosions, leaving ten dead and forty-five wounded. Again, paras had to restrain furious mobs. Bigeard and his men worked with alacrity, trying to find all the bomb caches they could, especially in the Casbah. Sauderers, plumbers, watchmakers, and tarring experts were particularly suspect, and questioning of such people led to big discoveries. In shops food packaging, cookie cases, even milk boxes might have explosive devices hidden in them. Empty vegetable boxes would be O.K. on top and at the bottom; in the middle of a stack, however, one might find arms of different sorts. In homes stairs often had one step that could be pried open and used as a bomb hideout. Searches rewarded only those who were thorough, and sometimes Bigeard's men went over the same ground a number of times. In three houses they unearthed twenty-five explosive devices, then *chez* Mustafa Bouhired (whose niece was Djamila) they went over a suspect wall several times, tipping their hat to a fine masonry job, before coming up with twenty-six more. They gave that street a new moniker—the Impasse de la Grenade. Bigeard's own patience was mirrored in that of his men, poring over a list of the city's masons—"Bigre, elle est longue!" They also checked a shorter list of unemployed masons, and one called in for questioning had cement spots on his uniform, odd for a man lacking work in his trade. That arrest of a man working for the FLN led to the center of its bomb network in Algiers. By February 19 Bigeard and his men had taken eighty-seven bombs, and over seventy kilos of dynamite, as well as a pile of detonators, and bombing attacks diminished significantly.[99]

The mason interrogated by Bigeard's lieutenant, Jacques Allaire, brought more human prizes, so much so that top FLN leaders prepared to flee the city. The mason mentioned work done at the Impasse Kléber for the "Bachaga Boutaleb." Bombs were then located there by Bigeard's men, while Boutaleb was in Paris. On his return he lied profusely, professing his love of France, and declaring that the bombs hadn't been there before his trip. But the dryness of the cache supported the mason's story—i.e., that he had built it two months earlier. Boutaleb began crying for a lawyer, and said he would only deal with another Knight of the Legion of Honor, like himself. He finally admitted that the FLN had threatened to kill him if he didn't keep the cache of bombs. Ironically, he had also been picked to go to France and talk peace with government officials there. The arrest of this two-faced fellow then made top FLN leaders in Algiers hurry their flight preparations—including Ben M'Hidi, planning to leave the Casbah for his old *wilaya* 5 (military district) in the Oranais country. Missing his connection en route, the latter moved to another hideout in a European part of Algiers.

As in Arthur Koestler's *Sleepwalkers*, searching for one thing scientifi-
cally led to an unexpectedly bigger discovery. Bigeard's men had gotten
the mason and that prevaricating *bachaga;* next came the trail of a couple
of brothers, one of whom was arrested and said nothing for over a week.
Then, fearing the incarceration of a younger brother he loved (still at
large), the oldest began singing. He was a real estate agent, and for almost
a year the FLN had used him to procure apartments in chic European
parts of town, hiding their leaders there. He handed over his address book
and Bigeard's men went first to a building on the Boulevard Saint-Saens,
showing the concierge a picture; but the man they sought had decamped.
They then went to the next address, and here came a real find. As luck
would have it, it was morning mail time for this apartment on the Rue
Claude-Debussy. The concierge mentioned a nice man named Antoine
Perez who lived here and worked at city hall, and who corresponded to
one of the photos she was shown. The postman then arrived with his
mail, and the concierge was instructed to make her normal rounds with
it, knocking at doors. The paras followed up the stairwell, receiving a
puzzled look from another regimental soldier there: as if to say, "What
are *you* doing here?" On the third floor the concierge tapped lightly at
Perez' door, and a man in pajamas opened up. It was Larbi Ben M'Hidi.

Here on February 23 was a major turning point in the Battle of Algiers—
the arrest of an FLN leader who conducted the entire orchestra of urban
terror! Ben M'Hidi was in fact the last member of the FLN's Comité
de Coordination et d'Execution (CCE) still in Algiers. The others had
headed either to the mountains or abroad (primarily Tunis). Ben M'Hidi
was one of the group's founding fathers, a rich kid—Castro also comes
to mind—who had forsaken a conventional career for a life of moralistic
violence. The 3d's operation was kept secret for about a week, and Bigeard
became an intimate of his opposite number, recognizing Ben M'Hidi's
fanaticism, but also his nobility. First he offered to remove cuffs in return
for cooperation, but the stubborn leader threatened to jump out a window.
For two weeks in prison the pair had coffee together and extended conversations, consuming days and sometimes nights. (Allaire would spell his
exhausted superior.) Bigeard was trying to play up Ben M'Hidi's differences with the captured Ben Bella, hoping he would turn, and work with
the French. He also wished to preserve him from the police, who were
dying to grill the man behind so much carnage in Algiers. But Ben M'Hidi
would not change hats for Bigeard or any French soldier. Instead, he
predicted that his side would win, but seeing ahead to the violence of

the liberators, predicted also that his own contingent would ultimately kill him.

Interrogating the FLN leader with this respect and tortoise-like patience, Bigeard felt a "current pass between us"; but Massu was growing ever more irritated. So were the "Special Services" people. Finally Aussaresses met Bigeard and his prize over morning coffee, realizing that Bruno was trying to save Ben M'Hidi's life. Aussaresses felt, however, that Bigeard had lost it ("perdait les pédales")! With a third week of Marcel's questioning on the horizon, a frustrated Massu, Trinquier, and Aussaresses met to discuss options. A trial seemed out of the question, as it would become a media and foreign policy extravaganza, and might impede the netting of other FLN leaders (papers found in Ben M'Hidi's apartment portending possibilities). Massu asked Aussaresses' opinion, and his forthright reply was that when it came to terrorism he didn't much care about ranks ("je ne suis pas plus impressionné par le caïd que par le sous-fifre"). He said French authorities had been busy interrogating all sorts of poor fellows working for Ben M'Hidi, and that the big fish shouldn't be spared. He knew police authorities were dying to "cook" the man and get him to talk; but Aussaresses believed they would obtain nothing. He therefore asked Massu if he could take care of the matter, and Massu promised to "cover" him.

Bigeard absented himself when Aussaresses' well-armed men arrived to take Ben M'Hidi from prison; but the 3d Paras were nonetheless instructed to present arms to the fallen leader, a "geste spéctaculaire et quelque peu démagogique," as Aussaresses viewed Bigeard's order. The men then sped off with their prisoner to a farm outside Algiers, set to shoot Ben M'Hidi dead if the FLN tried to spring him en route. In the farm house there was no torture, as has sometimes been alleged, but Ben M'Hidi was simply hung, and the official communiqué called it a suicide. The body was taken to the hospital for good measure. And his death dealt a large blow to the FLN in Algiers, making their prime focus return to the Atlas of the Blida region. Long after the dust had settled, however, even Godard, Massu's unsentimental chief of staff, would comment in his memoirs that had Ben M'Hidi remained in Bigeard's hands he would not have died.[100]

In a shaky way the French were close to winning this Battle of Algiers, using a network of informers, and now able to send many of their top soldiers back to the countryside. But allegations of heavy-handedness continued, especially with arrests of pro-FLN Communists Maurice Audin and Henri Alleg in June, the former disappearing and dying in mysterious circumstances, the latter tortured in prison. There were clergymen now helping the rebels, the press in Paris was having a field day, world opinion was roused, and the Fourth Republic was tottering.[101]

Alleg was the great catalyst here, and perhaps single-handedly, one of the key reasons France finally lost its colonial jewel. History, like life, is replete with paradoxes, and one in this war was a supposedly civilized country resorting to methods like torture in order to stymie uncivilized opponents who hadn't made Algiers and other cities the modern, well-functioning beauties they were; but who were ready to do anything to appropriate the lot. At one time people might have snickered at Jean Lartéguy using the analogy of "centurions" for his work on the French army trying to retain an empire. In 1958, when the U.S. edition of Alleg's *The Question* was published, the Americans, along with other nations, could take a self-righteous stance, for in those days there was little discord (or decadence) in the great capitals of the West, including New York.[102]

Henri Alleg, or Salem, was the grandson of Polish Jews who had emigrated first to England, then France. His family moved to Algiers in 1939 and he eventually became editor of *Alger républicain*, a daily giving the other side equal time. (We now know that the Communist Party did more than that—it vouchsafed FLN bombers et al. active aid and cover.) The newspaper was banned in September 1955, then a year later this Party member was forced into hiding to avoid imprisonment. In June 1957 he was arrested by members of the 10th Parachutist Division and taken to a camp, where he endured unspeakable torture (though he never mentions Aussaresses in his work). The word "torture" itself is too euphemistic; suffice it to say that a reader today might easily get through George Braziller's preface on how Alleg's account of this treatment made it to France, becoming a banned book that rapidly sold 150,000 copies, then was published in translation around the world. They might also read Jean-Paul Sartre's elegant introduction. But reading the book itself on what they did to various parts of his body is very difficult. The "centurions" had borrowed from the barbarian style, and in the Western world of the 1950s it couldn't be tolerated. This was the great dilemma in Algeria, and may yet become a dilemma again for the "civilized" world, or again, what remains of it.[103]

Bigeard would later remark that all French soldiers felt "splashed" by *La question*, "even those who, like myself, can affirm with head high that they never employed this kind of method." To put it in a nutshell, both

Massu and Bigeard fought like lions in Algeria, but there were some things, like systematic torture and brutality, which Bigeard did not favor, where Massu had no such scruples. In fact after the war had safely ended, Massu would himself put to bed any doubts about "la torture," categorically confirming its use. He would also continue declaring that the French were choirboys compared to foes who might lop off face parts, "quand ce n'est pas la verge, devenu le cadeau rituel des fellagas à leur 'frères' récalcitrants." Refuting Lamarck, he added that such appendages do not have a habit of growing back! In the renewed debate today, some argue that French authorities were at least trying to terrorize sources of terror, not innocent civilians.[104]

Even Massu, however, was prey to the ambivalence that wracked France's conscience when it came to Algeria—especially, concerning those it was protecting by such extreme measures: the *pieds noirs.* His view was that having attained a certain comfort, the latter had aroused Muslim jealousy of their refrigerators and other modern conveniences. The gulf had widened in other ways; the generation of *pieds noirs* he encountered in Algeria did not routinely know Arabic, as their parents had, and he felt that should have been remedied by compulsory teaching of the language in schools. He mentioned how his wife was criticized for worrying too much about the welfare of poor Muslims she encountered, and whom she tried to help. This included procuring clemency or at the least, fair trials for a number of known female terrorists, as well as secret meetings with women being hunted by security forces. Massu would also have liked more people to heed Lyautey's warning of 1920 (exactly a century after Jefferson's prescient words about American slavery)—that pan-Islam or pan-Arabism was a tidal wave with which one needed to reckon seriously.[105]

Debate soured the French air all through 1957—a kind of Dreyfus Affair over Algeria for intellectuals, including a searing division between those two *maîtres à penser,* Sartre and Camus. Sartre or de Beauvoir might look down on Camus, but he was the one who knew Algeria—the land where he was born in 1913 of a poor Alsatian-French worker, Lucien Camus, killed a year later on the Marne, and an illiterate Spanish mother who worked to the bone in "service." This was still that Bertrandesque age when *pieds noirs* disdained the finery of education, rolling up sleeves to make something of themselves and their surroundings. But despite growing up in a run-down section of Algiers, Camus himself became educated there—as a patronized scholarship holder at a bourgeois *lycée,* then due to tuberculosis, unable to mount higher in Paris. Joining the Communist

Party for a time in the '30s, Camus became a muckraking journalist for *Alger républicain*, fighting in his articles for Arab citizenship, campaigning for the Blum-Viollette reforms (allowing more Islamic votes), as well as for equal pay and equal rights, and the diminution of poverty in a series of articles on the misery of Kabylia.

To reiterate, Camus knew Algeria, including its Muslims, far better than his intellectual confrères minting aphorisms at Paris cafés. But in the Dreyfus-like atmosphere of 1957, the famed absurdist seemed to sit on the fence—favoring justice for both sides and an end to all violence. A year earlier he had gone to Algiers to promote a civilian truce and democratic confederation of opposing forces, speaking in a Muslim area, hooted at by irate *pieds noirs*, and finding his life endangered, but ironically protected by FLN. (Who were nonetheless busy at the time swallowing up Camus-like moderates on the Muslim side like Ferhat Abbas!)

After that harrowing experience, Camus kept silent on the Algerian issue, though privately he helped commute a number of death sentences imposed on terrorists. Receiving the Nobel Prize on the morrow of the Battle of Algiers, he made the famous statement, to the effect that he would defend his *pied noir* mother over justice. He also had the temerity to aver that the Russians and their cowed satellites were using the FLN to their advantage—that dictatorial tendencies were creeping into his native land. On Alleg he said he wanted investigations, but wouldn't sign a "Solemn Address to the President of the Republic"; on the late Communist mathematician Audin, formerly an instructor at the University of Algiers, and whose doctoral dissertation was defended *in absentia* before a large crowd at the Sorbonne—again, no attendance from Camus. Instead he quietly supported Marc Lauriol's plan for a Swiss-type federation of eight to ten self-governing territories in Algeria, clinging to the middle ground and pleasing no one. But he noted prophetically: "Tomorrow Algeria will be a land of ruins and corpses that no force, no worldly power will be able to restore in our century." Given today's situation, Camus' moderation has been perhaps vindicated.[106]

Returning from such divagations to Bigeard, he and his men had lasted in this tense Algiers of 1957 only three months. As noted, success made Massu slim down effectives there, taking the chase back to the mountains. But Massu also found his subordinate's warnings about the rebel movement's gravity too dire, taxing Bigeard with indiscretion. Before leaving the city in mid-March, Bigeard shot off a hot-blooded reply to his superior. Then the paratroop leader was dispatched to Paris to lecture top brass and younger pups at the Ecole de Guerre on his diagrammatic information-gathering techniques, and on the onerous tasks ahead in North Africa. Their applause only added to Bigeard's problems with superiors; he and Camus both had difficulty doing a job.

Near the end of March it was back to the fray for Bigeard, sent with his 3d RPC to the snows and cold rains of the Atlas Mountains for more operations. Compared to *ratissage* in Algiers this was his kind of war, and paradoxically safer, though the sight of soldiers with heads hacked off or intimates in their mouths revealed the continuing risks. But back in Algiers two assassination attempts aimed at the para leader with a celebrated face had barely and providentially missed. Out here, the general in charge allowed Bigeard to do as he wished, and the 3d managed to capture a top chemist who had fabricated bombs for Yacef, creating much of the capital's damage. He was found despite his phony Red Cross armband, and an infirmary full of medicines, under which lay explosives. The terrorist would later be judged and executed by others that summer of 1957. More operations with Bigeard's contingent split up into pursuing groups yielded results; however, he also knew that in Algiers a reduced regimental presence, and the use of trigger-happy new conscripts still posed problems. He also knew that jealous chiefs were giving him ever more difficult assignments out here, almost hoping perhaps that he would stumble and that his "star would dim." He could not stop thinking as well of the terrible divisions this conflict had now wrought at home in France, already fearing that he and his battle-weary men might be abandoned.[107]

Perhaps in reaction, he allowed his assistant, Lenoir, and Marc Flament, the *boutique's* talented photographer, to gather together an album of battle photos for a book called *Contre-Guérilla,* containing Bigeard's own from-the-hip comments on the endless marches and what it took to play this game. Along with fine photos the book would also contain summaries of operations, maps, and examples of Bigeard's complex *organigrammes* to ensnare FLN/ALN leaders. He and his 3d meanwhile recharged batteries after grueling operations (Atlas 1, 2, 3, 4, and Gérard 1), resting up on the base at Sidi-Ferruch by the sea. But on May 22 Salan sent them to an area south of Medea, where fellahin had ambushed a convoy the day before, killing fifteen and taking prisoners. These men had as much as a fourteen-hour start in their getaway, but Bigeard's instincts told him the rebels' direction. Curtly, he informed Salan that his *boutique* would migrate by night to a mountain area forty kilometers west of the original ambush site, and Salan assented. In Medea Bigeard spread out his map on a jeep, sending his captains in different directions, including old Indochinese associates and Dien survivors, Le Boudec and Allaire. He was gambling that Oued Boulbane was the rebel rendezvous point, but fanned out his companies over 100 square kilometers to build a larger, more flexible net. His hunches were indeed correct; however, the rebels were tipped off by a shepherd, and proved to be more fierce and numerous than his helicoptered troops planned. The first day of battle was a rough one, and as expected, the enemy tried unsuccessfully to break out at night. After three days of fighting the battle-hardened 3d had severely weakened this rebel unit, led by Si Azzedine, to the tune of ninety-six dead. They also freed five hostages. But some FLN, including Azzedine, managed to escape in the middle of the third night, and total victory eluded Bigeard. Detached observers might have seen in this a foreshadowing of France's ultimate fate in Algeria: if an elite unit like the 3d RPC, led by a great warrior like Bigeard, could not wipe out a rebel commando group, how was France going to win here?[108]

Eventually the majority of fighters in this *djebel* (mountain region) were out of commission, an important maquis area. And as usual, Bigeard's cap was off to courageous foes. But Algiers meanwhile was no more through submitting to terrorist attacks than today's Jerusalem; on June 3 three bombs placed in street lamps overlooking bus stops blew a large amount of office workers as well as schoolchildren into smithereens (seven dead, ninety-two wounded, some needing amputations). Then on Pentecost Sunday a few days later, a huge bomb exploded at a popular dance spot east of Agiers, the Casino de la Corniche, killing nine, and wounding at least eighty of the dancers and members of the orchestra. Placed beneath the bandstand, the explosive device killed the group's popular bandleader, leaving no trace, and the lead singer had both her legs ripped off. Massu, who lived nearby, arrived at top speed, and was freaked to see, among other things, a young girl of eighteen minus her legs, and lying there unconscious, blond hair plentifully daubed with blood. Salan arrived as well, and what provoked his nausea was seeing pieces of foot still in the shoes. Massu then erupted at Aussaresses, after it seemed he and his charges had won out here. A mob scene on the day of the funeral led to the blind killing of six people, the sacking of stores, and burning of automobiles. Aussaresses had to put on hold his ideas about hitting money sources for all this mayhem.[109]

In Indochina Aussaresses had been considered by some a simpy, egalitarian intellectual, and that egalitarianism had been telling him to take the battle to the métropole, especially against well-heeled French people who transported money for the acquisition of FLN arms and bombs. The term "suitcase carriers" became current later on, but there were already groups in France transferring much money for the terrorists. These sums were "purement et simplement rackettés sur le territoire métropolitain," as Aussaresses pungently puts it. The 400,000 or so Algerians working in French factories or commercial establishments either paid a monthly "tax" or were killed by machine guns or throat-slittings. This was what sectors of France's Left supported in the name of a brighter democratic-socialist future for Algeria. The most famous group of *porteurs de valise* was the Jeanson network, starting up with a summer, 1957 meeting between the FLN's Omar Boudaoud and Francis Jeanson. The thug and the philosopher got along well. Jeanson was the Marxist biographer of Sartre, and had become manager of Sartre's influential periodical, *Les Temps Modernes,* before a temporary break with the great existentialist. He brought on board a number of Sorbonne Trotskyists and Stalinists just getting used to the traumatic shock of Khrushchev's ideology shift. One militant in a Communist cell at the Sorbonne, Hélène Cuénat, became Jeanson's live-in aide. There were also priests involved, both in France and abroad. Villas were made available as safe houses for FLN, as were passports and identity cards to get them across the border, especially to Spain. But the main job for the Jeanson network was transporting shakedown money from provincial cities to Paris, at first in large valises. A rich banker's son and committed Communist, Henri Curiel, then used his father's contacts to telex the money to Swiss banks, sometimes waiting prudently for the exchange rate to improve! Cash was also used to remunerate people like Jeanson and his girlfriend for their pains, and to rent cars, find three-star hotels, and defray costs of meetings in plush cafés or restaurants. It seemed easier to melt into the population if one went around in style, but this was also an illustration of what one might call cashmere-sweater Bolshevism, the ready use of capitalist goodies and infrastructure one also wished to sabotage. Some in fact called these people *résistants de luxe.* As for Bigeard he feels that dubbing the *porteurs* Resistants at all would make a Jean Moulin turn over in his grave! But the resumption of terror in Algiers, requiring instant attention, and the impending end of his tenure (for which he was thankful) never allowed Aussaresses to mount operations against such money sources in the hexagon. Algeria remained problem enough.[110]

That summer, in fact, Bigeard penned a critique of the army's leadership there, especially its bureaucratic inertia. Yet those generals were forced to call back the 3d in the same eleventh-hour manner as people had once recalled Bugeaud or Gallieni—to the same sector of embattled Algiers. Bigeard at first refused Massu, then succumbed to orders, arriving back in the city July 20. He was stunned to see *organigrammes* he had left behind in March basically unaltered; his successors hadn't exactly slaved here! A second problem was Massu's temporary absence, and the need to take orders from Colonel Godard, which irritated him. Such orders weren't written out, so superiors could avoid responsibility for any problems incurred. But Bigeard continued to play a major role both in the beleaguered city, as in the *bled,* always giving 100 percent. Rapidly the 3rd RPC put a lot of bombers out of business, and the result was more pistol or grenade attacks, easier to handle, and less lethal. Bigeard notes that Germaine Tillion would take credit for this easing of FLN terror, due to her secret negotiations with Saadi Yacef, who would express the same thing in a celebrated film, *The Battle of Algiers.* Bigeard's view is that para pressure was the key factor involved. A high point came when his men snared two top FLN figures in a house in the Casbah, who came out pretending to surrender, but with bombs and grenades set to bring down the leopards. One was machine-gunned to death, the other hoisted by his own petard. Quite a number of former FLN now worked for the French side. One was a real prize in terms of what he could give Bigeard, and on the advice of Maurice Schmitt, a Dien Bien Phu alumnus, and later Army chief of staff, Bigeard leaked to the press that the man had escaped, allowing him to make a connection without media interference, and procure more surrenders.

Again, the 3d had done splendidly in this more restricted Second Battle of Algiers; but on August 10 Bigeard received a stinging letter from Massu, accusing him of insubordination. Pushed by the jealous Godard, Massu mentioned Bigeard's supposed vanity, menacing him with withholding promotion if he didn't cool down. He then decided to replace the successful 3d in that sector of Algiers with another paratroop regiment, the prestigious 1st REP under Colonel Jeanpierre, which after Bigeard's hard work, was able to nab Saadi Yacef himself. The latter turned out to be a profuse talker. His top gun, Ali la Pointe, and a number of other associates were then killed that October.[111]

In a number of books Bigeard salutes Massu's soldierly qualities, but also notes how a relationship he had once considered rock-solid had by then deliquesced. Was the imposing Massu now jealous of his subordinate's

renown? It did not help that Bigeard's *Contre-Guérilla* came out in August
1957, and that Colonel Charles Lacheroy of the Service d'Action Psychologique of the army had tried to censor the author's graphic realism about
endless marches, cloying thirst and ennui, and the omnipresence of death.
With something of a bumpkinish Burgundy accent, Lacheroy was nonetheless a keen student of both Communist and Islamic-Arab propaganda,
hiring teams to pore over newspapers, countering FLN propaganda with
his own on French beneficence, and studying public opinion in imitation
of America's Gallup Poll. He enjoined French *appelés* to bring the good
word back to France, and also urged Algerian Arabs not to give in to the
silence induced by fear of terror. But Bigeard would not keep *his* silence
either, holding fast to his prose in *Contre-Guérilla* and making only small
changes in a ringing conclusion. It was the first of a series of magnificent
picture books with Marc Flament photos, showing the unromanticized
reality of North African warfare. Bigeard admits, "I *had* become difficult
to command."[112]

At the time of this Second Battle of Algiers he was also plagued by
painful lumbago; yet his superiors sent him out again for more mountain
operations in late September. Orders from another general without sufficient field experience frustrated him, and journalists arrived too frequently
to watch and hype. In mid-October Bigeard's antiterror work southwest
of Algiers nonetheless earned the admiration of locals, though hunting
in dangerous caves and passes, and burying more paras seemed increasingly pointless. This was the era of "Maginotization" of frontier areas via
electrified wire, mines, and radar installations, dubbed the Morice Line,
after France's defense minister of the time. Completed that September,
the line hugged the Tunisian border from the Mediterranean right down
to the Sahara. But the Sahara itself was no longer safe, especially due to
a nascent oil boom there. One paradox was that just as French Algeria
was really taking off economically, still becoming for adventurous young
Frenchmen in the desert a new America, its military hold was tenuous,
mainly due to eroding support at home.

Bigeard and his men were then moved from this region 100 miles from
Algiers to Lyautey's Colomb-Béchar, some 600 removed from the turbulent capital. They would now have to chase hard-to-locate rebels over
huge expanses of desert, fighting sandstorms, and constantly frustrated
by the welcoming arms of Morocco's border. On October 20 members of
a company of Algerian camel corpsmen slaughtered over sixty soldiers
and cadres, including eight French officers, before deserting and joining

the FLN; then in early November, while troops vainly pursued them, the rebels returned and ambushed a convoy of oil exploration personnel, killing four geological prospectors and nine Legionnaires who were protecting them. All that remained were burned-out Land Rovers found in a desert area that had once seemed more secure than the high country. Salan duly asked Bigeard to embark on an operation against these deserters that would also protect oil company installations and personnel in an arid expanse almost the size of France!

Feeling wan, Bigeard wondered whether his vaunted *baraka* would remain intact. But after putting his foot down, he received what he wanted in terms of aircraft and land vehicles, and a parade of stirring desert scenery en route to the oasis of Timimoun got him going again. So did the feeling that an operation of this sort might avenge him with Massu and other army bigwigs. At oasis headquarters Bigeard met the French commandant there, whose planes shot at virtually anything that moved, and he wasn't impressed, particularly by the officer's lavish lifestyle, including servants Bigeard had trouble trusting.

In work on the French Resistance historians emphasize a necessary attribute for those in the movement: trusting one's instincts. And indeed, after arrests and the recovery of some stolen arms, Bigeard's hunches proved correct—servants and even the post's nurse were in the mix, and soon would have facilitated a massacre of Europeans there, as well as poisoning the head French military man. From these arrests, and from Flament's air photographs, rebel hideouts were located, and a 3d airborne operation combined with those by land companies converged for the kill. A tough fight ensued, dune to dune, as Bigeard recalls. In the next several weeks twelve of his crack men died. While headlines back in France and in Algiers continued splashing out his successes, and *Paris-Match* used Flament's combat pics, Bigeard kept being saddened by these human tragedies occurring around him. Could far-away journalists feel the passing of Staff-Sergeant Sentenac in this desert operation, a rare bird who had survived an escape attempt from Dien Bien Phu? Seven times wounded, possessor of thirteen *croix de guerre*—and now dead in this growingly unwinnable war! Could they feel the loss of men whose helicopters crunched the desert floor pursuing rebels in late November, motors apparently sabotaged? Or of choppers lost in sandstorms? Could they feel the hunger and thirst, weapons jammed with sand, jeeps breaking down, the constant fear? And the sheer fatigue of being helicoptered all over the place, trying to unearth the elusive; or worse, marching over interminable dunes, fighting hot blowing sand, or when up in the higher *djebel*, abrupt cold? Could they feel what it was like to lose men to mines, then be nitpicked for what successes they obtained by jealous brass like Château-Jobert?[113]

The peak of the whole operation occurred on December 7 when air reconnaissance revealed a human under an ersatz tree; Bigeard swooped, killing forty-five of the enemy and finally recovering the stolen materiel. He was legitimately proud of what he styled a military *coup de maître*. But a key problem of fighting at this point remained—a "whom-do-you-trust?" atmosphere, increasingly prevalent in Algeria, as rebels continued inflicting strong-arm tactics on fellow Muslims. Not to mention their courage, and better arms to bring down French aircraft. At the end of the year Bigeard's regiment received a gratefully accepted furlough back in Sidi-Ferruch; he himself had dropped six kilos and was dog-tired. Aged forty-one he was made a colonel at the start of 1958, youngest in France's army. The promotion had been supported by Generals Salan and Massu; yet his fissure with the latter failed to heal, particularly after Massu thrust an ill-conceived mission on Bigeard near the Tunisian border, which he flatly refused, angering the entire General Staff.[114]

Through February, under Vanuxem, Bigeard and his men were back up in the cold rain of the Nementchas, and he grew increasingly frustrated at seeing FLN cross the Morice Line back and forth into Tunisia. The main event that rankled was a murderous assault mounted from the border area, killing fourteen French soldiers and netting five French prisoners, whom Tunisian government authorities would not even try to free. When Resident Lacoste visited the frontier on February 7, Bigeard supported by his men told him bluntly that these rebels must be pursued, and tentative permissions were granted the next day. But a French airman exceeded his instructions, bombing the Tunisian border town of Sakiet-Sidi-Youssef, an ALN base. They obliterated the village, killing over seventy people, including women and children, and creating an international incident. This event occurred several weeks after France's interception of a Yugoslav ship en route to Casablanca, loaded with arms for the FLN, one of a series of interdictions of largely Soviet-sphere ships, and again, provoking international condemnations.[115]

At this juncture Massu wrote a patronizing army "recommendation" of Bigeard only read by the latter years later; supposedly buoyed by notes from an underling, Massu called Bigeard a publicity-struck, unbalanced man who needed to be watched, and one who might even be susceptible to French Communist Party influence! Ironically, Minister of Defense

Jacques Chaban-Delmas next summoned Bigeard to Paris, trying to persuade him to run for deputy in place of a recently deceased Communist, Marcel Cachin. The famed paratrooper demurred. But back in Algeria he confided his thoughts on the war to Lacoste, and the papers chatted it up, averring that Bigeard was making top army personnel fearful. Sure enough, General Gilles soon tried to transfer him to a position on Chaban's Paris staff. Bigeard refused, but newspaper articles predicted that he was not long for Algeria, and he himself knew that the usual limit for commanding a regiment was two years (he had had his for twenty-eight months).

In mid-March 1958 he was indeed forced to hand over his well-honed *boutique* to Colonel Trinquier, who swore he would retain the famed caps and mystique. Eyes became misty as Bigeard made a last speech to his paras, and he had to bite back his own welling tears. The celebrated 3d Colonial Regiment had lost 76 dead and 220 wounded, and he knew that he was legating what was left to another jealous man.[116]

Like a departing Bugeaud or Lyautey Marcel mounted the liner *Sidi-Ferruch* for a trip back to France; but on the quai a gaggle of journalists thronged him, including Serge Bromberger of the *Figaro*, Jean Lartéguy of *Paris-Presse*, and an admirer from *Le Monde*, Eugène Mannoni. Besieged in Paris as well by journalists who played up the army's internal divisions, Bigeard got away to Toul, where heavily-approving mail awaited him, but where his repose did not last long. A few days later Gilles called him back to Paris, asking him again to speak with Chaban. His assignment? To create a new, hands-on instructional school for paratroopers in Algeria, presumably to form new Bigeards. At first he refused categorically, but Gilles and Chaban pressed him, and finally he assented, guilty to be a professor, while his comrades were still risking lives in the field.[117]

He arrived back in Algeria April 20, 1958, but on the eve of a political volcano that would gravely affect France's divided Fourth Republic. It started with one ministry falling in mid-April, and negotiations with the FLN seemingly in the cards for a successor ministry under Pierre Pflimlin. Bigeard meanwhile set up his seaside school a few kilometers east of Philippeville at an old resort that included an Olympic-sized swimming pool. At least he would procure some fine instructors here. Trapp of Indochina, Clédic, formed by the great Brèche, Legionnaires with Indochinese experience, plus Lenoir and the ever-faithful Martial Chevalier signed on. Bigeard got his buildings finished quickly, and a first load of forty disillusioned or fearful students (of a contingent of eighty-six) arrived at the Centre d'Instruction de Jeanne d'Arc, full of book learning from

Paris' General Staff School or Ecole de Guerre. Here they would learn from a master about the experience of subversive warfare, not that this was the only such school in Algeria. Another farther along the coast near Oran, the Centre d'Instruction de Pacification et Contre-Guérilla d'Arzew, featured a curriculum of demanding first-aid and medical courses, shooting instruction, and lectures on psychology and organization of the FLN/ALN.[118]

Chaban's overarching idea was to put more spirit into an army of 440,000 (including Muslims adhering to the French side)—an army still having trouble with perhaps 25,000 armed rebels. Opening May 10 in front of journalists and the visiting Defense Minister, Bigeard's establishment seemed like it would be a success. Orders spewed forth—sport at 5 A.M., marching, plus Bigeard's promise that he could make these recruits paras within two weeks. History, however, was set to intervene. For rumors continued to fly that French diplomats would soon appease the enemy, and that there could be another Vietnam-type capitulation in Algeria. On May 10 the FLN announced their execution of three French soldiers held in Tunisia, pushing European settlers to the point of an explosion; and large sectors of the frustrated army as well.

On May 13 the bottom dropped out of the Fourth Republic's leaky ship with a revolt in Algiers of disgruntled settlers and soldiers, warning the French government that they wouldn't be sold out here. A huge crowd of *pieds noirs* and Muslims alike marched the 189 steps up to Algiers' Forum, singing the Marseillaise. Archives were thrown out the windows of government offices; anarchy was in the air. A Committee of Public Safety was formed, one of the last manifestations of France's revolutionary tradition, and called up by the applauding crowd to a balcony, Massu said he would head it. The Committee was a mixture of Massu's army colonels and civilians, and Massu knew he had crossed a Rubicon by becoming its leader. He wanted, however, to control an unruly situation, also favoring what newspaper publisher Alain de Sérigny had been calling for days earlier: the return to power of the one man who might save the situation and the French republic, the one to whom Massu had rallied when first he heard a scratchy radio appeal at an obscure post in Chad, June 1940: Charles de Gaulle. As for Salan, he was at first noncommittal, a Claudius behind the curtain, waiting for events to ripen before deciding to join up. Two days later he strode to the balcony, announcing his adherence to the Committee; he would later argue that he took the microphone merely to calm the crowds and mitigate a still riotous situation. He was also awarded special powers by a terrified Paris. But along with Massu he considered de Gaulle a kind of savior—the one shouted name from the crowds that could reassure nervous *pieds noirs* and Muslims alike.[119]

The moment was indeed revolutionary, especially May 16, with different ethnicities fraternizing, Muslim women ripping off veils, a happy, Flaubertian atmosphere (of *Sentimental Education*) in the Mediterranean air. This outpouring of Arabs from their *quartiers*, emerging by the thousands to hold hands with *pieds noirs*, was partially the result of seductive French promises and "stage management" by paras, trucking in demonstrators. But it also showed how the FLN might claim Muslim fears, but not always their deepest sympathies. One French commander of *zouaves* stationed in the Casbah, Captain Sirvent, exemplified the type many Arabs trusted. Born and raised in pre–World War II Algiers of Pyrenean parents, Sirvent had become a teacher in the Casbah's Rue Marengo, respected by Muslim parents, who wanted their charges to learn French. He then participated in the liberation of France, along with Algerian sharpshooters and Moroccan *tabors*. In 1956 he returned to Algiers, where he came to know artisans, workers, and *soukiers* of the Casbah like the proverbial back of his hand. Fluent in Arabic, he would crisscross Muslim sectors of the city on foot without arms. The foreign press could hardly believe the goodwill that people like this had helped create, especially given heavy FLN propaganda; but occur it did, most startlingly, and whether stage-managed or not, with a "Movement of Feminine Solidarity," bringing thousands of Muslim and European women out into an atmosphere of apparent harmony.[120]

In France, however, the atmosphere was very strained, with the Fourth Republic set to implode. The push for de Gaulle and a new republic came from patriotic pressure groups of unabashed French nationalists, frequently old Resistance comrades in associations like the Comité d'Action Nationale d'Anciens Combattants. Humiliations of the army, and the possible loss of a French Algeria made de Gaulle their man, and they organized pro-Gaullist demonstrations both before and after May 13 in Paris and Algiers alike. Against this background Bigeard simply wished to do his job, but it was difficult. Signs in Algeria's capital reading "Bigeard to Paris" or "Bigeard in Power," and even such scribblings found on the walls of his school,[121] undermined his position, as did exhortations of his assistant Lenoir for him to join the Committee of Public Safety in Algiers (other branches now springing up as well around the country). For once Bigeard stayed put, damned if he did and damned if he didn't.

His era of good feelings with Massu seemed entirely dissipated, and with forebodings of French doom in North Africa, Bigeard stuck to his training position. By mid-June it was graduation time—only 24 percent making it. Chaban was no longer in power to support the school, but Bigeard was pleased with the progress of his men, and also had some optimism concerning de Gaulle's arrival that June as last premier of France's Fourth Republic and soon, first president of a Fifth.

The press, however, remained a problem, even when supporters like Lartéguy came down for interviews. Promising not to publish revelations he heard, Lartéguy did exactly that, landing Bigeard in deep trouble with Salan and other brass he had criticized off the record. A specific reference to plush colonels of Algiers, contrasted to men fighting out in the elements was what hurt him most.[122] In Algiers Salan demanded a public denial, which his uppity subordinate refused. In August 1958 the irate commander in chief gave Bigeard two days to exit Algeria, making a gleeful press spit out yet more stories. Apparently Salan had also misunderstood Bigeard's intentions at the time of the Committee of Public Safety revolt, fearing mistakenly that he had something up his sleeve.[123]

So the paratroop ace found himself back in Lorraine mothballs during the crucial late summer and fall of 1958. That fall included the FLN's creation of a Provisional Government of the Algerian Republic (GPRA) in Cairo. It also included de Gaulle's Constantine Plan, in the short run bringing a substantial increase in Muslim deputies to the National Assembly, and announcing for the long run, more land for Muslim farmers, better wages, more modern accommodations, and enhanced schooling opportunities. Bigeard's own school continued running on the shores of the Mediterranean under a colonel he liked; but only in early December did Salan eat crow, just before his removal in favor of General Maurice Challe, inviting Marcel to return to Algeria as an aide to the recently promoted General Ducournau, who headed the 25th Parachutist Division.

Accepting, Bigeard arrived January 12, 1959, hoping for a better year and happy to be working for a man he held in high esteem. But Challe and others around him told Bigeard he was too good for such an assignment, informing him that he would instead replace a repatriated colonel who had been commanding in a sector headquartered at Saïda in the southern Oranais. Bigeard knew this was not a good region, and that via this appointment, the brass were probably trying to give him enough rope with which to hang himself! After a short bout of depression, he nonetheless made his way toward the godforsaken base, first meeting in Oran with General Gambiez, nicknamed "Nimbus," an old Lattrian who had lost a son at Dien Bien Phu and whom Bigeard respected. At Tiaret, 200 kilometers southeast of Oran, where rebels were busy setting off explosives, Bigeard then conferred with General Dodelier, another de Lattre acolyte.

Arriving in Saïda on January 25, 1959 (de Gaulle's Fifth Republic now in place), Bigeard received his umpteenth lackluster group to command, getting it rapidly up to speed in a Sahara rife with rebels. Daily, the French, as well as Muslim *harkis* (those loyal to France), were being found cut up on the roads. In the towns of the Oranais European settlers were also huddled in fear.

Despite what he could see down the line for Algeria, Bigeard worked his new regiment with daily exercise, sport, and marches. He wanted his men to be as tough as the rebels of this *wilaya*. Friendly Muslims, some released from prison and enrolled by Lieutenant Grillot, also followed Bigeard to an ultimately sad fate. The new leader set up several commando groups, and more successes via long night marches and chases ensued. The rebels began losing ground where they had formerly dominated. By the summer of 1959 things had gone so well here that Bigeard's men had managed to ensnare the top guerilla leaders in their hideouts, and ironically, the new commander in chief was also won over to methods Bigeard had proposed at least four years earlier, initiating the Challe plan. Its key facet was reduction of static troop emplacements in Algeria's cities, towns, and villages, and an increase in roving commando operations (shades of Bugeaud as well).[124] Bigeard says it would take a whole book just to describe combat operations of this one short period, and certainly the archives in France bear him out.

Defections of Muslim army personnel buoyed up his *commando musulman,* and though 800 francs a day was a compelling reason for these men to join up, there was idealism as well. These enrollees became indispensable aides for tracking, and for interrogations. Bigeard's people also taught them to pilot Piper Cubs and other aircraft. Muslim army men had to protect their own civilian *harkis* in a variety of villages across Algeria—people whose overriding fear was of nocturnal throat-cuttings. They worked closely with French soldiers, themselves trying to cling to ideals. In the preface to a published diary of the era, Jean Faure recalls the head of his company, one Captain Citerne, dubbed "the god of Agouni" by the Muslim population there. To Faure this Lorrainer was the perfect example of "the seductive and courageous French officer who acted on the rural terrain, at the head of his men." In the era of the Challe plan of searching out an increasingly well-armed enemy, it was certainly necessary to give the *harkis* sophisticated arms too. By infiltrating FLN networks, they brought in new recruits, though there was always the possibility of double-agentry. For all that, the many who were sincerely attached to France would pay a frightful price.[125]

Meanwhile, Bigeard's renown continued to spread, bringing visits from notables, including one from de Gaulle himself. Just when Challe's overall operations—including reinforcements to the Morice Line—seemed to portend military success, Le Grand Charles had decided to come down to Algeria with his own politically-imposed solutions perhaps already inside, if vaguely conceived. Bigeard's Saïda was first on his list of military units to visit. Soldiers there rapidly propped up photos, maps, and copies of terrorist network diagrams. In late August the president arrived, asking Bigeard to accompany him on a helicopter ride so that they might talk privately. But up in the chopper de Gaulle remained characteristically inscrutable. Bigeard gave the celebrated general his impassioned thoughts on the Algerian morass, mainly about winning over Muslims and unifying French leadership; however, de Gaulle's ears seemed plugged with desert sand.[126] His subsequent speech on September 16 mentioning "auto-determination" for Muslims would show which way the French wind was blowing at home.

Fighting, however, continued in Algeria, and more senseless deaths. One of Bigeard's top Muslim aides out on a Sunday drive with his daughter to attend a gypsy festival was shot in the back by FLN, dying in his daughter's arms. Then Colonel "Félix" Brunet, an old rival from Vietnam days, was killed at Colomb-Béchar—after 10,000 hours in the air, over 4,000 hours in battle engagements, and a legacy of innovation, especially in helicopter warfare. With a sense of the sacred, Bigeard placed Brunet's photo on his desk beside that of Sentenac—two men who had deeply touched his life. The beloved Ducournau would also die in a helicopter accident.[127]

With Saïda now purged of almost all its rebels, Bigeard left again to the applause of his men and civilians; but there would be other fires to put out, still a great number. In December 1959 he was sent to Aïn-Sefra to work in another vast area of mountains and arid valleys, and with 1,500 men under him. Then, when he made a hasty trip back to Lorraine, news of yet another death reached him—that of the man he had left in charge, Peretti, who crashed in his helicopter reconnoitering the Oranais. It was the same machine Bigeard had flown in many times. Coming right back,

Bigeard wondered whether his *baraka*, his long skein of good fortune would keep holding.[128]

The year 1960 would dawn with barricades, this time erected by paras in Algiers, and really the initial stages of what became the French "generals' revolt." Since becoming last premier of the Fourth Republic and first president of the Fifth, de Gaulle had played a subtle, erratic game, and for a year was truly all things to all people. Two days after taking power back in June 1958 he had made a first visit to Algiers, addressing a large throng with the enigmatic words "je vous ai compris!" which probably were never meant literally. The slangy sense of that phrase is not "I have understood you," but "I've got your number!" Most had expected de Gaulle to support a French Algeria, but he never quite said he would do that, and in his first year in office had begun exploring other options. By September 1959 he was ready to commit himself to the policy of Arab-Berber self-determination.

De Gaulle seems to have gradually realized that a majority of Algeria's Muslims (90 percent of the total population) wanted independence. Most didn't actively support the FLN, but to him, the fiction that Algeria was part of France would no longer work either. And rebel terror networks continued to keep many in a state of blackmailed fear. Consulting Algerian newspapers of the era, one finds numerous accounts of assassinations, terror bombings, and the like on any given day of the late '50s, and continuing into the next decade. *Pied noir* retaliation continued too, along with allegations of French torture which still agonized the home front, as in the case of a female bomber apparently violated in gruesome ways.[129] Like many of his generals, de Gaulle knew what it would take to keep Algeria French: a permanent army of occupation cresting up to 750,000 or even 1 million men, which would exhaust French resources and irretrievably split an already heart sore country. Unlike many army men, the president was not prepared to pay such a price. Once he pronounced the words "self-determination," any long-term hopes for an *Algérie française* were really gone.

The métropole basically greeted de Gaulle's views with calm—most French, according to polls, reconciled to the loss; but the reaction in Algiers was obviously different. There a conspiracy was hatched, led by the *pied noir* student leader Pierre Lagaillarde and a restaurateur-politician, Joseph Ortiz. The group received a boost from Massu, who gave an interview to a Munich newspaper, regretting that de Gaulle had (in his estimation) swung Left. Massu suggested that the army had made a big mistake helping him return to power in 1958, implying that the military leadership could no longer be relied on to support him.[130] When those remarks were published, de Gaulle drove Massu, the most famous general of the era, out of Algeria, and to an eventual command position in Europe.

That recall was the catalyst which then set off the reaction in Algiers. *Pied noir* leaders struck quickly in an effort to force de Gaulle's ouster, and establishment of a government committed unconditionally to a French Algeria. On January 23, 1960 barricades went up in Algiers, and military commanders had to decide whether to support these dissidents or the French government. General Challe, who had flown to Paris to argue vainly for Massu, reluctantly supported de Gaulle, sealing off affected sections of Algiers and ordering in paras and police. But Challe miscalculated, not realizing the extent to which these paras felt betrayed. When they didn't show up on schedule, the local police were massacred by *pied noir* fighters.

Most paratroop colonels were in fact sympathetic to this uprising, with three playing key roles—Antoine Argoud, Yves Godard, and Jean Gardes; what of Bigeard? Invited to join he said no, but let it be known that he *did* understand the army's frustration. His message on the subject hit the radio and printed press, and after the rebellion was quelled a week later, he was brought up on a Paris carpet by the current chief of staff, General Demetz, asking him more or less: Who do you think you *are?*[131] Almost comically General Gambiez then ordered Bigeard back to the southern Oranais, but found himself vetoed by the Defense Ministry: on February 1, 1960, Bigeard was removed for good from North Africa.

Shorn of its great paratroop leader, a lame-duck *Algérie française* would bump along, enduring a good deal during the next thirty months. Hélie de Saint Marc paints the period with poetic melancholy. Directive words from on high increasingly meant little, and while soldiers still placed hides in danger, de Gaulle seemed to be speaking out both sides of his mouth. At one point in 1960 he said the FLN flag would never fly over Algiers; but negotiations with antes constantly raised by the other side eroded the spirit of the French army. Saint Marc had believed in a future here— independence in progressive stages, some sort of accommodation between contenders, protection of numerous Muslims caught in a crossfire. Now he and many others felt cheated. He remembers that even in 1960 he could take a jeep out alone in formerly hostile areas, speaking to villagers, but knowing in his heart that they would be betrayed, and that France might indeed leave, dropping much of its soul and decency here. One army buddy talked of scared Muslims defecting back to the FLN, not wanting "les testicules dans la bouche." That man then raged that four years of hard, dangerous work were being blown to hell! By 1961 going out to die made no sense to a growing number of French soldiers. Those belonging to elite regiments like the 1st REP felt wounded inside. The many Legionnaires who had died perhaps in vain now inhabited Saint Marc's daily thoughts; not to mention hollow promises given to the Muslims. Having visited Israel, Saint Marc admired the cohesive spirit of their melting pot army in its youth; whereas the French military was now riven by searing divisions. Here was no rebel, in fact some soldiers found him too philosophical and liberal; but another, more serious army revolt *was* now afoot, and choices would have to be made. The putsch of April 1961 was supervised by four dissident generals: Salan and Challe, both recently retired from the army, Edmond Jouhaud, and Marie-André Zeller. Torn between obedience to an *engagement* he had made in the 1940s, and for which he had paid heavily, and the seductive words of a general he respected (Challe), Saint Marc committed—to one chance in a hundred, as he puts it, that France could somehow create a more equitable, just settlement in Algeria.[132]

But having already defused the January 1960 revolt by a combination of maneuvers and a captivating televised address, de Gaulle proved again that he functioned best in emergencies. Once more he took to the airwaves, drawing a painful portrait of events in Algiers. Then, speaking over the heads of the military leadership to soldiers listening on transistors in Algerian barracks, he drew the line: every possible means would be used to stop the putschists, and all French soldiers were forbidden to execute these dissidents' orders. In brief the French president was ordering soldiers to disobey their military superiors. This was later dubbed "the revolution of the transistors"; coupled with Interior Minister Roger Frey's dramatic arrest of several generals attempting to take Paris, using paras hidden in the woods outside the city, de Gaulle's moves destroyed the rebellion and in the process, many military careers.

Saint Marc says the few days of the putsch felt unreal. Soldiers who seemed committed suddenly wavered, and leaders of the revolt also underestimated new blood in the French army with no sense of prior abandonments—1940, Cao Bang, etc. Saint Marc's last night in North Africa was a bittersweet one. He thought of Don Quixote living for an ideal, however unrealistic; he remembers officers ripping off decorations, and Legionnaires cursing in a medley of European languages, some singing Piaf's "Non, je ne regrette rien." He himself "had accepted the possibility of losing it all, and I had." Meanwhile, the moralists were in high gear across the Mediterranean—that "clan of barkers beginning already to soil our motivations." Saint Marc paid up, succumbing to his arrest without flinching. Salan, somewhat unwillingly, and General Jouhaud went underground, henceforth key figures in the Organisation de l'Armée Secrète or OAS, a terrorist organization dedicated to preventing Algerian independence, including by assassination attempts on de Gaulle. Zeller put on mufti togs and disappeared into the crowds of Algiers; and among the dissident generals, only Challe did the right thing, flying to Paris to surrender.[133]

The road to French divestiture of Algeria was now clear, and de Gaulle moved swiftly down it. French and GPRA representatives met at Evian in late 1961 and early 1962, negotiating the terms of independence. Jouhaud was captured on March 25, 1962, Salan on April 20. Only the OAS had teeth left—one assassination attempt of August 22, 1962 nearly succeeding in killing de Gaulle. Sympathizers included former Resistance leaders of World War II like Soustelle, living in hiding, and Georges Bidault. And meanwhile, Muslim Algeria became independent on July 3 of that year, though destined to find no enduring stability.

In the short run alone there was much tragedy. First, there was a massive expropriation of the benefits of European modernity, a modernity soon to regress. Guy Méry, commander at the small town of Cassaigne, remembers the shock of the cease-fire, and the first FLN coming back from Tunisia July 5 with machine guns pointed, asking him how one ran the local *brasserie* and other industrial establishments there. Méry retorted that this was their concern now; such Khmer Rouge types would have to learn themselves to keep these enterprises going. In bigger cities local supporters of independence now cried out that they could take all the fine places on the Rue d'Isly or Rue Michelet in Algiers. Disappearances of Europeans mounted precipitously that fateful July, and were explained away by the usual gang of acquiescers in easier circumstances. The odd die-hard in this end-of-the line Algeria opened a bar at the usual hour, and was duly gunned down in a hail of bullets. Others were lynched, taken away to be dumped in water, or "emmurés." In Oran especially terrible massacres of *pied noirs* occurred, while what remained of a French army was hamstrung for lack of orders. It was the height of summer on a once thriving and beautiful Boulevard Gallieni or Square Lyautey. Frantically, Europeans bashed at the doors of the newspaper, *L'Echo d'Oran*, hoping for shelter, where Muslim employees also remained huddled inside. Outside, bloodthirsty screams and shooting punctuated sunny afternoons.

Could one make it to the Lycée Lamoricière, hopefully to be guarded? Or to the airport or quai? As for automobiles, the looters took those, as they took all else. At the great Oran synagogue on the Boulevard Joffre the rabbi tried repeatedly to reach the Bishop of Oran by telephone. When he finally got through, he was told flatly that there was nothing more to hope for here, and that people like them were abandoned. In places where they were guarded, *pieds noirs* exchanged horror stories. A young man had gone to breakfast at a restaurant on the Rue de la Fonderie. The other half-dozen patrons there were killed on the spot; somehow, he had managed to slip away. Others told of hangings they had witnessed that early July. Europeans still shivered as well behind the blinds of broiling apartments, awaiting the return of many who would never be heard from again. As in Oran, so in many other parts of Algeria: if one made it to the plane or ship clutching nothing but a bag and a few francs, then one was fortunate. So much for the "democratic-socialist" FLN Jeanson and other philosophical fat cats had aided in France. The smoking, sizzling shutdown of an entire civilization was the reality here.

And then there was the concomitant shame of the Muslim *harkis*, almost like the taste of desert sand in the mouths of departing French soldiers. Amid whirling governmental vicissitudes back home these soldiers *had* pledged their long-term protection. Jean Faure recalls banquets in camp with *harkis*, where the French would repeat such assurances, and where one Muslim fervently declared: "France is our mother and will never abandon us." Faure's comrades described the agonizing scene of leaving Agouni in Greater Kabylia (150 kilometers east of Algiers), driving away with *harkis* running desperately behind the trucks, fingers bashed as they tried to cling on and mount the vehicles. "We had made them promises," but had "delivered them up to a massacre" (eventually, of a good 150,000 souls), Faure concludes. Michel Alibert remembers the Algeria of 1956, when most everyone, including the Mitterands, had averred with total certitude that this would always be part of France. Then came the resultant *gâchis*, driving this truly fine Cyrien into revolt, a death sentence, and seven years of underground existence. René-Philippe Donely, born in 1937, and terribly marked by the 1940 defeat, felt that France and its *pieds noirs* had made Algeria prosperous, and sheds tears even now when he thinks of *harkis* getting intimates cut off by the FLN. He still avoids Algerian singers on French TV. The journalist Jacques Duquesne, far from an unqualified supporter of French policy during the war, remains disgusted as well by numerous tortures of *harkis* and their public execration—"castrated and dressed as women ... before being exposed in the villages ... [or] buried alive, head alone visible and covered with honey." As for Saint Marc? This Buchenwald survivor paid with almost six more years of French prison for joining the putsch, haunted inside by constant anguish as his lovely daughters grew up on the outside. He read much literature and history, saw iterative pictures in his mind of Muslim throats cut, discussed Camus with Jouhaud, and heard about the latter's grandparents who had come to Oranie full of hopes in 1848. He thought continually of all the courageous comrades he had left dead in Vietnam and Algeria. Having grappled since 1940 with the shattering of a known France at home, then abroad, and battling for an ideal, as he saw it, he would have to emerge (after two years in Buchenwald, fifteen in the French empire, and almost six more in another prison) to a more materialist, forgetful home front, following America's model.[134]

It was indeed the end of a certain ideal for a generation of French soldiers. When Saint Marc avers that a few sadists excepted, most soldiers in his generation *were* idealists—marked above all, by their country's 1940 collapse—it may be hard for baby boom historians to accept. But baby boomers are a different contingent—not so much chronologically, but qualitatively, historically. In the slightly older group there was still an almost puritanical devotion to something larger than themselves in places like Algeria. Certainly, some French soldiers used houses of prostitution there, but separation from Muslim women—encouraged by the Arab side—was largely observed by the French. As for the smoking of drugs, so much associated with America's Vietnam War a decade later, *kif* et al. were considered appropriate only for the indigenous down-and-out—not for soldiers to resort to when omnipresent cold, heat, thirst, or above all, fear got to them. (And as Alibert, among others, notes, on every single parachute jump of the hundred or so he took, one was scared!)

The ideal *had* died, and quickly. A few years before the putsch Saint Marc at the height of the Battle of Algiers would get away for a few hours when he could, deeply in love with a twenty-three-year-old named Manette, future mother of his children. They would find a secluded spot on the impossibly fragrant coast, swimming far out, then repair to a lovely seaside bistro to drink the bitter Algerian rosé that so much reminded them of the land itself. And they gazed at vines, and thought of their friends' fruit trees blooming on the former Mitidja swamp; and in the foreground, passing as they sipped, were Arab *burnouses* and French *képis,* and they heard French and Arabic promiscuously mixed, and yes, the latest Platters songs inside too; and they so wished that this Algeria could be made into a peaceful, thriving land of reconciliation for all. Dr. Pierre Godeau, author of an intelligent memoir on life in Algeria of the '50s, especially among Kabyles who esteemed his medical work on a variety of diseases, also writes movingly of the dénouement here. During the war he visited his cousin's farm 120 kilometers from Algiers, where "Charly" and workers who remained faithful to him spoke both French and Arabic. Parents and grandparents had worked this land since 1890, developed by the hard work of Charly's *pied noir* forbears. In the course of the conflict Charly and his hands held on, and partly because the FLN knew him and also realized he was armed and wouldn't go down easily (he had fought and been imprisoned by the Nazis in World War II), they allowed this *bagarreur*, his Arab pals, and twelve dogs to stay put. Finally, a year after the Evian Accords, a local FLN member warned that he would be imminently assassinated. Driving away and shot at, Charly ended up in France's Ardèche, and in the 1970s still smoked a pipe every night with Arabs who had come to the métropole with him. But reconciliation in Algeria itself? A dead issue, symbolized by Godeau's visit of 1987 back to a ruin of the old family farmhouse, ripped-out vines, and wheat fields left abandoned and fallow, before a new wave of violence made even such a visit impossible.[135]

The dream had ended bitterly, and Bigeard was probably fortunate to have left in 1960. Had he remained, he might well have supported Challe in 1961, though the impression lingers that he had more political savvy than that.

Discussing his hurt at being treated like an outcast in France, Bigeard's greatest memoir *(Pour une parcelle de gloire)* segues into a less vivid era he calls "The Fall . . . Oblivion . . . Serenity," stretching from February 1960 to its close in February 1973. That part commences with regret over the Algerian result—how militarily the war should have been easier to win than the Indochinese conflict; and reiterates the shame of enduring a forced leave of six months in France.

There ensued a string of less exigent positions for Bigeard, largely in the one-time colonies, the first of which was in La République centreafricaine (the former Oubangui-Chari) at the head of a regiment of Africans there. He was first taken to see Colonel Alain, the top gun in Bangui, who patronized Bigeard, telling him he was here to cool down! Shunted by plane to Bouar, he encountered a depressing area and *boutique,* but again obtained results with long jungle marches and the building of a pool, athletic facilities, and chapel. He knew he would be stuck here thirty months and decided to make the best of it. There was grumbling from the laid-back, but he received support from new friends like the French ambassador, and from David Dacko, the Republic's president, until overthrown by Bokassa. He also learned of the far-off generals' putsch, wondering where he might have stood on it, and felt saddened by the imprisonment, exile, or dismissal of men he knew so well—Botella, Lenoir, Brèche. But in a forbidding outpost he again fought to make his own circumscribed dreams come true, and left the area a success.

In February 1963 he returned on the *Jean-Mermoz* to a changed homeland—the era of "yé-yé" replacing a more sober postwar one dominated by the idea of national regeneration. Feeling suddenly on the old side, particularly with his stalwart mother dying in Lorraine, Bigeard made an effort to adapt to a more Americanized France: "So Gaby and I danced the twist," comments the great warrior laconically.[136]

General Le Puloch, the army's chief of staff in that period, now urged him to adapt to a more educated, globalized, nuclearized world, sending him to take courses at the Ecole Supérieure de Guerre in Paris. Bureaucracy had triumphed—the old nemesis of all our imperial greats. Bigeard, however, accepted, spending entire days reading, yet finding it hard to retain all this book learning. There was still the ritual of jogging at 6 A.M. in yawning Paris with its street sweepers and slouched espresso sippers; but Bigeard felt something like a volcano rumbling inside him. However, he kept his mouth shut, trying to adapt, and when Jules Roy's *Bataille de Dien Bien Phu* appeared in magazine chunks, with Bigeard's name prominently displayed, he felt somewhat vindicated. In Paris of the early '60s he had sometimes thought that all his experiences in Indochina, not to mention more recent ones in Algeria, were but a dream.

After a year of this academic existence Bigeard left with a certain ironic admiration for the hectic life of Parisians toddling back and forth on the subway each day, and went off to a new army position in Germany, where he met up again with Massu, at least outwardly loyal to de Gaulle, and with Martial Chevalier inevitably following. Then he was sent to command the 25th Paratroop Brigade in Pau, interrupted by a rapid return to Lorraine, where his dying mother asked about his general's stars, and her son lied to pacify her, saying he had indeed gotten his promotion. After working the Pau brigade up to his customary standards, Bigeard took over another paratroop aggregation in Toulouse, and in July 1966 was finally promoted at age fifty to the rank of brigadier general.

In February 1968 General Bigeard met President de Gaulle at the Elysée

Palace, considering the man a French monument, but still mindful of the price the French (and worse, loyal Muslims) had paid for his Algerian settlement. Thence back to Dakar, where he spent two years as head of French forces there, developing a fierce admiration for Senegal's intellectual president, Leopold Senghor. Here his old friend, Allaire, the one who had conquered polio and much else, and had been at his side with Ben M'Hidi, was blown on a parachute jump into power lines, lucky to be alive. In hospital Allaire devoured a French bestseller of the era, *Papillon*, supposedly an accurate memoir of an escape from Devil's Island, and urged Bigeard to start his own. Why not? It was the time, and in his usual expeditious way, Bigeard decided to begin, punching along into the Indochinese era, aided by Allaire on detail. And yet again, he had to leave a place where human attachments brought him tears.

Arriving back in Paris in July 1970, he would be kept there ten months as an aide to General Cantarel, the army's new chief of staff, and feeling the same as ever about working in a city "where one feels more isolated than in any African bush."[137] Then came a position in Madagascar in August 1971, where he assumed command of French forces in the southern Indian Ocean. Armed with his Algerian dossiers and a book contract, he would push ahead down here on his first great autobiographical book. He also had surging emotions entering his office in Tananarive, the former residence of a celebrated governor-general, and was quite overwhelmed to be Bigeard chez Gallieni! He thought that his predecessors of the colonial period had been great organizers and had put together large, romantic conceptions in places like this, however tenuous that presence now was.[138]

Again Bigeard did his current job well, working with forces spread out over a large area. After a year he returned to Paris to report on his progress, then regaining Madagascar in February 1972 (an aging lion now in his mid-fifties), decided to arrive back in style, parachuting into the ocean off Diego-Suarez. But this rather routine jump into a shark-filled sea became a disaster: fooling around a good forty meters above the ocean's surface, Bigeard mistakenly unhooked from his chute too early, probably fainted, and free-fell into the water, cracking three ribs, bruising his lungs, impairing his vision, and breaking his back.

Recovering, he watched from the sidelines as Madagascar chose a more radical, French-rejecting regime. In February 1973 he finished his marvelous memoir, much of it written on Gallieni's large wooden table, staring at photographs of Lyautey and his mentor hung on the wall, and thinking back to more than 100,000 kilometers he had himself marched; not to mention prison stints, escapes, wounds, and the many people he had met en route. He especially thought of the numerous comrades he had lost to the wars in Indochina and Algeria. Considering his thirty-seven years in the army (1936–73), he felt he had always tried to be in the midst of each crisis. But still, he couldn't help wondering what it had all been for, and why so many promising youths had been cut down so early in life. He even wondered whether the French causes for which he had fought so well were any better, deeper, or more valid than those of their opponents. He then dropped his pen in Tananarive on February 14, 1973, an appropriate place for us to close as well on this "last of the line" soldier abroad, cultured, tasteful, yet militarily magisterial. Bigeard's first memoir had ended in France's wheezing, final gasps of empire. Or *was* it all quite finished?[139]

CHAPTER NINE

"A Remnant Shall
Remain . . ."

WHAT IN FACT WAS LEFT of the great French colonial enterprise? Against the background of Algeria's final agony, de Gaulle, that Prince of Ambiguity, had still hoped to lead Greater France down the road to some form of grandeur and even resurrection. His goal? To create a nexus of relationships between métropole and former colonies along the lines of a commonwealth, which indeed occurred within a few short years. Some colonies remained departments of France itself; others were defined as "overseas territories"; most were independent, some with close ties to the métropole, others indifferent, a few overtly hostile.

When de Gaulle took power in 1958, he did so on the understanding that a referendum would decide on a new French constitution. That constitution of 1958 would substantially beef up the executive branch of government and weaken the legislature. Most analysts focus on its significance for the métropole, but de Gaulle also insisted on ratification by *all* of France's overseas possessions. That in itself was revolutionary: imagine the British Empire allowing self-governing dominions, to say nothing of its colonies, a vote on the complete overhaul of the home government! These votes within each French colony carried grave implications, for a majority of "nons" would constitute declarations of independence, which de Gaulle promised to honor.

On August 21, 1958, he flew to Africa for six days of colonial visits, during which he lobbied for acceptance of what became the Fifth Republic. Significantly, he chose Brazzaville for a major address of August 24, outlining options open to the colonies. A colony could vote for full incorporation into the métropole as a department of France; for continued existence

as a colony or territory; or for immediate independence. A vote for continued colonial status would not preclude eventual independence, for the
French Empire was soon to become the "French Community," a federal
system with its own parliament, from which any colony member might
withdraw. De Gaulle clearly underscored his preference against independence, outlining consequences for any colony voting "non": immediate
withdrawal of all French military, civil service, and commercial personnel;
immediate cancellation of all scholarships for that colony's students in
France; and immediate termination of all economic and commercial relations between colony and métropole. If, despite these warnings, a colony
chose independence, the government would offer no opposition.[1]

De Gaulle hoped to gain unanimous support for the Community concept, but he didn't receive it. On September 28 the AOF colony of Guinea,
led by Ahmed Sékou Touré, cast a resounding 95 percent "non" vote,
receiving full independence the next day.

All other French colonies, however, voted "oui," though their reasons
varied. Most wished for the moment to accept the new constitution and to
give de Gaulle's Community a chance. In Senegal an important percent-
age of public opinion seemed to support independence, but Léopold Senghor used his influence as head of the country's one real political party to
organize a 97.6 percent "oui" vote. France paid big money for Senegalese
groundnuts, and Senghor would not yet forfeit that relationship; besides,
he was an ardent Francophile who considered de Gaulle the greatest
"African" of the day, and the only completely nonracist Caucasian he had
ever known. Senegal's stance then snowballed into a "oui" vote in Sudan
(later Mali), since their vote for independence while Senegal remained with
France would cut off Sudan from the Dakar-Niger railway. Niger itself
eventually voted a 78 percent "oui," another response to Senegal's decision,
but due also to French electoral manipulation.[2] As for colonies like Côte
d'Ivoire, whose leader, Félix Houphouët-Boigny, was the first black African
ever to hold a portfolio in the French Cabinet, an immense affirmative
vote was a foregone conclusion.

Repercussions for lonely Guinea came instantly. Sékou Touré had believed that de Gaulle's threat of an instant pullout lacked substance, which
revealed his underestimation of the man's strength of will and convictions.[3] Touré ignored French officials who warned that the Algerian War
made it impossible for de Gaulle to show any flexibility on this issue; and
also, that virtually the entire French government supported a sharp distinction between colonies supporting the referendum and those opposing

it.[4] The result was a total French withdrawal from Guinea, and Touré then took over a presidential palace from which even telephones and light bulbs had been removed. More, all French police and medical personnel pulled out, all French public investment in Guinea ceased, and Paris pressured other nations to leave that vacuum intact. De Gaulle hadn't built a military and political career spanning half a century on sheer bluff, and neither for the first nor the last time, he showed it here.

As it turned out, however, the French Community idea was doomed. De Gaulle may have received his massive "ouis," but by Bastille Day, 1960 it became clear that most of those "oui" colonies now desired immediate independence. The president was not pleased, but the realist in him accepted this turn of events, working diligently to assure continuing cooperation between France and these newly independent states. By the time the Algerian War ended in July 1962, most of French Africa was free, and the French Community a dead letter. A new nexus of relationships would evolve to replace it.

Had de Gaulle in the end failed to hold to any fixed convictions? Perhaps, but convictions need not be inflexible in order to exist, and adaptability does not exclude sincerity. Once he concluded that the French Empire of the 1950s could not survive, representing a drain on French resources, he moved to excise this particular albatross from the neck of *la Grande Nation*. That ruthlessness astounded even one-time disciples like the former Algerian governor, Soustelle, as well as Michel Debré.[5] Unlike devotés of *Algérie française* such as Soustelle, or of *Algérie algérienne* like Sartre, de Gaulle had gone his own way. In fact he said he created the French Community to serve as an example for Algeria, which he hoped would evolve into an independent nation with close ties to the métropole.[6] In this way France could preserve influence over as many former imperial entities as possible, plus former departments. Such influence, he felt, would be crucial to its future as a great power both in Europe and in the world.

The actual result? By early 1960 the French Community was, as seen, a non-starter. Pressure from members like Madagascar and Mali for complete independence without forfeiture of Community membership persuaded de Gaulle to grant them a status he had denied Touré a year earlier. Quickly the Community disintegrated, as member after member demanded similar privileges. Though the Community served as a transitional institution between empire and cooperation, de Gaulle would have preferred a lengthier time lapse. Still he made the best of it, creating a Ministry of Cooperation to supervise aid programs and political relations between France and its former possessions. Financial and technical assistance were crucial to any future French influence overseas, and the Fifth Republic would prove generous in that regard.

Some in fact argue that France never decolonized economically in large swaths of its former empire. But despite institution of a common currency in Francophone Africa, the need for a kind of pan-African union there has been crucial, due to French (and British) creation of too many colonial entities ending up as small, economically non-viable nations. By about 1990 the French were also clearly tiring of economically propping up corrupt regimes, still dependent on them for resources. They began requesting more democratic accountability, not always forthcoming. In North Africa countries like Tunisia would come to France economically when the need arose, yet remain fairweather on human rights.

But all of course is not economic. The spread of Francophone culture has produced remarkable literature in the French language emanating from different countries drawn from the old empire. Senghor of Senegal is one among many who have shown this fecund hybridity in the language of Balzac and de Beauvoir. Francophone summits, and more recently, Francophone games have shown how that influence remains, though the impact of international French culture has been dogged since 1990 or so by limitations owing to resurgent Islam, and/or dictatorial regimes, not to mention American trends.[7]

When all is said and done, economics probably runs the show in what remains of a reciprocal relationship between France and its former colonies. As the 1990s dawned, Africa continued to serve as an indispensable source of raw materials for the métropole, an outlet for French development capital, and a large market for French manufactured goods, technological services, and expertise.[8] Here are some recent, but now approximate French dependency rates on African minerals: cobalt, 100 precent; uranium (vital for nuclear power plants), 87–100 percent; phosphate, 83 percent; bauxite, 68 percent; manganese, 35 percent; and copper, 32 percent. The métropole's principal trading partners in the early '90s were Cameroon, Congo, Ivory Coast, Gabon, Niger, Senegal, and Togo.[9] To summarize trends rather baldly, French financial aid to these countries had remained substantial till the late 1970s, when it dropped from 0.70 percent of metropolitan GNP to 0.47 percent. But in the mid-1980s it began rising again, and continued to do so into the '90s.

A significant military presence has also protected these economic interests, although the recent ending of French compulsory service has induced some change there. But in Francophone Africa the metropolitan army in recent memory maintained permanent garrisons totaling close to 8,000 troops, supplemented by a rapid deployment airborne force of 47,000 men, first created in 1983. Between 1963 and 1988, the French launched twenty military interventions into troubled African states, some well known, some nearly secret, and the trend has continued with varying intensity.[10]

French influence has also remained in other regions of the globe. Four former colonial possessions enjoy "departmental" status: Guyane, Guadeloupe, Martinique, and Réunion. Four others retain territorial status: French Polynesia, New Caledonia, Wallis and Futuna, and French Antarctic territories; while Saint-Pierre and Miquelon and Mayotte are classified as "territorial collectives." Together the group of ten are known as *départements et territoires d'outre-mer*, or the "DOM-TOMs"[11]

These DOM-TOMs are less important than Francophone Africa, though Guyane and French Polynesia have maintained high profiles, the former for its space launches, the latter for notorious French nuclear tests that took place within its borders. The sugar islands of Martinique and Guadeloupe now subsist primarily on bananas and tourism, while most French possessions feature high rates of unemployment and serious balance-of-payments problems. Strategically, the DOM-TOMs of less than 2 million inhabitants constitute the world's third largest maritime zone (more than 11 million square kilometers), giving France plenty of elbow-room in which to demonstrate its naval power.[12] De Gaulle's vision of revived French grandeur somewhat lives on in these DOM-TOMs, whose retention is more predicated upon strategic than economic necessities.

But in conclusion, let us not make proverbial molehills into mountains. France is largely a stay-at-home country now, and really like the entire West, now tries to hunker down and somehow fend off the ironic onslaught of a formerly imperialized world trying to crash *its* gates. Millions want to make it through the porous dykes, and in an age of cheap and quick air travel and overburdened immigration authorities, it is not so difficult. Paris is more and more full of Indochinese, Caribbean, Polynesian, or Indian/Pakistani faces, not to mention an increasing number of North Africans, all seeking a better life in Europe. Things have come full circle, but the past is worth remembering, if only for some of the truly great figures we have presented here. Will their influence rub off on future generations? It is doubtful, but new forms of venturesome courage will doubtless occur again. Hopefully there will be new historians to chronicle those sorties outward, which may, however, not be French ones!

Let us at least remember how comparatively decently imperial France once did by its extensive possessions, which in some cases have done worse since its departure. In cases like Vietnam (tardily appealing to French tourism), Cambodia, Madagascar, or Algeria, one might even wonder whether brief, relative French beneficence—or depending on one's point of view, nonbeneficence—was worth it.[13] Perhaps we should leave this issue to the philosophers, remaining historians of the "cultured force" shown by the empire's greatest representatives abroad. That character mixture should be recalled more readily than is usual in discussions of France's extensive imperial enterprises during the past few centuries.

Notes

PREFACE

1. Hélie de Saint Marc (with Laurent Beccaria), *Mémoires: les champs de braises* (Paris, 1995).
2. *The French Overseas Empire* (Westport, Conn., 2000).

INTRODUCTION

1. Christopher M. Andrew and A. S. Kanya-Forstner, *France Overseas: The Great War and the Climax of French Imperial Expansion* (London, 1981), 10.
2. A. S. Kanya-Forstner, *The Conquest of the Western Sudan: A Study in French Military Imperialism* (Cambridge, England, 1969), 8–9.
3. Antony Thrall Sullivan, *Thomas-Robert Bugeaud: France and Algeria, 1784–1849: Politics, Power, and the Good Society* (Hamden, Conn., 1983).
4. Jean-Pierre Bois, *Bugeaud* (Paris, 1997).
5. Kenneth J. Perkins, *Qaids, Captains, and Colons: French Military Administration in the Colonial Maghrib* (New York, 1981).
6. See Barrows, "Louis Léon César Faidherbe (1818–1889)," in *African Proconsuls: European Governors in Africa*, L. H. Gann and Peter Duignan, eds. (New York, 1978), 51–79; and "The Merchants and General Faidherbe: Aspects of French Expansion in Senegal in the 1850's," *Revue française d'histoire d'outre-mer* 61 (1974): 236–83.
7. Alain Coursier, *Faidherbe 1818–1889: du Sénégal à l'armée du Nord* (Paris, 1989).
8. See especially Marc Michel, *Gallieni* (Paris, 1989) and Jacques Bernhard, *Gallieni: le destin inachevé* (Paris, 1991).
9. André Le Révérend, *Lyautey* (Paris, 1983).
10. André Le Révérend, *Lyautey écrivain 1854–1934* (Gap, 1976).
11. William Hoisington, Jr., *Lyautey and the French Conquest of Morocco* (New York, 1995).

12. Daniel Rivet, *Lyautey et l'institution du protectorat français au Maroc 1912–1925* (Paris, 1996), 3 vols.

13. Pascal Venier, *Lyautey avant Lyautey* (Paris, 1997).

14. Moshe Gershovich, *French Military Rule in Morocco: Colonialism and Its Consequences* (London, 2000).

15. Douglas Porch, "Bugeaud, Gallieni, Lyautey: The Development of French Colonial Warfare," in *Makers of Modern Strategy: From Machiavelli to the Nuclear Age,* ed. Peter Paret (Princeton, 1986).

16. Douglas Porch, *The Conquest of Morocco* (New York, 1983).

17. Alice L. Conklin, *A Mission to Civilize: The Republican Idea of Empire in France and West Africa, 1895–1930* (Stanford, 1997).

18. Alice L. Conklin, "Boundaries Unbound: Teaching French History as Colonial History and Colonial History as French History," *French Historical Studies* 23 (2000): 215–38.

19. First quotation in Conklin, "Boundaries Unbound," 231; second and third in Conklin, "Colonialism and Human Rights, a Contradiction in Terms? The Case of France and West Africa, 1895–1914," *American Historical Review* 103 (1998): 420–21. Cf. also Daniel J. Sherman's review article, "The Arts and Sciences of Colonialism," *French Historical Studies* 23 (Fall 2000): 707–29. He comments: "It was only a matter of time before the 'cultural turn' manifested itself in the study of French colonial history" (707). One example of this melding is dissected by Richard Keller in "Madness and Colonization: Psychiatry in the British and French Empires, 1800–1962," *Journal of Social History* 35 (2001): 295–326. It is hard in fact to keep up with all the distinguished new contributions in French colonial history. Some recent examples blending new methodologies and use of interesting source material are David Henry Slavin, *Colonial Cinema and Imperial France, 1919–1939: White Blind Spots, Male Fantasies, Settler Myths* (Baltimore, 2001); Eric T. Jennings, *Vichy in the Tropics: Pétain's National Revolution in Madagascar, Guadeloupe, and Indochina, 1940–1944* (Stanford, 2001); and on the Algerian quagmire of the 1950s, James Le Sueur, *Uncivil War: Intellectuals and Identity Politics during the Decolonization of Algeria* (Philadelphia, 2001); and Matthew Connelly, *Diplomatic Revolution: Algeria's Fight for Independence and the Origins of the Post–Cold War Era* (New York, 2002).

20. Of course a major stimulus is the pioneering work of Jay Winter, *Sites of Memory, Sites of Mourning: The Great War in European Cultural History* (Cambridge, U.K., 1995), and his well-known series that is spawning a number of interesting studies melding cultural and military realms. One might also mention the evolution of purely military historians like Robert J. Young (see his *In Command of France: French Foreign Policy and Military Planning, 1933–1940* [Cambridge, Mass., 1978]), toward a biographical-cultural-military-diplomatic combination, seen in his *Power and Pleasure: Louis Barthou and the Third French Republic* (Montreal, 1991).

21. This is a main theme of Porch, "Bugeaud, Galliéni, Lyautey: The Development of French Colonial Warfare." Joffre was one ex-colonial who did not learn proper lessons abroad. Our long-held point of view on this figure goes well beyond (in documentation and depth) that of Pierre Miquel in *Le gâchis des généraux: les erreurs de commandement pendant la guerre de 14–18* (Paris, 2001).

22. See Chinua Achebe, *Things Fall Apart* (1958; reprint New York, 1994); Solomon O. Iyasere, ed., *Understanding Things Fall Apart: Selected Essays and Criticism* (Troy, N.Y., 1998); Ezenwa-Ohaeto, *Chinua Achebe: A Biography* (Oxford, 1997); and G. D. Killam, *The Novels of Chinua Achebe* (New York, 1969) on Achebe's influences, such as Graham Greene, Evelyn Waugh, and Joseph Conrad. Achebe's father was a Christian and mission teacher, so his son was looking back to his grandfather's world of the late nineteenth and early twentieth century. On Fanon see David Macey, *Frantz Fanon: A Biography* (New York, 2000). As has so often been the case with "rebels" who desire sweeping, violent change, Fanon grew up in a rather privileged, middle-class milieu, and by studying medicine in France after World War II, was part of a colonial elite.

23. See S. E Crowe, *The Berlin West African Conference 1884–1885* (London, 1942), 5, 194. See also Albert Michiels, *Notre colonie* (3d edition; Brussels, 1912) and J. Bertrand, *Le Congo belge* (Brussels, 1909); both Michels and Bertrand were professors at a Catholic Institute and the Ecole Normale of Charleroy, respectively. On Hobson and Lenin's purely economic emphasis as imperialistic motivation, see, among others, E. M. Winslow, *The Pattern of Imperialism* (New York, 1984), chs. 5, 7.

24. See T. Alexander Barns' *An African Eldorado* (London, 1926), with sad pictures of these creatures. On the paradox of elephants' ivory being used by Europe's cultured pianists, see Lewis Feuer, *Imperialism and the Anti-Imperialist Mind* (Buffalo, 1986), 43–44.

25. See Samuel H. Nelson, *Colonialism in the Congo Basin 1880–1940* (Athens, Ohio, 1994), Feuer, 40–43, and on Morel, William Roger Louis and Jean Stengers, eds., *E. D Morel's History of the Congo Reform Movement* (Oxford, 1968). The most damning treatment of Belgian brutality is Adam Hochschild's *King Leopold's Ghost: A Story of Greed, Terror, and Heroism in Colonial Africa* (Boston, 1998).

26. See Percival Spear, *A History of British India*, vol. 2 (Harmondsworth, U.K., 1965), ch. 10; Stanley Wolpert, *A New History of India* (3d edition; New York, 1989), 213–25; and Edward Thompson, *A History of India* (London, 1927).

27. See Spear, ch. 11 and Wolpert, 229–44.

28. Wolpert, 208–9.

29. J. H. Hutton, *Caste in India* (Cambridge, U.K., 1946), 97.

30. Harold R. Isaacs, *India's Ex-Untouchables* (New York, 1964), 27–32; Hutton, passim; and James M. Freeman, *Untouchable* (Stanford, 1979).

31. Leslie Palmer, *Indonesia* (New York, 1966), chs. 1–4, and Antoine Cabaton, *Java and the Dutch East Indies*, trans. Bernard Miall (London, 1911), ch. 2.

32. Paul Morand, *Nothing But the Earth*, trans. Lewis Galantiere (New York, 1927), 85, 90; Cabaton, *Java and the Dutch East Indies*, chs. 3–8; Palmer, ch. 6.

33. Ailsa Zainu'ddin, *A Short History of Indonesia* (New York, 1970), ch. 7 on "The Ethical Policy," and Bruce Grant, *Indonesia* (Harmondsworth, U.K., 1967), ch. 2.

34. Guy Hunter, *South-East Asia: Race, Culture, and Nation* (New York, 1966), 5.

35. See Virginia Thompson, *French Indo-China* (New York, 1942), ch. 1; Antoine Cabaton, *L'Indochine* (Paris, 1932), ch. 3; and D. G. Hall, *A History of South-East Asia*, 2nd ed. (London, 1964), chs. 9, 22.

36. See Edmund Roberts, *Embassy to the Eastern Courts of Cochin-China, Siam, and Muscat* (Wilmington, 1972; first published 1837), 220–21.

37. A. D. C. Peterson, *The Far East: A Social Geography* (London, 1957), 187.

38. Cf. Joan Peters' controversial *From Time Immemorial: The Origins of the Arab-Jewish Conflict over Palestine* (New York, 1993), on "Palestinian" incursions into a British and Jewish-improved Mandate area of the 1920s and 1930s.

39. Osbert Sitwell, *Escape with Me!* (London, 1940), 50.

40. See on French Vietnam the clear treatments in, among others, Charles Fisher, *South-East Asia: A Social, Economic, and Political Geography* (London, 1964), ch. 16, pt. 2; Charles Micaud, "French Indochina," in Lennox A. Mills, ed., *The New World of Southeast Asia* (Minneapolis, 1949), 216–45; and John F. Cady, *Southeast Asia: Its Historical Development* (New York, 1964), ch. 12, as well as relevant parts of sources listed earlier. On Vietnam since 1975 see Stanley Karnow's sketch in *Vietnam: A History* (New York, 1983), ch. 1. On French medical services, a qualifying point of view is presented by Patricia M. E. Lorcin, who finds that the French Medical Corps in Algeria, though rightly praised for its humanity and dedication, also helped "marginalize" the population by a certain categorization process. See her article "Imperialism, Colonial Identity, and Race in Algeria, 1830–1870: The Role of the French Medical Corps," *Isis* 90 (1999): 652–79. And on French education it is well to qualify, for while scholarships to institutions of higher learning might help bright students from colonial milieus, these same students were often unable to find professional positions upon graduation (due to both scarcity and discrimination), leaving them no opportunity to live out the sophisticated ideals their colonial educations promised. See Douglas Porch, "The 'Frontier' in French Imperial Ideology," *Journal of the West* 34 (1995): 20.

41. Sitwell, 54.

42. Sitwell, 54; Peterson, 184; Fisher, 537.

43. See especially personal accounts like Someth May, *Cambodian Witness* (London, 1986).

44. Cf. Max Beloff, who wonders how one could maintain that "Burma or the Sudan are better off now than when they were part of the British Empire?" (Beloff, "The British Empire," *History Today* 46 [February 1996]: 14). Of course one could to a degree say the same thing of former "mother countries" themselves! "Worse" is not simply found in the once colonized world—growingly urbanized, "re-religified," catching up to the West materially and medicinally; but in a Western world itself that has lost much of its old idealism and religiosity, once making it sure (some would say too sure) of values it was exporting. See among others on this theme, Samuel P. Huntington, *The Clash of Civilizations and the Remaking of World Order* (New York, 1996), ch. 4 ("The Fading of the West: Power, Culture, and Indigenization"). Anne McClintock's book, *Imperial Leather: Race, Gender and Sexuality in the Colonial Contest* (New York, 1995) might as easily deal with the West's sexualization, etc. in a *postcolonial* context or "contest," as she puts it. We have learned as well from the perceptive essay of Shashi Tharoor, "Global Insights: The Messy Afterlife of Colonialism," *Global Governance* 8 (2002): 1–5; Louise Yelin, "Postcolonial Criticism in the Era of Globalization," *Studies in the Novel* 34 (Spring 2002): 90–101; and Brian Keith Axel, "Colonialism and its Doubles," *Current Anthropology* 43 (February 2002): 197–200.

1. FRANCE'S FIRST EMPIRE

1. Albert Duchène, *La politique coloniale de la France: le ministère des colonies depuis Richelieu* (Paris, 1928), 5.

2. Jean Meyer, Jean Tarrade, Annie Rey-Goldzeiguer, and Jacques Thobie, *Histoire de la France coloniale des origines à 1914* (Paris, 1991), 139–40.

3. Rose Vincent et al., *The French in India* (Bombay, 1990), 28.

4. Vincent, 33.

5. Meyer, 141; Vincent, 38.

6. Vincent, 45.

7. Henry Dodwell, *Dupleix and Clive: The Beginning of Empire* (London, 1967), 8–12. For a justification of Peyton's bizarre conduct, consult his report to Corbett (First Lord of the Admiralty), P.R.O. Admiralty, 1–2288, November 28, 1746.

8. Vincent, 52.

9. Older biographies of Clive such as R. J. Minney's flowery *Clive* (New York, 1931) are generally unsatisfactory. One should consult A. M. Davies, *Clive of Plassey* (London, 1939) and Michael Edwardes, *Plassey: The Founding of an Empire* (London, 1969).

10. Gabriel Jouveau-Dubreuil, *Dupleix* (Pondichéry, 1941), 161–62.

11. Vincent, 54.

12. Vincent, 55–56.

13. See Louis Roubaud, *La Bourdonnais* (Paris, 1932), passim and 193–218. The book was written in the flush of France's Colonial Exposition of 1931, which brought forth a lot of other biographies of French colonial figures.

14. Vincent, 56–57.

15. Dodwell, 62.

16. Vincent, 57.

17. Dodwell, 108.

18. Dodwell, xvi, 113. Dupleix' defenders have alleged that his ultimate failure was due primarily to insufficient military support from France. The evidence indicates that he received approximately 2,500 reinforcements during the period 1750–53, 400 more than the total received by the British. Henry Dodwell's assertion that the British turned out to be better soldiers than the French simply echoes the judgment of Dupleix himself, who characterized French recruits as "rascals or children" (Dodwell, 82–83).

19. See similar remarks by Charles-André Julien, *Le Maroc face aux impérialismes 1415–1956* (Paris, 1978), 124 on colonial mandarins in the twentieth century.

20. See the final chapter of Virginia Thompson's *Dupleix and His Letters (1742–1754)* (New York, 1933), entitled "The Personality of Dupleix," 871–901, 895. See also the portrait of Dupleix in Alfred Martineau, *Dupleix et l'Inde française* (Paris, 1920).

21. On Lally see Trevor N. Dupuy, Curt Johnson, and David L. Bongard, *The Harper Encyclopedia of Military Biography* (Edison, N.J., 1992), 421. See also the views of Frederick Quinn in a pithy treatment of French India, given in *French Overseas Empire*, 80–83.

22. Dupuy, 421; Vincent, 62.

23. Carl L. Lokke, *France and the Colonial Question* (New York, 1932), 23–24.

24. See Lokke, 25–27 and Maureen Covell, *Historical Dictionary of Madagascar* (London, 1995), 45–46.

25. Philip M. Allen, *Madagascar* (Boulder, Colo., 1995), 32–33.

26. André Scherer, *Histoire de la Réunion* (Paris, 1965), 9–11.

27. Marius Leblond, *La Réunion* (Paris, 1956), 7; Scherer, 52–53; Quinn, 80–81. Quinn argues that Ile de France (or Mauritius) had a more limber economic base, due to spices like vanilla and nutmeg; but Richard B. Allen shows how sugar eventually predominated, with slave workers constituting some 75–85 percent of the island's population from the 1730s through to the early nineteenth century, and afflicted with high mortality rates. See Quinn, 79–80 and Allen, *Slaves, Freedmen, and Indentured Laborers in Colonial Mauritius* (Cambridge, U.K., 1999), ch. 1; as well as Deryck Starr, *Slaving and Slavery in the Indian Ocean* (London, 1998). When the British took over both "Mascareigne" islands, they tried to abolish slavery; but it continued illegally, along with a growth in indentured workers drawn from as far distant as China. It was la Bourdonnais who had first recommended sugar cane cultivation on Ile de France in the 1740s.

28. Martin and Harriet Ottenheimer, *Historical Dictionary of the Comoro Islands* (Metuchen, N.J., 1994), 51.

29. Ottenheimer and Ottenheimer, 52.

30. Marcus Franda, *The Seychelles* (Boulder, Colo., 1982), 6–7.

31. Franda, 9–11.

32. See Michael Ross, *Bougainville* (London, 1978), chs. 1–8.

33. Georges Hardy, *Histoire de la colonisation française*, 5th ed. (Paris, 1947), 106–7.

34. Quoted in Ross, 96–97.

35. Quoted in Ross, 125.

36. Henri Blet, *Histoire de la colonisation française* (Paris, 1946), 306–7.

37. See Ross, 157–62.

38. Robert S. Kane, *South Pacific A to Z* (New York, 1966), 160–61. On the origins of French interest in pestilential Guiana, see Quinn, 59–60.

39. Grey Dening, *Islands and Beaches* (Tuscon, 1993), 206–7; Gabriel Hanotaux and Alfred Martineau, eds., *Histoire des colonies françaises et de l'expansion de la France dans le monde*, vol. 4 (Paris, 1933), 464–67.

40. Lokke, 16. Quinn notes the comparative blindness of British negotiators as well as the British fear that the French sugar islands would glut London's market (Quinn, 71).

41. C. A. Banbuch, *Histoire de la Martinique* (Paris, 1935), 21–23.

42. Herbert Bolton and Thomas Marshall, *The Colonization of North America* (New York, 1921), 262.

43. Henri Bangou, *La Guadeloupe* (Paris, 1962), 104; Lokke, 65.

44. There is a large, interesting literature on Saint-Domingue and on slavery there before 1789. One might start with appropriate parts of Richard Graham, *Independence in Latin America: A Comparative Approach*, 2nd ed. (New York, 1994); then move to Herbert S. Klein, *African Slavery in Latin America and the Caribbean* (New York, 1986), 57; Robin Blackburn, *The Making of New World Slavery: From the Baroque to the Modern 1492–1800* (London, 1997), 290–91 on the *Code Noir* and

for the 1780s atmosphere, 450–51; Sue Peabody, *"There Are No Slaves in France":* *The Political Culture of Race and Slavery in the Ancien Régime* (New York, 1996), especially for issues involving those who returned with blacks to France; and then to monographs like Martin Ros, *Night of Fire: The Black Napoleon and the Battle for Haiti,* trans. Karin Ford-Treep (New York, 1994), 11–23; and Carolyn E. Fick, *The Making of Haiti: The Saint Domingue Revolution from Below* (Knoxville, Tenn., 1990), ch. 1. Fick has chilling detail on slave suicides, noting one slave master whose father "lost through poison over four hundred slaves in twenty-five years, and fifty-two more in only six months" (73). See also Quinn, ch. 3. On the intellectual effects at home raised by such colonial milieus, and especially putatively easy morals there, a lively debate over the virtues of "civilization" versus "savagery" engaged the pens of writers like Diderot. See among others, Anthony Pagden, *European Encounters with the New World: From Renaissance to Romanticism* (New Haven, 1993), 150–53.

45. Graham, 30; Ros and Fick, passim.

46. See Ros, 23–56.

47. Graham, 32. See also David P. Geggus, *Slavery, War, and Revolution: The British Occupation of Saint Domingue 1793–1798* (Oxford, 1982) on the growing British involvement here. The Frenchman who propelled the abolition of slavery in the part of Saint Domingue they held (August 29, 1793) is the subject of Robert Louis Stein's study, *Léger Félicité Sonthanax: The Lost Sentinel of the Republic* (Rutherford, N.J., 1985).

48. Useful accounts of these events are to be found in C. L. R. James, *The Black Jacobins,* 2nd ed. (New York, 1963), and Thomas O. Ott, *The Haitian Revolution, 1789–1804* (Knoxville, 1973); see also the vivid account in Ros, and on how the British perhaps unwittingly helped professionalize Toussaint and his forces, Geggus, ch. 15.

49. Hubert-Jules Deschamps, *Les méthodes et doctrines coloniales de la France* (Paris, 1953), 90–97; and Quinn, 72–77 on Louisiana. See also Frank W. Brecher, *Losing a Continent: France's North American Policy, 1753–1763* (Westport, Conn., 1998), who argues that French overconfidence and administrative stodginess helped doom its efforts in America. Stephen Greenblatt notes the superiority complex of *all* European peoples, not just the French in his *Marvelous Possessions: The Wonder of the New World* (Chicago, 1991). But in one of the richest chunks of Franco-American territory along the middle Mississippi, Carl Ekberg contrasts French (or Creole) tolerance to the rougher and readier Anglo-Americans who took over there. See Ekberg, *French Roots in the Illinois Country* (Urbana, Ill., 1998).

2. BUGEAUD AND THE CONQUEST OF ALGERIA

1. See Claude Martin's lucid *Histoire de l'Algérie française 1830–1962* (Paris, 1963) 7–115; Charles-Robert Ageron's much slimmer treatment, *Modern Algeria: A History from 1830 to the Present,* trans. Michael Brett (Trenton, N.J., 1991), chs. 1–2; and John Ruedy, *Modern Algeria: The Origins and Development of a Nation* (Bloomington, 1992), 1–60.

2. For example, Gordon Wright in his masterful *France in Modern Times* 5th ed. (New York, 1995), 121, calls Bugeaud "the most hated general in the service."

3. Sullivan in *Thomas-Robert Bugeaud* pointed the way, as noted, to positive revision in his slim, but solid biographical treatment; and then came the best biography to date, Jean-Pierre Bois' *Bugeaud*.

4. Roger Germain, *La politique indigène de Bugeaud* (Paris, 1955), 364, argues that once Bugeaud was highly considered, and then in more recent times, too "de-considered." He is the scholar who signals Bugeaud's fairness with tribal leaders—once "pacified"—and goes on to note: "C'est ce côté humain du maréchal, si sensible dans la protection des terres indigènes, qui risque de se trouver trop injustement éclipsé par sa renommée guerrière." Bugeaud really *did* care, argues Germain, about the social and economic life of indigenous people won over to the French cause.

5. Robert Forster, *Nobility of Toulouse* (Baltimore, 1960).

6. The surgeon's report from Warsaw, March 1807. No exact date appears in the archives of the Service Historique de l'Armée de Terre, Vincennes (hereafter SHAT): M.F. 42 (Maréchaux de France) Dossier Personnel de Bugeaud. See also in same file a letter from Major of 64th Infantry Regiment to War Min., January 17, 1808, on Bugeaud's health problems, which those above him might have seen as part of his decision to resign. And Bugeaud's own letter of retraction to War Min., January 30, 1808, saying he "burns" to get back into service and that the prior resignation should be ignored.

7. First quote in Henri H. Ideville, ed., *Memoirs of Marshal Bugeaud: From His Private Correspondence and Original Documents 1784–1849*, vol. 1, trans. and ed. Charlotte M. Yonge (London, 1884), 64; second letter 57–58; and quote in third, 67–68.

8. Biographical data to this point in Sullivan, 17–24; Bois, 19–96; Maurice Andrieux' beautifully written *Le Père Bugeaud 1784–1849* (Paris, 1951), 11–64; and ch. 1 of J. Lucas-Dubreton, *Bugeaud* (Paris, 1931), the latter more typical of the less substantial, belle-lettristic biographies that exist on Bugeaud. Others of this sort include Edouard de Lamaze, *Bugeaud* (Lyon, 1943), and slim treatments by Marshal Louis Franchet d'Espérey, *Bugeaud* (Paris, 1938), Albert Paluel-Marmont, *Bugeaud: Premier Français d'Algérie* (Tours, 1944); and among the first biographies, M. F. Hugonnet, *Bugeaud: Duc d'Isly, Maréchal de France* (Paris, 1859). See also Charles A. Julien, *Les techniciens de la colonisation* (Paris, 1947), 55–74. And Jean Gottman, "Bugeaud, Gallieni, Lyautey: The Development of French Colonial Warfare, in E. M. Earle, ed., *Makers of Modern Strategy: Military Thought from Machiavelli to Hitler* (Princeton, 1943), 234–59, as well as the summary of Bugeaud's Etat de Services in the War Min. files in SHAT: M.F. 42 Bugeaud.

9. See, for example, in SHAT: M.F. 42, a collective letter by infantry officers on Bugeaud to Louis XVIII, May 20, 1814, talking of their leader's probity, courage, and the general esteem in which they held him. There is also a whole file of letters to the war minister from his superior in Spain, the Duc d'Albuféra, a brigadier general who admired Bugeaud. In one such letter of May 18, 1815, he called Bugeaud "le premier colonel de l'armée sous tous les rapports." The oath

administered by Baron d'Oberlin de Mittersbach on induction into the order of Saint-Louis is also in this file.

10. See Bugeaud's elegant letter of justification for his rejoining Napoleon to M. le Duc de Bellume, president of "commission chargée de l'examen des officiers de l'armée," October 30, 1815, in SHAT: M.F. 42.

11. This of course fits with the thesis of Eugen Weber's pathbreaking *Peasants into Frenchmen: The Modernization of Rural France 1870–1914* (Stanford, 1976).

12. See ch. 1 of Sullivan, 24–35, for all of what precedes to here; Bois, ch. 3; and Andrieux, ch. 3. Bugeaud's letter to War Min., November 25, 1824, and to Son Altesse Royale Monseigneur le Dauphin of same date are in SHAT: M.F. 42.

13. In that beautiful handwriting of his, Bugeaud writes to War Min., August 19, 1830, citing his military background and how much he wants to contribute to French regeneration. In SHAT: M.F. 42.

14. For foregoing, see Lucas-Dubreton, ch. 3; and on the loss of children and illnesses of Madame Bugeaud, Bois, 113–15.

15. Lucas-Dubreton, 77.

16. The best account of this episode is in Bois, 182–97. In a published diary the doctor attending the duchess noted of Bugeaud: "M. Bugeaud est un homme excellent; ce farouche geôlier est plein de bonté, de faiblesse même, pour les femmes et les enfants" (Prosper Ménière, *La captivité de Madame la Duchesse de Berry à Blaye 1833*, vol. 1 [Paris, 1882], 67–68). On Bugeaud's reluctance to assume new positions, see his letter of April 5, 1832, to War Min. in SHAT: M.F. 42, begging not to receive employment except for an emergency, due to the state of his wife's health.

17. Quoted in Lucas-Dubreton, 97.

18. Bugeaud quoted in Andrieux, 131.

19. On this and aftermath see Lucas-Dubreton, 99–105; appropriate parts of Andrieux; and Bois, 197–201, though there are discrepancies.

20. Blanc quoted in Leo A. Loubère, *Louis Blanc* (Evanston, Ill., 1961), 11. Blanc added that dueling "does not avenge the outraged and sensitive man, but it shelters him against outrage."

21. Andrieux, 164–65; Bois, 201–8. It should be understood that Bugeaud was anything but a faithful presence in Paris; his dossier is peppered with requests for leaves to go back to Excideuil and with grants of those leaves. See e.g., Etat Major to War Min., September 27, 1834, in SHAT: M.F. 42, granting him a leave of two months back in Excideuil, starting October 1, to take care of personal affairs. His electoral fights, also quite acerbic and time-consuming, were another distracting activity, though they also permitted him time at home. See for same year, Bugeaud to War Min., July 3, 1834, on a hard campaign for reelection that he had just won.

22. See Sullivan, ch. 2.

23. For anecdotes on Bugeaud's arrival and the impression he made, see Germain Bapst, ed., *Le Marochal Canrobert: souvenirs d'un siècle*, vol. 1, 7th ed. (Paris, 1909), 252–69. See also Julien's chapter on Bugeaud in his *Techniciens de la colonisation*, and on Bugeaud's first campaigns, the clear account of Bois, 273–81.

24. To Thiers, Bugeaud wrote on August 10, 1836: "You scolded me harshly, my dear friend, for having made the mistake ... of expressing my opinion on Africa

at Algiers." But he went on to say that he just couldn't help himself. General Paul Azan, ed., *Par l'épée et par la charrue: écrits et discours de Bugeaud* (Paris, 1948), 23. Quote from the January 19, 1837 speech (Azan, 26).

25. Bugeaud's first quote in an extract from "Mémoire sur notre établissement dans la province d'Oran par suite de la paix (Juillet 1837)" (Azan, 34, 60). The best source of his long letters sent in this period from the camp at Tafna, then Oran to the Governor-General and to Paris authorities is Georges Yver, ed., *Documents relatifs au traité de la Tafna (1837)* (Algiers, 1924). For Bugeaud's admiration of Abd el-Kader as a "discipliner" of the Arabs see his letter to Governor-General Damrémont, May 25, 1837, 87 and one to the war minister, June 25, 1837, replying to critiques about "elevating" Abd el-Kader (Yver, 132–41).

26. See his letters in M. le Capt. Tattet, ed., *Lettres inédites du Maréchal Bugeaud Duc d'Isly (1808–1849)*, 171–75; February 3, 1839, letter to his friend Genty de Bussy on treating war as a "bagatelle," 187; July 4, 1839, letter to Genty on Lamartine, 188; and to Genty August 25, 1840, on "ces tribuns creux," 222.

27. Letter in Tattet, 199–200.

28. See in Maurice-Henri Weil, ed., *Oeuvres militaires du Maréchal Bugeaud Duc D'Isly* (Paris, 1883), 3, an astonishing work; see also Bugeaud's letter of January, 1828 and his "Essai sur quelques manoeuvres d'infanterie" (Weil, 5–27).

29. See, for example, "Sur quelques manoeuvres d'infanterie: réflexions suggérées par quelques événements de guerre" (Weil, 29–33, quote 29).

30. See in Weil, "Observations sur un article du *Spectateur* du 15 Sept. 1833," 35, 39; and "Principes physiques et moraux du combat de l'infanterie," 41–52, quote 45.

31. Weil, 51. See also "De l'application des manoeuvres de l'infanterie aux combats" (Weil, 53–66), and "De l'ordre de combat pour l'infanterie" (Weil, 67–70).

32. See "Du service des avant-postes et des reconnaissances en Afrique" (Weil, 77–88).

33. See "De la stratégie, de la tactique, des retraites et du passage des défilés dans les montagnes des Kabyles" (Weil, 89–97); "De l'enlèvement des corps attachés: dissertation" (Weil, 127–35); and "Essai sur les reconnaissances" (Weil, 137–43). In Algeria too, it was crucially important to bring the right equipment to the fray, developing, first off, a topflight breed of horses for the army. Vociferously Bugeaud argued the need for superbly trained cavalry—riders and horses working together in tandem. He preached the institution of "fermes de cavalerie," hoping to extricate soldiers from the sterility of garrison life and train them in the French countryside alongside their eventual steeds. He even broke down (like a good estate manager) exactly what it would cost to feed each man, the kinds of crops they could raise, and so on. See "De l'établissement des troupes à cheval dans de grandes fermes" (Weil, 163–78); and "Réflexions sur l'état actuel de la guerre en Biscaye et en Navarre" (Weil, 179–83). Douglas Porch argues that if there was something like a colonial school of warfare, "its founder was incontestably Marshal Thomas-Robert Bugeaud" (Porch, "Bugeaud, Galliéni, Lyautey: The Development of French Colonial Warfare," 378).

34. See "Mémoire sur notre établissement dans la province d'Oran par suite de

la paix" (Weil, 185–227, quote 223) and "De L'établissement de légions de colons militaires dans les possessions françaises du Nord de l'Afrique" (Weil, 229–49, quote 249). See also Victor Démontès, *La colonisation militaire sous Bugeaud* (Paris, 1918), which concludes Bugeaud's ideas were good ones, but that ultimately, those ideas had to lose out to civilian colonization. This would partly be because the *bureaux arabes* (see below) would be more and more under civilian, bureaucratic control after he left Algeria. These Arab bureaus, as we discuss, dealt with Muslim leaders, issues and problems. On the Arab bureaus see also Pier Paola Cossu, *I "Bureaux Arabes" e il Bugeaud* (Milan, 1974).

35. It was of course the July Monarchy that made the office of governor-general synonymous with autocratic command and control of a colony, and therefore of interest to someone like Bugeaud. See Kenneth Vignes, "Le Gouverneur General Tirman et le système de rattachements" (Paris, 1958), a doctoral thesis for the University of Paris, 10–11. For Valée (also spelled Vallée), see Girod de l'Ain, *Grands artilleurs: le Maréchal Vallée 1773–1846* (Paris, 1911). See also Georges Yver's introduction in Yver, ed., *Correspondance du Maréchal Vallée: gouverneur général des possessions de l'Afrique,* vol. 2 (Paris, 1950), and letters in that collection. See also Gabriel Esquer's introduction to Esquer, ed., *Correspondance du Maréchal Clauzel: gouverneur général des possessions françaises dans le Nord de l'Afrique (1835–1837),* vol. 1 (Paris, 1948). And on the terrible health problems of Valée's soldiers ("les fièvres et les moustiques sont plus redoubtables que les cavaliers de l'émir"), see Bois, 342.

36. See the portrait of Abd el-Kader given in Léon Roches, *Trente-deux ans à travers l'Islam (1832–1864),* vol. 1 (Paris, 1884), ch. 39, 153–427 passim. See also Moritz Wagner, *The Tricolor on the Atlas* (London, 1854), 354–62.

37. See Pierre Guiral, *Les militaires à la conquête de l'Algérie 1830–1857* (Paris, 1992), ch. 5 ("Le difficile appel à Bugeaud"); François Guizot, *Memoirs of a Minister of State* (London, 1864), 382–84; Raphael Danziger, *Abd al-Qadir and the Algerians* (New York, 1977), on the paradox of the French helping create Abd el-Kader's success; see also Bois, 295–316.

38. See Sullivan, ch. 3 for the clearest summary of these alternatives, and Bois, 317–44.

39. Proclamation (Azan, 80–81). One might note also his speeches in Chamber of 1840 (Azan, 61–71, 74–79). In a speech May 14, 1840, Bugeaud had asked what one would make of an admiral in a war anchoring his vessels on the coast and staying put. That would be the same as France holing up on the defensive in the big towns. Instead, "il faut une grande invasion en Afrique qui ressemble à ce que faisaient les Francs, à ce que faisaient les Goths; sans cela, vous n'arriverez à rien" (Azan, 79). On the tour of hospitals see Bois, 354, and on Bugeaud's attention to regional affairs in France ("Autrement dit, l'Africain n'efface pas le Périgourdin"), see Bois, 351.

40. For the preceding, one could start with appropriate parts of Sullivan, ch. 4, and of Bois, ch. 8, then sample Bugeaud's copious writings on these subjects. In one he noted "a European army [in Africa] finds itself in the situation of a bull assaulted by a multitude of wasps" (*L'Algérie. Des moyens de conserver et d'utiliser cette conquête* [Paris, 1942], 25). Canrobert remembers that Bugeaud's first talks to

troops revealed both a man of superior intellect and heart (German Bapst, 394). Good capsule portraits of Lamoricière and Changarnier are in Pierre Montagnon, *La conquête de l'Algérie 1830–1871* (Paris, 1986), 312; see also Bois, 389–90, 394.

41. See Bapst, 396, 397, 400, and on Tocqueville, André Jardin, *Tocqueville: A Biography*, trans. Lydia Davis and Robert Hemenway (New York, 1988), 318–20. Tocqueville did study the Koran, and at one time contemplated a thorough immersion in Arabic.

42. See Bugeaud's general order to the army of July 7, 1841, in Ideville, vol. 2, 29; and Ordre général August 8, 1841 (Azan, 94–95).

43. Tattet, 234–35.

44. Latter quotation in Ideville, vol. 2, 52 and other letters are in Azan. On the famous song having to do with Bugeaud's cap see Bois, 9–10 and Douglas Porch, *The French Foreign Legion* (New York, 1991), 79, as well as the display as one enters the Salle Bugeaud at the Musée de l'Armée (Invalides) in Paris. The song was regularly sung by French schoolchildren of the Third and Fourth Republic into the 1950s, making the name Bugeaud nationally recognizable for a long time.

45. There are some beautiful Arabic and French letters from such notabilities written to Bugeaud from this era in SHAT: M.F. 42. For Bugeaud's campaigns of 1841–42 and results see Bois, 407–30, and for the wall and ditch ideas in particular, 409–10.

46. See Centre des Archives d'Outre-Mer [hereafter CAOM]: 1H3: Correspondance 1833–1853 and Commission des interprètes 1842, containing a series of exhaustive and fascinating minutes from their meetings. In the sixth meeting of August 4, 1842, and the seventh of August 16 they modified both linguistic and "moral requirements."

47. On the relationship of Bugeaud and Soult see Jack Ridley, "Marshal Bugeaud, the July Monarchy and the Question of Algeria, 1841–1847: A Study in Civil-Military Relations" (Ph.D. dissertation, University of Oklahoma, 1970), 15, 35, 59, 63–64. See also CAOM: 1E210: Lettres de Bugeaud 1841–1847 for execution policies in Algeria, including numerous letters exchanged between General Négrier and Soult's office in Paris. (Typical: "Ce n'est pas sans un sentiment des plus pénibles que j'ai lu la dépêche" (Négrier to War Min., April 16, 1842). He goes on to say that in the Constantine area "le dernier Arabe, puni de mort, était un bandit coupable de quatorze meurtres.") See also CAOM: F80 561: Administration et affaires arabes: Prises sur l'ennemi; razzias 1840–1850 for numerous letter exchanges on that subject. On the latter Bugeaud fought for local initiative: "Toutefois je crois devoir vous faire observer qu'il y a dans ce pays des circonstances si variées qu'il me paraît convenable de laisser quelque chose à l'appréciation des généraux. Mais je pense dans tous les cas que la moitié des prises devrait entrer dans le trésor de l'état ou de la colonie, et que c'est sur l'autre moitié seulement qu'on pourrait laisser un peu à l'appréciation" (Bugeaud to Soult in ibid., March 22, 1841), only the beginning of a large correspondence between the two on the subject. Finance officers were also driven crazy having to provide lists of animals taken and how much they were worth, and to whom they were to be distributed. See, for example, in same file, the finance officer Appert in Algiers to the War Ministry, July 14, 1842, complaining that he just couldn't get the detail required

on *razzias*. On prisoner exchanges, etc. see CAOM: F80 562: Administration et affaires arabes: Prisonniers de guerres français et arabes 1837–47, again full of correspondence between Bugeaud and the War Ministry. One in his file of letters just on the ransoming problem sent to "M. le Maréchal" (Soult) is of July 19, 1841, where his anger comes through at already saying the same thing in earlier letters. There are also affairs of this sort in CAOM 1H4: Affaires indigènes: Correspondance concernant surtout la province de Constantine 1837–1847. For example, one involved an Arab who had stolen funds from fellow Muslims, was banished to Tunisia, and wanted to get back into Bugeaud's Algeria. Bugeaud found himself drawn into many of these affairs.

48. See in CAOM: 1H4 Bugeaud to Soult, August 10, 1843, on Algerian affairs generally, but mostly on Captain Rivet. Rivet's *Histoire du commandement du Maréchal Bugeaud de 1841 à 1847* is found in SHAT: MR (Mémoires et Reconnaissances) 882. Quote on Turks p. 230 of manuscript. Bugeaud also received many letters from his own subordinates, recommending appointments; for example, from Lamoricière, asking for promotion for a number of his soldiers, August 23, 1842 (Archives Nationales [hereafter AN]: AP 225 1–4: Papiers du Maréchal Bugeaud Duc d'Isly). In the same file Bugeaud wrote Soult, September 7, 1842, recommending the demotion or transfer of Commandant Bisson, supposedly a great inflator of his own qualities, but not good with his men.

49. Azan, 138, 139.

50. See Bugeaud to Genty November 17, 1843, and to d'Esclaibes, January 6, 1844 (Tattet, 265, 268). See also his letter to General de Bourjolly September 15, 1843 (Azan, 154–55). On his first trip Tocqueville too had noticed the divisions between government functionaries and/or colonists, and soldiers in Algeria (Jardin, 326–27).

51. See Sullivan, ch. 5; and Perkins, 13–16. Lamoricière had created the first *bureau arabe* in 1833, which was abolished, then became the *Direction des Affaires arabes* in 1837, which in turn was suppressed in 1839. In Bugeaud's scheme the Direction des Affaires arabes operated only in major cities or military divisions like Algiers and Oran, while the *bureaux* under them were strung out in smaller centers (Bois, 488–90). See also the excellent article by Abdelmajid Hannoum, "Colonialism and Knowledge in Algeria: The Archives of the Arab Bureau," *History and Anthropology* 12 (2001), 343–79.

52. See Bugeaud, *L'Algérie. Des moyens de conserver et d'utiliser cette conquête,* 9–10. Operating in the face of guards with guns, dogs, circled tents, such "virtuous thieves" seem to have some similarities to today's suicide bombers in the Middle East. See also "La Situation de l'Algérie à la fin de 1843" by Bugeaud posing as "un Touriste" (Azan, 158–63, quote 161–62); and on Abd el-Kader's brutality with chieftains Bois, 431. Oddly, even Victor Hugo saw whatever measures the French took as ones of civilization against barbarism. In a conversation with Bugeaud the famous writer noted: "C'est un peuple éclairé qui va trouver un peuple de la nuit" (Bois, 347).

53. "Proclamation de M. le Gouverneur Général à tous les chefs des Flissas, Aâmeraouas" and five other tribes *insoumis* (Azan, 168). See also Bugeaud's letter to Thiers February 29, 1844 (Azan, 164–66). On the Prince d'Aumale's capture of the *smalah* see Ridley, 67–68. Bugeaud truly admired him as a soldier. On

attaining the title of *maréchal de France* Bugeaud was pleased, but felt he had to do a lot more than his predecessor Valée, who was given the honor merely for a twenty-four hour stint taking Constantine, which Bugeaud would repeat (Bois, 436–38).

54. See Bugeaud's letter from the frontier to the Sultan of Morocco June 16, 1844 (Azan, 169–70; Bois, 439–40; Ridley, 75–80). Correspondence between Bugeaud and Abd el-Kader is in CAOM 1H3, including the emir's flowery letter back of February 10, 1844, translated by Roches.

55. See Bugeaud's letter on the Battle of Isly to War Min. (Soult), from his bivouac near Coudiat-Abd-er-Rahman, August 17, 1844 (Azan, 171–81, quote 176). One of the facets of Bugeaud's organization and planning skills was his ability to delegate, choosing talented subordinates like his aide-de-camp, Phocion Eynard, who procured information from Arab prisoners, khalifs, and a variety of commanders, then relayed it to Bugeaud. See AN: AP 230 2–3: Papiers du Général Eynard. On the fascinating career of Yusuf see Bois, 395–98.

56. See Louis' letter August 29, 1844, to Bugeaud (Ideville, vol. 2, 133–34). See also letter from Duke of Orleans to Bugeaud, August 31, 1844, talking of "orgueil national" from the victory (SHAT: M.F. 42). On the sultan's foot-dragging (and that of his son) see the copious correspondence exchanged between Bugeaud and these Moroccan leaders, complete with elegant Léon Roches translations of all the flowery Arabic formulae (CAOM: 1H3). See also on Treaty of Tangier Ridley, 81. A little like those who believed the dénouement of the 1990–91 Gulf War let Saddam Hussein off the hook, Bugeaud felt that Abd el-Kader could still find enough refuge to fight another day, and he was therefore far from satisfied with the treaty.

57. See Bugeaud speech in Azan, 190–202, quotes 193, 198. That first civilian administrator, an unfortunate named Léon Blondel, would be impelled to resign by Bugeaud in 1846, followed by a not very powerful Victor Foucher (Bois, 483). See the letter of congratulation mentioned from one Harispe to Bugeaud, August 25, 1844 (AN: AP 225 1–4). Harispe noted how this "éclatante victoire" had revivified "un bien ancien et bien tendre attachement." Bugeaud's admonition about Arab bellicosity was echoed in a famous statement of 1846 by Roches, who had certainly lived in the seraglio, so to speak, and warned the French: "Les Arabes vous détestent, tous sans exception; ceux que nous qualifions de dévoués ne sont que compromis; ils sont tous amis de l'indépendance qui est, pour eux, le désordre; ils sont tous guerriers; ils conservent au fond du coeur un levain de fanatisme" (in Bois, 525).

58. Letters in Ideville, vol 2, 32–33 (of 1841), and 89 (1843).

59. Quotes in Ideville, vol. 2, 168; Azan, 212. See also the standard biographies and military histories of Algeria for accounts of the atrocity. Bugeaud reminded Marshal Soult of his own past atrocities at Napoleon's Battle of Austerlitz, where he supposedly had cannoneers blow up the ice on a lake over which Russian soldiers were trying to flee (Bois, 456).

60. See his letter of October 6, 1845 (Azan, 225) and to Soult on same day from Excideuil (Azan, 226–31); and to Guizot October 6, 1845 (Azan, quote 232).

61. Bugeaud's proclamation to "Colons de l'Algérie" October 15, 1845, at Alger in Azan, 243–44 and letter to War Min., November 21, 1845 (Azan, 245–46). See

also discussion of Saint-Yon (Ridley, 108–9). Ridley calls 1845 the "most critical year of Bugeaud's tenure as Governor-General of Algeria" (Ridley, 112).

62. Letter to Gardère of March 22, 1846, in Ideville, vol. 2, 213–14. Bugeaud's precise knowledge of geography, of how many rations to give men, of who to delegate which leadership role are evident in his numerous letters to Pélissier during the operations of 1846, found in AN 235 1–6: Papiers du Maréchal Pélissier. Bugeaud kept warning Pélissier to protect loyal tribes, but to protect via a good offense against enemies.

63. See Bugeaud's letter to Guizot April 11 and 30, 1846 (Azan, 156, 256); and to Genty de Bussy February 8, 1845 (Azan, 285–87). On the Tocqueville delegation Jardin, 328–29, and for Tocqueville's ambivalence toward Bugeaud, see the 1846 Chamber debate in Alexis de Tocqueville, *Writings on Empire and Slavery*, trans. and ed. Jennifer Pitts (Baltimore, 2001), 117–28. On Lamoricière's schemes and the split with Bugeaud Ridley, 112–13; and Bugeaud, *Observations de M. le Maréchal Gouverneur-Général sur le projet de colonisation pour la province d'Oran par M. le Lieutenant-Général de la Moricière* (Algiers, 1847), quotes 8, 9, 21. See also his earlier work, *L'Algérie: des moyens de conserver et d'utiliser cette conquête*, where he remarked pithily: "Chaque Arabe qui s'enrichera deviendra notre partisan; c'est un ennemi de moins, et un allié de plus" (111). Bugeaud did concede that civilian colonization was all right for the big coastal cities and certain parts of the interior (and of course civilians there would learn to use arms). But the military colonists needed to be in frontier areas and near towns like Tlemcen, Mascara, or Medea. They also needed to build and expand their new villages and roads for defense (Ridley, 29–39).

64. See letter to Guizot in Ideville, vol. 2, 239 and quote 239; and letter to Thiers in Azan, 289–91. Meanwhile, the war minister truly saluted Bugeaud's great work in Algeria in a letter to Bugeaud of May 13, 1847, in which he said: "La France vous devra la création du plus grand établissement qu'elle ait encore formé hors de son territoire continental" (SHAT: M.F. 42).

65. First examples of Arab job-seekers: Mohammed be er-Roumili to M. le Maréchal Duc d'Isly, March 17, 1847 (knowing both Turkish and Arab languages) and Mohamed ben Hassen to Bugeaud, April 3, 1847, in Arabic with translation (CAOM: 1H4). For property claims see another Mohamed to Bugeaud, April 5, 1847, followed by a letter of the war minister to the Direction des Affaires Arabes de l'Algérie about such property reclamations (ibid.). See director of the Finance Administration (Algiers) to Bugeaud, January 30, 1847, on spurious claims, and Arabic letters sent to the King or to the War Ministry (ibid.). Other problems and affairs mentioned here are in CAOM: 1H6: Correspondance politique des affaires indigènes (including Correspondance arabe) 1845–1849. Bugeaud's correspondence on tribespeople attempting to return to Algeria from Morocco (e.g., February 2, 1847, to French Consul-General in Tangier and among other letters, consul to Bugeaud, March 29) in CAOM: 1H6. Bugeaud complained of the sultan's "incroyable apathie" in his letter of April 8, 1847, to the Consul (ibid.). The affair of distributing francs for Abd el-Kader's confiscated animals, reconfiscated by the French in CAOM: F80 561. Bugeaud wrote the War Min. March 25, 1846, on what an exhaustive, careful process this had to be. See also the problems of

distributing confiscated arms mentioned in letter from director of Finances (Algiers) to Bugeaud July 1, 1846, both in ibid. For the many forms Bugeaud's administration had to fill out in this era see AN: AP 225.

66. Farewell address in Ideville, vol. 2, 247–49 and letter to Roches of July 7, 1847, 263–66; *Memoirs of the Prince de Joinville*, trans. Lady Mary Lloyd (New York, 1895), 358–59; letter to General Charon July 8, 1847 (Tattet, 309). The capture and imprisonment of Abd el-Kader elicited a spate of poetry abroad by such as Thackeray and Lord Maidstone, and much English sympathy, in particular. Once he attained a well-heeled exile in Damascus, Abd el-Kader received visits from Richard and Isabel Burton, Byron's granddaughter, Lady Anne Blunt, and a number of other travelers. See Osman Benchérif, *The Image of Algeria in Anglo-American Writings, 1785–1962* (Lanham, Md., 1997), ch. 5.

67. Bugeaud to daughter September 3, 1847, in Ideville, vol. 2, 271; and second letter in vol. 2, 269, August 9, 1847. Oddly, Deputy Tocqueville's report of 1847 that voted a special appropriation but not Bugeaud's military colonization scheme was very supportive of the man, calling African war "a science for which everyone [now] knows the laws" and giving full marks to Bugeaud for "having understood, perfected and rendered comprehensible to all this new science." He also took his hat off to Bugeaud for instituting the *bureaux arabes*. See Tocqueville, "Rapport fait par M. de Tocqueville sur le projet de loi relatif aux crédits extraordinaires demandés pour l'Algérie" (Tocqueville, *Oeuvres*, 806, 810). Tocqueville also felt that the Bugeaud regime had been perhaps too liberal with Arabs—paying for pilgrimages or subsidizing construction. He himself preferred the independent Kabyles of the mountains.

68. For what precedes see Sullivan, chs. 6, 7; Bois, ch. 10; and Canrobert, vol. 1, 419–27. Reorganization of Algeria's government in 1847 also portended a more bureaucratized future (see CAOM: F80/1: Gouvernement de l'Algérie; F80/127, bulging with Arab dossiers; and F80/2043, another bulging carton, including increasing administration and creation of rules on polygamy).

69. Sherman Kent, *Electoral Procedure under Louis Philippe* (New Haven, 1937).

70. See *Mémoires de Caussidière*, vol. 1 (Brussels, 1848), 55–56. Caussidière himself called Bugeaud "le maréchal de la rue Transnonain" (55).

71. See Georges Duveau, *1848: The Making of a Revolution*, trans. Anne Carter (New York, 1967), 33–36; John G. Gallaher, *The Students of Paris and the Revolution of 1848* (Carbondale, Ill., 1980), 57–58; and *The Recollections of Alexis de Tocqueville*, trans. Alexander Teixera de Mattos (Cleveland, 1959), 43. See also Bugeaud to his colleague Léonce de Lavergne, October 19, 1848, a general narrative on the beginnings of the Revolution (Ideville, vol. 2, 306); and Bois, 530–37. There is some dispute as to whether Bugeaud, Bedeau, or both finally decided on a troop withdrawal.

72. Letters to Comtesse Feray, Bugeaud's daughter (Ideville, vol. 2, 315); to Gardère, March 29, 1848 (Ideville, vol. 2, 316–17); to Roches, May 4, 1848 (Ideville, vol. 2, 317–18); and to Col. Jamin July 4, 1848 (Ideville, vol. 2, 327–28); letter to Thiers, July 14, 1848 (Azan, 326–28); and letter to War Minister Charras (Tattet, 316).

73. *Recollections of Alexis de Tocqueville*, 73, 154, 181–82.

74. The Bugeaud manuscript on street warfare was finally published in a modern edition where he also discusses his former hesitations publishing this work (Maréchal Bugeaud, *La guerre des rues et des maisons* [Paris, 1997], quotes 105, 106). The present edition is largely a discursive preface by Maité Bouyssy. On his depressed state during this time see Bugeaud's letters to Genty of August 20 and September 23, 1848 (Tattet, 320–22, 334–35); see also Sullivan, 133–41 for what precedes. See also one of Bugeaud's election pamphlets, where he asked rhetorically: "Can I be the equal of your neighbor, Nicholas, who, instead of working like me from dawn to nightfall, spends half his time in the pub? . . . There will always be poor and rich, strong men and weak men, clever men and stupid men . . . spendthrifts and savers." The pamphlet appears in translation in Roger Price, ed., *1848 in France* (Ithaca, N.Y., 1975), quote 135. The Conseil de Guerre gave sentences of two years and two months to directors of *Le Républicain de Lyon,* a newspaper averring that Bugeaud wanted to destroy Lyon and massacre its inhabitants. See John M. Merriman, *The Agony of the Republic: The Repression of the Left in Revolutionary France 1848–1851* (New Haven, 1978), 38. Bugeaud's letter on improved stretchers of January 22, 1849, to War Min. (AN: AP 225 [2]).

75. On Bugeaud's death and burial at Invalides, see War Min. decree June 11, 1849, in SHAT: M.F. 42.

76. See Canrobert, chs. 1, 6.

77. Général Louis Jules Trochu, *Oeuvres posthumes,* vol. 2 (Tours, 1896), 309.

78. See quote in Trochu, vol. 1, 138; also 5–24, 60–61; and vol. 2, 133–42, 283–342.

79. Comte Pierre de Castellane, *Souvenirs de la vie militaire en Afrique* (Paris, 1856), 218.

80. Roches, *Trente-deux ans à travers l'Islam,* quotes, vol. 1, 428; vol. 2, 305, 317, and passim; and on Roches Blunt, ch. 12.

81. Lucien François de Montagnac, *Lettres d'un soldat: neuf années de campagnes en Afrique* (Paris, 1885), 194.

82. Letter to Uncle Bernard (ibid., 481–86, quote 486). Montagnac's critiques are echoed by a letter from Bugeaud's aide, Eynard, on one regiment decimated by hard fighting for a year and with numerous wounded, and needing some sort of reward (AN: 230 2–3, Eynard to Bugeaud, July 26, 1844).

83. Letters in Montagnac, 486–91, 491–500.

84. See nephew's preface to Montagnac, i–xxxiii.

85. See Porch, *French Foreign Legion,* ch. 4 ("La casquette du Père Bugeaud"), 75, 77, 88.

86. See François Maspéro, *L'honneur de Saint-Arnaud* (Paris, 1993), 200–15 and passim.

87. *Lettres du Maréchal de Saint-Arnaud,* vol. 1 (Paris, 1955), 325.

88. In *Lettres du Maréchal Saint-Arnaud* (letter of June 21, 1844), 537.

89. Quotes in letter to brother August 28, 1844, from Blida in *Lettres du Maréchal Saint-Arnaud,* vol. 1, 543, 544; second one in letter, vol. 2, 67.

90. Letter and quote in *Lettres du Maréchal Saint-Arnaud,* vol. 2, 68.

91. First quote in *Lettres du Maréchal Saint-Arnaud,* vol. 2, December 14, 1848, from Algiers to brother in Paris, 190; second in letter of June 4, 1849, vol. 2, 207.

92. In *Lettres du Maréchal Saint-Arnaud*, vol. 2, 212–14. Oddly, Bugeaud's wife who had suffered much ill health lived until 1874.

93. A useful account of post-Bugeaud Algeria to this point is Montagnon's *Conquête de l'Algérie 1830–1871*. On France's anti-Islamic bias that persisted after 1871 see Michael Willis, *The Islamic Challenge in Algeria: A Political History* (New York, 1996), 7; Rashid Messaoudi's ch. 1 in *Algeria: Revolution Revisited*, ed. Reza Shah-Razemi (London, 1997); and Ricardo René Larémont, *Islam and the Politics of Resistance in Algeria, 1783–1992* (Trenton, N.J., 2000), 39–50 on closings of Muslim schools and the use of a *Code de l'indigénat* to conscript Muslim Algerians into forced labor.

94. Older scholarship is often the clearest point of introduction, and for the fascinating, somewhat blundering nature of the French incursion into Tunisia, beating Italy to the punch, see Thomas F. Power Jr., *Jules Ferry and the Renaissance of French Imperialism* (New York, 1944), ch. 2. And for Algeria in its period of transformation from military to civilian control, see Vincent Confer, *France and Algeria: The Problem of Civil and Political Reform, 1870–1920* (Syracuse, 1966).

95. Maréchal Bugeaud, *Histoire de l'Algérie française*, vol. 1 (Paris, 1850), quotes 65, 134, 154, 155. Sullivan and Bois perhaps ignored this book because it isn't found in the catalogue of the Bibliothèque Nationale, and in the United States is located only in the Library of Congress and one other American university library. French quotations here best reveal Bugeaud's taste. On camels who could sense the onset of crippling sandstorms: "L'inquiétude se peint dans leurs regards; leurs narines se dilatent; enfin une heure ou deux avant que la tempête n'éclate, ils se couchent, subissent les plus mauvais traitements plutôt que de continuer à marcher, enfouissent leurs museaux dans le sable et restent dans cette posture, le dos tourné au vent." On France modeling the best of what Rome accomplished in North Africa, "la terre [ici] n'attend que la culture et ce que Rome a fait, la France peut le faire." Bugeaud writes of persecuted Christians of the second century A.D., taking refuge in "les cavernes les plus cachées, les sables les plus brûlants, les solitudes les plus horribles." On Romans of the falling empire who also later ran there, fleeing barbarians, "c'était la queue de l'épicuréisme romain, citoyens-rois déchus, mendiants déhontés, ayant abjuré leur dignité d'homme, étrangers à toutes les affections de famille, à tous les instincts moraux, vivant au jour le jour, sans souci, sans tracas, traînant insolemment leurs guenilles du *forum* dans les cirques et trouvant leur pâture à la table des riches ou dans les temples, comme les oiseaux de basse-cour dans les mangeoires des fermes." But they were countered by ascetics with a contrasting "tendance à l'isolement, de cette ardeur effrénée de vie contemplative ... depuis la simple privation des plaisirs mondains jusqu'aux plus dures macérations du cénobitisme, [avec] une indifférence totale pour les biens terrestres et une abnégation sans exemple dans les annales du monde." Bugeaud's marvelous scientific observations are indeed counterbalanced by deliciously sweeping generalizations, as on the Moors, once full of "mille brillantes qualités," yet now a people "peu industrieux, peu actif, peu entreprenant; mais, en général, hypocrite, intriguant et rusé, possédant ainsi les talents des êtres faibles." Or on the Kabyle-Berber: "Intrépide, mais attaché à son foyer; turbulent, mais laborieux; perfide, mais léger; indépendant, mais cupide" (French quotations 6–7, 16, 55, 57, 129, 130,

128 respectively). The generalization on Arab males (four loves) is on 140. It should be remembered that Bugeaud had truly contrasting parents in his lineage, and that via his mother, Françoise Sutton de Clonard, daughter of Thomas Sutton, Count of Clonard, and Phillis Master of Castletown, his Irishness helped create a paradoxical personality and *oeuvre*.

3. FAIDHERBE OF SENEGAL AND WEST AFRICA

1. See Leland C. Barrows, "General Faidherbe, the Maurel and Prom Company, and French Expansion in Senegal" (Ph.D. diss., UCLA, 1974), 3, 5. See also his articles "Louis Léon César Faidherbe (1818–1889)" in Gann and Duignan, eds., *African Proconsuls*, 51–79, and his "The Merchants and General Faidherbe."

2. Jean Martin, *L'empire renaissant: 1789–1871* (Paris, 1987), 218, 229; Martin Klein, *Islam and Imperialism: Sine-Saloum, 1847–1914* (Stanford, 1968), 61; Charles-André Julien, *Les constructeurs de la France d'outre-mer* (Paris, 1946), 237–38.

3. See, for example, Georges Hardy, *Faidherbe* (Paris, 1947), 9.

4. See André Demaison, *Faidherbe* (Paris, 1932), 4. And SHAT: M.F. (Maréchaux de France) 515 (Dossier personnel de Faidherbe): Min. of Commerce and of Travaux Publics to War Min. October 17, 1838, and Pref. of Nord to War Min., June 10, 1838, both strongly recommending Faidherbe. See notes of October 8, 1840, signed October 15 by the general *(commandant de l'école)*.

5. See Hardy, *Faidherbe* 14, 135–36, quote 135; as well as Coursier, 18–19, 25. Barrows disputes the fact that Faidherbe's paralysis stemmed from the Algerian battle. See "Louis Léon César Faidherbe (1818–1889)" in Gann and Duignan, eds., *African Proconsuls*, 53.

6. Letter of March 18, 1851, to mother in CAOM: 113 APOM 1–3 (Fonds Personnels: Archives Faidherbe, deposited there by the family in 1995).

7. See letter in CAOM: 113 APOM May 21, 1851, to mother in Lille from Bemi'Salah. See also letter of May 17, 1851.

8. Letter of May 31, 1851, to mother in CAOM: 113 APOM, from a bivouac; letter of June 2, 1851, to mother from a new bivouac, in same source.

9. See June 30, 1851, letter from another bivouac; letters from Bou Saada September 22 and October 30, 1851; letter from Sétif January 14, 1852; letter of February 20, 1852; and letter of February 25, all in CAOM: 113 APOM.

10. Sullivan, 167. Another difference from Bugeaud was Faidherbe's openness to the Left. See Hardy, *Faidherbe*, 147–49; see also an inspection report of 1848 signed by Chef de bataillon de génie, October 31, 1848, in SHAT: M.F. 515, which says that Faidherbe is "enclin au socialisme exagéré." The report also takes an ethical slam at the disease he contracted in Guadeloupe.

11. In CAOM: 113 APOM October, 1852—no day given.

12. Letter of November 18, 1852, in CAOM: 113 APOM.

13. As David Gamble writes in *The Wolof of Senegambia* (London, 1967), 17: "The history of the Wolof states [in what became Senegal] is a succession of conquests, invasions, rebellions, and usurpations."

14. John Barbot's account in *France and West Africa: An Anthology of Historical Documents*, ed. J. D. Hargreaves (London, 1969), 40.

15. On the history of the area see Michael Crowder, *West Africa under Colonial Rule* (Evanston, 1968); the compact summary in B. O. Oloruntimehin, *The Segu Tokolor Empire* (London, 1972), 26–33; and Léonce Jore, *Les établissements français sur la côte occidentale de l'Afrique de 1758 à 1809* (Paris, 1965), 80. Another clear introduction to this period is in Rita Cruise O'Brien, *White Society in Black Africa: The French of Senegal* (Evanston, Ill., 1972), ch. 1, quote 30–31. Adanson's book is *A Voyage to Senegal, the Isle of Gorée, and the River Gambia* (London, 1759). Great crocodiles, huge serpents a foot in diameter, endless fish off Gorée would have enthused the public (Adanson 128, 130, 178). Cf. the *métis* Abbé P. D. Boilat, *Esquisses sénégalaises* (Paris, 1853), viii: "There are few countries offering so many varieties of the human species ... so many matters for scientific research."

16. J. D. Hargreaves, *West Africa: The Former French States* (Englewood Cliffs, N.J., 1967), 78; Frédéric Carrère and Paul Holle, *De la Sénégambie française* (Paris, 1855), 94, 152, 170. On the problems of mining and selling Bambouk gold see Philip D. Curtin, "The Lure of Bambouk Gold," *Journal of African History* 14 (1973): 623–31.

17. See Jean Copans, *Les marabouts de l'arachide* (Paris, 1980), 94, quote 95. George Brooks mentions the term "l'arachidité" for Senegambia and an "overwhelming dependence on the peanut as the sole cash crop" (Brooks, "Peanuts and Colonialism: Consequences of the Commercialization of Peanuts in West Africa, 1830–70," *Journal of African History* 16 [1975], 54). See also Carrère and Holle, quote 84. Annual peanut exports from Senegal would soar from just under 15,000 tons in 1898 to 643,000 in 1939!

18. See Barrows, "General Faidherbe, the Maurel and Prom Company," part 1, 135, 232. Yves-Jean Saint-Martin in his readable *Le Sénégal sous le Second Empire* (Paris, 1989) says correctly that although Faidherbe did want to dominate the river with a series of French *comptoirs*, "there is no Faidherbe programme." His energy and improvisatory ability were most important (254, 239). A typical inspection report on Génie letterhead for 1854 in SHAT: M.F. 515 considers the thirty-six-year-old Faidherbe a fine officer in every way—intelligent and enthusiastic, and with a distinguished colonial record. See also in M.F. 515, Min. de la Marine et des Colonies to War Min., July 6, 1854 on the promotion, mentioning Faidherbe's *intrépidité* and *sang-froid* on his Algerian expeditions. And the Min. de la Marine et des Colonies report of October 23, 1854, on Faidherbe's appointment to governor, saying that he has remarkable qualities and can do more than engineering. See also CAOM: I 41 (Archives du Sénégal, Fonds ministériel: Correspondance général), Faidherbe to Min. de la Marine et des Colonies, May 24, 1855.

19. In a well-known quote Faidherbe said: "I don't like war, although I've waged it or *because* I've waged it during my life" (Coursier, 204); Mollien quoted in Donal B. Cruise O'Brien, *The Maurides of Senegal* (Oxford, 1971), 21.

20. For the foregoing see David Robinson, *The Holy War of Umar Tall: The Western Sudan in the Mid–Nineteenth Century* (Oxford, 1985); and Oloruntimehin, ch. 2.

21. Faidherbe, *Le Sénégal* (Paris, 1888), 164; and his letter to Min. de la Marine et des Colonies, October 1, 1855 (CAOM: I 41).

22. Faidherbe, *Sénégal*, 165.

23. Yves-Jean Saint-Martin, *L'empire toucouleur 1848–1897* (Paris, 1970), 73 (quote) and passim. Saint-Martin is much more pro-Faidherbe in his more recent book on Senegal, *Le Sénégal sous le Second Empire*.

24. Thierno Diallo, *Les institutions politiques de Fouta Djallon au XIXe siècle* (Dakar, 1972), 46–47, quote 46.

25. On Islamic moral standards Carrère and Holle were impressed by the fact that "a man cannot, during the absence of the husband, enter into the home of a married woman." Carrère and Holle, 130–31. On Faidherbe wanting to use Islam against animism, see William B. Cohen, *The French Encounter with Africans* (Bloomington, 1980), 257. For Eugène Mage see the handy abridged edition of his *Voyage au Soudan occidental (1863–1866)*, preface by Yves Person (1868; reprint Paris, 1980), xii, 303. The book was originally published in 1868.

26. For Boilat "the word *thiedo* is the opposite of *marabout;* it means a non-believer, an impious man, a man without faith or probity." These people, a kind of militia in the kingdoms of Cayor or Walo, lived off pillage. Boilat writes: "I have seen *thiedos* pass whole days drinking this horrible liqueur [eau de vie] and fall dead drunk" (*Esquisses sénégalaises*, 309). See also Faidherbe's very detailed letter to Min. de la Marine on these reconnoiterings on the river (CAOM: I 41). See also the laudatory article on Faidherbe of G. Cazavan in the *Journal du Havre*, October 8, 1855.

27. See Faidherbe, *Sénégal* 19, 139–52, quote 151; Barrows, "Louis Léon César Faidherbe (1818–1889)" in Gann and Duignan, eds., *African Proconsuls*, 58–59.

28. Robinson, *Holy War of Umar Tall*, 165, 191, 214; Oloruntimehin, 89.

29. Oumar Ba, ed., *La pénétration française au Cayor, I, 16 décembre, 1854–mai 28, 1861: collection de documents inédits pour servir à l'histoire de l'Afrique* (Dakar, 1976), 30, 63, 69. Cayor had its own authentic anti-Islamic forces or at least, it was opposed to a dominant brand of Islam. See Lucie G. Colvin, "Islam and the State of Kajoor: A Case of Successful Resistance to Jihad," *Journal of African History*, 15 (1974): 587–606. Printed copy of Faidherbe's speech at Banquet Offert par le Commerce à Monsieur le Gouverneur du Sénégal du 11 novembre 1855, sent back to Min. de la Marine (CAOM: I 41).

30. According to Barrows, "The war with the Trarzas seemed little more than a grand cattle rustle, [and] the French turned out to be the more effective rustlers." Barrows, "General Faidherbe, the Maurel and Prom Company," part 1, 286. He calls el-Habib a "regal cattle thief": 254. See also Faidherbe's Candide-like recitation in *Sénégal*. For example, "On the first of March [1855], to take vengeance for the treason of river inhabitants of Touareg, we burned the large villages of Ndombo, Ntiago, Keurmbay" (among others). In ten days, he goes on, the French took "2000 cattle, 30 horses, 50 donkeys." Not to mention 15 prisoners, 100 enemies killed, and a grand total of 25 villages burned! At first the French hadn't wanted to annex Walo, but after a good "razzia de boeufs" from the water and other fine actions, it just happened by December of 1855. See *Sénégal*, 131–35, 131.

31. First letter quoted in CAOM: I 41. Last one in paragraph is Faidherbe of June 10, 1857, to Min. de la Marine (CAOM: I 43, Archives du Sénégal: Correspondance). See also his letters in I 42 (Archives du Sénégal: Correspondance)

of February 3, February 11, March 8, April 6, April 18, May 5, May 29, June 4, September 13, among others in this huge file, where the flame of his obsession seems to burn! He would often sign these letters as "Le très-humble et très obéissant serviteur, le Gouverneur Faidherbe."

32. Robinson, *Holy War of Umar Tall*, 219, 231. See also his *Chiefs and Clerics: Abdul Bokar Kan and Futa Toro 1853–1891* (Oxford, 1975), chs. 2, 3; and Michel, 68–69.

33. CAOM: I 43. First quote in Faidherbe's obsessional sixteen-page account of July 19, 1857, to Min. de la Marine from Médine; second, Faidherbe to Min. de la Marine (another ten-pager) August 29, 1857; third, August 24, 1858, to Min. de la Marine; last letter, August 30, and long handwritten *mémoire* of Faidherbe October 1, 1858. See also Faidherbe's letter of May 12, 1858, to Min. de la Marine. G. Cazavan in *Journal du Havre* and other papers (October 14, 1858) also trumpeted the virtues and future of a pacified Senegal, the great river itself now an artery of peace and of progress.

34. First letter in SHAT: M.F. 515, as well as second, undated, 1858, signed "devoted cousin."

35. Hardy, *Faidherbe*, 140. On his ability at public relations with Paris, see Barrows, "General Faidherbe, the Maurel and Prom Company," part 1, 246–48.

36. One formula of politeness: on seeing someone, not "How are you?" but "Is your husband in peace? Your wife in peace? Are you really at peace?" Response: "True peace." Boilat, *Esquisses sénégalaises*, 364. Faidherbe also appreciated apothegms of the area: "A child from the first bed is not a son, but a civil war" (351). See also Henri Gaden, *Proverbes et maximes peuls et toucouleurs* (Paris, 1931).

37. Improved hygiene would also diminish the ravages of malaria in Senegal. See William B. Cohen, "Malaria and French Imperialism," *Journal of African History* 24 (1983): 23–36.

38. See François Renault, "L'abolition de l'esclavage au Sénégal: l'attitude de l'administration française (1848–1905)," *Revue française d'histoire d'outre-mer* 58 (1971): 5–81 and Barrows, "General Faidherbe, the Maurel and Prom Company," part 2, 499; part 1, 245. The school for "hostages" was an old African idea adapted by Europeans. Denise Bouche, "L'école française et les Musulmans au Sénégal de 1850 à 1920," *Revue française d'histoire d'outre-mer* 61 (1974): 222, and for Faidherbe's school policy in general 222–25.

39. Barrows, "General Faidherbe, the Maurel and Prom Company," part 2, 607, and see for one Senegalese area, Michael A. Gomez, *Pragmatism in the Age of Jihad: The Precolonial State of Bundu* (Cambridge, 1992), ch. 8.

40. On Jauréguiberry see Barrows, "General Faidherbe, the Maurel and Prom Company," part 2, ch. 18, and on *tirailleurs* 824. The "Senegalese sharpshooters" regiment would eventually become less attractive to Senegalese "softened by the comparative ease provided by urban life and discouraged by the inferiority status which they thought membership of the *tirailleurs* corps involved" (this by the late nineteenth century). "As a result the *tirailleurs sénégalais* gradually became Senegalese only in name." H. Oludare Idowu, "Assimilation in 19th Century Senegal," *Cahiers d'études africaines* 9 (1969): 208.

41. Barrows, "General Faidherbe, the Maurel and Prom Company," part 2,

41. On Dakar, see Jacques Charpy, *La Fondation de Dakar* (Paris, 1958) and Jean Delcourt, *Naissance et croissance de Dakar* (Dakar, 1981).

42. See Barrows, "General Faidherbe, the Maurel and Prom Company," part 2, 795–808, and ch. 22.

43. See interim governor Pinet-Laprade's letter on June 27, 1863, to Min. de la Marine (CAOM: I 49 Archives du Sénégal: Correspondance), expressing his hope that Faidherbe's arrival would calm things. And Faidherbe's September 11, 1863 letter to Min. de la Marine summarizing revolts, etc. (CAOM: I 50).

44. Barrows' quote in "General Faidherbe, the Maurel and Prom Company," part 2, 886. For Faidherbe's increasing inability to collect taxes in Casamance and elsewhere, and the need to revert to "voluntary contributions," see Christian Roche, *Histoire de la Casamance* (Paris, 1985), 121.

45. See Faidherbe to Min. de la Marine January 18, 1864 (CAOM: I 50). See also his letter of March 28, 1864, on how Jauréguiberry had given the Trarzas too many gifts and concessions, allowing them to recover their former arrogance. Other typical "shopping list" letters to Min. de la Marine include one of November 15, 1864, asking for support to build a new museum edifice in Saint-Louis; and one of December 20, 1864, asking for more boat-money. His letter of January 17, 1865, to Min. de la Marine seems almost frantic—Faidherbe wanted to leave behind a heritage of museum building, among other things that he fears the next administration might not sustain. His letter of January 28, 1865, mentions the possibilities of a zoo of rare animals (all in CAOM: I 50).

46. Faidherbe certainly played the health card to get the Algerian transfer. See in SHAT: M.F. 515 Faidherbe's letter from Lille to War Min., September 14, 1865, saying his doctors advised against a winter in the North of France, and so he wanted a *congé* in Algeria, with however, free passage down there for his wife, three children, and a houselady! There are a number of doctors' notes in here and other correspondence on other leaves, noting Faidherbe's chronic bronchitis. An inspection report here of 1868 notes Faidherbe's health as "fatiguée." See also in here, Gov. General of Algeria to War Min., August 4, 1870, on how he cannot extend Faidherbe's latest *congé de convalescence*, needing him to command a subdivision.

47. Bernard Grosbellet, *Le Moniteur du Sénégal et dépendances comme source de l'histoire du Sénégal au temps du premier gouvernement de Faidherbe (1856–1861)* (Dakar, 1967), 108.

48. Faidherbe, *Notice sur la colonie du Sénégal et sur les pays qui sont en relation avec elle* (Paris, 1859), 29–30, 47, quote 29. Cf. Boilat, in *Esquisses sénégalaises*, who says that Sérers don't attack bravely like Europeans, but go after women and children (125).

49. Faidherbe, *Chapîtres de géographie sur le nord-ouest de l'Afrique avec une carte des contrées à l'usage des écoles de la Sénégambie* (Saint-Louis, 1864), 12, 21, 33.

50. Coursier, 116–21.

51. Faidherbe, *Collection complète des inscriptions numidiques (Libyques) avec des aperçus ethnographiques sur les Numides* (Paris, 1870), 30 and passim.

52. Faidherbe, *Collection,* 50–53.

53. Faidherbe, *Vocabulaire d'environ 1500 mots français avec leurs correspondants*

en oulof de Saint-Louis, en poular (toucouleur) du Fouta, en soninké (sarakhollé de Bakel) (Saint-Louis, 1864), 52 and passim. Notice by the title how carefully he chooses which dialect to present his readers.

54. Faidherbe, *Le Zénaga des tribus sénégalaises: contribution à l'étude de la langue berbère* (Paris, 1877), 10, 29, and passim.

55. Faidherbe, *Essai sur la langue poul: grammaire et vocabulaire* (Paris, 1875), 4–7. The second edition is just about the same, but it is entitled *Grammaire et vocabulaire de la langue poul à l'usage des voyageurs dans le Soudan*, 2nd ed. (Paris, 1882). Cf. Henri Gaden, *Le poular dialecte peul de Fouta Sénégalais* (Paris, 1912).

56. Examples and quotes in Faidherbe, *Essai sur la langue poul*, 58–59.

57. Faidherbe, *Essai sur la langue poul* (first edition), two quotes 33, 34; 35–36, 52–56.

58. Faidherbe, *Essai sur la langue poul*, examples and quotes 21, 26. On the elegance of Poul poetry see Alfa Ibrahim Sow, "Notes sur les procédés poétiques dans la littérature des Peuls du Fouta-Djallon," *Cahiers d'études africaines* 5 (1965): 370–87. On different "myths" about the Peuls (or Fulani) going back at least to Mungo Park, see Paule Gérard Brasseur, "Le Peul imaginaire," *Revue française d'histoire d'outre-mer* 65 (1978): 535–42.

59. This is evident in the way he moves easily from ancient authors like Pliny or Plutarch to African ecological or ethnographic considerations in his "Mémoire sur les éléphants carthaginois," *Bulletin de l'Académie d'Hippone* 3 (Bône, 1867): 1–18.

60. On the Nord in the Franco-Prussian war and Faidherbe, see Coursier, ch. 8. See also Louis Gensoul, *Souvenir de l'armée du Nord en 1870–1871* (Paris, 1914). See also in SHAT: L.F. 6 (Armée du Nord: Correspondance) a typical letter by Faidherbe to War Min. in Bordeaux, December 16, 1870.

61. Louis Cadot, *La vérité sur le siège de Péronne: réponse au Général Faidherbe* (Paris, 1872), 24 and Coursier, ch. 9. See also letter of Chef d'Escadron Bonnault, an artillery commander, to Colonel de Villenoisy, January 11, 1871, on the results of Péronne, and a copy of Protocole de la Capitulation de Péronne of January 9 (SHAT: L.F. 6). On the battles of Vermand and Saint-Quentin, see Faidherbe's long report (signed Général en chef de l'Armée du Nord L. Faidherbe) of February 9, 1871 (SHAT: L.F. 6). There are many telegrams from railway or military personnel in this file, showing how seriously the Franco-Prussian War was taken that late in the Nord.

62. See Faidherbe, *Armée du Nord: réponse à la relation du Général Von Goeben pour faire suite à la campagne du Nord* (Paris, 1873), quote 16; and his *L'Armée du Nord en 1870–1871* (Paris, 1872).

63. See Jules Brenne, *Un mobile de l'armée de Faidherbe* (Paris, 1972), who describes the relationship between Faidherbe's scholarly side and his military abilities: "Faidherbe, very cultivated, was a superior mind . . . He had an incontestable authority. He showed a lot of skill in the command of a rather eccentric group" (146). See also Faidherbe, *Armée du Nord: réponse à la relation du Général Von Goeben*, 14.

64. Listening to friends, says Coursier, led Faidherbe mainly to "annoyance, attacks, slander" in the political world (Coursier, 205). On Gallieni and Lyautey

as war ministers, see Marius-Ary Leblond, *Gallieni parle* (Paris, 1920), 177–260 and Vladimir d'Ormesson, *Auprès de Lyautey* (Paris, 1973), 13–106. See also Faidherbe to War Min., April 18, 1871, asking to be put on *disponibilité* from the 25th (SHAT: M.F. 515). In same file see War Min. document of May 25, 1872, mentioning Faidherbe's recent scholarly expedition to Egypt.

65. See in SHAT: M.F. 515 the copious correspondence on all this, including War Min. note of October 22, 1872, putting him on Commission centrale des chemins de fer, in replacement of a dead general; Faidherbe's angry letter to Pres. of Republic, February 5, 1873, on revocation of street and place names and lack of medal; War Min.'s report of March 20, 1874, criticizing Faidherbe's views; and note of War Min. of February 13, 1879, noting that he had received above appointment for salary, since "il n'a aucune fortune." An earlier inspection report of Génie of 1851 in the same file mentions Faidherbe's debts going back to his time at school in Metz. Was he perhaps poor at managing finances?

66. See SHAT: M.F. 515, inspection-générale report for the Etat-Major of 1876 and the one for 1878, as well as notes of the War Min., such as March 3, 1880, on Faidherbe's paralysis.

67. See Coursier, ch. 11 and Barrows, "Faidherbe" in Gann and Duignan, eds., *African Proconsuls,* 76. See also Faidherbe's letters on Senate letterhead of July 23, 1884, to "Mes chers enfants," and one to his son-in-law of February 29, 1886, in which his handwriting grows larger and more scrawly (CAOM: 113 APOM). And from SHAT: M.F. 515, a note by Etat Major de l'Armée on burial in Invalides.

68. See Barrows, "General Faidherbe, the Maurel and Prom Company," part 1, 109; Coursier, 47–48; and Paul Gaffarel, *Le Sénégal et le Soudan français* (Paris, 1890), 18, 50–51. Gaffarel called this racial policy a failure.

69. In Joal (Sérer) only married people were fully clothed. Boilat, 104.

70. See Coursier, 102 and SHAT: M.F. 515—Faidherbe's letter to War Min. asking permission for marriage in 1858 (no date) and War Min. favorable reply on this *demande de mariage,* October 23, 1858. We also find his marriage act in here, as well as many other inspection notices.

71. See Faidherbe, *Sénégal,* 93–94. Umar Tall too reformed polygamy, getting one man down from 300 wives to the more usual four. On Cayor see Carrère and Holle, chs. 3, 4, 5. On the positive side they note quite an enlightened divorce policy: a woman's adultery was of course grounds, but only with seven honorable witnesses (26).

72. On the fear of colonial and commercial inundation of Morocco after World War I, see Lyautey's letters in André le Révérend, ed., *Un Lyautey inconnu* (Paris, 1980), 316, 386, and see Faidherbe, *Sénégal,* 485–86. By the late 1920s there were still only 7,700 French people in all of French West Africa. See Gershovich, 27.

73. Faidherbe, *Sénégal,* 478, 112–14, quote 114.

4. GALLIENI AND JOFFRE

1. Barriers between the colonial and metropolitan armies and mutual misunderstandings helped create this misestimation. Those barriers only started to evaporate in the immediate prewar period. See especially J. K. Munholland, "The

Emergence of the Colonial Military in France, 1880–1905" (Ph.D. diss., Princeton University, 1964), 302–39; and Douglas Porch, *The March to the Marne: The French Army 1871–1914* (Cambridge, U.K., 1981), 151–64. Porch uses the term "military apartheid" for the colonials (164). But see his somewhat different "Bugeaud, Gallieni, Lyautey: The Development of French Colonial Warfare," 376, 407.

2. On Gallieni's general reputation as a proconsul there is much fulsome praise. See, for example, Pierre Montagnon's *La France coloniale: la gloire de l'empire* (Paris, 1988) on the colonial enterprise as a whole: "Gallieni, le premier et le plus grand de tous les coloniaux français! Il les domine tous. Il est leur maître à tous." The rest, including his great disciple Lyautey, are considered to have a weak spot: "Lyautey est comédien, Faidherbe insatisfait, Bugeaud douteux, Brazza fragile, Mangin personnel, Marchand inconstant" (203). In B. H. Liddell Hart, *Reputations Ten Years After* (Boston, 1928), Hart also gave him very high marks both as a colonial and for his role in World War I (71–99). This unfootnoted portrait jibes with our opinion of Gallieni, especially in World War I. Virgil Matthews is also complimentary in his balanced article "Joseph Simon Gallieni (1849–1916)," in Gann and Duignan, eds., *African Proconsuls*, 80–108. Matthews gives less analysis of Gallieni's literary and military sides than we do and does not clearly link his colonial past with his World War I record. We also give much more space to the debate over the Marne. See also the unblushingly high opinion of Gallieni of Jean Gottmann, "Bugeaud, Gallieni, Lyautey: The Development of French Colonial Warfare," in *Makers of Modern Strategy,* ed. E. M. Earle (Princeton, 1941), ch. 10, compared with Porch's views in the later edition given above. Porch, *March to the Marne*, ch. 8 is best on the colonial army in general.

In the 6th edition of R. R. Palmer's and Joel Colton's standard text *A History of the Modern World Since 1815*, 2 vols. (New York, 1984), they omit Gallieni entirely and give Joffre full credit for ordering the counterattack "at exactly the right moment" (671). In Gordon Wright's *France in Modern Times*, 309, Joffre again gets high marks and Gallieni receives no mention. This, however, is not the case in Alfred Cobban's, volume 3 of the equally well known *A History of Modern France* (Harmondsworth, U.K., 1986), where according to the author, Gallieni started the counterattack and Joffre merely "let him loose" (111). In the late 1920s Liddell Hart had cleared up the problem, but as with his tank theories too few obviously read him: "Today . . . the world should recognize Gallieni, rather than Joffre, as the victor of the Marne" (*Reputations Ten Years After, 73*). To be fair, we should note that historians may be confused by estimates from intelligent, well-connected figures of the time such as Sir Edward Spears in his *Liaison 1914* (1930; reprint London, 1968). Spears says that Joffre was long aware of how the Marne would present an opportunity for counterattack and was simply "keeping his own counsel" until the right moment. Though Gallieni was "a fine and capable commander," Spears declares that "the Battle of the Marne was essentially Joffre's achievement" (336, 375, 435). Modern books on the Marne are unequal in value, but Georges Blond's confirmation of Gallieni's originality and preeminence over a weaker Joffre (at the Marne) may still be considered definitive. See Blond, *The Marne*, trans. H. Eaton Hart (Harrisburg, 1966), 102, 113. He does say that commanding a smaller army made things easier for Gallieni (111).

3. See Jean d'Esme, *Gallieni* (Paris, 1965), 17–27, a balanced "popular" biography. Roger-François Didelot's light if readable *Gallieni: Soldat de France* (Paris, 1947) says he would develop a "soul as inflexible as the marble [there]" (13). In *Gallieni* (Paris, 1959) Pierre Lyautey talks of the combined grace and wildness of the area (13). Pierre Gheusi, *Gallieni 1849–1916* (Paris, 1922), by a disciple, says Gallieni had a profile like the Pyrenees (7), though equating his Pyrenean background with Joffre's, as does Judith Cladel in *Le Général Gallieni* (Paris, 1916), 18 is misleading. The most scholarly biography, Michel's *Gallieni*, unfortunately has no notes, and similarity of taste accounts for a few quotes we have chosen in common from Gallieni's works. This is a fine book, and the best biography of Gallieni; but it seems to become somewhat cynical and to run out of gas by World War I. Clearer, more enjoyable, but less substantial (*except* on World War I) is Bernhard's *Gallieni*.

4. On languages see Michel, 30. On his Englishness cf. G. Blanchon (editor of the *Journal officiel*): "He has the aspect of an English officer." In his "Le Général Gallieni," *Pages actuelles* 16 (1915): 26.

5. There are some hagiographic exaggerations on Gallieni's incarceration. Pierre Lyautey writes: "In a few weeks, he will speak and write German fluently" (Lyautey, *Gallieni*, 21). The best summary of the influence of his captivity is in Bernhard, 17–19. In a letter to his father, he notes proudly: "We are not part of the capitulation of Sedan" (d'Esme, 32). Kitchener would share Gallieni's deep wartime reservations about offensives, and about Joffre. Like Gallieni he predicted early on that World War I would be a long one. See George H. Cassar, *Kitchener: Architect of Victory* (London, 1977), 230, 249, 270. The book makes some of the same claims for Kitchener as we make here for Gallieni.

6. Didelot in *Gallieni* calls his stay on Réunion "three years of paradise, dreaming, reflection" (45).

7. Most of the biographies mention these identifications.

8. For the foregoing see Michel, ch. 4 and most of ch. 5; Bernhard, 21–27, as well as appropriate sections of the older biographies and of Matthews, "Gallieni."

9. Gallieni, *Voyage au Soudan français (Haut-Niger et pays de Ségou 1879–1881)* (Paris, 1885), 36, 382, 427, 95, 15, 246–48, 134. On the background to problems and political configurations in the region see Robinson, *Chiefs and Clerics* and Oloruntimehin, passim; and Robinson, *Holy War of Umar Tall.*

10. Gallieni, *Voyage au Soudan français*, 136, 186, 195.

11. Gheusi, *Guerre et théâtre 1914–1918* (Paris, 1919), 272. Cf. Bianchon, "Le Général Gallieni," 28: "His art has been in choosing and employing men." And in a letter to J. Charles-Roux, September 26, 1902, in Gallieni's *Lettres de Madagascar 1896–1905* (Paris, 1928), 97, he himself wrote, referring especially to Lyautey: "Colonies are made with men, and these men, one takes them where one finds them." See, for example, Gheusi, *Guerre et théâtre*, 274: "The rivalries, the jealousies of the General Staff . . . shocked him . . . he had never wanted to face up to the baseness ("sonder la bassesse") of certain souls, nor the servility of perverse minds." Gallieni to J. Chailley, February 6, 1899, in his *Lettres de Madagascar*, 44.

12. Gallieni, *Voyage au Soudan français*, 145, 170, quote 133.

13. Gallieni, *Voyage au Soudan français*, 387, quotes 104, 209.

14. See d'Esme, 52–56; Michel, 88.

15. See Gallieni, *Voyage au Soudan français*, 222–25.

16. Gallieni, *Voyage au Soudan français*, 251–52, 352, quote 383.

17. See Gallieni, *Voyage au Soudan français*, 409–10, 421; Michel, 96; standard biographies, especially Bernhard, 27–33; and Kanya-Forstner, *Conquest of the Western Sudan*, 72–83, taxing Gallieni with a series of falsifications (to the sultan and then on the Treaty of Nango, to the French government), as well as anti-Islamic bias.

18. See Marius-Ary Leblond, *Gallieni parle*, vol. 1 (Paris, 1920), 238–39 (includes quote); Michel, 103–4 on his marriage; Bernhard, with Marthe Gallieni's quote 34, and appropriate sections of the older biographies, as well as Matthews, "Gallieni."

19. Michel, 113–20 and appropriate sections of the older Gallieni studies.

20. Joseph Gallieni, *Deux campagnes au Soudan français 1886–1888* (Paris, 1891), 107, 50, quotes 107, 121 (the latter also quoted in Michel, 122). On the slavery issue see Renault, "Abolition de l'esclavage au Sénégal," 5–81.

21. Gallieni, *Deux campagnes au Soudan français*, 51, quote 6.

22. See appropriate sections of the biographies, most clearly, Bernhard, 34–42. See also Gallieni, *Deux campagnes au Soudan français*, 84, 89, and Kanya-Forstner, *Conquest of the Western Sudan*, ch. 6 and beginning of ch. 7, where the term "Total Conquest" of the Sudan is used.

23. See Michel, 132; Bernhard, 42–43; Gheusi, *Guerre et théâtre*, 34 on Gallieni's modesty at the Ecole de Guerre; and on the falling-out with Archinard, Porch, "Bugeaud, Galliéni, Lyautey: The Development of French Colonial Warfare," 388; as well as Kanya-Forstner, *Conquest of the Western Sudan*, 198–99.

24. The clearest secondary source accounts in English on Ferry and the garnering of protectorates remain Power's *Jules Ferry and the Renaissance of French Imperialism*, ch. 7, and Virginia Thompson, *French Indo-China* (New York, 1942), ch. 2 passim. Both books again demonstrate that older and less cluttered is sometimes easier to follow. See also Karnow, ch. 2.

25. *Gallieni au Tonkin (1892–1896) par lui-même* (Paris, 1941), 12, ch. 10. And Paul Chack cited in *Gallieni au Tonkin*, 7.

26. See Michel, chs. 10 and 11; Bernhard, 44–59; appropriate sections of the older biographies; *Gallieni au Tonkin*, 39–43, 90; and J. Kim Munholland, "'Collaboration Strategy' and the French Pacification of Tonkin, 1885–1897," *The Historical Journal* 24 (1981): 629–50. The latter sees Vietnamese-Chinese enmity as an assist to Gallieni's success, but stresses also the transience of that success.

27. See Karnow, 115–18; and Thompson, *French Indo-China*, passim.

28. Michel, 107 and the recent, slim book by Charles-Armand Klein, *Gallieni: portrait varois* (Barbentane, 2003) on his domestic life here, before it became "the Riviera."

29. For the foregoing see Bernhard, 59–71; Stephen Ellis, *The Rising of the Red Shawls: A Revolt in Madagascar 1895–1899* (Cambridge, 1985), quote p. 102; Gallieni to Alfred Grandidier, letters of August 15 and October 25, 1896, in his *Lettres de Madagascar*, 3, 15; and Joseph Gallieni, *Neuf ans à Madagascar* (Paris, 1908), 12, quote 3. On the methods Gallieni used to deal with the revolt see also the

critical assessment of Ellis, "The Political Elite of Imerina and the Revolt of the *Menalamba:* The Creation of a Colonial Myth in Madagascar, 1895–1898," *Journal of African History* 21 (1980): 219–34. Ellis says the two men shot were innocent. Jennings is both negative and positive on Gallieni in *Vichy in the Tropics,* 33–35. The high cost of disease should also be figured into this discussion. Over 80 percent of Frenchmen in this campaign perished of it, asserts Douglas Porch in *The Conquest of the Sahara* (New York, 1984), 152. Good, general books on Madagascar include Arthur Stratton's *The Great Red Island* (New York, 1964) and Nigel Hesseltine, *Madagascar* (New York, 1971).

30. See Gallieni, *Neuf ans à Madagascar,* 50, 54–57; see also on Third Republic hygiene, Guy Thuillier, "Pour une histoire de l'hygiène corporelle: un exemple régional: Le Nivernais," *Revue d'histoire économique et sociale* 46 (1968): 232–53. On Gallieni's need to get out and see all areas under his command, see the excerpt from a previous inspection tour of April-May 1894 in Vietnam, in Hubert Deschamps and Paul Chauvet, eds., *Gallieni pacificateur: écrits coloniaux de Gallieni* (Paris, 1849), 142.

31. Gallieni to J. Charles-Roux, June 4, 1903, in *Lettres de Madagascar,* 114–15. On Malgache "wives" see Henry Charbonnel, *De Madagascar à Verdun: vingt ans à l'ombre de Gallieni* (Paris, 1962), 32–33.

32. See Maurice Gontard, "La Politique religieuse de Gallieni à Madagascar pendant les premières années de l'occupation française (1896–1900)," *Revue française d'histoire d'outre-mer* 58 (1971): 183–214; Gallieni's letter to Alfred Grandidier, June 1, 1904, on the *congréganistes* in *Lettres de Madagascar,* 152–53. Anticlerical French governments at home nonetheless allowed Catholic missionaries mostly free rein in the colonies, and just before World War I there were 70,000 to 90,000 pupils in missionary schools, learning both religion and elements of French patriotism in the colonial empire. Andrew and Kanya-Forstner, 41.

33. Jean Charbonneau, *Gallieni à Madagascar* (Paris, 1950), 24; Gallieni, *Lettres de Madagascar,* 39, 87–88; and Charbonnel, *De Madagascar à Verdun,* 76 ("the government demanded [pacification and organization] without money").

34. See Gallieni's *Rapport d'ensemble sur la pacification, l'organisation et la colonisation de Madagascar (octobre 1896 à mars 1896) (1899),* published by "governor-general of Madagascar."

35. Letter October 30, 1899, in Charbonneau, *Gallieni à Madagascar,* 140; Gallieni, *Neuf ans à Madagascar,* 147; and see also on this "public relations" trip, Tony Chafer and Amanda Sackur, eds., *Promoting the Colonial Idea: Propaganda and Visions of Empire in France* (Hampshire, U.K., 2002), ch. 2.

36. Lieutenant Paul Ellie, *Le Général Gallieni: Le Tonkin-Madagascar* (Paris, 1900), 43, 63; Capitaine X, *Voyage du Général Gallieni* (Paris, 1901), 2; and Charbonnel, *De Madagascar à Verdun,* 23.

37. Gallieni, *Neuf ans à Madagascar,* 161–67, 224–25; Charbonneau, 109–12. On Gallieni in Madagascar generally see Michel, chs. 12–15 and appropriate sections of the older biographies, as well as Matthews, "Gallieni."

38. Alistair Horne, *The Price of Glory: Verdun 1916* (London, 1964); A. J. P. Taylor, *Illustrated History of the First World War* (New York, 1963); and Barbara Tuchman, *The Guns of August* (New York, 1962).

39. See especially Otto F. Kernberg, *Narcissistic Personality Disorder* (Philadelphia, 1989) and *Severe Personality Disorders: Psychotherapeutic Strategies* (New Haven, 1984). See also James F. Masterson, *The Narcissistic and Borderline Disorders: An Integrated Developmental Approach* (Larchmont, N.Y., 1981), and most readably, *The Search for the Real Self: Unmasking the Personality Disorders of Our Time* (New York, 1988).

40. See Arthur Conte, *Joffre* (Paris, 1991), 24, among others.

41. G. Blanchon, *Le Général Joffre* in *Pages actuelles* 11 (1915): 1.

42. Louis Muller, *Joffre et la Marne* (Paris, 1931), 28. Muller was an ordnance officer under Joffre.

43. Emile Ripert, *Au Pays de Joffre* (Paris, 1918), 46. Other hagiographic biographical studies include Alexander Kahn, *Life of General Joffre: Cooper's Son Who Became Commander-in-Chief* (New York, 1915); Raymond Recouly, *Joffre* (Paris, 1931); and most substantial, Pierre Varillon, *Joffre* (Paris, 1956).

44. In French the "Ecole d'application de l'artillerie et du génie."

45. See General Joffre, *My March to Timbuctoo*, trans. Ernest Dimnet (London, 1915), passim, and on routs of enemy 144–45, 155–57, 168. On the whole series of episodes in Sudan discussed here the fundamental work is Kanya-Forstner's *Conquest of the Western Sudan*, 202–36, quote of Faure 263. See also Kanya-Forstner's "Military Expansion in the Western Sudan—French and British Style," 409–42.

46. See on all this Bernhard, 83–87, and the copious correspondence, reports, and directives in CAOM: Cartons 325 and 425 (Gouvernement de Madagascar), relating to Gallieni's work on the island.

47. See, for example, Conte, 81–88.

48. See CAOM: S.G. Madagascar 185 (Gouvernement de Madagascar) and SD 77, 78 on Diégo-Suarez (Province de Diégo-Suarez: Rapports politiques et administratifs (1900–1917)—which include Joffre's reports and letters.

49. Conte, 97.

50. See Michel, 241, 244, 246; Bernhard, 91–92, 284–85. To sample the clarity and taste of Gallieni's copious writing one could start with a potpourri like Deschamps and Chauvet, eds., *Gallieni pacificateur*.

51. Joseph Gallieni, *Un Noël au Soudan* (Paris, 1924).

52. Didelot, 195–96 is good on this. See also Michel, 262–67.

53. Charbonneau, 171–74; Leblond, vol. 1, 27–31, quotes 27 and 31.

54. See Leblond, vol. 2, 89–92; Michel, 258; Porch, *March to the Marne*, 172–73; and especially, Adolphe Messimy, *Mes souvenirs* (Paris, 1937), 69–79. Messimy praised Gallieni's "vivid imagination" and "very acute sensitivity," also his "very supple and inventive mind" (77). Messimy had become war minister in late June 1911 when the former minister, Maurice Berteaux, was killed watching an airplane "experiment" (70). Charbonnel says Gallieni also recommended Castelnau ahead of Joffre, but he was rejected for being clerical (243).

55. Even Joffre's assistant Castelnau noted bitterly: "It is very regrettable that Gallieni was not nominated generalissimo in 1912 because he had everything necessary for commanding.... He had learned in the colonies how to lead" (Leblond, vol. 1, 75). Liddell Hart remarks: "Gallieni's recommendation of his former subordinate was the one disservice he rendered to France and the worst to himself"

(*Reputations Ten Years After*, 78). The sacked Michel had also realized as early as 1911 that the German invasion route would come through Belgium. See among others, William Seaver Woods' sprightly *Colossal Blunders of the War*, 120. See also here Gallieni, *Les carnets de Gallieni* (Paris, 1922), 19, 22. He noted April 25, 1914, that Clemenceau was calling for him to take Joffre's place (25). On Joffre's girth see Horne, *Price of Glory*, 28–29; and Taylor, 82.

56. *Carnets de Gallieni*, 25, 29. Charbonnel says he would not even consider remarrying, despite names soon proffered by well-wishers (248).

57. See Messimy, 207–24. Gallieni only accepted the latter job when he received absolute authority to act in it. In connection with the post of *adjoint* (or assistant), Messimy notes "the glacial and almost hostile welcome" of Joffre (210). Poincaré's memoirs are much less useful and he demonstrates a certain snobbery toward Gallieni. See especially Raymond Poincaré, *Au service de la France: neuf années de souvenirs*, vol. 8 (Paris, 1931), ch. 3. He did concede that Gallieni was Paris' savior and that he was very popular with Parisians (253). On Gallieni's idea of offering the Germans Madagascar in exchange for the lost provinces and peace, see Bernhard, 102.

58. See Liddell Hart's chapter on Joffre in *Reputations Ten Years After;* Jules Isaac, *Joffre et Lanrezac: étude critique des témoignages sur le rôle de la 5è Armée (août 1914)* (Paris, 1922), critical of Joffre; W. A. Stewart's RAND study *Lanrezac, Joffre, and Plan 17* (Santa Monica, Calif., 1967), pro-Lanrezac, while mostly anti-Joffre; and for Belgian underestimation of an invasion, Archives du Ministère des Affaires Etrangères [hereafter MAE]: Papiers Klobukowski 60—a long report entitled "La Belgique et la Guerre".

59. *Les mémoires du Général Gallieni: Défense de Paris. 25 août-11 septembre, 1914* (Paris, 1920), 22. He wrote the book in 1915 and his children would publish it without altering the text. See also *Les Carnets de Gallieni*, 48 and appropriate sections of the biographies.

60. *Mémoires du Général Gallieni*, 30–35, 46–54, quotes 30; Leblond, *Gallieni parle*, vol. 1, 36–42.

61. *Mémoires du Général Gallieni*, 95–99, quotes 99, 143. See also Michel, ch. 18. Liddell Hart notes that G.Q.G. had gotten the German order for the shift southeast as early as September 2—a copy had been located in the wallet of a dead German officer! (*Reputations Ten Years After*, 84.) Gallieni's peremptory telephoning supposedly included a lapse in politeness. Instead of the normal "Hello, General" he used a more familiar "Hello, so it's you, Joffre" (Henri Isselin, *The Battle of the Marne*, trans. Charles Cornell [London, 1964], 123). Gallieni's reports, letters, and orders are in SHAT: GN52: Fonds Gallieni, including his letters of September 2, 1914, to Maunoury and to Joffre, and his *ordres généraux* no. 4 (September 3) and no. 5 (September 4). The air reconnaissace report by Pilot Chemet and Observer Capt. Allouch in a Blériot 296 is also in same file. To Sir John French Joffre had telegrammed September 2, 1914: "In view of the events of the past two days, I do not believe it possible at present to envisage an overall maneuver on the Marne with the totality of our forces." This damning telegram is in SHAT: 14N16: Fonds Joffre (Ordres et instructions 8 août 1914–26 sept. 1915). See also Liddell Hart, *Reputations Ten Years After*, passim. There is a lot of other archival evidence in the

files that indict Joffre. Joffre's archives are littered with the same gobbledygook on "morale" that the memoirs also contain. On September 6 in a *message téléphoné* to "gen. commandant la 3è Armée" he notes "l'indiscipline" and "des fautes graves," without of course specifying what they are: "Les Etats-Majors ne montrent pas assez d'activité. Les marches ne sont pas réglées soigneusement." We need extra effort in these times, he adds. Many such messages fill up the thick repository of his papers in SHAT: 14N16.

62. *Mémoires de Gallieni*, 162–80; Leblond, vol. 1, 49–56; Cladel, 10.

63. In SHAT: 14N16, we find his typical self-serving, general directives, such as a typed "note personnelle" of September 5, mentioning how the French must throw all "my" troops into battle "et sans réserve, pour conquérir la victoire."

64. Joffre is quoted in Gheusi, *Guerre et théâtre*, 67–68 (letter of September 7 from Joffre to Gallieni); *Mémoires de Gallieni*, 181, 193. On the lack of artillery (including shells) see P. A. Thompson, *Lions Led by Donkeys* (London, 1927), 103, and ch. 10 generally.

65. Gheusi, *Guerre et théâtre*, 244, 76; and Michel, ch. 18. According to Sir John French "The Aisne is a sluggish stream of some 170 feet in breadth, but, being 15 feet deep in the centre, it is unfordable." He goes on to describe the German position as dominating high ground, yet nicely camouflaged. See French, *The Despatches of Lord French* (London, 1917), 31. The broken ground of the banks and the steep wooded slopes are also approvingly described by Alexander von Kluck in *The March on Paris and the Battle of the Marne 1914* (London, 1920), 157.

66. Taylor, 23. At the time the President of the Republic in Bordeaux wondered as well about Joffre simply ending the pursuit. See his conversation with Colonel Emile Herbillon in Herbillon, *Souvenirs d'un officier de liaison pendant la guerre mondiale*, vol. 1 (Paris, 1930), 34–35. On the German occupation that resulted at least in part from Joffre's errors we have a useful study that shows how harrowing things became in Lille and other cities, towns, and villages of the French area held by the enemy through the war. Huge requisitions and food shortages, censorship, numerous imprisonments, and a drop in population remind one of the more celebrated Occupation one war later. See Helen McPhail, *The Long Silence: Civilian Life under the German Occupation of Northern France, 1914–1918* (London, 1999).

67. *Carnets de Gallieni*, 122, 130; *Le Temps* article of November 27, 1914. Sir John French was definitely bamboozled by his colleague Joffre, declaring that "the name of Marshal Joffre will descend to posterity with that battle [of the Marne] as one of the greatest military commanders in history" (French, *1914* [Boston, 1919], 143). Raymond Recouly, the journalist, was another in the Joffre camp who used panegyrics, noting that Joffre foresaw the Marne from August 25 and had "great moral elevation" (Recouly [Captain X], *General Joffre and His Battles* [New York, 1916], 13–14, quote 24). More even-handed is General René Alexandre in a postwar memoir: "Gallieni, Joffre, chacun à sa place, chacun dans son rôle, ont également mérité de la patrie" (Alexandre, *Avec Joffre d'Agadir à Verdun: souvenirs 1911–1916* [Paris, 1932], 143). More scandalously pro-Joffre given publication date and his scholarly background is Pierre Miquel's speech published as a short book: *Joffre: la volonté de vaincre* (Paris, 1984).

68. Martin S. Alexander, *The Republic in Danger: General Maurice Gamelin and the Politics of French Defence, 1933–1940* (Cambridge, U.K., 1992), 17.

69. Gamelin, *Manoeuvre et victoire de la Marne* (Paris, 1954), 10, quotes 192, 214.

70. One copy, unpaginated, in SHAT: GN55: Fonds Clemenceau.

71. MAE: Archives Diplomatiques 1005.

72. See Captain Pierre Lyet, *Joffre et Gallieni à la Marne* (Paris, 1938), vii–xii, quote xii. Joffre's narrative told to Bernard Desouches late in the war was then revised by Major Desmazes, chief of the marshal's personal staff and appeared in Marshal Joffre et al., *The Two Battles of the Marne* (London, 1927), 19, 29, 30, 34. In this narrative Joffre mentions Gallieni's name once (34). Charbonnel says that as late as the 1950s Gallieni's name was absent in classes given on the Marne at the Ecole de Guerre (292). See also the insufficiencies of Maxime Weygand's *Mémoires: idéal vécu* vol. 1 (Paris, 1953). And of course Joffre's own "memoirs" were ghostwritten by sympathetic subordinates and need to be used with caution. A handy English translation is *The Personal Memoirs of Joffre*, trans. T. Bentley Mott (New York, 1932). Henry Contamine in several confusing pages also reveals the bias of Lyet and the Service historique, as well as archival lacunae, yet will not commit himself clearly to a pro-Gallieni stand. See Contamine, *La victoire de la Marne* (Paris, 1970), 267–75.

73. Pierre B. Gheusi, *La gloire de Gallieni: comment Paris fût sauvé* (Paris, 1928), 92–94, 101 and Kitchener quote, 143. Gheusi notes an "offensive de fausses légendes," very much like Liddell Hart (49). Again, that legend has influenced more recent historians. Compare the pro-Gallieni Liddell Hart in the book cited above or in his *The Real War 1914–1918* (Boston, 1930) to, say, Corelli Barnett's *The Sword Bearers: Studies in Supreme Command in the First World War* (London, 1963), which gives Gallieni short shrift. As for von Kluck, his memoir on the Marne gives Gallieni prime credit for the turnaround, but bases it on what he heard and read (von Kluck, 115).

74. Adolphe Goutard, *La Marne: Victoire inexploitée* (Paris, 1968); *Mémoires de Gallieni*, 197, 195. Goutard's book has a preface by Liddell Hart, both averring that Joffre didn't know what he had. Goutard wrote also of the missed opportunities of 1940. Charbonnel's discussion (by a man on Gallieni's staff) is also very good (300–12), in which he begins a section on "The Campaign of Lies," including archive-destroying! Serving in a 1915 offensive with another great colonial, Marchand, Charbonnel astonished the latter with the truth of the Marne, vis-à-vis the "official version." (366). Even pro-Joffre historians like Robert B. Asprey in his *The First Battle of the Marne* (Philadelphia, 1962) acknowledge the missed opportunity. "Had the rupture between Kluck and Bülow been exploited . . . nothing in the world could have saved the German line" (163). General René Chambe is much firmer in his confirmation of Goutard, declaring that the lack of a young, vivacious leader and the inability or refusal to finish off Kluck's reeling left "sur place" were fatal to the French. Chambe, *Adieu cavalerie! La Marne, bataille gagnée . . . victoire perdue* (Paris, 1979), 281.

75. *Carnets de Gallieni*, September 3 and September 17, 1914 (95, 98, 99–111); December 2 (123) and December 9 (126), as well as January 17, 1915 (137) on Joffre. On not "making the hole," see Leblond, vol. 1, 78 (conversation of October 10,

1914). On Millerand, the war minister: "Very happy with himself" (*Carnets de Gallieni*, November 5, 1914 [117]). See also entry of November 21, 1914: "What guilty people our ministers and General Joffre!" (120).

76. In SHAT: 14N16.

77. Michel, 283; *Carnets de Gallieni*, 139, 141; and Horne, *Price of Glory*, 32.

78. On this period see Leblond, vol. 2, 57–78; on the Balkans, citing Joffre to Briand in March, 1915: "That's a personal ambition of Gallieni, who wants a command . . . I am sure of breaking through (*percer*) and of sending the Germans back home" (57–58). See also *Carnets de Gallieni*, 151–94 and Leblond, vol. 1, 79 (for the "folle ambition" quote). Michel says little about the Dardanelles conception before he gets to October 1915.

79. See especially Gallieni's wartime diaries *Carnets de Gallieni*, passim.

80. Blanchon, 23; Gabriel Hanotaux, *Joffre* (Paris, 1921), 59; Lieutenant Colonel Jean Fabry, *Joffre et son destin* (Paris, 1931), 54–57, 64; Gabriel Terrail, *Joffre: la première crise du commandement (novembre 1915–décembre 1916)* (Paris, 1919), 2; Henry Bordeaux, *Joffre ou l'art de commander* (Paris, 1933), 70, 88.

81. Both anecdotes and quotations in Jean d'Esme, *Le père Joffre* (Paris, 1962), 107–8.

82. René Benjamin, *Grandes Figures: Barrès, Joffre* (Paris, 1931), 195, 202; Emile Hinzelin, *Notre Joffre: Maréchal de France* (Paris, 1917), 8, 10. Cf. Blanchon, 26: "His life is regulated like a monk's." D'Esme, *Le père Joffre*, 245–46. Cf. B. H. Liddell Hart: "His staff learnt that it was better to sacrifice duty than to be late for meals, and only in emergency would they dare to disturb him after he had retired to bed at ten o'clock" (Liddell Hart, *Through the Fog of War* [London, 1938], 126). See also Contamine La Tour, *Joffre: sa vie, son oeuvre* (Paris, 1919), 38. Once he was taken to an ambulance to award a medal to a soldier blinded in battle. He then told the division general not to take him to such places again, for "I could never sign another attack order!" (Fabry, 16).

83. Alphonse Séché, *Le Général Joffre* (Paris, n.d.), 22; Owen Johnson, *The Spirit of France* (Boston, 1916), 187–88, 204.

84. *Personal Memoirs of Joffre*, vol. 2, 394, 341, 345.

85. Quotations in *Personal Memoirs* of Joffre, vol. 2, 352, 353; 359–60. Cf. A. J. P. Taylor: "He [Joffre] went on demanding just one more attack, convinced each time that it would be decisive. These so-called battles have no meaning except as names on a war memorial: 50,000 French lost in February, nibbling 500 yards forward in Champagne; another 60,000 lost at Saint-Mihiel; 120,000 lost in May near Arras" (62–63).

86. See SHAT: Etat-Major de l'armée. Service historique. *Les armées françaises dans la grande guerre*, vol. 2 (Paris, 1930), 453–81. See Joffre quoted 479.

87. In SHAT: 14N12 (Instructions diverses).

88. Joffre to War Min. October 3, 1915, in SHAT: 14N16.

89. See SHAT: 14N12, under "Instructions diverses." Joffre December 15 and 27, 1915, in *Armées françaises de la grande guerre*, vol. 3, 580–81. On Joffre's sweet-talking to Parliament during 1915, see *The Memoirs of Raymond Poincaré 1915*, trans. George Arthur, vol. 3 (London, 1930), passim.

90. People who said the right thing included General de Langle de Cary,

commander of the 4th army, in a secret report of November 12, 1915, on the Champagne offensives. One could also cite de Castelnau's report (October 27) of over forty pages long. The commander of the 8th Battalion of Chasseurs after Champagne (October 31) also retailed "Joffreisms" on morale, and how commanders must "require that soldiers carry their heads high," as if posture could defeat machine guns. Foch too was almost as adept as the master at such generalities. Reports in SHAT: 16N1974 (Journaux de Marche, World War I) and see also *The Memoirs of Marshal Foch,* trans. Col. T. Bentley Mott (Garden City, N.Y., 1931), passim.

91. Reports are in SHAT: 16N1974. See Méalin's dossier in SHAT: 3YB500 (Chasseurs à Pied 16th Battalion) and subsequent material in SHAT: 16N1974 and notes on Compagnon's career in G.D. 60213. Compagnon's report was of November 10, 1915. Since he was born in 1856 his "relève de fonctions" of February 2, 1917 might be laid to age. He spent some time in another position and in Algeria, and was completely retired in 1919.

92. Leblond, vol. 1, 88–94 and Michel on his hopes, 288–91.

93. Thierry's letter of January 13, 1916, in SHAT: GN52. So are Messimy's report and Gallieni's summary (February 21, 1916) of Favre's resolution.

94. During the fall of 1915 Generals French, Rawlinson, and Haig were *all* reluctant to help Joffre by attacking the German line at Loos. Recalling the entire tragic year of 1915, David Lloyd George discussed "that climax of stubborn folly—the Champagne attack, which was repelled with a loss of 200,000." He went on to note that "Joffre was at that time the unchallenged dictator as far as the War direction was concerned"—and of course anything but enlightened. See Robin Prior and Trevor Wilson, *Command on the Western Front: The Military Career of Sir Henry Rawlinson 1914–1918* (Oxford, 1992), 104–5; Philip Warner, *The Battle of Loos* (London, 1976), 6–7 and passim; and *War Memoirs of David Lloyd George 1914– 1915,* vol. 1 (Boston, 1933), quotes 352–53. The last two reports on the Dardanelles, labelled "secret," are found in SHAT: GN52. On Joffre and the fall 1915 Salonika campaign, very costly to the Serbs among many others, see Roy A. Prete's definitive article, "Imbroglio par Excellence: Mounting the Salonika Campaign, September–October 1915," *War and Society* 19 (May 2001): 47–70. Prete contrasts the stubborn Joffre to the prophetic Kitchener here.

95. Leblond, vol. 1, 109, 177–260; quote in Gheusi, *Guerre et théâtre,* 260; Michel, 293. The Foch anecdote is in Charbonnel, 416. Charbonnel was there as Gallieni's aide.

96. Leblond, vol. 1, 117, 129–31, 138. He says, "the colonies were the great school … (214). See also Leblond, vol. 2, 17–18; and Charbonnel, 405–7, 403, showing no paper on Gallieni's own desk and another reform he contemplated—better promotion procedures for officers.

97. Leblond, vol. 2, 174, and for doctors, fatigue, and so on, 82–174. On the plus side Gallieni was very proud of women working in munitions (127).

98. See Blond, 26, and on the declassing of Verdun and Joffre's betrayal of the conceptions of Rivières, H. E. W. Strachan, "Military Modernization 1789–1918" in *The Oxford History of Modern Europe,* T. C. W. Blanning, ed. (Oxford, 2000), 92–93, as well as standard biographical treatments.

99. See some of Gallieni's typical instructions on cutting bureaucracy in SHAT: GN52. For example, "instruction" of January 18, 1916, on "la décentralisation administrative et la simplification des écritures et de la correspondance."

100. *Personal Memoirs of Joffre*, vol. 2, 445, 447.

101. The easiness of that examination for, say, Parisians vis-à-vis those actually dying in the fog of Verdun or screaming at makeshift hospitals is well perceived by contrasting appropriate pages of Horne's *The Price of Glory* with those on the scene in wartime Paris given by Simone de Beauvoir in her *Memoirs of a Dutiful Daughter*.

102. See documents like his "Note au sujet de l'organisation du terrain en cours d'une bataille" and his "Note pour les Armées" of July 16, 1916, and a third one two days later, as well as many others in SHAT: 14N12.

103. Joffre's Ordre General no. 65 July 31, 1916, "SOLDATS de la République!" in SHAT: 14N12. A hard-hitting memoir written by Lieutenant-Colonel d'Artillerie B.H.M. riddles Joffre for his phoniness with soldiers: "Personne ne peut soutenir qu'il aimait le soldat ... Et il n'était pas aimé de lui; sur le front on était d'accord pour l'ignorer ..." (his ellipses). This memoir-writer considered Joffre "le chef qui a froidement présidé pendant deux ans à des hécatombes aussi sanglantes qu'inutiles" and a man "d'un profond égoïsme, d'une grande fatuité; et cependant dans le domaine stratégique, d'un savoir vague." *La vérité sur la guerre 1914–1918*, vol. 1 (Paris, 1930), quotes 41, 42, 45. Despite the veiled authorial name the book was published by the respected Paris firm of Albin Michel.

104. Leblond, vol. 2, 34–51, 177–89; Charbonnel, 409–10 on Clemenceau's admiration for Gallieni and distaste for Joffre.

105. Gheusi, *Gloire de Gallieni*, 160–61; Didelot, 240 on leaves and care of men; Leblond, vol. 2, 150–51, also cited by Michel, 304–35.

106. *Carnets de Gallieni*, 293, 297, 300, 301.

107. See D'Esme, *Gallieni*, 307–11; and Michel, 316–17, as well as the affecting memoir of Charbonnel, who stayed constantly by Gallieni's side during his last weeks and was plunged into depression by his death (Charbonnel, 433–50). He mentions how Gallieni's last testament, read aloud by André Maginot in the Chamber and sharply critical of Briand, continued to provoke posthumous controversy. On Gallieni in wartime our views and research predated a careful reading of Bernhard's biography, but among modern biographers he comes closest to our feelings about Gallieni versus Joffre, using some (but far from all) of the same material to buttress his position; however, we are the first to see Joffre as a clinical narcissist.

108. See, however, General Nivelle's reports in SHAT: 16N1977 with all the stock phrases like "un tel succès ne s'improvise pas." And "Les Adieux du Gen. Nivelle à son armée" of Verdun in the same file sound very much like Joffre: "L'expérience est concluante. Notre méthode a fait ses preuves." Again, the French army shows "son ascendant moral et matériel sur l'ennemi." There are many reports on Verdun in here, some over thirty pages. One witness writing on October 25 at Verdun's conclusion notes how in four hours Germany's work of eight months was undone!

109. *Personal Memoirs of Joffre*, vol. 2, 466–69. That Haig was pushed by Joffre to an early engagement on the Somme is the opinion of Robert Blake in his

introduction to *The Private Papers of Douglas Haig 1914–1919* (London, 1952), 53. Haig himself notes a red-faced Joffre outburst at the beginning of operations, followed by sweet apology: 154–55. He also notes that "the poor man cannot easily read a map" (154).

110. *Personal Memoirs of Joffre*, vol. 2, 477. Meanwhile other "Joffreistes" continued to churn out their own empty reports and instructions in the era of the Somme. Foch's typed plans before the battle began were very detailed and thick, and full of wind, such as, "A un tir de préparations, répondre par un tir de contre-préparations immédiat et plus violent que celui de l'ennemi" (Operation Orders in SHAT: 14N48: Fonds Foch, on the Battle of the Somme). Even after the massacre had decimated so many, Gen. Fayolle in his Note pour les Commandants de Corps d'Armée (October 29, 1916) was retailing more Joffreisms: "Ce qu'il faut assurer tout d'abord c'est la destruction de la première position, puisque c'est celle qu'il faut franchir avant de marcher à l'attaque de la seconde" (in SHAT: 14N48). See also Gen. Foch, Commandant le Groupe d'Armees du Nord to Commander of 6th Army, June 1, 1916, before the massacre: "Il est en autre indispensable que les actions offensives pour l'enlèvement des positions successives de l'ennemi soient nettement définies dans le temps et l'espace." See also secret note in ibid. on meeting of Foch, Gen. Rawlinson, and Gen. Fayolle June 16, 1916, and their sad attack plans. Incredibly Foch was still talking in October of "la rapidité avec laquelle seront renouvellées les actions offensives ... [pour obtenir] la désorganisation complète de l'ennemi" (October 17, 1916, Foch Note for Gen. Commander of 6th Army). If it were so easy, one wonders why it hadn't happened! But to be fair, Foch *was* starting to evolve in favor of sparing men and trying other things. But a fifty-one-page report issued after the debacle of the Somme by another Joffreiste ("approuvé par Joffre") on artillery use in the offensive (December 11, 1916) again talked patronizingly and unrealistically of experience, showing how well-prepared artillery attacks could lead to success against enemy positions! (SHAT: 16N1977).

111. See Maxime Weygand, *Mémoires: idéal vécu*, vol. 1 (Paris, 1953), 357–58; Gregor Dallas, *At the Heart of a Tiger: Clemenceau and His World 1841–1929* (London, 1993), 459; Jonathan Nicholls, *Cheerful Sacrifice: The Battle of Arras* (London, 1990) on how after Verdun "the French had finally ditched the solid old buffer, General Joffre, who by his uncontested leadership and prestige had for so long dominated the conduct of the war"; and *Personal Memoirs of Joffre*, vol. 2, 515–58, quote 559.

112. See *Personal Memoirs of Joffre*, vol. 1, 250 and also on the Gallieni phone call during the Marne, Henri Isselin, *The Battle of the Marne*, trans. Charles Cornell (London, 1964), 123. Cf. Tuchman: "Gallieni would not talk to anyone less than Joffre and Joffre would not come to the phone. He had an aversion to the instrument and used to pretend that he 'did not understand the mechanism.' His real reason was that, like all men in high position he ... was afraid that things said over the telephone would be taken down without his being able to control the [historical] record" (422–23).

113. *Personal Memoirs of Joffre*, vol. 2, 392–93, quote 392. Joffre also received decorations from colonial authorities like the Emperor of Annam in 1915. To the

Résident Supérieur of the French Republic of Annam Joffre replied March 18, 1915: "Je suis profondément touché de cette marque de sympathie et des appréciations flatteuses." (It was a beautiful decoration with gold on it and silk-sewn Chinese characters.) See also Res. Sup. of Annam to War Min. January 26, 1915 (from Hué). Both letters in CAOM: Amiraux 1881–.

114. See Painlevé to Joffre, April 13, 1917, and Tessan's report, as well as report from Etat-Major to War Min. April 14, 1917 (SHAT: 14N25, Mission du Maréchal Joffre aux Etats-Unis). See also *Notes d'un témoin: les grands jours en Amérique: mission Viviani-Joffre (avril–mai 1917)* (Paris, 1917), passim, headline quoted 154. Joffre's own recollections are in *Personal Memoirs of Joffre*, vol. 2, 568–80. Joffre's speeches translated into English are found in Francis Halsey, *Balfour, Viviani, and Joffre: Their Speeches and Other Public Utterances in America* (New York, 1917). It should be added that the mission was partly conceived to procure American loans for France. See Col. Red Reeder, *Bold Leaders of World War I* (Boston, 1974), 37.

115. See Tessan report in *Personal Memoirs of Joffre*, vol. 2, including Joffre quote.

116. See the many letters and telegrams in SHAT: 14N25, as well as General John Pershing, *My Experiences in the World War* (New York, 1931), quote 72, 97.

117. Conte, 429–32, quote 430.

118. Conte, 439.

119. See CAOM: 39621 (Fonds du gouvernement général de l'Indochine) on Joffre's visit, especially to Siam. See also SHAT: 14N46 (Fonds Joffre) on his trip to the Far East 1921–22.

120. All letters in SHAT: 14N46. American worship of Joffre was partly due to postwar books like Mary R. Parkman, *Fighters for Peace* (New York, 1919); Charles H. L. Johnston, *Famous Generals of the Great War* (Boston, 1919); Mary H. Wade, *Leaders to Liberty* (Boston, 1919); J. Walker McSpadden, *Boy's Book of Famous Soldiers* (New York, 1919); and Cora W. Rowell, *Leaders of the Great War* (New York, 1919), all with laudatory chapters on Joffre.

121. Conte, 461. On Joffre's composition of the memoirs, cf. Varillon, 596: "Comme il l'avait toujours fait, il parlait avec ses collaborateurs qui lui soumettaient un texte, il retouchait, allégeait, précisait." He even signed every manuscript page!

122. The poem begins:

> Petit Franc, les yeux clos, repose dans son lit
> Assise à son chevet, France, sa mère lit.
> Les veilles sur ses traits ont signé leur empreinte.
> Mais sa robuste foi, flamme jamais éteinte,
> Rehausse, dans les jours qu'assombrille le malheur . . .
> (Little Franc lies in bed, closing his eyes
> His mother, France, reads by his bedside.
> The wakeful nights have marked her face
> But the flame of her faith cannot be erased
> Shining all the brighter as evil darkens the days . . .)

All this material is in SHAT: 14N47 (Fonds Joffre).

123. See CAOM: 43572 ("Décès du Maréchal Joffre).

5. LYAUTEY

1. On Lyautey one could still start with the elegant older treatments of André Maurois, *Marshal Lyautey*, trans. Hamish Miles; London, 1931), which Lyautey sanctioned, and Sonia E. Howe, *Lyautey of Morocco* (London, 1931). General Maurice Durosoy's *Lyautey: Maréchal de France 1854–1934* (Limoges, 1984) is a relatively good introduction with many pictures. Gilbert Mercier, *Lyautey: le Prince Lorrain* (Jarville–La Malgrange, 1994) is useful for the copious pictures alone. Marcel Cordier, *Un grand Lorrain: Lyautey* (Saint-Seine-l'Abbaye, 1984) is slim. André le Révérend, *Lyautey* is balanced and solid, but his doctoral dissertation, "Lyautey écrivain 1854–1934," is much better documented. There is some biographical detail in Hoisington, *Lyautey and the French Conquest of Morocco*. Venier's *Lyautey avant Lyautey* is again best on this proconsul's early life and on his pre-Moroccan colonial activities. It entirely supersedes the misleadingly titled book by François Roux, *La jeunesse de Lyautey* (Paris, 1952). In the same year as Venier's book, Hervé de Charette brought out *Lyautey* (Paris, 1997), one of those French treatments with no bibliography and hardly any references, but clear and easy to read. Other, older biographical studies of Lyautey are noted below. Among the most hagiographic: Pierre Espérandieu, *Lyautey et le Protectorat* (Paris, 1947) and the well-written book of Henry-Louis Dubly, *Lyautey le magicien* (Lille, 1931).

2. The best source on Aunt Berthe is AN: 475 AP/243: Fonds Lyautey—"Souvenirs de famille," "Ma lignée maternelle." This same bulging carton contains a lot as well on his paternal side and influences. In terms of regionality his maternal side starting in Normandy always showed a rebellious, *frondeur* spirit, including a bout with Protestantism in the sixteenth century. Biographies above are also sources of preceding detail on Lyautey's life. Venier is the only one giving credence to another theory on Lyautey's health problems—that they might have stemmed in part from a tubercular lumbar condition (Venier, 27).

3. For an account of the early years of this elite Jesuit school, see John W. Langdon, "New Light on the Influence of the Jesuit Schools: The Ecole Saint-Geneviève and its Graduates, 1854–1913," *Third Republic/Troisième République* 1 (1976): 132–51. For Lyautey's background and young life to this point the best archival source is the Fonds Lyautey.

4. Quoted in Patrick Heidsieck, "Lyautey et les rapports Franco-Musulmans," *Etudes* (October 1954), 67. For other detail here see Lyautey's *Notes de jeunesse*, May 7, 1875, in *Rayonnement de Lyautey*, Patrick Heidsieck ed. (Paris, 1941), 47. There are biographies of key figures Lyautey knew, such as Bernard Auffray on the Margerie family in *Pierre de Margerie 1861–1942 et la vie diplomatique de son temps* (Paris, 1976).

5. See AN: 475/AP/10 (Fonds Lyautey): Etudes: dissertations et philosophies, etc. Quotations from his "Notes quotidiennes" at Saint-Cyr, May 26, 1875. The continual self-harassment is seen in his note of August 14, 1875, where he distinguishes between facility and intelligence, considering intelligence or understanding a higher quality. "Grand Dieu, je viens d'écrire ce qui précède au moment d'un examen de théorie, c'est à dire quand il me faut absorber en deux jours 800 pages ... pourvu que la facilité ne se venge pas de ce que je viens de sembler la

dédaigner." On Prosper Keller see Lyautey's note at Rethel August 10, 1877, noting that he had seen Prosper the night before. In his typically prolix way Lyautey writes: "Voilà un garçon qui est tout ce que j'aime, Dieu le sait, et je le persécute comme jamais personne, ou je me colle à lui de manière à l'encombrer de mon affection bruyante et expansive, je l'en fatigue, et le lendemain je l'assomme encore bien davantage en public par ... des coquetteries aussi ridicules qu'inutiles pour conclure le surlendemain par une tempête. Puis je reparcours le cycle."

6. Lyautey to his sister May 25, 1882 in his *Choix de lettres 1882–1919* (Paris, 1947), 3.

7. Letters of February 12, 1878 and December 14, 1880 to his father in *Un Lyautey inconnu: correspondance et journal inédits 1874–1934*, André le Révérend ed. (Paris, 1980), 5, 73, 75–76.

8. For quotations see Lyautey's letters to his father, March 23, 1881, and to de Margerie in Le Révérend, *Un Lyautey inconnu*, 87, 95; see also Hoisington, *Lyautey and the French Conquest of Morocco*, 2–4; as well as Venier, 37. A good source showing Lyautey's tireless linguistic work, including on Arabic, is AN: 475 AP/12 (Fonds Lyautey): Cahiers concernant l'apprentissage des langues étrangères, which contains more musty notebooks.

9. See SHAT: M.F.4 (Maréchaux de France) Lyautey dossier—Lyautey's letter of February 8, 1883, to War Min. asking for the leave in return for a detailed report, and see War Min. to Lyautey (in the 4th regiment of chasseurs), December 24, 1883, expressing their pleasure with the *mémoire* he had written and how well he had used his leave abroad.

10. In book form we have used the following edition, which also contains another of his key works: *Du rôle social de l'officier et du rôle colonial de l'armée* (Paris, 1946).

11. See SHAT: M.F.4 for representative reports by the *inspection générale;* for example, 1887 ("Il monte bien et vigoureusement à cheval"); 1888 ("Lyautey est plein d'entrain, d'un zèle exceptionnel, il a le feu sacré ... travailleur indefatigable"); 1890 ("beaucoup d'avenir"). See also in ibid., War Min. May 18, 1893, note for Direction de la Cavalerie (1ère Bureau), granting Lyautey the authorization to use the rest of a leave hitherto spent in Paris on a tour of Berlin, Bucharest, Budapest, Athens, Palermo, etc. For his celebrity deriving from "Du rôle social," see Venier, 46–48.

12. Letter of October 16, 1894 in Lyautey, *Lettres du Tonkin et de Madagascar (1894–1899)* (Paris, 1921), 12; and letter to Margerie, June 23, 1895, 212 and to Jacques Silhol, November 27, 1904, in *Vers le Maroc: lettres du Sud-Oranais 1903–1906* (Paris, 1937), 133. In the latter he attacked both ultramontanism and freemasonry. On the influence of de Lanessan and other colonial theorists on Lyautey, see Venier, 63–71.

13. CAOM: Etat-Major, Archives de l'Indochine (1–32), Lyautey's letter of January 16, 1896, to gen. commandant en chef des Troupes de l'Indochine, Hanoi.

14. See the standard biographies for this detail.

15. Lyautey letter of February 17, 1895 to his sister in *Lettres du Tonkin et de Madagascar*, 141.

16. Letters of February 23 and February 27, 1895 to his sister in *Lettres du Tonkin*

et de Madagascar, 148, 154, and standard biographies of Lyautey and Gallieni for other detail.

17. Letter of June 12, 1895 in *Lettres du Tonkin et de Madagascar,* 207 and letter of November 10, 1901 from Fianarantsoa in *Lettres du Sud de Madagascar 1900–1902* (Paris, 1935), 189, as well as standard biographies for other detail.

18. See Lyautey to his sister January 8, 1895 in *Lettres du Tonkin et de Madagascar,* 106; letter to Antonin de Margerie, March 7, 1895 in *Intimate Letters from Tonquin,* trans. Aubrey Le Blond (London, 1932), 156–57; Robert Garric, *Le Message de Lyautey* (Paris, 1964), 100; and Lyautey to Paul Desjardins, August 9, 1905 in *Vers le Maroc,* 228. For a critique of the Gallieni-Lyautey method of producing "security," see on disturbances in Madagascar during the 1890s, Ellis, "Political Elite of Imerina."

19. CAOM: E.M. Indochine (1–32). Col. Vallières to Gen. Commandant Hanoi, March 2, 1896 on Lyautey mission and March 22, 1896 on its successful conclusion. Lyautey's long report of his interview with Chinese authorities, dated March 30, 1896 is in the same source, as is the report on organization of territory and the treaty.

20. Lyautey to his brother March 9, 1896 in his *Intimate Letters from Tonquin,* 304.

21. Lyautey to his sister, March 9, 1898 in *Lettres du Tonkin et de Madagascar,* 565; and Venier, 91–104.

22. These themes came out in a speech he made in Paris, February 19, 1900 in AN: 475 AP 250 (Fonds Lyautey): Discours, allocations, toasts 1900–1916. Later speeches would contain the same message; for example, one he made at Oran, July 12, 1907 noting that North Africa is to the French "ce qu'est le Far West pour l'Amérique, c'est à dire le champ par excellence de l'énergie, du rajeunissement et de la fécondité." He went on to call the colonial life "la plus belle école de l'énergie," far from the "déchirements de la Métropole" (Lyautey, *Paroles d'action,* 52–54).

23. Lyautey, *Lettres du Sud de Madagascar,* 43.

24. Letter of Lyautey in *Lettres du Sud de Madagascar,* 130–31. Typical Lyautey speeches were one given at a *vin d'honneur* for the colonists in Fianarantsoa (October 1900), another at the inauguration of a nursery school there (August 1901), and another at the inauguration of a first French public school there (October 1901). See text of these speeches in AN: 475 AP 250.

25. First quotes in CAOM: SD95: Gouvernement de Madagascar. Commandement du Sud; see also *Lettres du Sud de Madagascar,* Lyautey's Rapport d'ensemble sur la situation politique en 1902, April 4, 1902.

26. First letter Gallieni to Lyautey of May 2, 1902 in CAOM: SD95; second letter, gov.-gen. to War Min., June 4, 1902, in SHAT: M.F.4; last letter in same source. On Lyautey in Madagascar generally, see Venier, ch. 3. An excellent comparision of Gallieni's and Lyautey's personalities is in AN: 429 Mi 1: Souvenirs du Général Aubert. Charles Aubert worked and fought in Tonkin and Madagascar under Gallieni, first protecting rail construction in North Vietnam from pirates, and later in Morocco under Lyautey. For him Gallieni was an operational genius, superior militarily to Lyautey, and in fact the "personnalité militaire la plus remarquable qui se pût rencontrer" (66). When it came to the Marne he would unambiguously

give full credit to Gallieni, believing it an "éclair de génie" (276). He concludes that one would have to be a great writer to "faire ressortir la qualité rare d'un Gallieni ... la hauteur de son génie" (315). In Lyautey he saw a fine administrator and someone of great courtesy and distinction, with the "goûts affinés d'artiste" (318). Aubert himself was lucky to be alive in the 1930s to produce this memoir in retirement, hoping that other shoulders would take on the Nazis. In his own cultured way he noted that "en 1930, 232 des nôtres [de Saint-Cyr] sont encore en ce bas monde." While "231 ont bouclé leur sac pour un monde réputé meilleur," many lost in colonial engagements.

27. See the standard biographies.

28. Theodore Zeldin, *France 1848–1945: Anxiety and Hypocrisy* (New York, 1981), 168. Lyautey's first important victory over Paris would be his final victory over Delcassé on the militarization of the Moroccan-Algerian border. See on this Kim Munholland, "Rival Approaches to Morocco: Delcassé, Lyautey and the Algerian-Moroccan Border, 1903–1905," *French Historical Studies* 5 (Spring 1968): 328–43.

29. Lyautey letter of February 9, 1895 in his *Lettres du Tonkin et de Madagascar*, 123; letters to his sister November 11, 1903 and November 20, 1903 in Lyautey, *Vers le Maroc*, 11, 28; and to Max Leclerc, 46.

30. See Nevill Barbour, *Morocco* (New York, 1966), chs. 1, 7; Porch, *Conquest of Morocco*, chs. 1–4; and Gershovich, ch. 2.

31. See Porch, *Conquest of Morocco*, relevant parts of chs. 4, 7.

32. See officer's report on Lyautey of 1904 in SHAT: M.F.4. "General Lyautey is a fine-looking man, with an agreeable, friendly face, a perfect *homme du monde*, very attractive in every way. A truly subtle mind; of superior intelligence; gifted with an extraordinary capacity for work.... He will be one of our most outstanding generals."

33. See early letters on all this to Margerie, November 18, 1880 and to his father, September 1, 1882 in *Les plus belles lettres de Lyautey*, Pierre Lyautey, ed., 21–24. At that time he was spending two to three hours a day on Arabic.

34. Letter of December 12, 1903, in Lyautey, *Vers le Maroc*, 135. This openness is another reason he was pro-Dreyfus earlier than most in his military caste. See Venier, 146–48. Cf. also Georges Hardy (who knew him well): "Lyautey a des amis de toutes opinions, de toutes confessions, de toutes races." And: "Nul ne fut moins chauvin" in Hardy, *Portrait de Lyautey* (Paris, 1949), 54–55, 59.

35. For the foregoing see Porch, *Conquest of Morocco*, ch. 12–14; Hoisington, *Lyautey and the French Conquest of Morocco*, ch. 2; Venier, ch. 5; and Ross E. Dunn, *Resistance in the Desert: Moroccan Responses to French Imperialism 1881–1912* (London, 1977). On the Glaouis see Gavin Maxwell, *Lords of the Atlas* (New York, 1966).

36. Cyril Connolly would also discuss the difficulties for "artists" like Lyautey who contemplated marriage: "The greatest charm of marriage, in fact that which makes it irresistible ... is the duologue, the permanent conversation between two people which talks over everything and everyone till death breaks the record ... but for the artist it may prove dangerous; he is one of those who must look alone out of the window, and for him to enter into ... the non-stop performance of a lifetime, is a kind of exquisite dissipation which ... is likely to deprive him of

those much rarer moments which are particularly his own" (Connolly, *The Unquiet Grave* [New York, 1945], 54).

37. See Le Révérend, *Lyautey écrivain*, 173–74 and his *Lyautey*, 334–37, 411–13.

38. See AN: 246 AP 45: Papiers Fortoul, Bourgoing, Lyautey 1895–1921.

39. Porch, *Conquest of Morocco*, 85–86; Christian Gury, *Lyautey-Charlus* (Paris, 1998).

40. See Porch, *Conquest of Morocco*, 131–32; Cecily Mackworth, *The Destiny of Isabelle Eberhardt* (London, 1951); and Sharon Bangert's preface to Eberhardt's diary, *In the Shadow of Islam*, trans. Bangert (London, 1993). The diary shows that Eberhardt also became a kind of feminist ahead of her time, wondering when her sex could cease being either slaves or idols.

41. Chamber of Commerce appreciation of Lyautey in SHAT: M.F.4. Lyautey himself showed a great awareness of the historical "lineage," giving the keynote speech at the inauguration of a monument for General Lamoricière in Tiaret, May 8, 1910. He saluted the creator of the *zouaves*, the first chief of the *bureaux arabes* in Algiers, and a great soldier who "loved war, but noble war." He went on: "Avec Bugeaud [Lamoricière] a été chef d'Ecole, de l'école glorieuse et bien française des chefs coloniaux avisés et clairvoyants" (AN: 475 AP 250).

42. Jean Martin, *L'empire triomphant: l'aventure coloniale de la France*, vol. 2 (Paris, 1990), 141. On Lyautey's rise to power in Morocco see Gershovich, ch. 2, and on the genesis of the protectorate idea, 22–23. A recent monograph by Paul Doury, *Lyautey: un saharien atypique* (Paris, 2002) argues that Morocco and the idea of modernization there changed Lyautey. Doury feels that Algeria, and in particular the Sahara, were Lyautey's first loves colonially.

43. See Hoisington, *Lyautey and the French Conquest of Morocco*, 42–73, quote (on Taza) 64. On the aggressive Mangin, whom Lyautey feared as a rival and as a "Napoleon" in Morocco, see Gershovich, 11, 94–100.

44. See texts of May 31 (for letter cited in previous paragraph from Fez); August 23, 1912, for latter quote in Pierre Lyautey, ed., *Lyautey l'africain: textes et lettres du Maréchal Lyautey*, vol. 1 (Paris, 1953), 30–31; April 23, 1913, from Rabat (264); preface in vol. 2 (Paris, 1954), i. For detailed plans creating the European city of Rabat, and Lyautey's very careful designations of what to preserve (from the sultan's gardens to the gate of the Casbah), see the file AN: 475 AP 114 (Fonds Lyautey) with a good deal on monuments, building, etc. It also contains a lot on which kind of cattle to import from where, which kind of merchandise to prohibit as imports, and all in all, indicates again the passage of Lyautey from a poetic youth to a more "prose-oriented" maturity here. Lyautey's love of fine horses, as well as his customary hospitality, resonated well with Maghreb inhabitants, according to Claude Farrère, *Lyautey créateur: notes et souvenirs* (Paris, 1955). Farrère noted that "tout le Moghreb a la passion des chevaux" (Farrère, 75).

45. See Porch, *Conquest of Morocco*, epilogue; Hoisington, *Lyautey and the French Conquest of Morocco*, ch. 5; and on Lyautey's "quest for a useful Morocco" Gershovich, ch. 4. One correspondent who heard a good deal about Lyautey's fears vis-à-vis wartime Morocco was Auguste Terrier, secretary-general of the Comité de l'Afrique française and then continuing his lobbying activities as director of the Protectorate Office in Paris during the war. Terrier maintained large

files of newspaper clippings related to the colony, and Lyautey used him for "damage control" with the Paris media for engineering contacts with the government, etc. An example of Lyautey's significant correspondence with Terrier on Moroccan problems in wartime is his letter of November 6, 1914, written during Zaïan operations. (Bibliothèque de l'Institut de France [hereafter BI]: Fonds Terrier [5903]). For typical clippings kept by Terrier see 5973. On the "politique du sourire," whereby Lyautey in wartime tried to give off an aura of things as usual, see among others, Farrère, 81. The "politique du sourire" was a Lyautey order for all in uniform, including his middle-aged "soldiers" that included "des bataillons de territoriaux du Midi ... de graves pépères de Marseille ou d'Ollioules aux bonnes gueules réjouies, aux ventres confortables, se dirigeant dans les postes de l'intérieur." Mounting expositions in wartime and having plenty of sugar available for tea (while it was lacking in France) was part of the same policy. See Guy Dervil, *Trois grands africains: dans l'intimité de Lyautey, Laperrine, Foucauld* (Paris, n.d.), quotation 202, 208.

46. See SHAT: 7N 2122: Section d'Afrique 1913–1915. War Min. to Lyautey, August 10, 1914. See in same source, Lyautey to Min. of Foreign Affairs, September 13, 1914 and September 28, 1914.

47. In SHAT: 7N 2122 see Lyautey to Bureau diplomatique, Bordeaux, October 7, 1914, and a longer, repetitive letter to Min. of Foreign Affairs, October 14; and Lyautey to Bureau diplomatique, October 19 and to Min. of Foreign Affairs, October 20, 1914. In AN: 475 AP/84 (Fonds Lyautey): Le Maroc: Documents généraux, there are a series of Lyautey letters to the War Ministry (from as early as August 27, 1914) on the need to make a good impression in Morocco when the European war denuded the protectorate of troops.

48. In SHAT: 7N 2122 see Lyautey to War Min., October 21, 1914. Lyautey's propping up of the Moroccan sultan as a centerpiece of his "Islamic policy" was countered by other French officers and bureaucrats, as he complained to Terrier in a letter of November 23, 1914 in BI: Fonds Terrier (5903). In the same letter he complained of his old anticolonial nemesis, Clemenceau.

49. Text of June 22, 1915 in Pierre Lyautey ed., *Lyautey l'africain*, vol. 2, 337; vol. 3, 14 (letter to Millerand); and see Lyautey speech of July 14, 1914 in his *Paroles d'action*, 113, 109. On Lyautey's opposition to the bill potentially offering citizenship to native soldiers see AN: 475 AP 84 (Fonds Lyautey): letters of Lyautey to minister of foreign affairs, June 15, 1915, and to the war minister June 16 and August 13 of that year. More decorations were fine, however!

50. See Maurois, 220–45; Le Révérend, *Lyautey*, ch. 17; Vladimir d'Ormesson's first-hand account *Auprès de Lyautey* (Paris, 1963), 13–106; another reminiscence by one of Lyautey's great diplomatic associates, Auguste de Beaupoil, Comte de Saint-Aulaire in *Au Maroc avant et avec Lyautey* (Paris, 1954), 241–42, noting his problem winning over parties or alliances versus isolated people; and Adrien Dansette, "Lyautey, Ministre de Guerre," *La Revue de Paris* (July 1964): 135–39. A typical fulmination of the period by Lyautey concerned "une de ces lamentables et stériles parlottes qu'on appelle un Conseil de ministres" (Pierre Lyautey, ed., *Lyautey l'africain*, vol. 3, 237 [letter to Gouraud, June 7, 1917]). See also SHAT: M.F.4 for his report on better organization of war and especially, use of aviation

as a military arm. On his ambivalent state of mind leaving Morocco behind in December, 1916 see his departing speech to French officers and functionaries of December 17 (AN: 475 AP 250).

51. Gershovich believes that the German threat was never as great as Lyautey supposed or alleged during the war (Gershovich, 107). He also offers a clear account of the evolution of the *Direction des affaires indigènes* in Morocco (84–87).

52. Letter in SHAT: M.F.4 (Barthou to President of the Republic). On Lyautey's economic compromises in Morocco, and a certain *sens unique* growth that favored France, see Rivet's *Lyautey et l'institution du protectorat français au Maroc*, passim. On the colonial literary explosion of the era see Roland Lebel, *Histoire de la littérature coloniale en France* (Paris, 1931). His celebratory conclusion sounds like pure Lyautey: "Colonial literature ... affirms itself in reaction against decadentism. ... It is a doctrine of action; it is, like the colony itself, a school of energy" (Lebel, 212). On Casablanca's prodigious growth, pushed by Lyautey, see Farrère, ch. 6; Henri Gouraud, *Lyautey* (Paris, 1938), 46; and Dervil, 177. All stress the initial objections Lyautey overcame. On a visit Max Leclerc saw Lyautey watching over Casablanca's development like a mother hen (Leclerc, *Au Maroc avec Lyautey* [Paris, 1927], 11–25).

53. In a monograph on one of Lyautey's trusted associates who helped run his administration when he was away, Bertrand Desmazières estimates that during the entire period from 1912–25 Lyautey spent as much as one-third to one-half of his time *outside* Morocco. See Desmazières, *Pierre de Sorbier de Pougnadoresse: le Colbert de Lyautey* (Paris, 1998), preface. A typed record of Lyautey's health problems accompanying a pension application by his widow in 1934 is in SHAT: M.F.4. A doctor's note of October 30, 1934 mentions seeing Lyautey during the war for crises of *angio-colite* with fever, shivering, etc. A health report of 1923 is in the same source. The letters to Castries noted here are also in M.F.4, with the last one dated February 1, 1924. The full correspondence is in AN: 220 Mi 1: Correspondance adressée au Colonel de Castries par le Maréchal Lyautey. It stretches from before World War I into the 1920s, but Lyautey's scrawled letters are hard to read here. He certainly felt close to Castries, close enough to unload his constant sources of chagrin, and over and over used the same formula in replies: "Votre lettre me touche bien." On French manpower in Morocco, see Gershovich, 79–81 and a series of letters and reports Lyautey sent to the War Ministry after 1918 in AN: 475 AP 84 (Fonds Lyautey).

54. See letters of September 25, 1925, and July 23, 1924 to Ormesson in Le Révérend ed., *Un Lyautey inconnu*, 316, 386. See also Guillaume de Tarde, "La Pensée politique de Lyautey," *Revue des deux mondes* (February 1960): 385–97, by Lyautey's key aide in the Secrétariat Général du Maroc 1914–20 and author of *Lyautey, le chef en action* (Paris, 1959). Charette concludes that Lyautey's ideas on Islam remain relevant in today's world (Charette, 305–6). On the possibility of a unified North African administration Lyautey wrote Terrier February 20, 1920: "Il me paraît de plus en plus nécessaire d'être aux aguets pour cette question de l'unification de l'Afrique du Nord" (BI: Fonds Terrier [5903]). For Lyautey's institutional set-up in Morocco, including the complex court system, the best accounts are in Alan Scham, *Lyautey in Morocco: Protectorate Administration, 1912–1925*

(Berkeley, 1970) and John P. Halstead, *Rebirth of a Nation: The Origins and Rise of Moroccan Nationalism, 1912–1944* (Cambridge, Mass., 1969), chs. 3–5. For an evaluation of the Native Policy Council see William A. Hoisington Jr., "Designing Morocco's Future: France and the Native Policy Council, 1921–25," *The Journal of North African Studies* 5 (Spring 2000): 63–108. Another of Lyautey's right-hand men in this era, besides Blanc, was Georges Hardy, Director-General of Public Instruction in Morocco and of course an admirer of his boss, whom he considered one of those "éclaireurs" qui "ont inspiré des conduites, raffermi des courages, indiqué des points de direction" (Hardy, *Portrait de Lyautey,* 19). On Hardy's importance running the educational service from 1920–26, especially in his pedagogical policies and ideas concerning Berbers and Arabs, see Spencer D. Segalla, "Georges Hardy and Educational Ethnology in French Morocco, 1920–26," (unpublished paper, 2002, kindly provided by the author), later published in *French Colonial History* 4 (2003): 171–90. One might also mention Lyautey's important role in a nascent film industry sprouting in Morocco during these years. See Slavin, *Colonial Cinema and Imperial France,* chs. 4, 6.

55. See in the AN: Fonds Lyautey *Souvenirs de famille: ma famille, historique, traditions, souvenirs,* including especially the part called "Mes atavismes au point de vue des opinions politiques"; and the separate manuscript there, "Crévic: la maison morte." He mentions being "crucified" by the loss in his letter to Terrier of September 26, 1914 (BI: Fonds Terrier [5903]).

56. See David S. Woolman, *Rebels in the Rif: Abd el Krim and the Rif Rebellion* (Stanford, 1968), 16; and for the effect of the Rif rebellion on Lyautey, Hoisington, *Lyautey and the French Conquest of Morocco,* ch. 9.

57. Woolman, 74–76.

58. Woolman, 79.

59. Woolman, 81–82, and for the entire Rif war Gershovich, ch. 5 is a good, more recent introduction. Lyautey partially looked down on the Spanish because of their dependence on English aid. He worried that the British might try to replace the Germans in Tangier, then worm their way via commerce and old intelligence agents into the French protectorate itself. See AN: 475 AP 84: his report of December 28, 1921 to the Minister of Foreign Affairs and letter to ibid., February 6, 1922.

60. Woolman, 164–70; and Anthony Clayton, *France, Soldiers, and Africa* (London, 1988), 108.

61. Quoted in Woolman, 170.

62. Woolman, 172.

63. Woolman, 174.

64. Woolman, 175–77.

65. Woolman, 178.

66. Woolman, 178, 201–2.

67. Woolman, 180–83. On Bournazel see Germaine de Bournazel, *Henry de Bournazel: le cavalier rouge* (Paris, 1979), using many of her husband's letters, and Jean d'Esme, *Bournazel, l'homme rouge* (Paris, 1952).

68. Clayton, 109.

69. Charles Julien, *Le Maroc face aux impérialismes, 1415–1956* (Paris, 1978), 125.

70. Jacques Benoist-Méchin, *Lyautey l'africain ou le rêve immolé* (Lausanne, 1966), 273. On the great differences between Lyautey and Pétain in Morocco see also Daniel Rivet, "Le commandement français et ses réactions vis-à-vis du mouvement rifain (1924–1926)," in *Abd el-Krim et la République du Rif,* Charles-André Julien ed. (Paris, 1976), 101–36. Rivet notes elewhere that Pétain, the "European," looked down on Lyautey militarily as "le maréchal de guerre nègre" (Rivet, *Le Maroc de Lyautey à Mohammed V: le double visage du protectorat* [Paris, 1999], 232–33). Colonel Serge-Henri Parisot, who arrived in Morocco seven years later, remains clearly pro-Lyautey. As he said, "Ce que nous les vieux 'Marocains' reprochent à Pétain, c'est la guerre européenne qu'il a livrée au Maroc." Interview with Parisot June 18, 2003. Parisot was also pro-Berber, praising their loyalty.

71. See Durosoy, *Avec Lyautey,* 190–91 and especially, an eyewitness account by the elegant Georges Catroux in his *Lyautey, le marocain* (Paris, 1952), ch. 9. Catroux was at the dinner with these two contrasting personalities—Lyautey "un être bouillonnant, enthousiaste, passionné, fervent, et, dans une certaine mesure, crédule, tandis que l'autre, le Maréchal militaire, avait depuis longtemps refréné ses impulsions juvéniles et s'était composé une âme de sage, prudent, positif, enclin au scepticisme et gouverné par la raison. On sentait ... qu'ils incarnaient deux types humains remarquables, mais essentiellement distincts l'un de l'autre" (228). Catroux goes on to mention the "night work" reference and how Pétain made a thinly-veiled jab at Lyautey's nocturnal habits, mentioning several of his top military associates who might not have been killed had they gotten more rest! (229–30). Another man who knew Lyautey very well, Hardy, recalls how "la journée faite ... Lyautey se retire chez lui et veille jusqu'à deux ou trois heures du matin. Il écrit, il dicte en marchant de long en large, en fumant à moitié d'innombrables cigarettes; c'est là sa façon de méditer, de digérer son action, de réviser ses règles de conduite, d'élaborer ses plans.... La nuit de Lyautey [est] ... une existence à part, avec un emploi du temps spécial, dans un plan qui ne se confond pas avec celui de ses occupations diurnes" (Hardy, *Portrait de Lyautey,* 31–32). See also Lyautey to Henry de Castries August 21, 1925, "la mort dans l'âme" and to Castries again September 28, 1925 on new military ideas opposed to his, as well as Lyautey's extensive report of September 24, 1925 on Pétain (SHAT: M.F.4).

72. See Scham's concluding chapter, and Halstead chs. 3–5, as well as ch. 6 on what he considered a revolution of rising expectations in Morocco. Catroux is again more personality-oriented on the succession problem, declaring that if Lyautey "leur laissait ses enseignements il ne pouvait leur laisser sa manière" (Catroux, *Lyautey le marocain,* 14). Dervil remembers a court atmosphere that no succeeding resident-general could reproduce. "Le Patron [Lyautey] aimait à recevoir, être entouré et les soirées à la Résidence étaient toujours fort élégantes et agréables." He recalls Lyautey with his "éternelle cigarette à la bouche" working the room, then getting away to his office to dictate at top speed or take care of other work matters, then reappearing to be the host again (Dervil, 186). Dervil also signals the importance of "la Maréchale" as a kind of Princess Eugénie, though also during the day promoting day care, soldiers' convalescent centers, libraries, and so on (Dervil, 193). See also Farrère, 115–17.

73. See memoir on this by Commandant G. Grand in SHAT: M.F.4.

74. See a letter of April 14, 1883, on hatred of disorder in Lyautey, *Lettres de jeunesse* (Paris, 1931), 80; and representative letters to War Min. November 28, 1925, on leave and October 9, 1926, on extension of it and wish to put together his archives in SHAT: M.F.4.

75. See his letters of August 6, 1919, and January 9, 1921, in Le Révérend ed., *Un Lyautey inconnu*, 290, 301 and quotes from the letter of December 9, 1918 in Pierre Lyautey ed., *Les plus belles lettres de Lyautey*, 129–30. Lyautey's speech in Thorey on staying strong is summarized in *Le Quotidien*, November 13, 1929.

76. See Lyautey letter to Vladimir d'Ormesson, February 9, 1927 in Pierre Lyautey ed., *Les plus belles lettres de Lyautey*, 147; and Ormesson, "La Dernière Victoire de Lyautey," *La Revue de Paris* (October, 1963): 1–9; as well as Patrick Heidsieck, "La Crise morale et religieuse (1875–1894)" in *Lyautey: Maréchal de France*, Heidsieck ed. (Paris, 1954), 40–58; and Heidsieck, *Lyautey* (Tours, 1950), ch. 8.

77. Lyautey's correspondence with Pierre is in AN: 475 AP 293 (Fonds Lyautey). Lyautey trusted his nephew totally, shown by the fact that he made him the executor of his will; but when Pierre was posted to Morocco under Poeymirau he says he received no special treatment (Pierre Lyautey, *Je les ai connus* [Paris, 1974], 34, 36). Like his uncle, Pierre became an indefatigable, though much more published writer.

78. On his work for the Colonial Exposition see his aide there, Hardy, *Portrait de Lyautey*, 244–45, who called Lyautey a "professeur de protectorat," little realizing that things would slide after this high point (245). See also Lyautey's letters to War Min., September 30, 1930 (SHAT: M.F.4). The biggest repository of his correspondence on it, as well as newspaper clippings is in AN: 475 AP 208 (Fonds Lyautey). See also the clear summary of Charette, 286–90; and with more emphasis on the "underside," Martin Evans, "Projecting a Greater France," *History Today* 50 (February 2000): 19–25. A flurry of publications on the French colonies also came out circa 1931. See, among others, Pierre Lyautey, *L'empire colonial français* (Paris, 1931), predictably celebrationist. But another published in the same year by Constant Southworth, *The French Colonial Venture* (London, 1931) is more cautionary, considering the French colonial empire on the whole unprofitable. One of the lasting effects of the "expo": Lyautey's "Zoo de la Coloniale." See Henry Thétard, *Des hommes, des bêtes: le zoo de Lyautey* (Paris, 1947).

79. The Lyautey version is found in a letter to A. M. Chailly, December 30, 1901, in his *Lettres du Sud de Madagascar*, 214; and in a letter to Gov.-Gen. Jonnart, December 31, 1905, in Lyautey, *Paroles d'action*, 44. The second version is in Raymond Betts, *Tricouleur: The French Overseas Empire* (London, 1978), 14. A typical Lyautey speech near the end of his life is on "union entre les races," "union entre les peuples," and last but not least, "union entre nous, Français"—quoted by Albert Paluel-Marmont in his *Lyautey* (Paris, 1934), 141.

80. To Louise Baignières February 13, 1933 in Le Révérend ed., *Un Lyautey inconnu*, 339. See also his letter to Heidsieck, December 15, 1933, in *Un Lyautey inconnu*, 343. Prefaces Lyautey wrote for a number of books in his twilight years indicate some of his concerns: for example, ones for Arsène Vauthier, *Le danger aérien et l'avenir du pays* (Paris, 1930) and in the same year, Marcel Jeanjean,

L'aviation (Paris, 1930); but also others on colonial themes, such as for Aimée Fauchère, *La France d'outre-mer illustrée* (Paris, 1931), or Paul-Louis Rivière, *Colonies: histoire des nouvelles Frances* (Paris, 1932). Prefaces by "M. le Maréchal Lyautey" obviously helped sell such books.

81. On the period of his life from 1925 see the general biographies, and the detail in Raymond Postal, *Présence de Lyautey* (Paris, 1941), and B. G. Gaulis, *Lyautey intime* (Paris, 1938), ch. 7.

6. HEIRS TO LYAUTEY

1. Among those who contributed to the war effort from the empire the group most lionized after the war was black Africans, especially the *tirailleurs sénégalais.* They seemed to have vindicated the predictions of Charles Mangin in his book of 1910 on the *force noire* as an antidote to French stagnation (not least in population). Between 160,000 and 170,000 *tirailleurs sénégalais* served in the war, and almost 30,000 black Africans died in the conflict. Though estimates vary, the empire as a whole gave as many as 800,000 to the war effort. See Nancy E. Lawler, *Soldiers of Misfortune: Ivoirien Tirailleurs of World War II* (Athens, Ohio, 1992), 2–22; Myron Echenberg, *Colonial Conscripts: The Tirailleurs Sénégalais in French West Africa, 1857–1960* (Portsmouth, N.H., 1991), ch. 3; and Martin Thomas, *The French Empire at War 1940–45* (Manchester, U.K., 1998), 10–11. One might also consult the pathbreaking study by Joe Lunn, *Memoirs of the Maelstrom: A Senegalese Oral History of the First World War* (Portsmouth, N.H., 1999).

2. Clayton, 6–7.

3. Julien, *Maroc,* 126 and Gershovich, ch. 5.

4. Clayton, 109; Woolman, 177.

5. Woolman, 193.

6. Clayton, 111.

7. Woolman, 215; Julien, *Maroc,* 127; Gershovich, 141.

8. See Walter B. Harris, *France, Spain, and the Rif* (London, 1927), 10–40, 318–29, quote 36 and Jack Cowart et al., *Matisse in Morocco: The Paintings and Drawings, 1912–1913* (New York, 1990), 94–95, including the painting mentioned and comments.

9. See General Antoine Huré, *La pacification du Maroc: dernière étape: 1931–1934* (Paris, 1952), passim.

10. Clayton, 116–19; Gershovich, 83 and ch. 5, especially 141–60; and Huré on Bournazel in ch. 14, and quote 193.

11. On the latter see William A. Hoisington Jr., "Cities in Revolt: The Berber Dahir (1930) and France's Urban Strategy in Morocco," *Journal of Contemporary History* 13 (July 1978): 433–48.

12. See Edouard Moha, *Histoire des relations franco-marocaines* (Paris, 1995), 149. On Moroccan-Arab resignation toward a whole variety of diseases (versus the attitudes of comparatively healthier Berber highlanders), Vincent Sheean, *An American among the Riffi* (New York, 1926), 98: "No matter how many thousands of them die of perfectly obvious endemic or epidemic diseases, you never can get [a Moroccan] Arab to admit that there was anything preventable or curable about

402   Notes to Pages 224–226

such a visitation. He will insist that Allah planned it all out." On this era see also the fine memoir of Georges Spillmann, *Souvenirs d'un colonialiste* (Paris, 1968), chs. 2–3, and the scholarly compendium of interviews woven into a monograph on what Morocco meant to the French who came there: Yvonne Knibiehler et al., *Des Français au Maroc: la présence et la mémoire (1912–1956)* (Paris, 1992). For a more ambivalent estimate, Jean and Simonne Lacouture, *Le Maroc à l'épreuve* (Paris, 1958), ch. 2.

13. See Guy Delanoë, *Lyautey, Juin, Mohammed V: fin d'un protectorat*, vol. 1 (Paris, 1988), preface. One should not think that the French won any final victory over "imperial diseases" in this era. A variety of respiratory illnesses, yellow fever, dysentery, and above all, malaria still killed regularly. As late as 1939 in Indochina malaria accounted for as many as 25 percent of all French deaths (Quinn, 191–92). On the insalubrious imperial background and gradual decline of deaths from disease, partly due to the victory of germ theory, see Philip D. Curtin, *Disease and Empire: The Health of European Troops in the Conquest of Africa* (Cambridge, U.K., 1998); and on the colonial Pasteur Institutes of the interwar era, Anne Marcovich, "French Colonial Medicine and Colonial Rule: Algeria and Indochina," in *Disease, Medicine, and Empire: Perspectives on Western Medicine and the Experience of European Expansion,* Roy MacLeod and Milton Lewis, eds. (London, 1988). In addition to medicine Lyautey helped launch a variety of scientific disciplines in Morocco, continuing there as in other colonial milieus during the interwar period—meteorological studies, an oceanographical service, geophysical observatories, etc. See Lewis Pyenson, *Civilizing Mission: Exact Sciences and French Overseas Expansion, 1830–1940* (Baltimore, 1993), ch. 5. The Lyautey-patronized Franco-Moroccan film industry that also continued through this period is given shorter shrift in David H. Slavin, "French Colonial Film before and after *Itto*: From Berber Myth to Race War," *French Historical Studies* 21 (Winter 1998): 125–55.

14. See Moha, 113–25, quotation on Saint 125; Col. Bel Madani, *Coupable de fidelité* (Paris, 1990), 45–65, quote on Noguès 64; and Bernard Lugan, *Histoire du Maroc* (Paris, 1992), ch. 11.

15. William A. Hoisington Jr., *The Casablanca Connection: French Colonial Policy, 1936–1943* (Chapel Hill, 1984), ch. 1.

16. Hoisington, *Casablanca Connection*, chs. 2–5. The whole issue of profitability of colonies is a complex one, though much studied. See, for example, Jacques Marseille's overview in "The Phases of French Colonial Imperialism: Toward a New Periodization," *Journal of Imperial and Commonwealth History* 13 (1985): 127–41. The rapid growth of skyscrapers in Casablanca was again due to a change from Lyautey's policy of harmonizing old styles with the new, in favor of modernism *tout court*. Lyautey's chief architectural planner, Henri Prost, gave way to more modernist planners in the late 1920s and 1930s. See Gwendolyn Wright, *The Politics of Design in French Colonial Urbanism* (Chicago, 1991), ch. 3, an excellent account containing numerous photographs of representative edifices in Morocco.

17. Meyer, et al., 204.

18. See Philip S. Khoury, *Syria and the French Mandate: The Politics of Arab Nationalism 1920–1945* (Princeton, 1987), part 1. The importation of cheap imperial cotton for use in French textile industries, and the improvement of an adverse

balance of trade (particularly vis-à-vis the Americans) was the postwar *idée fixe* of Albert Sarraut. See his *La mise en valeur des colonies* (Paris, 1923). On the stimulation of cotton production in French Africa during the 1920s and 1930s, particularly the Sudan, see Richard Roberts, "The Coercion of Free Markets: Cotton, Peasants, and the Colonial State in the French Soudan, 1924–1932," in *Cotton, Colonialism, and Social History in Sub-Saharan Africa*, Allen Isaacman and Richard Roberts, eds. (Portsmouth, N.H., 1995), 221–43, as well as appropriate parts of Roberts, *Two Worlds of Cotton: Colonialism and the Regional Economy in the French Soudan, 1800–1946* (Stanford, 1996).

19. Stephen H. Longrigg, *Syria and Lebanon under French Mandate* (New York, 1958), 152; Robert Aldrich, *Greater France: A History of French Overseas Expansion* (New York, 1996), 209–10; and Edmund Burke III, "A Comparative View of French Native Policy in Morocco and Syria, 1912–1925," *Middle Eastern Studies* 9 (1973): 175–86, arguing that the attempt especially by Gouraud to transplant Lyautey's Moroccan methods to Syria was doomed to failure, due to the inherent pride and nationalism of the mandate's inhabitants.

20. Clayton, 112; Longrigg, 148; Khoury, part 1, ch. 3; and a clear sketch in Philip K. Hitti, *Syria: A Short History* (New York, 1959), 242–44.

21. Longrigg, 153–54.

22. Longrigg, 154–59. Sarrail was also getting hammered at home, particularly by the Rightist French press. A sympathetic treatment of this man caught between extremes in the Levant is Jan Karl Tannenbaum's, *General Maurice Sarrail 1856–1929: The French Army and Left-Wing Politics* (Chapel Hill, N.C., 1974), ch. 10.

23. Aldrich, 211; Longrigg, 163–66.

24. Clayton, 112. The mandates are starting to receive increased scholarly attention, and with more limber emphases. A good example is Elizabeth Thompson, *Colonial Citizens: Republican Rights, Paternal Privilege, and Gender in French Syria and Lebanon* (New York, 2000).

25. Nicola Cooper, *France in Indochina: Colonial Encounters* (Oxford, 2001), 111. On the Popular Front and the empire, see Tony Chafer and Amanda Sackur, eds., *French Colonial Empire and the Popular Front: Hope and Disillusion* (London, 1999), especially Ghislaine Lydon's article in that collection, "Women, Children, and Popular Front's Missions of Inquiry in French West Africa" (170–87). See also Frederick Cooper, *Decolonization and African Society: The Labor Question in French and British Africa* (Cambridge, U.K., 1996), ch. 3 ("Reforming Imperialism, 1935–1940"). Resistance movements to forced labor were less overt than in an earlier era. A fine monograph on the most serious opposition to coerced labor round-ups in Africa (but for an earlier period) is Timothy C. Weiskel, *French Colonial Rule and the Baule Peoples: Resistance and Collaboration 1889–1911* (Oxford, 1980). On the fear of and restrictions on Islamic institutions one might begin with the Berber *dahir* of 1930 that had supposedly liberated 700,000 Berbers from sultanic rule, considering them a non-Islamic people, but leading to unrest in the entire Islamic world, according to Quinn (212). Allan Christelow notes that "French policy toward the official Islamic establishment in Algeria left a heritage of great bitterness" (Christelow, *Muslim Law Courts and the French Colonial State in Algeria* [Princeton, N.J., 1985], 265). There was more ambiguity in Senegal where

French citizens who were Muslims could use either French or Muslim law courts (by a decree of 1932). See Dominique Sarr and Richard Roberts, "The Jurisdiction of Muslim Tribunals in Colonial Senegal, 1857–1932," in *Law in Colonial Africa*, Kristin Mann and Richard Roberts, eds. (Portsmouth, N.H., 1991). See also Quinn, ch. 7 generally, Echenberg, ch. 4, and Thomas, 15–22, quote 20. Thomas tells us that even in advanced Senegal only 90,000 at most possessed the right of French citizens to vote (15). As for educational numbers in French West Africa of 1935, only 62,300 pupils attended primary schools and in French Equatorial Africa 15,877. See David E. Gardinier, "The French Impact on Education in Africa, 1817–1960," in *Double Impact: France and Africa in the Age of Imperialism*, G. Wesley Johnson, ed. (Westport, Conn., 1985), 334. See also Patrick Manning, *Francophone Sub-Saharan Africa 1880–1985* (Cambridge, U.K., 1988), 100–101 on the late establishment of higher primary schools in most of French West Africa during the 1920s. But again, too much French education might have incurred the wrath of anti-assimilationists!

26. On the background to and outcome of Mers el Kébir see Thomas, 51, and Charles W. Koburger's quirky but readable *The Cyrano Fleet: France and Its Navy, 1940–1942* (Westport, Conn., 1989), 13–30; and for the view of French Vichy naval authorities of the time, Adm. Paul Auphan and Jacques Mordal, *The French Navy in World War II*, trans. A. C. J. Sabalot (Annapolis, Md., 1959), ch. 13. Obviously there were longer-term reasons for French Anglophobia going back many centuries. A more recent one stemming from imperial issues is noted by Khoury: "France never forgave Britain for not halting the flow of men, arms, and money into Syria from Palestine, Transjordan, and Iraq during the Great Revolt [of the 1920s]" (Khoury, 583). On Noguès and Morocco during this period, Hoisington, *Casablanca Connection*, chs. 6, 7. Serge-Henri Parisot was bothered by Mers, but anything but pro-Vichy, and soon distinguished in the wartime Secret Services, eventually nabbing Joseph Darnand. Parisot interview, June 18, 2003, among other conversations.

27. Jean Lacouture, *De Gaulle: The Rebel, 1890–1944* (New York, 1990), 270–71.

28. Gerhard L. Weinberg, *A World at Arms: A Global History of World War II* (New York, 1994), 160.

29. See on careers from the Ecole Coloniale William B. Cohen, *Rulers of Empire: The French Colonial Service in Africa* (Stanford, 1971), 38–43.

30. See Brian Weinstein, *Eboué* (New York, 1972), 233–51 and Elie Castor and Raymond Tarcy, *Félix Eboué: gouverneur et philosophe* (Paris, 1984), passim.

31. Dorothy Shipley White, *Black Africa and de Gaulle* (London, 1979), 67–68; Lacouture, *De Gaulle*, 272.

32. White, 68; Lacouture, *De Gaulle*, 273; Jacques Soustelle, *Envers et contre tout*, vol. 1, *De Londres à Alger* (Paris, 1947), 124; Raoul Girardet, *L'idée coloniale en France de 1871 à 1962* (Paris, 1972), 198.

33. White, 71–73.

34. René-Marie-Edgard de Larminat, *Chroniques irrévérencieuses* (Paris, 1962), 132–33; and White, 72.

35. Robert L. Delavignette, "French Colonial Policy in Black Africa, 1945 to 1960," in *Colonialism in Africa, 1870–1960*, L. H. Gann and Peter Duignan, eds., vol. 2 (Cambridge, 1970), 255.

36. Michael Crowder, *West Africa under Colonial Rule* (Evanston, 1968), 486.

37. See Crowder, 487–88 and de Gaulle statement on Dakar in Lacouture, *De Gaulle,* 278, as well as Thomas, ch. 3 for its lasting significance. Koburger argues that a little more persistence might have given the Allies and Free French a victory, as the Vichy defenders were almost out of ammunition (42).

38. Thomas quote 83, and Crowder, 489. A sophisticated article on Boisson treats the difficulty of "placing" him ideologically, or awarding blame for all his wartime activities. See William I. Hitchcock, "Pierre Boisson, French West Africa, and the Postwar *Epuration*: A Case from the Aix Files," *French Historical Studies* 24 (Spring 2001): 305–41. Our chapter keeps revealing the divergences of Churchill and Roosevelt with de Gaulle, and Hitchcock shows here how they, along with Eisenhower, protested de Gaulle's arrest of Boisson, when it finally occurred.

39. Lacouture, *De Gaulle,* 280; Thomas, ch. 3.

40. Longrigg, 299.

41. Longrigg, 306.

42. Jean Meyer et al., 316.

43. Lacouture, *De Gaulle,* 263; Charles de Gaulle, *Lettres, notes et carnets,* vol. 3 (Paris, 1980), 309; and Georges Catroux, *Dans la bataille de Méditerranée: Egypte, Lévant, Afrique du Nord 1940–1944* (Paris, 1949), chs. 1–8. A recent view on Sir Harold MacMichael calls him a cynical man who cared little for Palestine, seeing it as one stop along the way in a colonial career that had already included positions in the British Sudan and Tanganyika. See Tom Segev, *One Palestine Complete: Jews and Arabs under the British Mandate* (New York, 1999), 416.

44. Weinberg, 230–31; Catroux, *Dans la bataille,* chs. 9–15.

45. Longrigg, 308–9.

46. Lacouture, *De Gaulle,* 301. De Gaulle later maintained that the guarantee was conditional. See also Thomas, ch. 4 on developments in the Levant and Gaullist tergiversations regarding independence.

47. Thomas, 106; and see Longrigg, 311–12. Algerians and especially *tirailleurs sénégalais* were a big part of that resistance (see Thomas, 107).

48. Weinberg, 231 and Longrigg, 313. Catroux believed Dentz led his zealous troops in a "quasi passive manner," remaining on the defensive (except for aircraft operations), when his modern tanks might easily have been used to skirt the invaders. Catroux did find that captured Vichy soldiers still felt that Pétain was correct and that de Gaulle was all wrong—a "tragique antinomie" (Catroux, *Dans la bataille,* 142, 145, see also ch. 18).

49. De Gaulle, *War Memoirs,* vol. 1 (London, 1955–59), 164. But see Koburger's cautionary view on repatriation of 33,950 French military personnel and civilians, requiring "twenty-one liner-voyages between Beirut and Marseilles, [and] testifying to the loyalty of the nine-tenths who refused to join the Free French there" (Koburger, 45).

50. On these issues see the monograph by A. B. Gaunson, *The Anglo-French Clash in Lebanon and Syria, 1940–1945* (London, 1987). See also Jean Meyer et al., 348, Longrigg, 316, and Catroux, *Dans la bataille,* ch. 23 ("Sur le Général Sir Edward Spears"), quote 198. Thomas confirms "Spears' dramatic conversion from chief protagonist to arch-antagonist of Free France" (112).

51. Lacouture, *De Gaulle,* 292; Clayton, 136, and on increasing black African conversions from Vichy toward the Free French side, Lawler, ch. 7 ("Changing Partners: From Pétain to de Gaulle").

52. White, 84. In all of World War II Echenberg estimates that the French had recruited a good 200,000 black Africans for duty (88). On the crucial role of countries in the African Empire in feeding wartime France see Koburger, 64.

53. On the Madagascar invasion and aftermath see Thomas, ch. 5 and Koburger, 46–47. The Madagascar fiasco ratcheted up Vichy's anti-English, anti-Gaullist propaganda. One aspect of that propaganda likened the English and their Gaullist "agents" to the persecutors of Joan of Arc, whose cult burgeoned in this period. See Eric T. Jennings, "Reinventing Jeanne: The Iconology of Joan of Arc in Vichy Schoolbooks, 1940–1944," *Journal of Contemporary History* 29 (1994): 711–34, and on the Madagascar invasion reinforcing the cult, 713. For Vichy's rule in Madagascar, "l'apogée d'un colonialisme pur et dur," but also of Vichy's persecution of enemies and institution of its own values, see Jennings, "Vichy à Madagascar: La 'Révolution nationale', l'enseignement et la jeunesse (1940–1942)," *Revue d'histoire moderne et contemporaine* 46 (octobre-décembre 1999): 729–46, quotation 730. As he has done for other parts of the French empire under Vichy, Jennings emphasizes Vichy's persecution of the French laic school, accent on physical culture, and so on. See also Jennings, *Vichy in the Tropics,* chs. 2–3. On the Legionnaires at Bir Hakeim see Porch, *French Foreign Legion,* 481–84.

54. There was haughtiness on the other side as well. Giraud would long hype his superiority to de Gaulle, declaring that "whether rightly or wrongly General de Gaulle was hardly accepted by the Army of Africa. For many ... he was the man of Dakar, and especially of Syria. Many men had fought hard in Syria against Gaullist troops, and kept a bitter memory of it." Giraud (a veteran of Morocco) also noted de Gaulle's lack of African military service (Giraud, *Un seul but, la victoire: Alger 1942–1944* [Paris, 1949], 32).

55. On the Allied invasion of North Africa and aftermath, including warfare in Tunisia, see Thomas, ch. 6; B. H. Liddell Hart, *History of the Second World War* (New York, 1971), chs. 21, 22; Koburger, ch. 4; John Keegan, *The Second World War* (London, 1989), ch. 18; and Henri Noguères, *Le suicide de la flotte française à Toulon* (Paris, 1961), 9.

56. White, 88 and Cohen, *Rulers of Empire,* 165–69. One of the present authors met the granddaughter of François d'Astier de la Vigerie on a plane to France. Her mother had been in the Resistance with Uncle Emmanuel in the Lyon area, and Jean Moulin allegedly ate at her mother's house the day before his arrest and subsequent torture to death at the hands of Klaus Barbie. Emmanuel would be called "le Baron Rouge" due to a second marriage with a Soviet woman and a conversion to Communism in the 1960s. At his funeral the woman on the airplane last saw de Gaulle, on whose knees she had sat as a little girl. Emmanuel had once dubbed Resistance "a childish and deadly game" (Patrick Marnham, *The Death of Jean Moulin: Biography of a Ghost* [London, 2000], 253).

57. White, 114–15. Summarizing the views of French Communists at the end of the war Edward Rice-Maximin notes: "Desiring to remain integrated in the mainstream of French political life, they also expected the colonies to remain a part of

a 'Greater France', possessing one hundred million souls (sixty million overseas and forty million in the Metropole), [but] in which the old colonial abuses would be eradicated and the overseas people allowed to share in all the benefits and reforms of a 'progressive and democratic' France" (*Accommodation and Resistance: The French Left, Indochina, and the Cold War 1944–1954* [Westport, Conn., 1986], 13).

58. White, 129 and Thomas, ch. 8.

59. Cohen, *Rulers of Empire*, 169. The inconsistencies would continue right after the war with the difficulty of defining key new words like "union," and with some leaps forward (the granting of French departmental status to Réunion, Guadeloupe, Martinique, and French Guiana), combined with efforts to hold the line in larger colonial entities (see Quinn, 224–25).

7. THE TWILIGHT OF FRENCH COLONIALISM

1. The latter figure, which seems somewhat exaggerated, is provided by Denise Bouche, *Histoire de la colonisation française*, vol. 2: *Flux et reflux, 1815–1962* (Paris, 1991), 415.

2. Bouche, 378.

3. The official name of this organization was Vietnam Doc Lap Dong Minh, or League for Vietnamese Independence.

4. Ellen J. Hammer, *The Struggle for Indochina 1940–1955* (Stanford, 1955), 12, 53–55, 58. Protectorates were ruled indirectly through local dignitaries, while colonies were ruled from Paris.

5. Hammer, 64. See also Charles Meyer, *La vie quotidienne des français en Indochine 1860–1910* (Paris, 1985) and appropriate parts of Philippe Héduy, *Histoire de l'Indochine: la perle de l'empire 1624–1954* (Paris, 1998).

6. Hammer, 15–18; Joseph Buttinger, *Vietnam: A Dragon Embattled* (New York, 1967), 235. The best discussion of Decoux' complexity and varying arguments on him is in Jennings, *Vichy in the Tropics*, ch. 8.

7. Hammer, 42–43; see also the clear account by a French veteran of the Indochina War, Olivier de Maison Rouge, *La Guerre d'Indochine 1945–1954* (Paris, 1989), 23–29. See too the interesting memoir of Decoux' diplomatic aide, Claude de Boisanger, *On pouvait éviter la guerre d'Indochine: souvenirs 1941–1945* (Paris, 1977), an indictment of French policy at the end of the war.

8. Hammer, 112–13, and Thomas, quote 216–17.

9. Joseph Buttinger's appraisal of Gracey's attitude is trenchant: "Gracey's simple political convictions excluded the possibility that an eastern country could cease to be a colony because unusual circumstances had led to the establishment of a native government and the proclamation of national independence" (Buttinger, 325). See also Karnow, 148–50.

10. Hammer, 116–20; Buttinger, 334–37. Karnow reminds us that calling a region "pacified" meant (given the opponent) that the French army would have to remain in place to hold it (Karnow, 150).

11. Hammer, 131; Buttinger, 340–44. An indictment of de Gaulle's dilatoriness in getting back to Indochina, and especially to the Tonkin of northern Vietnam,

thereby "making the bed" of the Viet Minh, is Alfred George, *Charles de Gaulle et la guerre d'Indochine* (Paris, 1974), quote 187. See also Pierre Lefranc, ed., *De Gaulle et l'Indochine 1940–1946* (Paris, 1982), a collective effort put out by the Institut Charles de Gaulle.

12. Hammer, 132; Bouche, 438.

13. Buttinger, 350–56; Hammer, 147; Karnow, 150–52.

14. Hammer, 152.

15. Hammer, 153 and Karnow, 150–57.

16. Buttinger, 373–79; Hammer, 154; and Karnow, 115, 141.

17. Jean Sainteny, *Histoire d'une paix manquée* (Paris, 1953), 167.

18. On Leclerc there are a number of biographical studies of varying quality, including General Adolphe Vézinet's, *Le Général Leclerc de Hauteclocque: Maréchal de France* (Paris, 1974); Jacques Béal, *Leclerc: vie et mort d'un croisé* (Paris, 1988), using the Leclerc archives; Maurice Cordier and Roger Fouquer, *Le Général Leclerc ou se commander à soi-même* (Paris, 1990), stressing his religiosity; General Jean Compagnon's hagiographic, *Leclerc: Maréchal de France* (Paris, 1994); and André Martel, *Leclerc: le soldat et le politique* (Paris, 1998). Leclerc was an aristocrat whose real name was Philippe de Hauteclocque, but he had taken the most common name in the village where he was raised, Leclerc.

19. Anthony Short, *The Origins of the Vietnam War* (New York, 1989), 50; Alexander Worth, *France 1940–1955* (Boston, 1956), 334; Hammer, 182–83.

20. Werth, 341–42; Hammer, 186–87.

21. See Buttinger, 681 for the contention that d'Argenlieu was simply carrying out the wishes of governments in Paris, and Karnow, 155–59.

22. Hammer, 194–95. There are a number of lively and interestingly researched points of view on Leclerc's actions and nonactions in Indochina presented in Guy Pedroncini and Philippe Duplay, eds., *Leclerc et l'Indochine: 1945–1947* (Paris, 1992), with contributions from a variety of scholars, journalists, and military men. One might also consult Sainteny's regretful account, *Histoire d'une paix manquée*, first published in 1953, then rereleased in the era of America's Vietnam War. A collection of primary sources from the Army archives at Vincennes on this all-important period is in Gilbert Bodinier, ed., *La guerre d'Indochine 1947: textes et documents* (Service Historique de l'Armée de Terre, Vincennes, 1989). Leclerc's careful attitude vis-à-vis Indochina was far different from his forthright Gaullist line during World War II. In a discussion with General Giraud, whom Leclerc tried to convert to that Gaullist line, calling anyone not supportive of de Gaulle a traitor, Giraud countered by asking whether Leclerc would use the guillotine in French villages on such traitors. "Parfaitement, mon Général, pas d'hésitation," he supposedly replied (Giraud, *Un seul but*, 175).

23. See Raymond Betts, *France and Decolonisation, 1900–1960* (New York, 1991), 80–81 and Karnow, 158–59.

24. Werth, 450–51, characterizes the MRP view on Vietnam as evidence of mental aberration, and (less charitably) suggests that many MRP backers were reaping substantial profits from the war.

25. Buttinger, 713–27; Werth, 452–53.

26. Porch, *French Foreign Legion*, 518; Werth, 454.

27. Betts, *France and Decolonisation*, 86–87.

28. See Marc Dem's bitter *Mourir pour Câo Bang: le drame de la Route Coloniale no. 4* (Paris, 1978); the spirited exposition and analysis of Porch, *French Foreign Legion*, 517–29; a pithier one in Karnow, 185; Saint Marc, 122–24; and another memoir on conditions along the road, Max Gaudron's *Légionnaire au Nord-Tonkin* (Paris, 1980), especially 151–56. See also the memoirs of the two column leaders, both with much prior colonial experience, particularly in Morocco, and both imprisoned after the disaster for four long years in horrid conditions: Colonel Marcel Le Page, *Cao Bang: la tragique épopée de la colonne Le Page* (Paris, 1981) and Colonel Pierre Charton, *RC4: Indochine 1950: la tragédie de l'évacuation de Cao Bang* (Paris, 1975). Another memoir by a soldier returning from this Vietnamese disaster area has some of the same resonance as those by soliders returning to a divided U.S. during the Vietnam War of the 1960s. Robert Gaget recounts his arrival in Marseille, and his astonishment at seeing Communist strikers on the docks carrying signs stigmatizing the French involvement in the colonies, as well as ones reading "Free Henri Martin," a man imprisoned on charges of sabotaging materiel designated for the French Expeditionary Corps in Indochina. He also encountered the plain indifference of young eaters, drinkers, and lovers, while survivors of Cao Bang were enduring brainwashing in Viet Minh camps (Robert Gaget, *Commandos parachutistes* [Paris, 1992]). Jean Ferrandi avers that these frosty welcomes in Marseille were an important reason for return trips to Indochina (Ferrandi, *Les officiers français face au Vietminh: 1945–1954* [Paris, 1966], 119). A clear and fair account of this parlous era for the French is also found in Alain Ruscio, *La guerre française d'Indochine* (Brussels, 1992), 146–55.

29. For historical studies of the Collège de Vaugirard, see two articles by John W. Langdon: "The Jesuits and French Education: A Comparative Study of Two Schools, 1852–1913," *History of Education Quarterly* 17 (Spring 1978): 49–60, and "Jesuit Schools and French Society, 1851–1908," *Indiana Social Studies Quarterly* 37 (Winter 1984): 31–44. And for the history of Sainte-Geneviève, Langdon, "New Light on the Influence of the Jesuit Schools."

30. Biographical studies of de Lattre include in English Guy Salisbury-Jones, *So Full of Glory* (New York, 1954), and in French, Jacques Dinfreville, *Le Roi Jean* (Paris, 1964), and a spate of quite recent ones—Bernard Simiot, *De Lattre* (Paris, 1994), Pierre Pellissier, *De Lattre* (Paris, 1998), and Bernard Destremau, *Jean de Lattre de Tassigny* (Paris, 1999). See also specialized articles, such as Don Alexander, "Repercussions of the Breda Variant," *French Historical Studies*, 8 (1974): 459–88.

31. Donald Lancaster, *The Emancipation of French Indochina* (London, 1961), 221.

32. Lancaster, 221, 225.

33. Lancaster, 225–30; Werth, 455.

34. Adjutant Roger Vandenberghe was one of the most interesting psychological cases to distinguish himself in this war. Abandoned with his brother by his mother, and barely literate, he came to Vietnam in February 1947 to "find himself" and became a kind of one-man band, almost seeking death, but punishing many Viet Minh en route, particularly after the loss of his brother in combat made him even more vengeful. Fighting with prized Vietnamese associates, in early January 1952 he augmented his troops with Viet Minh prisoners he thought he

could convert, and one brutally assassinated him, before fleeing back to the enemy. See the standard histories and Erwan Bergot, *Commando Vandenberghe: le pirate du Delta* (Paris, 1985).

35. Lancaster, 232, 236–42. On the impact of Bernard's death on his celebrated father, see Simonne de Lattre, *Jean de Lattre, mon mari,* 2 vols. (Paris, 1972). She herself writes emotionally of the death of her son, but in the context of what we discuss more fully in the next chapter—the many other deaths of a certain idealistic generation of soldiers here. She quotes Guy du Chaumont, who wrote just before being killed himself on the lower Mekong: "Tonight I think of all these dead I have seen in the mud, dust, or snow, all these French, German, Arab, Annamite dead . . . who all gave their lives to bring more happiness to the world" (vol. 2, 289). Lucien Bodard in his hysterical, novelistic *La guerre d'Indochine* (Paris, 1997, originally published in three separate volumes in the 1960s) devotes many pages to the oedipal triangle, whereby Bernard de Lattre, the sensitive son of a celebrated French general, was more drawn to his mother and vice-versa, yet felt he had to prove himself in Indochina. Pellissier notes that de Lattre never forgave himself for his son's death in the war (Pellissier, 13). On the same page he relates how apparently de Lattre asked his political associate Jean Letourneau just before he died whether he had made it to marshal of France, and if so, was he "the only one to be promoted"? Letourneau said yes, lying on both counts at that point. Bernard Simiot's final estimate of de Lattre places him simultaneously in the class of Lyautey and MacArthur (Simiot, 349). He certainly had some of the former's theatricality.

36. Just before he died, de Lattre warned his successor, Salan: "Vietnam is the army's great chance! If we lose here, everything will tumble. . . . We must not lose this war, Salan! If we do, it will continue in Tunisia, in Algeria, in all of Africa" (quoted in Georges Fleury, *La guerre en Indochine 1945–1954* [Paris, 1994], 490). But as noted, his larger legacy perhaps was his "selling" of a greater kind of Communist domino theory to the Americans. The English text of his appearance on NBC's "Meet the Press," September 16, 1951, shows this best. Asked if the fall of Indochina would mean the rest of Southeast Asia's loss, de Lattre replied: "Yes, I think so. . . . I think that there is not only a parallel to make between Korea and Indo China. It is exactly the same. In Korea you are fighting against Communists. In Indo China we are fighting against Communists. Korea War, Indo China War, it is the same war, the war of Asia" (quoted in Maréchal Jean de Lattre, *La ferveur et le sacrifice: Indochine 1951* [Paris, 1988], 448, a collection of his interviews, telegrams, and letters put together by Jean-Luc Barré). In an interesting book Antoine Colombani, a Corsican formerly attached to High Commissioner Letourneau's staff in Vietnam, blames both de Lattre and the Americans for seducing the French after the Cao Bang disaster into needlessly prolonging the war all the way down to Dien Bien Phu. See Colombani, *Vietnam 1948–1950: La solution oubliée* (Paris, 1997).

37. Porch, *French Foreign Legion,* 537; Maison Rouge, 168–77 on conditions in the Tonkin delta, though he also signals a higher degree of French stability southward in Annam and Cochin China.

38. Porch, *French Foreign Legion,* 556. In actuality Dien Bien Phu, as John

Prados explains, "was not even a real place. The name translates as 'large administrative center on the frontier'. There was no village called 'Dien Bien Phu'. Rather, a cluster of villages filled a large valley in northwestern Tonkin, close to the borders of both Laos and China" (John Prados, *The Sky Would Fall: Operation Vulture, the U.S. Bombing Mission in Indochina, 1954* [New York, 1983], 3).

39. See Prados, 15–16 and Yves Gras, *Histoire de la guerre d'Indochine* (Paris, 1992), 503–12. On Letourneau and the Fourth Republic's vacillation, the best account is in R. E. M. Irving, *The First Indochina War* (London, 1975). On growing opposition at home to the war in Indochina, Alain Ruscio has a scholarly, but rather turgid work on the most vocal and active contingent, the French Communists. See Ruscio, *Les Communistes français et la guerre d'Indochine* (Paris, 1985).

40. See Ruscio, *Guerre française d'Indochine*, 190–95, and the best book on actual conditions here, with numerous letters home cited, Roger Bruge, *Les hommes de Dien Biên Phu* (Paris, 1999), quote p. 92.

41. A good account of the battle is Jules Roy, *The Battle of Dienbienphu* (New York, 1965). The clearest textbook account of the prelude to Dien is in Maison Rouge, 222–46.

42. Hammer, 327–28.

43. Quotation in Short, 130. The best book on the idea of American intervention, "Operation Vulture," is Prados, *The Sky Would Fall.* See also Gen. Paul Ely, *Mémoires: L'Indochine dans la tourmente,* vol. 1 (Paris, 1964), ch. 3, and William J. Duiker, *U.S. Containment Policy and the Conflict in Indochina* (Stanford, 1994), ch. 5. Did the French Republic betray its soldiers in this entire enterprise? asks a one-time president of the national organization of Anciens Combattants d'Indochine et de Corée. "Yes!" replies Roger Delpey emphatically in the conclusion of his two-volume *Soldats de la boue,* vol. 2 (Paris, 1961), 387. The total human cost of France's attempt at holding Indochina, and especially Vietnam (or the previous Tonkin, Annam, and Cochin China) was a large one: the French Expeditionary Corps lost in total 75,194 men, of whom 20,685 were from France itself. The rest were from the Foreign Legion, almost half of it "Germanic" in origin (German, Austrian, Swiss), from Africa (mostly West Africa), and from North Africa (almost totally Moroccans and Algerians). The killing off of the cream of French officers, including many formed at Saint-Cyr, truly anguished those planning the army of the future. See Ruscio, *Guerre française d'Indochine,* 158–67 and the scholarly, statistical study by Michel Bodin drawn from his doctoral thesis, *Soldats d'Indochine 1945–1954* (Paris, 1997). Nearly half a million men had taken part in the war, including about 65,000 Legionnaires, 55,000 Africans, and some 116,000 North Africans from the Maghreb (Bodin, 6, and on the origins of Legionnaires, 85).

44. Julien, *Maroc,* 200, 204–5 and Hoisington, *Casablanca Connection,* ch. 8.

45. Julien, *Maroc,* 208.

46. Julien, *Maroc,* 208.

47. Aldrich, 291. El-Glaoui's Marrakech of this era remained, however, something of a paradise for French people living or stationed there. Before the mass onslaught of tourists in succeeding decades, Marrakech of the late 1940s was still "an extraordinary city. It was Baghdad in the time of the Caliphs" (Henri J. M.

Lombard, *Les jours ordinaires d'un "protecteur" au Maroc* [Nîmes, 1993], 27). A Frenchman who learned Arabic, Lombard and his wife lived in the Arab sector of the city.

48. Betts, *France and Decolonisation*, 100; Aldrich, 291.

49. The pledge was also a threat. Mendès-France stated that if the war were not terminated by July 20, 1954, he would resign. The French public, which was sick of Indochina, would have reacted strongly, and it is not inconceivable that the Fourth Republic might have collapsed four years before it actually did. In any event, few in Paris were inclined to call PMF's bluff, primarily since they believed it was not a bluff at all.

50. Julien, *Maroc*, 211 and on Juin's Morocco years, see his *Mémoires*, vol. 2 (Paris, 1960), 139–211.

51. Betts, *France and Decolonisation*, 100–2.

8. BIGEARD

1. A rare American article on Bigeard notes that his father was a pacifist railway worker, and that as a draftee Bigeard had at first refused to cut his hair (*Newsweek*, August 18, 1958, 45–46). An interesting evocation of Bigeard's youth parallel to a kind of popular history of the era's great people and events is in his *Le siècle des héros* (Paris, 2000), quote 102. He adds that he never realized then that he would one day spend so much time in Indochina, and without tuxedos and elegant women by his side! He also mentions how hard his parents worked, and how Léon Blum's vacations with pay didn't even affect their lives—there was too much to do at home (animals to feed, crops to raise in the garden). He says he remains antivacation to this day, and as for retirement, "C'est un mot que je déteste" (*Siècle des héros*, 115). In one phone conversation Bigeard said that "même dans mes périodes de gloriole je n'ai jamais reçu autant de courrier," requiring answers, and constant attention. Of this flurry of correspondence, as well as a thirteenth book in preparation, he said, "je travaille le Jour de l'An, je n'ai pas de Noël, pas de dimanche, je n'arrête pas" (phone interview February 8, 2002). In a subsequent talk he said in that brusque, warm brogue of his: "Si j'arrête, je meurs" (phone interview, March 15, 2002). In the book that then appeared only a couple of months after our interviews, Bigeard noted much the same thing as expressed on the phone—a symphonic theme and variations approach constant in both his conversations and books: "Je reçois des milliers de lettres qui expriment les vraies questions, les vraies craintes des Français. Jeunes ou vieux m'écrivent leurs angoisses" (*Crier ma vérité*, 13). And: "Pas de samedi, pas de dimanche, pas de jour férié ... [his ellipsis] les vacances, j'ignore ce que c'est. C'est ma vie. Si j'arrête je meurs" (256). In a letter to one of the present authors he noted (July 23, 2001) regarding nostalgia: "Le passé on s'y réfère, mais on ne vit pas avec."

2. For what precedes see opening chapters of Marcel Bigeard, *Pour une parcelle de gloire*, vol. 1, *Soldat inconnu* (Paris, 1975) and Erwan Bergot, *Bigeard* (Paris, 1988), 17–102, which offers valuable information based on interviews, primarily with Masbourian. See also Bigeard's *France: réveille-toi!* (Paris, 1997), 233–34, where he admits to having been "terriblement marqué" by his mother Sophie.

"Dominating my father by her size and authority, she commanded with no sharing her house, and elsewhere when she could. For her I always had to be first of the class." Marcel Cordier's thin, but interesting *L'héroïque Bigeard* (Le Coteau/Roanne, 1986) features photos of Bigeard not found elsewhere. He notes that Bigeard was four years Gaby's senior, while four years younger than his sister (17–18). "L'héroïque Bigeard" was a phrase taken from de Gaulle. Speaking of the latter, a vigorous rebuttal to the ineluctability of a French defeat in 1940 is Robert J. Young's book, *In Command of France*.

3. On leaving his wife at the Marseille quai, Bigeard writes: "Elle est enceinte. Je suis égoïste. Comme la plupart des hommes" (*Siècle des héros*, 188). An interview with Pierre Seigland outside the Château de Vincennes, February 22, 2002, gave valuable insights on a generation of Resistants of varying stripes who after fighting the Nazis in *maquis* operations, then decided to engage themselves in "Indo" rather than regain villages in Burgundy or the Bordelais.

4. On Leclerc, "un véritable seigneur," see Bigeard, *Ma guerre d'Indochine* (Paris, 1994), 12; and *Siècle des héros*, where he calls him "un homme de coeur" and a great leader. Bigeard also notes the tragedy of the plane crash that would kill Leclerc at age forty-five, occurring only a few kilometers from the place Lyautey had named Colomb-Béchar (197).

5. Bigeard, *Pour une parcelle de gloire*, vol. 1, 79, 80. See also his self-description—bare-chested in shorts, grenades on his belt, and his "carabine en bandoulière" (*Ma guerre d'Indochine*, 17). From the era of his first migration from Nice to Africa and thence to this point in his Indochinese adventures, see also Bergot, *Bigeard*, 107–83.

6. Bigeard, *Pour une parcelle de gloire*, vol. 1, 80. On this first "illusory period" of French reconquest in Indochina, an excellent interview with General Jean Compagnon notes how blithely the French of this era took back key points along the future death trap of Route 4, including Lang Son, and how much they were welcomed by Tonkinese inhabitants not yet won over by the Viet Minh, and still reeling from the Japanese. They were also welcomed by French people left over from the pre-1939 era here, and with whom there was much discussion of renewal. He also shows how the Viet Minh at first avoided heavy, pitched battles, preferring to gird themselves for another, more decisive day (SHAT: Fonds Privés. Histoire Orale. 3K11: Interview with Gen. Jean Compagnon [1997]).

7. Bigeard, *Pour une parcelle de gloire*, vol. 1, 84–85.

8. For the atmosphere in this era, see Bigeard, *Ma guerre d'Indochine*, 20.

9. For him that Vietnam would by and large remain the High Region. Bigeard writes that there "I knew my finest hours" and "left the best of myself" (*Ma guerre d'Indochine*, quotes 26, 30).

10. Bigeard, *Pour une parcelle de gloire*, vol. 1, 101.

11. He was also irritated by the relative silence of French newspapers on the heroic feats of his countrymen in Vietnam (Bigeard, *Ma guerre d'Indochine*, 38).

12. Bigeard, *Pour une parcelle de gloire*, vol. 1, 102.

13. See seductive recruitment posters, such as one in *Ma guerre d'Indochine*, 9, featuring a square-jawed Frenchman in beret: "Tu es un homme. Vas en Indochine défendre la liberté." And below those lines in capitals: "Tu deviendras un

CHEF!" According to Jean Compagnon he first sold Colonel Jacques Massu on the idea of making paratroop warfare central to the French effort in Indochina, during conversations they had at Lang Son in the summer of 1946. See SHAT: 3K11: Interview with Compagnon.

14. The fuller explanation: "I knocked them out in seconds, an unorthodox formula justifiable in that era" (Bigeard, *Pour une parcelle de gloire*, vol. 1, 104).

15. The *Pasteur* would go back and forth through the entire war, bringing new recruits to the fray in "Indo," then return hungrily for more (Bigeard, *Ma guerre d'Indochine*, 40).

16. In several of his books Bigeard likens the General Staff's methods to using "un marteau-pilon pour écraser une mouche," e.g., Bigeard, *Ma guerre d'Indochine*, 41.

17. Bigeard, *Pour une parcelle de gloire*, vol. 1, 112. Bigeard liked Paccioni's warmth, but owing to the latter's hardness of hearing, had to yell to be heard! Bigeard, *Ma guerre d'Indochine*, 44, and on the ambush, 45.

18. In the 1990s he confessed that "I wanted to go too quickly." Progressively he learned to prepare his moves more carefully (Bigeard, *Ma guerre d'Indochine*, 47).

19. Bigeard, *Pour une parcelle de gloire*, vol. 1, 125. Perhaps we are overemphasizing our "best and brightest" view, but the bean-counter's way of measuring intelligence and culture by the amount of degrees possessed will not do either. See for the latter Bodin, 155–56.

20. On the Meo see Norman Lewis' *A Dragon Apparent: Travels in Cambodia, Laos, and Vietnam* (London, 1982, originally published in 1951). He thinks they might have been of Esquimo origins, and had kept descending through mountain chains southward. "They are utterly independent and quite fearless ..." (Lewis, 279). Lewis says that the French had a kind of pecking order of who they liked here, with the Laotians, Thais, Cambodians near the top, and the Vietnamese at the bottom: "you never knew where you were with them, they suffered from an inferiority complex, concealed their true feelings, were cruel ... [and also refused] to go into a graceful decline" (Lewis, 152–53).

21. It was also the era of a scandalous trafficking of *piastres* and opium, provoking a government investigation in France. See Bigeard, *Ma guerre d'Indochine*, 50.

22. See Bigeard, *Ma guerre d'Indochine*, 52.

23. Cf. Peter Scholl-Latour, relating how angry French soldiers on leave were at "the sight of fat staff officers who spent the afternoons sunning themselves on the terrace of the Continental, knocking back brandies and soda. Then in the evening, to add insult to injury, these backroom boys would get off with all the best-looking Vietnamese tarts in the place." Scholl-Latour, *Death in the Ricefields*, trans. Faye Carney (London, 1981), 46–47. Of course Saigon was far more replete with corrupt possibilities than Hanoi.

24. Bigeard, *Pour une parcelle de gloire*, vol. 1, 131.

25. Bigeard, *Pour une parcelle de gloire*, vol. 1, 138. He was especially saddened by news of the Cao Bang-Lang Son disaster, which had decimated the marvelous paras of his 3d Battalion (see Bigeard, *Ma guerre d'Indochine*, 56). Pierre Seigland recalled that "Indo" news was generally about page five in French newspapers, but that Cao Bang had more resonance at home, constituting the first devastating

French defeat in Vietnam to that point (interview with Seigland, February 22, 2002). For the great soul-searching provoked by Cao Bang one should also consult SHAT: Fonds Privés. 1K 306: Papiers Alessandri. (Bigeard's nemesis took a major role in the operation as Commander of the Zone Opérationnelle du Tonkin, making the definitive decision to leave Lang Son in mid-October 1950.) And more poignantly, any researcher on Cao Bang should consult all the frantic reports in SHAT: 10H 1143: (Archives de l'Indochine) Dossiers Documentaires Concernant les Opérations: Cao Bang (septembre-octobre 1950). For the entire period in Bigeard's military career from the summer of 1946 through 1950 his *Pour une parcelle de gloire* remain fundamental, but clarified as well by Bergot, *Bigeard*, 183–255.

26. Bigeard, *Pour une Parcelle de gloire*, vol. 1, 145.
27. Bigeard, *Pour une Parcelle de gloire*, vol. 1, 146.
28. Bigeard, *Pour une Parcelle de gloire*, vol. 1, 149.
29. General Marcel Bigeard (with Patrice de Méritens) ed., *Lettres d'Indochine* (Paris, 1998). Letter of Jean-Claude Ballot to his brother, May 30, 1951, appears among a series (63–65). Ballot died in Algeria, fighting for the Legion.
30. Bigeard, *Pour une parcelle de gloire*, vol. 1, 149. Part of that sadness was due to disease. According to Commandant Vanuxem's journal the climate was "vraiment insupportable, même pour les habitants." In the mountainous north cholera raged; everywhere dysentery crippled soldiers and even the doctors who tried to cure them. French vaccinations increased apace, particularly against cholera (Bigeard, ed., *Lettres d'Indochine*, vol. 2 [Paris], 181–83).
31. Bigeard also felt himself different now—formerly a captain and "un peu chien fou," now heading an elite battalion as a major, and full of respect for a tough enemy and the losses it could inflict (Bigeard, *Ma guerre d'Indochine*, 70).
32. One reason Bigeard's men even had a chance for survival here was his orders for thorough, round-the-clock digging. "Digging one's hole is maybe what I first taught my paras. It avoids surprises and particularly, getting oneself foolishly killed" (Bigeard, *Ma guerre d'Indochine*, 78). Norman Schwartzkopf would also signal the lack of thorough digging as one reason for senseless deaths when the Americans took over in Vietnam.
33. See Bernard Fall, *Street without Joy: Indochina at War, 1946–1954* (Harrisburg, 1961), 61–66. See also SHAT: 7U 3037: Journal de Marche du 6ième Bataillion de Parachutistes Coloniaux, entry for October 20 and posthumous citations for Guérin and Letourneux. A sense of Viet Minh imprisonment comes from an account given by then Major Francis Turelier, incarcerated in Vietnam from July 5, 1947, to June 8, 1953. He started out tied to a post all night long, ravaged to the point of extreme bloodiness by mosquitoes he could not fend off. The next day he was flung into a cage with a Vietnamese priest who would not associate Marx with Christ, along with an interpreter about to be executed! There followed extensive, obligatory brainwashing sessions and poor nourishment (Bigeard, ed., *Lettres d'Indochine*, vol. 2, 238–39).
34. As usual Bigeard's French style on all this is inimitably terse. "Sommes proches du coma," he remarks laconically (*Ma guerre d'Indochine*, 82).
35. Bigeard, *Pour une parcelle de gloire*, vol. 1, 164, where he notes that his troops

were "drunk with fatigue." On General de Linarès, see Bigeard, *Ma guerre d'Indochine*, 84.

36. Bigeard especially notes positively the Saint-Cyrian assistant he had been given, Captain Tourret, a cool cucumber always wanting to stay behind with his men in the midst of ambushes. Summarizing Tulé Bigeard says: "We held due to heart and head," not numbers or amount of equipment (*Ma guerre d'Indochine*, 82–83).

37. Summaries of the Tulé (also Tu Lê) escape are in all the major histories, but the best secondary account is Alain Gandy's *Bataillon Bigeard à Tu Lê 1952: la légende des paras* (Paris, 1996). For decorations in Hanoi and the text of citations see SHAT: 7U 3037: Journal de Marche du 6ième Bataillion. Most of the men cited individually would be dead within a couple years. These included Lieutenant Michel Le Vigoureux, praised here for his courage, "sang froid" and "sens du terrain"; and Captain Paul Leroy, "qui après deux ans et demi passés en Extrême Orient dans des conditions souvent difficiles, n'a pas hésité à se porter volontaire pour un deuxième séjour" and who on the 21st and 22nd led courageous "combats retardateurs" allowing the battalion to reach the Black River. The Journal de marche du 6ième Bataillion also includes Bigeard's "Ordre du Bataillon no. 29" of October 31, including quotations ("qui ose gagne" and "il faut durer").

38. Fall, *Street without Joy*, 67–71. A subsequent report of Colonel Jacques Paris de Bollardière, Commander of Airborne Troops in Indochina (January 7, 1953), was critical of the entire Tulé conception and operation: "La préparation a été très brève, le briefing [sic] court et hâtif." Not to mention forbidding geography where a chain of granitic mountains often attained a height of 3,000 meters, and where "les rivières sont de véritables torrents . . . infranchissables aux époques de crues." And there were problems generally for aviators. See Bollardière's report in SHAT: 10H 1275 Dossiers Documentaires Concernant les Opérations: Thai Nguyen . . . Tu Lé (16 octobre 1952). In *Bataille d'Alger, bataille de l'homme* (Paris, 1972), Bollardière mentions the lure of "Indo" that had drawn this idealist there: "J'étais mystérieusement attiré par l'Asie dont la poésie avait enchanté mon enfance. Mon grand-père au moment de la conquête, puis mon oncle et mon père, avait foulé le sol d'Indochine. Mon père avait servi sous les ordres de Gallieni, qui, s'il était contraint d'attaquer un village rebelle, pensait déjà au marché qu'il faudrait y ouvrir et à la vie jaillissante qui l'animerait. . . . [Mon père] m'avait parlé bien souvent des rizières vert pâle, voilées de brume, des montagnes sauvages du Haut-Tonkin où il avait été blessé à trois reprises" (49).

39. Bigeard, *Pour une parcelle de gloire*, vol. 1, 173. The key battle of the era occurred at a huge French emplacement *cum* airport, Nasan (or Na San), before Dien Bien Phu, and perhaps unfortunately, a success for Gilles against Giap in "a real battle, not simply guerilla combat" (Bigeard, *Ma guerre d'Indochine*, 86). See also the report on the operation, December 10, 1952, in SHAT: 7U 30 26: Journal de Marche du 3ième B.P.C. (Bataillon Parachutiste Colonial) 1952–1953. That file contains numerous typed missives from Gilles, sent to a variety of battalions, including Bigeard's. The sense of fighting in a far-off land under difficult circumstances persisted while most French at home more or less ignored such matters. In fact that feeling had been there almost from the beginning. In a letter from

"Guy" of the 1st Tabors to his cousin he notes as early as 1947: "In France ... they ignore all the amplitude of these combats endured here, and don't talk enough of the heroic defense of certain positions attacked at 100 to one" (Bigeard, ed., *Lettres d'Indochine*, vol. 1, 55).

40. Bigeard, *Pour une parcelle de gloire*, vol. 1, 177. He spells Son La differently from other sources.

41. Bigeard, *Pour une parcelle de gloire*, vol. 1, 177.

42. Bigeard, *Pour une parcelle de gloire*, vol. 1, 178. He was on a brief roll when it came to good superiors. For a period of several weeks before that he and several other battalion leaders took their orders from Colonel Ducournau, "un diable d'homme qui veut être de toutes nos missions" (*Ma guerre d'Indochine*, 87).

43. Bigeard, *Pour une parcelle de gloire*, vol. 1, 180. Back again to knocking superiors, Bigeard mentioned one Colonel Dallier giving orders from the comfort of General Staff headquarters in Hanoi for a region much larger and more difficult than it appeared on his maps (*Ma guerre d'Indochine*, 89).

44. Bigeard, *Pour une parcelle de gloire*, vol. 1, 170. On new *Généchef* Navarre's almost risible lack of knowledge concerning an area where he would soon be making disastrous policy, see the Vietnam legend Brigitte Friang's *La mousson de la liberté: Vietnam, du colonialisme au stalinisme* (Paris, 1976), 17–18. And on the battalion's *prise d'armes* in honor of Navarre, SHAT: 7U 3037. The contrast between the militarily able and cultured Salan and the Joffre-like Navarre is clear in the former's writing on the dire situation in Vietnam. Salan's typed, unpublished book of over 200 pages called *Le Viet Minh mon adversaire* was finished just before he left his position and shows his seriousness and extensive knowledge of Vietnam. He had read his Mao carefully, knew a lot about Giap and his ability to hit weak points, and had great respect for an "adversaire redoubtable" (203). He knew the French would have no hope of remaining here on the cheap or by using half-measures. The archives also contain a curious brochure put out by Salan's Saigon office in 1952, aimed at soldiers and full of cartoons, as well as instructions to reduce the number of men in blockhouses, to get accurate information (and not to be fobbed off by disinformation), to hold needless fire, to fortify better and surround emplacements by a series of *périphériques*, to constantly check arms and always be ready for surprises, etc. See SHAT: Fonds Privés. 1K T220 (*Le Viet Minh mon adversaire*) and Archives de l'Indochine: 10H894 Organisation de la défense des territoires (1952–54), containing the brochure (completed November 20, 1952).

45. Bigeard, *Pour une parcelle de gloire*, vol. 1, 182.

46. Bigeard, *Pour une Parcelle de gloire*, vol. 1, 189. Bigeard realized by this time how fanatic Giap's Marxist charges were. Posters of Stalin and Mao were omnipresent; aside from a few elite para battalions, the French so far from home had nothing of the same fervor on the other side. He also knew from a dinner with Navarre how fatuous the new head commander was (*Ma guerre d'Indochine*, 92, 94). On exact troop numbers, maneuvers, losses, and enemy materiel gained in "Hirondelle," see the 6th's Journal de Marche in SHAT: 7U 3037 and best, an exhaustive file bulging with hundreds of telegrams marked "urgent" and with beautifully written reports on the operation. One by Colonel Bénet, Commandant

du Génie Opérationnel for Hirondelle (July 25, 1953), echoed Bigeard's humility here. In his conclusion he emphasized that "Dans l'opération 'HIRONDELLE' le Génie a pu obtenir un rendement exceptionnel, mais il est certain que les circonstances ont joué favorablement" (weather, height of rivers, absence of expected mines). He noted how "les Sapeurs ont travaillé de jour et de nuit," trying not to waste a minute. But again, one must *not* consider "ce rendement comme base de détermination de la vitesse de progression pour une opération future." Captain Carron de la Carrière's equally detailed, cultured report (from the branch of Appui Aérien, July 25, 1953) was also realistic on what worked, but also on what would need improving in future operations, especially concerning radio contacts, including the necessity of rapidly changing frequencies, and evacuations. One understands well how the underdog French of this era would embrace the underdog Israelis, both militaries combining Spartan and Athenian characteristics. Reports and telegrams in SHAT: Dossiers Documentaires Concernant les Opérations: Hirondelle (17–21 juillet 1953).

47. Bigeard's official report (Compte Rendu d'Opération) of November 25, 1953 is in SHAT: 10H 1144: Dossiers Documentaires Concernant les Opérations: Carnaval ... Castor (20 au 25 novembre 1953). One should also see the questionnaire on the operation sent by an American air attaché on preparations, tonnage dropped, parachutist effectives, dimensions of drop zones, utility of different airplanes, etc., and responses from Navarre's office, December 11, 1953. The latter mentioned great difficulties for the pilots and the small drop zones (both Natacha and Simone). As for para "accidents de saut," only two died jumping, and there were a few sprains or fractures, a "pourcentage faible." There is also a beautiful report with fine air photographs by General Gilles of November 25, 1953, showing the dried mud of rice fields in this season, forested heights, and the like. The report also notes customary morning fog here. All reports lamented the inability to use C 119's for drops of heavy equipment, due to topography and conditions. As usual Bigeard's own punchy prose from one of his books gives the best sense of these engagements. On fluttering downward, "I hear bullets whistling in my ears.... Every second counts." Partly the Viet presence there was a matter of luck—two of their battalions just happened to be engaged in a training exercise at the moment. But Bigeard says that Communist arms from Russia and China now made aviation (and airstrips) France's only point of technical superiority (*Ma guerre d'Indochine*, 93, 100).

48. Cogny's letters and reports are in SHAT: 10H 894. In one of August 17, 1953, he said that giving up Lai Chau unprovoked by the enemy would make the French lose face with Thai chefs, "lourd de conséquence dans ce Pays." We would be losing "nos amis les plus fidèles, ce qui lèvera les derniers scrupules de ceux qui le sont moins." He pleaded with Navarre to await events. "C'est pourquoi je vous demande instamment de *différer votre décision définitive*" (his emphasis). But Navarre's scribbled note on the letter demanded adherence to the plan. In a subsequent letter of August 5, 1953, Cogny declared that it was much harder and sillier to evacuate Lai Chau than Nasan, the "gouffre de bataillons." For the former "on prend des risques considérables, matériels et politiques." By December, however, Cogny was parroting the correct propagandistic line, noting how the Castor

of Dien was linked to the Pollux of Lai Chau and that this was our new strategy, making Dien the new capital of Thai resistance. Cogny report (Commandement des Forces Terrestres du Nord Vietnam) December 12, 1953, in SHAT: 10H 1178: Dossiers Documentaires Concernant les Opérations: Dien Bien Phu-études ... notes manuscrites des chefs et sous-chefs d'état-major (décembre 1953–mai 1954). Saddest are letters in this file from Thai chiefs pledging continued fidelity to the French (though plainly doomed). Bigeard knew in his bones too how wrong-headed this whole operation was. In some of his great engagements his men had held the heights over fixed Viet Minh emplacements; now the reverse would hold true (*Ma guerre d'Indochine*, 102). See also the day-by-day summary of operations in SHAT: 7U 3037: Journal de Marche. On protection of the South see a long, intelligent report by Commandant de Jacquelot of November 25, 1953, in SHAT: 10H894. According to Jacquelot the two main problems there were "une zone deltaïque très étendue (en gros trois fois la superficie de celle du delta du Tonkin)" and an enemy "assez insaisissable [qui] agit surtout par des mines, harcèlements et embuscades."

49. For his mindset at this time see *Ma guerre d'Indochine*, 109–10. The battalion's Journal de Marche also shows how frequent and serious firefights with the Viet Minh were in that first half of January 1954. They also mention picking up the wounded from other battalions during patrols (SHAT: 7U 3037).

50. Traditionally, protection of air bases like Cat Bi had been entrusted to North Africans, especially *tirailleurs marocains*, who by and large did a good job of it. The French often promised them rapid advancement in Indochina, set up Moorish cafés at bases, gave them time and space for religious ceremonies, and prominent roles in July 14 processions. See reports and correspondence in SHAT: 10H879: E.M.F.T.-3ème Bureau: Notes générales sur la défense des bases aériens ... Cat Bi, Langson, etc., 1949–53. See also files in SHAT: 10H2486: Organisation territoriale du Nord-Vietnam 1954, which show how frantically the French were moving men and materiel in this era, consolidating bases, and trying to detect mines and protect personnel on bases, including some American technicians. On "scary" air conditions General Guy Hinterlang recalls flying (or jumping) in dense fogs, the "crachin du Tonkin," which he says resembled "le crachin Breton" (SHAT: Fonds Privés. Histoire Orale: 3K8 Interview with Gen. Guy Hinterlang [1997]). On the story concerning Félix Brunet see Bigeard, *Pour une parcelle de gloire*, vol. 1, 214–15. See also the account in the battalion's Journal de Marche SHAT: 7U 3037. February had been an unusual month of no losses to the 6th, save the termination of seventy-three military contracts, including forty-eight *contrats autochtones*; March would be very different!

51. Bigeard, *Pour une parcelle de gloire*, vol. 1, 217. Bigeard evokes the state of mind of men, some near the end of their term in Indochina, all shoulder-to-shoulder, fanatically supportive of each other (*Ma guerre d'Indochine*, 112–13).

52. Bigeard, *Pour une parcelle de gloire*, vol. 1, 217. Bigeard quote on impression of death in *Ma guerre d'Indochine*, 114.

53. Bigeard, *Pour une parcelle de gloire*, vol. 1, 220. For a good capsule description of Castries and his career see Roger Bruge, *Les hommes de Dien Biên Phu* (Paris, 1999), 53. Olivier de Maison Rouge calls Castries a fine warrior, but not the

right man to command an entrenched camp; much better in his estimation was Colonel Vanuxem, then on an operation in the delta. Of course the original French estimate was that one Viet Minh division would arrive at Dien; instead there were four, necessitating a much quicker, more frantic and complete build-up (Maison Rouge, 236).

54. Langlais had mentioned the proverbial stubborn quality inherent in both his Breton origins and Bigeard's Lorraine roots. In fact both French regions were among the highest contributors of army personnel to the military effort in Indochina. See Bodin, 77–83. On what Bigeard's arrival meant to paratroopers of various units here, see Jean Collet's memoir, *Avoir 20 ans à Diên Biên Phu* (Paris, 1994): "[Bigeard's] savoir-faire as a winner, his faculty of adapting to conditions . . . make him miraculously place all combattants on an equal footing" (111). But Bigeard knew the realities were overwhelmingly against the French. Among other things the Chinese had taught the Viet Minh how to bury cannons around the fortress. They were taken out to pound down into the camp, then quickly buried again, so that French aviation couldn't reach them (Bigeard, *Ma guerre d'Indochine*, 118). The battalion's Journal de Marche mentions serious losses from the beginning, lack of materiel, and frantic *travaux défensifs* (SHAT: 7U 3037).

55. See Paul Grauwin, *Doctor at Dienbienphu*, trans. James Oliver (New York, 1955), 201. The book is full of poignant stories, such as on the orphan who had volunteered for the colonial paratroops, lost his arm, and was eventually killed at Dien. Grauwin had treated the boy and saved a beautiful sonnet he wrote before his untimely death. (Grauwin, 211–14). See also Bigeard, *Ma guerre d'Indochine*, 118, and Gen. Maurice Schmitt, *De Diên Biên Phu à Koweït City* (Paris, 1992), 33: "Je vis Grauwin en salle de triage, ne s'occupant de l'origine des blessés . . . mais uniquement de leur état. Calme, efficace, direct et même sachant plaisanter. . . . Un grand nombre de survivants de l'Indochine, des deux camps, lui doivent la vie."

56. Bigeard, *Pour une parcelle de gloire*, vol. 1, 236; and *Ma guerre d'Indochine*, 119–20 on the lack of generals here. The capsule portraits in Bruge's book of men with long histories of combat going back to the days of Resistance and dying at Dien make poignant reading. For example, the artillery commander, Charles Piroth, committed suicide by falling on a grenade to preserve his honor. He had been in Morocco, was wounded in World War II, then in postwar Indochina was again wounded in the arm, before being repatriated to France and having that arm amputated in March 1947. But he had returned, then found death in these ignominious surroundings (Bruge, 201). In addition to Le Vigoureux, Bigeard's Lieutenant Jacobs was also killed on March 28, along with four other noncommissioned officers, and eleven *hommes de troupe*. See battalion Journal de Marche entry in SHAT: 7U 3037. Viet Minh losses included 350 dead and 1000 "probably hors de combat." But again, they had far greater reserves in manpower. The 6th had absorbed a significant number of dead (46) and wounded (183) by the end of March, with worse to come.

57. Bigeard, *Pour une parcelle de gloire*, vol. 1, 241 and his *Ma guerre d'Indochine*, 123–24. "Très importantes pertes V.N." on the other side during "nettoyage" of Huguette 6 (noted April 3 in the Battalion's Journal de Marche) of course meant little. In SHAT: 7U 3037, also containing the 1st B.P.C. loss counts mentioned.

58. For his state of mind Bigeard, *Ma guerre d'Indochine*, 126.

59. Born in the West of France Gilles de Fromont de Bouaille had come out of Saint-Cyr in 1950, arriving as a lieutenant in Indochina in October 1952, and was soon known for his courage there. He had first jumped into Dien Bien Phu in "Castor" November 1953, then again with Bigeard March 16 (Bruge, 324).

60. See Bigeard, *Pour une parcelle de gloire*, vol. 1, 258, his *Ma guerre d'Indochine*, 129–30, 136, and the standard histories, as well as the vivid account in Prados' book, 178–79. The battalion had 268 men dead, wounded, or "disparus" in April (Journal de Marche entry for end of the month in SHAT: 7U 3037).

61. Bigeard, *Pour une parcelle de gloire*, vol. 1, 260. For the 6th "rump" *promotions exceptionnelles* of April 25 included Bigeard to lieutenant-colonel, and to the grade of captain, Francis de Wilde and René Lepage. See the battalion's Journal de Marche entries for April, including many citations as well in SHAT: 7U 3037. There is a particularly long list of *récompenses* noted for April 28. Cf. Bigeard, *Crier ma vérité*, 20: "Promu lieutenant-colonel à 37 ans, je suis le plus jeune à ce grade dans l'armée française. Cadeau dérisoire ... Je vois des centaines de camarades se laisser mourir sous mes yeux." Bigeard considered it a likely "promotion à titre posthume," costing the General Staff little, as did their promotions of Castries to general and Langlais to colonel (*Siècle des héros*, 218).

62. Bigeard, *Pour une parcelle de gloire*, vol. 1, 262. On Dien Bien Phu and its tragic dénouement we have benefited from a clear treatment by Williamson Murray, "Dien Bien Phu," in *MHQ: The Quarterly Journal of Military History* 9 (Spring 1997): 40–51; and from Porch, *French Foreign Legion*, chs. 24–26. For the whole war down to this crisis point we have also culled from Fall, *Street without Joy* and his *Hell in a Very Small Place* (Philadelphia, 1967); and Edgar O'Ballance, *The Indo-China War, 1945–54* (London, 1964), among other books.

63. Spelled as "Mo lae, Mo lae" (faster, faster) in Bigeard's *Ma guerre d'Indochine*, 134. Galard's nursing corps needs more study. There are radiant accounts from nurses in Bigeard ed., *Lettres d'Indochine*, vol. 2. As Simone Jeanselme, in Indochina over five years, notes: "Pour moi, l'Armée a été une grande famille, très chère à mon coeur, à qui j'ai consacrée ma plus belle jeunesse et mon idéal. ... car nous avons eu aussi dans ce pays extraordinaire de beauté, d'inoubliables et intenses moments de bonheur" (*Lettres d'Indochine*, vol. 2, 220–21). Suzanne Sancan wrote her brother (undated here) about Dien Bien Phu: "J'ai, une fois de plus, la vie que j'aime" (ibid., 221).

64. Bigeard, *Pour une parcelle de gloire*, vol. 1, 270 and see also his *Ma guerre d'Indochine*, 136. The 6th was formally dissolved at the end of May 1954. See last page of the Journal de Marche in SHAT: 7U 3037.

65. Bigeard, *Pour une parcelle de gloire*, vol. 1, 278.

66. The French for "lost" here is *paumé*, slang also conveying the sense of "sunk" (Bigeard, *Pour une parcelle de gloire*, vol. 1, 281).

67. On a trip to Indochina in 1994 Bigeard told a Vietnamese general: "Une scule banane par jour et tous mes camarades prisonniers ne seraient pas morts" (Bigeard, *Ma guerre d'Indochine*, 141). There were other death marches as well in various parts of the country. Guy Pontoizeau, another cultured soldier of that generation, was nabbed in Central Annam June 3, 1954, in great part due to the

overemphasis on Dien and then its fall, leaving soldiers in other areas of Vietnam outgunned. Twice grilled by educated, but cruel Viet Minh, he was tied to a tree, then marched 500 kilometers up toward the Annamite chain of mountains. En route thirst was so unbearable that men overcame their fear of dysentery by lapping from muddy puddles; hunger (given a ration of one bowl of bad rice per day) was constant, and feet were getting cut up by bamboo spines, bleeding and becoming infected, and always to the chant of "faster, faster." In the odd village one's clothes or gold chain could procure a banana or two, but once up in camp, more sadism reigned, and the death rate was high here too. Again, only the Geneva Accords saved this particular soldier. See Pontoizeau's nineteen-page report in SHAT: Fonds Privés. T595.

68. Another instance of Bigeard's bitterness extending into the 1990s occurred when President Mitterand visited Dien Bien Phu and sat next to a white-haired General Giap at a state banquet. Bigeard was invited to accompany Mitterand on the trip, but declined, noting that Giap was a great soldier, but that he had allowed at least 8,000 French prisoners of war to die in four months. As long as the regime was still Marxist, he would not go. Between the lines, however, he may also have been criticizing the former young politician Mitterand's easy opposition to the war from afar in Paris. See articles in the *Times* (London), February 17, 1993; and the *Los Angeles Times*, February 16, 1993. For Bigeard's state of mind before, during, and after the Dien Bien Phu debacle, his memoirs remain the best source, but see also Bergot, *Bigeard*, 255–362.

69. A good, comparative book ought to be done on this "packing up" phenomenon in places like Vietnam and Dutch Indonesia, and more generally, on history as a series of expropriations. The unusually thick file on all this for North Vietnam is SHAT: 10H 2252: Evacuation du Nord-Vietnam 1954–55. It includes cards that many Vietnamese tried to get for flight to the south, and long lists of those civilians, as well as much correspondence, most on the letterhead of Cogny's office of the Forces Terrestres du Nord Vietnam. The entire conflict had cost the French army (including of course recruits from the empire) almost 60,000 dead or missing. See Pierre Brocheux and Daniel Hémery, *Indochine: la colonisation ambiguë (1858–1954)* (Paris, 1994), 363. Bigeard remarks in *Crier ma vérité* that the scar of Dien and its aftermath never left him. As noted, his mother asked pointedly how he had become a prisoner, while "les plus hauts gradés ne m'avaient pas posé la question.... La Sophie tient à ce que je lui rende des comptes" (23, quote 21).

70. On his courses Bigeard would write of "salles de classes ennuyeuses, cours fumeux et théoriques. Rien à voir avec la pratique." He also felt himself an outsider amidst all these Cyriens and Polytechniciens (Bigeard, *Ma guerre d'Algérie*, 10). And more recently: "Les étudiants des grandes écoles me font sentir que je ne suis pas de leur monde.... Toute ma vie, je suis resté homme du peuple. C'est pour cela que je comprends les gens de la rue.... Je parle comme eux. J'écris comme eux. Directement, simplement" (Bigeard, *Crier ma vérité*, 21–22). Academic debates over the whole conception of Dien Bien Phu would of course continue for quite a time. The files in SHAT: 10H 1178 show how fearful and hesitant generals in charge were during the months preceding Giap's barrage, and how

they already seemed to envisage defeat in a variety of war game scenarios sketched in letters and reports. General Guy Méry in a recorded interview said he found the whole plan shocking from the word go. "Le site était très mal choisi" and the Viet Minh sure to annihilate it (SHAT: Fonds Privés. Histoire Orale. 3K4: Interview with Guy Méry [1996]). Another item in the *fonds privés* of April 4 again averred that the *cuvette* was a bad idea and that critiques of French artillery were misplaced. See SHAT: Fonds Privés. T 238. Lt.-Col. de Winter, *L'Artillerie dans la bataille de Dien-Bien-Phu*. In SHAT: 10H 1178 there is a poignant letter of 1963 from a Frenchman wounded at Dien Bien Phu, rebutting Jules Roy's published criticisms of Thai defections. He said his Thais—the same Montagnards Bigeard so valued—had fought bravely to the end (letter from Capt. Michel Désiré [of the Service Historique de l'Armée] to Jules Roy, November 8, 1963).

71. Bigeard, *Pour une parcelle de gloire*, vol. 1, 303; and see also his *Ma guerre d'Algérie*, 10–12. Reconstituting old battalions and regiments or reconstituting new ones after the debacle in Vietnam was a major undertaking. See SHAT: Fonds Privés. Histoire Orale. 3K6: Interview with General Bernard Saint-Hillier (1997).

72. Louis Bertrand, *Les villes d'or* (Paris, 1921), quote 32; Bertrand, *Le sang des races* (Paris, 1926), passim. In the former Bertrand equates lost cities with a civilization overwhelmed (the terms "city" and "civilization" of course related etymologically). He describes the frenzy of nineteenth and twentieth century pickers and shovellers to recover at least the ruins. Yes, "oubliées par l'envahisseur, après qu'il les eut copieusement pillées et dévastées, les villes romaines se sont enfoncées lentement sous la terre et les décombres" (185–86). Originally from Lorraine, Bertrand became a classics professor at the Lycée of Algiers in 1891, fell in love with North Africa, and on breaks traveled widely with cart-drivers for his material. Departing Algeria in 1897, he returned often through the 1930s. See Peter Dunwoodie, *Writing French Algeria* (Oxford, 1998), 83–108.

73. Gabriel Audisio, *Jeunesse de la Méditerranée* (Paris, 1935), 96, 98, 99, 112; and on Audisio Dunwoodie, 175–84. In his *Colonial Cinema and Imperial France* (ch. 1) Slavin stresses continuing *pied noir* support for limitations on Muslims, at least from the time of the Code de l'Indigénat implemented by the French Chamber after the Franco-Prussian War. He also stresses their antisemitism, though one still meets Algerian Jews who consider themselves *pied noirs*. One of the present authors interviewed one (Sarah C., May 2002), full of good things to say about French Oran before its demise.

74. See Camus, *The Plague* trans. Stuart Gilbert (New York, 1948), still a fine English rendition, Jacqueline Lévi-Valensi, *La Peste d'Albert Camus* (Paris, 1991), and Tony Judt's stimulating, "On 'the Plague,'" *New York Review of Books*, November 29, 2001, 6–9 (and also the preface for a new translation).

75. See Alistair Horne, *A Savage War of Peace: Algeria 1954–1962* (London, 1977), part 1. For detail on *pieds noirs* see Noël Moncade, *Les Français d'Algérie* (Paris, 1964), part 1; Pierre Mannoni, *Les Français d'Algérie: vie, moeurs, mentalités* (Paris, 1993), 6–7, 139–47; Daniel Leconte, *Les pieds-noirs: histoire et portrait d'une communauté* (Paris, 1980); and Joëlle Hureau, *La mémoire des pieds-noirs* (Paris, 1987), especially good on the life lived there after World War I. To hear the voice of a truly enlightened *pied noir* tracing his heritage back to Algeria of the 1850s on his

father's side and the 1830s on his mother's, see SHAT: Fonds Privés. Histoire orale. 3K38: Interview with Mario Favre (1998). Favre was educated both in Paris and Algeria in musical composition, but was also a writer, a businessman, and a prominent Resistant during the war. On divisions among Algerian Muslim leaders see Guy Pervillé, "The 'Francisation' of Algerian Intellectuals: History of a Failure?" in L. Carl Brown and Matthew S. Gordon, eds., *Franco-Arab Encounters: Studies in Memory of David C. Gordon* (Beirut, 1996), 415–45. See also SHAT: (Archives de l'Algérie 1945–67) 1H 1117/1: Action psychologique: documentation, études et schémas de causerie (1955–59) for documents on the elites, and also a marvelous, clear, enlightened report on the Kabyles, by a French officer who obviously admired them (*Etude sur quelques aspects de la psychologie kabyle*). The report notes "leur amère sagesse de pauvres gens," culling from their proverbs: "Si tu n'es pas un loup gare au loup"; "silence prime science"; and "la langue trop longue est mordue par les dents," among others. The author goes on: "Par point d'honneur, par gloriole, le Kabyle est prêt à se lancer dans les pire aventures et à commettre les pires excès. But at the same time "le Kabyle est ... un être lucide, d'un réalisme parfois brutal." One should finally note the problem of Arab antisemitism, mentioned by Giraud, 30–31, among other places.

76. Saint Marc, 185. Jean-Charles Jauffret takes issue with the thesis of putative tranquillity existing in Algeria until All Saints' Day, 1954 in "The Origins of the Algerian War: The Reaction of France and its Army to the Two Emergencies of 8 May 1945 and 1 November 1954," *Journal of Imperial and Commonwealth History* 21 (September 1993): 17–29. In a masterly study *Revolutionary Terrorism: The FLN in Algeria 1954–1962* (Stanford, 1978), Martha Crenshaw Hutchinson also dissects the long-term background to FLN terror, going back to a population explosion of the 1920s, growing urban origins of potential terrorists, and again, the influence of French army training and of France's stunning defeat by the Nazis in World War II (7 and passim).

77. Gen. Paul Aussaresses, *Services spéciaux: Algérie 1955–1957* (Paris, 2001), quotations 14, 25. Among the most objective Anglophone press articles on this first Aussaresses memoir were those by Keith Richburg in the *Washington Post*, June 18, 2001; Adam Shatz in the *Nation*, June 18, 2001; and Peter Gumbel in the *Wall Street Journal*, October 17, 2001. Aussaresses was retired from his army position, had to give up his *Légion d'honneur* decoration, and faced a criminal investigation suit. The question of this first book's "coauthorship" has been debated. Claude Ribes, sometimes identified as a coauthor, said Aussaresses composed a long manuscript by himself, based on conversations he had taped with Aussaresses, of which only the part on Algeria came to Librairie Perrin, the distinguished Paris publisher to which Ribes first brought Aussaresses. Subsequently Ribes did only some minor polishing, he said. See articles on this in *Le Monde*, November 26 and especially, November 28, 2001. Told-to and polished-up autobiographies in English by such notables as Hank Aaron, Brian Wilson, or General Schwartzkopf certainly reveal their authors' personality, and so does that of Aussaresses.

78. Aussaresses, *Services spéciaux,* 11–21.

79. For data to this point see Aussaresses, *Services spéciaux,* 23–47.

80. On the background and unfolding of the massacres, including el-Halia see

Aussaresses, *Services spéciaux,* 49–72. See also Jacques Soustelle, *Aimée et souffrante: Algérie* (Paris, 1956), ch. 6. Horne mentions another terrible massacre at Ain-Abid east of Constantine, where a *pied noir* family was slaughtered, including the hacking up of a baby put back into its disembowelled mother's opened womb (Horne, *Savage War of Peace,* 121). For this whole era we have also used Horne, part 1, ch. 6, 7, and appropriate parts of Edgar O'Ballance, *The Algerian Insurrection 1954–1962* (Hamden, Conn., 1967); John Ruedy's overview, *Modern Algeria: The Origins and Development of a Nation* (Bloomington, Ind., 1992); John Talbott, *The War without Name: France in Algeria 1954–1962* (New York, 1980); and Paul Henissart, *Wolves in the City: The Death of French Algeria* (New York, 1970). One should also mention the volumes on the Algerian war by Yves Courrière, noted in our bibliography and now somewhat in need of updating. In terms of Algerian terror the long-held French predilection for Kabyles of the mountains (really only one part of the Berber ethnic group) versus the Arabs would be blurred during this war, as even lowlander rebels took refuge in the mountains. For the French mythology of the good Kabyle and bad Arab see Patricia Lorcin's stimulating *Imperial Identities: Stereotyping, Prejudice, and Race in Colonial Algeria* (London, 1995). On Algerian terror producing massive counterterror see Jean-Jacques Servan-Schreiber's later lament, *Lieutenant in Algeria,* trans. Ronald Matthews (New York, 1957). Horne gives good data on FLN justification for murdering civilians as a response to the French army's notion of "collective responsibility," whereby they would round up villagers to cut trees and replace damaged telephone poles, etc. (Horne, *Savage War of Peace,* 113–22). He also notes significant "inside" help for the mine massacre (120).

81. Marcel Bigeard, *Pour une parcelle de gloire,* vol. 2, *La dernière des guerres* (Paris, 1975), 15. And in a more recent account: "Très vite je dynamise tous ceux qui m'entourent. . . . Je fais retailler les uniformes. Reserrer les pantalons, les vestes près du corps. . . . Pas de place pour les mous, pour les hésitants, ni pour la défaillance" (Bigeard, *Crier ma vérité,* 25).

82. Bigeard, *Pour une parcelle de gloire,* vol. 2, quotation 16, and see also his *Ma guerre d'Algérie,* 14, where he salutes Beaufre's "classe incroyable." In another book he remarks: "Beaufre sait de quoi il parle, il fut l'adjoint de De Lattre en Indochine et demeure notre plus grand penseur militaire de cette époque." He had also read his Mao and knew an army couldn't be everywhere against this type of foe (Bigeard, *J'ai mal à la France* [Paris, 2001], 103).

83. Horne, *Savage War of Peace,* 168 and on "immobilisme" Bigeard, *Ma guerre d'Algérie,* 19, and *Crier ma vérité,* 25–29. See also on night operations and his Lyautey-like views, *J'ai mal à la France,* 117–20. He felt the abrogation of the Arab bureaus had left a real void.

84. Bigeard, *Pour une parcelle de gloire,* vol. 2, 27. While interesting, the quotation is also somewhat misleading. Bigeard never underestimated opponents in Algeria. And as usual, he had to fight on two fronts—one being that of un-Beaufre-like superiors! For Opération Eventail, beginning December 7, 1955, and conceived to snare a top rebel leader, Si Messaoud, a general from France told Bigeard to use an army of 5,000 soldiers and much equipment. "Discussion de dandy dans un salon"—and yet another in the long line of Joffresque schemes hatched in an office. Of course it didn't work (Bigeard, *Crier ma vérité,* 32).

85. Quote Bigeard, *Pour une parcelle de gloire*, vol. 2, 40; see also his *Ma guerre d'Algérie*, 21–23. On helicopters Bigeard notes the improvements made by American manufacturers, but also the enemy's powers of adaptation, and how nothing could replace the human factor in this war (*J'ai mal à la France*, 106–14).

86. Bigeard, *Pour une parcelle de gloire*, vol. 2, 67, and *Crier ma vérité*, 43–44; and for his progress in Algeria to that point, Bergot, *Bigeard*, 365–97.

87. Bigeard quote, *Pour une parcelle de gloire*, vol. 2, 51. In this period he continued purging his ranks of unsuitable men, particularly bibulous captains: "on ne peut pas faire confiance à un officier qui boit" (*Ma guerre d'Algérie*, 28). On the journalists and the war in Algeria he notes their too often simplistic optic in favor of this or that good guy. The reason was that "la plupart des journalistes français regardaient les événements qui se déroulaient bien loin depuis leur confortable fauteuil à Paris." Had they really done their job in an objective manner "peut-être n'aurions-nous pas perdu cette guerre" (*J'ai mal à la France*, 122). Translation of the collective letter mentioned (February 26, 1956) is in SHAT: 1H 1117/1 and the long document on rebel atrocities is in SHAT: 1H 1092/1: Délégation Générale du Gouvernement en Algérie . . . : Documentation établie par le cabinet du ministre résidant sur le problème algérien (1956). The document also uses a sense of history—poor Turkish control of Algeria, the quadrupling of population under the French, etc.—to show French beneficence. Minister-Resident Lacoste witnessed horrors detailed above first hand. In the spring of 1957 he and a number of French journalists went to see an FLN massacre site of MNA adherents, dead with eyes hacked out, "sexe" in mouths, etc. Soon all major MNA leaders would be dead. See Jacques Duquesne, *Pour comprendre la guerre d'Algérie* (Paris, 2001), 54 and also his ch. 10 on the press. On the Jews cf. Horne, *Savage War of Peace*, 58–59, noting paradoxical support for the FLN, partly out of fear.

88. Quote in Bigeard, *Pour une parcelle de gloire*, vol. 2, 66–67. Again, the slangy prose on "Vanu" in a later book: "Un type pas facile qui ne fait pas la dentelle" (*Ma guerre d'Algérie*, 32).

89. Quote in Bigeard, *Pour une parcelle de gloire*, vol. 2, 71. He notes in *Ma guerre d'Algérie*, 33: "Rien de plus agaçant que ces hommes de bureau, qui viennent mettre le nez dans vos affaires!" And in a more recent account: "L'étau est bien serré. C'est le moment que choisit Vanuxem pour débarquer, frais toiletté, de son hélicoptère. Il me pose des questions qui m'exaspèrent. . . . Je sens la moutarde qui monte." Grabbing a microphone, Bigeard then called his company commanders together and invited Vanu to take over as their head! The latter backed off (Bigeard, *Crier ma vérité*, 54).

90. Quote Bigeard, *Pour une parcelle de gloire*, vol. 2, 72, and see *Ma guerre d'Algérie*, 34, and *Crier ma vérité*, 55.

91. Again, the punchy, oddly cultured Bigeard slang: "Engueulade des toubibs, furieux de ma petite échapée . . . rien à faire contre ces satanés médecins" (*Ma guerre d'Algérie*, 34). On his *baraka* generally: "Cent fois j'ai croisé la mort. Elle n'a pas voulu de moi" (*Crier ma vérité*, 19; and on the wound, 55–66).

92. These critiques would be remembered (Bigeard, *Ma guerre d'Algérie*, 36). The technicolor cover photo of Bigeard in the July 14, 1956 issue of *Jours de France* shows him clad in red beret, laden with medals and ribbons. The article is titled

"Premier Para du Monde," but gets at some of his contradictions, noting that "derrière un voile de sévérité," Bigeard has "une infinie bonté" and that "il n'aime pas la guerre et il le dit" (12–15, quotations 14). See also on the period from his wound through convalescence and the July 14 celebration, *Crier ma vérité*, 56–58.

93. On these "co-opting energies of the super-powers" Matthew Connelly argues that Dulles and Eisenhower understood far more about Nasser and Algeria than hitherto thought, and were not simply motivated by Cold War concerns. ("Taking Off the Cold War Lens: Visions of North-South Conflict During the Algerian War for Independence," *American Historical Review* 105 [2000]: 739–69). On Suez a good article describing "the shortest and possibly the silliest war in history" is Wilfrid P. Deac, "Operation Musketeer: Duel for the Suez Canal," *Military History* (April 2001): 58–64, quote 59. Bigeard adds: "A vrai dire, je n'ai pas manqué grandchose: quel foutoir ce Suez et quelle déception pour les généraux et pour mes hommes!" (*Ma guerre d'Algérie*, 42, and on the assassination attempt with photos 38, 40–41; *Crier ma vérité*, 62–63.) See also *Jours de France*, September 22, 1956 on "L'Homme à la baraka." The French army in one of its *schémas de causerie* put out by the Defense Ministry and intended for various commanders detailed Nasser's aims as leader of Pan-Islamism and a Pan-Arabic movement, and his efforts to destroy Israel and to take the Suez Canal. By getting close to the Soviets "Nasser s'est rangé du côté des loups. Il a introduit le loup dans la bergerie." Precise notation of losses on all sides is also included here (SHAT: 1H 1117/D1).

94. An irony in the Lacoste appointment was that this Socialist was appointed in order to promote a tougher Algerian policy, replacing the old Gaullist Catroux, who favored decolonization! Bigeard gives his fullest accounts of the Battle of Algiers and his role in it in *J'ai mal à la France*, 134–44 and *Crier ma vérité*, 68–76; and see Horne, *Savage War of Peace*, ch. 9, still the best secondary source account in English. The irony of a strong-armed "grève scolaire" was that in this autumnal period of French Algeria, Muslim children had been flocking to schools. From 1944 to 1954 numbers roughly tripled, due to hunger for French culture, diplomas, and social promotion, but also to family allowances and other benefits that were linked to school attendance. See "schéma de causerie" of late December 1956 intended for army commanders (SHAT: 1H 1117/D1).

95. Aussaresses, *Services spéciaux*, 90.

96. Aussaresses, *Services spéciaux*, 91–95, quotes 91, 93.

97. Aussaresses, *Services spéciaux*, quotes 96, 97, 99, and see also 106.

98. The growing crisis in Algiers was covered by *Jours de France*, January 19, 1957; and for the simultaneous bombing of the cafés on Algiers' Rue Michelet on January 26, see *Paris-Match*, February 9, 1957. By this time the FLN had announced that the French Army's next Dien Bien Phu would indeed be on the Rue Michelet. Bigeard's quotation in *Pour une parcelle de gloire*, vol. 2, 102–3. See also his *Ma guerre d'Algérie*, 46, where he calls this "un sale et dur épisode qui ne vaudra jamais pour moi le vrai combat du djebel.... Tout est bon pour le combattant révolutionnaire et nationaliste: immoralité totale, cruauté sans nom qui écoeure les chefs les plus endurcis." See *Crier ma vérité*, 68–69 and also Schmitt in *De Diên Biên Phu*: "La 'bataille d'Alger' n'est pas un bon souvenir pour le régiment, je le constate. Comme le terroriste a toujours raison et le policier systématiquement

tort on retient la répression et non l'attentat terroriste.... [Mais] il faut en avoir ramassé les débris humains pour en parler" (87). As we will see, Bigeard's relationship with Massu would soon break down here, but Salan "a été toujours chic avec moi. Il m'a souvent confié des missions très difficiles," believing that Bigeard had a sixth sense about dangers. During the Battle of Algiers they would dine together and Salan would quiz Bigeard on all its ramifications (Bigeard, *De la brousse à la jungle* [Paris, 1994], 196). On the breaking of the strike Aussaresses' account in *Services spéciaux*, 137–42 should somewhat revise Douglas Porch's view of the French secret service during the Algerian Revolt given in his *The French Secret Services: From the Dreyfus Affair to the Gulf War* (New York, 1995). He calls Trinquier "France's greatest theorist of counter-insurgency" (383), but one can hardly blame Porch for the fact that Aussaresses' name doesn't even appear in the index, nor in Horne's account. Aussaresses was no household name until the twenty-first century, in good part because he had shunned publicity (due to his position), that is, until the end of his life approached.

99. Bigeard, *J'ai mal à la France*, 147–49, quotation 148, and *Crier ma vérité*, 83–84. Aussaresses notes also that FLN arms caches were often "emmurées." He adds that the way to tell whether an unemployed mason was in the bomb trade was to check his hands (Aussaresses, *Services spéciaux*, 180). See also Horne, *Savage War of Peace*, 184, 193, and on the stadium bombs, coverage in *Paris-Match* of February 23, 1957.

100. See Horne, *Savage War of Peace*, 195, 201 and for Bigeard in Algeria through this episode, Bergot, *Bigeard*, 398–439. On Ben M'Hidi see Aussaresses, *Services spéciaux*, 161–71, quotes 165, 167, 168, and Bigeard, *Crier ma vérité*, 88–115. The latter includes Bigeard's account of his recent meeting with Ben M'Hidi's sister, still a top FLN figure. Bigeard has also reconstituted his conversations in prison here, and Ben M'Hidi's views, like hers, have a similarly simplistic quality. Ben M'Hidi talked about a free, democratic Algeria that would surely result if the French gave it up; but obviously history has proven otherwise. Apparently Ben M'Hidi's last words to Bigeard were: "Je vous estime beaucoup, mon colonel" (99). See also Yves Godard, *Les trois batailles d'Alger*, vol. 1, *Les paras dans la ville* (Paris, 1972), 300; and *Ma guerre d'Algérie*, 50. Godard's book is breezy, yet intelligent on the terrorist underworld in Algiers. In this book he plays down the amount of heavy-handedness imputed to French investigators. He also includes copies of Bigeard's complicated diagrams, outlining the rebel network in Algiers.

101. See Gandy, *Salan* (Paris, 1990), ch. 12. For a scholarly study of the torture issue see Rita Maran, *Torture: The Role of Ideology in the Franco-Algerian War* (New York, 1989). A passionate anti-Massu diatribe is Jules Roy's *J'accuse le Général Massu* (Paris, 1972). Admitting that the FLN also slit throats and tortured, he nonetheless calls Massu the "gravedigger of Algeria while supposedly defending it" and a man who stained the army with his "legal crimes" (90–112, quotes 90, 112). Fanon was another key figure in the antitorture campaign, having treated victims of it as a psychiatrist. See among others, Macey, passim. A French "Safeguard Commission" was launched to investigate charges of torture April 5, 1957, producing its first report that September, which was leaked to *L'Express* magazine and brought "isolated incidents" to world attention.

102. American critiques of French policy in Algeria came from people like labor boss George Meany and Senator John F. Kennedy. For the latter's views see Irwin M. Wall, *France, the United States, and the Algerian War* (Berkeley, 2001), 85–86, 240, 243. Of course the FLN were now lobbying in the States, working the campuses, etc. (Horne, *Savage War of Peace*, 244–47).

103. See Henri Alleg, *The Question* (New York, 1958)—preface by George Braziller, who published the American edition, and introduction by Jean-Paul Sartre. On Alleg's background see Raphaël Delpard, *Vingt ans pendant la guerre d'Algérie* (Neuilly-sur-Seine, 2001), 127–28.

104. Bigeard, *Siècle des héros*, 232 (and he adds in *J'ai mal á la France* [133] that in thirty years of army work "je n'ai jamais torturé qui que ce soit"); Jacques Massu, *La vraie bataille d'Alger* (Paris, 1971), 167–68, quote 168. A marvelous description of Massu is in Geoffrey Bocca, *The Secret Army* (Englewood Cliffs, N.J., 1968): "This massive officer, with his cowboy strut, his Cyrano de Bergerac nose, his face like one carved out of Mount Rushmore . . . [had] a toughness and tolerance for pain . . . so legendary as to be scarcely believable." Wounded in World War II by a German bullet that pierced through his leg, "he cauterized the wound by jabbing his burning cigarette into the hole." And "more incredible, after accusations had been published that his paratroops were torturing suspects, it was revealed by correspondents of the responsible conservative press that Massu had tried all the same tortures on himself first to see how much they hurt." These included "the *gégène*—French army slang for the field telephone, which could be adapted to send electric shocks through a suspect's genitals" (Bocca, 22–23). Aussaresses tells us, however, that Massu used his own "courtesans" to give him a rather light amount of shock (*Services spéciaux*, 156).

105. Massu, *Vraie bataille d'Alger*, 52–54, 313–19. Massu was not as far removed generationally from Lyautey as one might think; he fought in Morocco when Lyautey was still alive. The influence of his wife, Suzanne, on such ambivalence was undeniable. Of Jewish extraction Suzanne Rosambert had first married another French Jew, Henri Torrès, and both had had to flee to the United States during the war. But Suzanne returned to work with General Leclerc's division as "Toto," then took some of her group of "Rochambelles" to French Indochina after the war, where she met Massu (Aussaresses, *Services spéciaux*, 96–97, 181–83). As the latter notes: "Mme Massu avait une grande influence sur le général. . . . Elle estimait que la clémence à l'égard de certaines poseuses de bombe servirait peut-être à gagner la sympathie des femmes algériennes" (182). On her wartime background and on Indochina, including her courtship by Massu, see Suzanne Massu, *Quand j'étais Rochambelle* (Paris, 1969) and *Un commandant pas comme les autres* (Paris, 1971). One might add that the Massus adopted two Muslim children who would give them grandchildren. The most influential and prestigious army critic of Massu's policies, and of torture particularly, is Paris Bollardière in his *Bataille d'Alger, bataille de l'homme*. His critiques included as well a growing anticolonial and antiwar stance. As he put it: "La guerre n'est qu'une dangereuse maladie d'une humanité infantile qui cherche sa voie. La torture, ce dialogue dans l'horreur, n'est que l'envers affreux de la communication fraternelle. Elle dégrade celui qui l'inflige plus encore que celui qui la subit" (Bollardière, 11–12). In this

book Bollardière mentions his great respect for Massu's courage, yet traces the history of his opposition to the latter's policies from January 1957 (see 92–94).

106. The best introductions to this subject are David Schalk's *War and the Ivory Tower: Algeria and Vietnam* (New York, 1991), ch. 3, and the chapter on Camus in Tony Judt's *The Burden of Responsibility: Blum, Camus, Aron, and the French Twentieth Century* (Chicago, 1998), quote 120. See also Morvan Lebesque, *Albert Camus par lui-même* (Paris, 1963) with much material on Camus' Algerian background. We have also learned from an illuminating undergraduate essay on Camus (Harvard, 2001) by Heather Langdon, "All Silent on the Algerian Front?" Important primary source collections, showing the development of Camus' thoughts on Algeria, include Jacqueline Lévi-Valensi and André Abbou, eds., *Cahiers Albert Camus 3: Fragments d'un combat 1938–1940* (Paris, 1978). Camus' break with Sartre had already started in the early 1950s, after the former published his book *The Rebel* (*L'homme révolté*), critical of such historical events as the French Reign of Terror, well ahead of its time, and again, only tardily vindicated by a French academic establishment that finally began looking more objectively (circa 1990) at a hitherto iconic Revolution. On French-Protestant intellectual divisions of this era see Geoffrey Adams, *The Call of Conscience: French Protestant Responses to the Algerian War, 1954–1962* (Waterloo, Ont., 1998). James Le Sueur in his *Uncivil War*, ch. 5, nicely delineates intermediate, conciliatory positions of Jean-Jacques Servan-Schreiber and Germaine Tillion in this intellectual "Dreyfus Affair" atmosphere. Joël Roman also warns against "une mémoire manichéenne" (Roman, "Repères: Les Oppositions à la guerre d'Algérie," *Esprit* 7 [2001]: 209).

107. Bigeard, *Ma guerre d'Algérie*, 52. On Massu's transfer of the 3d to the Atlas, Bigeard remarks: "Drôle de cadeau. Les massifs de l'Atlas regorgent des cachettes. Le froid, la neige, l'importance des dénivelés sont autant d'obstacles" (*J'ai mal à la France*, 129). On the two assassination attempts in Algiers Bigeard's various books are silent. But according to Aussaresses, the FLN wanted to nail him on the streets, and in the first attempt, the killer was given a description that included blond hair, camouflage outfit, solid physique, how many stripes Bigeard wore, and so on. Bruno and "Prosper" Mayer were walking together on the streets one day, both answering roughly the same physical description, and both wearing a uniform with five military stripes (*galons*). The assassin hesitated. Bigeard and Mayer were out of cigarettes, abruptly changed direction to find a *tabac*, and while the assassin waited for them to come out, a patrol came by to ruin the whole thing. Soon after, in a second attempt, a group of killers gunned down a sergeant-major who resembled Bigeard (Aussaresses, *Services spéciaux*, 123). Bigeard's most recent account of the chemist's arrest is in *Crier ma vérité*, 121.

108. See *Ma guerre d'Algérie*, 58–62 and *Crier ma vérité*, 122–28. In Operation Agounnenda Bigeard concedes the rebels' tenacity, despite the fact that "mon pifomètre ne m'a jamais trahi" (*Crier ma vérité*, 124). He believes, however, that the 3rd did creditably in this forbidding region of "immenses massifs montagneux, de crêtes violentes, de torrents et d'oueds," compared to an Algerian army that would fight murderous Islamic guerillas (some trained in Afghanistan) here almost a half century later—with armaments improved, but morale, courage, and planning still counting as well (*Crier ma vérité*, 130–31, quote 130).

109. Aussaresses, *Services spéciaux*, 187–88; Bigeard, *J'ai mal à la France*, 153. See also "Les Jours de Colère" in *Paris-Match* of June 22, 1957, including pictures of the damage and of surging, revengeful crowds. Salan's squeamishness about bombs had probably been intensified by a bazooka explosion at his office on the Rue d'Isly January 16, 1957, only twenty minutes after he went out. The explosion was not the work of FLN, as was first believed, but of disgruntled European "ultras" lodged in a nearby apartment building, supposedly fearing a Salan-engineered sellout here. One was a Dr. Kovacs, and another Philippe Castille, who worked for Renault in Algiers, had the bazooka fabricated and launched it. The latter took out a poor officer seated at Salan's desk! Salan would be persuaded for years—even after fruitless investigations in Paris—that this "Bazooka Affair" reached up to the highest political strata, including de Gaulle himself. See Alain Gandy, *Salan*, ch. 11 and Aussaresses, *Services spéciaux*, 84, 129–36.

110. On the *porteurs de valises* see Hervé Hamon and Patrick Rotman, *Les porteurs de valises: la résistance française à la guerre d'Algérie* (Paris, 1979), quote 87. The authors show how Sartre got back together with Jeanson and his network early in 1959, hoping that an FLN victory would lead to that democratic-socialist future for Algeria mentioned (ch. 10). See also Aussaresses, *Services spéciaux*, quote 185 and Bigeard, *J'ai mal à la France*, 173. If he found these so-called "resistants" repulsive, Bigeard had more admiration for the concerns about Algeria of a Servan-Schreiber, who had actually served there (168). The Réseau Jeanson would be brought to trial with much publicity in 1960. And as Soustelle remarks, "à l'audience, leurs avocats faisaient l'apologie de la trahison et l'on voyait les accusés hilaires, saluer de la main leurs 'supporters', bourgeois cossus et femmes élégantes, qui les soutenaient de leurs applaudissements" (Jacques Soustelle, *L'espérance trahie (1958–1961)* [Paris, 1962], 194–95). It should also be noted again that the FLN in France, as in Algeria was still busy purging members of rival groups perceived as too moderate, especially Hadj's MNA. Another autobiographical book by Aussaresses that appeared at the end of 2001, on his secret service career before Algeria, has a more anodyne feel to it, yet at the end gets in one last series of rejoinders to his army of critics: "Qu'auriez-vous donc fait à l'homme qui savait que la terreur s'abattrait sur Manhattan, qui savait où, quand et comment mais qui refusait de parler? Qu'auriez-vous fait si votre enfant avait été là-bas?" He goes on to note that "tous ces gens, qui prennent de fait le parti des égorgeurs et des poseurs de bombes, n'ont jamais été accusés d'apologie du terrorisme tandis qu'ils m'accusent, moi, de faire l'apologie de crimes de guerre. Crimes de guerre?... Le plus grand crime de toutes les guerres n'est-il pas la guerre elle-même?" And finally: "En ce qui me concerne, j'ai simplement voulu dire—sans complaisance—que la torture et les éxecutions sommaires avaient *systématiquement* été pratiquées en Algérie, sur ordre de la République française" (Aussaresses, *Pour la France: service spécial 1942–1954* [Paris, 2001], 269–70). This second book was published by another prestigious Paris publisher.

111. See among several Bigeard accounts of this era his *J'ai mal à la France*, 154–58. Two months earlier (June 1, 1957) Massu had been very complimentary of Bigeard, calling him in an *ordre du jour* the "seigneur de l'Atlas" (133). Bigeard's *j'accuse*-type open letters on slackness in the army hierarchy fighting terror helped

put him in troubled waters. He was truly angered by this sloppy *fonctionnarisme*, as he called it, undoing his 3d's prior efforts in Algiers. See Bigeard, *Crier ma vérité*, 138.

112. Last quote in Bigeard, *Pour une parcelle de gloire*, vol. 2, 132, and for period leading up to this parlous moment, Bergot, *Bigeard*, 439–63. Massu would praise Bigeard with one hand—extolling his "innate gift for command" and noting the affection and respect all had for him; but take away with the other, calling him something of a *caïd* in Algeria (Massu, *La vraie bataille d'Alger*, 111). Salan would also salute Bigeard's work in this era, including his information-gathering diagrams, yet point to his "very individual ideals [and] a certain egocentricity" (Raoul Salan, *Mémoires: fin d'un empire*, vol. 3 [Paris, 1972], 155). Bigeard's first picture book (with Lenoir and Flament), *Contre guérilla*, was, as noted, published in Algiers, 1957; then followed (in the editions we have used) another book containing artistic Flament photos, *Aucune bête au monde* (Paris, 1959), dedicated to Sentenac; and finally, *Piste sans fin* (Paris, 1963) with a Bigeard poem on the "Piste où l'on vit intensément / Piste qui ne mène nulle part / ... Piste que l'on hait / ... Piste cruelle, où tu succombes à quelques heures de ta libération." (In yet another military-imperial figure art paradoxically emerged here, as well as from his associates.) For Lacheroy see his revealing interview of 1997 in SHAT: Fonds Privés. Histoire Orale: 3K18, and a variety of interesting documents put out by his office in SHAT: 1H 1117/1. The one on cowed Arab silence in Algeria would certainly not be amiss in our era of political correctness, and it almost has the appearance of a catechism. Lacheroy says: "Le silence est stupide. Le silence est contre nature.... Les bêtes ne parlent pas. Que seriez-vous si subitement vous étiez condamné au silence? Si vous deveniez muet? Vous seriez des morts en mouvement." Without words, he goes on, "Ce serait un monde mort. Un monde ou le bien et le mal se confondraient. Un monde offert aux voleurs et aux tueurs.... C'est ce que veut la rebellion barbare stupide. Elle veut le silence. Elle coupe les langues. Elle a fait tuer les chiens." Near the close this catechistic chant becomes a kind of ode to enlightenment: "Le Silence, c'est les ténèbres. La Parole, c'est le jour. Le Silence, c'est la nuit." The document is dated August 4, 1957. Lacheroy's autobiographical account, *De Saint-Cyr à l'action psychologiqe: mémoires d'un siècle* (Panazol, 2003), came late to us. Of this man nearing age 100 Serge Parisot said (June 18, 2003): "Il a toute sa tête." Of Massu Parisot commented: "C'était un très brave soldat," but no intellectual! We should note that Parisot's recorded interviews at the "Histoire Orale" branch of Vincennes were useful for us as well (going back to Morocco of the early '30s). Massu's have a tone of no-nonsense directness.

113. For operations from late September, 1957 to this point see Bigeard, *Crier ma vérité*, 158–65. The assessment of his then subordinate, and later the Army's chief of staff at the time of the Gulf War, Schmitt: "On ne l'a pas assez dit[:] s'il fut parmi les chefs les plus exigeants, Bigeard fut aussi parmi les plus économes de nos soldats" (*De Diên Biên Phu*, 95). Even Salan bypasses the cost to French soldiers in his account of Bigeard's work here. See Salan, vol. 3, 221–28. See also the stirring photos of a dying Sentenac in the desert, November 21, 1957, included in Bigeard's *Ma guerre d'Algérie*, 82–83, and the most poignant one also in *Crier*

ma vérité, and still on Bigeard's desk in the twenty-first century. On trusting one's instincts people who were in the Resistance say it best, such as Hélie de Saint Marc: "Il fallait apprendre un autre langage que celui des mots. Jauger son interlocuteur en un éclair, lancer l'hameçon ou se rétracter, savoir d'emblée où l'on mettait les pieds, flairer la tension ou la peur—cet art ne s'apprenait nulle part" (Saint Marc, 64).

114. "Cette fois, rien ne va plus entre nous.... Mes déconvenues avec Massu s'estompent ... [et] mon prestige n'a jamais été aussi grand en France" (Bigeard, *Ma guerre d'Algérie,* 90, 92, and on his military *coup de maître,* 88). See also *Crier ma vérité,* 169–70.

115. As Irwin Wall and others have showed, the Americans were an important part of the condemnatory brigade. On the significance of Sakiet-Sidi-Youssef for the French future in Algeria, and for that of the Fourth Republic, see Adams, 109–10. In terms of arms shipments Porch shows how ideologically promiscuous money and/or arms providers to the FLN were—Russian Communist satellites or semisatellites, Egyptians, and even former Nazi SS involved from their lairs in a variety of countries (Porch, *French Secret Services,* 370–71). Porch is correct here in averring that French agents were overmatched. See also Bigeard, *Crier ma vérité,* 170–71.

116. Bigeard, *Ma guerre d'Algérie,* 92. He quotes from his last *ordre du jour* to the 3d in *Crier ma vérité,* 172: "Vous étiez ma vie, ma joie, mes espoirs." Trinquier's ambivalence toward Bigeard is seen in his own writing. In one book he concedes that Bigeard had "made [of this regiment] a war machine of redoubtable precision.... Of his paras, of his officers, he had known how to make supermen, almost stars forcing the admiration of the crowds when they marched ... singing in the streets of Algiers.... For [these paras] Bigeard was a God, the God of war come down to the earth ... [and] they would have followed him to the ends of the earth." But a page later he says that "the press was at [Bigeard's] service and had succeeded in making him a great national star." Trinquier also plays up Bigeard's connections with military bigwigs like Gilles and notes that even Paris ministries treated him like royalty. "This strange adulation flattered Bigeard and served him; he used it without limit. Never had anyone seen in the army a chief of such a subaltern rank occupy such a large place, scorning ... the most elementary rules of discipline" (Roger Trinquier, *Le coup d'état du 13 mai* [Paris, 1962], 68–70). On Trinquier's own paratroop credentials see his *Le premier bataillon de bérets rouges* (Paris, 1984), and for a rather positive assessment of his takeover from Bigeard, Schmitt, *De Diên Biên Phu,* 96. On Massu's absurd fear of Bigeard's "Communism" the accused recalls: "Communiste Bigeard? Oui, sans le savoir, j'ai été soupçonné de l'être. Je contestais, je ruais dans les brancards, je ne filais pas droit comme on l'aurait voulu. Donc j'étais suspecté d'être communiste!" (Bigeard, *Crier ma vérité,* 70). He only read Massu's precise words in his *dossier* in 1974, when he attained a governmental position: "Pourrait devenir dangereux si le Parti communiste se l'attachait," said Massu in one evaluation of Bigeard (April 9, 1958) (quoted in *Crier ma vérité,* 129).

117. Bigeard considered Chaban a master salesperson possessing great charisma. See *Ma guerre d'Algérie,* 94 and *Crier ma vérité,* 173.

118. See Bigeard, *Ma guerre d'Algérie,* 94 and SHAT: 1H 1115: Centre d'Instruction de Pacification et Contre-Guérilla d'Arzew ... 1957–1961. Again, all the seriousness and culture one finds here even in the medical/first aid courses astounds, not to mention the large amount of detail found in diagrams relating to the FLN organization. Among articles students read was one by the old novelist Jules Romains (from an issue of *L'Aurore,* March 1958), prophetic on American views of the French struggle. Terror? "Rien n'est en réalité plus facile." He warned the Americans that only regimes that respond in kind can defeat it, and that they were in actuality more vulnerable than the French!

119. See Trinquier, *Coup d'état,* ch. 6; Gandy, *Salan,* ch. 13; Salan, vol. 3, 293–94; O'Ballance, *The Algerian Insurrection,* ch. 4–5; and Martin, *Histoire de l'Algérie française,* part 4, ch. 7. Salan says he too "crossed his Rubicon" on May 13, leaving the "discipline" (of army and political strictures), but also following de Gaulle, who later turned out to be a liar! (Salan, vol. 4, 261–62). Massu avers that Salan carefully waited a couple days past the May 13 explosion. See his *Torrent et la digue: Alger du 13 mai aux barricades* (1972; reprint, Paris, 1997), chs. 1–3. De Gaulle's words at the time were of course seductive to those who saw him as a savior. In a speech of May 19 he declared that he belonged to no party or organization, and on June 6 at Oran he would say what he said so many times: "La France est ici pour toujours." See these extracts in SHAT: 1117/D1 and in 1117/D3: Action psychologique dans les centres d'hébergement ... 1957–1958.

120. On the "stage-managing" of the French see the balanced account of Adams, 119–23. On Sirvent see, among others, Massu, *Le torrent et la digue,* 85–117. On FLN/ALN propaganda efforts to deny any French beneficence or French-Muslim cooperation, and which had its effect on the foreign press in Germany, Italy, Spain, and an often gullible United States, see SHAT: 1H 2586/2: Renseignements sur la rébellion: Propagande du Front de Libération Nationale (1954–1961). The thick dossier notes amateur ALN/FLN documentary films, some produced in Cairo, for international distribution, as well as phony, staged photographs of bereavement sent in variations to different foreign newspapers or magazines, or to Cairo for distribution to the UN. The psychological offensive included multiple accusations of the "Christianizing French" (including in their liberation of Muslim women). There are also tracts here that were sent to French educational institutions, for example, the Lycée Voltaire in Paris. There are appeals to FLN going to France to spread the word to army *appelés.* The many tracts distributed in Algeria were generally in French and Arabic. There were also radio broadcasts. To which the French tried as best they could to counterpropagandize, to detoxify and intoxify as they put it, partially by listing the many achievements of French engineering, and the creation of an Algerian nation from a place "restée anarchique, puis dominée imparfaitement par les Turcs." The latter quote is in a document found in another good archival file both for this propaganda and for French counterpropaganda, though in a slightly earlier period: SHAT: 1H 1103/2: Plan de protection de l'Afrique française du Nord contre la guerre froide (1955–1956). See also the many French tracts and posters that might now be collectors' items in SHAT: 1117/2: Action psychologique: panneaux-photos, tracts et affiches, films (1957–1961), showing Nasser as a Hitler, FLN leaders as "scorpions vénimeux", fellahin

terrorists as locusts taking schools, sons, harvests, and leaving only a vale of tears, Ferhat Abbas and others living well in foreign palaces, etc. The countertheme was one of belonging to a "nation" of fifty-five million Frenchmen; but even this propaganda war was one the French could not win, and not simply due to the ineluctability of decolonization. The greater the brutes, the more vociferous, long-winded, and ultimately meretricious the propaganda—so it often seems. There are also pictures of men lacking noses or lips found in these files. The file also has many examples of tracts aiming to seduce *harkis*, painting the blissful future of decolonization claiming the world.

121. Bigeard, *Pour une parcelle de gloire*, vol. 2, 199, and *Crier ma vérité*, 175. On the role of old Resistants and *anciens combattants* in the advent of de Gaulle see the recorded interview with Maître Jean Baptiste Biaggi in SHAT: Fonds Privés. Histoire Orale: 3K20. Biaggi had been shot in the stomach during the 1940 campaign, took part in the Resistance before his arrest by the Gestapo in 1943, and now played a key role in mobilizing the opinion of the many ex-Resistants he knew, favoring the return of de Gaulle. As for what kind of *Algérie française* they envisaged, there were divisions, and de Gaulle himself in a famous line would reject the concept of total integration, declaring that his home village of Colombey-les-Deux-Eglises should not become Colombey-les-Deux-Mosquées (cited in the Biaggi interview). In Algiers the main Gaullist proponent was Léon Delbecque.

122. Lartéguy later made Colonels Bigeard and Ducournau the joint model for Colonel Raspéguy in *The Centurions*, arguably the best novel to come out of the Algerian War. His series of articles appeared in *Paris-Presse*, May 1958.

123. Bigeard knew he had gotten under "Papa Salan's skin" with his "critiques directes sur la façon dont on mène la guerre. . . . Ce qui est sûr, en tout cas c'est que Salan n'a pas trouvé ma salade à son goût." See *Ma guerre d'Algérie*, 100–1; also *Crier ma vérité*, 175. Bigeard's removal from Algeria made the American press as well (see articles on it in both *Time* and *Newsweek* of August 18, 1958). The former notes that Bigeard read a prepared statement in Paris, then pleaded with masses of reporters: "Don't make me say anything else, or you'll have me in the cooler" ("No Time for Soldiers," *Time*, 23). *Newsweek* quotes his words on comfortable superiors: "The colonels have got to get out and march with their men, and not circle overhead in their helicopters. . . . Rebel commanders get the same pay as their men; they go on foot like the men and don't bring any wives" ("A Hero Casualty," *Newsweek*, August 18, 1958, 45).

124. Hélie de Saint Marc remarks: "Nous vivions le plan Challe comme une aventure militaire originale. Pour la première fois, le succès semblait à notre portée" (Saint Marc, 241). Bigeard also notes that he and his men were dealing much more now with notables like mayors, and with ordinary people—increasingly social and economic in focus, in addition to military. And that of course sounds Lyautesque (*Ma guerre d'Algérie*, 106–12). On his sadness regarding his *harkis* and their vulnerability to score-settling, see *Crier ma vérité*, 179–80.

125. Catherine Wihtol de Wenden noted in 1993 that "there are few serious studies of the *harkis*," including the fortunate ones who ultimately made it to France. See her article "The Harkis: A Community in the Making?" in *French and Algerian Identities from Colonial Times to the Present*, A. G. Hargreaves and M. J.

Heffernan, eds. (Lewiston and Lampeter, 1993), quote 189. Works on them have certainly been appearing since then. Jean Faure's book is entitled *Au pays de la soif et de la peur: carnets d'Algérie 1957–1959* (Paris, 2001), 15–19, quotations 15. Faure remarks: "J'ai perdu des dizaines d'amis [in Algeria]. Jamais je n'ai ressenti autant la sincérité, la générosité de l'amitié que pendant cette époque" (19). And yes, there were the *gégène* and water, but very little sadism for the sake of sadism. Faure would have a lot of trouble fitting in back in France, though this native of the French Alps would eventually become Senator of France's Isère department, then Vice-President of the Senate. On double-agentry see Porch, *French Secret Services*, 388.

126. Bigeard was at first reduced to little boyhood by de Gaulle's presence, then handed him two full dossiers containing his ideas for a new Algeria. See *Ma guerre d'Algérie*, 118 and *Crier ma vérité*, 183–85. Jacques Soustelle makes the plausible case that de Gaulle's old emphasis on tank warfare put him out of touch with the antiguerilla techniques of a younger contingent of colonels in Algeria. See Soustelle, *Espérance trahie*, 87–90. He also felt that de Gaulle patronized *pieds noirs* and Muslims alike, that he understood nothing of a "southern" mentality, and that his one obsession was regaining France's power in Europe (*Espérance trahie*, 104, 250). "Pour lui, les Musulmans n'étaient que des 'clochards' dont la France n'avait pas à s'embarrasser; les Européens, des sujets indociles et agités" (250). Soustelle says de Gaulle also wanted to do the great, ahistorical thing in Algeria, giving it independence it had never had in a long past dominated by Carthaginians, Romans, Vandals, Byzantines, Syrian Arabs, Cordovan Arabs, Turks, and French (275). In Wall, passim there is, however, a strong argument made that de Gaulle always wished to retain a "French Algeria." A fine article on de Gaulle and his famed nose as a bonanza subject for the era's cartoonists and satirirsts is Christian Moncelet's, "Guerre d'Algérire," *L'Esprit créateur* 41 (Winter 2001): 9–18. As for Bigeard, despite former frustrations with de Gaulle, he mentioned him positively in our March 15, 2002 phone interview, noting the absence of such a man in today's political arena.

127. On Bigeard's trusted aide, Zga, see photo in *Ma guerre d'Algérie*, 113, and on death 122.

128. Bigeard called the helicopter accident "un choc terrible ... d'autant que Peretti ... était devenu ma seconde moitié." The newspapers had been chatting up the "fameux team Bigeard-Peretti" (*Ma guerre d'Algérie*, 124; and see also *Crier ma vérité*, 187).

129. Bocca, 38–39. See Simone de Beauvoir and Gisèle Halimi, *Djamila Boupacha* (Paris, 1962) for graphic reportage on torture that was translated abroad and had great influence. On the home front's importance militarily, cf. Maurice Schmitt: "Certes sur le terrain la guerre est gagnée. Mais la guerre révolutionnaire ne se gagne pas seulement sur le terrain. Elle se gagne ou se perd ailleurs. Or en métropole l'opinion évolue, de plus en plus lassée, travaillée par une intelligentsia et un parti communiste ... [pour qui] l'Algérie doit être indépendante et marxiste" (*De Diên Biên Phu*, 101–2). Most persuasively, Matthew Connelly confirms that the FLN won by diplomacy (including with the United States), and by propaganda, when it was actually losing militarily (Connelly, *Diplomatic Revolution*, passim). The idea of an independent "Algerian nation" had come almost by serendipity,

distrusted by people like Ferhat Abbas, who hardly spoke Arabic at all. Connelly
also traces the FLN's legacy in all this to future Middle Eastern terrorist groups
(*Diplomatic Revolution,* 10 and passim).

130. Horne, *Savage War of Peace,* 357. See also Merry and Serge Bromberger et
al., *Barricades et colonels: 24 janvier 1960* (Paris 1960). Massu would aver after de
Gaulle's death that the latter had played a "double game" from the start. And he
notes that de Gaulle had been downright chicken about Muslim *harkis* recruited
to the French side; asked on his tour of French army posts in Algeria whether that
should continue, *le grand Charles* supposedly gave no answer, and of course they
were later slaughtered. Massu's own justifications for his harsh policies in Algiers
also continued. One must "know that the Algerians are capable of anything.…
That's why we sometimes used brutal methods with them; they acted like savages
from the beginning." See Jacques Massu with Alain-Gilles Minella, *Avec de Gaulle:
du Tchad 1941 à Baden 1968* (Paris, 1998), 85–88, quotes 85, 88.

131. Words that got him in trouble included: "les hommes des Barricades re-
présentent effectivement le peuple d'Algérie" and "ils n'ont agi que par désespoir"
(Bigeard, *Ma guerre d'Algérie,* 128). In *Crier ma vérité,* 188 Bigeard admits from
the vantage point of 2002 that "je n'ai pas encore toute la maturité voulue pour
comprendre ses salades politiques." Among political types who supported the
disaffected military, one could mention Georges Bidault, who had taken over de
Gaulle's Conseil National de Résistance in 1943, after Jean Moulin's murder, and
Jacques Soustelle.

132. Saint Marc's conversation and quotation 258. Soustelle adds that de Gaulle
had missed a glorious chance to make the Challe plan work by negotiating with
true Arab leaders inside the country, who still valued his prestige, rather than with
the *émigrés* of the Gouvernement Provisionnel de la République Algérienne
(GPRA). These men in Tunis and Cairo had been won over (as de Gaulle himself
knew) to Soviet and/or Chinese tutelage (Soustelle, *Espérance trahie,* 198). One of
the great paradoxes of the era was that just as France seemed to be withdrawing
from Algeria, it also seemed to retain its "Saharan dream," committing to the
extension of infrastructure there and the protection of oil exploration personnel.
This was in fact the end of a dream within a dream, but in 1961 there was still a
large official correspondence on sewers, rail lines, blueprints for army bases and
police stations, and a definite worry about "importantes agglomérations pétro-
lières," some with several thousand employees. As late as June 1961 a decree instituting new Saharan departments within an equally new Région Militaire du Sahara
indicated that die-hard, ant-like French optimism and hope for the area. Since
1957 the FLN had been extending its terror to this part of Algeria, particularly by
pressuring nomadic populations. See the excellent files in SHAT: 1H 3365: Commandement du génie auprès du commandement interarmé au Sahara (CIS.);
quote in letter from le Préfet des Oasis to M. le Colonel Commandant la Zone
Est Saharienne September 25, 1961. See also 1H 3234: CIS 1èr Bureau: Organisation du Commandement militaire au Sahara 1958–1962 (with many urgent telegrams on assassinations and security needs), and the decrees of 1961; as well as
files on more restricted areas, such as 1H 3339: Secteur de Touggourt: Opérations
1956–1962.

133. See Horne, *Savage War of Peace*, 446–60 and Saint Marc, ch. 12, quotations 266, 270. Soustelle dismissed the idea that Challe, in particular, ever wanted to take Paris. As for associating members of the OAS who had often fought in the Resistance, and were later supported by many of Algiers' formerly left-wing Jews numbering some 130,000, with Nazis, Soustelle finds this a repulsive analogy (*Espérance trahie*, 242–48). Challe's account, partly composed in prison, is *Notre révolte* (Paris, 1968). For this era see also John C. Cairns, "Algeria: The Last Ordeal," *International Journal* (Spring 1962): 87–97. Among those imprisoned for life, then amnestied in 1968 by the supple de Gaulle, one of the most bitter memoirs was composed by Colonel Antoine Argoud, who in his account calls de Gaulle who had seduced the army in 1958 an "imposter" (Argoud, *La décadence, l'imposture et la tragédie* [Paris, 1974]). As for Salan, one version argues that he wished to emulate Challe and surrender, but was supposedly kidnapped to transient safety by a wealthy *pied noir* (Bocca, 73–74).

134. Guy Méry's second interview of 1997 in SHAT: 3K4 reveals how he flouted orders disallowing the evacuation of *harkis*. He contrasts the army's "ouf" of relief when the Vietnam era ended with guilt over Algeria's end which, he said, would take a good ten years to get over. On other aspects of the end of *pied-noir* Algeria see the moving account by Gérard Isräel, *Le dernier jour de l'Algérie française: 1er juillet, 1962* (Paris, 1962), ch. 7; and an equally moving diary of the mounting anarchy from the end of 1960, Francine Dessaigne, *Journal d'une mère de famille pied-noir* (Paris, 1972). See Saint Marc, chs. 12 and 13 on his revolt, incarceration, and liberation; Faure, 20; and interviews with Alibert and Donely in Delpard, 265–74 and 247–56; quote in Duquesne, 255. Soustelle's third book on Algeria, *La page n'est pas tournée* (Paris, 1965), was finished "somewhere in Europe." Guilt remained in the gut of a generation of French soldiers. As Hélie de Saint Marc notes: "Nous avons contracté envers l'Algérie une sorte de dette." For the many soldiers of this sort going back to the good life in France was no easy matter. Along with the *rafle* of Jews at the Vél d'Hiver in Paris during World War II, Saint Marc considers the abandonment of the *harkis* among the most sordid chapters in France's history. Saint Marc quote 222, and see his caption on a *harki* soldier, mentioning the Vél d'Hiver (290). Even Raphaël Delpard, who generally bats from the other side of the plate on the Algeria issue, makes no bones about the tortures reserved for many Algerian Muslims, citing a French agent, himself tortured by FLN, who saw what happened to the *harkis*: "Ils les égorgeaient ou leur ouvraient le ventre, les pendaient par les pieds, allumaient un feu et les faisaient rôtir comme des animaux." Delpard also mentions them having *les couilles* cut off, and of course the French didn't do such things, never disemboweled. Does one fight a raging fire with fire of one's own? Or with white gloves? The dilemma continues to rage in France. See Delpard quotation 281, and ch. 19. Claude Martin also concludes his history of French Algeria regretfully: "Only the European population of Algeria resisted the abandonment of a land it considered its own. It was not one of the least successes of French Algeria that it had assimilated this population formed of French, Spanish, and Italian contributors, who constituted a new Latin-ethnic group. . . . Its work, accomplished under the shadow of French swords . . . had contributed a good deal toward creating the cities and agricultural

domains that visitors admired. . . . The French government sacrificed them, as it sacrificed—in the literal sense of the word—Muslim auxiliaries in the French army" (Martin, *Histoire de l'Algérie française,* 482–83). In the archives one sees FLN propaganda challenging the "Frenchness" of Ortiz, Lopez, etc. They had no trouble turning the Rue d'Isly into the Rue Ben Mehidi Larbi and La Place Bugeaud into La Place Emir-Abdelkader (Cordier, *Héroïque Bigeard,* 105). One also gets a pathetic visual sense of how much France created in photographs of modern hospitals, including one in the Bône area, the Centre d'Hospitalisation, opened in 1961 (due to its emphasis on tuberculosis, dubbed the "Preventorium") (Hubert Cataldo, *Bône, 1832–1862, et Hippone la Royale* [Montpellier, 1986], unpaginated photographs).

135. Saint Marc, 225–29, and on "le deuil de notre idéal" 303, as well as personal conversations; Pierre Godeau, *Une aventure algérienne* (Paris, 2001); and Delpard for Adilbert's fear of parachuting, 269. Before going to Algeria as a young doctor Godeau had been prepped along with other medical students by Colonel Lacheroy in 1954: "C'était un orateur exceptionnel, il incarnait un idéal, il avait vécu dans son âme et dans sa chair ce qu'il nous décrivait. Nous l'écoutâmes dans un silence religieux" (Godeau, 26). Tragedies mentioned here did not occur only in Algeria during this period. David Slavin gives the most graphic account in English of police massacres of demonstrators in Paris, and of unexplained "disappearances" during the fall of 1961. See Slavin, *Colonial Cinema and Imperial France,* 1–3 and ch. 1, passim.

136. Bigeard, *Pour une parcelle de gloire,* vol. 2, 286.

137. Bigeard, *Pour une parcelle de gloire,* vol. 2, 318.

138. Only later did he notice how many similarities there had been in his own colonial "style" with Lyautey's, in particular. Lyautey knew one couldn't run a foreign country like a French department, "which I will discover in my turn many years later." Lyautey would call colonial soldiers teachers, architects, and agronomists rolled into one, exactly what he, Bigeard, tried to do in his own colonial assignments, he says. Lyautey (like Bugeaud) lightened packs carried, and Bigeard too wanted his men to fight in simple, unencumbered attire. Finally, Lyautey found as war minister that he was "submergé par des tâches inutiles, des rendez-vous stériles, et des réunions sans fin. . . . Pas mon style. Pas celui de Lyautey non plus" (Bigeard, *Siècle des héros,* 34–35, 51, 64). See also Cordier, *Héroïque Bigeard,* 54, noting Bigeard's appearance at Thorey for ceremonies commemorating the fiftieth anniversary of Lyautey's death.

139. For Bigeard's era from the end of his Algerian involvement to February 1973 see Bergot, *Bigeard,* 463–532 and of course appropriate pages of *Pour une parcelle de gloire,* vol. 2. But Bigeard himself was anything but done at this point; as seen, rolling over and playing dead was never his style. So we should note that in 1974 he became a *général de corps d'armée,* commanding the 4th military region in Bordeaux, and in January 1975 Giscard d'Estaing's secretary of state for defense in the cabinet of then-premier Jacques Chirac (a post from which he resigned the following year). In 1978 he became deputy for Meurthe-et-Moselle (Lorraine), representing for ten years the *Union pour la démocratie française.* He was also, from 1978–81, president of the National Defense Commission of the National

Assembly. He covers these political years of the 1970s, '80s, and early '90s in a remarkable published diary, *De la brousse à la jungle*. Much like a Gallieni he remarks: "En Indochine, je montais une attaque en quelques minutes. Ici, il faut des jours simplement pour se dire qu'on va se rencontrer." *De la brousse à la jungle*, 102. Bigeard took many tiring trips all over the world, then returned to Paris—with "ses servitudes, son rythme, ses interviews, ses dîners, cocktails, débats" (110). In this milieu he realized one had to "peser ses mots, s'étudier, utiliser la langue de bois" (112). The brush had been tough, but the political menagerie was worse! On the fall of Giscard: "Malheureusement dans la jungle, il faut parer toutes les attaques, même les plus basses" (161).

And yet Bigeard has continued to write and speak out copiously on issues that matter—nothing smaller in subject matter than the destiny of France and really, of the West. When one of the present authors wrote him for a second time in the spring of 1997, he received a surprisingly prompt reply, and many to follow from this thronged individual, inundated with correspondence. Obviously the old cliché still applies—and indeed, always did in the case of our great colonials: ask a busy person ... That reply of 1997 came on one photocopied interview of Bigeard in *L'Evénement du jeudi* for April 17–23, 1997, and another in *Pèlerin Magazine* of April 25, 1997 on the reverse side. On the front page of the copy Bigeard hastily scribbled that he had just published his latest book, *France: réveille-toi*, noting that "I am drowning under hundreds of letters, and each week [spend] three days in Paris! Radio, télé, etc." Then on returning to peaceful Lorraine, he encountered a "courrier infernal plus visites, téléphone ..." At eighty-one he figured he might just die standing up! He signed off decently: "Let's stay in touch. Votre vieux para."

The interview in *L'Evénement* with France's most decorated living soldier is as slangy, practical, and plain-speaking as are his memoirs, mentioning his admiration for politicians who take chances, including women like Margaret Thatcher or Golda Meir. (He feels, by the way, that Israel is "the only modern country where warriors are always heroes for the people. Maybe simply because they *are* the people" [Bigeard, *Siècle des héros*, 251].) Bigeard's feeling at the turn of the century was that France had lost its "punch," and that an extremist like Le Pen could only do as well as he did because the other political stripes failed to address national issues that truly mattered. Then came the media blitz on *la torture*, including an utterly baseless allegation by Louisette Ighilahriz against Bigeard (first made public by *Le Monde*, June 20, 2000); and Bigeard felt he had to fight his own battles by writing on the subject, first in *J'ai mal à la France* (2001), then more completely in *Crier ma vérité* (2002). As she became more famous in the media, partly propelled by Communists of *L'Humanité*, Ighilahriz got deeper and deeper into the muck of absurd contradictions and lies. But the press largely fell down on the job of fact-checking. On *France-Inter* and later in her book that appeared in the spring of 2001, she said she had been arrested September 27, 1957, in Algiers, and that Bigeard and Massu began visiting her cell three weeks later, around October 20. As noted, Bigeard wasn't even in the capital during this period. Instead, he was busy fighting in forbidding rural terrain. In the original *Le Monde* article Bigeard supposedly abused Ighilahriz in her cell; but in her book that came out in June, 2001 she changed her story and said that Bigeard never laid a hand on her. Just before the appearance of that book *Le Nouvel Observateur* published an extract, in which Ighilahriz said she recognized the famed Bigeard by his green beret. In fact he and his men wore only red berets! The book's editorial staff got wind of this error, and on their pages she duly recalled a red beret. The best analysis of all these changes and lies is in Bigeard, *Crier ma vérité*, ch. 8; but archival and press sources of the era confirm the fact that he was simply not in Algiers at the time.

Meanwhile, Bigeard kept receiving huge piles of correspondence. Yet after the appearance of *J'ai mal à la France* in 2001 a third letter was answered just as promptly by the "vieux para," again, on a photocopy of a book review of his new offering; and after that a fourth (on photocopies, including a complimentary letter from Giscard), and a fifth, and a half dozen to come, always amazingly prompt.

It is somewhat sad that a man in his mid-eighties had to take on the untested moralists substantially without help. (With, however, the waters of potential barbarism continuing to lap higher and higher.) One wonders again how these people will do when truly tested. The generation of Bigeard's grandchildren *does* have more equitable instincts, and their interest is one reason why books on French Indochina and Algeria clutter bestseller tables at French bookstores (cf. also movies like *Pearl Harbor* or *We Were Soldiers,* which were hits there, as well as chez nous). But by and large this generation doesn't have what the French so aptly call *le verbe,* the linguistic sophistication to jump in and defend such as the Bigeards. Speaking of *le verbe* one last time concerning our proconsuls and those in their lineage, Bugeaud, Faidherbe, Gallieni, Lyautey, and yes, Bigeard all obviously had it—in the suit of spades! And in Bigeard's case that has continued to the present. Frying in unprecedented August, 2003 heat (as bad as anything experienced in Senegal, North Africa, or Indochina, according to Gaby Bigeard on the phone), her eighty-seven-year old husband Marcel still kept at his latest *oeuvre,* refusing vacations, and with this current example of *le verbe* in action slated to appear sometime in 2004. His concern for France still emerged in hurtling, torrential comments, as did the desire to live always for today, with a citation of MacArthur's favorite poem about youth as a state of mind.

9. A REMNANT SHALL REMAIN

1. White, 200–1; Aldrich, *Greater France,* 302.

2. White, 209.

3. Touré's stance won him tremendous popularity in Africa at the time, but Guinea has experienced deep economic problems since independence.

4. White, 210.

5. Some argue that de Gaulle was influenced by *cartierisme,* the idea of journalist Raymond Cartier that France should divest itself of empire and withdraw into the métropole; but this influence, if it existed, has never been adequately explored. See Raymond Cartier, "Attention, la France dilapide son argent!" *Paris-Match,* February 29, March 7 and 14, 1964. Cf. Edward Peter Fitzgerald in "Did France's Colonial Empire Make Economic Sense? A Perspective from the Postwar Decade, 1946–1956," *The Journal of Economic History* 48 (June 1988): 373–85. On

de Gaulle's ending of an empire that cost too much he sees "no small irony that these historic decisions were taken by an old soldier who despised economic theory and who had been swept into power by a colonial uprising that acclaimed him as the empire's savior" (Fitzgerald, 385).

6. Pierre Viansson-Ponté, *Histoire de la République Gaullienne,* vol. 1 (Paris, 1971), 95.

7. For the foregoing, journalistic articles are best. We have consulted relevant ones in *The Guardian* (London), October 2, 1986; *The Guardian,* May 24, 1989; *Africa News,* February 26, 1990; *The Independent* (London), March 3, 1990; *BBC Summary of World Broadcasts,* March 31, 1990; *The Guardian,* June 6, 1990; *The Economist,* January 29, 1994; *Africa News,* October 31, 1994; *The Times* (London), October 11, 1996; *Africa News,* March 5, 1997; and *The Independent,* March 11, 1999, among others.

8. Guy Martin, "France and Africa," in *France in World Politics,* Robert Aldrich and John Connell, eds. (London, 1989), 106.

9. Martin, "France and Africa," 106–8.

10. Martin, "France and Africa," 115; White, 246.

11. John Connell and Robert Aldrich, "Remnants of Empire: France's Overseas Departments and Territories," in Aldrich and Connell, eds., 148–49.

12. Connell and Aldrich, "Remnants of Empire," 148.

13. Despite continuing French aid and investment, and a branch of the Institut Pasteur there to fight disease, Madagascar still suffers from great poverty. There has of course been much emigration to France through the 1990s and into the new century. See articles in *Le Monde,* September 5, 1997, May 6, 1999, and March 14, 2001. As for Vietnam, the French adopted many children from there during the 1990s, until a review of corrupt procedures suspended operations for a time in 1999. The first official visit to France from the secretary-general of the Vietnam Communist Party in the spring of 2000 was greeted with protests by France's Vietnamese community (similar to the way Cuban exiles in Miami have felt about Castro). The president of the Comité Vietnam pour la Défense des Droits de l'Homme (in France) published a White Book on Vietnam of the year 2000, calling attention to the existence of 150 prisons or camps still featuring "re-education" to handle dissidence, and another 600 planned for construction! Meanwhile, the Vietnamese Communist leader promised France more modernization and openness. See article on this in *Le Monde,* May 27, 2000, and on adoptions, article in *Le Monde,* July 4, 2001. For French-Algerian relations since independence, see Phillip C. Naylor, *Decolonization and Transformation* (Gainesville, Fla., 2000).

Bibliography

PRINCIPAL ARCHIVAL SOURCES

For more precise files, numbers, and descriptions within some of general appellations below, please see Endnotes.

Centre des Archives d'Outre-Mer

Administration et affaires arabes: Prises sur l'ennemi; razzias 1840–50
Administration et affaires arabes: Prisonniers de guerre français et arabes 1837–47
Affaires indigènes: Correspondance concernant surtout la province de Constantine 1837–47
Amiraux
Archives Faidherbe: Fonds Personnels
Archives du Sénégal: Fonds Ministériels
Correspondance politique des affaires indigènes (including correspondance arabe 1845–49)
Fonds du Gouvernement Général de l'Indochine
Gouvernement de l'Algérie
Gouvernement-général de l'Algérie: Correspondance 1833–53
Gouvernement de Madagascar
Lettres de Bugeaud 1841–47
Province de Diego-Suarez; rapports politiques et administratifs (1900–17)

Service Historique de l'Armée de Terre, Vincennes

Archives de l'Algérie 1945–67 (1H)
Archives de l'Indochine 1867–1956 (10H)
Armée du Nord: Correspondance
Chasseurs à Pied 16ième Bataillon
Fonds Clemenceau

443

Fonds Foch
Fonds Gallieni
Fonds Joffre
Fonds Privés (1K)
Fonds Privés. Histoire Orale (Témoignages Oraux)
Journal de Marche du 6ième Bataillon de Parachutistes Coloniaux
Journal de Marche du 3ième Bataillon de Parachutistes Coloniaux 1952–53
Journaux de Marche (World War I)
Maréchaux de France: Dossier personnel de Bugeaud
Maréchaux de France: Dossier personnel de Faidherbe
Maréchaux de France: Dossier personnel de Lyautey
Mémoires et Reconnaissances (contains General Rivet's *Histoire du commandement du Maréchal Bugeaud de 1841 à 1847*)
Ministère de la Guerre, Etat-Major de l'Armée. *Les armées françaises dans la Grande Guerre.* Paris, 1930
Section d'Afrique 1913–15

Archives Nationales

Correspondance adressée au Colonel de Castries par le Maréchal Lyautey
Fonds Lyautey
Papiers Fourtoul, Bourgoing, Lyautey 1895–1921
Papiers du Général Eynard
Papiers du Maréchal Bugeaud Duc d'Isly
Papiers du Maréchal Pélissier
Souvenirs du Général Aubert

Archives du Ministère des Affaires Etrangères

Archives Diplomatiques
Papiers Klobukowski

Bibliothèque de l'Institut de France

Fonds Terrier

PRINTED SOURCES

Note: We have not listed magazines and newspapers here that are cited in the Endnotes.

Achebe, Chinua. *Things Fall Apart.* 1958. Reprint, New York, 1994.
Adams, Geoffrey. *The Call of Conscience: French Protestant Responses to the Algerian War, 1954–1962.* Waterloo, Ont., 1998.
Ageron, Charles-Robert. *Modern Algeria: A History from 1830 to the Present.* Translated by Michael Brett. Trenton, N.J., 1991.

Ain, Girod de l'. *Grands artilleurs: le Maréchal Vallée 1773-1846.* Paris, 1911.

Aldrich, Robert. *Greater France: A History of French Overseas Expansion.* New York, 1996.

————— and John Connell, eds. *France in World Politics.* London, 1989.

Alexander, Don. "Repercussions of the Breda Variant." *French Historical Studies* 8 (1974): 459–88.

Alexander, Martin S. *The Republic in Danger: General Maurice Gamelin and the Politics of French Defence, 1933–1940.* Cambridge, U.K., 1992.

Alexandre, René. *Avec Joffre d'Agadir à Verdun.* Paris, 1932.

Algeria. Direction de l'agriculture, du commerce et de l'industrie. *La colonisation officielle de 1871 à 1895.* Tunis, 1928.

Alleg, Henri. *The Question.* Translated by John Calder. New York, 1958.

Allen, Philip M. *Madagascar.* Boulder, Colo., 1995.

Allen, Richard B. *Slaves, Freedmen, and Indentured Laborers in Colonial Mauritius.* Cambridge, U.K., 1999.

Andersson, Nils. "La résistance à la guerre d'Algérie: le rôle de l'édition." *Les Temps modernes* 56 (2001): 305–26.

Andrew, C. M., and A. S. Kanya-Forstner. *France Overseas: The Great War and the Climax of French Colonial Expansion.* London, 1981.

Andrieux, Maurice. *Le père Bugeaud 1784–1849.* Paris, 1951.

Argoud, Antoine. *La décadence, l'imposture et la tragédie.* Paris, 1974.

Asprey, Robert B. *The First Battle of the Marne.* Philadelphia, 1962.

Audisio, Gabriel. *Jeunesse de la Méditerranée.* Paris, 1935.

Auffray, Bernard. *Pierre de Margerie 1861–1942 et la vie diplomatique de son temps.* Paris, 1976.

Auphan, Adm. Paul, and Jacques Mordal. *The French Navy in World War II.* Translated by A. C. J. Sabalot. Annapolis, Md., 1959.

Aussaresses, Gen. Paul. *Pour la France: services spéciaux 1942–1954.* Paris, 2001.

—————. *Services spéciaux: Algérie 1955–1957.* Paris, 2001.

Axel, Brian Keith. "Colonialism and its Doubles." *Current Anthropology* 43 (February 2002): 197–200.

Azan, Paul. *Sidi-Brahim.* Paris, 1905.

Azan, Paul, ed. *Par l'épée et par la charrue: écrits et discours de Bugeaud.* Paris, 1948.

Ba, Oumar, ed. *La pénétration française au Cayor.* Dakar, 1976.

Banbuch, C. A. *Histoire de la Martinique.* Paris, 1935.

Bangou, Henri. *La Guadeloupe.* Paris, 1962.

Bapst, Germain, ed. *Le Maréchal Canrobert: souvenirs d'un siècle.* 7th edition. Paris, 1909.

Barbour, Nevill. *Morocco.* New York, 1966.

Barnett, Corelli. *The Sword Bearers: Studies in Supreme Command in the First World War.* London, 1963.

Barns, T. Alexander. *An African Eldorado.* London, 1926.

Barrows, Leland C. "General Faidherbe, the Maurel and Prom Company, and French Expansion in Senegal." Ph.D. dissertation, UCLA, 1974.

Barrows, Leland C. "Louis Léon César Faidherbe (1818–1889)." In *African Proconsuls:*

European Governors in Africa. Edited by L. H. Gann and Peter Duignan. New York, 1978.

Barrows, Leland C. "The Merchants and General Faidherbe: Aspects of French Expansion in Senegal in the 1850s." *Revue française d'histoire d'outre-mer* 61 (1974): 236–83.

Beauvoir, Simone de, and Halimi, Gisèle. *Djamila Boupacha.* Paris, 1962.

Beloff, Max. "The British Empire." *History Today* 46 (February 1996): 13–20.

Benchérif, Osman. *The Image of Algeria in Anglo-American Writings, 1785–1965.* Lanham, Md., 1997.

Benjamin, René. *Grandes Figures: Barrès, Joffre.* Paris, 1931.

———. *Les paroles du Maréchal Joffre.* Paris, 1929.

Benoist-Méchin, Jacques. *Lyautey l'africain ou le rêve immolé.* Lausanne, 1966.

Bergot, Erwan. *Bigeard.* Paris, 1988.

———. *2è classe à Diên Biên Phu.* Paris, 1988.

———. *Commando Vandenberghe: le pirate du Delta.* Paris, 1985.

Bernhard, Jacques. *Gallieni: le destin inachevé.* Paris, 1991.

Bertrand, J. *Le Congo belge.* Brussels, 1909.

Bertrand, Louis. *Le sang des races.* Paris, 1926.

———. *Les villes d'or.* Paris, 1921.

Betts, Raymond. *Tricouleur: The French Overseas Empire.* London, 1978.

———. *France and Decolonisation, 1900–1960.* New York, 1991.

Bigeard, Marcel (with Marc Flament). *Aucune bête au monde.* Paris 1959.

Bigeard, Marcel. *Crier ma vérité.* Paris, 2002.

———. *De la brousse à la jungle.* Paris, 1995.

——— (with A. Lenoir and Marc Flament). *Contre-guérilla.* Algiers, 1957.

———. *France: réveille-toi.* Paris, 1997.

———. *J'ai mal à la France.* Paris, 2001.

——— (with Patrice de Méritens), ed. *Lettres d'Indochine.* Vol. 1. Paris, 1998.

——— (with Patrice de Méritens), ed. *Lettres d'Indochine.* Vol. 2. Paris, 1999.

———. *Ma guerre d'Algérie.* Paris, 1994.

———. *Ma guerre d'Indochine.* Paris, 1994.

——— (with Marc Flament). *Piste sans fin.* Paris,1963.

———. *Pour une parcelle de gloire.* 2 vols. Paris, 1975.

———. *Le siècle des héros.* Paris, 2000.

Blackburn, Robin. *The Making of New World Slavery: From the Baroque to the Modern, 1492–1800.* New York, 1998.

Blanchon, G. "Le Général Gallieni." *Pages actuelles* 16 (1915).

Blanning, T. C. W., ed. *The Oxford History of Modern Europe.* Oxford, 2000.

Blet, Henri. *Histoire de la colonisation française.* Paris, 1946.

Blond, Georges. *The Marne.* Translated by H. Eaton Hart. Harrisburg, 1966.

Blunt, Wilfrid. *Desert Hawk: Abd el Kader and the French Conquest of Algeria.* London, 1947.

Bocca, Geoffrey. *The Secret Army.* Englewood Cliffs, N.J., 1968.

Bodard, Lucien. *La guerre d'Indochine.* Paris, 1997.

Bodin, Michel. *Soldats d'Indochine 1945–1954.* Paris, 1997.

Bodinier, Gilbert, ed. *La guerre d'Indochine 1947: textes et documents.* SHAT: Château de Vincennes, 1989.

Boilat, Abbé P. D. *Esquisses sénégalaises.* Paris, 1853.

Bois, Jean-Pierre. *Bugeaud.* Paris, 1997.

Boisanger, Claude de. *On pouvait éviter la guerre d'Indochine: souvenirs 1941–1945.* Paris, 1977.

Bolton, Herbert, and Thomas Marshall. *The Colonization of North America.* New York, 1921.

Bordeaux, Henry. *Joffre ou l'art de commander.* Paris, 1933.

Bory, Paul. *Les explorateurs de l'Afrique: Nachtigal, Galliéni, Stanley, de Brazza, Samuel Baker, Georges Révoil, etc.* Tours, 1889.

Bouche, Denise. "L'école française et les Musulmans au Sénégal de 1850 à 1920." *Revue française d'histoire d'outre-mer* 61 (1974): 218–55.

———. *Histoire de la colonisation française.* Vol. 2, *Flux et reflux, 1815–1962.* Paris, 1991.

Bournazel, Germaine de. *Henry de Bournazel: le cavalier rouge.* Paris, 1979.

Boyd, Richard. "Tocqueville's Algeria." *Society* 38 (September/October 2001): 65–70.

Brasseur, Paul Gérard. "Le Peul imaginaire," *Revue française d'histoire d'outre-mer* 65 (1978): 535–42.

Brecher, Frank W. *Losing a Continent: France's North American Policy, 1753–1763.* Westport, Conn., 1998.

Brenne, Jules. *Un mobile de l'armée de Faidherbe.* Paris, 1972.

Brocheux, Pierre, and Daniel Hémery. *Indochine: la colonisation ambigue (1858–1954).* Paris, 1994.

Brooks, George. "Peanuts and Colonialism: Consequences of the Commercialization of Peanuts in West Africa, 1830–70." *Journal of African History* 16 (1975): 29–54.

Bromberger, Merry and Serge et al. *Barricades et colonels: 24 janvier 1960.* Paris, 1960.

Brown, L. Carl, and Matthew S. Gordon, eds. *Franco-Arab Encounters: Studies in Memory of David C. Gordon.* Beirut, 1996.

Bruge, Roger. *Les hommes de Dien Biên Phu.* Paris, 1999.

Bugeaud, Thomas-Robert. *L'Algérie: des moyens de conserver et d'utiliser cette conquête.* Paris, 1842.

———. *La guerre des rues et des maisons.* Edited by Maité Bouyssy. Paris, 1997.

———. *Histoire de l'Algérie française: précédée d'une introduction sur les dominations carthaginoises, romaines, arabes et turques.* 3 vols. Paris, 1850.

———. *Observations de M. le Maréchal Gouverneur-Général sur le projet de colonisation présenté pour la province d'Oran par M. le Lieutenant-Général de La Morcière.* Algiers, 1847.

Bugnet, Charles. *Le Maréchal Lyautey.* Tours, 1946.

Burke, Edmund III. "A Comparative View of French Native Policy in Morocco and Syria, 1912–1925." *Middle Eastern Studies* 9 (1973): 175–86.

Buttinger, Joseph. *Vietnam: A Dragon Embattled.* New York, 1967.

Cabaton, Antoine. *L'Indochine.* Paris, 1932.

———. *Java and the Dutch East Indies.* Translated by Bernard Miall. London, 1911.

Cadot, Louis. *La vérité sur le siège de Péronne: réponse au Général Faidherbe.* Paris, 1872.

Cady, John F. *Southeast Asia: Its Historical Development.* New York, 1964.

Cairns, John C. "Algeria: The Last Ordeal." *International Journal* (Spring 1962): 87–97.

Camus, Albert. *The Plague.* Translated by Stuart Gilbert. New York, 1948.

Capitaine X. *Voyage du Général Gallieni.* Paris, 1901.

Carrère, Frédéric, and Paul Holle. *De la Sénégambie française.* Paris, 1855.

Cassar, George H. *Kitchener: Architect of Victory.* London, 1977.

Castellane, Pierre Comte de. *Campagnes d'Afrique, 1835–48. Lettres adressées au Maréchal de Castellane par les Maréchaux Bugeaud, Clauzel, ... etc.* Paris, 1898.

Castellane, Pierre de. *Souvenirs de la vie militaire en Afrique.* Paris, 1856.

Castor, Elie and Tarcy, Raymond. *Félix Eboué: gouverneur et philosophe.* Paris, 1984.

Cataldo, Hubert. *Bône, 1832–1962, et Hippone la Royale.* 2 vols. Montpellier, 1986–87.

Catroux, General Georges. *Dans la bataille de Méditerranée: Egypte, Lévant, Afrique du Nord 1940–1944.* Paris, 1949.

———. *Lyautey, le marocain.* Paris, 1952.

Caussidière, Marc. *Mémoires de Caussidière.* Brussels, 1848.

Chafer, Tony, and Amanda Sackur, eds. *French Colonial Empire and the Popular Front.* New York, 1999.

———. *Promoting the Colonial Idea: Propaganda and Visions of Empire in France.* Hampshire, U.K., 2002.

Challe, Maurice. *Notre révolte.* Paris, 1968.

Chambe, René. *Adieu cavalerie! La Marne, bataille gagnée ... victoire perdue.* Paris, 1979.

Charbonneau, Jean. *Gallieni à Madagascar.* Paris, 1950.

———. *La jeunesse passionnée de Galliéni: les années d'apprentissage d'un grand chef.* Bourg-en-Bresse, 1952.

Charbonnel, Henry. *De Madagascar à Verdun: vingt ans à l'ombre de Gallieni.* Paris, 1962.

Charette, Hervé de. *Lyautey.* Paris, 1997.

Charpy, Jacques. *La fondation de Dakar.* Paris, 1958.

Charton, Pierre. *RC4: Indochine 1950: la tragédie de l'évacuation de Cao Bang.* Paris, 1975.

Christelow, Allan. *Muslim Law Courts and the French Colonial State in Algeria.* Princeton, 1985.

Cladel, Judith. *Le Général Galliéni.* Paris, 1916.

Clayton, Anthony. *France, Soldiers, and Africa.* London, 1988.

Cohen, William. B. *The French Encounter with Africans.* Bloomington, Ind., 1980.

———. "Malaria and French Imperialism." *Journal of African History* 24 (1983): 23–36.

———. *Rulers of Empire: The French Colonial Service in Africa.* Stanford, 1971.

———. "The Sudden Memory of Torture: The Algerian War in French Discourse." *French Politics, Culture, and Society* 19 (2001): 82–94.

Colombani, Antoine. *Vietnam 1948–1950: la solution oubliée.* Paris, 1997.

Colvin, Lucie G. "Islam and the State of Kajoor: A Case of Successful Resistance to Jihad." *Journal of African History* 15 (1974): 587–606.

Compagnon, Jean. *Leclerc: Maréchal de France.* Paris, 1994.

Conklin, Alice L. *A Mission to Civilize: The Republican Idea of Empire in France and West Africa, 1895–1930*. Stanford, 1997.

———. "Boundaries Unbound: Teaching French History as Colonial History and Colonial History as French History." *French Historical Studies* 23 (2000): 215–38.

———. "Colonialism and Human Rights, a Contradiction in Terms? The Case of France and West Africa, 1895–1914." *American Historical Review* 103 (1998): 418–42.

Connelly, Matthew. "Taking off the Cold War Lens: Visions of North-South Conflict during the Algerian War for Independence." *American Historical Review* 105 (2000): 739–69.

———. *Diplomatic Revolution: Algeria's Fight for Independence and the Origins of the Post–Cold War Era*. New York, 2002.

Connolly, Cyril. *The Unquiet Grave*. New York, 1945.

Contamine, Henri. *La victoire de la Marne*. Paris, 1970.

Conte, Arthur. *Joffre*. Paris, 1991.

Cooper, Frederick. *Decolonization and African Society: The Labor Question in French and British Africa*. New York, 1996.

Cooper, Nicola. *France in Indochina: Colonial Encounters*. Oxford, 2001.

Copans, Jean. *Les marabouts de l'arachide*. Paris, 1980.

Cordier, Marcel. *Un grand Lorrain: Lyautey*. Saint-Seine-l'Abbaye, 1984.

———. *L'héroïque Bigeard*. Le Coteau/Roanne, 1986.

Cordier, Maurice, and Fouquer, Roger. *Le General Leclerc: se commander à soi-même*. Paris, 1990.

Cossu, Pier Paola. *I "Bureaux Arabes" e il Bugeaud*. Milan, 1974.

Courrière, Yves. *Les feux du désespoir*. Paris, 1971.

———. *Les fils de la Toussaint*. Paris, 1968.

———. *L'heure des colonels*. Paris, 1970.

———. *Le temps des léopards*. Paris, 1969.

Coursier, Alain. *Faidherbe 1818–1889: du Sénégal à l'armée du Nord*. Paris, 1989.

Covell, Maureen. *Historical Dictionary of Madagascar*. London, 1995.

Cowart, Jack et al. *Matisse in Morocco: The Paintings and Drawings, 1912–1913*. New York, 1990.

Croidys, Pierre. *Lyautey, bâtisseur d'empire*. Paris, 1943.

Crowder, Michael. *West Africa under Colonial Rule*. Evanston, 1968.

Crowe, S. E. *The Berlin West African Conference, 1884–1885*. London, 1942.

Cruise O'Brien, Donal B. *The Maurides of Senegal*. Oxford, 1971.

Cruise O'Brien, Rita. *White Society in Black Africa: The French of Senegal*. Evanston, 1972.

Curtin, Philip. *Disease and Empire: The Health of European Troops in the Conquest of Africa*. Cambridge, U.K., 1998.

Curtin, Philip D. "The Lure of Bambouk Gold." *Journal of African History* 14 (1973): 623–31.

Dallas, Gregor. *At the Heart of a Tiger: Clemenceau and His World, 1841–1929*. London, 1993.

Dansette, Adrien. "Lyautey, Ministre de Guerre." *La Revue de Paris* (July 1964): 135–39.

Danziger, Ralph. *Abd al-Qadir and the Algerians.* New York, 1977.

Davies, A. M. *Clive of Plassey.* London, 1939.

Dawbarn, Charles. *Joffre and His Army.* London, 1916.

Deac, Wilfred. "Operation Musketeer: Duel for the Suez Canal." *Military History* (April, 2001): 58–64.

De Gaulle, Charles. *Lettres, notes et carnets.* Paris, 1980.

———. *War Memoirs.* 3 vols. London, 1955–59.

Delanoë, Guy. *Lyautey, Juin, Mohammed V: fin d'un protectorat.* Vol. 1. Paris, 1998.

Delavignette, Robert L. "French Colonial Policy in Black Africa, 1945 to 1960." In *Colonialism in Africa, 1870–1960.* Edited by L. H. Gann and Peter Duignan. Cambridge, 1970.

Delcourt, Jean. *Naissance et croissance de Dakar.* Dakar, 1981.

Delpard, Raphaël. *Vingt ans pendant la guerre d'Algérie: générations sacrifiées.* Paris, 2001.

Delpey, Roger. *Soldats de la boue.* 2 vols. Paris, 1961.

Dem, Marc. *Mourir pour Câo Bang: le drame de la Route Coloniale no. 4.* Paris, 1978.

Demaison, André. *Faidherbe.* Paris, 1932.

Démontès, Victor. *La colonisation militaire sous Bugeaud.* Paris, 1918.

Dening, Grey. *Islands and Beaches.* Tucson, Ariz., 1993.

Dervil, Guy. *Trois grands africains: dans l'intimité de Lyautey, Laperrine, Foucauld; souvenirs personnels.* Paris, n.d.

Deschamps, Hubert-Jules. *Les méthodes et doctrines coloniales de la France.* Paris, 1953.

———. *Le Sénégal et la Gambie.* Paris, 1964.

Deschamps, Hubert-Jules, and Paul Chauvet, eds. *Gallieni pacificateur: écrits coloniaux de Gallieni.* Paris, 1949.

Desmazières, Bertrand. *Pierre de Sorbier de Pougnadoresse: le Colbert de Lyautey.* Paris, 1998.

Dessaigne, Francine. *Journal d'une mère de famille pied-noir.* Paris, 1972.

Destremau, Bernard. *Jean de Lattre de Tassigny.* Paris, 1999.

Diallo, Thierno. *Les institutions politiques de Fouta Djallon au XIXè siècle.* Dakar, 1972.

Didelot, Roger-François. *Gallieni: soldat de France.* Paris, 1987.

Dinfreville, Jacques. *Le Roi Jean.* Paris, 1964.

Dodwell, Henry. *Dupleix and Clive: The Beginning of Empire.* London, 1967.

Doury, Paul. *Lyautey: un saharien atypique.* Paris, 2002.

Dubly, Henry Louis. *Lyautey le magicien.* Lille, 1931.

Duchène, Albert. *La politique coloniale de la France: le ministère des colonies depuis Richelieu.* Paris, 1928.

Duiker, William J. *U.S. Containment Policy and the Conflict in Indochina.* Stanford, 1994.

Dunn, Ross E. *Resistance in the Desert: Moroccan Responses to French Imperialism 1881–1912.* London, 1977.

Dunwoodie, Peter. *Writing French Algeria.* Oxford, 1998.

Dupuy, Trevor N., Curt Johnson, and David L. Bongard. *The Harper Encyclopedia of Military Biography.* Edison, N.J., 1992.

Duquesne, Jacques. *Pour comprendre la guerre d'Algérie*. Paris, 2001.

Durosoy, Maurice. *Avec Lyautey*. Paris, 1976.

———. *Lyautey: Maréchal de France 1854–1934*. Limoges, 1984.

Duveau, Georges. *1848: The Making of a Revolution*. Translated by Anne Carter. New York, 1967.

Eberhardt, Isabelle. *In the Shadow of Islam*. Translated by Sharon Bangert. London, 1993.

Echenberg, Myron. *Colonial Conscripts: The Tirailleurs Sénégalais in French West Africa, 1857–1960*. Portsmouth, N.H., 1991.

Edwardes, Michael. *Plassey: The Founding of an Empire*. London, 1969.

Ekberg, Carl J. *French Roots in the Illinois Country: The Mississippi Frontier in Colonial Times*. Urbana, Ill., 1998.

Ellie, Paul. *Le Général Gallieni: Le Tonkin-Madagascar*. Paris, 1900.

Ellis, Stephen. "The Political Elite of Imerina and the Revolt of the *Menalamba*: The Creation of a Colonial Myth in Madagascar, 1895–1898." *Journal of African History* 21 (1980): 219–34.

———. *The Rising of the Red Shawls: A Revolt in Madagascar 1895–1899*. Cambridge, U.K., 1985.

Ely, Gen. Paul. *Mémoires: L'Indochine dans la tourmente*. Vol. 1. Paris, 1961.

Esme, Jean d'. *Gallieni*. Paris, 1965.

———. *Bournazel, l'homme rouge*. Paris, 1952.

———. *Joffre*. Paris, 1953.

———. *Le père Joffre*. Paris, 1962.

Espérandieu, Pierre. *Lyautey et le Protectorat*. Paris, 1947.

Evans, Martin. "La Lutte continue . . . ? Contemporary History and Algeria." *History Today* 47 (1997): 10–12.

———. *The Memory of Resistance: French Opposition to the Algerian War (1954–1962)*. New York, 1997.

———. "Projecting a Greater France." *History Today* 50 (2000): 19–25.

Fabry, Jean. *Joffre et son destin*. Paris, 1931.

Faidherbe, Louis Léon. *L'armée du Nord en 1870–1871*. Paris, 1872.

———. *Armée du Nord: réponse à la relation du Général Von Goeben pour faire suite à la campagne du Nord*. Paris, 1873.

———. *Chapitres de géographie sur le nord-ouest de l'Afrique avec une carte des contrées à l'usage des écoles de la Sénégambie*. Saint-Louis, 1864.

———. *Collection complète des inscriptions numidiques (libyques) avec des aperçus ethnographiques sur les Numides*. Paris, 1870.

———. *Essai sur la langue poul: grammaire et vocabulaire*. Paris, 1875.

———. *Notice sur la colonie du Sénégal et sur les pays qui sont en relation avec elle*. Paris, 1859.

———. *Le Sénégal*. Paris, 1888.

———. "Mémoire sur les éléphants carthaginois." *Bulletin de l'Académie d'Hippone* 3 (Bône, 1867): 1–18.

———. *Vocabulaire d'environ 1500 mots français avec leurs correspondants en oulof de Saint-Louis, en poular (toucouleur) du Fouta, en soninké (sarakhollé de Bakel)*. Saint-Louis, 1864.

———. *Le Zénaga des tribus sénégalaises: contribution à l'étude de la langue berbère*. Paris, 1877.

Fall, Bernard. *Hell in a Very Small Place*. Philadelphia, 1967.

———. *Street without Joy*. Harrisburg, 1963.

Farrère, Claude. *Lyautey, créateur: notes et souvenirs*. Paris, 1955.

Faure, Jean. *Au pays de la soif et de la peur: carnets d'Algérie 1957–1959*. Paris, 2001.

Ferrandi, Jean. *Les officiers français face au Vietminh: 1945–1954*. Paris, 1966.

Feuer, Lewis. *Imperialism and the Anti-Imperialist Mind*. Buffalo, 1986.

Fick, Carolyn E. *The Making of Haiti: The Saint Domingue Revolution from Below*. Knoxville, Tenn., 1990.

Figuéras, André. *Lyautey assassiné: la question marocaine*. Paris, 1958.

Fisher, Charles. *South-East Asia: A Social, Economic, and Political Geography*. London, 1964.

Fitzgerald, Edward Peter. "Did France's Colonial Empire Make Economic Sense? A Perspective from the Postwar Decade, 1946–1956." *The Journal of Economic History* 48 (June, 1988): 373–85.

Fleury, Georges. *La guerre en Indochine 1945–1954*. Paris, 1994.

Foch, Ferdinand. *The Memoirs of Marshal Foch*. Translated by T. Bentley Mott. Garden City, N.Y., 1931.

Forster, Robert. *The Nobility of Toulouse in the Eighteenth Century*. Baltimore, 1960.

Franchet d'Espérey, Louis. *Bugeaud*. Paris, 1938.

Franda, Marcus. *The Seychelles*. Boulder, Colo., 1982.

Freeman, James M. *Untouchable*. Stanford, 1979.

French, John. *The Despatches of Lord French*. London, 1917.

Friang, Brigitte. *La Mousson de la liberté: Vietnam, du colonialisme au stalinisme*. Paris, 1976.

Gaden, Henri. *Le Poular dialecte peul de Fouta Sénégalais*. Paris, 1912.

———. *Proverbes et maximes peuls et toucouleurs*. Paris, 1931.

Gaffarel, Paul. *Le Sénégal et le Soudan français*. Paris, 1890.

Gaget, Robert. *Commandos parachutistes*. Paris, 1992.

Gallaher, John G. *The Students of Paris and the Revolution of 1848*. Carbondale, Ill., 1980.

Gallieni, Joseph. *Les carnets de Gallieni*. Paris, 1922.

———. *Deux campagnes au Soudan français 1886–1888*. Paris, 1891.

———. *Gallieni au Tonkin (1892–1896) par lui-même*. Paris, 1941.

———. *Lettres de Madagascar 1896–1905*. Paris, 1928.

———. *Les mémoires du Général Gallieni: défense de Paris. 25 aôut–11 septembre 1914*. Paris, 1920.

———. *Neuf ans à Madagascar*. Paris, 1908.

———. *Un Noël au Soudan*. Paris, 1924.

———. *Rapport d'ensemble sur la pacification, l'organisation et la colonisation de Madagascar (Octobre 1896 à Mars 1898)*. 1899.

———. *Voyage au Soudan français (Haut-Niger et pays de Ségou 1879–1881)*. Paris, 1885.

Gamble, David. *The Wolof of Senegambia*. London, 1967.

Gamelin, Maurice. *Manoeuvre et victoire de la Marne*. Paris, 1954.

Gandy, Alain. *Salan*. Paris, 1990.

———. *Bataillon Bigeard à Tu Lê 1952*. Paris, 1996.

Garric, Robert. *Le message de Lyautey*. Paris, 1964.

Gaudron, Max. *Légionnaire au Nord-Tonkin*. Paris, 1980.

Gaulis, B. G. *Lyautey intime*. Paris, 1938.

Gaunson, A. B. *The Anglo-French Clash in Lebanon and Syria, 1940–1945*. London, 1987.

Geggus, David P. *Slavery, War, and Revolution: The British Occupation of Saint-Domingue, 1793–1798*. Oxford, 1982.

Gensoul, Louis. *Souvenir de l'armée du Nord en 1870–1871*. Paris, 1914.

Georges, Alfred. *Charles de Gaulle et la guerre d'Indochine*. Paris, 1974.

Germain, Roger. *La politique indigène de Bugeaud*. Paris, 1955.

Gershovich, Moshe. *French Military Rule in Morocco: Colonialism and Its Consequences*. London, 2000.

Gheusi, Pierre B. *Galliéni 1849–1916*. Paris, 1922.

———. *La gloire de Gallieni: comment Paris fût sauvé*. Paris, 1928.

———. *Guerre et théâtre 1914–1918*. Paris, 1919.

Girardet, Raoul. *L'idée coloniale en France de 1871 à 1962*. Paris, 1972.

Giraud, General Henri. *Un seul but, la victoire: Alger 1942–1944*. Paris, 1949.

Godard, Yves. *Les trois batailles d'Alger*. Vol. 1, *Les paras dans la ville*. Paris, 1972.

Godeau, Pierre. *Une aventure algérienne*. Paris, 2001.

Gomez, Michael A. *Pragmatism in the Age of Jihad: The Precolonial State of Bundu*. Cambridge, U.K., 1992.

Gontard, Maurice. "La Politique religieuse de Gallieni à Madagascar pendant les premières années de l'occupation française (1896–1900)." *Revue française d'histoire d'outre-mer* 58 (1971): 183–214.

Gottman, Jean. "Bugeaud, Gallieni, Lyautey: The Development of French Colonial Warfare." In *Makers of Modern Strategy: Military Thought from Machiavelli to Hitler*. Edited by E. M. Earle. Princeton, 1943.

Gouraud, Henri Joseph Eugène. *Lyautey*. Paris, 1938.

Goutard, Adolphe. *La Marne: victoire inexploitée*. Paris, 1968.

Graham, Richard. *Independence in Latin America: A Comparative Approach*. 2nd edition. New York, 1994.

Grandidier, Guillaume. *Galliéni*. Paris, 1931.

Grant, Bruce. *Indonesia*. Harmondsworth, U.K., 1967.

Gras, Yves. *Histoire de la guerre d'Indochine*. Paris, 1992.

Grauwin, Paul. *Doctor at Dienbienphu*. Translated by James Oliver. New York, 1955.

Greenblatt, Stephen. *Marvelous Possessions: The Wonder of the New World*. Chicago, 1991.

Grosbellet, Bernard. *Le Moniteur du Sénégal et dépendances comme source de l'histoire du Sénégal au temps du premier gouvernement de Faidherbe (1856–1861)*. Dakar, 1967.

Guiral, Pierre. *Les militaires à la conquête de l'Algérie 1830–1857*. Paris, 1992.

Guizot, François. *Memoirs of a Minister of State*. London, 1864.

Gury, Christian. *Lyautey-Charlus*. Paris, 1998.

Hall, D. G. *A History of South-East Asia*. 2nd edition. London, 1964.

Halsey, Francis W. *Balfour, Viviani and Joffre: Their Speeches and Other Public Utterances in America . . .* New York, 1917.

Halstead, John P. *Rebirth of a Nation: The Origins and Rise of Moroccan Nationalism, 1912–1944.* Cambridge, Mass., 1969.

Hammer, Ellen J. *The Struggle for Indochina 1940–1955.* Stanford, 1955.

Hamon, Hervé, and Rotman, Patrick. *Les porteurs de valises: la résistance française à la guerre d'Algérie.* Paris, 1979.

Hannoum, Abdelmajid. "Colonialism and Knowledge in Algeria: The Archives of the Arab Bureau." *History and Anthropology* 12 (2001): 343–79.

Hanotaux, Gabriel. *Joffre.* Paris, 1921.

Hanotaux, Gabriel, and Alfred Martineau, eds. *Histoire des colonies françaises et de l'expansion de la France dans le monde.* 5 vols. Paris, 1933.

Hardy, Georges. *Faidherbe.* Paris, 1947.

———. *Histoire de la colonisation française.* 5th edition. Paris, 1947.

———. *Portrait de Lyautey.* Paris, 1949.

Hargreaves, A. G., and M. J. Heffernan, eds. *French and Algerian Identities from Colonial Times to the Present.* Lewiston and Lampeter, 1993.

Hargreaves, J. D. *West Africa: The Former French States.* Englewood Cliffs, N.J., 1967.

———, ed. *France and West Africa: An Anthology of Historical Documents.* London, 1969.

Harris, Walter B. *France, Spain and the Rif.* London, 1927.

Harrison, Christopher. *France and Islam in West Africa, 1860–1960.* Cambridge, U.K., 1988.

Héduy, Philippe. *Histoire de l'Indochine: la perle de l'empire 1624–1954.* Paris, 1998.

Heidsieck, Patrick. *Lyautey.* Tours, 1950.

———. "Lyautey et les rapports Franco-Musulmans." *Etudes* (October 1954): 62–69.

Heidsieck, Patrick, ed. *Lyautey: Maréchal de France.* Paris, 1954.

———. *Rayonnement de Lyautey.* Paris, 1941.

Hélias, Pierre-Jakez. *The Horse of Pride: Life in a Breton Village.* Translated by June Guicharnaud. New Haven, Conn., 1978.

Henissart, Paul. *Wolves in the City: The Death of French Algeria.* New York, 1970.

Herbillon, Emile Emmanuel. *Souvenirs d'un officier de liaison pendant la guerre mondiale.* 2 vols. Paris, 1930.

Hesseltine, Nigel. *Madagascar.* New York, 1971.

Hinzelin, Emile. *Notre Joffre: Maréchal de France.* Paris, 1917.

Hitchcock, William I. "Pierre Boisson, French West Africa, and the Postwar *Epuration*: A Case from the Aix Files." *French Historical Studies* 24 (Spring, 2001): 305–41.

Hitti, Philip K. *Syria: A Short History.* New York, 1959.

Hochschild, Adam. *King Leopold's Ghost.* New York, 1998.

Hodeir, Catherine, and Pierre, Michel. *L'Exposition coloniale.* Paris, 1991.

Hoisington, William A., Jr. *The Casablanca Connection: French Colonial Policy, 1936–1942.* Chapel Hill, N.C., 1984.

———. "Cities in Revolt: The Berber Dahir (1930) and France's Urban Strategy in Morocco." *Journal of Contemporary History* 13 (July, 1978): 433–48.

————. "Designing Morocco's Future: France and the Native Policy Council, 1921–25." *Journal of North African Studies* 5 (Spring, 2000): 63–108.

————. *Lyautey and the French Conquest of Morocco*. New York, 1995.

Horne, Alistair. *The Price of Glory: Verdun 1916*. London, 1964.

————. *A Savage War of Peace: Algeria 1954–1962*. London, 1977.

Howe, Sonia E. *Lyautey of Morocco*. London, 1931.

Hunter, Guy. *South-East Asia: Race, Culture, and Nation*. New York, 1966.

Huntington, Samuel P. *The Clash of Civilizations and the Remaking of World Order*. New York, 1996.

Huré, Gen. Antoine. *La pacification du Maroc: dernière étape, 1931–1934*. Paris, 1952.

Hureau, Joëlle. *La mémoire des pieds-noirs*. Paris, 1987.

Hutchinson, Martha Crenshaw. *Revolutionary Terrorism: The FLN in Algeria 1954–1962*. Stanford, 1978.

Hutton, J. H. *Caste in India*. Cambridge, U.K., 1946.

Ideville, Henri H., ed. *Memoirs of Marshal Bugeaud: From His Private Correspondence and Original Documents 1784–1849*. 2 Vols. Translated and edited by Charlotte M. Yonge. London, 1884.

Idowu, H. Oludare. "Assimilation in 19th Century Senegal." *Cahiers d'études africaines* 9 (1969): 194–218.

Irving, R. E. M. *The First Indochina War*. London, 1975.

Isaac, Jules. *Joffre et Lanrezac: étude critique des témoignages sur le rôle de la 5ième Armée, août 1914*. Paris, 1922.

Isaacman, Allen, and Roberts, Richard, eds. *Cotton, Colonialism, and Social History in Sub-Saharan Africa*. Portsmouth, N.H., 1995.

Isaacs, Harold R. *India's Ex-Untouchables*. New York, 1964.

Israël, Gérard. *Le dernier jour de l'Algérie française: ler juillet, 1962*. Paris, 1972.

Isselin, Henri. *The Battle of the Marne*. Translated by Charles Cornell. London, 1964.

Iyasere, Solomon O., ed. *Understanding Things Fall Apart: Selected Essays and Criticism*. Troy, N.Y., 1998.

Jacques Béal. *Leclerc: vie et mort d'un croisé*. Paris, 1988.

James, C. L. R. *The Black Jacobins*. 2nd edition. New York, 1963.

Jardin, André. *Tocqueville: A Biography*. Translated by Lydia Davis and Robert Hemenway. New York, 1988.

Jauffret, Jean-Charles. "The Origins of the Algerian War: The Reaction of France and Its Army to the Two Emergencies of 8 May 1945 and 1 November 1954." *Journal of Imperial and Commonwealth History* 21 (September 1993): 17–29.

————. *Soldats en Algérie, 1954–1962: expériences contrastées des hommes du contingent*. Paris, 2000.

Jennings, Eric T. "Reinventing Jeanne: The Iconology of Joan of Arc in Vichy Schoolbooks, 1940–44." *Journal of Contemporary History* 29 (1994): 711–34.

————. "Vichy à Madagascar. La 'Révolution nationale', l'enseignement et la jeunesse (1940–1942)." *Revue d'histoire moderne et contemporaine* 46 (octobre–décembre, 1999): 729–46.

————. *Vichy in the Tropics: Pétain's National Revolution in Madagascar, Guadeloupe, and Indochina, 1940–1944*. Stanford, 2001.

Joffre, Joseph. *My March to Timbuctoo*. Translated by Ernest Dimnet. London, 1915.
———. *1914–1915; la préparation de la guerre et la conduite des opérations*. Paris, 1920.
———. *The Personal Memoirs of Joffre*. Translated by T. Bentley Mott. New York, 1932.
Joffre, Joseph et al. *The Two Battles of the Marne*. London, 1927.
Johnson, G. Wesley, ed. *Double Impact: France and Africa in the Age of Imperialism*. Westport, Conn., 1985.
Johnson, Owen. *The Spirit of France*. Boston, 1916.
Joinville, Prince de. *Memoirs of the Prince de Joinville*. Translated by Lady Mary Lloyd. New York, 1895.
Jore, Léonce. *Les établissements français sur la côte occidentale de l'Afrique de 1758 à 1809*. Paris, 1965.
Jouveau-Dubreuil, Gabriel. *Dupleix*. Pondichéry, 1941.
Judt, Tony. "On the 'Plague.'" *New York Review of Books*, November 29, 2001: 6–9.
———. *The Burden of Responsibility: Blum, Camus, Aron, and the French Twentieth Century*. Chicago, 1998.
Juin, Maréchal Alphonse. *Mémoires*. Vol. 2. Paris, 1960.
Julien, Charles. *Les constructeurs de la France d'outre-mer*. Paris, 1946.
———. *Le Maroc face aux impérialismes 1415-1956*. Paris, 1978.
———. *Les techniciens de la colonisation*. Paris, 1947.
Julien, Charles-André, ed. *Abd el-Krim et la République du Rif*. Paris, 1976.
Kahn, Alexander. *Life of General Joffre: Cooper's Son Who Became Commander-in-chief*. New York, 1915.
Kane, Robert S. *South Pacific A to Z*. New York, 1966.
Kanya-Forstner, A. S. *The Conquest of the Western Sudan: A Study in French Military Imperialism*. Cambridge, U.K., 1969.
———. "Military Expansion in the Western Sudan—French and British Style." In *France and Britain in Africa*, Prosser Gifford and W. Roger Louis, eds. New Haven, 1971.
Karnow, Stanley. *Vietnam: A History*. New York, 1983.
Keegan, John. *The Second World War*. London, 1989.
Keller, Richard. "Madness and Colonization: Psychiatry in the British and French Empires, 1800–1962." *Journal of Social History* 35 (2001): 295–326.
Kent, Sherman. *Electoral Procedure under Louis Philippe*. New Haven, 1937.
Kernberg, Otto F. *Narcissistic Personality Disorder*. Philadelphia, 1989.
———. *Severe Personality Disorders: Psychotherapeutic Strategies*. New Haven, 1984.
Kessel, Patrick. *Moi, Maréchal Bugeaud: un soldat de l'ordre*. Paris, 1958.
Khoury, Philip S. *Syria and the French Mandate: The Politics of Arab Nationalism 1920–1945*. Princeton, 1987.
Killam, G. D. *The Novels of Chinua Achebe*. New York, 1969.
Klein, Charles-Armand. *Gallieni: portrait varois*. Barbentane, 2003.
Klein, Herbert S. *African Slavery in Latin America and the Caribbean*. New York, 1986.
Klein, Martin. *Islam and Imperialism: Sine-Saloum. 1847–1914*. Stanford, 1968.
———. *Slavery and Colonial Rule in French West Africa*. Cambridge, U.K., 1998.

Kluck, Alexander von. *The March on Paris and the Battle of the Marne 1914*. London, 1920.

Knibiehler, Yvonne et al. *Des Français au Maroc: la présence et la mémoire (1912–1956)*. Paris, 1992.

Koburger, Charles W., Jr. *The Cyrano Fleet: France and Its Navy, 1940–1942*. Westport, Conn., 1989.

Lacheroy, Charles. *De Saint-Cyr à l'action psychologique: mémoires d'un siècle*, Panazol, 2003.

Lacouture, Jean. *De Gaulle: The Rebel, 1890–1944*. New York, 1990.

Lacouture, Jean and Simonne Lacouture. *Le Maroc à l'épreuve*. Paris, 1958.

Lamaze, Edouard de. *Bugeaud*. Lyon, 1943.

Lancaster, Donald. *The Emancipation of French Indochina*. London, 1961.

Langdon, Heather. "All Silent on the Algerian Front?" (unpublished undergraduate essay, Harvard University, 2001).

Langdon, John W. "Jesuit Schools and French Society, 1851–1908." *Indiana Social Studies Quarterly* 37 (Winter 1984): 31–44.

———. "The Jesuits and French Education: A Comparative Study of Two Schools, 1852–1913." *History of Education Quarterly* 17 (Spring 1978): 49–60.

———. "New Light on the Influence of the Jesuit Schools: The Ecole Sainte-Geneviève and Its Graduates, 1854–1913." *Third Republic/Troisième République* 1 (1976): 132–51.

Larémont, Ricardo René. *Islam and the Politics of Resistance in Algeria, 1783–1992*. Trenton, N.J., 2000.

Larminat, René-Marie-Edgard de. *Chroniques irrévérencieuses*. Paris, 1962.

La Tour, Contamine. *Joffre: sa vie, son oeuvre*. Paris, 1919.

Lattre, Maréchal Jean de. *La ferveur et le sacrifice: Indochine 1951*. Edited by Jean-Luc Barré. Paris, 1988.

Lattre, Simonne de. *Jean de Lattre, mon mari*. 2 vols. Paris, 1972.

Lawler, Nancy E. *Soldiers of Misfortune: Ivoirien Tirailleurs of World War II*. Athens, Ohio, 1992.

Lazard, Didier. *Max Lazard, ses frères et Lyautey: lettres, 1894–1933*. Neuilly, 1990.

Lebel, Roland. *Histoire de la littérature coloniale en France*. Paris, 1931.

Lebesque, Morvan. *Camus par lui-même*. Paris, 1963.

Leblond, Marius-Ary. *Gallieni parle*. Paris, 1920.

Leblond, Maurice. *La Réunion*. Paris, 1956.

Lebon, André. *La pacification de Madagascar, 1896–1898*. Paris, 1928.

Leclerc, Max. *Au Maroc avec Lyautey*. Paris, 1927.

Leconte, Daniel. *Les pieds-noirs: histoire et portrait d'une communauté*. Paris, 1980.

Lefranc, Pierre, ed. *De Gaulle et l'Indochine 1940–1946*. Paris, 1982.

Le Page, Marcel. *Cao-Bang: la tragique épopée de la colonne Le Page*. Paris, 1981.

Le Révérend, André. *Lyautey*. Paris, 1983.

———. *Lyautey écrivain 1854–1934*. Gap, 1976.

———, ed. *Un Lyautey inconnu*. Paris, 1980.

Lesourd, Paul. *Bugeaud, le soldat-laboureur*. Paris, 1943.

Le Sueur, James D. *Uncivil War: Intellectuals and Identity Politics during the Decolonization of Algeria*. Philadelphia, 2001.

Lévi-Valensi, Jacqueline. *La Peste d'Albert Camus.* Paris, 1991.

Lévi-Valensi, Jacqueline, and André Abbou, eds. *Cahiers Albert Camus 3: fragments d'un combat 1938–1940.* Paris, 1978.

Lewis, Norman. *A Dragon Apparent: Travels in Cambodia, Laos, and Vietnam.* 1951. Reprint, London, 1982.

Lichtenberger, André. *Bugeaud.* Paris, 1931.

Liddell Hart, Basil H. *History of the Second World War.* New York, 1971.

———. *The Real War 1914–1918.* Boston, 1930.

———. *Reputations Ten Years After.* Boston, 1928.

———. *Through the Fog of War.* London, 1938.

Lloyd George, David. *The War Memoirs of David Lloyd George, 1914–1915.* Boston, 1933.

Lokke, Carl N. *France and the Colonial Question.* New York, 1932.

Lombard, Henri J. M. *Les jours ordinaires d'un "protecteur" au Maroc.* Nîmes, 1993.

Longrigg, Stephen H. *Syria and Lebanon under French Mandate.* New York, 1958.

Lorcin, Patricia. *Imperial Identities: Stereotyping, Prejudice and Race in Colonial Algeria.* London, 1995.

———. "Imperialism, Colonial Identity, and Race in Algeria, 1830–1870: The Role of the French Medical Corps." *Isis* 90 (1999): 652–79.

Louis, William Roger, and Jean Stengers, eds. *E. D. Morel's History of the Congo Reform Movement.* Oxford, 1968.

Lucas-Dubreton, J. *Bugeaud.* Paris, 1931.

Lugan, Bernard. *Histoire du Maroc.* Paris, 1992.

Lunn, Joe. *Memoirs of the Maelstrom: A Senegalese Oral History of the First World War.* Portsmouth, N.H., 1999.

Lyautey, Hubert. *Choix de lettres 1882–1919.* Paris, 1947.

———. *Du rôle social de l'officier et du rôle colonial de l'armée.* Paris, 1946.

———. *Intimate Letters from Tonquin.* Translated by Aubrey Le Blond. London, 1932.

———. *Lettres de jeunesse.* Paris, 1931.

———. *Lettres du Sud de Madagascar 1900–1902.* Paris, 1935.

———. *Lettres du Tonkin et de Madagascar (1894–1899).* Paris, 1921.

———. *Paroles d'action.* Paris, 1927.

———. *Vers le Maroc: lettres du Sud-Oranais 1903–1906.* Paris, 1937.

Lyautey, Pierre. *L'empire colonial français.* Paris, 1931.

———. *Gallieni.* 4th edition. Paris, 1959.

———. *Je les ai connus.* Paris, 1974.

———, ed. *Les plus belles lettres de Lyautey.* Paris, 1962

———, ed. *Lyautey l'africain: textes et lettres du Maréchal Lyautey.* Paris, 1953.

Lyet, Pierre. *Joffre et Gallieni à la Marne.* Paris, 1938.

Macey, David. *Frantz Fanon: A Biography.* New York, 2000.

Mackworth, Cecily. *The Destiny of Isabelle Eberhardt.* London, 1951.

MacLeod, Roy, and Milton Lewis, eds. *Disease, Medicine, and Empire: Perspectives on Western Medicine and the Experience of European Expansion.* London, 1988.

Madani, Col. Bel. *Coupable de fidelité.* Paris, 1990.

Mage, Eugène. *Voyage au Soudan occidental.* Paris, 1980.

Maison Rouge, Olivier de. *La guerre d'Indochine 1945–1954*. Paris, 1989.

Mann, Kristin, and Richard Roberts, eds. *Law in Colonial Africa*. Portsmouth, N.H., 1991.

Manning, Patrick. *Francophone Sub-Saharan Africa 1880–1985*. Cambridge, U.K., 1988.

Mannoni, Pierre. *Les Français d'Algérie: vie, moeurs, mentalités*. Paris, 1993.

Maran, Rita. *Torture: The Role of Ideology in the French-Algerian War*. New York, 1989.

Marnham, Patrick. *The Death of Jean Moulin: Biography of a Ghost*. London, 2000.

Marseille, Jacques. "The Phases of French Colonial Imperialism: Toward a New Periodization." *Journal of Imperial and Commonwealth History* 13 (1985): 127–41.

Martel, André. *Leclerc: le soldat et le politique*. Paris, 1998.

Martin, Claude. *Histoire de l'Algérie française 1830–1962*. Paris, 1963.

Martin, Jean. *L'empire renaissant: 1789–1871*. Paris, 1987.

Martineau, Alfred. *Dupleix et l'Inde française*. Paris, 1920.

Maspéro, François. *L'honneur de Saint-Arnaud*. Paris, 1993.

Massu, Jacques (with Alain-Gilles Minella). *Avec de Gaulle: du Tchad 1941 à Baden 1968*. Paris, 1998.

Massu, Jacques. *La vraie bataille d'Alger*. Paris, 1972.

———. *Le torrent et la digue: Alger du 13 mai aux barricades*. Monaco, 1997.

Massu, Suzanne. *Un commandant pas comme les autres*. Paris, 1971.

———. *Quand j'étais Rochambelle*. Paris, 1969.

Masterson, James F. *The Narcissistic and Borderline Disorders: An Integrated Developmental Approach*. Larchmont, N.Y., 1981.

———. *The Search for the Real Self: Unmasking the Personality Disorders of Our Time*. New York, 1988.

Matthews, Virgil. "Joseph Simon Gallieni (1849–1916)." In *African Proconsuls: European Governors in Africa*. Edited by L. H. Gann and Peter Duignan. New York, 1978.

Maurois, André. *Marshal Lyautey*. Translated by Hamish Miles. London, 1931.

Maxwell, Gavin. *Lords of the Atlas*. New York, 1966.

May, Someth. *Cambodian Witness*. London, 1986.

McClintock, Anne. *Imperial Leather: Race, Gender and Sexuality in the Colonial Contest*. New York, 1995.

McPhail, Helen. *The Long Silence: Civilian Life under the German Occupation of Northern France, 1914–1918*. London, 1999.

Ménière, Prosper. *La captivité de Madame la Duchesse de Berry à Blaye. 1833. Journal du docteur P. Ménière . . .* 2 vols. Paris, 1882.

Mercier, Gilbert. *Lyautey: le Prince Lorrain*. Jarville–La Malgrange, 1994.

Merriman, John M. *The Agony of the Republic: The Repression of the Left in Revolutionary France 1848–1851*. New Haven, 1978.

Messimy, Adolphe. *Mes souvenirs*. Paris, 1937.

Meyer, Charles. *La vie quotidienne des français en Indochine, 1860–1910*. Paris, 1985.

Meyer, Jean et al. *Histoire de la France coloniale des origines à 1914*. Paris, 1991.

Michel, Marc. *Gallieni*. Paris, 1989.

Michiels, Albert. *Notre colonie*. 3rd edition. Brussels, 1912.

Mills, Lennox A., ed. *The New World of Southeast Asia*. Minneapolis, 1949.

Minney, R.J. *Clive*. New York, 1931.

Miquel, Pierre. *Le gâchis des généraux: les erreurs de commandement pendant la guerre de 14–18*. Paris, 2001.

———. *Joffre: la volonté de vaincre*. Paris, 1984.

Moha, Edouard. *Histoire des relations franco-marocaines*. Paris, 1995.

Moncelet, Christian. "Guerre d'Algérire ..." *L'esprit créateur* 41 (2001): 9–18.

Montagnac, Lucien François de. *Lettres d'un soldat: neuf années de campagnes en Afrique*. Paris, 1885.

Montagnon, Pierre. *La France coloniale: la gloire de l'empire*. Paris, 1988.

Morand, Paul. *Nothing But the Earth*. Translated by Lewis Galantière. New York, 1927.

Muller, Louis. *Joffre et la Marne*. Paris, 1931.

Munholland, J. Kim. "Collaboration Strategy and the French Pacification of Tonkin, 1885–1897." *The Historical Journal* 24 (1981): 629–50.

———. "The Emergence of the Colonial Military in France, 1880–1905." Ph.D. dissertation: Princeton University, 1964.

———. "Rival Approaches to Morocco: Delcassé, Lyautey, and the Algerian-Moroccan Border, 1903–1905." *French Historical Studies* 5 (Spring 1968): 328–43.

Murray, Williamson. "Dien Bien Phu." *MHO: The Quarterly Journal of Military History* 9 (Spring 1997): 40–51.

Nelson, Samuel H. *Colonialism in the Congo Basin, 1880–1940*. Athens, Ohio, 1984.

Nicoll, Edna L. *A travers l'exposition coloniale*. Paris, 1931.

Nicholls, Jonathan. *Cheerful Sacrifice: The Battle of Arras*. London, 1990.

O'Ballance, Edgar. *The Algerian Insurrection 1954–1962*. Hamden, Conn., 1967.

———. *The Indo-China War, 1945–54*. London, 1964.

Ohaeto, Ezenwa-. *Chinua Achebe: A Biography*. Oxford, 1997.

Oloruntimehin, B. O. *The Segu Tokolor Empire*. London, 1972.

Ormesson, Vladimir d'. *Auprès de Lyautey*. Paris, 1973.

———. "La dernière victoire de Lyautey." *La Revue de Paris* (October 1963): 1–9.

Ott, Thomas O. *The Haitian Revolution, 1789–1804*. Knoxville, 1973.

Ottenheimer, Martin, and Harriet Ottenheimer. *Historical Dictionary of the Comoro Islands*. Metuchen, N.J., 1994.

Pagden, Anthony. *European Encounters with the New World: From Renaissance to Romanticism*. New Haven, 1997.

Page, Melvin E. et al., eds. *Personality and Political Culture in Modern Africa: Studies Presented to Professor Harold G. Marcus*. Boston, 1998.

Palmer, Leslie. *Indonesia*. New York, 1966.

Paluel-Marmont, Albert. *Bugeaud, premier Français d'Algérie*. Tours, 1944.

———. *Lyautey*. Paris, 1934.

Paris de Bollardière, Jacques. *Bataille d'Alger, bataille de l'homme*. Paris, 1972.

Parkman, Mary R. *Fighters for Peace*. New York, 1919.

Peabody, Sue. *"There Are No Slaves in France": The Political Culture of Race and Slavery in the Ancien Régime*. New York, 1996.

Pedroncini, Guy, and Philippe Duplay, eds. *Leclerc et L'Indochine 1945–1947*. Paris, 1992.

Pellissier, Pierre. *De Lattre*. Paris, 1998.

Perkins, Kenneth J. *Qaids, Captains, and Colons: French Military Administration in the Colonial Maghrib, 1844–1934*. New York, 1981.

Pershing, John J. *My Experiences in the World War*. New York, 1931.

Peters, Joan. *From Time Immemorial: The Origins of the Arab-Jewish Conflict over Palestine*. New York, 1993.

Peterson, A. D. C. *The Far East: A Social Geography*. London, 1957.

Poincaré, Raymond. *Au Service de la France*. Paris, 1931.

———. *The Memoirs of Raymond Poincaré 1915*. Translated by George Arthur. London, 1930.

Porch, Douglas. "Bugeaud, Gallieni, Lyautey: The Development of French Colonial Warfare." In *Makers of Modern Strategy from Machiavelli to the Nuclear Age*. Edited by Peter Paret. Princeton, 1986.

———. *The Conquest of Morocco*. New York, 1983.

———. *The Conquest of the Sahara*. New York, 1984.

———. *The French Foreign Legion: A Complete History of the Legendary Fighting Force*. New York, 1991.

———. *The French Secret Services: From the Dreyfus Affair to the Gulf War*. New York, 1995.

———. "The 'Frontier' in French Imperial Ideology." *Journal of the West* 34 (1995): 16–22.

———. *The March to the Marne: The French Army 1871–1914*. Cambridge, U.K., 1981.

Postal, Raymond. *Présence de Lyautey*. Paris, 1941.

Power, Thomas F., Jr. *Jules Ferry and the Renaissance of French Imperialism*. New York, 1944.

Prados, John. *The Sky Would Fall: Operation Vulture, the U.S. Bombing Mission in Indochina, 1954*. New York, 1983.

Prete, Roy A. "Imbroglio par Excellence: Mounting the Salonika Campaign, September–October 1915." *War and Society* 19 (May, 2001): 47–70.

Price, Roger, ed. *1848 in France*. Ithaca, N.Y., 1975.

Prior, Robin, and Trevor Wilson. *Command on the Western Front: The Military Career of Sir Henry Rawlinson 1914–1918*. Oxford, 1992.

Pyenson, Lewis. *Civilizing Mission: Exact Sciences and French Overseas Expansion, 1830–1940*. Baltimore, 1993.

Quinn, Frederick. *The French Overseas Empire*. Westport, Conn., 2000.

Recouly, Raymond. *General Joffre and His Battles*. New York, 1916.

———. *Joffre*. New York, 1931.

Reeder, Red. *Bold Leaders of World War I*. Boston, 1974.

Renault, François. "L'abolition de l'esclavage au Sénégal. L'attitude de l'administration française (1848–1905)." *Revue française d'histoire d'outre-mer* 58 (1971): 5–81.

Rice-Maximin, Edward. *Accommodation and Resistance: The French Left, Indochina, and the Cold War*. Westport, Conn., 1986.

Ridley, Jack. "Marshal Bugeaud, the July Monarchy and the Question of Algeria, 1841–1847: A Study in Civil-Military Relations." Ph.D. dissertation, University of Oklahoma, 1970.

Riéthy, J. *Histoire populaire du Général Faidherbe.* Paris, 1901.

Ripert, Emile. *Au pays de Joffre.* Paris, 1918.

Rivet, Daniel. *Lyautey et l'institution du protectorat français au Maroc, 1912–1925.* 3 vols. Paris, 1996.

———. *Le Maroc de Lyautey à Mohammed V: le double visage du protectorat.* Paris, 1999.

Roberts, Edmund. *Embassy to the Eastern Courts of Cochin-China, Siam, and Muscat.* Wilmington, 1972.

Roberts, Richard L. *Two Worlds of Cotton: Colonialism and the Regional Economy in the French Soudan, 1800–1946.* Stanford, 1996.

Robinson, David. *Chiefs and Clerics: Abdul Bokar Kan and Futa Toro 1853–1891.* Oxford, 1975.

———. *The Holy War of Umar Tall: The Western Sudan in the Mid–Nineteenth Century.* Oxford, 1985.

Roche, Christian. *Histoire de la Casamance.* Paris, 1985.

Roches, Léon. *Trente-deux ans à travers l'Islam (1832–1864).* 2 vols. Paris, 1884–85.

Roman, Joël. "Repères: les oppositions à la guerre d'Algérie: le rôle de l'édition." *Esprit* 7 (2001): 209–12.

Ros, Martin. *Night of Fire: The Black Napoleon and the Battle for Haiti.* Translated by Karin Ford-Treep. New York, 1994.

Ross, Michael. *Bougainville.* London, 1978.

Roubaud, Louis. *La Bourdonnais.* Paris, 1932.

Roux, François de. *La jeunesse de Lyautey.* Paris, 1952.

Rowell, Cora. *Leaders of the Great War.* New York, 1919.

Roy, Jules. *The Battle of Dienbienphu.* New York, 1965.

———. *J'accuse le Général Massu.* Paris, 1972.

Ruedy, John. *Modern Algeria: The Origins and Development of a Nation.* Bloomington, 1992.

Ruscio, Alain. *Les Communistes français et la guerre d'Indochine 1944–1954.* Paris, 1985.

———. *La guerre française d'Indochine.* Brussels, 1992.

Sainteny, Jean. *Histoire d'une paix manquée: Indochine 1945–1947.* Paris, 1967.

Saint-Arnaud, Jacques Leroy de. *Lettres du Maréchal Saint-Arnaud.* Paris, 1855.

Saint-Aulaire, Auguste. *Au Maroc avant et avec Lyautey.* Paris, 1954.

Saint Marc, Hélie de (with Laurent Beccaria). *Mémoires: les champs de braises.* Paris, 1995.

Saint-Martin, Yves-Jean. *L'empire toucouleur 1848–1897.* Paris, 1970.

———. *Le Sénégal sous le Second Empire.* Paris, 1989.

Salan, Raoul. *Mémoires: fin d'un empire.* Vols. 2, 3, 4. Paris, 1971, 1972, 1973.

Salisbury-Jones, Guy. *So Full a Glory.* New York, 1954.

Sarraut, Albert. *La mise en valeur des colonies.* Paris, 1923.

Schalk, David L. *War and the Ivory Tower: Algeria and Vietnam.* New York, 1991.

Scham, Alan. *Lyautey in Morocco: Protectorate Administration, 1912–1925.* Berkeley, 1970.

Scherer, André. *Histoire de la Réunion.* Paris, 1965.

Schmitt, Maurice. *De Diên Biên Phu à Koweït City.* Paris, 1992.

———. *Alger, été 1957: une victoire sur le terrorisme.* Paris, 2002.

Scholl-Latour, Peter. *Death in the Ricefields*. Translated by Faye Carney. London, 1981.

Schrader, Charles. *The First Helicopter War: Logistics and Mobility in Algeria, 1954–1962*. Westport, Conn., 1999.

Séché, Alphonse. *Le Général Joffre*. Paris, n.d.

Segalla, Spencer D. "Georges Hardy and Educational Ethnology in French Morocco, 1920–1926." *French Colonial History* 4 (2003): 171–90.

Servan-Schreiber, Jean-Jacques. *Lieutenant in Algeria*. Translated by Herbert Matthews. New York, 1957.

Shah-Razemi, Reza, ed. *Algeria: Revolution Revisited*. London, 1997.

Sheean, Vincent. *An American among the Riffi*. New York, 1926.

Sherman, Daniel J. "The Arts and Sciences of Colonialism." *French Historical Studies* 23 (Fall, 2000): 707–29.

Short, Anthony. *The Origins of the Vietnam War*. New York, 1989.

Simiot, Bernard. *De Lattre*. Paris, 1994.

Singer, Barnett. "Lyautey: An Interpretation of the Man and French Imperialism." *Journal of Contemporary History* 26 (1991): 131–57.

———. "A New Model Imperialist in French West Africa." *The Historian* 56 (1993): 69–86.

———. "Colonial Background and Leadership in World War I: The Tragic Case of Gallieni." *Biography* 18 (1995): 1–30.

———. "Mon Général: The Case of Joseph Joffre." *American Scholar* 65 (Autumn, 1996): 593–99.

Singer, Barnett, and Langdon, John. "France's Imperial Legacy." *Contemporary Review* 272 (May, 1998): 231–37.

Sitwell, Osbert. *Escape with Me!* London, 1940.

Slavin, David Henry. *Colonial Cinema and Imperial France, 1919–1939: White Blind Spots, Male Fantasies, Settler Myths*. Baltimore, 2001.

———. "French Colonial Film before and after *Itto*: From Berber Myth to Race War." *French Historical Studies* 21 (Winter, 1998): 125–55.

Soustelle, Jacques. *Aimée et souffrante: Algérie*. Paris, 1956.

———. *Envers et contre tout*. Vol. 1, *De Londres à Alger*. Paris, 1947.

———. *L'espérance trahie (1958–1961)*. Paris, 1962.

———. *La page n'est pas tournée*. Paris, 1965.

Southworth, Constant. *The French Colonial Venture*. London, 1931.

Sow, Alfa Ibrahim. "Notes sur les procédés poétiques dans la littérature des Peuls du Fouta-Djallon." *Cahiers d'études africaines* 5 (1965): 370–87.

Spear, Percival. *A History of British India*. Vol. 2. Harmondsworth, U.K., 1965.

Spears, Edward. *Liaison 1914*. London, 1968.

Spillmann, Georges. *Souvenirs d'un colonialiste*. Paris, 1968.

Starr, Deryck. *Slaving and Slavery in the Indian Ocean*. London, 1998.

Stein, Robert Louis. *Léger Félicité Sonthanax: The Lost Sentinel of the Republic.* Rutherford, N.J., 1985.

Stewart, William A. *Lanrezac, Joffre, and Plan XVII*. Santa Monica, Calif., 1967.

Stora, Benjamin. *Histoire de la guerre d'Algérie (1954–1962)*. 1995. Reprint, Paris, 2002.

Stratton, Arthur. *The Great Red Island*. New York, 1964.

Sullivan, Antony Thrall. *Thomas-Robert Bugeaud: France and Algeria, 1784–1849*. Hamden, Conn., 1983.

Talbott, John. *The War without a Name: France in Algeria 1954–1962*. New York, 1980.

Tannenbaum, Jan Karl. *General Maurice Sarrail, 1856–1929: The French Army and Left-Wing Politics*. Chapel Hill, N.C., 1974.

Tarde, Guillaume de. *L'enseignement de Lyautey*. Paris, 1942.

———. *Lyautey, le chef en action*. Paris, 1959.

———. "La Pensée politique de Lyautey." *Revue des deux mondes* (February 1960): 385–97.

Tattet, M. le Capitaine, ed. *Lettres inédites du Maréchal Bugeaud, Duc d'Isly (1808–1849)*. Paris, 1923.

Taylor, A. J. P. *Illustrated History of the First World War*. New York, 1963.

Terrail, Gabriel. *Joffre: la première crise du commandement (novembre 1915–décembre 1916)*. Paris, 1919.

Tharoor, Shashi. "Global Insights: The Messy Afterlife of Colonialism." *Global Governance* 8 (2002): 1–5.

Thétard, Henry. *Des hommes, des bêtes: le zoo de Lyautey*. Paris, 1947.

Thomas, Martin. *The French Empire at War 1940–1945*. Manchester, U.K., 1998.

Thompson, Edward. *A History of India*. London, 1927.

Thompson, Elizabeth. *Colonial Citizens: Republican Rights, Paternal Privilege, and Gender in French Syria and Lebanon*. New York, 2000.

Thompson, P. A. *Lions Led by Donkeys*. London, 1927.

Thompson, Virginia. *Dupleix and His Letters (1742–1754)*. New York, 1933.

———. *French Indo-China*. New York, 1942.

Thuillier, Guy. "Pour une histoire de l'hygiène corporelle: un exemple régional: le Nivernais." *Revue d'histoire économique et sociale* 46 (1968): 232–53.

Tocqueville, Alexis de. *Oeuvres*. Edited by André Jardin. Paris, 1991.

———. *The Recollections of Alexis de Tocqueville*. Translated by Alexander Teixera de Mattos. Cleveland, 1959.

———. *Writings on Empire and Slavery*. Translated by Jennifer Pitts. Baltimore, 2001.

Trinquier, Roger. *Le coup d'état du 13 mai*. Paris, 1962.

———. *Le premier bataillon de bérets rouges*. Paris, 1984.

Trochu, Louis Jules. *Oeuvres posthumes*. Tours, 1896.

Tuchman, Barbara. *The Guns of August*. New York, 1962.

Varillon, Pierre. *Joffre*. Paris, 1956.

Venier, Pascal. *Lyautey avant Lyautey*. Paris, 1997.

La vérité sur la guerre, 1914–1918. 2 vols. Paris, 1930.

Vézinet, Adolphe. *Le Général Leclerc de Hautelocque: Maréchal de France*. Paris, 1974.

Viansson-Ponté, Pierre. *Histoire de la République Gaullienne*. 2 vols. Paris, 1971 and 1976.

Viereck, George Sylvester. *Glimpses of the Great*. New York, 1930.

Vignes, Kenneth. *Le Gouverneur Général Tirman et le système de rattachements*. Paris, 1958.

Vincent, Rose et al. *The French in India.* Bombay, 1990.

Wade, Mary. *Leaders to Liberty.* Boston, 1919.

Wagner, Moritz. *The Tricolor on the Atlas.* London, 1854.

Wall, Irwin M. *France, the United States, and the Algerian War.* Berkeley, 2001.

Warner, Philip. *The Battle of Loos.* London, 1976.

Weber, Eugen. *Peasants into Frenchmen: The Modernization of Rural France, 1870–1914.* Stanford, 1976.

Weil, Maurice-Henri, ed. *Oeuvres militaires du Maréchal Bugeaud, Duc d'Isly.* Paris, 1883.

Weinberg, Gerhard L. *A World at Arms: A Global History of World War II.* New York, 1994.

Weinstein, Brian. *Eboué.* New York, 1972.

Weiskel, Timothy C. *French Colonial Rule and the Baule Peoples: Resistance and Collaboration 1889–1911.* Oxford, 1980.

Werth, Alexander. *France 1940–1955.* Boston, 1956.

Weygand, Maxime. *Mémoires: idéal vécu.* Paris, 1953.

White, Dorothy Shipley. *Black Africa and de Gaulle.* London, 1979.

Willis, Michael. *The Islamic Challenge in Algeria: A Political History.* New York, 1996.

Winslow, E. M. *The Pattern of Imperialism.* New York, 1984.

Winter, Jay. *Sites of Memory, Sites of Mourning: The Great War in European Cultural History.* Cambridge, U.K., 1995.

Wolpert, Stanley. *A New History of India.* 3rd edition. New York, 1989.

Woods, William Seaver. *Colossal Blunders of the War.* London, n.d.

Woolman, David S. *Rebels in the Rif: Abd el Krim and the Rif Rebellion.* Stanford, 1968.

Wright, Gordon. *France in Modern Times.* 5th edition. New York, 1995.

Wright, Gwendolyn. *The Politics of Design in French Colonial Urbanism.* Chicago, 1991.

Yelan, Louise. "Postcolonial Criticism in the Era of Globalization." *Studies in the Novel* 34 (Spring 2002): 90–101.

Young, Robert J. *In Command of France: French Foreign Policy and Military Planning, 1933–1940.* Cambridge, Mass., 1978.

———. *Power and Pleasure: Louis Barthou and the Third French Republic.* Montreal, 1991.

Yver, Georges, ed. *Correspondance du Maréchal Vallée: Gouverneur général des possessions françaises dans le Nord de l'Afrique (1835–1837).* Paris, 1948.

Yver, Georges, ed. *Documents relatifs au Traité de la Tafna (1837).* Algiers, 1924.

Zainu'ddin, Ailsa. *A Short History of Indonesia.* New York, 1970.

Zeldin, Theodore. *France 1848–1945: Anxiety and Hypocrisy.* New York, 1981.

Index

467